BRESCIA COLLEGE LONDON CANADA
FIDES ET VERITAS

The Netherlandic Presence in Ontario

Pillars, Class and Dutch Ethnicity

Frans J. Schryer

Wilfrid Laurier University Press

This book has been published with the help of a grant from the Humanities and Social Sciences Federation of Canada, using funds provided by the Social Sciences and Humanities Research Council of Canada.

Canadian Cataloguing in Publication Data

Schryer, Frans J.
The Netherlandic presence in Ontario : pillars, class and Dutch ethnicity

Includes bibliographical references and index.
ISBN 0-88920-262-1 (bound)

1. Dutch – Ontario. 2. Immigrants – Ontario. 3. Dutch Canadians – Ontario.* I. Title.

FC3100.D9S37 1998 305.83′9310713 C96-931981-9
F1059.7.D8S37 1998

WILFRID LAURIER UNIVERSITY PRESS
Waterloo, Ontario, Canada N2L 3C5

Cover design: Leslie Macredie

Cover art: Huibert Sabelis, *Objects of My Heritage*, 1993.
Acrylic on canvas. (Used by permission of the artist.)

Printed in Canada

To my parents
who struggled to improve their lives
yet continue to give so much of themselves to others
and
in memory
of all the postwar immigrants of their generation
who have since passed away

Contents

List of Figures

List of Tables

Foreword

The term pillars was coined as an English equivalent of the word *zuilen* (supports or pillars), which refers to the major segments of Dutch society, each with its own institutions based on religious or non-religious principles. With the population movement from the Netherlands to Canada between 1947 and 1958, at least two *zuilen* were transported and partly reassembled on Canadian soil. Other Dutch people came as "unattached" immigrants, leaving their pillars behind. However, all but one of the pillars started to crumble in the sixties in both Europe and Canada.

The Dutch society they left behind was stratified along class lines, with its own status distinctions based on speech, family background and education. Such distinctions cut across the pillars. Stretching the metaphor further, each pillar had many tiers, with tiers at the same level displaying the same colour. Immigrants who had occupied higher positions in Dutch society often displayed their colours, especially when interacting with each other. Eventually the colours faded, or were camouflaged in the Canadian context. Distinctions based on gender, age and region of origin were likewise altered and partly replicated in North America.

My portrayal of Dutch immigrants can be compared to creating a painting or producing a film; however, it is impossible to keep the brushstrokes within a single frame, or to create a single plot. Although my story deals primarily with the cohort that came after World War Two, one cannot totally ignore the "old-timers" who came to Canada from the Netherlands before the War or the smaller contingent of more recent Dutch immigrants. Nor can we overlook the inevitable contact between Dutch-Canadians and their Flemish cousins from Belgium, or the connections between Dutch newcomers in Canada and the descendants of Dutch immigrants living south of the border.

Dutch-speaking immigrants quickly became an integral component of an officially multicultural, albeit predominantly English-speaking, society.

Simultaneously, men and women of diverse backgrounds struck out in different directions, becoming different types of Canadians in terms of religious affiliation, identity, political loyalty and occupation. The transformation of immigrants into Canadians of Dutch descent epitomizes both change and continuity. To capture such a multidimensional process requires different lenses, each zooming in on the changing social landscape from different angles, then putting together a relatively sharp picture. But it is difficult to capture Dutch-Canadian reality through consecutive sketches or snapshots—not even by highlighting one region. What I will present, through constantly rearranging the basic patterns, more closely resembles a revolving kaleidoscope. No doubt rough brush-strokes will miss finer details, and the picture may occasionally become blurred. I hope that I have at least prepared the way for others to carry on with a task that will never be completely finished.

Preface

One might expect a book about an ethnic group written by one of its members to project only a positive image. Such books often describe high-profile people; anyone who became a movie star, a business tycoon or a well-known writer is included regardless of whether or not that person identifies with the ethnic group in question. Another tendency is to portray one's own group as subject to more discrimination than others. My book was written from a more critical perspective and will not ignore the Dutch-Canadian community's "dirty laundry." However, readers looking for gossip will be disappointed; the names of most people interviewed are excluded. Yet no attempt was made to disguise people in the public eye or whose stories have already been told.

Readers holding a fixed image of the typical Dutch-Canadian person should be forewarned. Women and men of Dutch background do not make up a single, cohesive group. Moreover, the nature of being "Dutch" has become transformed, and will continue to change over time. People originating in the Netherlands (or Holland) define themselves in different ways; some even deny the existence of a Dutch-Canadian culture. You will learn about the constant tensions among competing religious, ethnic, linguistic, regional, national and class identities.

I am both insider and outsider, born and raised in the Netherlands yet with most of my education and work experience in a non-Dutch environment. To better understand Dutch-Canadians, I had to take a more active part in the Dutch-Canadian community. Apart from conducting interviews, I occasionally wrote articles for the Dutch-Canadian bi-weekly newspaper (*De Nederlandse Courant*), attended Dutch social events, and became involved in the Canadian Association for the Advancement of Netherlandic Studies, first as a member and then as national secretary. My research not only affected my professional activities, but part of my profession (academia) became part of what I examined (see chapter 16). I also decided to speak more Dutch to my parents, which became a source of amusement or surprise for my brothers and sisters, and to visit old family acquaintances. Readers familiar with the social science literature will recognize this form of observation and participation as the first stage in doing ethnography (literally, "writing about people").

Apart from my own interpretation, this study reflects the insights and opinions of other writers, and many interviewees, making it difficult to draw a hard-and-fast line separating what is personal and what is "scientific." Furthermore, the investigative process itself can alter the identities of the people whom the social scientist tries to study as objectively as possible. The act of interviewing and writing about an ethnic group, especially one's own, might strengthen (or weaken) that group or modify how it is defined. I offer no apologies.

I began collecting data on August 8, 1988, during a conversation with a fellow passenger on a return flight from Amsterdam. The plan for a book was conceived in the fall of 1989, while living in Sudbury, and the writing endeavour started two years later, after moving to Kitchener. Teaching duties and other obligations made it necessary to put off further writing until 1993. A manuscript was submitted that summer, but it took another three years of evaluation and revision before it went to press. During those last three years, I made additional fieldtrips and came across additional information. Last-minute additions brought the story up-to-date as of the winter of 1997.

Much of the research was financed through a grant from the Secretary of State's Multicultural Directorate, which paid for travel, phone calls and photocopies. The Social Science and Humanities Research Council covered additional expenditures, including the hiring of Kitty DeVoogd as a part-time assistant for several months. Additional interviews were conducted under the auspices of St. Willibrord Credit Union (in London). They covered the travel and subsistence costs incurred while interviewing and tape-recording their charter members. The University of Guelph enabled me to carry out research during several research and development semesters. I am indebted to all these institutions that facilitated my investigations with no obligation other than writing up the results.

This book would not have come to fruition without the criticism, cooperation and hospitality of many people. Apart from recounting their stories, we often exchanged views on a wide range of topics. I am particularly grateful to a number of people in the city of London, including Tom and Ann VandenMoer and John Strijbosch, who opened their homes to me on numerous visits. In the Toronto area, Marten Mol introduced me to key people and generously escorted me on initial visits to various locations, including visits to Holland Christian Homes, the headquarters of the

DUCA Community Credit Union and the Holland Marsh. Alfons H. M. Claus van Banning, former Vice-Consul for Social and Emigration Affairs, Consulate General of the Netherlands, generously gave me access to his library and personal files. Two people went out of their way in performing the tedious but necessary task of helping me trace kinship connections and find maiden names from membership lists; Ann van Boxmeer in Wyoming and Margaret Hendrickx in Warwick. Copies of a number of interviews or sections from my book were sent to informants who made corrections, or provided additional written information. I want to thank Jules Fryters of Acton, Frieda Leenders of Erin, Rimmer Tjalsma of Mississauga, John Koeslag in Quadville and Dick de Man of Willowdale. People who invited me to stay for lunch or dinner are too numerous to mention, though I wish to acknowledge their kindness.

Four paid assistants helped me in the laborious task of seeking documents, listening to tapes, making photocopies, or adding up columns from computer printouts of census data: Krystyna Henke, Eric Schryer and Stephen and Emily Schryer. Additional data were collected by Margaret Vanderschot, Lisa Dent-Couturier and Michael Fallon, all of whom conducted interviews as part of a separate research project on Dutch-Canadian farmers. During the five years of my research project, I met various undergraduate and graduate students at Guelph who were investigating aspects of the Dutch community: John McMurdo, Joanne Van Dijk, Fiep de Bie, Michael Fallon and Joyce VanderVliet. Their research papers or dissertations, cited in the footnotes and bibliography, provided further information and insights. I want to thank Herman Ganzevoort and other (anonymous) readers, plus several colleagues who commented on earlier drafts of my manuscript, especially Dr. Henri van Stekelenburg. Marie Puddister's skills in map-making and Carroll Klein's painstaking copy editing also contributed to the production of this book. Finally, I acknowledge the encouragement and assistance of two people—Franciscus Leonardus Johannes Schryer and Theodora Schryer (neé Makovitz). They provided the initial contacts, read sample chapters and corrected my misspelling of Dutch words. To them, my parents, I dedicate my book.

While this book was in the process of being written and published I discovered that at least a half a dozen people whom I interviewed have since passed away. Others who told me their stories may never have the opportunity to see the work which could not have been produced without their contributions. That realization fills me with sadness. Hopefully this book will help to keep alive the memory of that entire generation of postwar immigrants who did so much to make Canada what it is today.

Chapter 1

Introduction

People from the Netherlands have been coming to Ontario since before Confederation. The Dutch-Canadian presence today, however, is the outcome of more recent events. Approximately 200,000 Dutch immigrants came to Canada between 1946 and 1990.[1] Since most of them arrived prior to 1958, my book deals primarily with the cohort who came during that first decade, many of whom are still alive today. At the time of departure, they shared a common citizenship. They had all been taught the history, together with the patriotic songs, which make up part of Dutch political culture.[2] The postwar Dutch immigrants had also experienced five years of Nazi occupation or heard many war stories while growing up during the decade following World War Two. Despite these common elements, Dutch immigrants were a diverse group. A sizable minority felt more comfortable speaking the Frisian language or some Dutch dialect. Many were farmers and working-class people, but there were also professionals and business owners. A few had aristocratic connections. These different Dutch immigrants represented the major Dutch religious denominations, with a smattering of socialists or liberals with no church affiliation. Moreover, some were born, or had spent a part of their lives, in Dutch colonies, principally the Dutch East Indies (now Indonesia). They too spoke Dutch, and had attended Dutch schools prior to emigrating to Canada (usually via Holland). Once we include the Dutch Jews who survived the Holocaust, Dutch-Canadians represent a heterogenous population.

Dutch-Canadians have been labelled an "invisible" minority.[3] Postwar Dutch immigrants did not form block settlements or conglomerate in inner-city neighbourhoods. They were relatively well-educated compared to their counterparts from some other parts of Europe. Even Dutch rural

---

Notes to this chapter are on p. 326-29.

immigrants had been exposed to a highly urbanized, industrial society. Taking into account the reputation and social conditions of their country of origin, it is easy to understand their geographical dispersal, linguistic assimilation and economic integration. Surveys, especially those focusing on language retention, indicate that compared to other immigrant populations, Dutch-Canadians have one of the lowest ethnic identity retention rates, especially in the second and third generation.[4] Although they comprise one of the larger groups of postwar immigrants, the Dutch do not have a national ethnic organization. Moreover, a surprisingly large number of Dutch-born immigrants became involved in politics, without drawing attention to their ethnic origin (see chapter 19).

But there is more to the Dutch-Canadian reality than what one would expect. While few postwar immigrants today use the Dutch language at home, many continue to read Dutch. After three decades—long after the influx of Dutch immigrants slowed down to a trickle—there are three Dutch-language newspapers. The Dutch-Canadian consumer market makes up a well-established niche for specialty foods and objects (wall tiles, posters and copper trinkets) which serve as symbols of ethnic identity. Dutch-Canadians have also maintained beliefs or values not immediately apparent to outsiders; van den Hoonaard calls this phenomenon "silent ethnicity."[5] Other aspects of the Dutch presence are more conspicuous. One component of the Dutch-Canadian population, namely the orthodox Calvinists, are characterized by social cohesion and institutional completeness[6] going well beyond the second generation. Their churches, schools and nursing homes can be seen all over southwestern Ontario, in parts of British Columbia and in pockets of the prairies (see chapter 9). Additional evidence also contradicts the belief that the Dutch have not left much of an imprint on Canada's ethnic landscape. Two large credit unions in Ontario—with no religious connections—were founded and are still run by Dutch-Canadians (see chapter 15). Many people, including Dutch-Canadians, are not aware that half a dozen formerly Irish-Canadian Catholic villages in southern Ontario were transformed into de facto Dutch parishes in the fifties (see chapter 8). When a heritage museum organized an exhibit dealing with postwar Dutch immigrants in Lambton county in 1996, attendance jumped from several people a day to over 600 per week.[7] And a Frisian (Dutch) picnic held near Paris, Ontario, annually draws over a thousand visitors. In light of the surveys on Dutch ethnicity, the counter-evidence of a strong Dutch-Canadian presence raises the question why Dutch immigrants did not blend in more. This question can only be answered by taking into account the interrelationships among demographic factors, values and patterns of social interaction.

Diversity and Continuity

My study will demonstrate that the migration of a large number of people with a common national background can result in considerable social continuity even when these immigrants do not exhibit a strong national or ethnic identity. In the case of the postwar Dutch immigrants, much of the behaviour, and many of the values and habits prevalent in the Netherlands at the time of emigration, re-emerged in southwestern Ontario. Moreover, these social patterns were replicated by the next, Canadian-born generation. Dutch-Canadians who do not identify with their ethnic heritage might not be aware of such continuity. People associated with Dutch-Canadian religious institutions (mainly Reformed) would not seem Dutch to researchers looking for overt ethnic symbols. Nevertheless, their offspring are likely to marry someone from the same national background. A high rate of endogamy, together with the persistence of group boundaries based on common beliefs, leaves the door open for a subsequent revival of ethnic identity. Dutch immigrants who were not associated with ethnic clubs or Reformed denominations joined organizations or churches most closely resembling their equivalents in the Netherlands (see chapter 7). Their integration into Canadian society was still shaped by the homeland's social structure and their children's social trajectory echoes that of the parents.

The interaction of Dutch immigrants from diverse backgrounds did result in some groups being defined in explicit ethnic terms, especially in larger urban settings. However, only a small percentage of people of Dutch birth or recent Dutch origins became actively involved in urban Dutch-Canadian communities, whose long-term viability depends on the periodic influx of newcomers and visitors from Europe. While continuing to be "very Dutch" in some respects, their members represent a cosmopolitan lifestyle. Their children do not remain active in Dutch-Canadian community events, much less marry into their own ethnic group, although they are more likely than their non-urban counterparts to know the Dutch language (see chapter 11).

Ontario: A Case Study

This book complements earlier studies by paying more attention to cultural pluralism among Dutch-Canadians.[8] Such a perspective requires a broad, sweeping approach, taking into account both Canada's regional diversity and the disparate nature of the Dutch-Canadian population. Ideally all of Canada should have been included. However, the detailed analysis required of ethnographers and social historians dictates a more in-depth case study approach. To combine the two strategies required making hard decisions. I opted for a narrower geographical range, zooming in on the province of Ontario. The emphasis on Ontario excludes the treatment of ethnic dynamics in other parts of Canada (particularly Quebec). Nonetheless, Ontario exhibits enough internal, sub-regional variation to be fairly representative of Canada as a whole.

Ontario has become home to more than half the Dutch-Canadian population. According to the 1986 population census, there were 171,150 people of Dutch descent in Ontario, 40 percent of whom listed Dutch or Frisian as their mother tongue. The overwhelming majority are offspring of the approximately 50,000 immigrants who came between 1947 and 1958. Most of these new Canadians are concentrated in a narrow band running through southwestern Ontario (see chapter 6). That region also provided a fertile ground for the replication of Dutch cultural and social patterns, as we shall see later. I suspect that a similar phenomenon occurred in other pockets of Dutch concentration in British Columbia and perhaps other parts of Canada. However, my generalizations for Ontario remain to be tested outside of Ontario (see Conclusion).

Theoretical Orientation

The research resulting in this book was guided by a set of conceptual tools developed by Pierre Bourdieu,[9] whose career has been dedicated to breaking down the disciplinary boundaries among history, literature, ethnography and sociology.[10] His approach resembles that of Norbert Elias who influenced Dutch social scientists.[11] Bourdieu uses many technical terms derived from different disciplines, ranging from philosophy to economics. I do not intend to discuss his work at length, but a brief outline of his key concepts and assumptions is warranted since much of his perspective is reflected in this book.

The main term used by Bourdieu is that of 'habitus,' which refers to partly unconscious dispositions, inculcated through upbringing and education. Such dispositions, including expectations and habits, are normally shared by people from the same generation who occupy similar positions in the social structure.[12] Anthropologists might use the term subculture.[13] However, 'habitus' is more than just an alternative label. Bourdieu's approach aims to overcome the gap between two types of social research—that which puts too much emphasis on structure (hence determination) versus one which focuses on human agency (voluntarism).[14] He also rejects the Cartesian split separating the realm of the human mind from the body, since Bourdieu sees social categories as literally embodied in the form of 'habitus'; people of contrasting ages and gender, or varied social class and ethnic backgrounds have a different bearing or 'hexis' ingrained in their deportment, speech and even physical appearance.[15] In this book I will use the word disposition, or dispositions, in the same sense as 'habitus.'

In Bourdieu's work, human beings are sometimes depicted as players who use strategies in competing in various spheres of social life to which he refers as 'fields.'[16] One could think in terms of various games, each with its own reward structure and unwritten rules, which may change from time to time though improvisations. Following Bourdieu's metaphor, the players intuitively know how to "play the game," although they may not have an explicit knowledge of the rules nor an equal say in how the rules are changed.[17] From the standpoint of the social system as a whole, different social 'fields' may overlap, but they can also be hierarchically ranked. Some people may even be completely excluded from certain 'fields' in which case they could form their own separate, albeit less prestigious versions.

Bourdieu is particularly interested in how these and other forms of social inequality are maintained through distinctions, demarcating such social divisions as gender, class, age, region, "race" and ethnicity.[18] All of these divisions, based on 'classifications' can become the basis for the formation of 'classes' or social groups.[19] 'Classes,' in this sense, have to do with how people interact on the basis of how they see themselves and each other while 'fields' define institutionalized human activities: the economy, sports, politics, religion and education. The various social 'fields' and 'classes,' with which we come into contact through upbringing and education, jointly mould people's predispositions to act in certain ways, which in turn reproduces the social structure. People's dispositions, usually acquired early in life, thus become attuned to various 'fields' of action, which give us that sense of familiarity associated with the taken-for-granted world of "common sense" and thereby reproduces the social structure.[20] Bourdieu's conceptual framework also treats different aspects of society as dimensions of a complex topology of 'social space,' whose logic goes beyond the material interests rooted in the process of material production.[21]

Since 'classes' and 'fields' can be treated as relatively stable sets of relations which are replicated over time, Bourdieu has been accused of placing more emphasis on continuity than on change. However, his approach, known as 'generative structuralism,' does not ignore improvisations and strategies, as indicated in the metaphor of social life as a game. A new generation never displays exactly the same dispositions as their elders, even in seemingly stable societies. Furthermore, new 'classes' and 'fields' can come into being at any time, and old ones are constantly becoming further differentiated as people compete for power and prestige within various spheres of action. People continually jostle to improve or maintain their positions in this multidimensional 'social space' or to prevent others from doing so. The most common strategy is to redefine group boundaries. Social actors frequently disagree about the significance of religious versus regional identity or whether they should join together on the basis of common economic interests, gender or a shared language. According to Bourdieu, social structures are the outcome of such struggles over meaning and resources. Moreover, he acknowledges various levels of discrepancy between people's expectations and social structures no longer corresponding to their dispositions. Such divergence, especially those resulting from conquest, colonialism or migration, involves contradictions whose resolution may culminate in new social configurations.[22]

In my study, a flexible application of Bourdieu's conceptual framework helped me to examine why and how Dutch immigrants reproduced the social structure of their homeland, while simultaneously modifying their behaviour and attitudes in a new social and cultural context. Bourdieu's insights also helped to make sense of why recent immigrants from the Netherlands, with a whole new set of dispositions reflecting a different Dutch society, have so little in common with their compatriots who arrived just after World War Two.

Following Bourdieu's line of thinking, ethnic relations, like other aspects of social structure, are created and recreated through linguistic interactions among people struggling for 'symbolic power.' Mental categories and claims can become self-fulfilling prophesies, culminating in new ethnic groups and even whole nations. The creation of ethnic groups involves both subjective realities (representations)—expressed in spoken and written language—and the actions and cultural artifacts that form part of observable (objective) reality. These two aspects of social reality are complexly interrelated. The complexity increases when large numbers of people, associated with distinct cultural traditions, come into close contact. Hence we must examine how Dutch immigrants from diverse backgrounds saw themselves, how others saw them, as well as what they actually did and with whom they associated. Nor can one ignore how reading and writing about Dutch-Canadians became an integral part of the process of ethnogenesis.[23]

This book will demonstrate how the diverse forms of social behaviour of Dutch immigrants in Canada were generated by dispositions corresponding to the Dutch system of class stratification (chapter 12) and gender (chapter 13), as well as the various Dutch 'fields' (religion, economics and politics) which did not operate in the same way in Europe as in North America. However, before proceeding to outline the methodology used to generate the data needed for my study, we need to look more closely at ethnicity itself. Indeed, Bourdieu has written little about ethnic relations or ethnic identity per se, nor have many scholars applied his perspective to ethnic studies.[24]

Ethnicity and Ethnic Relations

Ethnicity, as a dimension of social differentiation, is invariably associated with cultural or linguistic diversity. Most ethnic groups and their corresponding categories—such as Dutch, Frisian, Macedonian or African Canadian—came into being through contact among people who had previously belonged to distinct societies, separated by geography. Such ethnogenesis is often a direct consequence of large scale migration or conquest. Distinct ethnic groups also emerge when culturally diverse populations, sharing a common territory, coalesce against inhabitants of an adjoining territory. Such a process occurs during the process of nation building, culminating in state borders. Moreover, any group whose members reinterpret old values, or invent new customs, may create further ethnic diversity within the borders of existing nation states. Such distinct intranational ethnic groups can survive over long time periods, notwithstanding dramatic changes in, and even the virtual disappearance of, the contrasting traits originally used to distinguish such ethnic groups.[25] Some authors even argue that ethnicity, as a form of social differentiation, may increase despite cultural homogenization in today's world of mass communication and increasing population movements.[26]

Social relations defining interactions among ethnic groups can be conceptualized in terms of boundaries. According to Frederick Barth, ethnic boundaries are perpetuated over time, irrespective of the cultural content associated with distinct ethnic groups.[27] Thus, North American native peoples continue to interact with Euro-Canadians as separate ethnic groups even when they have adopted the English language, Christianity and European clothes. Likewise, the defining traits of French Canadian Quebeckers versus "English" Quebeckers have changed over time; language is still important, but the ethnic dynamics revolve less around religion or place of origin. However, the strength and permeability of ethnic group boundaries vary over space and time, and one cannot exclude the possibility of the total disappearance of an ethnic group within a specific society.

Members of ethnic groups make subjective claims based on geographical origins, a common belief system, kinship ties or shared grievances. The permutations and combinations are almost endless. However, taken-for-granted ethnic categories may not correspond to the actual distribution of cultural traits or even social position as defined by outsider observers. For example, not all Mennonites speak low German or drive horses and buggies. Not all Englishmen in Canada are rich. Divergence between the distribution of distinctive cultural traits and membership in ethnic groups is especially prevalent during the initial phase of ethnic group formation or the early stages of the resurrection of old ones. The same dynamic applies to regionally based groups, which can be seen as variants of ethnicity. Pierre Bourdieu cites the emergence of Occitanie, a region in France, whose inhabitants claim to speak a separate language called Occitan. According to outside observers, no such language exists, since "Occitan" consists of diverse dialects of French. Nevertheless, such regional or ethnic claims, together with the display of cultural objects serving as symbols, can create the very social phenomenon denied by the objective critic who can only see such claims as delusion.[28]

Similarly, a Dutch ethnic group exists in contemporary Canada by virtue of the fact that people talk and write about it, even though the number of people speaking Dutch is declining. Nor does it matter that Dutch-Canadians no longer have much in common with people living in the Netherlands. The act of representation can lead to the constitution of an ethnic group regardless of the degree to which the objective traits used to identity such a group are associated with members of that group. Even cynical social scientists, interested in disproving an ethnic group's existence, may inadvertently help to strengthen a nascent ethnic group. A growing awareness of an ethnic group generates forms of behaviour and the creation or recreation of cultural traits which serve as markers for group boundaries. However, the strategy whereby claims lead to ethnic groups does not always work, nor do they continue indefinitely, once generated.

It is not easy to identify the causal chain explaining the relative strength of ethnicity as a principle of social interaction. Attempts at accurate prediction are doomed to fail, given the extremely complex nature of ethnic dynamics under constantly shifting social conditions. Understanding how ethnic or racially defined groups arose in the past is an equally daunting task, even where there is a clear association among phenotype, shared cultural traits, occupation and the distribution of property.[29] By identifying common economic interests, researchers can often go a long way in explaining the appearance or decline of ethnic boundaries. Yet even where overt class conflict takes on the form of ethnic cleavage, members of a subordinate ethnic group rarely all belong to the same economic class.[30]

In looking at the place occupied by people of Dutch descent in Canada's system of stratification, one would not find a strong association between class position and ethnicity. Dutch-Canadian men and women are neither underrepresented or overrepresented in most levels of the economic class structure (see chapter 19). A low correlation between economic position and national origin can account for the weak political presence of the Dutch as an ethnic group in Canada. Indeed, the manner in which postwar Dutch immigrants became integrated into the Canadian economic class structure goes a long way in helping us to understand why a Dutch ethnic 'class' is so poorly developed. At the same time we cannot ignore the importance of intra-ethnic class dynamics, together with gender, region and religion, in shaping the way that Dutch immigrants and their offspring competed for both economic power and status in a multicultural, but Anglo-dominated society. We will see how Dutch dispositions ('habitus'), together with the way they formed their own groups through social representation, can explain why some Dutch immigrants defined themselves in primarily ethnic terms, while others emphasized their membership in a separate religious group (albeit one with strong Dutch connections) and still others rejected or denied their Dutch heritage altogether.

Methodology

In my study of Dutch-Canadians, I used different techniques to generate the data.[31] My background research was largely qualitative in nature. I read everything I could find about the Netherlands and about Dutch-Canadians. Next, I visited the major regions of Ontario, including the North. These early trips took me to numerous farms, villages and cities. These preliminary trips were followed by an examination of the 1986 population census. Print-outs of statistical data pertaining to the distribution of people reporting Dutch as ethnic descent and mother tongue were compared to my own impressions of where the Dutch were located, and what other people told me. Only then did I select specific parts of Ontario for more detailed investigation. Extensive open-ended interviews were combined with genealogical investigations, and the examination of material available in local or personal archives. I attended public functions to observe and meet as many people as possible. Numerous hours were spent browsing through documents housed in the Archives of Ontario and listening to cassette tapes collected by the Multicultural History Society of Ontario. That task was made easier by a recently completed inventory of Dutch-Canadian papers.[32] The archival research resulted in several binders of photocopied letters, newspaper clippings and notes.

The bulk of my data consists of typed fieldnotes based on open-ended interviews with 636 Dutch-Canadians.[33] Most people were interviewed in their homes or workplace, although I conducted some phone interviews. Representatives and members of organizations, and people of various class backgrounds, political persuasion and religious (or non-religious) affiliations were targeted. Interviews were usually set up beforehand by phone or letter, but I did short interviews on the spur of the moment.[34] The selection process was based on the "snowball" technique for picking a non-random stratified sample.[35] I used both English and Dutch during these interviews. Sometimes I initiated the interview in Dutch to see how people would respond, but on most occasions I played it literally by ear. Although informants were aware that I could speak and understand Dutch, the social context determined which language was spoken (see chapters 11 and 12).[36] Occasionally people would converse in a Dutch dialect (most of which I could understand), and I would try to modify my speech pattern to conform to theirs.

The fieldwork phase of my empirical research was conducted in several stages. For example, when I reached the 433 mark in my interviews, I ascertained that at that point I had contacted people living in thirty different counties of Ontario, plus a handful of informants from outside the province.[37] Apart from a small percentage who were born in Canada, these people came from every province or region in the Netherlands except Flevoland. There were 14 people from Indonesia and 12 from Flanders (in Belgium). I then did a breakdown in terms of the age, sex, occupation, time of immigration, religious background, church membership (if any) and sub-ethnic categories.[38] In the light of this quantitative examination of the first phase of my interviews, I diagnosed which categories of people or places with a Dutch presence were over- or underrepresented in the fieldnotes, in order to proceed with maximum variety sampling.[39] I had not interviewed enough Frisians (especially Catholic Frisians), Dutch people resident in eastern Ontario or Dutch-Indonesians who were not born in the Netherlands. Women were also underrepresented. I kept those gaps in mind as I looked for additional contacts and proceeded with more participant-observation and interviews. In the end I questioned over 200 more individuals. Well into the writing-up stage, I conducted additional interviews or contacted people to whom I had spoken one or two years before. I stopped when I was satisfied that I had obtained as much information as possible from a fairly representative set of people.

The ensuing written records varied in length from half a page (for less than 10 percent) to between 12 to 25 pages of text (for a dozen key informants). In terms of the nature of the interviews, about half of them consisted of a complete life history combined with a wide-ranging conversation on a variety of topics. Such in-depth interviews, often done in stages, lasted anywhere from three to nine hours. The rest were either shorter interviews on very specific topics, or partial life histories. The latter included conversations with spouses (where one person played a more dominant part of an interview) or with unexpected visitors drawn into a formal interview. Some of these interviews were tape-recorded and transcribed, but the vast majority resulted in written accounts based on notes taken while listening. A laptop computer enabled me to reconstruct my interactions, based on a combination of memory and handwritten notes, usually within several hours of the interview (and never more than a full day), resulting in over two thousand pages of single spaced, typed text. These fieldnotes, some of which appear as "interludes" in the second part of this book, are in the voice of the person with whom I spoke. Roughly two thirds of the resulting text is in English and the rest is in some version of the Dutch language as spoken in Canada. These notes also were classified according to themes and topics. I also subscribed to all three Dutch-Canadian newspapers, paying special attention to (and filing) any articles dealing with or written in Canada.

Overview and Organization

This book is divided into three parts. Three background chapters in the first part, based on secondary sources, provide an outline of the genesis of the Dutch nation, and describe Dutch society, with its "pillar" system, at the time of emigration. The actual emigration experience, from the perspectives of both countries, is also included. Readers looking for additional information about these and other topics can consult the scholarly books cited in the endnotes.

A longer second part, comprising chapters five through seventeen, deals with the history and contemporary situation of postwar Dutch immigrants in Ontario and their immediate descendants. This is where I present most of my ethnographic and historical data. Dutch-Canadian reality is examined from the standpoint of class, language, business, politics, regionalism, gender and religion. The reader will get an account of the multifaceted nature of people of Netherlandic descent. Part two also covers diverse topics, ranging from the early process of adaptation to Canadian society to the rise and decline of Dutch-Canadian clubs. Tracing social ties and historical connections will occasionally lead us to the United States and other parts of the world. Since the central focus is on tracing the trajectory of the cohort of people who arrived between 1947 and 1958, this part will end with a chapter on the elderly, many of whom today live in retirement homes. Short passages selected from my fieldnotes and archival collection appear at the end of each chapter. These excerpts serve several functions: to illustrate general trends, to add a more subjective, personal perspective and to include odd cases that do not fit into the overall pattern. The latter serve as reminders of the often messy, unpredictable nature of social reality.

The third part, which becomes more interpretative and speculative, consists of three chapters. Here the reader will again see a general picture of the postwar Dutch immigrant population, within the broader context of Canadian society. Chapter 18 deals with altered dispositions, with emphasis on the identities and perceptions of that original cohort of Dutch immigrants. How *the Dutch* are perceived by others, including how they fit into the "vertical mosaic," will be covered in chapter 19, to be followed by a more theoretical chapter. That final chapter will scrutinize some of the literature on immigration and ethnicity from a Bourdieuan perspective, in the light of my case study of Dutch immigrants in Ontario.

Part One

Shifting Ethnicity

Chapter 2

Dutch Ethnicity: Genesis and Transformation

People from the Netherlands have been a part of North American history since the earliest contact between Europeans and native peoples. Yet the Dutch and their country are relatively unknown. The stereotypes about them vary. They are supposedly Protestants who quickly integrate. Yet Dutch Protestants set up their own churches, while an equally large number of Dutch Catholics rapidly integrated into multiethnic parishes. Another image of the Dutch is that they are rich; such names as Van Horne or Roosenveld are associated with the most prominent families in North America. But Dutch women are also known as cleaning ladies. Most North Americans are confused about the differences among the Dutch, Hollanders, Frisians and Flemish. These diverse groups of Netherlanders came to North America during various time periods and for different reasons, which raises questions of historical continuity and of the extent to which different immigrants from the Low Countries came into contact with one another. Yet ethnic or national groups are usually portrayed as homogeneous, stable entities.

Professional historians contribute to the social construction of such homogeneous ethnic groups, but we cannot ignore the process whereby postwar immigrants who became amateur historians have resurrected earlier Dutch settlers as a way of defining their place in Canadian society. Starting in the sixties, stories about early Dutch-Canadians started appearing in the ethnic press and became topics of discussion for Dutch-Canadian cultural and academic organizations. If it had not been for the writings of postwar Dutch immigrants, the Dutch background of Thomas Edison, or the fact that first surveyor-general of British North America, Samuel Holland, was born in the Netherlands would have remained mere

---

Notes to this chapter are on p. 329-33.

footnotes in specialized monographs.[1] Historical data pertaining to early Dutch settlers would still be buried in little-known archives or as genealogies and family histories. Such archival material and folk memories make up the "raw material" for constructing *the Dutch* as an ethnic group in North America. However, it would be naive to make too stark a contrast between a "real" history of the Netherlands and an "artificial" historiography of Dutch North America. We cannot leave out the equally arbitrary nature of the original emergence of a separate Dutch nationality.

The Genesis of *the Dutch*

The locus and meaning of a Dutch identity have changed over time. A Dutch "culture," centred in Antwerp (in present-day Belgium), appeared only around the middle of the fifteenth century.[2] The focus of "Dutchness" subsequently shifted north to Holland, a region under the jurisdiction of its own count.[3] The seventeenth century, known as the *Gouden Eeuw* (Golden Age), was one of overseas expansion and increased political prominence for a new republic established in that region. From their base in Holland, merchants spread out to establish forts and colonies throughout the world. Despite wars and internal squabbling the seventeenth century was one of prosperity. Spices, cocoa and other produce flowed in to be processed and reexported. Dutch merchants controlled the timber trade and fisheries in the North Sea and the Baltic, and the expansion of polders allowed agricultural production to expand. The Netherlands, particularly the region known as Holland, had a large middle class of wealthy farmers, small town notables and guild craftsmen. Visitors were amazed at the efficient transportation canals, the high status of women (for the time), and the clean streets. Prominent Dutch painters like Rembrandt put their stamp on Western Europe. The seventeenth century is thus seen as the essence of Dutchness. Even today, this Golden Age is a key symbol in the portrayal of *the Dutch*.[4]

Ironically the Dutch nation came about as a result of actions by foreign rulers. A sense of nationhood emerged only after different parts of the Low Countries became a single administrative and territorial unit. Between 1385 and 1433, Germanic people living in the regions of Flanders, Brabant, Holland, Zeeland and Limburg, together with the French-speaking inhabitants of what are today Belgium and Luxembourg, became subjects of the duke of Burgundy.[5] At that time the eastern half of the Low Countries still paid homage to the German emperor, subject to the regulations of the imperial Diet. These two administrative territories, plus Friesland (formerly a small kingdom on its own), were brought together under Charles V of Habsburg who became both king of Spain and German emperor.[6] Thus came into being the "Seventeen Provinces of the United Netherlands."[7] Charles's son, Philip, was raised in the Low Countries—he even spoke a form of Dutch and had blond hair—but his father sent him to Spain to become the new head of a Spanish empire.

Historians have written about the religious and economic factors that triggered a widespread, popular revolt in the Netherlands against their Spanish king. This rebellion, followed by an 80-year war, ended with the recognition of an independent country, ruled by an alliance of various groups.[8] The main factions were the military, with noble connections, and the regents, or city rulers. The latter, who could be described as merchant capitalists or patricians, organized the Dutch East Indies company with its seafaring empire.[9] For several hundred years, members of these upper classes were in charge of a very decentralized country where people from different regions continued to speak their local ("low" Germanic) languages.[10] The development of a single national identity involved the gradual imposition of one official language (*nederlands*). Equally important was the official Dutch history, which excluded Low Germanic-speaking people outside the national borders who were exposed to the influence of High German.

A central myth that defines who the Dutch are is their presumed common descent from an obscure tribe of antiquity known as the Batavians.[11] This Batavia myth allowed the Dutch nation to project its historical roots further back in time. The name was also used by a short-lived republic (1794-1806) set up by a Dutch patriot faction around the time of the French Revolution, and for a town founded by Dutch land speculators in the Genesee region of New York in the early 1900s.[12] Dutchness is also equated with the physical geography of the Low Countries, especially in the northern and western sections where the North Sea has played tug-of-war with the land for centuries. The constant struggle against inundation, and the gradual process of land reclamation through polders, provides the mystique of what it means to be Dutch, and the "essence" of Dutch character. Even the farmers who inhabit the hilly region in the east have learned to portray themselves as members of a maritime nation lying below sea level. Another ingredient of national identity is loyalty to the House of Orange-Nassau, the military leaders during the revolt against the Spanish. The fact that the original home of this minor branch of the European nobility was located in Germany, and that the first William of Orange (the "Father of the Fatherland") preferred to speak French, is irrelevant. The House of Orange[13] (and the orange colour of its banner) became as typically Dutch as raw herring, windmills and wooden shoes. In the early part of the nineteenth century, the Netherlands established a monarchy headed by this aristocratic family when they crowned another William of Orange as king.[14] Although closely linked with Calvinism, the House of Orange became a symbol of national independence and unity for people of all religious persuasion, including Dutch Catholics. You can thus imagine the surprise of Roman Catholic Dutch immigrants when they encountered anti-Catholic Orange parades and Orange lodges in Ontario in the early 1950s.[15]

The tendency to define *Dutchness* in terms of a common language, geography and religion is problematic. It is true that the most consistent opposition to Spanish rule came from the Calvinists, but their original stronghold was in Flanders, not Holland.[16] Staunch Catholics also fought against the Spanish yet continued practising their religion, and Dutch Catholics writers and painters helped to develop a national culture.[17] The Calvinists were themselves divided between a liberal wing and an orthodox wing (see chapter 3). But the meaning of Dutch ethnicity is not to be equated with Christianity. Historians have traced the development of an international Dutch Jewry, based in the Netherlands. Merchants of Sephardic Portuguese background adopted both the language and the lifestyle of Dutch burghers and built a synagogue with the same architectural splendour as their Christian counterparts.[18] Such interplay among linguistic, ethnic and religious elements is no different than the shifting and often contested definitions of what it means to be a "real" American or a "genuine" Canadian.[19]

Unlike the Dutch republic, where both the upper and lower classes were *Dutch*, a more complex form of identity emerged in the southern part of the Low Countries (today's Belgium). After the borders of the Dutch republic were established in 1648, with the signing of the Peace of Munster,[20] the common people of the Flemish provinces continued to speak a kind of Germanic language similar to that of their northern counterparts. However, their masters and rulers increasingly resorted to French. With the reshuffling of borders after the 1815 Congress of Vienna, all the Low Countries (including Luxembourg) were reunited, which made the reunited Kingdom culturally more diverse. However, a larger, ethnically more diverse Dutch nation did not last long because a rebellion in the Flemish provinces resulted in a second nation state (Belgium), internally divided by a linguistic line separating Dutch and French speakers. The original Dutch republic (now a kingdom) became more cohesive and culturally homogeneous. Subsequently foreign newcomers became Dutch through a process of linguistic assimilation and identification with their new homeland, just like people from across the world today become British, American or Canadian.

"Dutch" Categories

Up to now I have been using the English word "Dutch" because that is how people from the Netherlands are portrayed in the English-speaking world. Nowadays most Dutch people also use the term to identity themselves when speaking English to outsiders. However, native Dutch speakers refer to their homeland as *Nederland* and to themselves as *Nederlanders*. Their official language, which is also spoken and recognized in the northern part of Belgium, is known as *Nederlands*.[21] The use of this and other labels reflects an ongoing struggle over group boundaries. Postwar Dutch immigrants in Canada felt ambivalent about the word "Dutch" because it sounded like the Dutch word for German (*duits*), which is *deutsch* in the German language.[22] Among European Dutch people, there is a similar ambiguity concerning the word *hollands*. The Netherlands as a country is frequently equated with Holland, which technically comprises only two of its seven provinces. Frisians and people from other provinces of the Netherlands object if people from the western provinces refer to them as *hollands*.[23] The controversy over such categories indicates that nationhood took a long time to develop and is always open to contestation. Even today there are signs of regionalism. A weak separatist movement exists in the province of Friesland, where inhabitants still remember that they once had their own kings whose sphere of control stretched from the coast of southern Holland to Denmark. Nevertheless, Holland's dominance over the rest of the Netherlands is well-entrenched.

Netherlanders Abroad

The diverse trajectory of emigrants from the Netherlands becomes apparent upon comparing different parts of the world where ethnic and racial identities of populations resulting from colonization or colonialism display great variation. For example, the colonial rulers in the former Dutch East Indies (today Indonesia) did not impose the Dutch language as an obligatory standard of communication.[24] They also intermarried and accorded Dutch citizenship status to Eurasians. Such relative racial and cultural tolerance stands in stark contrast with the intolerance of Dutch settlers towards the inhabitants in South Africa, where they imposed strong sanctions against intermarriage.[25] Yet in both regions, a minority resulting from miscegenation adopted the Dutch language. The preservation of so-called "racial" purity through endogamy, the survival of the languages of the Low Countries and the evolution of Dutch cultural traits vary independently. The Cape Coloured in South Africa continue to speak a Netherlandic language referred to as Afrikaans, although they do not consider themselves, nor would they be labelled by others, as Dutch.[26] In contrast, many Eurasians from the former Dutch East Indies who moved to North America or Europe do identify themselves as Dutch or *Nederlands* (see chapter 10). And a small Eurasian ethnic minority in Sri Lanka (formerly Ceylon) are referred to as "Dutch burghers" even though they speak English and do not identity with Holland. The arbitrary and relativistic nature of the broader category of "Dutch," like all other social labels, becomes even more apparent in the case of the Caribbean, where some islands are still politically tied to the Dutch state. In Bonaire and Curaçao, Dutch-speaking and Dutch-educated African Caribbeans could be classified as more "Dutch" than many acculturated Dutch-Canadians who rarely use the Dutch language.[27] On the other hand, some people from the Dutch West Indies also speak a creole language of their own. Ethnicity and nationality, like language, gender or regionalism, are open to different interpretations which must be explained in their proper social and historical context. It is necessary to distinguish the ethnic dynamics resulting from the imposition of a national identity resulting from a process of primary state formation from those associated with international migration or the subjugation of people through colonialism or colonization.

Netherlanders in North America

Books dealing with the Dutch in North America invariably begin with a reference to Henry Hudson, who charted the North Atlantic coast, including Hudson Bay, while searching for a northwest passage to the Indies.[28] Yet Hudson was English! His ship's crew, like that of most of the Dutch merchant fleet, was an assortment of men of various nationalities. Hudson's name is also associated with the Hudson Valley, the narrow strip of land stretching from Long Island to Albany. The most important urban centre of that region, once known as New Netherlands, was New Amsterdam, now New York City. Ironically, its first settlers, placed there by the Dutch West Indies Company, were not Dutch but French-speaking people (the Walloons).[29] They were followed by Dutch-speaking immigrants who traded furs and supplied guns to the Iroquoian confederacy, or Six Nations people. However, the Dutch settlements along the Hudson and Delaware Rivers were soon hemmed in by faster-growing English colonies on both sides, and New Amsterdam was taken over by the English in 1664. Today the only signs of a former Dutch presence in New York are the names of streets and neighbourhoods.[30]

The American Revolution resulted in the first significant entry of people of Dutch descent into Canada, when Dutch-Americans loyal to the British Crown had to choose sides. Those who did not want to support the rebels fought on the side of the British, and later joined other United Empire Loyalists in Canada. These Dutch loyalists ended up in the Bay of

Quinte, along the north shore of the St. Lawrence river, in the Eastern townships of Quebec or in the Maritime provinces. In the nineteenth century a few well-connected and wealthy families also emigrated to Upper Canada directly from the Netherlands.[31] However this numerically small contingent of early Dutch-Canadians did not leave a durable legacy. To find a stronger Dutch presence in North America during the nineteenth century we must again look to the United States. However, it would be useful to first examine the social and political conditions in Europe that motivated people to emigrate.

The united kingdom of the Netherlands, which emerged after the Napoleonic Wars, was quite different from the Dutch republic of the "Golden Age." Starting in the 1820s, agriculture declined as a result of the imports of cheap grain from America. Simultaneously the mechanization of industry in the southern Netherlands (now Belgium) hurt the artisan-based manufacturing of the towns of Holland. People also experienced a loss of religious freedom. The appointment of a prince of Orange as monarch went hand in hand with the restoration of a state-sponsored Reformed Church. Dutch Catholics, who had been granted complete freedom of religion after the French Revolution, were again relegated to the status of second-class citizens. New sects of orthodox Calvinists also suffered persecution. Both the Catholics of Brabant, then the most impoverished Dutch region, and Dutch orthodox Calvinists became the most enthusiastic emigrants. However, their respective patterns of emigration were distinct. A comparison of the distinct trajectories of these two groups of immigrants to the United States can throw light upon the contrasting patterns of Dutch immigration and identity formation which would later be replicated in the Canadian context.

Dutch Calvinists and Catholics in the U.S.A.

The person responsible for organizing the block settlement of Dutch Catholics in the nineteenth century was Van den Broek. One of many Dutch-speaking missionary priests in North America, he brought large numbers of Dutch settlers to Wisconsin.[32] His efforts resulted in a Dutch presence still visible in the countryside around La Chute. Most of the Dutch people who settled in that part of the West, starting in 1848, were from the eastern part of the province of Noord Brabant and the northern part of Limburg. Both regional and kinship ties played a major part in bringing in these and other Dutch immigrants.[33] However, these Catholics in Wisconsin never formed an ethnic parish, and Van den Broek used to hear confession in four or five different languages. The preponderance of rural Dutch Catholic immigrants from the eastern half of Brabant, and the multiethnic nature of parishes established by Dutch priests in North America are typical features that later reemerged in Ontario (see chapter 8).

The origin and subsequent development of nineteenth-century Dutch Calvinist settlements requires a somewhat longer story. Their original U.S. founders were Albertus Christiaan Van Raalte and Hendrik Pieter Scholte, dissenting Calvinist ministers who brought their followers to America about the same time as the Dutch Catholics were settling in Wisconsin.[34] Within two generations, Dutch Calvinist settlements, with their own ministers, lawyers and craftsmen, were flourishing in Michigan and Iowa. Their presence was more visible than that of their Catholic counterparts since Dutch-American Calvinists maintained a unique way of life and married their own kind. Although they did become increasingly incorporated into American politics, people from these ethnic enclaves in the Midwest established a separate Christian Reformed Church which later had close links with its Dutch counterpart, the *Gereformeerde Kerken* (see chapter 3). From their original bases in the Midwest, orthodox Dutch-American Calvinists gradually spread out all over the continent. Dutch-American ministers from that denomination, who still spoke some Dutch, subsequently played a key role in assisting postwar Dutch immigrants in Canada. Indeed, Dutch-American Calvinists were to play a major part in shaping this unique brand of Protestantism in Canada (see chapter 9).

Calvinist dissenters and rural Catholics were not the only Dutch immigrants in North America. Together they represented about a third of the total Dutch immigration prior to 1880.[35] The history and subsequent fate of other types of Netherlanders is not as easy to establish, since the religious groups, especially those who founded rural colonies, left more records and were able to perpetuate a group identity. Other kinds of Dutch immigrants were more likely to end up in the industrial cities of America, especially in the central and eastern U.S.,[36] yet no matter how strong their national identity or knowledge of the Dutch language, their children were likely to marry across ethnic lines. Nevertheless, all Dutch immigrants, including the Calvinists, eventually underwent a process of linguistic assimilation, as reflected in the declining readership and eventual loss of most Dutch-language newspapers which flourished in the States in the late nineteenth century.[37]

We should not overlook the predominantly Catholic Flemish who also emigrated to the United States in large numbers. Indeed, these Flemish-North Americans ended up dominating the Dutch-language press, long after the Dutch press founded by immigrants from the Netherlands had disappeared; the *Gazette van Detroit*, which resulted from the amalgamation of several smaller Catholic Flemish-American newspapers, is still published today.

Large-scale Dutch and Flemish migration continued until the end of World War One. Between 1890 and 1914, the opening of land in the far

West attracted both Dutch-Americans and new immigrants from the Netherlands.[38] Some Dutch-American farmers settled in the western provinces of Canada, where Reformed churches were established for the first time. During this period, immigrants started arriving in Western Canada directly from the Netherlands as part of a settlement scheme sponsored by the Canadian Pacific Railway.[39] In the United States, the booming industries of Chicago also attracted Dutch immigrants at the turn of the century. Their arrival invigorated a Dutch-Canadian Catholic community already established in that city. For example, Dutch-Catholic immigrants in Rosemond, in southern Chicago, asked for a Dutch priest and called their parish St. Willibrord[40]— a typical Dutch-Catholic name we will encounter later (see chapter 8).

The Dutch in Canada

After 1921 the United States imposed a quota system on immigration. During the twenties and thirties Canada thus again received more immigrants from the Netherlands and Belgium. Starting in 1925, both the CNR and CPR promoted homesteading in Western Canada, resulting in Dutch-Catholic "colonies" in British Columbia, Alberta and Manitoba.[41] In Ontario, Dutch-Calvinist congregations were established in Chatham, Hamilton and Sarnia.[42] In the thirties, at the height of the depression, a group of Dutch immigrant families created their own settlement in the Holland Marsh, which did not take long to mushroom into a prosperous market-gardening region. However, these largely Calvinist Dutch immigrants in the twenties and thirties were numerically insignificant compared to the large number of Flemish (and some Dutch) Catholics in southwestern Ontario. Initially most of these Flemish newcomers came as temporary migratory workers to harvest sugar beets or tobacco, arriving in the spring, and returning to Belgium in the fall (see chapter 10). Many who came later stayed and bought land; hence that part of rural Ontario today still has a Flemish presence.[43]

With the outbreak of World War Two, immigration from the Netherlands ceased. A few Dutch Jewish refugees made their way into Canada just before the War started. Some Dutch businessmen, who regularly made trips to Canada, were left stranded.[44] The crown princess Juliana and her daughter Beatrix, both of whom would later become Dutch monarchs, spent the war years in Ottawa. Dutch men who joined the war effort in Britain underwent military training in Stratford.[45] However, only after the War ended, did tens of thousands of Dutch immigrants from all walks of life stream into Canada. Nowadays, Americans of Dutch descent who want to read Dutch language newspapers, or to meet "real" Dutch people, look towards Canada.

Chapter 3

Dutch Society and the Pillar System

To understand any group of immigrants, we need to examine their country or region of origin. A central thesis of this book is that postwar immigrants from the Netherlands replicated many structural features of Dutch society, despite a high level of linguistic assimilation and weak ethnic identity. Hence this chapter explores the various 'fields' of action characteristic of Dutch society during the fifties and sixties: its politics, the economy and religious institutions. Social stratification, gender and regional or sub-ethnic variations are included to give a more complete picture of the dispositions associated with its overlapping sub-groups. These dispositions—as well as those shared by a whole generation with a common citizenship—are the outcome of previous social configurations. We will therefore look at the broad outlines of Dutch society and at how the actions and perceptions of a diverse group of Dutch citizens were historically generated. In so doing I will also take into consideration the issue of how or if one can identify a Dutch national culture and identity.

Dutch Society

The Netherlands is similar to other European nations, with a constitutional monarchy, analogous to that in Britain, and numerous political parties running the spectrum from right to left, just like in Italy. Its combined free-enterprise and state-planned economy resembles Sweden. Like other countries, there is a mix of Catholics, Protestants, other ethno-religious minorities and people without religious affiliation; but Dutch society also has unique features. Throughout this century, its major social groupings have been segregated to a greater degree than in any other Western democracy. Each grouping not only has its own churches, but separate

---

Notes to this chapter are on p. 333-39.

school systems, its own hospitals, newspapers and radio stations, and even labour unions. Such institutional segregation, or *verzuiling*, has been labelled pillarization by English-speaking social scientists.[1] To explain how this system functions requires an examination of the connections between politics and religion, and how both relate to social class.

Around the time of massive emigration to Canada, after World War Two, the main *zuilen*, or pillars, were the Roman Catholics, orthodox Calvinists (*gereformeerden*), mainstream Calvinists (*hervormden)* and the neutral (non-denominational) bloc. The latter encompassed a variety of smaller religious or political groups. Not all of the *zuilen* or blocs were equally prominent. The first three were almost synonymous with the largest religious denominations as well as being closely identified with their respective political parties. The neutral, or "general," bloc was not as cohesive, nor did it operate as a single entity, although its members sent their children to public schools referred to as *openbaar*.[2] Groups who identified with the neutral bloc did not like the notion of an institutionally segmented society. They were thus united more in their opposition to the system as a whole than through a cohesive philosophy. The neutral bloc also included Dutch Mennonites and Jews, plus those who did not want to identify with any religion.[3] Some political groups, including the socialists—many of whom were secular humanists—likewise closely identified with neutral educational institutions and civil organizations. The same holds true for a smaller liberal group, which supported a conservative, free-enterprise party. They included businessmen with no religious affiliations or with only loose ties with established churches.[4]

People belonging to the major Dutch groups or pillars lived in separate worlds. Their children did not associate with "others" who attended different schools and joined only youth organizations connected with their own *zuil*. A young person was thus more likely to meet, and eventually marry, someone holding similar religious or non-religious views. There were separate health care organizations—the Catholic White-Yellow Cross, the Protestant Orange-Green Cross and the non-aligned Green Cross—and even segregated goat-breeding organizations! Dutch people might only shop in a store or work for a boss from the same denomination. Indeed, unless they belonged to the same pillar, neighbours avoided each other. People belonging to different denominations were aware of each others' presence and could cooperate if necessary. However, members of some groups might never socialize with people outside their own bloc. Only among the intellectual and political leaders of the respective groups would one find a sense of social cohesion, or friendships, that cut across denominational and ideological boundaries.

The History of the Dutch Pillar System

The Netherlands is well known for its tolerance, a tradition going back to the Dutch republic when persecuted Protestant sects and Jews from other parts of Europe fled to the Netherlands. The Dutch ruling regents (see chapter 2), themselves Calvinists, were not adverse to reaching a detente with powerful Catholic families who wielded considerable influence. This pragmatism in religion and politics took other forms, especially in the nineteenth century,[5] eventually culminating in the classic pillar system described above. In tracing the history of Dutch society, we must also be aware of two crosscutting social rifts going back to the "Golden Age": tensions between liberal and orthodox Calvinists and the opposition of Catholics and Protestants. Nor can we ignore the influence of secular humanism, with its roots in both Catholicism and Calvinism.

Historically, the wealthiest families in the Netherlands were associated with more liberal forms of Protestantism. Dutch Jews and Mennonites (*doopsgezinden*), well established in the Netherlands by the early seventeenth century, were also overrepresented among the better-educated and more prosperous segments of the population. However, members of both these minorities have never had a high profile in national politics. In contrast, an alliance of two other religious minorities, Catholics and Calvinist dissenters within the Dutch Reformed Church, initiated a political struggle which culminated in the pillar system. This struggle was partly influenced by class because at one time or another members of both these groups were economically deprived and subject to religious discrimination. What united them was an aversion to a state which they saw as too secular.

Dutch Calvinism

The nature and history of Dutch Calvinism, or Reformed churches, is complex and controversial. For much of its history, the Dutch Reformed Church was a state institution. Yet from its inception, Dutch Calvinism has been the site of diametrically opposed currents. One wing embodies a humanist tradition within Christianity going back to Desiderius Erasmus; the other represents a stricter, more puritanical strain whose roots can be traced back to the Swiss reformer Calvin himself.[6] Chapter 2 mentioned how a group of militant Calvinists played a leading role in the war against Catholic Spain. Calvinism and politics became even more closely intertwined once the Dutch republic consolidated its power. Initially the ruling city merchants and nobles joined the Calvinist ranks wherever the Calvinist minority was already strong. In these regions in particular, Calvinist beliefs served as a rallying force that united all classes in opposition to the

Spanish rulers. From this struggle emerged a strong Reformed Church, whose members were the only ones technically eligible to hold public office in the republic.[7] However, even before the threat of war was over, internal religious differences came to the fore.

The principal dispute involved an academic debate between Franciscus Gomarus and Jacobus Arminius. The former, leader of the Gomists, insisted on doctrinal purity, while the latter espoused a more flexible interpretation of church doctrine. The latter, the Arminians, who proclaimed their views in the 1610 Remonstrance, followed a more lenient form of Calvinism.[8] This controversy provided the symbols used by opposing political factions. The city regents (or ruling merchants) were more sympathetic to the Arminians, as was their main representative, the senior statesman Oldenbarneveld. The Gomists (orthodox Calvinists), allied themselves with prince Maurice of Orange, who ran the military. By 1618 the factional conflict among Dutch Calvinists came to a crisis, around the same time that Oldenbarneveld arranged an unpopular truce with Spain. The Gomists called a synod in Dordrecht (also known as Dort Synod) to resolve the theological controversy, culminating in the expulsion of Arminians from the Reformed Church. In a parallel political coup, Oldenbarneveld was executed. The next year the Arminians started their own Brotherhood of Remonstrants—the first open split in the Reformed Church.[9]

Yet religious orthodoxy did not always dictate state policy. The ruling regents were more flexible than Church leaders. For the Dutch merchant elite, tolerance was a way of assuring the social peace necessary for commerce to thrive. For example, in the southern provinces, citizens had only to declare they were Reformed even if they continued to practise the Catholic religion. Moreover, throughout the eighteenth century, Dutch Calvinism was increasingly influenced by the ideas of the French Enlightenment.[10] Under a short-lived Batavian republic and the subsequent domination by the French under Napoleon, the Reformed Church lost most of its privileges. By the turn of the century, secular state institutions, including non-religious schools, were firmly rooted. All churches, including a now politically weakened Reformed Church, had to operate as private institutions.

Politics and religion again became intertwined after the expulsion of the French. When William I became the first Dutch monarch, he reopened the States-General with a prayer and provided salaries to Calvinist ministers. In 1816 the king remodelled the Reformed Church,[11] which brought a storm of protest from orthodox Calvinists. Stirring of unrest developed into an open secession in 1834 called the *Afscheiding* (Separation). Led by dissident ministers, local congregations held their own general synod to restore the old faith. These dissenters saw themselves as the authentic Reformed Church, now purified and restored.[12] However, the king would not give them permission to hold services unless they registered as a new and separate denomination. Many seceders migrated to the United States (see chapter 2), although some gave in to the government and were officially registered as Christian Seceded Congregations.[13]

The split among Dutch Calvinists in the nineteenth century was more than just a theological squabble. The preceding half century had witnessed a general economic decline compounded by a falling standard of living. Since the official church was seen as an integral component of the ruling elite, poorer and lower-middle-class people used the religious secession to protest an unjust state of affairs.[14] The ongoing movement for reform resulted in a second schism called the *Doleantie*, the Dutch word for "grieving." This split took place when the issue of state funding for denominational schools was being hotly debated.[15] As their movement spread, another group cut loose their ties with the official Dutch Reformed Church (*De Nederlandse Hervormde Kerk*) and also went back to the original Dort church order (of 1816). In 1892, the two secessionist churches united under the name *De Gereformeerde Kerken*,[16] although not all congregations resulting from the earlier splits joined them. The man who orchestrated the union, a clergyman by the name of Abraham Kuyper, was elected prime minister in 1901. This statesman, who formed a political alliance with the Catholics to fight for state funding for both Catholic and "bible" schools, is considered to be the father of the Dutch pillar system. His brand of neo-Calvinism emphasized the need for Calvinists to apply their religious principles to all walks of life and to transform society and culture at large by setting up their own political, economic and cultural institutions.[17]

The *Gereformeerde Kerken* grew rapidly during the next sixty years, although their membership never reached more than ten percent of the population. They nevertheless remained a cohesive segment of Dutch society, whose political influence outweighed their numerical size. These neo-Calvinists voted en masse for the Anti-Revolutionary Party, a party going back to the middle of the nineteenth century, which still existed in 1960. However, there were numerous smaller denominations left over from earlier secessions, and others have since disowned the *Gereformeerde Kerken*.[18] Such Calvinist splinter groups, some of which established their own political parties, could be considered additional "subpillars." These smaller denominations, like the broader divisions within Dutch Calvinism, were later replicated in the North American, and especially Canadian, contexts (see chapter 9). In contrast, members of the once state-supported Reformed church (*hervormden*) constitute one of the larger blocs, making up about a quarter of the Dutch population.[19] This umbrella denomination has various loosely affiliated liberal branches, whose members are more likely to support the neutral pillar.[20] We will later see how they were predisposed to join the United Church once they landed in Canada.

Dutch Catholicism

Dutch Roman Catholics, with their own sub-culture, represented one of the most cohesive social groups in Western Europe prior to 1970.[21] Not only did they have a strong sense of group identity but they rarely married outside the faith. For half a century, Catholics supported their own political party en masse.[22] The clergy maintained a united front by socially isolating their parishioners from contact with Protestants. This was the case long before the emergence of the pillar system, when they were still subject to restrictions under Calvinist rulers. Catholics were technically not allowed to hold civic posts, or join guilds. Moreover, Catholics were underrepresented in the more prestigious professions. Dutch Catholics not only felt isolated from the rest of the republic, which treated them like second-class citizens, but they kept Rome at a distance. Secular priests were particularly jealous of their autonomy against the intrusions of religious orders from outside the country. Yet there was a contradiction between the zeal of the Dutch Catholic clergy who played a leading role in the Counter-Reformation, which meant to rid the Church of corruption, and the pragmatism of this same clergy in dealing with Calvinist authorities.

For several centuries, Dutch priests struggled to retain the traditions of Roman Catholicism in the face of a state-sponsored Reformed Church. In the northern and western provinces, overwhelmed by Calvinism, only committed Catholics remained. In the still predominantly Catholic provinces of Noord Brabant and Limburg, priests imparted a purified form of Catholicism.[23] At the same time they cooperated with non-Catholic civil authorities with the expectation that all of the Netherlands would eventually return to the "true faith." With the establishment of the Batavian republic after the French Revolution, Catholics were granted full civil rights. However, both Rome and the Dutch clergy were leery of secular liberalism and its potential erosion of religious dogma, so few Catholics got involved in public life. Indeed, the reestablishment of the Roman hierarchy in the Netherlands was delayed by several decades due to opposition from both Calvinist purists and secular Catholic priests who wanted to maintain their local autonomy.[24]

Ironically, in 1853 Dutch Catholics again got their own bishops, originally expelled by the Dutch republic, under a government dominated by liberals. These secular statesmen hoped to integrate Catholics into Dutch society. Liberal Catholics, in favour of a more open society, welcomed such developments in the hopes that such integration would further emancipate Catholics as individuals. Nevertheless the isolationist and purist tendencies of the Dutch Catholic Church reasserted themselves when more traditional Catholics joined forces with orthodox Calvinists, both of whom opposed the secular and humanistic trends of the ruling class. After setting up their own parochial schools in 1888, a movement of Catholic emancipation took the form of building its own lay organizations. In 1918 the Netherlands got its first Catholic prime minister and other important public posts began to be occupied by Catholics. The period following World War One saw the full-fledged development of a series of Catholic institutions on the national level, which went hand in hand with a flourishing of Dutch-Catholic literature and a sense of pride known as the "Rich Roman Life."[25] During this period, Catholics continued to be divided along regional lines, and by class cleavages; yet a high degree of unity was maintained under a church hierarchy that supported a variety of educational and other services catering to the needs of its diverse constituencies.

In setting up its own pillar, modern Dutch Catholicism paralleled the emergence of an equally isolationist orthodox Calvinist way of life. While the humanist strain within Dutch Catholicism had earlier influenced liberal Calvinism, the influence went in the other direction in the nineteenth century. The Dutch Catholic Church emulated the political tactics and the strict puritan spirit of Calvinism, even though it disagreed with the content of Calvinism on theological grounds. The Catholic Church in the Netherlands differed from its counterpart in Belgium or Germany in other ways; its bishops have always acted in unison on the national level. The collegiality of the Church hierarchy was an important factor in reinforcing the cohesion and unity of the Catholic bloc.[26] Since the formation of the Dutch pillar system, based on a political alliance between orthodox Calvinists and Roman Catholics, the latter became equal players in all 'fields.' With the setting up of Catholic universities, the previous underrepresentation of members of this pillar in both the economic and political arenas became insignificant.[27] Dutch Catholics also became unanimous in their support of the House of Orange.

Social Stratification

Apart from its religious divisions, Dutch society, especially in the fifties, had an elaborate system of class distinctions, with an emphasis on status—*standsverschil.*[28] Distinctions based on education and occupation (and religion to some degree)[29] were particularly pronounced, and there was little interaction between manual and white-collar workers. Such social distinction penetrated every conceivable facet of life, even in the smallest villages. In the fertile clay regions of the countryside, there was a huge social gap between the *herenboeren* (gentlemen farmers) and their *pachters* (renters) and the *landarbeiders* (farm day-labourers). The latter were not allowed to eat at the same table as their employers, much less attempt to marry "up."[30] Independent or landed farmers in turn ranked higher than factory workers. Going the other way, all farmers were perceived as "lower class" in comparison with "sophisticated city people."[31] Family connections were equally important, especially among upper-class persons who would point out that they came from "good families."[32] A more subtle distinction consists of a kind of reverse snobbery—accusing someone of being *burgerlijk* or *kleinburgerlijk* ("conventional," "philistine"). This elitist label is used by the intelligentsia, especially people portraying themselves as artistically inclined, to place greater weight on education and "breeding" than wealth. The same term might be used by people with aristocratic connections to distinguish themselves from monied families of more lowly origins.[33]

While marked differences in social status (*stand*) coloured all aspects of social interaction, overt class discrimination was frowned upon.[34] Although people openly displayed their religious affiliation, it was impolite to openly discuss class differences.[35] Yet everyone knew exactly where they "stood" in the elaborate system of social ranking in Dutch society through reading such cues such as accent, name, oblique references to one's schooling or knowledge of music and art.[36] People who did not share the same class background were expected to "keep their distance," even if they belonged to the same region, and subtle sanctions were applied against those who did not "know their place."[37]

This system of social stratification is manifested in spoken language. One way of indicating that something is "upper class" is through use of the adjective *deftig* or *sjiek* ("respectable," "distinguished"). People with higher education, capable of using formal speech, are *ontwikkeld* ("cultured," "educated"). An equivalent expression is *beschaafd* ("cultivated," "refined"). A "proper" manner of talking and writing is particularly important. Slightly different pronunciations, such as that of the province of Brabant, is acceptable as long as the right vocabulary and grammatical conventions are observed. But "real" provincial dialects or working-class speech used to effectively shut the door to many professions and better-paid salaried positions. Moreover, although the official language is based on the speech patterns of the western provinces, even there pronunciation and syntax vary considerably within urban areas. The pronunciation considered most prestigious is that of the urban upper classes, and a knowledge of foreign languages has long been a sign of social standing. People who do not live up to these speech standards nor a middle-class lifestyle are referred to as *ordinair*, which has pejorative connotations.[38] Rural and working-class people have internalized this dichotomous view by contrasting their own *plat hollands* ("low" Dutch) to *beschaafd nederlands* (cultured Dutch).

Both the vocabulary and speech patterns of standard Dutch reflect the hegemony of the bourgeois culture that developed in the part of the Netherlands known as Holland. The language of the Hollanders holds sway even in the province of Friesland, which has its own literature. However, Gramsci's notion of hegemony does not refer to a static, permanent state of affairs. Rather hegemony refers to an ongoing process which includes contestation or counter-hegemony.[39] For example, there has always been a nationalistic current among the Frisians, and Frisian is today again recognized as an official minority language within the Netherlands.[40] Speakers of other forms of Dutch likewise question the legitimacy of the national standard of their elites. When conversing with each other, members of economically subordinate classes might refer to more educated, upper-class people's manners and speech as *bekakt* ("posh" or "toffee-nosed," with the connotation of "la-de-da").[41] However, a trend towards the validation of either the Frisian language or regional variations of Dutch did not have a major impact on Dutch society until well after the exodus of the majority of postwar emigrants.

The Dutch system of social stratification and its corresponding linguistic distinctions were perpetuated through schooling.[42] Although all Dutch schools received state funding, some were considered more prestigious. For example, one of the educational institutions in the town of Baarn was considered to be *the* primary school for all of Holland. The secondary school system was even more hierarchical. Its academic programs used to be divided into categories of increasing status: the *Muloschool* (school for more general secondary education), the *Hogere Burgerschool*, or HBS ("High Citizen School") and the *Gymnasium*, a school that emphasized the classics.[43] The university system in turn catered to a small percentage of the population.[44] We must keep this Dutch society of the fifties in mind when looking at postwar immigrants in Ontario.

Despite the pervasiveness of such class distinction, Dutch society has remained largely free of violent social conflict. The continuity of a stable society, and the absence of overt class strife, can be attributed to the late development of industrial capitalism, which resulted in a weaker urban working class.[45] Even when the working class did develop as a political force, the proletariat was organized along the lines of the pillar system. Class tensions existed within each of the three main blocs, but most workers belonged to denominationally based trade unions whose leaders gave their support to their respective religiously based parties. These parties in turn followed middle-of-the-road or slightly left-leaning policies. Only the numerically smaller liberals and socialists represented clearly class-based political groupings. Arend Lijphart has suggested that this crosscutting or overlap of class boundaries and denominationally segregated grouping kept conflict to a minimum.[46]

Gender

Sexual inequality, and the low visibility of women in the public sphere, does not differ greatly between the Netherlands and North America. However, Dutch women are more likely to become full-time homemakers after marriage.[47] This is as true today as it was in the past.[48] Female participation in the Dutch labour force is still lower than in North America.[49] Gender lines are also not drawn in exactly the same way on the two continents. While Dutch women are less involved in the public sphere and in waged labour, there is actually less social segregation by gender in the Dutch home compared to the Canadian home. Dutch women have full control over the kitchen, as in other societies, but men and women spent more time together during and after meals. Although men tend to dominate conversations in the presence of strangers, and in public settings, Dutch couples jointly participate in all social activities involving extended family members, neighbours and friends. During adult gatherings, men and women tend to stay in the same room. Such a lack of marked gender segregation, especially in the home, applied to Dutch households of various class standings. There was thus more overlap in the social worlds of men and women.[50] Dutch men and women also had to consult each other on money matters.

Regional and Ethnic Diversity

Despite common national institutions, plus a uniform system of class distinctions and gender inequality, Dutch society displays strong regional differentiation (see figure 1). Dutch people often depict people from provinces other than their own in terms of stereotypes. The *Drentenaars* (people from Drenthe) are labelled as taciturn, introverted and "hard." People from Gelderland are considered to be more enterprising than their counterparts from Noord Brabant. Similar comparisons are made between people within the same province. In Limburg, people from the south may be depicted as better off than those from the north, who supposedly have an inferiority complex.[51] However, people from each province and sub-

Figure 1
The Netherlands

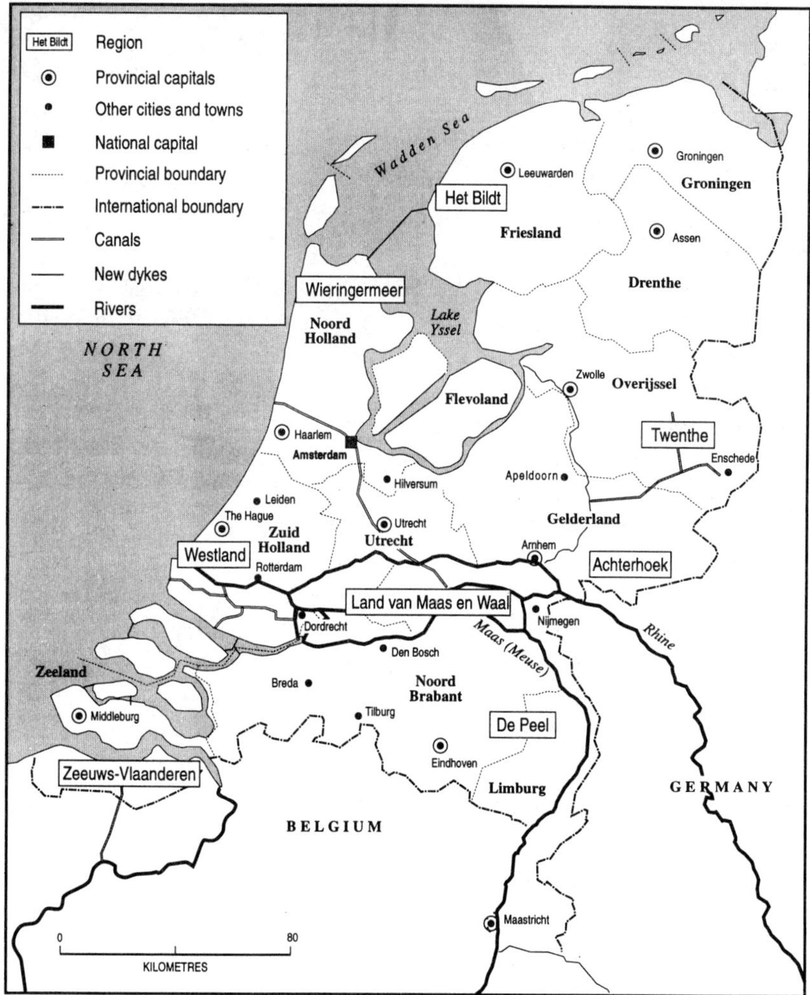

region portray themselves in a more positive light. Indeed, regions like the Peel (in Eastern Brabant and part of Limburg), Twenthe (in Overijssel) or the Achterhoek (in Gelderland) can be socially more significant than their respective provinces.[52] There are even further distinction on the local level. Up until two generations ago, most rural villages had unique local customs, including the wearing of folk costumes, as well as their own dialects, which people spoke at home. Many polders or small pieces of countryside also had strong local identities, even if their inhabitants were divided along class or religious lines.[53] However, Dutch regions displayed variance in level of class differentiation and rural-urban mix. Consequently, some regions or even towns had greater social cohesion than others. People born and raised in such regions were more likely to get together in the Canadian context (see chapter 10).

Sub-national differences also come into play. Friesland has a separate language called Frisian which resembles old English.[54] While all Frisians learn Dutch from an early age, they not only have a strong provincial identity but also a separate national one. Frisians can often be identified by their surnames, which frequently end in *ma* or *stra*.[55] Frisians are proud of their history as a nation, going back long before the birth of the Dutch state (see chapter 2). They consider themselves to be distinct, even more so than people who speak dialects of Dutch. However, Dutch sociologists have argued that the most pronounced ethnic and regional cleavage is not between Frisians and non-Frisians, but between the southern provinces of Noord Brabant and Limburg and the rest of the country.[56] Indeed these two provinces continue to show signs of forming a separate, regionally based subculture.[57]

Ethnic or cultural diversity also reflects colonial connection, especially the long-standing contact with the Dutch East Indies. Chapter 1 mentioned interracial unions. In the past, Dutch nationals stationed in Indonesia, even those of higher rank, married native woman or took them as concubines.[58] Dutch-Indonesians include the offspring of European colonists and members of the Javanese aristocracy, or other non-Europeans. Before World War Two, members of such families frequently visited the Netherlands or received their education in Europe. Moreover, people from other national origins who lived in Indonesia (e.g., French and German, as well as Chinese and Arabs) became Dutch nationals. Their offspring, usually the result of intermarriage with colonial settlers or officials, became part of a separate Dutch-speaking ethnic group. In Dutch, they were known as *Indisch*, and they experienced various degrees of prejudice directed against people with a different skin colour.[59]

While constituting a high-status minority in Indonesia, the Dutch-Indonesians were internally stratified, depending on level of education, income and whether or not their families owned plantations.[60] Occupational ranks ranged from professionals, through white-collar workers to skilled craftsmen. Historically people belonging to this sub-ethnic category had close contact with the Netherlands.[61] Many families, especially in The Hague and Amsterdam, had an *Indische* connection.[62] Apart from native Dutch-Indonesians, members of the Dutch armed forces, career diplomats or colonial administrators used to spent time abroad. Other professionals and business people also travelled to *Indië* (Dutch East Indies) with their families. They would normally come back to the Netherlands, although some preferred to stay in Indonesia. Such Dutch-speaking people with an Indonesian connection represent part of the diversity within Dutch society.

Is There a National Dutch "Culture"?

Culture, as a concept used in anthropology, usually refers to a coherent pattern in ways of thinking and acting, or a shared way of life.[63] For many contemporary social scientists, *a* culture also implies stability, permanency and homogeneity.[64] By using this term, anthropologists can explain the behaviour and attitudes of people in terms of a set of unwritten rules. However, discovering the "basic rules," or describing *the culture* of a particular society—what "really" makes people Dutch—is problematic. Given the diversity of religious traditions, customs and even different languages, one wonders if such an endeavour is even possible. Yet for most people, academics and non-academics alike, the expression "Dutch culture" implies an essence, something all Dutch people have in common. Presumably Dutch culture is something the Dutch have had since the birth of their nation.

Attempts to discover and explain a "culture" are an example of objectivism.[65] According to Bourdieu, such an objectivist perspective implies an outsider's position, or a theoretical stance by someone who does not have a stake in the "game." In the case of Dutch society, "objective" observers have already "figured out" the Dutch way of life. In fact, booklets and magazines put out by the Dutch government—designed to explain the Dutch to the rest of the world—are often written by foreigners.[66] The fact that the accounts of scholars have been incorporated as part of the official discourse of the Dutch state illustrates the 'theory effect' of social science,[67] whereby social science constructs themselves become a part of the distinctions that shape social reality. The rest of this chapter will present such an objectivistic interpretation of the culture of the Netherlands, based largely on several books written by non-Dutch scholars. These scholars have not only learned the Dutch language but have read more original sources than I will ever hope to accomplish.[68] Indeed, most of what I learned from these authors about the basic traits or "rules" of Dutch culture made sense in the light of personal experience and my knowledge of Dutch history and society.[69] However, the reader should be aware that the version of Dutch culture I am about to present, like ethnicity itself, is a product of past struggles for control over meaning as well as an ongoing process of constituting social relations through discourse; it is constantly changing, even though it is typically presented—and believed to be—something that remains the same over time.

What follows is thus a useful, albeit objectivist, account of Dutch "culture" around the time postwar immigrants landed in Canada. While it glosses over many local variations (the "sub-cultures") and the contested and often ambiguous nature of both norms and social institutions, such an account does provide insights into a more broadly defined Dutch 'habitus' shared by a diverse group of people born, raised and educated within a society characterized by the pillar system. This 'habitus'—the mindset, collective memories, body language and habitual behaviour shared by most postwar Dutch immigrants regardless of gender or class standing[70]—subsequently shaped, and to some extent continues to influence, the construction of "Dutch-Canadians" as a social phenomenon.

Family and Household

Dutch households are supposed to create a special atmosphere of cosiness and security. The Dutch word for that atmosphere (*gezellig*) is difficult to translate but easy to recognize as soon as you step into a Dutch house or apartment: lots of bric-a-brac, carpets and pictures; an arrangement of chairs and tables allowing for maximum interaction; and many, many indoor plants. The physical setting of the home plays an important role in shaping the dispositions of Dutch people,[71] or the way their "culture" gets embodied. Such dispositions include a concern for orderliness, privacy, respectability, discretion and seclusiveness. The Dutch sociologist Johan Goudsblom has suggested a convergence between this prevailing family style and the broader Dutch social structure: "But it is plausible that two typically Dutch features, the burgher inheritance and the tenacity of religious divisions, are connected with the strongly introverted family culture."[72] Standard household objects also serve as symbols of Dutch culture. The "typical" Dutch room has some Delft blue plates or tiles, usually hanging on the wall, decorative pieces of copper, table coverings that look like carpets and lace curtains at the top edge of all windows.

A tradition that reinforces the value of family cohesion is the manner of celebrating birthdays. To forget a single birthday of one's relatives and close friends is to break a norm of social etiquette. People automatically show up on one's birthday, without invitation, but the "birthday person" is expected to act as host or hostess. As a handy reminder of this important social occasion, every Dutch household has a birthday calendar. On December 5 everyone in the Netherlands also celebrates a kind of national birthday party dedicated to *sinterklaas*, a solemn-looking man dressed as a bishop with his mitre and staff. Despite the obviously Roman Catholic appearance of this Dutch Santa Claus, it is a purely secular family feast where presents are exchanged. This ritual involves the exchange of poems, teasing and criticizing one another. Even very strict Calvinists celebrate this secular feast, which is separate from more solemn and sober Christmas celebrations.

Dutch society draws a strict line between the household, as the private domain, and the rest of the world. The household is the main setting for social interaction outside the world of work. Market research, and United Nations statistics, indicate that people in the Netherlands spend more money on magazine subscriptions, videos and CDs than on public entertainment. Popular at-home activities, in order of importance, are reading, watching television and listening to the radio or stereo.[73] Such primacy of the private sphere ("home life"), as opposed to the public sphere, presumably goes back to the early seventeenth century.[74] Although the nuclear family (*het gezin*) is important—with the mother at the centre—contact with the extended family and in-laws is equally valued. Extensive social interaction and frequent visiting is possible due to the small size of the country and easy communication, which adds to the *gezelligheid*. Neighbours or friends drop by for morning coffee or afternoon tea, which follow a schedule as predictable and regular as the national train service. In contrast, casual acquaintances are rarely invited to one's home. People do not extend dinner invitations to newcomers or virtual strangers as in the case of North America. Daily meals are strictly family occasions and everyone sits around the same table. In the evenings, when close friends meet for entertainment and conversation, adults and children keep apart.

In this family setting, children pick up basic dispositions: male authority, affection and deference.[75] Scholars who examine childrearing and family socialization in the Netherlands have observed a tendency to combine indulgence, love and attention with an emphasis on self-discipline and "not wasting time." As a result, or so the theory goes, Dutch men or women end up having a strong work ethic combined with an overdeveloped guilt complex. Hierarchical relations between parents and children are also inculcated, forming the basis for the combination of paternalistic control and a high level of class-consciousness and formality so characteristic of Dutch society. In the past, working class and rural youth were expected to contribute money earned outside the home to a common budget controlled by the parents. Theoretically, this expectation even applied to wealthy, upper class families.[76] People are not supposed to waste anything; they are expected to be frugal. Dutch adults seem to have a down-to-earth attitude towards sex and other bodily functions; their humour tends to dwell on scatological themes. The picture just outlined corresponds reasonably well to my own image of most older Dutch people, including those who emigrated to Canada after World War Two.

Dutch people are supposed to be preoccupied with cleanliness, if one is to go by a common stereotype. In the past, foreign observers were amazed at the amount of time Dutch women spent washing windows and floors. Even sidewalks and brick-paved streets were given a weekly scrubbing. This ritual is still found in smaller towns in the Netherlands today. Simon Schama has traced this obsession with cleanliness back to the birth of the Dutch republic, and interprets it as part of the moral imperative of a new nation who needed to show the rest of Europe that its citizens were a chosen people.[77] I think scrubbing and washing are as much a manifestation of the desire to demonstrate one's moral superiority vis-à-vis fellow Dutch. Yet the Dutch are not as conscious as North Americans about personal hygiene.[78]

Interpersonal Relations

Shifting the focus from the household to the social interaction of people in a broader arena, we can explore another norm. Although the Dutch are generally private people, it is not considered impolite to "stick your nose in someone else's business." They expect everyone to be subject to scrutiny. This norm is also reflected in the physical structure of houses; the curtains of living room picture windows are left open to allow bypassers and the people who dwell inside to be constantly aware of each other's presence. The Dutch excel at avoiding being "outdone" in the latest fashion in cars, hobbies or interior decorating, indicating a strong social pressure resulting in uniformity. Another kind of conformity relates to people-made urban and rural landscapes. There are strict regulations to ensure a harmonious and orderly arrangement of houses and streets, and green belts between cities. Architectural styles and exterior colours are not supposed to clash, and even park trees are carefully trimmed and manicured. The physical landscape reveals the same attention to detail and order associated with the classical Dutch paintings or the typical Dutch living room. Huggett even suggests that this emphasis on minute detail is part of a broader cultural pattern of hair-splitting, which leads to numerous religious sects and splinter parties in politics.[79]

How do we then conciliate an emphasis on conformity and order, and the corresponding conservatism, with the reputation of the same Dutch society for religious tolerance and hospitality to refugees? How can we reconcile the bourgeois nature of Dutch society with its humane and sometimes radical tendencies? Are the Dutch schizophrenic or is there some underlying logic, or a cohesive set of rules, that can explain the apparent dual nature of Dutch culture? Since I am myself a product of a Dutch upbringing, I prefer the latter explanation, especially the one presented by an English scholar, William Shetter.[80] The two basic and interconnected rules of the Dutch way of life, according to Shetter, are as follows: "tolerate different fundamental beliefs, but be less tolerant of deviations from universal standards of social behaviour."[81]

Rule One

People in the Netherlands are expected to be restrained and respectful in their interpersonal relations. One should not probe into the personal life or basic beliefs of someone who is not a close friend. Open displays of emotion are frowned upon. This reserve creates the impression of a lack of sympathy. Shetter argues that such reserve allows people with fundamentally different systems of belief to get along with each other. These rules of behaviour are reflected in the Dutch language, which includes the use of separate second-person pronouns (*u* and *jij*). The use of *u* (like *vous* in French) is used to maintain distance and formality with both strangers and people in positions of authority.[82] The use of the "proper" Dutch language is another way of expressing social distance. Even people who already speak standard Dutch (*nederlands*), distinguish a more formal and informal manner of speech. The formal mode, usually reserved for written communication, is also used for speeches and prayers.[83] Unlike North America, such formality is observed during both public and smaller, private meetings or gatherings.

Like the Scots, the Dutch are often portrayed as extremely stubborn people with strong opinions. They are also disputatious. How can we reconcile such traits with the first "rule" of tolerance and respect for different points of view? The answer: the rule does not mean one has to like the opposing point of view, nor that people holding the same basic view cannot quibble endlessly over minor nuances. Ironically, the fact that people are so committed to their beliefs makes it all the more necessary to argue about them. One can easily find examples of hair-splitting among Dutch Calvinists, but the generalization applies to Netherlanders of any political or philosophical persuasion. In fact, vehement debates even occur in the middle of family dinner conversations, giving the impression that the Dutch are always arguing or "shouting at" each other.[84] The Dutch have strong opinions, a trait closely related to individualism and independence. Yet, "arguing" or disagreeing does not break the ties of loyalty that bind family members, a religious faction or the same political party together. Affective ties and rational disputation often coexist.[85] But it is a matter of when and with whom you can argue—that is what the "rules" are about.

Rule Two

Shetter's second rule has to do with intolerance of deviations from universal standards of civility. Strangers who are "too friendly," or "too forward" are likely to receive the cold shoulder or be ostracized. People with different customs and strange ideas will generally be tolerated but held at a distance. The "cold" Dutchman, however, will also go out of his or her way to help such strangers, if they perceive a miscarriage of justice or a need for compassion. Nonetheless, "other people," especially "other" types of Dutch people, are expected to follow the same code of public conduct, which includes obeying the proper rules of civility, etiquette and formality. When someone does not, it becomes not only a right but a duty to point out the errors of the transgressors. This cultural "rule" especially applies to breaches of public conduct or appropriate dress. It is not unusual to see someone on the street being given a "friendly reminder" by a complete stranger that they have just dropped a piece of garbage on the street. In some cases, the criticism or ridicule can become nasty and boorish. This is where you see the Dutch, especially those who are overpreoccupied with small details, at their worst; such self-designated guardians of public order comprise a small but vocal minority. Other Dutch people are likely to regard these boorish champions of Dutch "culture" with amusement, or shake their heads.

The two basic rules, especially as applied to people from different pillars, involve being simultaneously discrete and observant. In train stations, the market or the street, people are not supposed to refer to which category of Dutch society they belong. Everyone is expected to be courteous yet maintain their distance, and one cannot publicly disparage any of the pillars or refer to class differences. At the same time, Dutch people can recognize slight differences in dress or behaviour indicating to which *zuil* someone belongs. For example, married Catholics wear their wedding ring on their left hand, the Calvinists on the right hand. In the past, all one had to do was take a glance to see what kind of a newspaper someone was reading or to what kind of radio program they were listening to figure out to which groups they belonged. This information is important, since one would normally not go out of one's way to be friendly with strangers except if they belonged to the "right" category.[86]

In general, Dutch people do not easily make new friends, even when they share the same religious affiliation. Friendship in Dutch culture is not defined in the same way as it would be in Latin cultures; people only become "friends" after a long period of social contact.[87] Hence Dutch people become suspicious when someone claims to be "your friend" after only a short period of acquaintance—which brings us back to the first rule about keeping one's social distance. This disposition is consistent with the Dutch system of religious and political segregation. However, it would be unwise to equate the Dutch norms for social interaction too closely to the pillar system. Other forms of reciprocal toleration existed prior to this system. One could raise the question whether the same "rules" still apply to Dutch society today, at a time when the parallel institutions associated with segregated social blocks are all but gone.

The reader will notice that I did not address the issue of whether the Dutch national culture exists only in the Netherlands, or in any part of the world where people identify themselves as Dutch. Can someone speaking only English partake of "Dutch culture"? What happens when a pattern of thinking or set of dispositions are modified due to colonization or emigration, as in South Africa or North America, or when national borders get moved, giving rise to a new government, as with Belgium? What will happen as the Netherlands gets increasingly incorporated into a new united Europe? In that case, will future scholars continue to talk about a broader national Dutch culture or will we then have to deal with a whole new "European culture"—or a Dutch sub-culture? How many connections must we find before we can talk about a "Dutch" culture worldwide? There is no definitive answer to any of these questions.

Scholars construct models to capture the social relations and cultural myths that are both part and parcel of the same social reality; yet researcher and informant often share a common discourse. The objective and subjective components of ethnicity are part of a single social reality (see Introduction). Academic writers must be vigilant lest their representation of social reality become another aspect of myth making, and thus a part of the social phenomena under investigation.[88] This caveat applies as much to social scientists as it does to professional historians or specialists in language and literature. Part two of this book will strive to go beyond such cultural reproduction to achieve a more nuanced yet still comprehensive understanding of the postwar Dutch immigrants and their descendants. However, we must first look at the economic and political situation in both Canada and the Netherlands around 1945, in order to better understand the broader economic and political backdrop to a series of events resulting in a massive population movement of an entire cohort of people from one continent to another.

Chapter 4

Postwar Migration: From Holland to Canada

Newcomers from the Netherlands constituted the first of several streams of European immigrants who came to Canada at the end of World War Two. The arrival of close to a thousand Dutch war brides in 1946 was followed by an influx of farm hands. In the smallest villages, Canadians became aware of the presence of these "foreigners" in their midst. Together with other postwar immigrants, these newcomers changed the face of Canada. Tastes in food, music and landscaping were altered within two decades. This transformation of Canadian society was particularly noticeable in southern Ontario, which had hitherto been very British and Protestant in orientation.

In 1946, the ethnic character of Ontario was largely defined by the Anglo-Celtic mix found in the British Isles.[1] Catholicism was confined to a minority of French-speakers, and pockets of Irish-Canadians in the Ottawa Valley or other rural or urban enclaves. Apart from native peoples, the Belgians in Elgin and Haldimand counties, Finns in Northern Ontario, and the German Mennonites in the Waterloo area constituted the only significant "others." Canadians of German descent had to keep a low profile, especially in Kitchener (once known as Berlin). There was open discrimination against Jews[2] and the few Ontarians of African or Asian background were conspicuous only by their lack of social visibility. New immigrant groups, including the Dutch, had to find their place in this "vertical mosaic," a term coined by John Porter to describe a British-dominated Canadian society characterized by ethnic stratification.[3] The postwar Dutch must be placed in this broader context. Their presence reinforced existing stereotypes but radically altered other images. Newcomers from the Netherlands had to cope with what their Canadian neighbours thought

---

Notes to this chapter are on p. 340-42.

of them, while native-born Canadians had to adjust to the Dutch, who by 1961 represented the fourth largest immigrant ethnic category.[4] Starting in the late forties with numbers in the hundreds, then thousands, the yearly influx of people from the Netherlands grew to tens of thousands, to peak at over 20,000 in 1952 and 1953.[5] They landed in all parts of Canada, although more than half came to southern Ontario or ended up there after several years.[6] The Dutch presence first became noticeable in key agricultural regions. However, by the mid-fifties, a variety of different occupations were well represented. The flow of Dutch immigrants declined during the rest of the decade, peaked again at just under 12,000 in 1957 and diminished rapidly throughout the 1960s.

Planned Migration?

The population movement from the Netherlands to Canada was directed and promoted by the governments of the two countries. This bilateral intervention makes Dutch emigration to Canada unique. What prompted their respective governments to act the way they did has been the object of controversy. According to William Petersen, the influx of postwar Dutch immigrants was the outcome of rational state planning, albeit one based on irrational impulses.[7] In contrast, Abe Tuinman points out that the postwar policies of both governments were not guided by any consistent ideological position. He mainly attributes this surge of Dutch migration to a unique set of circumstances.[8] Both authors recognize the role played by chance. To understand the Dutch-Canadian population movement, we thus need to examine many factors. In the case of the Netherlands, it is important to take into account the psychology of a population that had undergone a traumatic period of foreign occupation, followed by a difficult period of economic reconstruction and increasing state intervention. For Canada, and particularly Ontario, the postwar economic situation and policy debates also determined what kind of people were admitted. A historical analysis which takes into account the combined effects of these economic and ideological factors in both countries can tell us why so many people from the Netherlands ended up making their homes in Canada. At the same time, we must remember the role played by key persons who made the right contacts at the right time.

Canada

Immigration policy just after the War was restrictive, and only close relatives were allowed in. Politicians were worried immigrants would jeopardize the economic security of returning war veterans starting new careers, or looking for jobs. However, there were no impediments to the entry of farm hands. According to Petersen, the decision to admit Dutch agrarian immigrants was consistent with a long-standing policy to fill up the empty spaces in Canada with northern Europeans.[9] People from the Netherlands, a country perceived to be essentially Calvinist, fulfilled the cultural and the economic needs of a Canada still dominated by an elite largely of English origins. Dutch Catholics could be accommodated in Quebec. The Dutch government at that time was interested in promoting the emigration of farmers who faced a shortage of land; indeed the Netherlands was the first country to promote this type of selective emigration after the war.[10] In 1946, Dutch officials sent Tuinman to Canada to make enquiries. This resulted in the Netherlands-Canadian Settlement Scheme. According to this agreement, only Dutch agriculturalists could emigrate to Canada, as long as farm sponsors in Canada were willing to provide a guaranteed job and lodgings for a year.

Canada's postwar immigration policy reflects the outcome of negotiations among diverse groups. The decision to admit farm hands and sponsored relatives was the outcome of conflicting views, resulting in a compromise solution.[11] Farm immigrants would not immediately compete for either industrial or white-collar jobs, the social background of the Dutch would enable them to "fit in," and they might eventually become part of the labour pool needed in a growing economy after demobilization was completed. In fact, at the time Dutch agriculturalists were admitted, Canada was already making the transition from a mainly agricultural and resource-based nation to an industrial society. By the end of World War Two, most of the better quality arable land had been cleared and the more dynamic sectors of Canada's rural economy (especially in the North) were lumbering and mining, not agriculture. Most of the Dutch, even those who became full-time farmers, came to regions like southwestern Ontario, which were a far cry from "empty," and which also had the highest level of industrialization and urbanization. At least one thing went "according to plan"—nearly half the postwar Dutch agrarian immigrants stayed in agriculture. However, rather than clearing uncultivated land, they displaced existing farmers.

The takeover of farms by Dutch immigrants, often within several years of arrival, must be seen in the context of broader economic forces. In the forties and fifties, industries in Sarnia, Windsor, Toronto and Hamilton were attracting increasing numbers of rural people. Returning war veterans were more interested in working in the city than going back to the family farm, and prices for farmland were depressed. Dutch farmers were able to step in and occupy this niche at just the right time. However, the ongoing trend of industrialization, especially during the Korean War boom, meant a need for more urban craftsmen and factory workers than farmers. Canada's immigration policy therefore changed in the fifties. After 1952, the government started to admit large numbers of tool-and-die-makers, electricians and construction workers. This change in immigration policy is reflected in statistics regarding the types of people who emigrated in successive years. Between 1948 and 1955 the proportion of Dutch immigrants who worked in agriculture declined from almost 100 percent to just under 20 percent, while the percentage of Dutch immigrants who found jobs in industry rose from a low of 4.8 in 1948 to a high of 32.8 in 1954, then tapering off to 25.8 percent for 1955.[12]

Canada continued to receive many immigrants from Europe in the late fifties, but by the middle of the sixties Canadian employers had to start looking wider afield for new sources of skilled as well as unskilled labour. The government's immigration policy consequently underwent another transformation and the country opened its doors to the rest of the world. However, while removing most of the barriers previously erected against non-Europeans, the emphasis was placed on immigrants with higher levels of education and capital to invest. Even white Europeans found it hard to emigrate to Canada unless they had money. In any case, few people from the Netherlands came to Canada in the seventies. The eighties and nineties saw an upswing of Dutch farm immigrants who came with sufficient means to buy prime agricultural land, while urban areas continued to receive a smattering of newcomers from Holland, ranging in occupation from nannies to physicians. These recent immigrants find a Canadian society very different from that of the fifties—one characterized by official multiculturalism and a much larger presence of "visible minorities" from all corners of the globe.

The Netherlands

The dynamics of Dutch emigration are more complicated. Despite a high population density, Holland had not previously seen the massive out-migration experienced by countries such as Italy or Sweden. Moreover, the Netherlands experienced a high growth rate in the number and size of towns without the changing dispositions usually associated with urbanization. Prior to 1960, its population was more religious than their neighbours, and Holland continued to have the highest birth rate in Western Europe. Such indicators of "traditionalism" were maintained (or had eroded less) due to several factors: the commercial versus industrial nature of capitalist development in the past; the co-existence of intensive agriculture alongside manufacturing; and flat terrain, which facilitated communication among town and country. All these factors allowed for the maintenance of strong family bonds.[13] The low level of "urbanism" (as opposed to urbanization) was encouraged by religious and political leaders, both Catholic and Calvinist.[14]

However, the postwar period witnessed growing tension between the need for ongoing industrialization and the goal of reinforcing community and family bonds. Rebuilding after the devastation resulting from five years of Nazi occupation put strains on economic resources; flooded polders had to be drained, factories and houses rebuilt. Scarce resources were diverted towards a military campaign to reestablish colonial rule in the Indonesian archipelago. When the Netherlands lost the "Dutch Indies" in 1950, a lucrative source of revenues disappeared and numerous expatriates and Dutch-Indonesian families moved to the Netherlands.[15] The country was faced with a dilemma. Only accelerated industrialization, including farm mechanization, would halt the decline in living standards; yet too rapid economic plus demographic growth might erode traditional values and disrupt social stability. Initially the Dutch government, consisting of a Labour-Catholic alliance, did not have a consistent plan.[16] However, trade unions, farm organizations and immigration societies pressured the government to pursue a vigorous migration policy.[17] The idea was to reduce population pressure in densely populated rural areas, which would minimize the outflow of unskilled workers to the cities.

The Dutch government's interest in promoting emigration coincided with the willingness of several countries, especially Canada, to admit farm immigrants. Starting in the late forties, emigration "fever" hit with a vengeance. People everywhere wanted to start new lives in Brazil, South Africa, Australia, New Zealand, the United States and Canada; indeed, between 1946 and 1982 well over 500,000 people emigrated. Canada received more of these Dutch migrants than any other country: 185,000, or 35 percent of the total Dutch emigration to all parts of the world.[18] However, Holland could not afford to export dollars, and severe restrictions were placed on the amount of money that could be taken out of the country. Any emigrant who sold a farm or a business, or had savings, was allowed to buy clothing and household goods, but capital had to remain in Dutch banks. The Dutch government allowed every adult to take with them only a hundred dollars. Before 1952, emigrants had to pay most of their moving costs (including their passage); but restrictions were gradually lifted and, starting in 1956, full passage was paid for all wishing to leave the country.

In looking at Dutch emigration, we should not underestimate the role played by organized religion in a society characterized by pillarization (see chapter 3). Before 1947, the Dutch Catholic hierarchy was reluctant to promote the exodus of its parishioners to Canada or Australia, which were considered to be Protestant countries. In contrast, Dutch Calvinists knew that a nucleus of like-minded (Christian Reformed) church communities existed in Canada and would be willing to receive them. Like their predecessors a hundred years earlier, orthodox Calvinists saw a move abroad as a migration by divine appointment.[19] During the first couple of years, Calvinist agrarian emigrants outstripped their Roman Catholics counterparts. However, the Dutch Catholic clergy was worried about the weakening of religious bonds among rural people resulting from a shortage of land. They witnessed rural migration to port cities like Rotterdam, where church attendance declined rapidly. Gradually they came to believe that Catholic emigrants might even be able to carry out an apostolic mission. Jan de Quay, an influential Catholic layman, also promoted Catholic emigration. A former social science professor and governor of Noord Brabant from 1946 to 1959, De Quay served as chair of the national Emigration Council in the fifties. He pointed out that Catholic immigrants could be easily absorbed into the already existing Canadian Catholic Church and argued that they would better integrate into Canadian society than Calvinist immigrants.[20] Starting in 1951, emigration of Dutch Catholics started to surpass that of their Reformed counterparts.

In the mid-fifties, when out-migration was still seen as an important contribution to help alleviate many social and economic ills associated with the period of postwar reconstruction, emigration started to drop. Worried about this decline, the Dutch government provided financial incentives for those who wished to emigrate. The proportion of people leaving from the industrial western part of the country soon outstripped those originating in eastern rural regions.[21] However, with an upswing in the economy following the Marshall plan, leaving one's homeland became less attractive. The yearly average rate of emigration fell from 31,779 during the fifties, to 11,049 in the sixties, and to 4,813 in the seventies.[22] By the eighties about a thousand people were leaving for Canada every year. During the sixties, the Netherlands had itself started to face a labour shortage and had become a country of net immigration, as they received "guest workers" from southern Europe, Morocco and Turkey.

Why Emigrate?

This question has no easy answer. We need to distinguish between what various Dutch immigrants tell others, what they believe themselves, and the perspectives of "outsiders." Some scholars put more emphasis on the relative causal weight of "objective" factors, such as class membership and demographic trends. Others want to know the "subjective" dimensions or personal motives. Historians are more sensitive to changes over time, pointing out that Dutch immigrants who came immediately after the

War did so for reasons quite different from those who came later. We cannot exclude the "silenced stories," which people would not admit in either public or private. Aritha van Herk has raised this issue. How many jilted lovers or children who could not get along with their parents emigrated to Canada?[23] Given my primary interest in exploring the collective self-image which has become part of the creation of the Dutch-Canadian reality/fiction, I paid close attention to the verbal statements of people I interviewed, most of whom arrived in Canada between 1947 and 1957.[24] There was remarkable consistency in the type of answers people gave to questions about why they left and chose Canada as their destination. The same reasons come up time and time again in publications about Dutch immigration to Canada.[25]

The Trauma of the War and Its Aftermath

One of the reasons for emigration was the bitterness left in the wake of death and destruction associated with the German occupation. Others resented the people who had held positions of power during the Nazi occupation, but who continued to function as politicians or civil servants after liberation. This theme is mentioned in memoirs written by older Dutch-Canadians and in stories written down verbatim by other researchers.[26] Dutch civilians who took personal risks by helping the underground, or by hiding Jews and allied soldiers from the German occupying forces, were more likely to emigrate if they felt they had not been rewarded for their heroism.[27] A more common reason for emigration was the poor economic situation of the Netherlands after the War. Not only was there a severe housing shortage, but people who wanted to start farming on their own could neither rent nor buy land. In some regions, land had already been divided up into tiny parcels, and the criteria for farming in newly developed polders were stringent. One had to have operating capital, technical training and the right connections. Even the fertile new polder regions developed just prior to the War were filling up fast. Farmers could not own land there. There was a lack of jobs in the cities.

The disillusionment of those who survived the War in Europe was matched by the bitterness of civilians interned in Japanese prisoner-of-war camps in Indonesia during and even after the War. Not only were families separated, but those who survived suffered from malnutrition and abuse in squalid camps. When these people returned to the Netherlands, they found that people at home were too preoccupied with their own bitter memories to pay much attention to these expatriates. Within a few years, after the short-lived war of independence in Indonesia, they were joined by Dutch-speaking Indonesians who were expelled or who did like the government of this newly emerging nation. These refugees and immigrants from the former Dutch East Indies often had a hard time adapting to life in Europe. Although they had not all enjoyed the same social status, they had had secure jobs or property. Many were used to open spaces, and to having servants and big houses. In the postwar Netherlands, former functionaries or professionals were demoted or opened up family restaurants.[28] Many chose to emigrate again.

Creeping Socialism

Another reason frequently given for emigrating is "creeping socialism,"[29] or the increasing bureaucratization of Dutch society after the War. Families with few or no children were not allowed to occupy large apartments or houses even if they were the owners. Compared to other European countries, there were more zoning and building regulations. Entrepreneurs had to pass exams and apply for numerous licenses before they could start their own businesses. People pointed out to me that the Dutch government that came to power after World War Two came increasingly under the influence of a small group of dedicated socialists who had been active in the underground resistance movement against the Nazis.[30] While sympathetic to the socialists' role in fighting against the Germans, deeply religious people did not like the secular nature of the socialist ideology. With the emergence of the Cold War, prospective Dutch emigrants were also worried that "the communists" might take over.

Such statements must be put into a broader perspective. The Dutch are not opposed to government regulation on principle. The Netherlands has a long-standing tradition of centralized planning and state control. The physical survival of the country, a third of which is below sea level, requires a complex, bureaucratic system for controlling the flow and level of water.[31] At the same time, people in the Netherlands are not inherently cooperative or submissive to authority, since the Dutch are individualistic and hold strong opinions (see previous chapter). For people whose aspirations for social advancement were thwarted, further government regulations outweighed the benefits derived from restrictions on individual initiative. These people preferred the option of emigration.

My hunch is that the people who benefited most from the welfare state in the Netherlands—those who held steady, secure jobs, single mothers and the elderly—were less likely to see a better future abroad. However, young people, even those with secure jobs, were often dissatisfied. The Netherlands had a well-developed program of apprenticeship for training young workers. But even after full certification, pay scales did not reflect ability or the quality of work. The government, in cooperation with the labour movement, passed laws that adjusted salaries according to age, marital status, number of children and place of residence.[32] Such laws reflected a philosophy that workers should be remunerated as much on the basis of need as effort, a policy that reflected a belief in the importance of reinforcing traditional communal and family values. This was a situation in which those with strong religious convictions agreed with socialists. Nonetheless, even for young couples or single people who believed in the ethical principles of Dutch society, the chance for a well-paid job abroad offered an attractive alternative.

Lack of Space and Family Dynamics

A broad range of people cited lack of personal space as a reason for leaving the Netherlands, where houses and apartments are small due to high urban densities; hence the appeal of the open expanses of Australia or North America, where one could move about freely without constantly bumping into people. This factor continued to be an important reason given for emigrating, even after the economic problems of the Netherlands had been overcome. Indeed, a strong desire for "room" explains the tendency of Dutch people abroad to look for big houses with gardens and to avoid city centres. At the same time the Dutch prefer to combine "open spaces" with the comforts and conveniences offered by small towns (see chapter 6).

Apart from land shortage and lack of jobs, family dynamics played an important role. Many young people, especially those from rural areas, emigrated because that was the only way they could settle down on their own. However, couples were usually required to get married first and spend their honeymoon on the boat trip to Canada. Other engaged couples were allowed to leave together with the stipulation that they would get married within three months of arrival. Another reason given for emigrating was to avoid social stigma when one member of a couple had married someone of the "wrong" social class or religion.

The vast majority of postwar Dutch immigrants came as already well-established families with children. Canadian rural sponsors preferred Dutch families with teenage children who could work as farm hands. Families with older children who could work were in a particularly good position to save up money to buy a farm. Immigrants with teenage offspring rationalized the move by stressing they were "doing it for the future of their children." However, older children with a circle of good friends did not always appreciate their parents' decision to emigrate. Frequently, teenagers who did not adjust well experienced personal difficulties and ended up resenting their parents (see next chapter). Whether or not they, or younger children, would have been better off if they had remained in the Netherlands is hard to say. Certainly, belief in a better future for their offspring provided the moral justification that Dutch parents needed to uproot themselves. The decision to emigrate created other kinds of tensions. Often the husband was more interested in emigrating than his wife or vice versa. Needless to say, the woman usually had less of a say in the matter than the man (see chapter 13). Elderly parents of Dutch emigrants were also opposed to the idea of their children and grandchildren disappearing forever into the wilds of Canada.[33]

Immigration Fever and the Image of Canada

One could add numerous items to the list of reasons why postwar immigrants were motivated to leave the Netherlands. Whatever the motivation or underlying socio-economic factors, the momentum was built up and reached a critical level where it seemed that almost everyone was talking about emigrating. This immigration "fever" lasted for almost a decade. Both Dutch-Canadians and people who remained in the Netherlands frequently mention that many people emigrated just because it was "the thing to do." When asked why they chose Canada as opposed to other countries as their country of destination, the picture becomes clearer. The United States still had a quota system, which restricted the number of people who could enter from any one country. Given the long waiting list, Canada was the closest and best alternative destination. Compared to Australia or Brazil, the trip to Canada took less time, and Canada already had some Dutch settlements. Various people I interviewed also mentioned being impressed by what they had read about Canada.[34] Moreover, most immigrants had at one time or another received favourable impressions of Canadian soldiers who entered the Netherlands with the Allied forces in 1945. The Canadian soldiers seemed strong, healthy and friendly. They were generous with their cigarettes, and most importantly, they were part of an army of liberators and not an occupying force. Many Canadian soldiers ended up marrying the young women they met in Holland.[35] The overall impression of Canadians in the postwar Netherlands was thus favourable. Over the next few decades, after a period of massive population movement, Canada continued to be seen in a good light, but more on the basis of impressions of the many Dutch people who had already become well established in their new homes.

The Institutions Responsible for Immigration

Going back to before the War, private, denominationally based Dutch emigration societies associated with the main Dutch pillars provided information and advice to prospective emigrants. In Canada, similar organizations were founded to assist in the settlement process of immigrants. In 1947 the Christian Reformed Church, which had its headquarters in Michigan, set up a Canadian Immigration Committee. It worked through an extensive network of "home missionaries." Dutch Catholic immigrants were initially channelled through the Catholic Immigration Aid Society, established in 1950. The smaller Immigration Committee for Canada of the Reformed Church of America was started that same year.[36] All of these associations worked closely with the Dutch embassy in Ottawa, which took care of citizens who had no religious affiliation.

The person who played a leading role in coordinating the postwar Dutch immigrants was Dr. A.S. Tuinman, the agricultural attaché of the Dutch embassy posted in Ottawa in 1946.[37] His office received the files of prospective Dutch immigrants from the Netherlands Emigration Service, which passed the information on to the Canadian superintendent of settlement. Once employers were found, the prospective immigration candidates were approved by the Immigration Service of the Department of Mines and Resources, which then notified the Canadian Embassy in the Hague and the Dutch emigration officials. Next, the person or family who wanted to emigrate to Canada received a letter telling them to report in at The Hague for a compulsory medical check. The Netherlands Emigration Service booked passage and provided the name and address of the Canadian sponsor.

Although relatively straightforward in terms of the legal procedures, the logistics of shipping thousands of Dutch families to various destinations sometimes ran into snags. The search for sponsors and the reception of immigrants were largely handled by the private immigration organizations set up in Canada. Although each organization hired full-time fieldmen (and they were all men) to oversee the placements, much of the work was done by volunteers and there were inevitable breakdowns in communication. Dutch immigrants sometimes arrived at the end of a long journey by train from Halifax or Montreal to find no one waiting for them, or to discover that their luggage had ended up in the wrong town. In some cases, a new sponsor had to be located at the last minute. There were also misunderstandings among the three denominationally based immigration societies, but in 1955 they set up a coordinating body, the Canadian Netherlands Immigration Council (CNIC). By this date, most immigrants did not start off on a farm and were sponsored by fellow immigrants living in town, or came with job offers. Nevertheless, not all Dutch immigrants knew where to go when they got off the boat or arrived at a train station. Fieldmen working for different churches, often Dutch immigrants themselves, picked up stranded newcomers and provided temporary lodgings when necessary.[38] Together with other immigrants, they helped to set up houses to act as reception centres in cities like London and Toronto. In other places they would put people up in their own homes.[39] By the early

1980s, the CNIC had for all practical purposes disbanded. Any additional newcomers either came on their own or were sponsored by relatives. In the case of new farm immigrants who were allowed to come to Canada because they were willing to invest their money here, various real estate agents started playing a more prominent role.[40]

Another institution that has had many dealings with Dutch immigrants over the years is the consulate. The consuls in both Ottawa and Toronto organized social events and kept in contact with what was happening in the growing Dutch-Canadian community (see chapters 12 and 16).[41] A network of honorary vice-consuls in smaller towns and cities also acted as advisors to Dutch immigrants scattered throughout the province, especially when Canadians of Dutch descent needed special assistance. They provided their own office space and secretarial help in return for a small percentage of the processing fee on the renewal of Dutch passports. These vice-consular offices still exist today. However, all of these institutions were more relevant for Dutch-Canadians during their first few weeks in Canada, or in cases of emergencies or trips back to the old country. Once settled, the new Canadians had to cope on their own.

Old-timers versus Newcomers

Postwar Dutch immigrants inevitably met the small number of prewar Dutch immigrants who had already been integrated into Canadian society.[42] Known as "old-timers," the prewar immigrants had to polish up their rusty Dutch to communicate with the newcomers. These old-timers also provided advice, although a few did not want anything to do with "the immigrants." The relationship between the two groups was ambivalent. Old-timers had experienced great difficulties during the Great Depression and some of them, especially farm immigrants who had first settled in Western Canada, were real pioneers. Even earlier city immigrants, who eventually found steady jobs or ran small businesses, knew what it was like to go hungry or depend on welfare. These prewar immigrants had little patience for what they saw as spoiled postwar newcomers who came with their crates full of clothes and furniture, or whose travel costs to Canada were subsidized either in whole or in part. Postwar immigrants, in turn, resented what they saw as the haughtiness or arrogance of the old-timers.

The interaction between the old-timers and the postwar immigrants can be compared with that which took place between the Dutch who came in the fifties and more recent immigrants from the Netherlands. Immediate postwar rural immigrants argue that the farmers who have been coming into Canada over the past decade "have it too easy." They resent the fact that such newcomers can buy their farms right away, complain that they drive up the price of land and predict that newcomers will quickly go bankrupt. The older immigrants whom I interviewed commented that the newcomers "are not real immigrants."[43] In contrast, recent immigrants, with their own difficulties and anxieties, sometimes find they are not welcomed by the old immigrants. Except for chance encounters, those who came in the fifties are even less likely to socialize with recent Dutch immigrants who are in turn forming their own networks of social interaction. People who grew up or lived in the Netherlands in the sixties and seventies consider postwar Dutch-Canadians "old-fashioned and traditional." The two groups have little in common since they do not have the same dispositions.

Immigrants often come in waves. If the peaks in the waves are close enough together, new immigrants and those who came before them blend together. In the case of the Dutch, there was one large influx that lasted from 1947 until 1957, with a gradual tapering off in the sixties. The much smaller waves (one in the twenties and another starting in the mid-eighties) were close enough in time to allow for at least some interaction between well-established Dutch-Canadians and new Dutch immigrants (see chapter 16). However, the cohort that came in the fifties—with their pillar mentality—still sets the tone of the debate about what it means to be Dutch-Canadian.

Part Two

Transported Pillars (with Fieldnote Interludes)

Chapter 5

Adapting to Ontario

Initially postwar Dutch immigrants arriving in train stations throughout the province were objects of curiosity. Often they were equated in peoples' minds with political refugees from Eastern Europe (displaced persons).[1] Some Canadians viewed newcomers who did not speak English with contempt, or ignored them altogether. When it came to individual encounters, the experience of Dutch-Canadians was more positive. Canadians who had been in Holland during the war went out of their way to be friendly to Dutch immigrants. Indeed, they were quite generous and helpful; many a Dutch immigrant who was stuck with a flat tire or ran out of gas was amazed at how Canadian neighbours and even complete strangers would help.[2] On the other hand, when renting a house or buying their first car, immigrants might encounter con-artists who preyed on naive newcomers.[3] This chapter will introduce the Dutch-Canadians at the point of entry and a decade beyond, using case studies to illustrate how individuals or individual families adjusted to a new way of life and simultaneously formed bonds with fellow Dutch-Canadians.

Immigrants arriving in the forties and fifties faced many problems, including a shortage of cash.[4] A language barrier presented what seemed like insurmountable obstacles. The task of finding a stable source of income—locating a job, starting a farm or setting up a business—usually involved moving to a new location within two years of arrival. Some immigrants moved to a different farm or town from where they first landed; others had to go further afield before they "stayed put." During those crucial first years, Dutch immigrants learned to communicate in a new language, although it took some longer than others. The experiences of rural immigrants were different from those of city immigrants, although one

---

Notes to this chapter are on p. 342-45.

should not draw too sharp a line between them. Many city people started off working on farms, while farm immigrants often ended up in urban settings. Indeed, their common plight as newcomers to a strange country drew them together. For a while, differences in occupation and class status became less relevant (see chapter 12), although religious divisions continued to play a major role in how Dutch immigrants interacted with both Canadians and with each other (see chapter 7).

Learning English

Some Dutch immigrants already had a working knowledge of spoken English, reinforced through previous contact with Allied soldiers (see chapter 4) or listening to short-wave radio broadcasts. However, most did not, even after taking last-minute crash courses. Even high school graduates had a purely theoretical understanding.[5] Like other newcomers, most of the Dutch immigrants learned through a process of trial and error, although some attended evening language courses. Most men, as well as unmarried women entering the labour force, learned or improved their English in the workplace, while adult women who stayed at home picked it up from their school-age children or by watching television. How quickly and how well Dutch immigrants learned a new language depended on age and what they had learned prior to emigration. They were all able to express themselves in English after less than a decade in Canada. However, many Dutch-Canadians today still speak with a noticeable "accent,"[6] a source of frustration or embarrassment in a society where one's manner of speaking is still a part of a system of ethnic stratification (see chapter 12).

The Farm Immigrants

The farm immigrants came into close social contact with their sponsors before they could communicate effectively. What transpired during the first year of working in agriculture varied greatly. According to a standard contract, each family received $48 a month plus a house to use in return for doing chores in the barn and helping out in the fields.[7] How this arrangement worked out depended on the personality and economic backgrounds of both immigrants and employers. Although farm immigrants were for the most part genuine country people, a few sponsors were disappointed to discover that their new farm hand did not have prior experience. Sometimes the Canadian employer might be a bachelor with a drinking problem and a tiny operation, while his Dutch farm hand had been a prosperous, independent farmer at home. In other cases, a Dutch farm hand might end up as one of several employees working for an innovative Canadian farmer on a modern, efficient operation.

The stories told by Dutch immigrants include both acts of great kindness and outright exploitation. Jaap De Boer is an example of someone who was lucky. A former farm manager with a wife and two young children, Jaap emigrated in 1949. In Montreal they were personally greeted by their employer, a wealthy engineer of Scottish descent who owned a beef farm in the Laurentians. The family moved into a house with large closets filled with linen and dishes, running water and electricity. They could keep all the eggs they wanted and Jaap was allowed to use the horses to go to town. Within two years his salary was raised to $80 a month. During the third year, the family moved to Norwich, in southern Ontario, where a niece's husband got Jaap a temporary job in a factory. Within a year, he became a foreman for $165 a month on a farm near Innerkip, where he was allowed to grow his own hay for the two heifers he brought with him. Five years later he bought a farm, under the condition that he continue to look after the cattle of his former employer. His salary paid off the farm in instalments. Jaap continued to build up his own herd of dairy cattle and eventually bought more land. Meanwhile Jaap's wife picked tobacco so they could buy home appliances.[8]

Another family, a couple with ten children who emigrated in 1952, represents the opposite extreme. The father, who grew up on a farm near Leiden, had already moved into a Dutch urban environment, but saw no future for his children. Their second oldest son, who came along reluctantly, told me their story in the company of his now-elderly mother. They all started working in a dairy and cash-cropping operation in Linwood, near Kitchener. That farm was one of ten owned by an executive of a major U.S. airline. The owner, who bought and sold land for speculative purposes, kept his farms in minimal working condition. The Dutch immigrant family, with five able-bodied workers, received $150 a month, with none of the extra benefits originally promised. They were cheated by the farm manager and, to make things worse, the fieldman who had found their sponsor pocketed $10 a month. These injustices made them leave the farm before the year was over and they moved to Wingham, where the father and sons started working in factories and the only daughter got a job working in a store. A year later they all moved to Plattsville, closer to the Kitchener job market, and the father returned to doing odd jobs for local farmers. At one point he even ploughed by hand for a Mennonite farmer. His next job was working in a fruit orchard near Vineland. With the help of the children, this couple eventually bought a small fruit farm in Virgil for $30,000. The family sold the farm 12 years later for a small profit, only to witness the new owner in turn sell the land for three times as much.[9]

Another hard luck story involves a family sponsored by a farmer in Lucan, near London, in 1950. When their crate of personal belongings was delivered a month after their arrival, the farm owner noticed that his farmhand had brought over a large number of carpentry tools. From that day on, instead of working in the fields, the Dutch immigrant and his sons had to start building a circular stairway in the farmer's home, plus a new barn. When the barn was finished, he hired out the Dutch boys and their father to various neighbours. The farmer charged a dollar an hour for their skilled labour, but the Dutch family was still paid the original $45 a month. Their sponsor would drive them to their work site, bring them home for lunch, and then drive them off for another shift which often lasted until late into the evening hours. This situation ended when neighbours notified immigration authorities.[10]

Most cases lay somewhere in between these extremes. However, even when treated fairly, living conditions in rural Ontario were primitive by European standards. Canadian farmhouses in the late forties were not painted and did not have plumbing or electricity. The Dutch family was often given a small, wooden-frame building without insulation or a converted chicken coop. Adaptation was especially challenging for women who had small children and little contact with neighbours. Isolation and lack of public transport further restricted the limited autonomy of immigrant women who were used to easy access to stores within walking or bicycling distance in the old country. Dutch families, spread out over a wide area, also found it difficult to get together in a place of worship of their choice and depended on rides to church from neighbours or employers. Others had to venture long distances in rusty old cars over gravel roads filled with potholes.[11] The first winters were particularly hard. On the other hand, food was inexpensive. Although themselves poor, farm sponsors often helped out their Dutch employees. Some Canadian farm couples, if they were older or did not have children, ended up handing over their entire farm operation to the family they had sponsored in return for a small down payment and a private mortgage at 5 percent interest!

Not all Dutch rural immigrants worked in agriculture or on only one farm. Sometimes the parents would stay with their sponsor, while their children were sent off to earn money in town or on other farms. Older children were often joined by their mother in such seasonal activities as blocking beets or working in tobacco fields. In parts of southwestern Ontario, both men and women worked part-time in local canneries. In this way, the family could earn extra money to start saving. In some cases, the family would quit the farm as soon as they found better-paid work in a nearby factory, realizing they were not legally bound to stay with their farm sponsor for an entire year. Most of the Dutch agrarian immigrants aspired to start farming on their own, but they soon discovered that Canadian factory workers received good wages. An industrial job made it possible to more quickly save money needed to start farming. Such immigrants bought a piece of land and an old house to start farming part-time. Sometimes a mother or an older son were put in charge of such operations while the father worked elsewhere. The majority of full-time farmers whom I interviewed had thus spent some time working in the city. However, not all Dutch immigrants who initially dreamed of owning farms became independent farmers. Some decided to set up non-farm businesses. An even greater number did not want to give up a steady and secure source of salaried income for the risks and hard work involved in farming on their own. However, even if they did not become full-time farmers, Dutch rural immigrant families invariably bought houses with big yards where they could plant their own vegetables and flowers.

The immigrants who stayed in rural Ontario continued to interact with non-Dutch neighbours. After overcoming the initial language barrier, a process of mutual adjustment was marked by ambivalence on both sides. Protestants welcomed the Dutch with open arms, but their enthusiasm waned when "the nice Dutch families" turned out to be "Papists." Even when religious differences did not get in the way, the Dutch were seen as having strange customs, such as putting carpets on their tables, cutting down trees in the fence rows, speaking in loud voices and taking religion too seriously.[12] At the same time rural Canadians admired their work ethic, but were puzzled about how their Dutch neighbours got ahead so quickly. These quaint families with their funny clothes at first looked undernourished and spoke little or no English. The Dutch seemed to eat nothing but potatoes, and the women spent endless hours scrubbing windows. You can imagine the surprise of Canadian farm sponsors when a huge crate appeared on the doorstep several weeks or months later. Out came brand new bicycles, furniture and clothing—sometimes a prefabricated house! These were the goods each immigrant was able to ship over with whatever money was left over after selling the home farm, or cashing in their life savings before emigrating (see chapter 4). A year or two later, the Dutch family bought a farm and before you knew it, they had planted flowers all over the front yard and were fixing up the old barn.

Regional Case Studies

The Dutch had a hard time explaining who they were and where they had come from. In Simcoe county, where Dutch immigrants started off living and working on farms in and around the village of Stroud (south of Barrie), Canadians who dominated community life looked upon their Dutch hired hands with a mixture of pity and condescension; many a Dutch family, struggling to get established, would receive a food basket at Christmas or a loan from the local credit union. The Dutch men, some of whom had been village notables or prosperous farmers in the old county, had to swallow their pride. They were not used to working as hired hands or being seen as "the poor." Their Canadians neighbours in turn could not understand why Dutch families did not accept their offer to join the local Presbyterian church. The Dutch Calvinists wanted to set up their own churches, and about half the Dutch immigrant families around Stroud were Dutch Catholics![13] After several years, these Dutch Catholic farm families moved to Phelpston, on the other side of Barrie. Phelpston had once been a thriving Irish-Canadian settlement, but many farmers there had gone bankrupt during the War. The Dutch immigrants were able to buy rural properties for low prices, and more farm families followed, in search of affordable farms. In Phelpston they had access to a Catholic church and a separate school. These Dutch farm families worked hard, took jobs on the side, and started building up their own family farms. In one decade, the poor Dutch immigrants who had landed in Stroud—subject to charity handouts—had turned into "those rich Dutch buggers who take over our land."[14] Dutch Protestant farmers established farm operations around the villages of Thorton, Alliston and Stayner.

The picture of the successful Dutch-Canadian farmer has become an image firmly planted in the minds of Canadians of both Dutch and non-Dutch descent. It is true that many Dutch-Canadian farm immigrants ended up among the most prosperous full-time farm operators in Ontario (see chapter 19). However, not all Dutch farm immigrants represent success stories. Some of those who took the risk of becoming "their own boss" ended up selling their farms. Moreover, some of those who survived continued to struggle right up to retirement. A Dutch-Canadian farmer on Wolfe Island told me he stayed in farming "because I am not smart enough and young enough to do anything else."[15] Even farmers who built up successful commercial farms later wondered if all the hard work and sacrifice was really worth the effort.[16] Moreover, the offspring of farm immigrants often received little education because they had to work out or help on the family farm.[17] When they entered adulthood, many of them were able to set up their own farm operations with their parents' help, but those who did not become farmers had few skills to offer in an increasingly competitive job market. They joined the unskilled labour force of the small towns and cities of Ontario.

From Farm to City in Canada: Wellington County

The move from country to town replicated what was already taking place in the Netherlands at the time of postwar emigration.[18] Wellington county can serve as a case study of Dutch rural-urban migration, simultaneous with the takeover of existing farms by Dutch rural immigrants. A large number of rural Dutch immigrants, many from the province of Drenthe, started off as farm hands or tenants in the area of Guelph (Wellington county). Within a decade of their arrival, these predominantly Dutch Calvinist immigrants founded two Reformed churches (affiliated with different denominations) in the village of Drayton. Forty years after the first Dutch family landed in this area, a quarter of the total population of the township of Maryborough, which includes the villages of Drayton, Moorefield and Rothsay, was of postwar Dutch descent.[19] However, many of these Dutch-Canadians had only indirect ties with the farming community. By 1986, 27 percent of the inhabitants in the village of Drayton (not including people living in the surrounding countryside) were of Dutch descent.[20] This trend towards urban occupations can be more clearly detected in the transfer of people to the county seat, Guelph.

Few Dutch farmers became established in the rural area surrounding the city of Guelph, where people of Dutch descent constituted between 2 and 5 percent of the largely rural townships of Puslinch, Eramosa, Erin and Nichol in 1986. The agrarian immigrants who had originally started working as hired hands in this region moved to the Drayton area to start their own farms.[21] However, the city of Guelph itself pulled in Dutch farm immigrants who had originally landed in townships in the northern part of Wellington county. Various industrial plants, two hospitals, the city works department and a major reformatory were the major employers of Dutch agrarian immigrants who became janitors, assembly-line workers, guards and gardeners. The University of Guelph also employed rural Dutch immigrants to work on its experimental farms, as lab assistants or as part of its staff of maintenance workers. The city attracted other Dutch immigrants who came directly from Dutch towns and cities or who had first landed in other parts of Canada.

The influx of agrarian immigrants into Guelph, mostly of Protestant background,[22] stimulated the growth of three Dutch Calvinist churches: Christian Reformed, Canadian Reformed and the Reformed Church. However, these congregations, did not remain rural for long. Within a decade farmers came to represent a tiny minority in these three congregations, which today have several hundred families, or close to a thousand people. John Derksen, who served as minister of the First Christian Reformed Church of Guelph from 1956 to 1977, witnessed the transition of his congregation from a predominantly rural to an urban church.

> In 1957, most members of my congregation lived in the countryside, outside the city, and that was true for the Kitchener-Waterloo church too. The second generation started moving to town to find work and many people also

moved in from places like Listowel. It was the same industrialization process I saw in the Netherlands after the War.[23]

The process of adaptation and adjustment to both rural and city life did not always go smoothly. While Canada was a land of opportunity, Dutch agrarian immigrants got ahead by working long hours, which meant that children did not get as much attention as they deserved. Older children first had to leave their friends behind, and worked hard to help their parents. The resulting emotional and financial hardships were particularly difficult for orthodox Calvinist families who needed to make sacrifices to build churches and support their own schools; it was not unusual for them to give 10 percent of their income to the church.

The psychological pressures were particularly felt by young couples who had been teenagers when they came to Canada. In the Guelph area, about a dozen such young people became alienated and left their churches in order to join a religious cult. This cult, initiated by a young Dutch immigrant, was part of a broader charismatic movement that cut across all denominations. Its emphasis on a direct experience of religion conversion and messianic zeal appealed to a generation of transplanted young Dutch-Canadians brought up in a religion that was too rational and did not meet their emotional needs. Henk Katerberg, who came to Canada as a young teenager with his widowed mother, was in his early twenties when he left the Christian Reformed Church in 1969 and began recruiting members for such a charismatic group in the Guelph region. He was trained as a carpenter in Holland and was already working as an independent contractor when his life changed dramatically.[24] This visionary persuaded a small group of young Dutch-Canadian couples to sell their belongings and set up a small commune, just outside Guelph, which they called the Elora Fellowship.[25] As a result of this charismatic movement, both Dutch Calvinist congregations lost members.[26]

The City Immigrants

Starting around 1952, an ever-increasing number of people emigrated directly from the Netherlands to Canadian urban centres (see chapter 4). We can again use the city of Guelph as an example.[27] Apart from the ongoing influx of Dutch from its rural hinterland, Guelph received skilled workers, small businessmen and a few professionals who used to live in small towns and cities in the Netherlands.[28] Consequently, the make-up of the Dutch-Canadian population of Guelph became more diversified. By 1970, it had a physician who was trained in the Netherlands, several Dutch professors who worked at the University of Guelph and about a dozen stores and other types of businesses run by Dutch-Canadians. Others entered the work force as sales clerks, nurses, secretaries and skilled labourers. In 1986 the total number of Canadians of Dutch descent still represented fewer than 3 percent of the fast-growing city of Guelph,[29] but in numerical terms, there were over two thousand Dutch-Canadians living within the city boundaries, compared to fewer than 200 in the village of Drayton.

The Dutch-Canadian population of Guelph and other cities became more varied in terms of religious affiliation. An increasing number of Dutch-Canadians who had belonged to more liberal urban churches in the Netherlands entered directly into mainstream Canadian churches. At least one non-Dutch Protestant church in Guelph even got a minister trained in Holland (see chapter 7). Moreover, the city started to receive Dutch immigrants who were Catholics and people with no religious affiliation. These diverse immigrants started coming into contact with each other through a purely secular Dutch-Canadian club, which organized dances and cultural events (see chapter 16).

On average, city immigrants were better educated than their rural counterparts.[30] They had technical training, or knew about bookkeeping and other business skills. Some who had run businesses in the Netherlands came to Canada with the aspiration of setting up similar businesses, even if they had not done well at home. Numerous bakers who ran the plethora of corner-store pastry shops in the Netherlands moved to Canada because they were being squeezed out in the process of concentration and mechanization (see chapter 14). Many of them were unable to fulfil their dreams in Canada, although most did eventually find some form of employment related to their own trade (see chapter 19).[31] Others started their own bakeries and one even became a millionaire after introducing new varieties of cookies and pastries that appealed to the Canadian palate. Nevertheless, the typical city immigrant was more likely to be a semi-skilled worker who also became a salaried employee in Canada. Such urban workers came from all over the Netherlands and from a variety of religious (or non-religious backgrounds). In Ontario, most ended up in larger Metropolitan centres.

In larger urban settings, Dutch immigrants were likely to rub shoulders with other newcomers of various ethnic backgrounds. Unlike their rural counterparts, the typical city immigrants had less face-to-face contact with "real Canadians" on a social level. In the larger, more impersonal, urban context, newcomers from the Netherlands were likely to be perceived, and learned to see themselves, as part of a broader immigrant population, while simultaneously setting up more specialized ethnically defined organizations. However, many Dutch families who settled on the outskirts of large cities encountered the same problems of physical hardship and isolation as those who lived on farms. Women raised in a Dutch urban, middle-class environment had to become very resourceful. For example, one educated city woman with five children had to boil well water and then pour it into a bathtub as the only way of doing her laundry in a small four-room house without running water located in the vicinity of the town of Pickering. When her husband lost his first job, she took a low-paid job in a local community hospital in Ajax, leaving her oldest child in charge of the younger children. She also worked part-time as a cleaning lady in a nearby farmhouse, something she had to confess in a letter to a wealthy aunt in the Netherlands who asked in a letter whether her niece had "found a girl to help in the house."

Dutch Immigrants in Northern Ontario

Immediate postwar Dutch-Canadians first arrived in the farm country and cities of southern Ontario. However, some eventually moved to northern Ontario. A more detailed examination of the regional municipality of Sudbury, with its outlying villages (Coniston, Lively, Blezard Valley, and Chelmsford) can throw further light on the development of a small Dutch-Canadian community in this part of the province. Nowhere in the region of Sudbury do Dutch-Canadians today represent more than 1.5 percent of the total population,[32] nor is there a Dutch store or a church with strong Dutch connections. Nonetheless, even though the region of Sudbury only has approximately 200 Dutch-Canadian families, a large proportion of first generation Dutch immigrants know each other. These Dutch-Canadians make up an informal network of contacts with a modest level of cohesion.[33]

Dutch immigrants started moving to Sudbury around 1950, mainly from other parts of Ontario. At that time the city was a service centre for a booming, but polluted mining zone;[34] wages were high, especially in mining and construction. The Dutch immigrants who initially came to Sudbury were single men, or men who left their families in southern Ontario. They came to earn money, not to settle down. I have met at least a dozen Dutch-Canadians in southern Ontario who at one time or another worked in Sudbury on a temporary basis to save enough earnings to make down payments on farms in southern Ontario, or in the Ottawa Valley. By the mid-fifties, the first Dutch-Canadian couples settled in the city and started renting out rooms to other newcomers of Dutch background.[35]

Although the majority of Dutch immigrants stayed in Sudbury for only a year or two, an increasing number obtained full-time jobs working for Inco (formerly the International Nickel Company) or Falconbridge. Some worked underground while others got jobs in the smelters. These men sent for their wives or fiancees from southern Ontario or took a trip to Holland to get married. Such couples bought or build their own homes, preferably on the edge of a lake or near a wooded area, in nearby villages or what were then the outskirts of Sudbury. For example, one young couple from the province of Noord Brabant built a house near Whitefish, along highway 17, a fifteen-minute drive from Sudbury. He worked in the mines while she got a part-time job in one of the hospitals. There were a few other Dutch families nearby, but their closest neighbours were French-Canadians, and the francophone women insisted that she teach them her still-broken English. This Dutch family also owned a small woodlot where they put up a trailer camp, which provided extra income for their children who worked there during the summer.[36] Most Dutch immigrant families in the Sudbury area settled just north of the city, in places like Val Caron and Chelmsford, where many established hobby farms.

The vast majority of Dutch-Canadians who stayed in Sudbury were Catholics. Not that Dutch Calvinists had an aversion to living in Northern Ontario. On the contrary, a rural settlement of Dutch Calvinists was established around the same time near Thunder Bay.[37] A small group of Dutch Calvinists also attempted to found an agrarian settlement near the town of Cochrane.[38] It just so happens that no Reformed minister ever came to Sudbury, nor was there ever an attempt to set up their own congregation there. In contrast, Sudbury already had a large Catholic population, albeit French-speaking, and the Catholic bishop for the diocese of Sault Ste. Marie (to which Sudbury belongs) recruited a Dutch priest from the Netherlands to come to Northern Ontario.[39] This bishop, who had previously visited the Netherlands, found Father Kaptein, a former Trappist monk originally from the Achterhoek region. Father Kaptein arrived in 1952 to minister to the Dutch immigrants. The Dutch Catholic immigrants in the Sudbury area, mainly from the provinces of Noord Brabant and Limburg, used to attend his masses in Christ the King Church and they formed their own choir.[40]

Although the Dutch in Sudbury were spread out over a large area, they kept in touch with one another. A group of young men who worked at the Creighton mine even formed their own soccer team. As their families started growing, the older children also mingled; a Dutch-Canadian farmer in the valley built on his property a race track that became a focal point for young people from all over northeastern Ontario. Those who lived and worked in the city organized a social club in the late sixties, after they received a visit from a Dutch-Canadian in southern Ontario who offered to provide cheap charter flights to the Netherlands for members of such clubs.[41] Although the Dutch priest played a minor role in such organizations, these largely secular activities attracted Dutch-Canadians who were not of Catholic background (see chapter 16).[42] As Sudbury grew, new economic opportunities enabled some men and women to go into business on their own. Some started selling real estate, while others opened up nurseries or became contractors. One newcomer, who came in the seventies, set up a fish restaurant. The most successful business was founded by a young man whose father owned a candy store in the city of Leeuwarden, in Friesland. Today he owns a chain of convenience stores called Skippy Milk. This young man started off working in the tobacco fields near London in 1949 and then joined a group of bachelors looking for work in the mines in Sudbury. After working in the mines, he got a job as an assistant to an engineer, worked his way up to supervisor of Coniston's sewage department and then moved to Chelmsford to become a store manager.[43]

The upward mobility of earlier immigrants caused jealousies and frictions with those who came somewhat later and who wanted to emulate their example. According to one informant, such frictions were the main cause for the Dutch club's breakup. In the sixties and seventies the occasional Dutch newcomer still came to Sudbury, but they had little to do with one another or with the older immigrants, even if they were aware of their existence. Several Dutch professors were recruited to Laurentian University directly from Europe, and a single mother, who initially emigrated to Canada in 1940 at the age of seven, came to work as a scriptwriter for the local radio station. Eventually she set up her own business. In 1991, the original core of postwar Dutch immigrants was getting older and met each other only at occasional weddings or funerals. Father Kaptein was the chaplain of a largely Italian-Catholic parish in Coniston. The offspring of the remaining Dutch immigrants have since scattered throughout the region, and their descendants are gradually being absorbed into either the English- or French-speaking populations of Northern Ontario.

A small number of Dutch people, some of whom started working in the bush, also ended up working and living in such mining towns as Elliot Lake, Timmins and Kirkland Lake. However, unlike people of Finnish and Swedish descent,[44] Dutch-Canadians never comprised a large proportion of northerners (see chapter 6). Those who stayed usually maintained contact with Dutch-Canadian friends or relatives either in the Netherlands or in southern Ontario. Unlike many places in southern Ontario, the Dutch-Canadians "in the north" have remained largely unnoticed.

In general, the postwar Dutch immigrants who ended up in Ontario adapted well to Canadian society, regardless of their background or time of arrival. Even first-generation Dutch immigrants consider themselves to be "ideal Canadians," with a low level of ethnic identity retention (see chapter 18). Their successful transition to a new country should not come as a surprise given the high level of education and the standard of living of northwestern Europe (see chapter 19). Nevertheless, these same Dutch immigrants inadvertently replicated many of the social structures and cultural values of their country of origin, notwithstanding a rapid process of linguistic assimilation and economic integration. The dispositions they had acquired in the Netherlands were for the most part in tune with the social structures of Canadian society, thus enabling most men and women to transfer the 'social' and 'cultural capital' they had already acquired at home, school or place of work. Their greatest drawback, which often prevented Dutch immigrants from eventually finding a position in Canadian society higher than what they could have reached at home, was the right kind of 'linguistic capital' (see chapter 12). Moreover, even when they had acquired or improved their English, a Dutch 'habitus' was not always suitably aligned to match all 'fields' of social action, particularly when it came to religion and politics. The process of immigrant adaptation sometimes required creative solutions and modifications of both ingrained dispositions and patterns of social interaction. At the same time, despite a conscious effort to become "typical Canadians" (see chapter 18), postwar Dutch immigrants ended up replicating many of the patterns of thought and action they brought with them from the Netherlands. Such social and cultural continuity can even be detected in the spatial distribution of Canadians of Dutch descent once they had finally "settled down."

Fieldnotes Interlude

5.1 *Excerpt from an interview with a real estate agent, conducted on July 2, 1990, in Sudbury*

I come from Pijnacker, which is near Delft. There was no high school in that place, so I attended the HBS in Rotterdam, as one of a few girls from that village to get that kind of education .... I was 19 years old when my husband proposed to me. He didn't really propose, but asked me whether I wanted to go and join him in Canada, just two weeks before he left to go back to Canada. My parents said there was no way I could go to Canada, at least not until I was 20 years old, but I did go. I turned 20 when I was on the boat. I did not realize then that my future husband did not have a penny to his name.... Although my father had paid the full fare, they put me on an old train [in Halifax], with smoke flowing into the windows and that is how I arrived in Clarkson.... Then I realized I had married a total stranger, whom I had only gone out with for two weeks. After we got married, we rented a house—that was from June to August. It was a decent house, but it was owned by a Dutch couple and we paid for their insurance plus rent—$40 a month. But when they returned, my husband announced that we had to look for another place to stay. Would you believe that he was 31 years old at the time and did not have a penny? Only a car on payments. So we had to start looking for an apartment. Later on we rented a place which had an outdoor toilet and there were rats that used to crawl up and down the stove. It had no refrigerator. It was part of an old estate, a farm house owned by a Dutchman. He had bought a huge old house and rented out two parts to Dutch families, then put up another couple in a converted chicken coop. We lived in what used to be the horse stable. That is why there were so many rats. The summers were hotter then and we all ran out of water when the well ran dry. How could the landlord do that to his own people? We lived along highway 2, between Clarkson and Oakville.

. . . I used to pick strawberries for 5 cents a quart. That was when I already had a baby—I had my first baby after 10 months and then another. I had three while we were still living in Clarkson and altogether I had five babies in five and a half years. My husband worked as a mechanic. But he became sick and they had to take him to a hospital in Toronto, because they didn't have the facilities for what he had in Oakville. He had already been telling other people where he worked that they should be getting some health insurance—like the Blue Cross—but everyone was young and thought that was not necessary. . . . We had to pay a lot for the doctor's bills. It took five years to pay it all off. You automatically paid off your bills—it was not a question of filing for personal bankruptcy. . . .

5.2 *Excerpts from "First Impressions of an Immigrant Family," by W.J. Pluim, Brantford, Ontario, Christmas 1984 (written for his children and grandchildren)*

Though I don't claim to be an author, I am going to try to put some sort of story together about the time when we first set foot on the shores of our glorious Canada, starting at the landing place (Quebec City). I am not going into detail about the boat journey. . . . There we were with nine of us, on a strange continent and a strange land. It was a moment never to forget, some 30 years ago. The stewardess had given us some valuable instructions and advice about what to do first. Accompanied by the older children (Mom stayed behind with the younger kids, surrounded by all kinds of luggage), I went out to buy some food, as we had still a long journey ahead of us. . . .

After a rather long wait, which caused quite some pressure on Mom's and my nerve system, the long train arrived which would bring us to the first big city, Montreal. It's hard to describe our feelings of that immigrant train ride. As it was still daylight, the countryside which we rode through had naturally our full attention. We noticed the busy railway crossings, and highways filled with all sorts of cars. . . . We saw the first ciotheslines, which were criticized by Mom as not being too clean, according to Mom's Dutch standards. You see, the first judgement is not always the right one, as we learned after some months. There are a lot of neat and clean Canadians also.

. . . I don't remember how long it took to reach Montreal. We got out of the train, gathered our flock, and were bussed to another station to begin our final ride to Brockville, or as we first thought, Prescott. The Kleiboers, who sponsored us, had been waiting at the Prescott station, but seeing the train go by, hurried to Brockville to fetch us. We got out, went to the waiting room and stood there forlorn, and the only thing we could do was just wait. After about half an hour the Kleiboers were there with three cars to drive us to our final destination. It was about 3 a.m. It took another hour and a half and everything came to a full stop. . . .

It was August 1, 1954, 4:30 a.m. We were treated with good homemade soup, though we were not too hungry, because of the commotion and emotions we had experienced since we left Holland July 23. After some chatting, we were accompanied to our house and fell exhausted on our makeshift beds. . . .

5.3 *Excerpt (translated) from an interview, conducted in Dutch, on November 11, 1988, in Brantford, with a retired school custodian (and author of the passage quoted in 5.2 above)*

We came from Epe, in the Veluwe, and emigrated to Canada in 1954. In the Netherlands we ran a furniture store, which we sold before we came here. I was a furniture dealer, so you might be thinking, "why did you decide to emigrate?" Well, in the first place, I saw no opportunities to expand my business and I did not foresee any possibility for my children in that. Secondly, we were much too busy with that business, and we (and that includes my wife) were not able to pay enough attention to the children. Around that time a lot of other small business people left—it was a kind of emigration sickness. At that time we already had seven children and one was also born in Canada—that was our surprise gift. It was not easy the first couple of years but I can't say I regretted coming here; maybe it was irksome sometimes but there were never any regrets.

Chapter 6

The Spatial Distribution of Dutch-Canadians

In my interviews, I often heard comments referring to the geographical dispersion of Canadians of Dutch descent. Many people were convinced that "one is likely to encounter a Dutch person anywhere in Ontario," and that Canadians of Dutch background are evenly distributed among the rest of the population. Another image of *the Dutch* in Ontario is that they are primarily farmers or people involved in farm-related activities living in rural areas. This chapter will subject both of these images to closer scrutiny on the basis of data already collected in large-scale surveys conducted by Statistics Canada. I will first map out the patterns of spatial distribution of Dutch-Canadians and then explain such patterns in term of the dispositions or habits shared by postwar immigrants who came from the Netherlands.

Social geographers have long been aware of the close association between spatial and social relationships, especially when it comes to looking at ethnicity.[1] The challenge is to find the links, through a careful analysis of general census data. In the case of Ontario, the most recent figures available at the time of my study were those of 1986.[2] That census, which forms the basis for this chapter, contained questions about ethnic origin and mother tongue, broken down into rural and urban areas. The basic patterns of geographical distribution of Dutch-Canadians have not undergone major changes since that time.[3] Thus, unless otherwise specified, the present tense will be used. Unfortunately the 1986 census did not include a question concerning religious affiliation, so it was impossible to systematically incorporate this variable, so important for explaining the behaviour of Dutch-Canadians. However I was able to estimate the proportions of neo-Calvinists in most areas by extrapolating from other sources that enumerated members of various Reformed denominations.[4] All of the quantitative

Notes to this chapter are on p. 345-49.

data pertaining to spatial clustering were also interpreted in the light of data collected through oral interviews, plus observations made during fieldtrips.

Dutch-Canadians in the Population Census

The official population census data does not support the view that Canadians of Dutch descent are proportionally represented in all regions of Ontario. Rather, they exhibit a unique pattern of spatial distribution. The vast majority of Canadians of Dutch descent reside within a narrow band from Sarnia to Bowmanville, with noticeable pockets of concentration both within and outside of that band. On the other hand, the image of the Dutch as predominantly rural does come somewhat closer to reality. If we use the official Census Canada definition of rurality as any locality with fewer than 10,000 people, almost half, or 47.12 percent of all people of Dutch descent in Ontario live in rural regions.

Before examining and interpreting the census data, we must first distinguish between percentages and absolute numbers. While the total number of people in most rural townships is quite low, the proportion of Canadians of Dutch descent in these same townships may be relatively high. We can get a visual image of these two dimensions of spatial distribution by comparing two maps of southern Ontario, one portraying the Dutch in terms of percentage of total population in each area and the other as absolute numbers (see figures 2 and 3). The boundary lines indicate either rural townships or the division between urban and rural zones (including those within large Metropolitan areas). The maps also show all villages and towns (or cities) if they appear as separate census units with a significant Dutch presence (in terms of either percentages or absolute numbers). Numbers and letters on these maps correspond to place names included in various tables in this chapter.

Rural Townships

The majority of people living in most "townships" or "rural areas" are directly or indirectly involved in the agricultural sector or resource-extraction industries. In twelve such rural census divisions, Dutch-Canadians constitute over 15 percent of the population. Table 1 lists these units in decreasing order of importance. The rural townships with the highest percentages of Dutch-Canadians—Adelaide, Warwick and West Williams—are located in the area between London and Sarnia. In all three of them, people of Dutch descent constitute more than a quarter of the total population. By adding in the rural census units where the Dutch make up more than 10 percent of the population, the number goes up to

49,[5] and if the cut-off point is dropped to 5 percent, we get 135 townships with a "Dutch presence." Thus, in almost a third of the rural townships in Ontario, one out of every 20 persons is of postwar Dutch background.

Figure 2
Distribution of Dutch-Canadians in Southern Ontario (percentage of population)

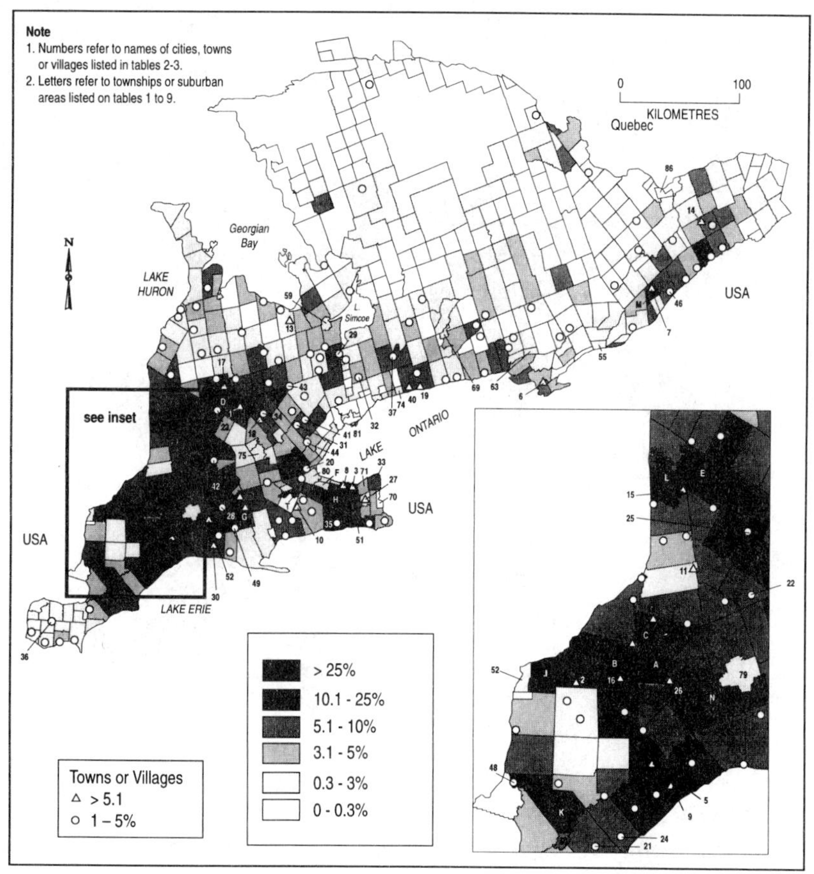

When we look at where exactly rural Dutch-Canadians are located, we notice that they are almost completely absent in the Canadian shield. There, very small numbers of them constitute below 1 percent of the population in most districts or counties.[6] These figures demonstrate that Dutch-Canadians are not well represented in areas whose economies revolve mainly around mining, logging, trapping and tourism, as opposed to dairying or agricultural production. The image of the Dutch as basically agricultural is thus essentially correct. However, the pattern of spatial distribution of Dutch-Canadians within both rural and urban areas shows further variation.

Figure 3
Distribution of Dutch-Canadians in Southern Ontario
(absolute numbers)

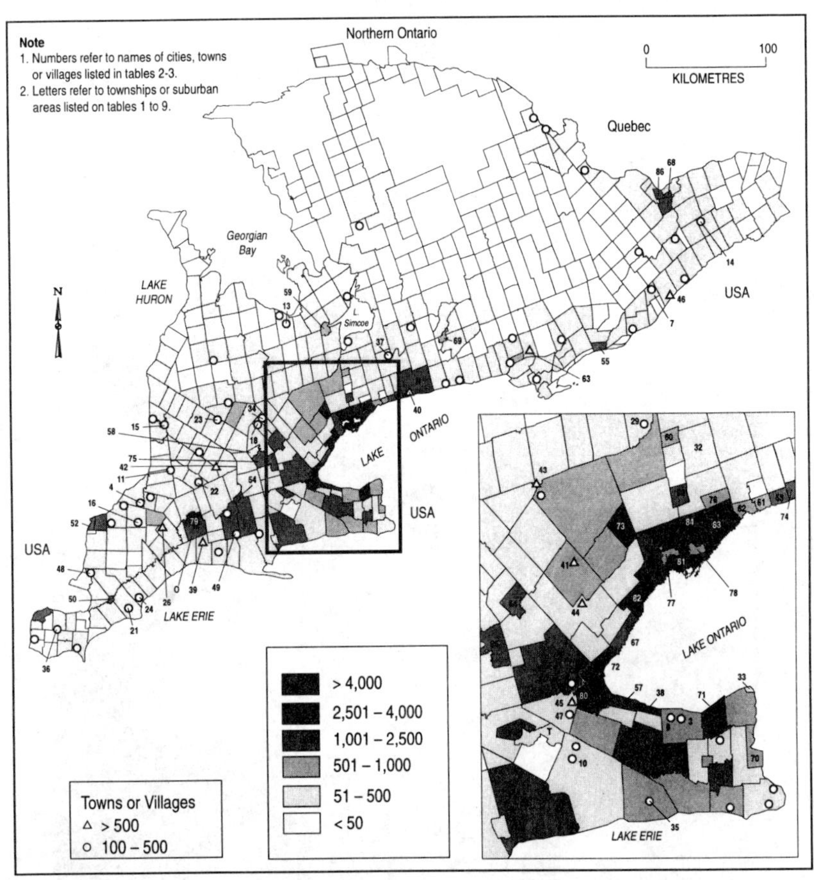

Villages and Small Towns

Settlements with the legal status of village may have anywhere from a couple of hundred to over two thousand inhabitants. Technically these villages are all considered "rural," which implies farming, although their inhabitants are as likely to work in a variety of other occupations, or for schools or other public institutions. Dutch-Canadians, who constitute more than 3 percent of the population in 27 such villages, consist of a mixture of farmers, retired farm couples and the young people who have "moved to town" to work in stores, garages or feed mills.[7] All of these villages with a Dutch presence are located in townships already identified as having a significant number of rural Dutch-Canadians. Indeed, in all but two cases, the Dutch population of the surrounding countryside outnumbers that of the villages both in relative proportion and absolute numbers. This is the case even for localities where less than 3 percent of the population is of Dutch descent.[8]

Table 1
Rural Census Divisions with a Significant Dutch Presence (letters in brackets shown in figures 2 and/or 3)

Name of census division (with county, district or regional municipality)	Percentage of Dutch descent
Adelaide township (Middlesex) [A]	28.93
Warwick township (Lambton) [B]	28.81
West Williams township (Middlesex) [C]	27.72
Maryborough township (Wellington) [D]	23.15
Hullet township (Huron) [E]	23.06
Rural part of the town of Grimsby (Niagara)[F]	20.25
Rural part of Norwich township (Oxford) [G]	19.57
Rural part of West Lincoln township (Niagara) [H]	17.78
Rural part of the township of Sarnia (Lambton) [J]	16.70
Rural part of the town of Chatham (Kent) [K]	16.39
Township (not the town) of Goderich (Huron) [L]	15.67
Rear of Yonge and Escott (Leeds and Grenville) [M]	15.21
Delaware township (Middlesex) [N]	12.60

Dutch-Canadians who live in and around such villages may be almost all Catholics or all Calvinists. An example of a small population centre with mainly Dutch Protestants is Drayton in Wellington county, discussed in the last chapter.[9] Another is Athens, in the eastern Ontario county of Leeds and Grenville, which has a Christian Reformed church and a Christian school which serves the 200 Dutch-Canadian inhabitants of the township Rear of Yonge and Escott, including the hamlet of Addison.[10] An example of a predominantly Dutch Catholic presence is Arkona, in Lambton county. This village has only 430 people, 15 percent of whom are Dutch-Canadians. The fact that only 15 percent of those in turn have Dutch as their mother tongue indicates that Arkona has a younger Dutch- Canadian population, consisting of the offspring of Dutch postwar immigrants who settled down in the townships of Bosanquet, Plympton and Warwick.[11] Arkona is also the original rural centre of St. Willibrord Credit Union, which used to have both an ethnic (Dutch-Flemish) and a religious (Catholic) bond (see chapter 8). Today this village still has one of the main rural branches of this credit union, and a hall set up by Dutch Catholic immigrants, some of whom still live in or close to places like Thedford, Forest and Grand Bend (see inset in figure 2).

A short drive from Arkona, just south of highway 402 in Warwick township, lies Watford. In absolute numbers, Watford only has 75 Dutch-Canadians; however, this village serves as a service centre to a large, predominantly Catholic Dutch-Canadian farm population. Indeed, 28.81 percent of the township of Warwick, including the hamlet with that name, is of Dutch descent. Several years ago Watford received its own branch of a formerly Dutch-Canadian credit union. However, although the majority of the farmers who live near Watford are Dutch-Canadian Catholics, there are also Dutch Protestants (mainly Christian Reformed), who own businesses in downtown Watford. They attend church in the nearby village of Wyoming (township of Plympton), which represents the rare case of a small rural settlement where there is about an equal representation of Dutch Catholics and Dutch Protestants.[12]

The concentration of Dutch-Canadians in all of the villages so far mentioned corresponds fairly well to where I have been told one would find "lots of Dutch." A Dutch presence is also noticeable in Chesterville, Winchester and Iroquois (in Stormont, Dundas and Glengarry united counties); Stirling and Frankford (Hastings county); Lucan (Middlesex); West Lorne (Elgin county); Elora (Wellington) and Blythe and Kintail (both in Huron county).[13] All of these settlements are surrounded by pockets of Dutch-Canadian farmers. Villages where the Dutch constitute more than 10 percent are Bloomfield in Hallowell township (Prince Edward county), and Wardsville in Mosa township (Middlesex county). Moreover, numerous villages or hamlets that are not listed as separate census divisions, and hence do not even appear on the two maps, also have a significant Dutch-Canadian presence.[14] These are subsumed under their respective townships or the rural component of more urbanized townships.

Similar patterns of rural Dutch settlement, with a corresponding presence of Dutch-linked institutions, can be found in census divisions labelled as "towns" with fewer than 10,000 inhabitants. Very small towns (with fewer than 5,000 people) are often indistinguishable in size and appearance from officially designated "villages." Table 2 lists such small towns where either more than 3 percent of the population is of Dutch descent or where there are at least 100 Dutch-Canadians. Ten of the "villages" with lower absolute numbers, but higher percentages, were added to this table if they appeared as separate census units. Beamsville has the largest number of Dutch-Canadian inhabitants in absolute numbers (455), while Drayton has the highest percentage (17.19). All of the towns or villages listed in table 2 service a Dutch-Canadian farm population representing more than 10 percent of the total population of their respective rural surroundings. Even when the percentage of that Dutch farm population goes well below 10 percent, there are still more Dutch-Canadians (in absolute numbers) in their surrounding rural hinterland than in nearby towns and villages. The only exceptions are St. Marys, Exeter and Ridgetown, but each of these towns still acts as a service centre for at least a hundred Dutch-Canadian farmers in its respective township.[15]

Table 2
Small Towns and Villages with a Significant Dutch Presence—Under 4,999 Inhabitants (numbers in brackets shown in figures 2/3)

Name (and jurisdiction)	No. of Dutch Canadians	Percentage of people of Dutch descent
Drayton (Wellington) [1]	190	27.14
Wyoming (Lambton) [2]	300	17.19
Vineland (Niagara) [3]	385	17.12
Arkona (Lambton) [4]	65	15.12
Wardsville (Middlesex) [5]	45	12.50
Bloomfield (Prince Edward) [6]	80	12.03
Athens (Leeds and Grenville) [7]	115	11.39
Beamsville (Niagara) [8]	455	9.81
West Lorne (Elgin) [9]	120	9.02
Hagersville (Haldimand-Norfolk) [10]	180	7.78
Exeter (Huron) [11]	285	7.67
Park Hill (Middlesex) [12]	100	7.52
Stayner (Simcoe) [13]	125	6.67
Winchester (Stormont, Dundas & Glengarry) [14]	130	6.58
Clinton (Huron) [15]	185	6.09
Watford (Lambton) [16]	75	5.98
Harriston (Wellington) [17]	95	5.16
Elora (Wellington) [18]	135	5.13
Newcastle (Durham) [19]	85	5.06
Flamborough (Hamilton-Wentworth) [20]	210	4.76
Blenheim (Kent) [21]	195	4.53
St. Marys (Perth) [22]	210	4.26
Listowel (Perth) [23]	200	4.07
Ridgetown (Kent) [24]	110	3.60
Mitchell (Perth) [25]	100	3.44

In most of these villages and towns, the ethnic presence becomes visible in a literal sense since one is prone to encounter Dutch-Canadian or Dutch-linked institutions. In their downtown cores one would come across a Dutch delicatessen, one or two Reformed churches, or a Catholic church where a large proportion of members are of Dutch descent. You might also come across a Dutch retirement home and perhaps a Dutch-Canadian social club or annual festival (see chapters 16 and 17). A good example of the latter is the town of Clinton, which is surrounded by townships with a considerable number of farmers of Dutch background.

Table 3
Towns with a Significant Dutch Presence—Between 5,000 and 9,999 Inhabitants (numbers in brackets shown in figures 2/3)

Name of Town (and jurisdiction)	No. of Dutch Canadians	Percentage of Dutch descent
Strathroy (Middlesex) [26]	845	9.58
Pelham (Niagara) [27]	580	6.46
Ingersoll (Oxford) [28]	350	4.22
Bradford (Simcoe) [29]	330	3.78
Aylmer (Elgin) [30]	275	5.32
Acton (Halton) [31]	275	3.75
Whitchurch-Stouffville (York) [32]	245	3.47
Niagara-on-the-Lake (Niagara)[33]	215	4.12
Fergus (Wellington) [34]	205	3.33
Dunville (Haldimand-Norfolk) [35]	195	3.81
Essex (Essex) [36]	190	3.18
Port Perry (Durham) [37]	170	3.36

Table 3 lists towns with a total population of between 5,000 and 9,999 inhabitants. Like very small towns, they are all located in rural townships whose Dutch-Canadian population surpasses that of the town itself. The only exception is Strathroy whose 845 Dutch inhabitants surpass the Dutch rural population of the township over which it has jurisdiction. However, the figures on the proportion of Dutch living in the town of Strathroy as opposed to the township of Adelaide are misleading, since Strathroy lies on the boundary between the townships of Caradoc and Adelaide whose combined population of Dutch-Canadian rural dwellers goes well beyond 1,000. Dutch farmers from the townships of Adelaide, Caradoc and the township of Metcalfe all come to Strathroy to attend churches or do their shopping.

Unlike very small towns and villages, towns in this category have a large proportion of Dutch-Canadians who first came to Canada as city rather than farm immigrants,[16] even though all of these towns are technically designated as "rural" population centres. Consequently, one is likely to find the same mix of occupational groupings as in the old country.

Urban Areas

According to the 1986 Canada Population Census, urban census divisions have populations of over 10,000 people. For this section, I selected those which had at least 500 people of Dutch descent or those where the proportion of Dutch-Canadians is at least 3 percent. The Dutch-Canadian population of these urban centres goes up gradually from several hundred, for some of the medium-sized towns, to a maximum of 6,700 for large cities. I further broke these urban centres down into five sub-categories according to their total population. These sub-categories of urban areas appear in tables 4 to 8, each of which includes an additional column indicating the proportion of people of Dutch descent who report Dutch as their their mother tongue (DMT). The urban centres in each table are also listed in order of decreasing overall numerical importance in terms of absolute numbers of Dutch-Canadians. Some of the medium-sized and larger towns listed in tables 4 and 5 are still surrounded by predominantly rural, agricultural townships, although only Milton and Sarnia have more Dutch-Canadians living on surrounding farms than in town.[17] The rural counterpart of all other towns and cities, including Guelph, were insignificant in comparison to people who pursued completely urban occupations. However, we should keep in mind that these city dwellers include Dutch-Canadians originally placed on farms, but who then came to town as a result of the rapid process of rural-urban migration (see previous chapter).

Table 4
Urban Centres with a Significant Dutch Presence—Medium-sized Towns between 10,000 and 29,999 Inhabitants (numbers in brackets shown in figures 2/3)

Name	Population	Percentage	Proportion (DMT)
Grimsby [38]	1115	7.36	52.91
St. Thomas [39]	975	3.45	35.90
Bowmanville [40]	755	5.86	33.11
Georgetown [41]	660	3.29	46.21
Stratford [42]	655	2.49	35.88
Orangeville [43]	600	4.19	20.00
Milton [44]	595	2.61	31.09
Dundas [45]	580	3.21	31.03
Brockville [46]	520	2.51	43.27
Ancaster [47]	470	3.61	46.81
Wallaceburg [48]	460	4.10	38.04
Tilsonburg [49]	340	3.21	36.76

More than half of the towns and cities counted as urban census divisions form part of larger urban-industrial conglomerations. The largest urban band, the Golden Horseshoe, stretches from Grimsby to Bowmanville and includes such cities as Hamilton, Burlington, Oakville, Mississauga, Metropolitan Toronto, Whitby and Oshawa (see inset in figure 2). Although Dutch-Canadians represent a very small proportion of the population of such larger urban areas, four urban belts actually have more Dutch-Canadians in absolute numbers[18] than all the rural regions and small towns of the province put together.

Looking at table 4, you will note that the medium-sized town (between 10,000 and 29,999 inhabitants) that has the most Dutch-Canadians is Grimsby. It also has the highest percentage; 7.36 out of every hundred inhabitants is Dutch-Canadian. In fact, as late as the mid-sixties one could often hear more Dutch than English spoken in its downtown core. In 1986, Grimsby still had the highest proportion of Dutch-Canadians who reported a Netherlandic language as mother tongue.[19]

Table 5
Urban Centres with a Significant Dutch Presence—Large Towns between 30,000 and 59,999 Inhabitants (numbers in brackets shown in figures 2/3)

Name	Population	Percentage	Proportion (DMT)
Chatham [50]	2330	5.69	36.48
Welland [51]	2105	4.78	8.55
Sarnia [52]	1445	2.93	35.99
Whitby [53]	1325	3.21	44.53
Woodstock [54]	1100	3.06	46.82
Kingston [55]	1060	2.00	26.89
Richmond Hill [56]	1015	2.31	39.90
Stoney Creek [57]	1015	2.46	35.47
Waterloo [58]	915	1.57	37.70
Barrie [59]	825	1.73	52.12
Newmarket [60]	700	2.08	41.43
Ajax [61]	660	2.17	40.15
Pickering [62]	625	1.61	45.60
Belleville [63]	595	1.67	26.05

Table 5 lists the next category of urban centres, the large towns with a total population between 30,000 to 59,999 people. At this level of population size, five urban centres still have the legal status of town instead of city. Chatham has both the highest percentage (5.69) and highest absolute number of Dutch-Canadians (2,330). There are several Reformed churches, a downtown "Dutch store" and numerous Dutch businesses. For example, in 1991, eight contractors of Dutch descent were listed in the yellow pages of the phone book for Chatham.[20]

Cities included in the next level, designated as "small cities," appear in table 6. Only Oakville still has the legal status of town. Among these small cities, with a population of between 60,000 and 99,999, the one that ranks the highest is Guelph, where 2,110 Dutch-Canadians make up 2.74 percent of the city's population. Close to a thousand of these Dutch-Canadian Guelphites (42.18 percent) report Dutch as their mother tongue, and about a hundred of them regularly read one or more of the three Canadian newspapers written in the Dutch language.[21] Sudbury and Sault Ste. Marie, with only 345 Dutch-Canadians each, were not included in this table because they did not meet the minimum cut-off of 500 people, or 3 percent.

Table 6
Urban Centres with a Significant Dutch Presence—Small Cities between 60,000 and 99,999 Inhabitants (numbers in brackets shown in figures 2/3)

Name	Population	Percentage	Proportion (DMT)
Guelph [64]	2110	2.74	42.18
Cambridge [65]	1515	1.92	32.34
Brantford [66]	1410	2.00	28.72
Oakville [67]	1315	1.72	59.32
Nepean [68]	1230	1.53	46.34
Peterborough [69]	840	1.40	42.86
Niagara Falls [70]	580	.84	57.76

Table 7 lists the medium-sized cities, with populations of between 100,000 and 199,999. This category still includes one legally designated town (Markham). The biggest Dutch presence is found in St. Catharines, with 4,485 Dutch-Canadians constituting 3.68 percent of the city's population. This percentage is slightly higher for Burlington (3.75). Both of these urban centres are surrounded by rural townships with significant proportions of Dutch-Canadians, which is an indication that the influx of rural Dutch-Canadians who started off working on farms located close to cities made a significant contribution to the growth of the population of Dutch descent in such urban centres in southwestern Ontario.

On the average, the number of Dutch-Canadians in the large cities of over 200,000 inhabitants is not much higher than that of medium-sized cities. However, in most of the nine urban centres under this category, listed in table 8, people of Dutch descent represent an insignificant minority representing below 1 percent. The only large cities with a somewhat higher proportion of Dutch-Canadians are Hamilton, with 1.42 percent, and the city of London with 2.52 percent. Again, these are the only large cities surrounded by rural areas or townships that also have a significant proportion of Dutch-Canadians (i.e., more than 3 percent). The larger percentage in the case of London also corresponds to higher absolute numbers, since more people of Dutch descent live there than in any other census division in Ontario.[22]

Table 7
Urban Centres with a Significant Dutch Presence—Medium-sized Cities between 100,000 and 199,999 Inhabitants (numbers in brackets shown in figures 2/3)

Name	Population	Percentage	Proportion (DMT)
St. Catharines [71]	4485	3.68	38.57
Burlington [72]	4215	3.75	35.54
Brampton [73]	3400	1.95	35.74
Oshawa [74]	2300	1.91	39.78
Kitchener [75]	2020	1.35	33.66
Markham [76]	940	.87	42.55
Thunder Bay	760	.71	40.79
York [77]	630	.56	35.71
East York (borough) [78]	545	.54	35.78

Of course, if we add up all the Dutch-Canadians in Metropolitan Toronto combined (including Mississauga), this Metropolitan centre ranks at the top, with nearly 17,000 Dutch-Canadians. Including Brampton would bring the total well over this number. Thus, although the Dutch may not be as "visible" in the largest urban belt in proportional terms, they are certainly important as a potential market for any businesses catering to the Dutch-Canadian population (see chapter 14). A good indicator of the economic importance of this ethnic presence is the number of Dutch delicatessen stores, travel agents or other ethnic businesses that advertise in the Dutch-Canadian press. Of the 30 stores that placed ads in one or more of the ethnic newspapers in 1992, six were located in the Greater Toronto region and another five in the Hamilton area, including Grimsby and Burlington.[23]

Within the boundaries of all these urban zones, we can detect another pattern of spatial distribution. For instance, in the case of the city of Sarnia, the Dutch presence was (and still is) more noticeable in a neighbourhood close to the exit from Sarnia to London than in the downtown core. A similar Dutch concentration in the suburbs or outskirts can be detected in bigger cities; according to the ethnocultural data base for Hamilton, Dutch immigrants are more heavily concentrated in the suburbs and nearby towns.[24] One is also likely to find Dutch-Canadian institutions in urban fringes, especially if they are contiguous with concentrations of rural Dutch. This is the case for the town of Ancaster (part of Hamilton-Wentworth), which also has about the same number of Dutch-Canadians as its rural counterpart.[25] Likewise, the township of Sarnia has almost exactly the same number of Dutch as the city of Sarnia itself. However, we need to be careful in how to interpret such figures for urban-rural ratios in this fuzzy zone between urban and rural regions.

Table 8
Urban Centres with a Significant Dutch Presence—Large Cities with over 200,000 Inhabitants (numbers in brackets shown in figures 2/3)

Name	Population	Percentage	Proportion (DMT)
London [79]	6700	2.52	38.58
Hamilton [80]	4325	1.42	40.23
Toronto [81]	3775	.60	38.81
Mississauga [82]	3545	1.08	43.28
Scarborough [83]	3265	.61	40.58
North York [84]	2990	.55	46.15
Etobicoke [85]	2405	.80	44.70
Ottawa [86]	2200	.74	44.09

The Semi-urban Fringe

The townships or rural zones of towns located on the edges of urban expansion are rapidly becoming transformed into suburbs and industrial parks. Such suburban development might engulf small towns where the Dutch had already settled before the rapid expansion of Metropolitan regions. Canadians of Dutch descent living in such semi-urban areas represent a mixture of city and rural immigrants and their descendants. Moreover, many of these areas have only recently gone from being predominantly rural-agricultural to becoming an integral part of urban conglomerations. A list of such intermediate rural-urban zones includes the rural zones of several towns that are quickly becoming satellite cities of larger Metropolitan centres. Unlike typical rural townships, which rarely have more than 5,000 inhabitants, these semi-urban census units (in many cases still labelled as "rural" in the 1986 census) have between 12,000 and 21,000 people. Two smaller semi-urban census units listed as townships, but where the Dutch constitute more than 10 percent of the total population, are included in this ambiguous category.

Table 9
Ambiguous ("Semi-Urban") Census Divisions
(letters in brackets shown in figures 2/3)

Name (census category)	Total Population	Total Dutch	Percentage (DMT)	Proportion
Westminster [O] (township)	5,865	1935	32.99	7.49
Flamborough [P] ("rural")	21,493	2390	11.12	30.54
Newcastle [R] ("rural")	17,272	1285	7.44	40.47
Nanticoke [S] ("rural")	12,457	1080	8.67	29.63
Onondaga [T] (township)	1,357	175	12.90	28.37

The Anomalies of Westminster and Onondaga

In 1986, Westminster had about 6,000 inhabitants, compared to an average of 2,000 for rural townships in the rest of Middlesex county. At that time Westminster was already well on its way to becoming part of the suburban fringe of the city of London. Indeed, it had actually been upgraded into a town (with a rural component) just prior to 1986, and was absorbed into the city of London in 1992. Unlike most other townships, the close to 2,000 Dutch-Canadians in this former township in 1986 were also much younger (probably second and possibly third generation), because the people reporting Dutch as their mother tongue was under 10 percent. This number stands in stark contrast with figures for more established Dutch-Canadian localities (rural or urban), where the proportion of people reporting Dutch as their mother tongue is usually around 30 or 40 percent.

At first glance, it appears that the spatial distribution found in Westminster is similar to that of towns and villages that saw an influx of young Dutch-Canadians from nearby rural areas in the fifties and sixties. Such an influx happened in Drayton (see chapter 5). However, by the seventies and eighties the dynamics of rural-urban migration underwent changes; younger, better-educated Dutch-Canadians in rural townships either stayed on the farm or moved straight to larger towns or cities,[26] while older, retired Dutch-Canadian farmers began moving to nearby villages and small towns (see chapter 17). In contrast, on the fringes of large cities one was more likely to find an influx of younger people from both rural and urban backgrounds.

The Dutch-Canadian population of the former township of Westminster (including the town of Lambeth) is of comparable size to that of Sarnia or the rural section of Flamborough, bordering on Hamilton. However, unlike the latter two areas, there have never been churches or other institutions with Dutch connections in Westminster, nor is this area perceived as one "with a lot of Dutch people." Yet, according to the 1986 census, 32.99 percent of the population of this township listed "Dutch" as their ethnic background! This statistical finding presents an anomaly that had to be investigated. On the basis of a half-dozen phone calls and additional interviews, I was able to ascertain that the Dutch-Canadians in Westminster are a combination of young professional couples buying the new homes now being built in this area, and the offspring of rural Dutch-Canadians moving closer to the city.[27] There are also apple orchards owned by younger Dutch farmers, several contractors, and small Dutch-Canadian businesses recently established in the township. Even the former part-time mayor, Ben Weel, is a Dutch immigrant.[28] Yet the high proportion of people of Dutch descent in Westminster does not represent the outcome of a deliberate choice to live close to people of the same ethnic origin. On the contrary, the people whom I contacted there were astonished at the high percentage of Dutch-Canadians.

London and its rural hinterland, which once included Westminster, received a large number of Dutch Catholic immigrants in the fifties; they set up a credit union that still has a strong Dutch-Canadian flavour today (see chapter 15). The London area also saw the arrival of a significant number of postwar Calvinists (Reformed), who came to represent 24.43 percent of the Dutch-Canadian population of Middlesex county.[29] It so happens that neither of these sub-groups established institutions anywhere in Westminster; one of the main centres of Dutch Catholic immigrants was located in Delaware, just outside the borders of Westminster, while Dutch-Canadian Calvinists established their Reformed churches in other parts of the city and outskirts of London. People in Westminster who have maintained ties to both of these religious communities thus belong to quite different sub-segments of the Dutch population. Furthermore, Dutch-Canadians in Westminster who might be interested in socializing with members of their own ethnic group, regardless of religious affiliation, can join a club built by Dutch immigrants on the outskirts of another part of London. Similarly, anyone who wants to buy Dutch delicatessen goods can easily drive the short distance to one of two Dutch stores located in the city of London. Straight geographical proximity of people from the same national background therefore does not automatically mean a strong sense of local ethnic identity, especially when they are such a diverse grouping.

A similar anomaly was detected in the census division of Onondaga (Brant county), close to Brantford. About 12 percent of the population of that township is of Dutch descent, even though this part of the county likewise lacks a reputation for having a Dutch presence. However, the underlying dynamics of this spatial distribution are different from those of Westminster. There is a greater ratio of Dutch-Canadians living in the rural sector, and the smaller number of Dutch-Canadians who live in Onondaga are also somewhat older than in the case of Westminster, since 18 percent of Dutch-Canadians report Dutch as their mother tongue. Nevertheless, Onondaga can be used to further illustrate the point that spatial proximity by itself does not necessary lead to ethnic solidarity. At various times in the past, Dutch-Canadian farmers from a variety of backgrounds, and with connections to other communities, bought farms in Onondaga.[30] Moreover, families belonging to different churches had little need to get together; Dutch Calvinist immigrants could easily attend one of several Reformed churches in nearby Brantford, while Dutch Catholics already had contacts with Dutch priests in the village of Caledonia and Hagersville just to the south, in Haldimand county (see chapter 8).[31] However, before we further interpret these patterns of spatial concentration of Dutch-Canadians, we need to again look at the province as a whole.

The Data for Northern and Central Ontario

With the exception of a few tiny pockets, Dutch agrarian immigrants did not settle down to farm outside the Ottawa and St. Lawrence Valleys. Most of Northern and central Ontario, with few people of Dutch descent (see above), shows quite a different form of spatial distribution from southern Ontario; indeed, the ratio of urban-to-rural Dutch is inversely proportional to that of southern Ontario. We can take the districts of Algoma and Nipissing as examples. The cities of North Bay and Sault Ste. Marie have 195 and 345 Dutch-Canadians respectively, with only one or two families of Dutch descent in their corresponding rural regions. This is also the case for towns further north, such as Timmins, Dryden and Fort Frances. Only when agriculture or cattle raising is possible does the southern pattern of urban-rural ratios show up in the north. For example, in rural portions of the flatter arable land around Verner (on the north side of Lake Nipissing) there are more Canadians of Dutch descent than in the nearby towns of Cache Bay and Sturgeon Falls. Similar agricultural pockets with rural Dutch can be detected in the districts of Cochrane and Thunder Bay. The Dutch tendency for people who belong to the same religion to live in the same place also shows up; while Dutch-Canadians in the rural pockets near Thunder Bay are mainly Calvinists, most Dutch farmers in the district of Nipissing or Sudbury are Catholics.

Within somewhat larger northern cities, Dutch-Canadians also tend to live mainly on the outskirts, the same as in southern urban zones. Thus, in the regional municipality of Sudbury the number of Dutch-Canadians in such nearby communities as Lively, Hagar, Copper Cliff, Azilda, Chelmsford, Val Caron and Blezard Valley is about the same as than that of the city of Sudbury itself.[32] This finding is consistent with the portrayal of Sudbury presented in the previous chapter.

Cottage Country

Another variation of the distribution of rural versus urban Dutch-Canadians is found in cottage country: Manitoulin Island, the Bruce peninsula, the Kiwarthas and the Muskokas. In all these areas, the Dutch proportion of the population is very small; yet whenever the census divisions distinguish between a rural area and its corresponding township, the Dutch are about equally distributed in both. For example, in the Muskokas, we find approximately the same number of Dutch-Canadians in the town of Gravenhurst as in its rural district.[33] In general, Dutch-Canadians are thus just as likely to end up living in towns as in isolated cottages in these middle parts of Ontario.[34]

My explanation for this spatial distribution in cottage country is as follows. Older Dutch-Canadians who have done well economically bought summer cottages, like their Canadian neighbours. These would be included in the rural sections of the townships mentioned above. Simultaneously, other Dutch-Canadians (both young and old) who used to live in other parts of the province, have invested in small hotels or resorts, or have retired in resort towns. However the few Dutch-Canadians who live in this central part of the province have little in common and are even less likely to get together, since members of different religious persuasions and regional origins already have their respective ties to relatives and friends in southern communities. I further hypothesize that both northern and central Ontario probably have a higher proportion of Dutch-Canadians originally associated with the "neutral pillar," who are less likely to have contacts with people of similar ethnic background (see next chapter). The decision of these people to live in more isolated areas could be seen as a deliberate reaction against—rather than an unconscious attempt to imitate—the Dutch patterns of intense social interaction along pillar lines. Lately a number of recent Dutch immigrants with money have also come to cottage country because they see this as a good investment.[35]

An Interpretation: Dutch-Canadian Dispositions

The picture that emerges from the census data is that Canadians of Dutch background are not evenly distributed over the province, nor are their numbers proportional to the population as a whole. If Dutch-Canadians as a group were really "typically" Canadian, as many believe they are (see chapter 18), there would be more people of Dutch descent living in Northern Ontario. In the south, the percentages of Dutch living in the countryside, and the proportion of first-generation members in the suburbs would also be much lower. This unique form of spatial distribution[36] reflects the dispositions shared by immigrants with a common upbringing and national origin, dispositions that shape peoples' daily practice and that generate the regularities captured through the use of statistical techniques.[37]

Shared values, perceptions and habits account for the configuration of people in space, since people with similar skills and expectations are more likely to recognize, and take advantage of, opportunities available in certain localities or geographical settings.[38] Such dispositions, or 'habitus,' both facilitate and constrain the physical movement and subsequent settlement patterns of immigrants when they find themselves in a new country. Hence Dutch immigrants with prior experience and familiarity with commercial agriculture gravitated towards those regions best suited for that type of farming, resulting in the overrepresentation of Dutch-Canadians in rural townships with good land, located close to urban markets (see chapter 19). It is more challenging to determine how dispositions shared by a diverse group of immigrants of common national origin can account for the overall patterns of distribution of Dutch-Canadians. That is why we need to take into consideration the national "culture" of the Netherlands, which cuts across the divisions of gender, generation and religious affiliation.

The high ratio of Dutch-Canadians in the outskirts of urban zones as well as agricultural regions is consistent with the Dutch tradition of urbanism without urbanization. In chapter 4 we saw that the Netherlands is one of the most urbanized countries in Europe, but without the typical "urbane" characteristics of large Metropolitan centres. The Netherlands had (and still has) an "urbanized" countryside and "rural" towns and cities with green belts and suburban garden plots. Most Dutch people have an aversion to crowded city centres, yet they still want the conveniences of easy access to shopping and other services. Even Dutch farmers prefer to live close to a school and church, or other institutions of their choice, depending on their religious or philosophical convictions. People brought up in the Netherlands were also used to a good system of transportation. To some extent then, the spatial distribution of the Dutch in Ontario replicates settlement patterns based on expectations formed in the Netherlands.

The availability of jobs and affordable land suitable for commercial agriculture, plus a small-town atmosphere, jointly determined where Dutch immigrants from both urban and rural background were likely to end up in Ontario. More specific dispositions based on occupation and religious upbringing accounts for further variations within the main pattern of spatial distribution. Dutch agrarian immigrants interested in becoming commercial farmers preferred the fertile soil of the St. Lawrence Valley, although they could manage in small agricultural pockets in other parts of the province, but only if necessary. A large number of rural Dutch immigrants also gravitated towards small towns or the outskirts of larger cities, where they could engage in part-time farming or set up nurseries. This tendency for the Dutch to live in the suburbs has been noticed by other studies, such as one based on 1976 data for the city of Windsor (not mentioned so far):[39] "Dutch-background residents are concentrated in the upper-middle class sections of the city, in Sandwich South, (the part that was formerly Sandwich East), combining urban occupations with gardening."[40]

Dutch city immigrants, especially skilled labourers, were likewise attracted to urban areas experiencing economic growth, yet they too wanted to have gardens and access to open spaces. They found this combination, plus access to the modern services and the religious institutions they wanted, on the outskirts of large cities or in smaller cities and towns.[41] Consequently, urban and rural immigrants from the Netherlands ended up in the same small towns and urban fringe areas, albeit sometimes for somewhat different reasons.[42]

The large percentage of mainly younger Dutch-Canadians in places like Westminster and other new semi-urban zones illustrates the reproduction or continuity of Dutch spatial distribution over several generations, despite a low level of ethnic identity retention. Like their elders, younger Dutch-Canadians from diverse religious backgrounds ended up in similar places, since rural and urban proclivities, as well as modified dispositions originally manifested in Dutch national "culture," reinforced each other. As noted above, the offspring of farm immigrants now tend to move to somewhat larger, nearby urban centres, where they are more likely to find jobs, while their urban counterparts are more likely to move to newer urban areas with affordable housing once they get married and obtain full-time employment. Westminster, a still rural-oriented area on the outskirts of a city experiencing both economic growth and housing development in the eighties, acted as a pole of attraction to young Dutch-Canadians from different backgrounds.

One could argue that the movement of second-generation immigrants to the suburbs is typical of all immigrant groups who experience a process of generational upward social mobility. However, what is unique to the Dutch is that a high proportion of even older, first generation Dutch immigrants ended up on the outskirts of cities throughout Ontario. In fact, the much younger make-up of Dutch-Canadians in the township of Westminster (as indicated by a low proportion of Dutch-speakers) represents the exception rather than the rule. The propensity of first-generation Dutch immigrants to live in the suburbs or city fringes can be demonstrated by comparing different sections of any large city in Ontario in terms of the proportions of Dutch-speaking Canadians versus those only of Dutch descent, with the latter representing the vast majority of second and third-generation Dutch-Canadians (see chapter 11). Thus, in the city of Toronto proper (largely comprising the downtown core), 38.81 percent of Dutch-Canadians report Dutch as their mother tongue, compared to 46.15 percent in North York and 44.70 percent for Etobicoke.[43] This higher proportion of people with Dutch as their mother tongue in the suburbs indicates that the Dutch-Canadian presence in the outskirts of cities is not the result of the gradual, and usually inter-generational, dispersion of an ethnic group that originally settled in the centre of the city.[44]

Despite such common patterns or convergence in spatial distribution for the Dutch as a whole, we should not overlook internal variations, including spatial segregation based on class background. Some evidence for the latter comes from the 1976 survey of Windsor previously mentioned: "Working class Dutchmen live along Dougall Avenue bounded by the CPR and in old Sandwich East, south of the CN railroad."[45]

Given the pillar system of the Netherlands, we should also be on the lookout for spatial patterns reflecting religion. We already encountered this phenomenon for villages or rural areas mentioned earlier in this and previous chapters. Dutch Catholics and Dutch Calvinists tended to group together with people "of their own kind" even within the urbanized belt stretching from Oshawa to Hamilton. For example, west of Toronto, most Dutch Catholics ended up in a narrow strip running from Milton, through Palermo, to Bronte. In contrast, there is a heavier concentration of Dutch Calvinists in a roughly triangular area which goes from Orangeville to Georgetown to Acton. Similarly, one is more likely to find Dutch Calvinists to the east of Oshawa (Bowmanville) then in the western part (Whitby and Pickering).[46] Not only did sub-groups of Netherlanders often end up in different places in Ontario, but the contrasts in subsequent patterns of social interaction—both in their relationships among themselves and with Canadian society at large—were as great among people belonging to different religious sub-categories as between Dutch and non-Dutch Canadians. The exact nature and implications of such Dutch intra-ethnic differences, based on religion, will be examined in the next three chapters.

Fieldnotes Interlude

6.1 Excerpt (reconstructed) from a conversation with a Dutch-Canadian farmer, near Chesterville [Stormont, Dundas and Glengarry United Counties], July 2, 1991

Yes, there are lots of Dutch farmers in the Chesterville area. I farm together with my sons. . . . My son lives in the farm house next door, but we have also bought other farms nearby. One piece of land is 2 km from the barn and the other 3km. . . .

There are other Dutch farmers; over there [as he pointed in the distance] there is another Dutch farmer and beyond that one—you can just see the blue silo sticking out behind that other farmhouse—another Dutch farmer, as is the one on the other side. Our farms here go from road to road. To use one expression that isn't maybe so nice: "it smells of Dutch around here." I think about 60 percent of the farmers around here are Dutch. . . .

6.2 Excerpt from a conversation with a retired steel worker at Inco, just outside Sudbury, April 10, 1991

We have noticed that there are a lot more Dutch people in parts of southwestern Ontario and some of the people from the same village we came from live there. There were four families from the same place. I remember we used to sit in the same pew at church when I was young. They settled in Gads Hill, which is close to Stratford. That was not really a village but more like a crossroad and that was the name on the sign.

6.3 Excerpt (translated) from an interview (in Dutch) with a retired nurse who lives on a farm near Landsdowne [Leeds & Grenville United Counties], July 13, 1990

Formerly there were a lot of Dutch vegetable gardeners who had come together in the region of Picton but a lot of them later moved to other places. . . .

We came here in 1954 and there were two other Dutch farm families here. We were the only Dutch Catholics in the parish, and we also knew Martin, who had been in Quebec for a while. He came four years later. A few more couple moved in later, but I do not think that we were more than 4 percent of the parish here. There was more of a concentration of Dutch Catholics in Chesterville; about 40 families settled there, and also in Spencerville. In the past, all of the Irish lived on the other side of the road (across from where we are) and the English and Scottish Protestants lived here. In fact, the previous owner of this farm was really not supposed to ever sell this land to Catholics, but he was glad when we were able to do so. . . .

6.4 *Excerpt from an interview with a Dutch-Canadian woman, on her farm near Landsdowne [Leeds & Grenville United Counties), July 13, 1990*

There are also a lot of Dutch in Maitland. I would say the majority of people of that town is of Dutch background and they have both a Christian and a Dutch Reformed church. There are many Dutch-Canadians in Prescott and Brockville too. In Brockville we had a Dutch-Canadian club, but there were no Reformed people in that at all. . . . I came to Canada in 1952 with my husband, who was an engineer. When we arrived there was an economic slump and no jobs, so we moved to Maitland where they had just built a Dupont plant. We were one of the first Dutch immigrants who arrived there. Those who were there already included a station engineer and several other families. Maitland was not a big farming community but a lot of Reformed people ended up living there and more people moved in later. They had two chemical plants there. New industries also made it possible for Brockville and Prescott to grow from small villages to respectable-sized towns. The Dutch immigrants in Maitland came from all over, including Friesland and Groningen and there were also people from the Gelderse *achterhoek*. Many of them also worked for Russell and Pear Lumber. A lot of Dutch people who came to Maitland used to live in Windmill Avenue, near the school, and many of them were *boerenknechten* (farmhands) from Friesland. But the Frisian man we knew was a real farmer. His son now has a delicatessen. I would say that about 90 percent of the Dutch immigrants in Maitland came from farms in Holland.

Chapter 7

Dutch-Canadian Pluralism

A one-page spread in the Guelph daily newspaper features the local Dutch population.[1] A series of articles deals with various topics: Dutch food, the Reformed churches, how the "Dutch came first" after the War, a Dutch club, the Dutch roots of the Christian Heritage Party, the local John Calvin Christian School, and the monthly meeting of the *Wapenbroeders* (Dutch War Veterans) in a nearby city. The photo illustrations consist of a replica windmill and two members of the Dutch club dressed up as *sinterklaas* and *zwarte piet*.[2] This newspaper coverage exemplifies how the same institutions and organizations grouped together in the official records of Canada's multicultural bureaucracy are likewise subsumed under a single ethnic umbrella in the mentality of Canadian journalists and the broader public.[3] It is true that Canadians of Dutch background share much in common, perhaps more than they might be willing to admit. However, portrayals of *the Dutch* in Canada gloss over or ignore intra-ethnic diversity.[4] Dutch immigrants brought up under the Dutch "pillar" system, with its contrasting religious values and social expectations, headed in quite different directions to became distinct Canadians.[5]

This chapter will introduce each of the major and minor groupings of Dutch-Canadians, following a division similar to that found in the Netherlands in the forties and fifties. In the Netherlands, Dutch Catholics and orthodox Calvinists had the greatest degree of institutional completeness and the strongest sense of group identity prior to 1960. People associated with these two blocs had the greatest propensity to reproduce the Dutch social and political system in Ontario. The history of these two major groupings will require more in-depth treatment in chapters 8 and 9. How-

---

Notes to this chapter are on p. 349-54.

ever, we should not forget the pillars that were not as strong or that did not get transplanted in Canadian soil.

To some extent Dutch-Canadians of diverse backgrounds did create common institutions. We will examine such all-encompassing Dutch-Canadian institutions later (see chapter 16). However, starting in the early fifties, the three main Dutch religious groupings each had their own emigration societies (see chapter 4). This pattern of segregation and parallel institutions continued to shape identities and dispositions in a Canadian context. To some extent, immigrants of different religious backgrounds settled in different parts of Ontario (see previous chapter). However, even in places with a concentration of diverse Dutch-Canadians, people with different belief systems rarely socialized. Sometimes they were, and still are, oblivious of one another's existence. Thus, one Frisian Calvinist family who bought a farm close to Phelpston (outside of Barrie), had no contact with the Catholic Dutch farmers who lived in the same township. Instead, they travelled to Barrie for both church services and social events. In the village of Wyoming (near Sarnia), Dutch Catholics and Dutch Calvinists likewise kept apart. A Catholic Dutch-Canadian who participated in a study of postwar immigrants from the Netherlands in the St. Marys area noted that "I find still that I am more likely to make friends with a Canadian, regardless of religion, than with another Dutch person whose religious background is different from mine."[6] Even when Dutch immigrants of different backgrounds came into contact with each other because of work or business, they would rarely visit each other. Marriage or dating with people from the "wrong" group was unheard of.[7] Canadians not of Dutch background were often not aware of the extent of such internal divisions.

Statistical Information Relating to Ontario

A rough estimate of how many people were associated with the broader categories of Dutch society can be made on the basis of the 1980 census for Ontario, which included a question on religion. A little over a third of those reporting Netherlandic/Dutch as ethnic origin were placed in the category of "Other Protestant." Assuming that "Other Protestant" refers to Reformed denominations in the case of the Dutch, this census category corresponds to orthodox Calvinists. The approximately 5 percent of Dutch-Canadians listed as Presbyterians would probably belong to this same category. About one-fourth of the Dutch respondents declared themselves to be Catholics, while people with no religious affiliation, comprising around 8 percent, represented the core of the "neutral" pillar. Another approximately 15 percent of Dutch-Canadians, who joined the United Church,[8] would be the rough equivalent of the more liberal Calvinists (*her-*

vormden) for reasons which will become clearer later. The remainder (a little over 10 percent), are harder to pinpoint. Dutch-Canadians who declared themselves to be Anglicans, Baptists, Pentecostals or members of other religions were less likely to report Dutch as mother tongue. This finding suggests that those religious affiliations are overrepresented among second or third generation Dutch-Canadians or the more distant descendants of earlier Dutch immigrants. Smaller groupings, such as ***doopsgezinden*** (Mennonites) would also fall under this "miscellaneous" category. Dutch Jews—practically exterminated during World War Two—made up a minuscule .2 percent of the Dutch-Canadian population in Ontario.

Provincial figures average out regional variations. The small number of Dutch people of Jewish background ended up mainly in greater Toronto. Likewise, Dutch Catholics are more likely to be found in the London area, while people listed under "Other Protestant" are overrepresented in the Hamilton-Wentworth region and the Niagara peninsula.[9] Nonetheless, the overall provincial figures are not out of line with Canada as a whole.[10] The rough breakdown of each of these categories in Ontario is also consistent with the Dutch government's figures on emigrants to Canada, released in 1956. According to the Netherlands Emigration Service, the percentage of postwar Dutch emigrants to Canada of Catholic background varied from a low of 17.8 percent in 1949 to a high of 34.6 percent in 1955. People of Reformed affiliation (*hervormden*) constituted anywhere from 23.6 percent (in 1948) to 30 percent (1949), while orthodox Calvinists (*gereformeerden*) represented anywhere from 26.4 percent (in 1954) to 45.4 percent (in 1951). Other denominations ranged between 1.6 to 3.3 percent, while people with no denominational affiliation made up between 3.6 (in 1950) to 15.4 percent (in 1948) of Dutch emigrants to Canada.[11]

Compared to the relative proportion of these categories in the Netherlands (in 1947), the orthodox Calvinists were overrepresented among the emigrants since they constituted a small minority of 9.7 percent in the Netherlands. In contrast, people without church affiliation, were underrepresented; they constituted 17 percent of the total Dutch populace, but only 8 percent in Ontario. Catholics and members of the Reformed church were both slightly underrepresented in Canada. These major categories included in the Dutch statistics represent the vast majority of Dutch-Canadians. Unfortunately, we cannot do a similar breakdown of the numerically smaller groupings that are almost impossible to detect in official census records. Statistical information on emigrants from the Netherlands likewise excludes all postwar Dutch-speaking emigrants from Belgium (the Flemish) and Dutch people who came to Canada directly from other parts of the world. However, the statistical absence of smaller groups that fall just outside the fuzzy boundaries of the Dutch ethnic 'class' does not mean we can afford to dismiss their presence or social significance.

Major and Minor Groupings

The groupings of Dutch society cannot be directly equated with membership, or non-membership, in North American religious denominations. Many people who were not religious in the Netherlands became involved in church life after emigrating. Nor did Dutch Protestants always end up in the closest equivalent of a North American Reformed denomination. Nonetheless, the vast majority of postwar immigrants and their offspring gravitated to people with similar dispositions, even if only on the basis of common upbringing. Thus, ex-Catholics of Dutch origin often become friends and even marry though they no longer go to church. The same thing would hold true for former Dutch Calvinists.[12] Indeed, a person's background shapes the way he or she sees the world. One's worldview, as well as general demeanour, is bound to play an important role throughout life, even when that person is no longer affiliated with a religious institution. In the case of closed or more exclusive groups, former members may associate with people from the same background simply because they have had few opportunities to get to know anyone else. We thus need to examine how members of each group interacted with people "of their own kind" and with other Canadians.

The Liberal Reformed Dutch-Canadians

The liberal Reformed immigrants, especially *hervormden* with higher education, came the closest to fitting the stereotype of the "ideal immigrant" in WASP-dominated Ontario. Together with *remonstranten* and members of the *Protestantenbond* (see chapter 3), they represent a more cosmopolitan trend within Dutch Protestantism. The value system of people brought up as *hervormd* made it easier for them to join mainstream Protestant denominations in Canada, especially if their background was urban middle class. People originating in small towns or farming communities who were *hervormd* would not have had much exposure to the English language, and their religious values were more traditional. Their lifestyle and value system were nonetheless similar to those of Protestants in small-town or rural Ontario. They, too, did not have much difficulty "fitting in." The successful assimilation of these Dutch Protestants was further facilitated by ecclesiastical policy. Prior to 1950, the *Hervormde Kerk* advised its members to join the United Church upon arrival in Canada. Not until several years later did the Reformed Church of America (the closest equivalent to the Dutch Reformed Church) send fieldmen to Canada. Even then, few congregations were founded. Consequently many townspeople, and quite a few independent farmers who belonged to this Dutch denomination, joined the United Church, which operated in most towns and cities in Ontario.

The proportion of Dutch-Canadians belonging to the United Church ranges from 10 to 15 percent, and church members of Dutch background are spread out all over Ontario. Indeed, almost all United congregations have anywhere from a few to a dozen Dutch-Canadian families.[13] Such families of Dutch background recognize each other, but are not perceived as an ethnic bloc; they were quickly accepted and became involved at all levels of the church.[14] Their offspring attended public schools and universities, and rarely married into their own ethnic category.[15] These liberal Protestants, or people of *hervormd* background, had few difficulties adapting to a Canadian lifestyle because they were already accustomed to separating their religious practices and beliefs from other aspects of social life. Indeed, in the Netherlands, liberal Calvinists with a higher level of education often identified themselves with the "neutral" sector. Moreover, *hervormd* professionals looking for the Canadian equivalent of a prestigious church could always join a more "up-scale" United congregation.[16]

The rapid integration of most *hervormden* into a Canadian "mainstream" denomination is a good illustration of how the dispositions of this segment of the Dutch population were well matched for at least one well-established religious 'field' of Canadian society. Only more conservative *hervormden* would not feel "at home" in Canadian Protestant denominations due to the stricter rules followed in the small rural congregations they had left behind. This segment of people of *hervormd* background would be more likely to join a "Dutch" church (mainly Christian Reformed).[17] However, the vast majority of non-orthodox Dutch Calvinists integrated quickly into the mainstream Protestant sector of small-town and rural Ontario.

Social Acceptance in Durham

Albert John Koeslag, a farmer with a medium-sized mixed operation in Laren (Gelderland), first came into contact with Canadians in April of 1945, during the liberation of Holland. He emigrated in 1948 and settled in the area around Durham, where the family joined the Knox United Church. They had been *hervormd* and had no interest in joining the Christian Reformed Church. Although they helped a few other Dutch families get farm sponsors, and kept in touch with relatives in the Netherlands, they had more social contacts with already well-established Canadians of British origin. They also received a lot of attention and recognition as a result of the family's prior involvement with the Canadian army.[18] When the Koeslag family's oldest son, John, married the woman to whom he was engaged prior to emigrating, their wedding was attended by the RCAF officers they had helped during the War. This son, who had already finished a program at a Dutch agricultural college prior to emigration, became a high school teacher in the town of Durham between 1955 and 1967, after two further years of study at the Ontario Agricultural College in Guelph.

We can learn a lot about the social acceptance of such Protestant Dutch-Canadian families by looking at the gossip columns of local newspapers.[19] For example, visits from Mr. and Mrs. Kessler, the parents of John's wife, were regularly reported in the local press, starting in 1957. We learn that the Kesslers had entertained allied troops in their home in Holland. John's father-in-law, a University of Leiden graduate, was a member of a prominent family that included the founder of Shell Oil; Mrs. Kessler had studied voice and piano at the Amsterdam conservatory. During one of their trips to Canada, this older couple provided the music for a meeting of the Grey county chapter of the Imperial Order of Daughters of the Empire, held at John's home. The Koeslags, who were themselves actively involved in community affairs, became completely integrated into Canadian society.[20] Even those who married Dutch spouses after arriving in Canada had little contact with other Dutch-Canadians apart from their relatives. For example, the high school teacher (John), did not get to know any other Dutch-Canadians when he moved to Barrie to teach at a nearby military base. After retirement he moved to a remote part of central Ontario.[21]

Notwithstanding their incorporation into mainstream Protestant congregations in small towns, people like the Koeslags did not abandon all aspects of their ethnic heritage. Indeed, middle-class Dutch immigrants who came to Canada when they were adults often retained their ability to read and write standard Dutch, even if they rarely had the opportunity to speak Dutch (see chapter 11). Nor did they abandon their nationally based ethnic identity. For example, members from several Dutch-Canadian families in Durham sang the Dutch national anthem when they joined their Canadian neighbours in celebrating the anniversary of the liberation of Holland in 1970. A photograph of the new Minto-Clifford Central Public School taken in 1966 also shows a picture of *sinterklaas* as part of their display.[22]

Apart from their personal ethnic identity, mainstream Protestants of Dutch background retained other deeply ingrained dispositions, although they might not acknowledge the extent to which their values and habits survived their transformation into "typical Canadians." Even successful, well-integrated first-generation Dutch-Canadian couples who are liberal Protestants, including professionals, continued to be "Dutch" at some level. An anecdote from another part of Ontario illustrates this point. In the fifties, a half dozen Dutch couples joined the United Church in Beamsville because they did not want to join any of the Reformed churches located nearby. The reasons given were similar to those I have heard in other places—"Dutch" churches were for "farmers," and prone to "gossip and in-fighting." Yet 30 years later, when theological controversies engendered considerable debate and controversy in Beamsville's United congregation, the most vociferous spokesmen on both sides of the debate were these same Dutch people who had earlier joined the congregation to get away from such "squabbling."[23]

The "Neutrals"

The "neutral" block in Dutch society was a more amorphous category partially overlapping with other sectors (see chapter 3). Apart from liberal Protestants, this pillar included people with no religious affiliation, and nominal Catholics. In the Canadian context, some of these people, who had not been church-goers at home, ended up joining mainstream Canadian churches. Others became part of the secular stream found in the bigger cities of Canada.[24] In many respects, these "neutrals" were similar to liberal Reformed in terms of how they adapted to their new environment. They became well integrated into Canadian society and sent their children to public school. However, not all member of the "neutral" pillar became part of a homogeneous, largely secular crowd. Members of specific Dutch sub-groups, such as card-carrying humanists and socialists looked for, and eventually found, their own niches (see interlude 7.3).[25]

The Dutch "neutral" pillar has so far been portrayed as non-religious. Indeed, orthodox Calvinists and more traditional Catholics portray members of that segment of Dutch society as "Godless" and anti-religious. However, the Dutch term "neutral" (*neutraal*) has another connotation: non-partisan or someone in favour of a school system that accommodates pupils from all religious backgrounds. In fact, identification with that label allowed religious minorities, such as modern Dutch Mennonites[26] or Jews, to preserve their own social networks in a society dominated by Calvinists and Catholics. When people who had belonged to these minorities emigrated to Canada, they too found their own niche and preserved their own group identity and cultural values.

Dutch Jews[27]

At home the Jewish community had a more complex and ambiguous relationship with the rest of Dutch society than Dutch Catholics or people belonging to dissident Calvinist groups.[28] One cannot deny the presence of anti-Semitism within Christianity, including its Dutch version.[29] At the same time Dutch people of a variety of religious persuasions assisted and hid Jews at great personal risk and economic sacrifice during the Nazi occupation. This combination of prejudice, ambivalence and respect was reproduced in a North American context. It is difficult to estimate exactly how many Dutch-Canadians of Jewish background there are in Ontario today.[30] Dutch secular Jews, who might define Jewishness as a cultural heritage, would not necessarily declare they are Jewish by religion. If we go according to the 1980 census, it looks like there were only about 20 Jews of Dutch descent in Toronto.[31] However, using a broader definition including anyone of Jewish background, there must be at least several hundred first- and second-generation Jewish Dutch-Canadians in the greater Toronto area.[32] All of them became aware of considerable anti-Semitism in Toronto and other parts of Ontario.[33] One Jewish Dutch immigrant who started working in a bank faced discrimination when his fellow employees discovered his Jewish background. They could not understand that one could be Dutch and Jewish at the same time.[34] One Dutch Jew joined the Anglican church as a way of becoming socially accepted.[35]

Newly arrived Jewish immigrants presented themselves to fellow Dutch immigrants either as practising Jews or secular humanists. The latter would normally not talk about their Jewish background. However, given the slight nuances in accents and mannerism, and the way Dutch people recognize each other through surnames, Dutch people would soon discover someone's religious background. Nonetheless, the Dutch-speaking Jewish minority became an integral component of an emerging urban Dutch-Canadian community. In the Toronto area, a handful of both secular and religious Jews played an active role in Dutch-Canadian organizations, including a large credit union (see chapter 15). These Jewish Dutch immigrants became part of a close-knit social network of largely middle-class urban Dutch-Canadians.[36] They also had as much, if not more, social contact with other Dutch-Canadians as with native-born Canadians. In fact, orthodox Dutch Jews had difficulties getting accepted by their non-Dutch counterparts in Toronto because of cultural differences.[37] The largely prewar Jewish immigrants, who had come predominantly from Eastern Europe, could not understand how someone who did not speak Yiddish and who had a very Dutch-sounding name could possibly be a Jew—even if the Dutch Jew was more orthodox.[38] Such intra-religious tensions continue. I once asked a non-Dutch member of the Jewish community in Toronto whether he knew any Dutch Jews. He replied, "Yes, and they are very dogmatic and legalistic."[39]

The vast majority of the non-Jewish Dutch immigrants who live in rural Ontario have had no contact with Dutch Jews since coming to Canada. Of numerous people I interviewed on farms or rural villages, all but one told me they had never met Dutch Jews in Canada. However, the broader Canadian Jewish community is certainly not oblivious of the Dutch-Canadian presence in Ontario. On several occasions postwar immigrants, usually of a humble rural background, have received special recognition from the Israeli government and the international Jewish community for their heroism in hiding Jews during the War. In his book *Quiet Heroes*, André Stein writes the following with regard to a list of rescuers presented at a 1984 conference in Washington on "righteous Gentiles":

> There were more Dutch people among them than any other nationality. Furthermore, many of these Dutch people had resettled in Ontario, mostly in small towns and rural communities. It turned out that most of them were born and raised in the northern Dutch province of Friesland."[40]

Over the last decade or so, Dutch-Canadian Jews have become increasingly more visible to the broader Dutch-Canadian community, as they became a topic of discussion in the Dutch-Canadian ethnic press, Reformed churches, and conferences organized by Dutch-Canadian intellectuals.[41] In this climate of self-reflection, a number of Dutch-Canadians who were brought up in a Jewish environment, are now reclaiming their religio-cultural identity.[42]

The Orthodox Calvinists

The Dutch orthodox Calvinists (mainly *gereformeerden*) warrant special attention because of their high profile. I have found no strong evidence that members of this sub-group are more or less likely to stress their Dutch heritage than other Dutch-Canadians. Yet, unlike other segments of the Dutch immigrant population, the Calvinists achieved a high level of institutional completeness. They built their own churches and started their own schools, social organizations and a myriad of other institutions.[43] Since the orthodox Dutch Calvinist grouping is more "visible" and displays a high level of group cohesion and endogamy, they are more likely to survive as a separate group within the North American context than any other category of people with Dutch connections. Despite linguistic assimilation, the orthodox Dutch Calvinists have replicated a worldview, and a pattern of internal tensions, typical of the Netherlands (see chapter 9). They thus illustrate a close connection between religious and ethnic boundaries.[44] To properly explain this sub-group requires a chapter all by itself.

However, not all the immigrants who were brought up as *gereformeerd* became part of the Reformed community in Canada. Many Dutch orthodox Calvinists who came into contact with pentecostal forms of Christianity, might find religions with a greater emphasis on evangelism more appealing than the rationalism of Dutch Calvinism. Younger Reformed Dutch-Canadians who felt alienated or cut off from their own religious grouping often made likely converts. In chapter 5 we saw an example of this happening in Wellington county, where a charismatic movement won a significant proportion of converts from both the Christian Reformed and Reformed congregations in the city of Guelph. Some orthodox Calvinists refused to join Reformed congregations for other reasons. Some newcomers, especially those of low socio-economic status, wanted to "get ahead" in Canada as quickly as possible; for them, joining any of the Reformed churches, which were perceived to be Dutch, was seen as a barrier to success. Others also did not "fit in," even if they were not ashamed of their ethnic background. Reformed Dutch-Canadian churches counted members with a variety of socio-economic backgrounds. Even orthodox Calvinists who had run small businesses or who were professionals in the Netherlands usually encountered at least one or two people from the same region and class background. However, anyone who was an oddball—for example, an insurance agent from Rotterdam among a group of Frisian-speaking farmers—might be tempted to join a Canadian church, as long as that church was perceived to be strict enough for their liking.[45] For those looking for a "Canadian" church that was still Reformed, the choice was Presbyterian.

Dutch-Canadians in the Presbyterian Church

The Presbyterian Church has a natural affinity with the Reformed church since it is also Calvinist in orientation. Social historians have commented on the similarities between the dispositions of people in Scotland and the Netherlands in terms of their austerity and independence.[46] However, while some orthodox Calvinists joined the Presbyterian Church in Canada, many found the Presbyterian churches in Canada either too "liberal"[47] or too "Scottish" for their liking. That might explain why such a small percentage of postwar Dutch immigrants became Presbyterians. Nevertheless, unlike the case of the United Church, whose Dutch-Canadian constituency is fairly evenly distributed throughout Ontario, the Dutch do constitute an ethnic cluster in some Presbyterian congregations. For example, in Fergus there are seven Dutch-Canadian families who constitute a "Dutch" network in a congregation that still has a strong Scottish flavour.[48] In Chesley (in Bruce county), the Dutch are likewise associated with only one of three Presbyterian churches, which seem to be divided along ethnic lines.[49] At the same time the Presbyterian Church in Canada has several ministers of recent Dutch descent,[50] including Tony Plomp, their first national moderator born in the Netherlands.

Apart from receiving postwar Dutch Calvinist immigrants—including a few *hervormden*—there are other connections between the Presbyterian Church and Dutch-Canadian Reformed churches. Although the Presbyterian Church was even less interested in attracting immigrant families than the United Church, it did recruit at least one Dutch minister directly from the Netherlands to minister to potential Dutch-Canadian members.[51] However, once in Canada, this immigrant clergyman ended up serving mainly non-Dutch congregations. Not until relatively late in his career did he came into more extensive contact with Dutch-Canadians, when he was occasionally invited to preach to Christian Reformed congregations.[52] Thus, while a certain level of compatibility and historical connections—and pure chance—can account for a modest influx of postwar immigrants into this denomination, the dispositions of orthodox Dutch Calvinists were more in tune with a parallel religious 'field' (especially the institutions of the Christian Reformed community) already well established in North America.

The Roman Catholics

For the most part, Dutch Catholics have been absorbed into the North American version of Roman Catholicism, although the parishes they joined in Canada had few or no previous Dutch connections. However, compared to their Protestants counterparts, Dutch Catholic immigrants were more likely to come into contact with diverse, multicultural congregations.[53] Like other Catholic immigrants, those of Dutch background were inclined to vote Liberal while Protestants gave greater support to the Conservative Party.[54] Dutch Catholics, who were more lax in such matters as social drinking and dancing, also became more involved than their Calvinist counterparts in ethnic cultural clubs which organize dances and take part in multicultural events (see chapter 16).[55] Yet, while they usually made up a minority within most Canadian congregations (like the Dutch liberal Protestants), Dutch Catholic immigrants represented a high percentage, sometimes even a majority, in some rural parishes. While the situation changed rapidly with the influx of Catholics of other nationalities, Dutch-Canadian Catholics ended up constituting more than half the population in some parts of rural southwestern Ontario. In such, Dutch Catholic immigrants also married within their own ethnic group. For this reason the Dutch-Canadian Roman Catholics—who have been neglected by social historians—will have to be scrutinized in more detail in the next chapter.

Summary and Broad Comparisons

While all Dutch immigrants experienced rapid linguistic assimilation, they went in different directions. In Ontario, like the rest of English-speaking Canada, most Dutch immigrants were absorbed into one of three broad segments that continue to define social interaction in the North American setting. The majority of people in North America still belong to either the Roman Catholic, the Protestant or the Jewish bloc.[56] However, it would be misleading to compare Dutch-Canadians who have a Christian background simply in terms of a Catholic versus Protestant dichotomy. Not all Dutch Calvinists had the same dispositions or values, and we cannot generalize about the way they became inserted into Canadian society. Indeed, in terms of a continuum of social integration, the liberal versus orthodox Calvinists appear at opposite ends, while the other groupings would fall somewhere in between. The more liberal Dutch Protestants (mainly *hervormd*) integrated most quickly and were more readily accepted. They have become the most "invisible." The "neutrals" and the majority of Dutch Catholics also integrated very rapidly.

However, if "integration" means fitting into an ongoing North American trend towards increasing secularization, then a large number of Dutch-Canadians did not integrate very much. Dutch orthodox Calvinists reinforced and redefined a form of "traditional" puritanism in Ontario society. They did this by expanding a small religious denomination founded by Dutch orthodox Calvinists in the United States as well as founding their own (see chapter 9). Orthodox Calvinists also created a host of new institutions that left a small but durable imprint on Canadian society. They have consequently become highly "visible," although not in the sense of skin colour, dress code or speaking a different language. The influence of this sub-grouping has been disproportional to its smaller numerical weight. Orthodox Calvinists thus constitute the only "transported" pillar that has endured the test of time.

The minor groupings are not include in this broad comparison because they were not big enough. If they had been numerically stronger, would Dutch Mennonites, Dutch Jews or Dutch-Indonesians as distinct sub-groups have significantly modified Canadian society? I will not speculate, although the readers can draw their own conclusions on the basis of more information to come (see chapter 10). Yet even in generalizing about the major groupings, much internal diversity is glossed over.

A minority of Dutch Catholics have preserved, and in some cases revived, more traditional and close-knit ethnic parishes. In a half dozen parishes, the Dutch-Canadian Catholic grouping is even more close-knit and cohesive than many orthodox Calvinist communities. Dutch-Canadian Catholics have also had an impact in a broader regional setting, but in ways that are no longer obvious. This is why Dutch Catholics, in their totality, occupy a somewhat lower position on the ladder of "integration" than either the "neutral" wing or the more liberal Protestants. This may come as a surprise. The existence of a unique Dutch-Canadian presence of Catholic origin in Ontario represents the remnants of a largely unsuccessful transplanting of the Dutch Catholic version of the Dutch system into Canada. But that is a story by itself.

Fieldnotes Interlude

7.1 Excerpt (translated) from an interview with a Dutch-Canadian physician in a small town in southwestern Ontario, October 22, 1989

I was *hervormd* and joined the United Church in this town. Many Dutch intellectuals who came to Canada did not want to join the Christian Reformed Church because they saw that only farmers belonged to that denomination. But I got along well with my Dutch patients who were of farm background because of my rural experience during the War, when I had to go underground in Groningen. . . . You know, it is funny; there are eight Dutch ministers in this town and they all became my patients. However, we never spoke about religion. I don't know if they would have come to me if this town had had a physician who was also Reformed (*gereformeerd*). But maybe then they would have needed eight physicians!

I can see why someone might get the impression that all the Dutch people in this area are Reformed [*gereformeerd*]. I have met some Dutch Catholics too, but you can count them on your fingers. They also chose me as their doctor. But the Reformed form the vast majority around here.

7.2 Excerpt from an interview with a Dutch-Canadian woman (retired from farming), in Wyoming, June 4, 1991

We had two neighbours. One was a Dutch Protestant and the other did not go to church anywhere. There was not much social contact and we had more to do with the Canadians than with the Dutch Protestants. For example, we once had to walk to church because of a flat tire. It was a Canadian who picked us up and the Christian Reformed neighbour passed us. In the beginning we felt that the Dutch Protestants were more against Catholics than Canadians of different backgrounds. There is still a bit of that. For example, we have a big choir and we have sung in their church but not the other way around.

When our youngest son died in 1982, lots of people of the community attended the funeral but no one came from the Christian Reformed Church. But I think there is more communication today than in the past and some working together. I find they are willing to talk to you and be friendly when we meet in town, but there is not much social interaction in other places. They have their own ideas and are very strict.

7.3 Excerpt from an interview with a Dutch-Canadian truck driver, in Guelph, March 27, 1990

I came from Kapelle, in Zeeland, and had never been to any big city before coming here. When I got to Canada I worked on different farms, especially in the tobacco country. I actually arrived in Hamilton and was sponsored by the Reformed church, although I didn't know that until I came here. I can't really say I go to church any more, but my wife does attend the Reformed church. She takes her mother there, who lives upstairs in the house here, and does it for her.

My father in Holland was a socialist and he belonged to the NVV [a non-aligned labour union] and he was also a member of the *Partij van de Arbeid* [the Dutch Labour Party]. . . . I remember how my father and a group of friends used to meet after church and how opposed they were to Colijn [a conservative Dutch prime minister]. Some of those people, who sympathized with the socialists, were *gereformeerd* (orthodox Calvinists). I also knew a *gereformeerde*, when I lived in Stratford, who openly supported the NDP and he even did some campaigning for them. He would rarely go to the meetings although he did help out whenever they needed someone, but he was opposed to the NDP stance on abortions. . . . over time I have come across many other Dutch immigrants in the labour movement or who supported the NDP. For example, I remember a Dutchman on the provincial council, who was a member of the Automakers in London. I know another Dutchman involved in the NDP who lives in Aylmer. He came from a section of Groningen where the communists were very strong and where they even had a seat on the town council. That man in Aylmer used to vote for the communists in the Netherlands. They were also members of the *Hervormde Kerk* (Reformed Church)—at least his father was—but they were not really church-going types.

I became actively involved in the NDP about ten years ago, although I used to vote NDP long before that. I think I joined the NDP when I lived in Stratford, in 1969. In Huron county I got involved in the National Farmers Union, when I tried my hand at farming. There were lots of Dutch farmers involved in that union and they were mainly Catholic farmers, from the Ashfield area, north of Mitchell. There were also a few Protestants. . . .

Chapter 8

The Fate of the Catholic Pillar

Dutch Catholic immigrants usually found parochial schools and a church to their liking, although it was difficult to confess to a parish priest who could not understand Dutch. There were no Canadian equivalents for Dutch Catholic lay organizations. They could join the Knights of Columbus, but there were no Catholic labour or farmer unions, nor an Ontario counterpart to the French-Canadian *caisses populaires* (credit unions), which resembled Dutch Catholic cooperative banks. When a group of Dutch priests set up institutions for Dutch Catholics in one part of Ontario, they received grass-roots support. However, their vision of how to organize immigrants—which reflected assumptions inherent in the Dutch pillar system—clashed with the political realities of Canadian society. Not only did they confront a still largely Protestant-dominated provincial government, but the immigrant priests did not take ethnic and political divisions within the Canadian Catholic hierarchy into account. While their labour resulted in the clustering of Dutch Catholics in several pockets of rural Ontario, the mission of transplanting the Dutch model in Canada failed. Nor could they stem the centripetal forces that drove Catholics from different regions and classes apart.

Upon arrival, Dutch Catholics had access to services not that different from those in the Netherlands; prior to the sixties, Latin was the liturgical language in Catholic churches worldwide, and separate schools received state support as they did at home. However, they still had to adapt to an English-speaking environment.[1] As we saw in the last chapter, Dutch Catholics were generally absorbed into existing Canadian parishes and their children tended to marry outside their ethnic group. Unlike Catholic immigrants from other countries, the Dutch did not set up special

---

Notes to this chapter are on p. 354-58.

"ethnic" parishes. However, we must take local variation into account. The presence of Dutch Catholics did not go unnoticed in many small towns and villages that saw an influx of Dutch immigrants in the late forties and fifties; by the 1960s, Dutch families equalled or outnumbered their Canadian-born Catholic neighbours in many rural parishes.[2] For example, the Dutch farm immigrants on Wolfe Island were originally all Catholics, and they had their own priest. Also, in a number of localities in southwestern Ontario, a religious order of Dutch priests actively promoted Dutch Catholic immigration.

The ethnic mix of parishes receiving large numbers of Dutch immigrants in the early fifties changed rapidly throughout the late fifties and sixties, when the inflow of Dutch newcomers was overtaken by a larger wave of Italians, Portuguese and other European Catholic immigrants. This happened even in towns where the Dutch already constituted a significant component of the local congregation. For instance, in Strathroy, the Dutch started arriving in 1949; by 1953 they comprised the majority of a small congregation. However, with the arrival of Portuguese immigrants in Strathroy, resulting in the expansion of one parish into two, the Dutch became a minority, although they still make up almost half the congregation in All Saints parish.[3] Only in various rural parishes in the counties of Lambton, Middlesex and Perth do the Dutch remain predominant; they also still constitute more than half the Catholics in Ingersoll, in Oxford county. A Dutch Catholic presence can similarly be detected in Winchester and Chesterville, in Stormont county, south of Ottawa.[4] In such parishes, Dutch Catholics are more likely to intermarry and retain a separate identity right up until the third generation.

The Dutch-Canadian Rural Parish in Ontario

To some extent, postwar Dutch Catholic rural immigrants followed a pattern established by block settlements of ethnic groups who emigrated to Ontario at an earlier time. In the forties and fifties, Protestants and Catholics operated in separate social worlds, much as in the Netherlands at that time, and Catholicism was associated with specific ethnic labels. Some Catholic parishes in rural Ontario had previously been French-speaking, while the English-speaking ones were often dominated by Irish-Canadians—in the Ottawa Valley, Landsdowne (near Kingston) and parts of southwestern Ontario. In Middlesex and Oxford counties, people referred to the "Roman" line, a string of predominantly Catholic settlements of Irish descent stretching from Ingersoll (close to Woodstock) to Dublin (in Perth county). These parishes had difficulties surviving in the fifties, given a rapidly dwindling rural population and low birth rates. Thus the Canadian clergy encouraged the settlement of Dutch Catholic families who were looking for land in the fifties.

In parishes with educated, middle-class English-speaking leaders, rural Dutch Catholic immigrants kept a low profile, although they provided the volunteers for choirs and served in the kitchen and as members of clean-up crews.[5] In other places Dutch Catholic immigrants themselves played a leading role. Dutch immigrants were largely responsible for starting separate schools in Stayner, Kingsbridge (north of Goderich), Thamesford, Brussels and Kintore.[6] In still other parts of rural Ontario, the efforts of a combination of Dutch priests, plus farm immigrants who had played a prominent role in the public sphere in the Netherlands, resulted in a virtual takeover of the hitherto weak and disorganized parishes. The strong presence of these Dutch Catholic immigrant farm families alarmed their English-Canadian Protestant neighbours, especially in regions with a strong tradition of Orange lodges.[7]

Dutch immigrants intermarried in rural parishes where they constituted a majority. This first happened during the initial contact period, when young people making the adjustment to a new language and way of life felt more at ease with members of the opposite sex who belonged to their own ethnic group. However, in a few localities the trend of marrying spouses of Dutch Catholic background continued into the second generation of the now English-speaking Dutch-Canadians. This pattern of endogamy among some Dutch-Canadian Catholics does not per se reflect a strong preference for spouses of Dutch background. Although Dutch immigrant parents thought it would be "nice" if their son or daughter married someone who was also "Dutch," it was considered much more important that they marry someone who was Catholic. On the provincial level, and certainly in urbanized areas, a consistent pattern of ethnic group endogamy did not become widespread among Dutch Catholic immigrants, in contrast to the orthodox Calvinists (see chapter 9). Rather, the chances of marrying someone whose parents were also Dutch Catholic immigrants were higher in areas where a large percentage of students in primary, and later, secondary schools belonged to the same ethnic group and religion.

In some rural areas, the majority of Catholic primary school students were still Dutch-Canadians at the time this research was conducted. In the Catholic school in Park Hill, which draws pupils from the surrounding rural areas, over 90 percent of the students were of Dutch descent in 1990.[8] The percentage of Dutch students attending the Catholic school in Arkona numbered around 80.[9] In other places Dutch children used to form the majority of pupils not too long ago. In St. Joseph's school in Uxbridge, which was not an area of heavy concentration for Dutch Catholics, about half the student population were children of Dutch immigrants.[10] Another example is the Holy Rosary School in Wyoming. Based on figures in a 1964-65 school yearbook, 50 percent of all students in grades 1, 2 and 3 were children of Dutch immigrants.[11] The percentage for grades 5 and 6 was even higher; 24 out of 44 students were Dutch.

Social contact among young people with the same ethnic background attending these schools was not the only factor that led to endogamy among some Dutch Catholics. An equally important criterion for mate selection was farm background. Only in places where most full-time farmers also happen to be Dutch Catholics do we find de facto "Dutch-Canadian" parishes. A good illustration of a strong Dutch presence is Our Lady Help of Christians parish, in the village of Watford. According to a young third-generation Dutch-Canadian woman in that part of the countryside, over 90 percent of the parish and the student population attending St. Peter Canisius school (which serves the same parish) are still "Dutch" today.[12] The same young woman, whose father was only five when he came to Canada, speaks no Dutch, but when I asked her how many of her friends were Dutch, she answered "between 80 and 90 percent." In order to get a better picture of the recent history as well as the ongoing connections between the Catholic Dutch-Canadian rural families in this area, I conducted a long interview with one of her neighbours, who lives just inside of the boundary of St. Christopher, another parish dominated by Dutch-Canadians.[13]

St. Christopher parish serves Roman Catholics living in the townships of Bosanquet and Warwick (Lambton county). According to a written parish history, the present church building in the town of Forest dates from 1893. This parish, which used to include Grand Bend on Lake Huron, had been served by priests stationed in Sarnia or London up until 1939.[14] Although the church obtained its own resident priest at that time, it was still a small parish, but one covering a large geographical area. Only after 1949 did the parish start to grow, with the first arrival of a large number of immigrants from the Netherlands. These Dutch Catholic families organized a Catholic primary school, St. Mary's, on the 6th line of Warwick township in 1964.[15] The 1989 St. Christopher yearbook lists 382 families. Of these, 195 are Dutch-Canadian couples or, in a few cases, couples with one partner of recent Dutch background. Although the Dutch represent only a little over 50 percent of that parish, the proportion is close to 70 percent if we look only at those who had a rural address (particularly in the vicinity of Arkona).[16] The names of several large extended Dutch-Canadian families appear more than four times in the same yearbook: Boere (7), De Groot (5), Devet (5), Koolen (6), Rombout (5), Van Bree (7), Vandenberg (7), Van Engelen (8), Van Kessel (5) and Vanos (9). This list does not include a half dozen other big "clans" with only four family units in this parish, but who are well represented in other parts of southwestern Ontario. These families are all descended from postwar farm immigrants, some of whom already knew each other in the Netherlands.[17] Within one generation they all became part of a cohesive rural community, bound together through kinship ties.

Figure 4 shows the extent of kinship ties, especially among Dutch Catholic farm families. The three brothers at the top, whose parents (now deceased) emigrated to Canada in the late forties, all live in or near the village of Arkona. The married offspring of this family, labelled "A," plus their spouses, are included. The rest of the letters represent other surnames (maiden surnames in the case of women). Figure 4 also indicates places of present or original residence other than Arkona.[18] Almost all the couples shown in the figure are full-time and, in some cases, part-time farmers. You will notice that in several cases, brothers and sisters married siblings from another family, creating an even denser network of kinship ties.[19] No members of this family network have yet married outside their ethnic group, although other families in the parish of St. Christopher have at least some Canadian in-laws. Figure 4 also shows how this family in Arkona formed links through marriage with other Dutch-Canadian families in nearby towns and villages.[20]

Figure 4
Kinship Network of a Dutch Catholic Family in Arkona

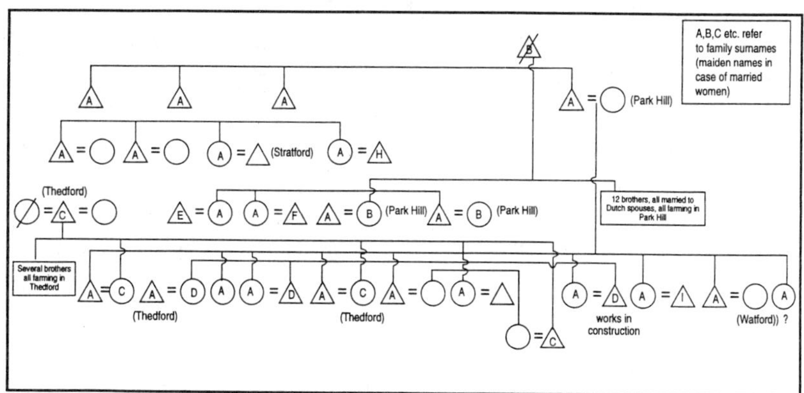

Family connections link Dutch-Canadian Catholic farmers to small business operators, teachers and other professionals in larger towns or in the city of London. Although some non-farm relatives also have spouses of Catholic Dutch background, they are more likely to marry outside their ethnic group. The children of younger and more educated Dutch-Canadians will in turn have looser ties with their own ethnic group, unless they enter occupations that will bring them into direct contact with the

Dutch farming community. Marriage to non-Dutch spouses is also more prevalent when male family members enter other occupations—such as welding, carpentry or construction work—which requires residence in or constant commuting to nearby cities. Figure 5 illustrates a typical pattern of ethnic intermarriage for several interconnected families in Wyoming, near Sarnia.[21] Such exogamy (marrying outside one's group) increases in areas with a lower concentration of Dutch-Canadians.

Figure 5
Kinship Network of a Dutch Catholic Family in Wyoming

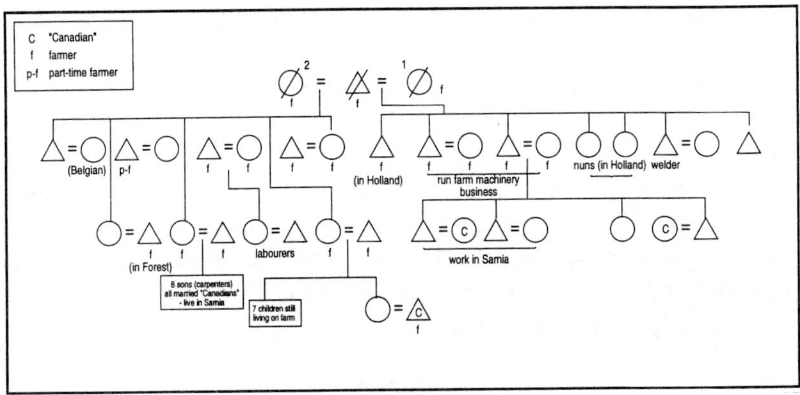

The high level of concentration of Dutch-Canadian Catholics in the diocese of London, which includes all of the rural areas so far described, is not the result of coincidence or purely economic factors. The social infrastructure that brought these families of the same ethnic and religious background together was put into place by a group of Dutch immigrant priests belonging to the Sacred Heart religious order. Although they collaborated with their Canadian counterparts, these Dutch priests coordinated the placement of postwar Dutch immigrant farmers, and provided the support needed for the initial period of transition to the Canadian way of life. They provided at least some cohesion among Catholic Dutch-Canadians.

The Role of the Sacred Heart Fathers

The Sacred Heart fathers (*congregatie van het Heilig Hart* or *SCJ*) is an international religious order founded in France. In the nineteenth century they sent a small group of priests to Western Canada; some of these priests eventually moved to Montreal. The order's Father General later rebuilt their "province" in Canada, this time with Dutch priests who had their own centre in the Netherlands. By 1949 there were only three of them in Canada and they had close links with a larger province in the

United States.[22] The national council of bishops invited his Dutch Sacred Heart order to send more Dutch priests to Canada when the former became aware of the special needs of Dutch Catholic immigrants. Anne van de Valk, a Dutch schoolteacher who had already accompanied immigrants from her native province of Noord Brabant on boat trips to Canada during the late forties, played a key role in bringing these needs to the Canadian bishops' attention. She spoke English and ended up staying in Ottawa to work as secretary to the Canadian Conference of Catholic Bishops (CCCB). Father White, then director of immigration and rural settlement for the diocese of London, was another key player.[23] This Canadian priest persuaded the bishop of London to appoint a Sacred Heart father to work full time with Dutch immigrants throughout the large diocese of London.[24] The order then purchased an old homestead with a house and 360 acres of land in the village of Delaware. This site became the nucleus of a new parish within the diocese of London, run by Dutch priests but meant for all Catholic families who lived in the area, regardless of ethnic origin.[25] Like the postwar Catholic lay immigrants from the Netherlands, these Dutch priests brought with them the assumptions and values of the Dutch pillar system.

In the Netherlands, the Sacred Heart fathers specialized in ministering to socially disadvantaged groups, including people displaced by war and the families of seamen. Jan van Wezel and Martin Grootscholten, who had both worked in Rotterdam, were interested in ministering to the immigrants flocking to Canada. Those priests gained their first Canadian experience in Delaware in the early fifties, and subsequently worked with Dutch immigrants throughout the diocese and beyond. About a dozen additional Dutch Sacred Heart priests, later put in charge of parishes in other parts of Ontario,[26] joined them in the mid-fifties. Some of these priests, including fathers Grootscholten and van Wezel, eventually returned to the Netherlands to retire, but the rest stayed in Canada. These Sacred Heart fathers carried out a variety of tasks. For example, John Meendering was pastor for seven years in Uxbridge, and worked in many other places where there were Dutch immigrant families.[27] He also served as bursar for the order, first in Delaware and later in Ottawa, site of another minor seminary, before retiring in Caledonia (near Hamilton), where the Sacred Heart order is in charge of St. Patrick's parish.[28]

Sometimes the Dutch priests had to interrupt their work to serve their order in other parts of the world. Thus, Father Falke twice left Canada for several years to work in Uganda. In Ontario, he not only spent time in the parishes run by his order (including Uxbridge) but also taught in their minor seminary in Delaware.[29] Like the other Dutch priests of his order, he also performed his pastoral duties in predominantly non-Dutch parishes. For example, Father Falke spent 12 years at St. Monica in Nepean (part of Ottawa). There only about a dozen out of approximately 500 families were Dutch-Canadian, although he considered them among his most loyal parishioners. Such personal contacts with small groups of Dutch Catholics throughout the province helped to reinforce an emerging network of Dutch Catholics. Father Falke later moved to Toronto, where the Sacred Heart fathers still run the very large parish of St. Joan of Arc today.[30]

While Dutch-Canadian Catholic families throughout Ontario thus had sporadic contact with Dutch clergy, the Sacred Heart order had their greatest impact in the London region. Apart from saying mass and hearing confessions in Dutch, they organized youth clubs, an annual picnic at Delaware and became involved in a credit union for Dutch Catholics. Father Grootscholten, who came to Canada in the mid-fifties, acted as advisor for these Dutch Catholic organizations. He also supervised an immigrant reception centre, located in downtown London, which later served as a residence for young Dutch-Canadian women who found jobs in the city. Another activity was to organized dances where young immigrants could socialize with other Dutch Catholics, as part of a deliberate policy to foster marriages among the offspring of young first generation Dutch Catholics.[31]

Van Wezel, in charge of all immigration matters in the diocese of London in 1950, played a prominent part in implementing a vision that echoes the Dutch pillar system. His first task was bringing Dutch Catholic agrarian immigrants together, preferably in already existing parishes; for example, he personally supervised the reception of numerous Dutch immigrant families from Gelderland and Brabant in Kinkora (near Stratford). He wanted to help them settle down on their own farms as soon as possible so that their numerous children would be more likely to stay put and further strengthen bonds within the Catholic community. Catholic farm immigrants who had smuggled in money (inside the leg of a chair or the back of a painting) entrusted this to van Wezel, out of fear that this "black" money might be confiscated if it were deposited in the bank.[32] More importantly, this priest helped set up a Dutch Catholic credit union, called St. Willibrord, which became the focus of further social bonding among Dutch Catholic immigrants living in the London-Sarnia-Grand Bend triangle (see chapter 15). Not only did he do the initial homework for setting up this credit union, but he led negotiations with the Cooperative Dutch Farmer's Bank (*Co-operatieve Centrale Boerenleenbank*) who still held the assets of Dutch farm immigrants.[33] The reputation of van Wezel and the institutions set up by the Sacred Heart fathers attracted numerous Dutch Catholic immigrants to the London area. Lonely Dutch-Canadian Catholics, who first landed in the Maritimes or the prairies, flocked to join their friends and relatives in the London area. Soon there were thousands of them.[34]

Van Wezel hoped that his experiment with settling Dutch-Catholic farming families in the diocese of London could be replicated elsewhere. He initially received support from Bishop Cody of London. The bishop encouraged him to go to Ottawa in 1952 to better coordinate his work with the Department of Immigration, and thus channel Dutch Catholic immigrants to other areas that needed new parishioners. In Ottawa, Bishop Vanier invited van Wezel to set up a national centre for Dutch immigration. However, neither the Dutch Catholic hierarchy nor the Canadian government was willing to finance a Bureau of Catholic Immigration, since both were opposed to what might become predominantly Dutch parishes in Canada. In the meantime, Father van Wezel was sent to work in an Irish-Canadian parish about 50 miles from Ottawa.[35] Nonetheless, van Wezel decided to still focus his attention on national coordination in Ottawa. When he complained about the lack of services for Dutch Catholic immigrants, some resources (including a car) finally came his way via the International Catholic Immigration Council in Geneva.[36] However, despite all his efforts van Wezel's vision was not to come to pass.

The Collapse of the Dutch Catholic "Pillar" in Canada

Between 1952 and 1954, van Wezel sought sponsors for Dutch Catholic immigrants and arranged placements for Dutch priests in various parishes. In 1953, he joined forces with representatives of the two Calvinist immigration organizations already operating in Canada so that they could coordinate their activities. This became the CNIC mentioned in chapter 4. However, his attempt to promote a province-wide league of Dutch Catholic credit unions, an extension of St. Willibrord's in London, was a disaster. In the Netherlands, the Catholic Immigration Central supported van Wezel's idea of promoting a Catholic cooperative bank in Canada and they agreed to pay the salary of Niko van Wijk, a former inspector for the Dutch *Boerenleenbank* to help in the setting up of more branches of Dutch Catholic credit unions. However, although other credit unions were started by Dutch people throughout Ontario (see chapter 15), petitions initiated by van Wezel were systematically turned down.[37]

In a taped interview recorded later in his life, van Wezel provided his version of this failure. He claimed that the official in charge of approving the original charter for St. Willibrord Credit Union for the diocese of London was biased.[38] Van Wezel also suspected that Tuinman, the Dutch agricultural attaché in Ottawa, used his political influence to prevent the formation of a Dutch Catholic credit union league to prevent any further pillarization in the Canadian context. He thus accused Tuinman of imposing a "neutral" policy, whereby Dutch immigrants from different denominations were deliberately exposed as much as possible to people of opposing religious affiliations.[39] Such opposing visions resulted in tensions between Tuinman and all three of the denominationally based immigration societies. Van Wezel lodged a complaint in The Hague, via the Dutch Catholic Peoples' Party (*Katholieke Volkspartij*).[40] Nevertheless, it was too late to salvage the plan for a Dutch-Canadian Catholic credit union league.[41]

The difficulties faced by Father van Wezel illustrate the incompatibility of Canadian and Dutch socio-political structures. His plan for a separate Dutch Catholic credit union league implied collaboration between a Dutch Catholic organization and the government of Ontario, something inconceivable for either side. Even when the *Boerenleenbank* extended credit to the Catholic credit union in London in 1956, all financial transactions were channelled through the Dutch embassy,[42] resulting in delays and further frictions. Unlike the orthodox Reformed sector, which received financial assistance from the Christian Reformed Church based in Michigan, and could thus maintain some degree of independence, Dutch Catholic immigrant clergy and laymen in Canada had neither the financial resources nor the external support they needed to expand their base in London. Canada also did not have a united national Catholic hierarchy which might have provided the moral support for a Dutch-Canadian ethnic pillar.

While the bishop of Toronto was in favour of inviting Dutch priests to work in parishes with Dutch Catholic immigrants, Bishop Ryan of Hamilton was adamantly opposed to anything that smacked of ethnic parishes.[43] Moreover, the bishops of Quebec wanted van Wezel to set up his immigration centre in Montreal, which was already the location for SCER (Societé Canadien d'Etablissement Rural).[44] However, van Wezel preferred Ottawa because it was bilingual and the site for all the other immigration offices with jurisdiction on a national level.[45] In the taped interview mentioned above, van Wezel recalled a confrontation with Cardinal Léger of Quebec, in which Léger accused him of "sending all of those good Catholic families to the pagan regions of Canada."[46] Matters came to a head when Cardinal Léger complained to Cardinal McGuigan of Toronto that van Wezel was sowing discord between the English and French-speaking bishops. In 1957, van Wezel had to step down as director of the Central Bureau, which was thus effectively disbanded.[47]

Other Dutch Religious Orders

Several other Dutch Catholic religious orders came to operate in Ontario. In 1955 Bishop Cody of London invited the brothers of St. Louis, members of a teaching order, to his diocese. At first they lived in the house of the Sacred Heart order in Delaware, but then established their own communal residence in Aylmer, which lasted until 1967. The members of this religious order later joined the staff of a new Catholic High School in St. Thomas. Soon afterwards they took charge of St. Patrick's High School in Sarnia and set up their own centre and communal residence.[48] Like other Catholic orders, the brothers of St. Louis operated on an international scale. Their centre in Sarnia also served as a training centre for Dutch brothers to get English-language education diplomas so they could teach in other parts of the British Commonwealth. Apart from sporadic contacts, the brothers stationed in Sarnia did not specifically cater to the needs of the Dutch immigrants in Ontario.[49] A similar attempt by a group of Dutch nuns to establish their own house in the London area failed. Six came to Ontario, under the auspices of the Sacred Heart priests in Delaware, but they spent most of their time serving St. Peter's Seminary and King's College in London and eventually returned to the Netherlands (see chapter 13).[50]

Informal Networks

Notwithstanding strong bonds among Dutch-Canadian Catholics in the London area, no permanent Dutch Catholic institutions developed anywhere in Ontario. For about a decade, a group of Dutch Catholics undertook their own annual pilgrimage to the Martyrs' Shrine in Midland. That was organized in the fifties by a Dutch priest from the province of Zeeland.[51] The only other quasi-formal organization is a group of first-generation Dutch Catholic immigrants who formed a committee, "The Friends of Titus Brandsma," to keep alive the memory of a Dutch priest beatified in 1985.[52] All other social interaction among Dutch-Canadian Catholics—again all first generation—occurs on the local level, where groups of Dutch Catholic members in the same city or the same parish get together informally as friends to play cards or attend dances. Such networks may or may not coincide with a common membership in a secular Dutch club (see chapter 16).

The composition of such informal networks are shaped by social class or region of origin. For example, about a half dozen well-educated Dutch-Canadian Catholic couples in Metropolitan Toronto still keep in touch.[53] Such networks often coincide or overlap with more broadly based non-denominational ethnic groups. For example the middle-class Dutch

Catholics mentioned above are all associated with or actively involved in a number of Dutch-Canadian associations (see chapter 12). However they would rarely mention that they are Catholics in public to other Dutch immigrants from different backgrounds. They do not belong to the same parish nor do they share the same neighbourhood. The only thing they have in common is a shared class disposition, or a "way of thinking" and a sub-identity representing the tradition of rational Catholicism typical of the Netherlands (see chapter 3). In Scarborough, another small group or "clique" of Dutch Catholics, without ethnic club connections, constitutes a separate and unrelated network of friends who socialize among themselves within a large multicultural parish. In most other Catholic churches in Ontario, the majority of Catholics of Dutch background do not have much contact with each other. Many will even deny that there is a "Dutch" presence, even if Dutch-Canadians are overrepresented in choirs or on parish councils. A good example would be the Catholic churches in Aurora.[54] Almost all of their offspring have married spouses of non-Dutch, but frequently Catholic, background. Such Catholic families are just as assimilated and integrated as the liberal Protestants who were described in the previous chapter.[55]

Like the rest of Canada, rural and small-town Catholics of Dutch background are more conservative than their urban counterparts. They have become actively involved in the pro-life campaign, alongside non-Dutch Canadians and even Dutch-Canadian Calvinists. One small group has gone even farther and joined a small "underground" offshoot of the Roman Catholic Church which no longer recognizes the Pope. They are the followers of the late Bishop Lefèbre in Europe. These rebel Catholics still celebrate the mass in Latin and refuse to accept any of the liturgical changes introduced in the sixties.[56] When I first started investigating this small group of approximately 25 people in southwestern Ontario, an informal spokesman told me that he just "happened" to be of Dutch background. Further enquiries resulted in the discovery that more than half of the families involved in this split-off group are Dutch-Canadians.[57]

Except for a few parishes in parts of rural Ontario, the Dutch Catholic presence in Ontario, as an ethnic phenomenon, has all but disappeared. Dutch Catholics have not left any permanent institutions or organizations, except for in the region of London.[58] Many people are aware that the core of the large St. Willibrord Community Credit Union is still composed of first- or second-generation Dutch-Canadian Catholics, even though this institution is now officially a credit union without ethnic or religious bonds (see chapter 15). However, at least one of their branches (Sarnia) today has a predominance of Dutch-Canadian Calvinists members. Another branch even has a manager who belongs to the Christian Reformed Church. Times have changed!

Fieldnotes Interlude

8.1 Excerpts from an interview (partly translated from Dutch) with a retired couple in Aurora, March 28, 1993

The man: When we came here, they had a small ***noodkerk*** (temporary church). It was built around 1953 or 1954. Before that date, they used to hold mass in the pastor's house. They never had Dutch priests in this parish but sometimes they came from Uxbridge so that people could do confession with them. . . . First we used a building owned by St. Michael's College, which also owned a farm where all of those Dutch families lived. The parishioners bought the other house for the pastor and the first church was built in 1953. In 1950 there were only around thirteen families, but our parish grew rapidly and today there are 2000 members. Yes, originally about half were Dutch, and the Dutch immigrants did a lot to get a separate school. Many had come from Noord Brabant and I remember a family from Gelderland but they later left to go to Richmond Hill. We also had a lot of young single people.

The woman: I have a younger sister who teaches in the Catholic high school, and a brother too. My youngest sister in only four years older than my daughter and she married someone of German background . . . . none of our children married Catholics and most of them do not attend church any more. Yes, in the Netherlands hardly anyone goes to church any more either, but those we still know who come here to visit find that there is more regard for religion in Canada.

8.2 Excerpt from an interview with a Dutch-Canadian manager of a branch of St. Willibrord Credit Union, June 29, 1990

My parents arrived in Canada in January of 1952. My father started working for Ingersoll Machine in 1953. At that time there were only a few Dutch immigrants in the Ingersoll area. Actually my parents came here with two other Dutch families, from the same neighbourhood in Tilburg [in Brabant], but one of them later moved to Delaware. For the next two or three years, additional immigrants from the same area in Holland arrived and they were a kind of a nucleus. They used to attend the Dutch picnic in Delaware. Later on there were quite a few other Dutch families in Ingersoll. They all knew each other and it grew. I would say that they represented a significant core of people in our church. There were not that many Dutch as in other places, but they were big families and they took quite a few pews in the church.

The Catholic church in Ingersoll used to be mainly Irish; the rural Irish Catholic families were the core group [he mentioned some names] before they were infiltrated by the Dutch. This was true in Beachville as well. The other major immigrants that came into the parish were the Italians, but they came a bit later. But I would say that in Ingersoll the Dutch still outweigh the Italians. In contrast, in Strathroy, the Portuguese and the Dutch are more in competition; they are about even.

... my kids all attended the separate school in Thamesford. They had a strong Dutch contingent, but a lot of the other kids were already second or third generation at that time. Most of them got married to local Canadians. We were with seven kids at home, but it is funny, most of them ended up marrying spouses of Dutch background. My oldest brother already had a Dutch girlfriend when he emigrated and he later married her. Of the other six, only two married Canadians who were not of Dutch background. My next two sisters met their future husbands when they attended social events at a Dutch-Canadian youth club on Ann Street, in London. Yes, that is also how she got her job with the credit union.

.... my son—he just graduated from high school—his friends used to talk about a "Dutch" group and an "Italian" group when they were attending that school. Most of his friends, who are also second or third generation make jokes about where they are from. When I was growing up, we didn't do that, or else kids would refer to "dirty Dutchmen" or use other derogatory terms. That is no longer the case.

8.3 *Excerpts from section entitled "St. Michael's Farms," from* Hendrika and Her Family, *a family history written and printed by John van Bakel (Quadville, 1980)*

During the summer months student priests from St. Michael's College spent their vacations working on the farm. Often at night or on the weekends they would all come over to our place and have a party or have a sing-song.... Dad worked for St. Michael's farms for about a year when it came up for sale (p. 61)....

During the next few years we had many weddings on the farm including these: Frank and Riet Donkers, Mary and Tony Brinke, John and Truus Rutten, Mieske and Betsie van den Broek, Ted and Annie Baks, Toni and Walter Chlon, Martin and Mary Koks, Len and Jane Mennen, Harry and Nelly Koks (p.68).... Peter Donkers and his family lived in one half of the middle house. They later built their own house on the D.F.R.B. sideroad, where they still live today... After most of her children got married, Mrs. Koks moved into the second half of the middle house. Lena Koks married my brother Harry, and John Koks, her brother, became my best friend. John and Truus Rutten lived in the middle house as well.... John worked for Murray Associates, along with most of the farm residents..... When my sister Mary married Tony Brinke, they moved into the cottage. Shortly afterwards the Nabuurs family arrived from Holland and had no place to live. Tony and Mary moved in with us at home, to make room for this large family .... Harry and Lena lived here until they bought their present residence on the Aurora sideroad (pp. 70-72).

8.4 *Excerpt based on a transcription of a tape-recorded interview with a second-generation, Dutch-Canadian manager of a credit union in Lambton county, July 7, 1990*

You see, with me—having a Dutch background, and being of a Dutch Protestant background [Christian Reformed]—well, when I first started working for St. Willibrord [credit union], I never realized there were so many Dutch Catholics. I had always associated Dutch with being mostly Protestant. I knew there were some Dutch Catholics because there were some in Clinton, but it amazed me and it really impressed me how many there were in this area. And they're very strong..... the support St. Willibrord had from the Dutch Catholics, that really impressed me; and also, the connections—how many of them are interrelated. If you look at this area—Watford, Park Hill, Strathroy—a lot of these people come from the same part of Holland and a lot of them are relatives going back to four generations, and that is what I found very interesting. You see, I know more of the backgrounds of a lot of Dutch Catholics than of Dutch Christian Reformed. And I get that from working with St. Willibrord . . .

8.5 Excerpt from an interview with a Dutch-Canadian woman from Wyoming

I believe the separate school was started by several Canadian families but the Dutch got very involved. I remember our oldest daughter started attending and that was in 1957. Initially there was a lot of opposition to the school; some of the Irish were opposed because they liked the idea of having a single community school for everyone. But the Dutch Catholics were very determined and there were also so many of us that we had more votes. Our neighbours, who were not Catholics, were quite upset about us starting the separate school. They used to hold picnics at the old schoolhouse but didn't invite us any more. There were actually more Dutch Protestants in this area but they set up their own church and later their own school as well.

Chapter 9

The Reformed Pillars

Dutch Calvinists belong to the same branch of Protestantism as Presbyterians of Scottish descent. Technically both are Reformed Churches.[1] Nonetheless, only a small proportion of postwar Dutch immigrants became Presbyterians (see chapter 7), since the dispositions of orthodox Dutch Calvinists were incompatible with mainstream North American Protestantism. Reformed churches are also close-knit; their members generally intermarry, as indicated by the preponderance of Dutch surnames in membership directories.[2] Yet Dutch-linked Reformed denominations in Ontario are not officially "Dutch," nor do they carry Dutch labels, with the exception of one obscure sect. Moreover, one cannot say that these denominations present a common front, or project a single image to outsiders; indeed they are highly divisive. This chapter will nevertheless examine all such Reformed denominations with Dutch connections together, a procedure consistent with the inclination of Dutch-Calvinist scholars themselves to refer to all these denominations as a single Reformed family.[3] However, more Liberal Dutch Calvinists, especially those who joined Canadian mainstream Protestant churches, are not included in this chapter.[4]

The Dutch-linked Reformed community in Ontario comprises a de facto transplanted Dutch pillar, albeit with modified institutions and labels. Initially, postwar Dutch Calvinist immigrants conceived their social and religious life in terms of Dutch categories, such as the contrast between *hervormd* and *gereformeerd* (see chapter 3). Even when such categories lost their relevance, values and habits found in the Netherlands at the time of mass emigration survived, as did a unique form of fissioning. Not only did the dispositions of members of this sub-group influence how they interacted with fellow immigrants and other Canadians, but they forged a

Notes to this chapter are on p. 359-68.

separate religious 'field' whose internal dynamics as part of a broader 'social topology'—to use another phrase from Bourdieu—strongly resembles its historical Dutch counterpart in all but name, despite formal links with an American equivalent and the use of the English language.

The Divisible Minority

Despite past schisms, the majority of orthodox Calvinists in the Netherlands had crystallized into stable denominations that maintained the allegiance of entire families for generations. Figure 6 shows the genealogy of most of them, with both Dutch and English names. When postwar Dutch Calvinists emigrated, they looked for approximate equivalents. However, Reformed churches with a Dutch connection rarely corresponded exactly with their Dutch counterparts, resulting in renewed tensions. The closest North American equivalent to the *Gereformeerde Kerken*, the largest orthodox Dutch denomination, was the Christian Reformed Church (CRC), founded by Dutch seceders who emigrated in the nineteenth century. However, the *gereformeerden* represented a somewhat different version of orthodox Calvinism referred to by some scholars as neo-Calvinism. Unlike the earlier Dutch Seceders who founded the CRC (see chapter 3), the Dutch neo-Calvinists believed in active involvement in worldly affairs, including a different notion about the relationship between their church and the rest of society.[5]

Postwar immigrants from a variety of Reformed denominations initially entered the Christian Reformed Church. Some families were able to join existing congregations founded during the interwar period—in Hamilton, Chatham, Sarnia and the Holland Marsh. In the rest of Ontario, however, orthodox Dutch Calvinists had to organize prayer groups on their own.[6] They received visits from American ministers, who served as fieldmen in charge of helping to settle Dutch immigrants (see chapter 4). These ministers, known as home missionaries, had huge territories.[7] Although most of them spoke some Dutch, albeit with an English accent, they had to cope with linguistically diverse congregations, including some where the majority spoke Frisian at home and after church services. Moreover, the early congregations' membership fluctuated, since so many Dutch immigrant farm workers had short-term contracts. Nevertheless, a network of fledgling congregations gradually spread throughout southern Ontario.[8] As more stable congregations became established a shortage of Dutch-speaking clergy made it necessary to "call" ministers directly from the Netherlands. Although usually conversant in English, these Dutch ministers had to adapt to the North American way of life and also learn to cater to the special needs of the immigrants arriving on a daily basis.

Figure 6
Reformed Denominations and Their Origins (with Their North American Equivalents)

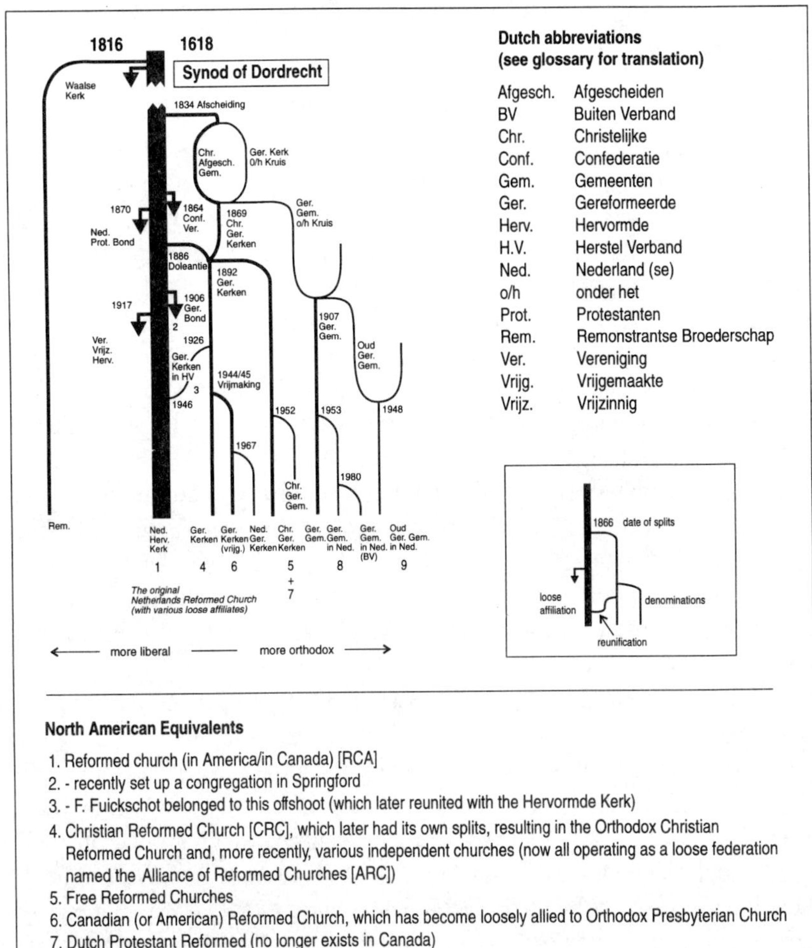

During the early years of adaptation and adjustment to Canadian society, CRC congregations were characterized by a spirit of cooperation, and their members temporarily put aside their internal differences. Nevertheless, before long, tensions resulting from diverse denominational backgrounds reappeared. Prior to 1950, the only option for more orthodox Calvinists brought up in conservative, rural *hervormd* congregations and unable to adjust to the United Church (see chapter 7) was to join the CRC. Such members still insist today that this American-based denomination is not the same as the *Gereformeerde Kerken*. They resent it when that Dutch label is used. Another source of tension was memories of a recent (1944) schism within the Dutch equivalent of the CRC in the Netherlands, resulting in the *Gereformeerden Kerken Vrijgemaakt Artikel 31* (Liberated Reformed, Article 31). When members of this group emigrated to Canada, the issue of their relationship with the CRC had not yet been resolved,[9] and some refused to hand over their papers.[10]

In the early fifties, the U.S.-based Reformed Church in America also entered the domain of immigration to set up a separate denomination for people from *hervormd* background. They appointed a director, Harry Zegerius, an American-Dutch minister, who used Hamilton as his headquarters. He personally received immigrants at his home and visited fledgling congregations. Like their CRC counterpart, the Reformed church hired a fieldman coordinator, Jan Heersink (also living in Hamilton), to receive the Dutch newcomers who landed in Halifax and Montreal. Heersink had recently served as the mayor of Steenderen; at that time he was the youngest mayor in the Netherlands.[11] Rimmer Tjalsma, another recent Dutch immigrant, was likewise hired because he was well educated and spoke English. Tjalsma grew up in Rotterdam, where his father had been a minister in the *Remonstrantse Broederschap*.[12]

Although the first Reformed congregations were set up in Toronto and Hamilton, they soon took root in farming communities such as Drayton. There Berend Flinkert, who later became one of the biggest milk producers in Ontario,[13] was the local congregation's kingpin. Initially he helped to set up a CRC in Harriston; with the promotion of the Reformed Church, he started a congregation in Drayton. Later, other farm families of *hervormd* background in the area came directly into a new Reformed congregation in Drayton.[14] Today they have large congregations in Woodstock, Exeter, Fruitland and Wainfleet. With an increasing presence of this denomination, Dutch immigrants in many parts of southwestern Ontario had a choice between two Reformed churches with Dutch connections. Still, the Reformed Church in America (now the Reformed Church in Canada) never gained the same stature as the CRC. By 1987, they had 15 congregations in Ontario, organized into a single administrative unit (classis), including Winnipeg, Manitoba.[15] In contrast, by the late 1980s the CRC counted 126 organized churches, with a total of 50,000 people,[16] spread out over six classes (Chatham, Hamilton, Huron, Niagara, Quinte and Toronto).[17]

The emergence of separate Reformed churches represents the continuation of Dutch denominational loyalties in a Canadian context. Notwithstanding some collaboration, such as in running a summer camp, there were frictions. For example, Reformed Church members were not as keen about supporting a Christian school in Drayton as were their CRC counterparts. Such tensions, which also existed within the same denomination, could only be held in check by a skillful minister.[18] Yet continued unity depended mostly on demographic factors. There were simply not enough immigrants in eastern, central and Northern Ontario to found separate denominations. In contrast, in regions with a heavy concentration of Dutch immigrants, separate Dutch Calvinist denominations and sects were almost inevitable, given prior dispositions. The area between Toronto, Hamilton and Woodstock was especially ripe for a proliferation of "Dutch" churches.[19]

Like the CRC, these new denominations introduced English-language services as soon as possible,[20] but they were careful to adopt English names that could not be identified with those of rival churches with Dutch connections. Thus *Christelijk Gereformeerd* ("Christian Reformed") became Free Reformed so as not to be confused with the CRC (Christian Reformed Church). The "article 31" church, whose Dutch name included the adjective "freed" (or "liberated') became the Canadian Reformed Church in Canada (see figure 6).[21] However, these smaller denominations only represent a small percentage of the Dutch-Canadian Calvinist population. The Free Reformed today has churches in Chatham, Exeter, St. Thomas and Dundas, while the somewhat larger Canadian Reformed Church comprises about a dozen congregations in different places in Ontario.[22] These small Ontario churches maintain links with sister congregations in other provinces, especially in Western Canada. Yet despite their small size and limited budgets, both denominations run their own private primary schools. The Canadian Reformed Church has even established its own theological college in Hamilton. An even smaller denomination, with no overriding hierarchy at all, is the Netherlands Reformed Congregation (*Gereformeerde Gemeenten*). This is the most extreme manifestation of orthodox Calvinism in Ontario, and the only sect that has a dress code and opposes vaccinations. This sect became firmly established only in Norwich and Ancaster, although services are held in rented accommodations in Bradford, St. Catharines, Hamilton and Unionville.[23]

The Dutch Calvinist scene becomes more complicated when we add the various sub-groups within the denominations listed above. Initially members of one conservative sect, which still operate under the umbrella of the *Hervormde Kerk* in the Netherlands, joined the Reformed Church in Woodstock. However, more recent immigrants of the same persuasion are now conducting services in Springford, just south of Woodstock. In Holland, they are known as *gereformeerde bonders*, but they have nothing to do with the Dutch church that bears that same name; nor can one equate them with a community church in Salford that earlier split off from the

Netherlands Reformed congregation in Norwich.[24] This proliferation of Dutch Calvinist churches creates confusion even in the minds of Calvinists themselves. The vast majority, including those who speak Dutch, are only vaguely familiar with the presence of these sub-groups. This particularly holds for members of the two larger denominations (Reformed and CRC) who lump the stricter sects under the Dutch category *zwarte kousen kerk* (black stocking church). However, regardless of internal rivalries, this complex community shares a common heritage, although rival denominations play down such affinity.[25]

Kinship Patterns

Many Protestant churches in North America have grown through proselytization. In contrast, Reformed churches have expanded mainly by recruiting members from within, through an effective system of formal socialization.[26] Despite internal divisions and a low level of spatial concentration, they have grown and prospered due to their internal organization, which facilitates social interaction and intermarriage among young people. According to a sociological study of a CRC community in Chatham, frequent family church attendance, youth clubs and visits by other church members are strongly correlated with a preference for dating within the same denomination.[27] During the sixties and seventies, it was almost inconceivable that a young man or woman would marry someone not of Dutch Calvinist background.[28] The resulting kinship network looks much like that of the rural Dutch Catholic enclaves described in the last chapter. However, unlike the Catholic case, the patterns of marriage among Dutch Calvinists have continued over more generations in both rural and urban settings. Indeed, the entire Reformed Dutch community constitutes an extensive network of people on the provincial and even national levels, with conferences, summer camps and other institutional links. Consequently, even in urban settings, the level of endogamy is unusually high.[29] These orthodox Calvinists resemble what sociologists label a "closed" society; people participate only in the organizations, clubs and even sport teams connected with their faith community.

Today an increasing number of young Dutch-Canadian Calvinists are marrying outside their ethnic group. Yet even in such cases, non-Dutch spouses usually convert. Figure 7 shows one family network. The elderly couple at the top still lives on a farm near Alliston. They came to Canada in 1949 and all their children attended public schools since no Christian schools had yet been established anywhere they previously lived. By 1991, at the time of the interview, three children and one of two grandchildren were married to non-Dutch spouses. This high level of marriage outside the Dutch-Canadian Calvinist community is more the exception than the rule. Still, all the non-Dutch spouses joined the CRC to which their in-laws belonged, even if the mixed couple ended up in the city. This trend towards increasing interethnic marriages in Reformed churches is reflected in the yearbook of a larger urban centre. Thus, the membership list for the Emmanuel CRC in Hamilton for 1991 shows that 30 out of 242 members (around 13 percent) did not have Dutch names.[30] The entry of non-Dutch members means greater exposure to in-laws and relatives from other churches, which is bound to result in greater tolerance for interreligious marriages. Even older people are now mellowing, and might say, "well, at least they are marrying someone who is a good Christian."

Figure 7
Kinship Network of a Reformed Family in Alliston

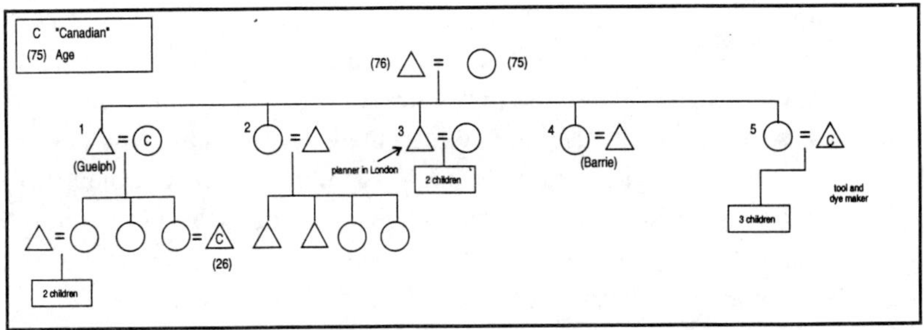

Notwithstanding an increasingly cosmopolitan character, especially in the larger denominations, most Reformed churches continue to be close-knit. In smaller splinter groups, one must not only marry a Reformed Christian but one who is a member in good standing from the same sect or denomination. Regardless of such internal differences, the various kinds of orthodox Calvinists or Reformed Dutch as a whole represent a continuum that goes from more open to highly inbred, with great diversity in levels of tolerance towards outsiders. Such diversity is found both within and among different denominations. Orthodox Dutch Calvinists thus constitute a single, largely Dutch-Canadian network of social interaction sharing a common set of symbols and the same kinds of institutions. In the language of Bourdieu, they form single 'fields,' where people sharing a common discourse and with the same 'stakes' struggle to impose their definitions of Calvinism. While members of its sub-components draw strong group boundaries, they are all interconnected. We can illustrate such connections by again looking at the kinship network of the 76-year-old man from Alliston depicted in figure 7. The second daughter's father-in-law used to be Netherlands Reformed. Likewise, a nephew (a brother's son) who recently immigrated to Canada started another group of *bonders*

in Canada.[31] All these people, though theoretically members of rival denominations, share common kinship and ethnic bonds, which are reinforced through a separate school system and other institutions.

The Dutch Calvinist "Pillar" in Ontario

Despite the important role played by the American-based CRC, the overwhelming presence of postwar Dutch immigrants gave its Canadian branch a unique character.[32] Unlike their American counterparts, the Dutch immigrants of orthodox Calvinist leaning brought with them the political tradition known as *verzuiling* or pillarization (see chapter 3). The largest group of orthodox Calvinists (*gereformeerden*) were particularly committed to this ideal.[33] In each area of social life they are supposed to first isolate themselves, produce a coherent philosophical position and then reenter the broader social and political arena.[34] This neo-Calvinist philosophy had limited impact in the United States where both the more established, older Reformed Church (RCA) and the CRC had both become an integral part of broader American society.[35] The notion of separate Christian- (Reformed-) based institutions was strange and unacceptable.[36] In contrast, the Dutch model of denominationally based economic or political institutions took firmer root in Canadian soil; within a decade, orthodox Calvinist immigrants had not only established their own schools, but their own newspapers, high schools, a labour organization (CLAC), a research institute for Reformed studies, a farmers' association, old age homes, a professional and business association, their own health and psychological counselling services and a myriad of smaller organizations. In the seventies, the Reformed community founded Redeemer College, a residential college for students wanting to go beyond the secondary level.[37]

Lay immigrants founded Reformed institutions throughout Ontario. However, we cannot ignore the Dutch immigrant ministers who provided guidance for the rapidly growing CRC denominations. Aileen van Ginkel has shown that congregations which today have a strong presence of such Dutch-linked Christian organizations originally had Dutch-trained, as opposed to American, ministers.[38] These Dutch ministers and laymen laid the groundwork for a unique Dutch-Canadian version of the Reformed tradition in North America. However, when Dutch-Canadians tried to join forces with other Protestant Canadians, cultural differences got in the way. The primary schools established by Dutch Calvinists can illustrate such differences.

Christian Schools and the Reformed Dutch Culture

Discrepancies in worldviews did not become apparent until Dutch Calvinists came into close contact with Canadian society. Schools based on Reformed principles are an important facet of the Calvinist community. Although they lack a radically distinct curriculum,[39] the schools introduce children to a Reformed perspective and ensure they will meet students from like-minded families. Parental, as opposed to state, control is an important component. Unlike the Netherlands, such Christian schools were not eligible for government funding in Ontario, and immigrant families had to make financial sacrifices. Despite these difficulties, by 1990 Christian schools were seen all over southern Ontario.[40] In the fifties, these privately funded schools were run by and for Dutch immigrants. Today, the staff and the majority of students still have Dutch surnames, but an increasingly number of children of non-Dutch and non-Reformed families are attending these schools. The mixture varies from place to place.[41] In 1989, about 90 percent of the pupils in the Holland Marsh school were of Dutch background,[42] and the percentage is close to 100 for Christian schools set up by smaller Reformed denominations, such as the one in Guelph set up by Canadian Reformed parents or a Free Reformed Christian school in Ancaster.[43] In contrast, in a CRC-linked school in Rexdale, about a third of the pupils are neither of Dutch nor of Reformed background, although all the teachers are Dutch-Canadian.[44] For the rest of Ontario, the proportion of non-Dutch pupils is between 30 and 60 percent.[45]

Collaboration between Dutch Calvinists and Protestants not of Dutch descent has not always proceeded smoothly. While alike in their beliefs, cultural differences can get in the way when it comes to developing a standard education policy.[46] For example, although not adverse to the use of physical punishment, Dutch Calvinists are more tolerant of misbehaviour among young people.[47] The Dutch accept a "rebellious stage" and believe that a child or teenager will eventually "turn out alright."[48] In contrast, their North American counterparts see rowdiness as a manifestation of evil. Moreover, unlike some North American evangelists, Dutch neo-Calvinists do not see smoking as sinful, nor are they adamant prohibitionists. While excessive drinking is frowned upon, they allow liquor during social gatherings among church-minded people.[49] In contrast, Dutch Calvinists are more preoccupied about how often one has to attend church, and in the early fifties they were not allowed to play soccer on Sunday.

The motives of Dutch-Canadian parents for sending children to Christian schools are different from those of other parents. While anxious for their children to succeed in a competitive job market, orthodox Dutch Calvinists expect these schools to reinforce the Reformed heritage. Whereas non-Dutch Protestant families send their children to these schools because "they are strict," Christian Reformed parents have a greater personal emotional investment in their schools. Church elders and ministers want their members to support such schools in order to ensure that the orthodox Calvinist community retains a distinctive set of values.[50] School attendance, especially where there is an overwhelming Dutch presence, thus accentuates the Reformed community's isolation from the larger society.[51] The fact that students can continue their education beyond high school in a Reformed environment further increases the likelihood that young orthodox Calvinists will meet future spouses from the same ethnic and religious background.[52]

Other Reformed Institutions

A de facto ethnically based separate (Reformed) school system is not the only institution that contributes to institutional completeness. Special counselling services and retirement homes are equally important. Chapter 17 will deal with the latter. However, not all Reformed institutions in Ontario are equally well known or have the same level of support; while still important for their symbolic value, two other Reformed institutions cater to a small proportion of the Dutch-Canadian Reformed population, while several others serve a constituency which is primarily of non-Dutch and non-Calvinist background. However, despite the great differences amongst all these institutions, they share one common feature. They all implement neo-Calvinist principles within a Canadian setting.

The Christian Farmers Federation of Ontario (CFFO)

Various Christian farmers associations started as an attempt to set up a Canadian equivalent to the Dutch Protestant Farmers' Association (*De Boeren en Tuinders Bond*). Representatives of four associations (Wyoming, Woodstock, Forest and Strathroy) met in 1954 to create a federation, although that lasted only two years.[53] However, members of local associations continued to meet to discuss farming, buy fertilizers in a cooperative fashion and disseminate information about farming techniques.[54] The idea of a federation was resurrected in 1961, when a much larger number of local groups met in Woodstock. They hired a part-time field organizer in 1966, although several locals continued to operate in a completely independent fashion.[55] Their executive, made up of family farmers, continued to meet throughout the decade, and in 1971 they hired a full-time secretary-manager.[56]

While theoretically open to a broader membership, the CFFO continues to be 95 percent Dutch-Canadian and Reformed. Yet their leadership has gradually been transferred from the first generation to a younger group of second- and third-generation farmers.[57] In terms of policy, the

CFFO believes strongly in the family farm and their long-term vision is "a blend of entrepreneurial and co-operative agriculture" and proper stewardship of the land.[58] However, while the CFFO has become well known among policy makers and academics, its membership has remained small. The number of farm members grew rapidly from about a hundred to 600 members in the seventies, but by 1988 the organization still had only 625 farm members.[59] Almost all of these farmers, plus their entire executive, belong to Reformed denominations.[60]

The Canadian Reformed Christian Business and Professional Association (CRCBPA)

A new organization within the Reformed community (founded in 1984), CRCBPA's membership, which had reached over 400 by 1990, ranges from owners of small businesses (less than 20 employees) to more prominent business entrepreneurs such as Bill Voortman (of Voortman Cookies) and Bill Harkema (who used to run a fleet of trucks). About 15 percent are professionals. They call themselves Reformed Christians rather than Christian Reformed, since many do not belong to the CRC. Like the CFFO, they recruit their members from different Reformed denominations and there are a few Presbyterians who happen to be Dutch-Canadians.[61] The older members tend to join out of loyalty to the Reformed community, while the second-generation members tend to see the organization more as an internal support group. Their greatest support lies in the Burlington-Hamilton area, but the CRCBPA also has members in major cities throughout southwestern Ontario.[62]

The Christian Labour Association of Canada (CLAC)

Many Dutch Calvinists immigrants who arrived after the war had been employees in the Netherlands, affiliated with a denominationally based labour union, the CNV (*Christelijke Nederlandse Vakbond*). In 1952, former members of this Dutch union, got together with a handful of other young immigrant workers in Sarnia to form the Christian Labour Association of Canada.[63] They were not all workers, nor did all Dutch Calvinist employees want to unionize. Their common goal was to set up a Christian labour movement based on Kuyperian principles, along the lines of similar labour unions in the Netherlands and other European countries.

As in the case of the unsuccessful attempt to set up a Dutch-Canadian Catholic credit union league (see last chapter), a pillar mentality brought Dutch Calvinists into direct conflict with the Canadian state. Indeed, it took over a decade of battles in the courts before any groups of workers affiliated with the CLAC won the right of certification in Ontario. The first unsuccessful attempt to get official recognition involved a group of 16

Dutch-Canadian employees in a printing plant in Hamilton set up by two Dutch investors.[64] The legal stumbling block was the wording of their proposed constitution, which would not allow non-Christian workers to join. The organizers involved in setting up this union eventually modified their position to conform to Canadian labour laws.[65] However, the process of changing their constitution, and the subsequent change in policy and tactics, became the object of bitter infighting. Once they received the legal right to organize workers in 1963,[66] the CLAC was led by a group of younger Dutch-Canadians of Calvinist background. They moved the organization in quite a different direction than its founders had anticipated. In 1988, only 20 of the 300 companies with CLAC workers were owned by Dutch-Canadians, and the proportion of CLAC-organized workers of Dutch background was even smaller.[67]

The CLAC's history illustrates a clash of principles between Dutch-Canadian Calvinist leaders and both the government and established labour union leaders. Dutch Calvinist immigrants could not accept the closed shop with its checkoff system, which did not allow workers in the same plant to join the union of their choice or to opt out of union membership altogether. They also did not like the confrontational tactics associated with established unions. Dutch immigrants saw North American unions as "neutral" (i.e., anti-religious) institutions. They therefore thought it unfair to force workers to pay union dues to an organization if they disagreed with its principles. But unlike other conscientious objectors, who were eventually allowed to have their dues transferred to a charitable cause, they wanted to set up their own unions.

While initiated by Dutch Calvinists of working-class background, the first serious attempts to establish a Christian labour union in Canada involved a professional Dutch labour union organizer. In 1952, Frans Peter Fuykschot was commissioned by a European-based labour federation to promote Christian-based unions in Canada. He had already become actively involved in the Dutch Calvinist labour union (the CNV) when he started working fulltime for them in 1938.[68] At that time his religious affiliation was with a small group within the *Gereformeerde Kerken* called *Herstel Verband*, which wanted to return to the *Hervormde Kerk*. His somewhat more liberal views on interchurch cooperation, combined with a more cosmopolitan and sophisticated lifestyle, eventually put him at odds with more orthodox Calvinists.[69] Shortly after his arrival in Hamilton, in 1952, Fuykschot was elected national secretary and edited their newsletter, *The Guide*. His vision was to work with a broad range of people, but he realized that he had to begin with Dutch Calvinists.[70] He remained strongly committed to the goal of forming a Christian labour union, but was willing to make compromises to get legal recognition.

Between 1952 and 1958, support for the CLAC within the Reformed Dutch community grew rapidly,[71] but every request for certification was turned down. A suggestion by their Canadian legal advisor that the CLAC drop all reference to the Bible resulted in a bitter dispute. Fuykschot and a majority in the national executive were in favour of making this change. They argued that the CLAC's Christian nature would be safeguarded by keeping a short reference to the application of Christian principles in one article of their constitution.[72] Vehement opposition came from spokespersons for the Dutch-Canadian Calvinist community, who condemned the national executive's "un-Christian" and "Canadian" way of thinking.[73] Fuykschot's main opponent was Gerald Vandezande, a man who was later to become an intellectual leader of a more radical Reformed faction. At that time, Vandezande took the "hard-line" position. This disagreement about how to apply the principles of Dutch Calvinism to labour issues in a Canadian setting resulted in a split in the CLAC.[74] At their sixth national convention in September 1958, the proposed changes in the CLAC constitution were defeated when the majority of delegates voted against the motion. The national executive, including Fuykschot, resigned. Together with a splinter group of dissatisfied members, they set up a rival Christian National Trade Union and Fuykschot became its executive secretary. However, three years later he died in a car accident, and the new union (CNTU) never grew beyond a few hundred members.[75]

Certification was not granted until 1963 after yet another change in the wording of their constitution.[76] The CLAC was finally able to represent workers as an official bargaining unit, although they had to work in a climate of hostility and ridicule from the big unions. Over the next two decades, they not only grew, but their membership changed drastically. Initially, workers organized under the CLAC umbrella were Dutch-Canadian employees in construction, trucking, brick-yards and glass. Often a Dutch-Calvinist owner might be instrumental in getting the union established.[77] Under a new generation of young Dutch-Canadians leaders, the CLAC organized workers in retirement and nursing homes, most of whom were women neither of Dutch nor Calvinist background.[78] However, the CLAC is still run by a leadership steeped in the Kuyperian neo-Calvinist tradition.[79]

Citizens for Public Justice (CPJ) and the Institute for Christian Studies (ICS)

Another example of a Reformed organization is Citizens for Public Justice, whose public affairs director, Gerald Vandezande, we have met before. Like the CLAC, this organization underwent a transition from one defending the rights of the Dutch-Calvinist community to one with a broader mandate to change public policy in Canada. In the seventies this organization started tackling such issues as alternative energy policies and native land claims.[80] By the late eighties, they had become a diverse ecumenical group with over two thousand supporters.[81] Today, the CPJ collaborates with the Canadian Conference of Catholic Bishops and the Mennonite Central Committee in fighting for justice.[82] However, their leadership is still Dutch-Canadian Reformed.[83]

The Office of Citizens for Public Justice is located in an old stone building on College Street that bears the inscription "Institute of Christian Studies." Located close to the University of Toronto, the ICS is the only postgraduate institution in Ontario that came out of the Reformed community. Officially registered in 1967,[84] it obtained a charter to grant its own degrees in 1983.[85] However, this institution has had a stormy history. Initially younger members, who were the product of a Calvinist offshoot of the students movement in the late sixties, antagonized the older leaders of the Reformed community.[86] Many of these young researchers graduated from Trinity Christian College in Chicago, the same independent Reformed college where an organizer now working for the CLAC also got his degree.[87] In 1988 its 30-odd students came from all over the world; three of the Canadian students were of Dutch-background and only one was Christian Reformed. They were taught by eight faculty members, of whom three were second-generation Reformed Dutch-Canadians. Two others had a distant Dutch-American background and three had no Dutch connection whatsoever. They included philosophers, historians and experts in education.[88]

The Institute of Christian Studies represents a dilemma for radicals who share a vision of implementing a left-wing version of the Kuyperian model.[89] While successful in gaining the attention of non-Dutch Christian social activists, they depend on the financial and moral support of a more traditional Dutch-Canadian constituency. Yet their attempts to implement changes within the Reformed educational system have been met with internal opposition, which in turn weakens their support base. Consequently, the institute has become somewhat marginalized, and an increasing number of Dutch Calvinists either disapprove or are no longer aware of its existence. Such internal tensions and controversies have recently escalated within the Reformed community.

Renewed Social Tensions

Notwithstanding an emphasis on conformity, the Dutch Calvinist community is far from homogeneous. Even orthodox Calvinists represent an uneasy alliance among neo-Calvinists, who believe in social involvement in the broader society; more pietistic Calvinists, who want to isolate themselves from the secular world; and "doctrinalists." Each of these streams in turn displays a conservative and a revisionist version.[90] Moreover, the same tensions that exist in society as a whole are mirrored in the Reformed churches. Reformed organizations take opposing sides on such political issues as farm subsidies, immigration policy and foreign aid. Likewise, some people disagree about what form Christian education should take, and whether or not the Kuyperian neo-Calvinist tradition should be emphasized. There are even church members who have criticized the policy of establishing separate Christian schools, arguing that the Ontario school system was already Protestant in orientation when they arrived, not "neutral" or irreligious as in the Netherlands.[91] Even people who support the school system cannot always see eye to eye. Thus, soon after the first Christian high school was established in Woodbridge in 1969, its entire teaching staff was fired. The controversy started when a teacher, Albert Witvoet, wanted to use *Catcher in the Rye* as a grade 12 text.[92] A group of largely Dutch-born immigrant parents, who wanted greater control over the school, confronted the teachers.[93] Today some loyal members are criticizing the church from a feminist perspective (see chapter 13). Yet vocal opponents of such changes sincerely believe that they are "preserving the heritage."

Neo-Calvinists face a dilemma. To keep their pillar strong requires mechanisms of socialization—the schools—which are rooted in a highly endogamous ethnic community; a large number of students and almost all teachers still carry Dutch names. At the same time, the inclusion of non-Dutch members, which requires compromise and accommodation, is bound to dilute the typically Dutch forms of Calvinism that inspired such a vision in the first place. The Calvinist immigrant parents who made great sacrifices to establish their Christian schools did so because of their commitment to a model of denominationally linked schools modelled after the Dutch pillar system. However, the radical teachers whom the parents opposed were equally inspired by a Dutch neo-Calvinist vision that emphasizes social action. There is also a growing gap between the intellectuals, who want to perpetuate the Kuyperian vision, and their Dutch-Canadian constituency, who no longer know much about Kuyper and his ideas.[94] Indeed, the whole Reformed community is today seeing a growing rift between "liberal" and "traditional" factions, involving both political and theological tensions. To some extent, the conflict reflects rural-urban differences[95] as well as a generation gap between first- and second-generation Dutch-Canadians with different dispositions.

For the first several decades, internal tensions were kept in check through the fissioning of larger CRC congregations.[96] Younger couples might set up a new church even before the old one was filled up, taking with them more liberally oriented older couples. Each group would in turn call a minister of their liking. It was thus possible to have some level of intra-denominational diversity.[97] However, by the eighties, signs of an open rift appeared. The first rift occurred when the Reverend Harry van Dijk protested against an article passed at a synod meeting. He left the Toronto congregation he had served to set up his own denomination called the Orthodox Christian Reformed Church in Listowel. Several ministers who followed his lead were expelled. For several years, few families followed their lead, but another orthodox group of "concerned" citizens was formed in the late eighties. This group, still within the Christian Reformed fold, started their own newspaper and cancelled their subscriptions to the *Calvinist Contact*, which was taking a "middle-of-the road' position between the two feuding factions.[98] In this period of increasing polarization, the smaller Canadian Reformed church took steps to ensure that their own members would not be tainted with what they perceived as the growing influence of secular humanism.[99] Although most Reformed denomination in Ontario had at this point been thoroughly Canadianized, internal dissension took a typical Dutch Calvinist form.

Dutch-style Dissension

The church structure and dogmas of the Reformed churches presents another dilemma for Dutch Calvinists who trace their roots back to the Reformed church set up in the Netherlands at the end of the sixteenth century. Reformed congregations, including those set up by the Dutch in North America, all recognize—or want to return to—the confessional form and articles of principle outlined at the Dort Synod of 1618 (see chapter 3). Since the original Dutch Reformed church represents the "true" form of Dutch Calvinism, any decision to secede or split off from an established church that claims to be the continuation of the original Church should only be done after a great deal of soul-searching, since unity should be maintained if at all possible.[100] Concurrently, since no authority can stand above God, it is also the duty of a congregation to leave a broader church association if those making decisions on behalf of the entire church go against basic principles. Likewise, representatives of the synod have the obligation to expel heretics in order to defend the faith.

The first step in an escalating dispute is for a dissenting faction to initiate a "movement" to reform the church from within. Such a movement may become institutionalized and turn into a permanent sub-group.[101] When a dispute turns into a real split, the faction in charge of the established church will invariably accuse the dissenters of being schismatic. Such accusations can result in the dismissal of a minister considered to be too critical of the established church. However, dissenting ministers will invariably back up their criticism with references to the documents already mentioned. A dissenting minister and his followers, who may argue that the church has become too "hierarchical," will claim that they represent the true Reformed heritage.[102] In most cases, however, they are more likely to set up one or more completely independent, separate congregations. Theoretically they may still go back, but reunification is rare.

In terms of the underlying social dynamics, Dutch Calvinism revolves around a strong sense of loyalty reinforced by an intensive process of socialization within the Dutch family (see chapter 3). Membership in the extended family and membership in a particular church become almost synonymous when people marry within their own faith community, which is a norm among Dutch people of all Reformed persuasions. This sense of family loyalty runs counter to the breach of unity represented by a schism. Whichever minister or group of laymen triggered the last split technically betrayed the norm of church unity, which is based on the notion that the church should be like one big family. Every new church thus needs to work hard to create new loyal supporters who will in turn pass on their convictions to their offspring. Yet feelings of anger and bitterness between the original factions may run high for years, even for generations, making a possible reunification very difficult.

Whenever Dutch Calvinists feel that they must abandon the Calvinist church in which they have been brought up—let us call it church A—they will inevitably start a new church (B) rather than join some other denomination or Calvinist community church (C). This happens even if they recognize that denomination (C), resulting from an earlier split, may better fit what they perceive as the appropriate level of strictness or purity of doctrine. Yet the propensity towards always starting yet another Reformed church has continued. Dissident members—who now become (B)—usually remember when the other group (C) originally broke away from church (A), which they must now reluctantly abandon. Thus the people leaving church (A) may still harbour lingering feelings of resentment against those whom they have now come to resemble (C). For this reason, dissidents would never really "feel at home" in another, already existing Calvinist church, no matter how close that other church comes to their ideal of the appropriate level of orthodoxy. For similar reasons, it is equally difficult for members of any existing Reformed congregation to receive, as new members, people once associated with rival congregations. The exact wording of small theological differences and the corresponding nuances in church procedure have usually already become too wrapped up with one's sense of identity and loyalties.[103] Given these social dynamics, it is doubtful that dissatisfied conservative CRC members in Ontario would switch allegiance to a rival orthodox denomination.[104] Their Dutch Calvinist heritage is too deeply rooted, the memories of recent splits too bitter.

The Alliance of Independent Churches

The nineties witnessed a deepening rift within the Reformed Dutch-Canadian community around the ordination of women, the teaching of evolution in the Christian schools and the increasing liberalization of lifestyle. In 1992, a general synod of the CRC decided not to allow the ordination of women, although any women serving as deacons could continue to serve without ordination. The liberals were disgruntled, but decided to bide their time. Their opponents decided that matters had gone too far. One by one, more conservative congregations split off to form their own Independent Christian Reformed Churches which formed a loose federation or alliance which includes orthodox Christian Reformed churches. Some congregations, such as the one in Ancaster, which still recognized the legitimacy of synod, became independent community churches within the Christian Reformed umbrella. They still appeared in the 1993 yearbook. Other congregations, such as the ones in Dundas or Hamilton Mountain left altogether.[105] As during earlier controversies, some people became fed up with the internal bickering and switched their allegiance to non-Dutch Protestant churches.[106]

Dutch Calvinists have not yet resolved the tensions associated with the contradictions between the Dutch and North American models of how society should operate. This became apparent with the Reformed labour movement. The largely Dutch-Canadian Reformed community is also constantly losing members, in part because of the proselytzing of North American evangelicals who represent an alternative source of 'symbolic power' in the religious 'field.'[107] Nonetheless, if we count all the Reformed denominations together, the overall membership is expanding. This trend will probably continue for some time.[108]

The Reformed community today resembles its counterpart in the Netherlands fifty years ago.[109] Stricter denominations, which have all but disappeared in the Netherlands, are alive and well in Ontario.[110] At the same time, the larger denominations are engendering their own internal splits along the lines of earlier schisms in the Netherlands. Such splits and the discourse used to justify them also replicate the Dutch model. Orthodox Dutch-Canadian Calvinists have thus reproduced the world view and institutions of their ancestors, especially in southwestern Ontario. This socio-cultural continuity illustrates the force of ingrained values and expectations, even after people have become immersed in a different country.[111] The orthodox Calvinist pillar has survived within the Canadian context, albeit full of cracks and fissures.

Fieldnotes Interlude

9.1 *Excerpt from an interview with a retired factory worker, in the Holland Marsh, September 19, 1989*

We came to Canada in 1949 from Groningen. I was orthodox *hervormd*, but since they did not have my church here, I joined the Christian Reformed Church. . . . I know Gerald Vandezande quite well. I also knew his grandparents because we came from the same region. In fact, his mother used to be my girlfriend and I once told him that. . . . yes, I am acquainted with the CLAC and sat on their board of directors and used to send them contributions. But no workers around here were ever organized as far as I know. I used to go to their conventions too.

9.2 *Excerpts from an interview with a Christian Reformed woman who lives outside of Kingston, December 20, 1989*

My Canadian neighbours still say that the First CRC is Dutch, but that is no longer true for the new, Second Christian Reformed Church we built. We have 10 members out of the 40 who are not of Dutch descent, and a lot of the other members are second-generation people who can't speak or understand any Dutch. Also, more than half of the students who attend our Christian school are non-Dutch. . . . it is very important for Christians to work together, but we have to reach out more. The Dutch Christian Reformed were initially quite clannish, but that is because we felt intimidated and we didn't know the language well. But now that we are strong, we should reach out more and work with other Christians. . . . I represent the seniors of the First Christian Reformed Church and had to convince them to help participate in setting up a retirement home that was not officially Christian [there were not enough people to set up a Christian Reformed home]. But I pointed out what a wonderful opportunity that gave us to bear witness to the Christian faith. Every Sunday, when our members return from services, we provide coffee in the lounge [of Dutch Heritage Villa] and invite all of the other residents to join us, which they do . . . it became a tradition.

9.3 *Excerpt from a conversation (in Dutch) with an importer (liberal Dutch Protestant) in Toronto, December 7, 1988*

I had a lot of girls working in my office who were Christian Reformed and who could no longer speak Dutch. I once asked some of them if they would ever consider going out with a young man if he did not belong to their religion. They answered that it was impossible; that they would never agree to go on a date, and that they would not feel the least bit of attraction towards boys who were not Christian Reformed.

Chapter 10

Regional and Inter-National Networks

This chapter looks through another set of lenses at the Dutch-Canadian landscape. We have seen how economic forces and religious affiliation shaped patterns of settlement and social interaction. Regional ties likewise brought people together, even if they did not share a common religious or political affiliation.[1] Dutch immigrants came from 11 provinces, each characterized by sub-regional diversity (see chapter 3). Moreover, many Dutch-speaking postwar immigrants originated in Belgium or former Dutch colonies. The latter had already become separate "ethnic" groups within the Netherlands, just like the Frisians. We could call them ethnic groups within ethnic groups, or groups occupying an ambivalent place in a shifting social continuum where the "typically" Dutch merge into something else. These sub-groupings, as well as networks based on a home town or a geographical region, mostly cut across the Dutch pillars.

Shared dispositions derived from a common region or sub-national identity can give rise to further distinctions. Such secondary lines of division were reactivated in Canada, sometimes involving less visible connections among women. Social ties based on a common geographic/sub-ethnic origin frequently evolved into reunions or clubs which stimulated long-term friendships. In some cases, regionally based networks became relevant to the economic sphere, as entrepreneurs used such networks to recruit workers, form partnerships or attract customers. The boundaries of such regional or sub-ethnic 'classes' might not be as salient as those based on gender and economic class. Yet whatever their specific dynamics, relations based on regionalism cannot be left out.

Not all sub-ethnic or regional groupings were equally represented in the postwar flow of emigrants to Canada. Dutch-speaking Belgians, or

---

Notes to this chapter are on p. 369-76.

Flemish, were far outnumbered by people from the Netherlands. People from the Dutch provinces of Zeeland and Limburg were also under-represented. Moreover, the outflow of people even within provinces varied. Thus Dutch-Canadians from Noord Brabant are more likely to have come from its eastern half.[2] Other areas of Brabant more likely to export emigrants to Ontario included its southwestern corner (below the cities of Breda and Tilburg), and the narrow strip of land between the Maas and Waal Rivers. Likewise, many immigrants from Drenthe came from the region between Hogeveen and Meppel, while Achterhoekers were overrepresented among immigrants from Gelderland (see figure 1 in chapter 3).[3]

Dutch emigrants from the same province, or even town, sometimes settled in the same place in Ontario. For instance, numerous people who were born and grew up in the village of Koekange in Drenthe landed in Drayton.[4] Likewise, the majority of Catholic immigrants in Park Hill and Arkona, in Lambton county, came from the vicinity of Alphen, Baarle Nassau and Chaam (Brabant).[5] A coterie of families from this last region, who already knew each other in the Netherlands or had attended the same agricultural school,[6] were instrumental in starting up the St. Willibrord Community Credit Union in the diocese of London (see chapter 15)—a little bit of Brabant in rural Ontario!

The phenomenon of direct transplanting also occurred in the case of city immigrants. In London, the Loyens and Willems, prominent names in the construction business, were bricklayers in Tilburg who employed many people from their home province.[7] Such enclaves in the house building industry, based on regional networks, are found in other cities. In Chatham, Ben Bruinsma started building houses soon after he arrived in 1947. Trained as a carpenter in Friesland, he had extensive experience in demolition, and used previous business connections to sponsor other Frisians to come to Canada to work for him. Gradually these men went into business on their own and in turn sponsored others from their home region.[8] Today, a handful of Frisian-Canadian contractors dominate house-building, general contracting and excavating in the region of Chatham.[9] Despite such local clustering, immigrants from the same Dutch province or region were more often dispersed all across Ontario. Nevertheless, geographical dispersal did not prevent people with a common regional or sub-ethnic origin from seeking out friends and relatives—or even strangers—once in Canada.

The Frisians

According to John Kralt, there were about 10,000 Frisians in Canada in 1976, although not all reported Frisian as their mother tongue.[10] Despite such small numbers, the Frisians have kept a strong sense of identity. Although most are Calvinists, religion is not the basis for their cohesion; I have come across self-proclaimed Catholic Frisians[11] and Frisians without religious affiliation throughout Ontario. Initially some Frisians clustered together, within Ontario Reformed congregations, especially around Bowmanville and between Simcoe and Paris; later such local areas of concentration became poles of attraction for occasional gatherings of Frisians from a variety of backgrounds. Thus, a large park near Paris is the site of an annual Frisian picnic.

The driving force behind this annual reunion is Luit Miedema, who lives in Waterford (near Simcoe).[12] He emigrated in 1950 with the intention of farming, but became a butcher instead. A decade later, Luit started the first annual Frisian reunion, drawing people from all over the province. The first time 500 people showed up, and by the mid-eighties they were attracting up to 3000 people.[13] Apart from organizing the annual picnic, this Frisian-Canadian butcher set up a folk theatre group, which performed plays in Frisian. The actors were local farmers who used to perform three days at a time in many places in southwestern Ontario.[14] The plays were part of a fundraising campaign for Christian high schools being established in areas with a concentration of Dutch Calvinists.[15] However, the audiences attending such plays were often not aware that the actors included Catholic Frisians who lived in the same vicinity as Luit.[16] These Frisian plays were being performed in the eighties, when a new Dutch consul of Frisian descent in Toronto gave the group moral and financial support. Nevertheless, the plays ceased in 1983, when not enough young Frisian-speaking players could be found to replace those becoming too old. The long duration of the Frisian folk plays, and the continuation of a well-attended Frisian reunion, are remarkable given the absence of formal recognition by the multicultural establishment. Although probably better preserved as a home language than Dutch, there are no heritage classes in Frisian nor are Frisians listed in official directories of ethnic groups.[17] Nonetheless, Frisian-Canadians keep their heritage alive in Ontario.[18]

Another magnet is their national sport, *kaatsen*.[19] Soon after coming to Canada, Frisians got together to play in different localities, and by the mid-fifties a group of men founded a *kaats* tournament in the Halton region. They played on Sunday afternoons, first in Terra Cotta and then in Lowville (near Oakville).[20] Around the same time a group of stricter Reformed Frisians in the Strathroy and Sarnia area ran a *kaats* tournament on Saturdays. They became aware of each others' presence when players met at their annual picnic in Paris. That event was always scheduled on 1 July (or the closest Monday), which allowed people of different religious persuasions, as well as purely secular people, to take part.[21] Starting in

1978, a tournament of rotating games for all Frisians grew into the Ontario Kaats Federation, which still operates today.[22] There are six tournaments, sponsored by businesses whose owners are of Frisian descent.[23] Apart from the occasional players who only show up once a year in Paris, they have twenty-five dues-paying members who are active players throughout the summer.[24]

Most Frisian-Canadians present themselves to others as Dutch immigrants. The only visible signs of a sub-ethnic identity are wall tiles with Frisian sayings or the use of typically Frisian first names such as Sipke, Poppe or Rennie. Nevertheless, Frisian immigrants are more likely than other Netherlanders to preserve a sense of belonging to both a region and a "people" who have long struggled to maintain their distinctiveness. A small core group of Frisian immigrants are fiercely nationalistic, even in a Canadian context.[25] More typically, Frisians and non-Frisians have a kind of joking relationship.

Other Provincial and Regional Networks

Frisians are not the only group to hold annual reunions. People from the province of Zeeland used to get together at Springbank Park near London.[26] They once had 200 people, with an average turnout of around 40.[27] A more popular get-together is the "Grunniger" picnic in Rockwood, organized by people tracing their roots back to Groningen. Harry Klungel, from the Exeter area, has been in charge since 1973. Average attendance is 200 people, who come from all over southern Ontario, including the Holland Marsh, Hamilton, London, Oakville, Woodstock and Guelph.[28] When I attended the sixteenth reunion on June 17, 1989, only about 60 people showed up because of inclement weather. I observed a range of ages, and overheard a mixture of English, Dutch and the *gruningse tael* (the dialect of that province). Apart from sharing a meal and socializing, such games as *plankje lopen* were organized for both kids and adults.[29]

Other reunions, or special "days," have been held on a more sporadic basis. For about ten years, people from the region of Twenthe (in Overijssel) who settled on farms near St. Marys and Goderich, gathered at an annual summer reunion,[30] as did people from the Wieringermeer.[31] Similarly, a Mr. de Kort used to organize an annual picnic for the Andijkers, which was held in Aylmer.[32] Sometimes people from the same province or region would also get together for special "evenings" in conjunction with a more general Dutch club. Club The Netherlands in St. Catharines organizes yearly or bi-yearly get-togethers for people from Drenthe, Overijssel, Noord Holland and Brabant.[33] Other regional networks take the form of informal visits among friends and relatives. For example, while there has never been any formal social gathering for people from the province of Limburg, they do keep in contact in other ways. Those whom I first met in Toronto told me about a couple they knew in Hamilton, who in turn recalled the Limburgers with whom they socialized on a regular basis, a group consisting of eight families in Stoney Creek, Grimsby, Beamsville and Dunville.[34]

People from the same region form networks within church congregations or in specific towns. Calvinists still comment on how people from different regions (including the Frisians) used to "flock" together. Catholic immigrants are likewise conscious of regional differences. Dutch Catholics in a parish in Phelpston are about evenly divided between Brabanders and Gelderlanders. Such regional differences were accentuated in the mid-fifties, with the influx of city immigrants from the western provinces. For example, tradesmen and small business people from Noord Holland, Zuid Holland and Utrecht started coming into the city of Guelph, where they encountered a large population of earlier farm immigrants from the eastern Netherlands.[35] Such east-west splits made the Dutch-Canadian community more fragmented. Even people from the same urban centre, such as Rotterdam, might have more to do with one another than with people from other Dutch cities.[36] Localism or regionalism could thus repel immigrants from the same country.

Regionalism can be a source of unity or cohesion as well as division. In most cases Dutch-Canadian local and regional networks cut across religious and class lines; as many Catholics as Protestants used to attend the Zeeland reunion,[37] and prominent businesspeople who performed skits at an Achterhoek reunion rubbed shoulders with farmers and factory workers.[38] High status persons, who normally used the more prestigious standard Dutch obtained through formal education, were able and willing to use their regional dialect in this context, regardless of the shame or prejudice otherwise associated with the use of a "dialect" in other settings (see chapter 12).

The Brabanders

Immigrants from Noord Brabant must be treated as a separate category. Brabanders are not only predominantly Catholic, but a numerically much larger regional grouping. For example, in 1952 alone, 2,235 people emigrated from this province, almost a third of whom worked in agriculture and horticulture.[39] They make up a majority of Dutch-Canadians in some parts of rural Ontario (see chapter 8) and formed small clusters in many other townships.[40] Brabanders have a strong presence in major cities too, since half of those from a farming background turned to carpentry, worked in auto plants or became contractors (see chapter 19).[41] Brabanders maintained strong ties with each other in both rural and urban Ontario, and were sometimes resented by other Dutch immigrants who found them "too cliquish." Brabanders in turn may detest "northerners" with their haughty attitude and "high Dutch."[42] It does not matter if such northerners are also Catholics. This division reflects a similar north-south distinction in the Netherlands (see chapter 3). Yet despite their strong regional identity, Brabanders did not organize formal picnics or annual reunions in the fifties, since they preferred to keep each others' company through frequent home visits.[43] Later they got together with people from a particular city, such as Tilburg, or rural towns, such as St. Oedenrode and Gemert.[44]

Home-town Reunions

Many people from Brabant felt great loyalty toward the villages or towns where they were born. This can be illustrated through a series of home-town reunions in the late eighties and early nineties. The first home-town reunion involved people from the two villages of Mariahout and Lieshout. Mariahout is unique since it dates back to only 1933, as a result of the expansion of Dutch agriculture into former heathland. Its inhabitants not only had a strong sense of cohesion, but they were already disposed to moving off in search of new land. After the War, a third of its inhabitants emigrated to Canada, yet they kept in close contact with their home town. When Mariahout celebrated its fiftieth anniversary in 1983, their Dutch-Canadian friends were invited to attend the ceremonies.[45] In 1984 the Canadians invited their hosts to a Mariahout get-together in Canada, and they have continued to hold reunions in alternate years since that time.[46] Most of these former *Mariahoutenaars* are farmers, with a few tradesmen and business people, including Bill Brouwers of Oakville, whom we will meet in chapter 16.[47] One person involved in running these reunions, a woman who lives on a farm in Erin, organized a similar reunion for her husband's home town of Boekel. Figure 8 shows the location of these and other villages in East Brabant mentioned in this section.

Freda Leenders (née Vander Zande) was approached by a group of people in Boekel when she and her husband made a return visit on their twenty-fifth anniversary. In conjunction with a committee from Boekel and the nearby hamlet of Venhorst, they compiled a list of names and got to work. A year later, 50 people flew to Canada. They were accompanied by a film crew from a Dutch company (Den Blok), who produced a documentary. A couple of hundred people converged on the Leenders' farm, and then attended a mass in Georgetown. Parts of the Dutch film made on this occasion were subsequently transformed into a four-and-a-half-hour video of conversations with former inhabitants of Boekel, interspersed with panoramic views of farmland and well-known Ontario landmarks.[48] These taped interviews are a good indication of the geographical and occupational distribution of these largely agrarian immigrants, most of whom were middle aged or retired when they appeared on camera during the 1990 reunion.[49] With the exception of two people—an elderly woman who had been a social worker before emigrating and a retired priest now living in Ottawa—the people portrayed in the film were from a farm background and most either had farmed or were still farming in both eastern and southwestern Ontario.[50] Home-town reunions were also held for people from Uden, who have met twice, and Bakel, all towns in eastern Noord Brabant. Such reunions were the catalyst for bigger festivals for all Brabanders, which were open to a more general public (see chapter 16). One such festival, held in Hamilton in 1991, featured a special musical quartet, which had participated in the Boekel reunion.[51] The mailing list used to contact people for this event was compiled by combining people who had attended the previous home-town reunions with new names. These people in turn have relatives or friends who came from other towns in Brabant.

Figure 8
Eastern Part of Noord Brabant

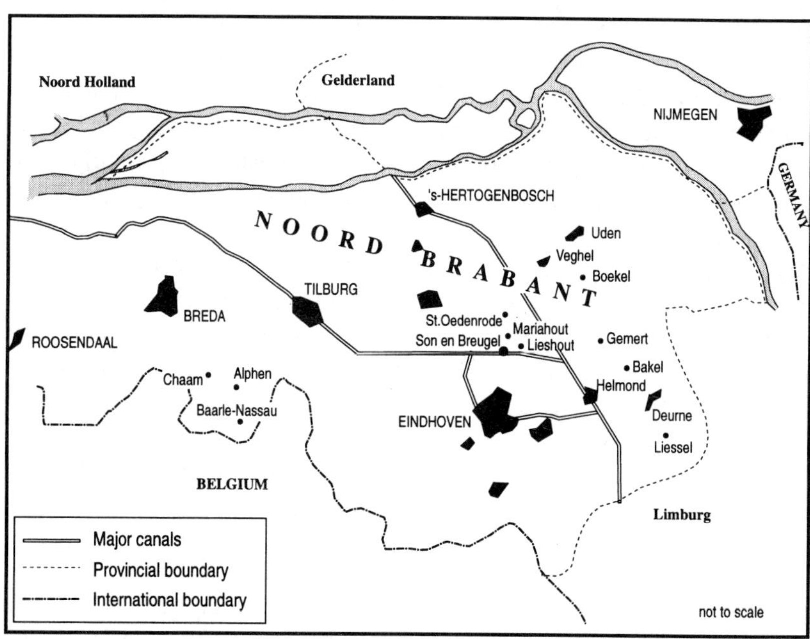

A Comparison of Home-town Reunions

People with roots in agriculture are more likely to organize local reunions than people who grew up in Dutch cities or heavily urbanized regions. I will therefore compare the home-town reunions of East Brabanders described in the last section with that of a group of people from a village in the region of Holland. Such a comparison can demonstrate how social bonds based on a common geographical origin must be reinforced by ties of kinship and common occupation.

Noordwijkerhout: A School Reunion

People originating from villages without the strong local and kinship bonds found in places like Mariahout were not as likely to get together in Canada to celebrate common links with their place of origin. Nevertheless, relatives or schoolmates from the same locality might become reunited as a result of special efforts. Martin Van Denzen, who lives in Toronto, decided to host such a reunion for a group of people from Noordwijkerhout (Zuid Holland),[52] which also happens to be the home town of Bill Vander Zalm, the former premier of British Columbia. An examination of that home-town school reunion can provide insights into the career paths of immigrants from a village very different from Mariahout or Boekel.

Immigrants from Noordwijkerhout were dispersed all over Canada.[53] Unlike the independent farmers of Noord Brabant, most postwar immigrants from Noordwijkerhout were offspring of day labourers. The Van Denzens were one of the poor families from the same neighbourhood as the more prosperous Vander Zalms. Like Mariahout, Noordwijkerhout is a predominantly Catholic village with a sense of cohesion, more so than other places in the more industrialized western Netherlands.[54] However, unlike Mariahout, Noordwijkerhout was more stratified along class lines; there was little social contact between the Vander Zalm family, who lived in a free-standing house, and the Van Denzens and other working-class neighbours. Although their children played together, the parents had little in common. However, even emigrants from the same class background in such villages had little opportunity or desire to seek each other out in Canada unless they ended up in agriculture. Noordwijkerhout had already started to make the transition to a more mobile, urban-industrial society, thus making its citizens less predisposed to farm on their own and more likely to end up in Canadian cities. These speculations are born out by looking at what happened to some of these emigrants, who had the opportunity to meet each other 30 years later.

Martin Van Denzen emigrated in 1957, at the age of 17. Together with a cousin, who found an advertisement for gardeners in Toronto, he departed with the permission of his parents.[55] He met his wife from Limburg on a return visit. Around 1970, Martin's father, still living in Holland, came for a visit. Since this visit coincided with his sixty-fifth birthday, Martin and his wife decided to hold a surprise reunion of emigrants from Noordwijkerhout living in Ontario. Few people who emigrated from this Dutch village had kept in contact with each other after they landed in Canada, nor did they all know Martin Van Denzen. The only family contact was Martin's brother, who worked for Stelco in Sault Ste. Marie. Martin's wife used her experience working in personnel to trace down the names and addresses of men from Noordwijkerhout who had attended the same school as her father-in-law. They managed to get in touch with a dozen of his old classmates from grades five or six. Their guests had a great party, with lots of reminiscing. However, they never got together again. Apart from sharing a home village, the emigrants from Noordwijkerhout ended up in different cities and in different occupations. Unlike the rural immigrants from villages in Noord Brabant, they had little in common.[56]

Home-town Family Reunions

Another home-town network coincided with family bonds based on a common surname. There are examples of large extended family reunions in both the Netherlands and North America.[57] However, rarely have Dutch family names continued to be so closely associated with a place as the Rodenburg family, which traces its roots back to Overschie, an old polder near Rotterdam.[58] In 1989 several members of this family put out the first issue of a bilingual Dutch-English family newspaper called the *Rodenburger Courant*, in order that all the dispersed members of the family, on both sides of the ocean, could keep in touch.[59] Again, we can see how the institutionalization or continuity of Netherlandic regional group identities abroad, no matter how tenuous, require the intersection of more than just one dimension of social reality. However, such continuity in regional bonding is more likely to happen in the case of much larger areas which have a quasi-national status, even if such regions fall outside the borders of the Netherlands.

The Flemish Connection

Flemish immigration to Ontario goes back to the turn of the century, when Dutch-speaking immigrants from Belgium outnumbered those from the Netherlands (see chapter 2). Flemish-Americans started moving to southwestern Ontario, especially in the Wallaceburg area, after 1902, with the development of sugar beet production. They were soon joined by people coming directly from Flanders. Until the outbreak of the World War One, this migration resulted in a Flemish corridor stretching from Wallaceburg, through Chatham, up to Leamington.[60] Canadians of Flemish descent still live in this area today. Since no French-speaking Walloons came into this region, Belgian became synonymous with Flemish. With the subsequent introduction of flue-cured tobacco, Flemish immigrants moved to a new region, stretching from Aylmer to Simcoe. Their centre for socialization became Tilsonburg, where hundreds of Flemish used a local dance hall to play music and listen to plays.[61] Starting out as share farmers, many of them survived the depression and ended up owning their own farms by the time the postwar immigrants arrived.[62] By 1980 people of Flemish descent constituted about 30,000 Canadians in southern Ontario.[63]

Relations between Dutch and Flemish Immigrants

The Dutch and Flemish, who share a common official language in Europe, continued to rub shoulders in the North American setting. There are few differences between the Dutch and Flemish on both sides of their shared international border; Belgium also has a region called Brabant and the Dutch province of Zeeland has a sub-region called Zeeuws Vlaanderen (Flemish Zeeland) with very close ties to Belgium.[64] Minor linguistic and cultural variations did not prevent social contact in the Canadian context, albeit with minor tensions expressed through friendly rivalry and joking. The Canadians they encountered were usually not aware that these two immigrant groups represented different nationalities. The ethnic boundaries between the Dutch and the Belgians are less clear-cut in other ways. Some postwar "Dutch" emigrants to Canada, who originally came from towns near the Belgian border, were actually born in Belgium; the reverse is also true. Hence these two ethnic groups in Canada, representing different nationalities, might each claim the same celebrity as a "native son."[65] Starting in the fifties, Dutch and Flemish immigrants also established ethnically mixed social clubs; the Belgian-Dutch Association in Wallaceburg, the Benelux Club in Stratford and the Canadian Belgian-Dutch Club in Chatham each include both Dutch and Flemish immigrants and their offspring (see chapter 16).

The relative proportion of Dutch to Flemish in Ontario varies according to time and region. Before the War, Dutch Catholic immigrants from Zeeuws Vlaanderen and Noord Brabant joined the mainly Flemish "swallow migration" to Ontario. A tiny minority among Dutch-speaking newcomers, they were swamped by their Flemish cousins. Prewar Dutch Catholic immigrants encountered Flemish-dominated parishes in La Salette, Delhi and Blenheim, where they received help and advice from Flemish priests of the Capuchin order. These priests, who set up their own parish in Blenheim in the twenties, catered to the Flemish and to the less-numerous Dutch immigrants in both Essex and Kent counties, and in the new tobacco-growing regions in Elgin and Norfolk.[66] However, marriages between Belgians and Hollanders were rare in Ontario prior to 1945.[67] This situation changed in the postwar period, when the prewar situation was reversed. Starting in 1948, Flemish immigrants in Ontario were absorbed into the Dutch-dominated postwar immigration wave.

Initially Dutch and Flemish postwar immigrants came to the same beet- or tobacco-growing regions mentioned above.[68] Their turnover was high because these workers, who aspired to own their own farms, soon moved to other parts of Ontario, especially Huron, Middlesex or Lambton counties, where land was less expensive. Both Dutch and Flemish postwar immigrants were better educated than their prewar counterparts. If they did not have enough savings to start farming on their own, they moved closer to bigger cities such as London or Windsor to earn higher wages. Dutch immigrants who stayed in the older Flemish regions were influenced by the Belgian presence. Thus, Dutch immigrants joined a Belgian club set up by Flemish tobacco farmers in Delhi.[69] However, in the rest of Ontario, a minority of Flemish postwar immigrants became members of Dutch-Canadian communities and institutions. For example, most of the Flemish members recruited by St. Willibrord Credit Union—officially set up for both Dutch and Flemish immigrants—were married to Dutch immigrants.

The Flemish parents of Jose Cozijn, the first woman manager of St. Willibrord Credit Union, landed in London in 1951. Here they bought a house together with a Dutch immigrant couple. Most of the other immigrants they encountered were also from the Netherlands, and Jose, then a young woman, married a Dutchman.[70] Almost all members of the Benelux Club they joined were Dutch-Canadians, although the board of directors included a mixed Belgian-Dutch couple who still run a small business in Stratford. Madeleine Visser recalls when she moved to nearby Kinkora in 1956, where her parents bought a farm. They were the only Flemish family in that village, and the nearest Flemish family lived in Mitchell. Of her eleven siblings, one brother married a Flemish woman, but another brother and two sisters married Dutch immigrants.[71] In the region west of London there was a somewhat larger Belgian presence, but they too became a part of the postwar Dutch-Canadian community through intermarriage.[72]

Transitions from Prewar Flemish to Postwar Dutch

In some places with a prewar Flemish presence, the Dutch practically "took over" in a nearly undetectable process of ethnic transition. Angelina Leugenhagen arrived in Sarnia in 1950. After a stint as cleaner and dishwasher, this newly arrived Flemish immigrant moved into hairdressing, and two years later she set up her own beauty salon. When Angelina founded the Belgian-Canadian-Dutch Club,[73] all 18 members were either prewar or postwar Flemish, with the exception of one lone Hollander. Few Dutch immigrants joined her club because almost all of the newly arrived Dutch immigrants whom Angelina knew were Calvinist girls who were not allowed to attend dances, a central club activity (see chapter 16). About a decade later, a group of mainly Dutch Catholic immigrants asked Angelina Leugenhagen to represent the local Flemish community in setting up a branch of St. Willibrord Credit Union. The Flemish presence in Sarnia was then still quite important. However, throughout the sixties and seventies, an increasing number of postwar Dutch immigrants joined both the club and the credit union, until they formed an overwhelming majority in both organizations.[74]

A more sudden shift from a Flemish to an overwhelming Dutch presence took place in a credit union in Blenheim. Originally set up by Capuchin priests, St. Mary's Parish Credit Union was run by mainly Flemish prewar immigrants. Only one member, of English descent, was born in Canada.[75] In contrast, most Dutch Catholic immigrants in the same region joined St. Willibrord Credit Union's Chatham division, whose part-time commuting manager was a postwar Dutch-Canadian farmer in Blenheim.[76] Despite a further influx of Dutch Catholic farm immigrants in the region, the religious and ethnic composition of the parish credit union did not change much, even after St. Mary's was transformed into the Blenheim Community Credit Union. The board of directors was still dominated by Flemish old-timers. However, the status quo changed completely when they were amalgamated with the larger and now more powerful St. Willibrord Credit Union. After a takeover in 1980, all but one board member stepped down. At this point the Dutch-Canadian man who had hitherto served as manager for St. Willibrord's Chatham branch started running day-to-day operations when that branch, including staff, was transferred to Blenheim. The new board members, plus local delegates representing their board in London, were likewise postwar Dutch immigrant farmers.[77]

The County of Perth

The town of St. Marys and its rural hinterland epitomizes the relationship between postwar Dutch- and Flemish-Canadians in another region of Ontario which had few prewar Flemish-Canadians. Although Belgians worked in the local flax industry in the twenties, they disappeared after this industry pulled out during the recession.[78] After 1945, only ten Flemish families moved into the St. Marys region. In 1990, a study of postwar immigration from the Netherlands to this region was carried out under the auspices of the St. Marys Museum.[79] While the project's focus was more on the Dutch, two Flemish farm women participated in the project as resource people and volunteers. During an exhibit, which came out of the research project, one of these Flemish women set up a display case with a map of Belgium. The emphasis was on the bilingual and bicultural nature of Belgium. However, her heritage is not likely to be preserved in the next generation, even in a rural farm environment. The four daughters of the Flemish woman at the St. Marys exhibit have all married spouses with no Flemish or Dutch connections, and only one continues to live in the area.

Flemish-Canadians in the Urban Environment

A national (Belgian), rather than a Flemish identity, is likely to be displayed in a more urban setting. For example, at a multicultural festival in Brantford, the Dutch and the Belgians were represented in separate "villages," or displays.[80] In larger cities, the Flemish are also more likely to set up their own clubs rather than join Dutch-Canadian ones.[81] Thus, in Toronto a Belgo-Canadian Club was organized by Yvonne Kennedy, who came to Canada as a war bride. The few remaining non-agrarian Flemish postwar immigrants in the city of Hamilton joined this social club in Toronto, when their own organization was disbanded in the seventies.[82] However, as in the case of the Dutch, more recent, younger Flemish newcomers are not likely to show much interest in the clubs set up by earlier immigrants. Instead, they set up their own ethnically based Belgian Business and Professional Association in Toronto,[83] which has recently started to develop close ties with its Dutch-Canadian counterpart.[84]

Shifting Ethnicity

Canadians of Flemish descent, like the Dutch, have gone in different directions. The Flemish illustrate the fluid nature of ethnic boundaries and how members of a social group sharing a common language can follow different trajectories, depending on the wider social context. In regions that received immigrants from Belgium in the twenties, Flemish-Canadians see themselves more as Netherlandic (in the broader sense) than as Belgian. Although predominantly English-speaking today, they still want to preserve their cultural heritage, which includes the Dutch language. In fact, in Essex county, there was more interest among Flemish-Canadians than among Dutch-Canadians in Dutch language classes.[85]

In contrast, descendants of prewar Flemish immigrants who landed and stayed in Quebec or the capital region have not only become Francophones but nationalistic, even *separatistes*, Quebecois.[86] Although seemingly opposites, the more conservative Flemish-Canadians in Ontario and their left-wing counterparts in Quebec share a common disposition of fierce nationalism born out of an earlier struggle for ethnic autonomy in the European context. However, not even acculturated, younger Francophones of Flemish descent necessarily lose their Flemish identity. For example, Cornelius Jaenen, a historian at the University of Ottawa, is writing an ethnic history of the Belgians in Canada, together with another Flemish-French-Canadian from Montreal.[87] These Flemish-Canadians are writing about the once Dutch-speaking Belgian-Canadians in French!

Dutch Indonesians in Ontario

Dutch-speaking people from Indonesia represent another form of indeterminacy when it comes to ethnic boundaries. Dutch-speaking people with an Indonesian connection are not counted as a separate category in the Canadian census, nor do they easily fit into any of the ethnic or racial labels found in North America. Many would be considered Eurasians, or members of a "visible minority." However, there is no consistent association with phenotype (physical appearance) and identity or cultural traits. Some Dutch-Indonesians may be quite European (Dutch) in language and culture, but "look" Chinese or Arabic; others may identify themselves as non-European yet be taken for "Dutch."[88] In the case of these Dutch-speaking people, who lived in the Indonesian archipelago, we can appreciate the tremendous internal diversity that may be found even among a numerically small ethnic sub-group. A high proportion of Dutch-Indonesians emigrated to North America or Australia via the Netherlands, although most ended up in places like Hawaii or Los Angeles. Here we will only look at those who came to Ontario as part of the postwar immigration that took place between 1946 and 1957. These immediate postwar Dutch-Indonesian immigrants were later joined by other Indonesian emigrants who may or may not have had a Dutch connection.

Chapter 3 included the historical background of the Dutch-speaking people from the former Dutch East Indies. People have been travelling back and forth between Europe and what is now known as Indonesia for such a long time that the Dutch and Dutch-Indonesians have become both genetically and culturally intertwined. As in the case of Dutch Jews, the level of prejudice and discrimination against Dutch-Indonesians has mostly been kept within bearable limits. However, there was enough of a stigma attached to being "part Indonesian" in the Netherlands that some people of Indonesian descent opted to hide or deny their ancestry. But the social and cultural dynamics associated with the long history of Dutch colonialism in Asia, and its subsequent breakup, are more complex than what has so far been presented. For example, we must keep in mind the different dispositions between postwar immigrants who were born in or lived in Indonesia prior to 1950 and more recent refugees who entered the stream of Asian immigrants entering Canada after 1980.

The little-used English word "Dutch-Indonesian" is a rough translation of the Dutch word *Indisch* (see chapter 3), which is still used by some Dutch-Canadians. This label, subject to different interpretations, can be used to categorize other people, as well as being a means of self-identification. As an ethnic distinction that underscores Dutch colonial connections, *Indisch* refers to three overlapping categories: Indonesian families whose ancestors originally came from Europe; Dutch citizens who were either brought up or spent considerable time in the former Dutch East Indies; and "racially mixed" people in the Netherlands who can trace their ancestry to the former Dutch East Indies. None of these categories is incompatible with being Dutch (*Nederlands*). However, unlike Dutch people who have never been to Indonesia, people who identify themselves as *Indisch* do not necessarily make the racial distinction noted above.[89] A new word, which is used by some "Dutch-Indonesians" in both North America and Europe, is "Indo." This post-colonial label emphasizes the unique nature of a group of people who are neither Dutch nor Indonesian, yet have their own identity. It is difficult to calculate the number of Indos and/or *Indisch* even if one were to conduct a survey, because any estimate would depend on one's definition.[90] When I asked a Dutch-Canadian artist who identified himself as Indo to estimate the numbers of Dutch-Indonesians in Ontario, using a broad definition, he suggested around 3,000.[91]

In looking at Dutch-Indonesians as a category or a social group we can start by examining how they are perceived by others. Dutch-Canadians born and raised in the western part of the Netherlands or in an urban setting usually "know" who is Dutch-Indonesian, on the basis of both cultural and culturally defined physical traits. Even if the *Indisch* connection is not immediately apparent, first generation Dutch-Canadians, especially those brought up in a more cosmopolitan urban environment, will find such a connection by making inquiries about personal history and family background. In contrast, rural Dutch-Canadians might have never met anyone who is *Indisch* in the Netherlands, much less in Canada. Such Dutch-Canadians, originally brought up in small Dutch villages, might never know that an elderly "Chinese" owner of a restaurant in a small town in Ontario might speak better standard Dutch than they do. Other Dutch immigrants identify anyone who spent some time in the former Dutch East Indies, either in the army or in a prisoner-of-war camp, as "Dutch-Indonesian."

The way people are labelled by others may not be the same as how they see themselves. In my research I have come across people who find it difficult to accept the assertion of an "oriental-looking" person that they are Dutch. On the other hand, a well-meaning but naive Dutch immigrant might inadvertently offend someone by calling them *Indisch*. Such persons, whose ancestors might have come from Indonesia, might prefer the label Dutch or Netherlandic, especially if they grew up in Holland. They are particularly likely to reject such a label when faced with prejudice. In contrast, other Dutch-Indonesians, from diverse backgrounds, identify themselves positively as Indos. Dutch-Indonesians who grew up abroad, but later married Dutch-born spouses, tend to emphasize the Dutch rather than the Indonesian connection. However, they would still see themselves as different from other Dutch-Canadians. A close-knit network of such people in Toronto regularly socializes.[92] Nevertheless, Dutch-Indonesians and Netherlanders are strongly bound together in the Canadian context. Dutch-Indonesians are bound to meet immigrants from the Netherlands almost anywhere in Ontario, whether via a church, a club or an informal network of friends and relatives.

The Rijsttafel Connection

Apart from a common language, national identity and a shared history, ethnic food binds people together. Most Dutch immigrants had developed a taste for Indonesian food, especially an elaborate multicourse meal known as *rijsttafel*.[93] Dutch-Canadians who were unable to cook such dishes themselves could not find Indonesian food in Ontario prior to 1960, and after that only in restaurants in a few places, including Toronto. Dutch war veterans' reunions in Canada first brought together Dutchmen and Dutch-Indonesians. Not only had some Dutch veterans married Dutch-Indonesian women, but many "racially mixed" Dutch-Indonesians, who later ended up in Canada, had been in the Dutch armed forces.[94] Indonesian food is a popular dish for any such gathering. Another social network revolving around the *rijsttafel* involves Dutch diplomats posted in Canada, who have contacts with Dutch-Canadian businessmen, professionals and academics. Such "upper-crust," well-educated, Dutch-Canadians include a fair share of Dutch-Indonesians, or people with Dutch-Indonesian connections. This connection is especially evident to any "outsiders" who join the group. For example the non-Dutch wife of a former consul in Ottawa, who had attended numerous social functions in places like Calgary, Toronto and Montreal, once asked her husband if all Netherlanders in Canada came from Indonesia![95]

Formal Organizations

Some Dutch-Indonesians belong to larger, international organizations whose headquarters are located in the Netherlands or in the United States. They have a bilingual newsletter called *Magazine Mousan*, and one can buy bumper stickers which read *Ik ben Indo, ik blijf Indo* (I am Indo, I remain Indo). However, there are also Canadian organizations for Indos, including a former club that grew out of more informal gatherings. The history of that Club (Insulinde), set up in Toronto by Winnie Olenroot-Macaré,[96] can be used to illustrate the heterogenous and quickly changing nature of overlapping ethnic groups.

The transformation of the Insulinde Club reflects broader changes in the Dutch-Indonesian network. In the fifties and sixties, all of its members were *Indisch* who had arrived directly from the Netherlands. Postwar immigrants with an indirect connection to Indonesia, often through marriage, also used to attend. Their identification as *Nederlanders* with an Indonesian connection and the use of Dutch held them together. In the late sixties and seventies more and more people who came directly from Indonesia attended such gatherings. These new immigrants included people of Chinese or mixed Chinese descent who had been persecuted under Suharto.[97] The original Dutch-Canadian couples, including most mixed couples, initially continued to attend "Indonesian" gatherings. However, gradually the more "European" Dutch-Indonesians started dropping out because they no longer "felt at home."[98] Around the same time, the arrival of additional newcomers from Indonesia to the Toronto area led to the formation of an Indonesian-Canadian Association and many Eurasian Dutch-Indonesians who belonged to the Insulinde Club joined it as well. Although their newsletter is printed in *Bahasa Indonesia*, the official language of Indonesia, older members speak or understand Dutch. However, the Dutch-Indonesians who learned the older trade language (*maleis*) cannot read modern *Bahasa Indonesia*. The next generation, growing up in Ontario, will have to communicate in English, even if they have been exposed to other languages such as *Bahasa Indonesia*, Mandarin or Dutch.

A few recent immigrants from the Netherlands have also joined this new association. Willem van der Griff, a Dutchman who moved to Canada after he retired in 1980, became a member soon after he arrived. This man is married to a "Dutch burger" from Sri Lanka, whom he had met when his battalion, originally stationed in Indonesia, fled to what was then called Ceylon. The "Dutch burgers" are a "racially mixed" but westernized ethnic minority in Sri Lanka, descended from the Europeans who worked for the Dutch East Indies Company before that island was taken over by the British (see chapter 2). Today the "Dutch burgers" of Sri Lanka speak English. This couple also spent some time in Curaçao, in the Dutch West Indies, where she read about the earlier Insulinde Club of Toronto in a newsletter. They joined both organizations as soon as they landed in Canada.[99]

Although the original Insulinde Club was disbanded in the early eighties, Winnie continued to organize an annual picnic in Pelco Park, near Milton. The picnic I attended on June 19, 1989, consisted of some old club members, including the Van der Griffs, Dutch-Canadian immigrants who had never attended the picnic before and the Dutch representative for Martinair. Several people who were not Dutch-Indonesians came after hearing about the picnic at the annual consular reception in Toronto in honour of the queen's birthday about a month earlier. The turnout at the picnic was around 50 people. Several women visiting from Indonesia sold drinks and food at a table set up in the park. More Dutch than English was spoken at this gathering, but people kept switching back and forth from one language to another.[100]

The Indonesian-Canadian Association is not the only organization that includes members with Dutch connections. There is also an Indonesian Catholic Organization (with largely Chinese connections) and a senior citizens club, INCASEC (Indonesian Canadian Senior Citizens). The majority of members in the latter are Protestants (from various denominations), but one member and a past president are Muslims. They have also had Catholic members.[101] Indeed, there is a great deal of overlap in all three organizations. All of these Indonesian organizations advertise for both their businesses and social and fund-raising activities in the *Nederlandse Courant*. The old connection between the Netherlands and Indonesia is thus alive and well in Toronto. In fact, when the Dutch consul-general addressed the Indonesian-Canadian Association's opening meeting a couple of years ago, he spoke in Dutch and received thunderous applause.[102]

Informal Networks: A Case Study

Dutch-Indonesians who belong to formal organizations are also connected to an extensive informal network of friends and relatives. One way to gain insights into how such networks come into being is through a life history. Huibert Sabelis, who identifies himself as an Indo, can serve as an illustration. He has many Dutch-Indonesian acquaintances and, like Winnie Olenroot, is well known in the Toronto Dutch-Canadian community. His story also illustrates the presence of racial prejudice. Huibert arrived in Canada in 1963 at the age of 21.[103] His father was a Dutch-Indonesian of Frisian and Indonesian descent. In Canada he could pass as someone from anywhere in the Mediterranean or the Near East.[104] Huibert's first wife was also Dutch-Indonesian. Her skin colour was darker and she had Southeast Asian facial features, which made her conspicuous when they started living in rural Ontario.[105]

The Sabelis couple travelled to Canada by boat, landing in Montreal. Huibert had received training as a baker and pastry chef, but started doing odd jobs. His first offer of a steady position brought them to Ayton in Grey county. Here they got their first taste of discrimination when they could not find a place to live. A subsequent move to Mount Brydges was their first immersion in a Dutch-Canadian community, since all thirty co-workers and his boss were Dutch immigrants belonging to the Christian Reformed church. At church, people stared at his wife, and at work he was often forced to do overtime against his will. The next decade, spent in the London area, was an uphill struggle to make a living, with periods of unemployment. Around this time Huibert and his wife met their first close friends, including Dutch-Indonesians. Although they did not join a Dutch-Canadian club operating in London, Huibert did get a small loan from St. Willibrord, and they sought out a Dutch family physician. Their life insurance agent was a Dutchman who had come from Indonesia. In London, Huibert started to meet other Indos, the beginning of an extensive network that expanded to Waterloo, Woodstock and Toronto.

Huibert Sabelis, who had always seen himself as an artist,[106] started his professional art career when he sold several india ink sketches—depicting Indonesian scenes—to the owner of a donut shop where he worked part-time. His increasingly busy life resulted in the breakup of his marriage. While still recovering from the trauma of the divorce, Huibert moved to Toronto, where he boarded with a Dutch-Indonesian family he first met in London. Around that time Dutch clubs were springing up all around the province. That is how he met John Macaré, the brother of Winnie Olenroot-Macaré (see above). John was dating a Filipina. She and a group of other Filipina seamstresses who had received their training in Holland were then working in Toronto. These women, some of whom had picked up the Dutch language, and the Dutch-Indonesian men they dated, formed their own branch of a Dutch-Canadian Entertainment Club, which organized charter flights (see chapter 16). Huibert met more Indos and Filipinos, but also got to know the heterogenous Dutch- Canadian community of Toronto. He made more Dutch friends, but was also exposed to prejudice; upon entering a Dutch social function in Brampton, with Winnie's brother and the Filipina he later married, someone suggested that all the *zwartjes* (blackies) sit together in their own corner. Today Huibert is listed as a professional artist in the membership booklet of the Netherlands Luncheon Club. Starting in the early nineties, he set up an Indo club and took over the organization of the Dutch-Indonesian picnic.[107]

Huibert Sabelis is typical of Indos who lived for only a short time period in Indonesia. However, even among Eurasians born and raised in Asia, there are differences in attitudes and values. Some Indos now in Ontario initially emigrated to Dutch New Guinea (now Irian Jaya), as part of an ill-fated postwar project to set up a separate state in this outer island of the Indonesian archipelago. These people were pioneers who had to learn practical trades, as opposed to those who stayed in Java as clerks or office workers.[108] The former consider themselves to be different from Indos who first emigrated to the Netherlands.

Like the Flemish, Dutch-Indonesians have multiple identities. Indos also faced discrimination from native Ontarians and, to a lesser extent, from other Dutch immigrants. At the same time, Dutch Indonesians and the role of the Dutch in Indonesia have become popular topics for scholarly discussion and news coverage in the Dutch-Canadian press or at learned conferences.[109] The presence and portrayal of Dutch-Indonesians, together with Dutch Jews, serve a symbolic function in defining *the Dutch* as a people who once had an important international presence. Yet members of the Indonesian group are aware that their children will not maintain the diverse contacts and unique identity of their parents. Despite the saying on the bumper stickers produced by their organization, the categories of Indo and *Indisch* will eventually disappear since the Dutch East Indies no longer exists. One of the elderly Dutch-Indonesians whom I interviewed designates his group as the "last generation."

Most Dutch sub-identities are a temporary phenomenon. The few remaining annual regional reunions are slowly petering out. Even the recent successful home-town reunions of Brabanders are basically a first-generation affair. Ironically, only the younger people in Mariahout have become the driving force in keeping up contacts with their former townspeople in Canada. Their older Dutch-Canadian counterparts are quite conscious that they better get in as many reunions as possible before their time is up. They know the link will break with the next generation. One or two children might possible make a visit to their grandparents' birthplace out of curiosity, but would not identify strongly with a particular Dutch town or region, even if they were to preserve a broader Dutch ethnic identity. Only the Flemish and perhaps the Frisians might establish more stable and longer-lasting networks.

Dutch-Canadian ethnicity involves at least two forms of diversity and competing interpretations of cultural discourse: pillarization versus sub-ethnic or regional particularities. In this chapter we emphasized sub-ethnic variation. Many Flemish and Dutch-Indonesian immigrants became part of a more broadly defined Dutch-Canadian or Netherlandic group, just like Frisians and people from very diverse regions within the Netherlands. At the same time all of these sub-groups forged their own ties with other national, ethnic or religious groups. The Canadian mosaic displays fuzzy edges, with colours and patterns blending. The kaleidoscope keeps turning.[110]

Fieldnotes Interlude

10.1 Excerpt from an interview (in Dutch) with a Dutch-Canadian war veteran, in Chatham, December 1, 1989

Some people who are *Indisch* don't want to recognize their background. My ex used to say that she only happens to have brown skin (*bruin velletje*), but I always told her that she was *Indisch* inside of her head because she had a different way of thinking. My daughters are 25 percent *Indisch*, but they won't let you say that. One time my daughter came into the office where I worked and a Dutchman who worked there as gardener made the remark "*daar gaat een Indisch meisje want haar moeder is Indisch* [there goes an *Indisch* girl, since her mother is *Indisch*)." She got really angry and told him she was a hundred percent Dutch. That happens a lot with children of people who are *Indisch* who have never lived in Indonesia.

10.2 Translations from excerpts of an interview (in Dutch), with additional observational notes [in brackets], with a woman in Sarnia, June 3, 1991

. . . when I first came here in 1950, Sarnia was a small city. I felt more at home here than in the States because it seemed more European—at least half European—and I wrote to the consul in Detroit asking for permission to emigrate to Canada. He explained I could not get the proper papers without my husband who was in Belgium, so I wrote my husband and told him to change his papers so he could go to Canada instead of the United States. He came in July, a couple of months later, and came here with our daughter. Before that I could not work here. [*note*: She had travelled to North America to visit an uncle who lived in Wisconsin]. . . . I started cleaning floors, like everyone else who is an immigrant and my second job was washing dishes at the Colonial Hotel. Then I got into hairdressing and eventually started by own business . . . a lot of my customers were Dutch girls but not necessarily Catholic. Later I had Greta working for me and she was a Dutch Protestant. She later became engaged to ____ who had lived in Indonesia.

. . . marriages between Dutch and Belgians became more prevalent after we started our social club. Before that Belgians only married Belgians and Dutch married Dutch. But the Dutch Protestant girls I knew would not go to our club because they were not allowed to dance and I used to talk to Greta about that. Their religion forbad dancing because they saw it as something sexual, but I once told her that dancing was a gift from God and that dancing made me feel happy; if you saw it as sexy, then it was all in your mind. . . . as I said, I got along with the Protestants because they were my customers or employees, but I found that the Hollanders would try to poke fun of the way I spoke. In Holland, the Dutch thought that speaking with their *harde gee* [a gutteral "g" sound] made them more important and they would poke fun of the Flemish we spoke. However, I remember how the wife of their minister once heard me speak Flemish [she recounted how the minister's wife was intrigued when this Flemish woman sang her a traditional Flemish folksong]. Afterwards the minister himself came to see me because he really liked what I used to sing and he made an appointment for his daughter to get her hair done with me as well.

. . . once Brother Peter [a member of a Dutch religious order in Sarnia] made a comment on my speaking Flemish and said it was impossible to understand. But I pointed out to him that I had learned to speak proper Dutch (*Nederlands*) and even knew how to take dictation in Dutch shorthand.

10.3 Excerpt from same retired farm woman from Wyoming, quoted in fieldnote interlude 8.5

One day, Mrs. Raaymaker and myself were in the Dutch store and we heard some people speaking Dutch and thought it might be nice to also speak some Dutch to some people we met there. But they were Frieslanders and they said "oh—Hollanders" and were not interested in talking to us.

. . . we once made a trip to Wisconsin together with my brothers-in-law from Ottawa. They accompanied someone originally from Boekel, a Rooiackers, who wanted to visit a relative there who had come to the Boekelse reunion here in Ontario. That place in Wisconsin had all kinds of Dutch street names from when people from our province settled there a hundred years ago. People there regretted that their parents and grandparents had not written down their history and we have to make sure that we don't lose ours—our history of how we came to Canada.

Chapter 11

Language Retention

The retention of languages other than English is seen as an indicator of ethnic or regional identity in most of North America. Speaking a "foreign" language is invariably associated with being an "immigrant," or with membership in an exotic ethnic enclave.[1] One measure of language retention is the proportion of an ethnically defined population speaking their language as mother tongue. According to the 1986 census, the percentages for Dutch-Canadians in various counties in Ontario were between 30 and 40 (see also chapter 6).[2] The only ethnic category ranking lower was Scandinavian (22 percent).[3] Another measure is the numerical differences between people using a language at home versus those reporting the same language as mother tongue. On that scale, Dutch-Canadians (Netherlands) showed negative 75 percent.[4]

In the case of Canadians of Dutch descent, a reported low rate of language retention is consistent with their rapid assimilation and low level of ethnic identity. However, the phenomenon of language use among immigrants and their descendants is too complex to measure through the rather crude notion of a single "mother tongue" ascribed to a very diverse population. A single number representing language retention for a group as a whole glosses over the issues of how variations connected to age, gender, region and other social variables effect trends in language loss and retention. It is equally important to look at the process whereby different Netherlandic languages (and regional dialects) were lost, and in some cases revived, in separate social contexts.[5] The official survey data must therefore be interpreted in the light of qualitative research on both spoken and written discourse.

Notes to this chapter are on p. 376-79.

The Survival of Netherlandic Languages

The population census does not contain any figures on the use of written as opposed to spoken language. Chapter 1 mentioned that the Dutch-Canadian community has maintained three Dutch-language newspapers, which seems to indicate that a relatively high level of reading might coincide with a low level of spoken Dutch. Quantitative data focusing on linguistic identity in specific localities may also contradict the picture derived from aggregate-level analysis. For example, according to a recent sociological study, the Dutch in Toronto had "relatively high proportions of second- and third-generation members with at least some knowledge of their ethnic language."[6] It is thus necessary to look at different aspects of language retention.

Not all Dutch-Canadians who emigrated as adults retain fluent use of Dutch. Fewer still have passed it on to their offspring. However, "Dutch" mother tongue as reported in the census is not always synonymous with official *Nederlands* (see chapter 3). Adult immigrants learned to communicate in standard Dutch through school or church, but this "high Dutch" was often a second language. Their younger children, whether born in Canada or in Europe, did not have much exposure to this version of Dutch unless taught at home. We must therefore first examine actual mother tongue usage, regardless of whether this happens to be Dutch, one of its regional variations (or dialects), some form of Flemish, or a version of Frisian.

Which language ends up being used at home depends in part on the parents' attitudes.[7] Another factor responsible for language retention is the presence of relatives. Children who interacted with grandparents retained their ancestral language. In contrast, if a husband and wife came from different provinces, with different forms of speech, they would find it easier to use whatever was the official language. Such couples made the transition to English much earlier. The parents might come from opposite sides of the country and not understand each other's home language: in one case the father was Frisian and the mother from Limburg. When they met in Canada, they communicated in a combination of standard Dutch and English. Even if one or both parents taught their own mother tongue to the children, home languages other than English frequently fell by the wayside unless early exposure was reinforced through ongoing contact with relatives or neighbours. Since frequent visits back to the old country were out of the question for most postwar immigrants, such linguistic contact was more likely to occur where Dutch immigrants from the same home region kept in contact in Canada. The importance of frequent social interaction outside the immediate family can be illustrated by the childhood of Hermina Joldersma, who later became a professor of Germanic languages at the University of Calgary.

Hermina's parents emigrated from the eastern part of the Netherlands, her father from Drenthe and her mother from Overijssel. They met and married in Ontario (in 1951) and bought a farm in the Niagara peninsula, where Hermina was born and brought up. She grew up in an extended family, consisting of a broad network of relatives within driving distance. Her maternal grandparents lived in a separate section of their farmhouse.[8] The predominant language, both at home and at numerous family gatherings, was the dialect of Holten, her mother's home town. Years later Hermina Joldersma wrote,

> "Holtens plat" was more than just a language: rather, it represented an entire culture to which we children (my two brothers and I) were proud to belong. So I would remember how I would identify myself if I were ever to visit Holten: "Ik ben de dochter van Trui van Willem van Lambooy'[9] (Lambooy being the farm name, not the family name, which was Beldman). Through listening to our grandparents visit with other people from Holten who had immigrated to our part of Southern Ontario, we got to know the town of Holten as though we had lived there ourselves.[10]

Such continuity of a mother tongue happened in places with a concentration of immigrants, particularly in rural enclaves.

Linguistic retention was lower in regions where immigrants were isolated from each other. An almost complete loss of mother tongue occurred in Blenheim, in Kent county, where a man arrived with his parents when he was nine years old, in 1947. This young immigrant had attended three years of primary school in Noord Brabant, and later married a Dutch-Canadian woman. But when I interviewed him in 1990, he told me not to ask him to speak Dutch, because he had not spoken it for years. Their family had only spoken English from the day they arrived, because at that time they were the only Dutch immigrants around.[11] They were part of a handful of early postwar Dutch immigrants who integrated on their own, several years prior to an influx of other Dutch immigrants into southwestern Ontario. Even today there is a difference in speech habits between this man's family and the later arrivals from his home region, including his own in-laws, and several nephews who were more "Dutch" since they maintained their mother tongue.[12] Such examples where people stopped speaking some version of Dutch within the first year of arrival are rare. The typical scenario is a gradual process of transition, with the replacement of more and more Dutch words and expressions for English ones. Even the language used among close friends and family invariably became transformed into a creole of Dutch, Dutch dialect and English.[13]

The Survival of Dutch Dialects

In some cases dialects of Dutch survived up to the second generation. Indeed, their pronunciation and vocabulary have been preserved to a greater extent than in the Netherlands.[14] People in the rural Netherlands are surprised when a young cousin from Canada arrives for a visit, speaking what they perceive as "authentic" village speech. Dutch linguists even visit Ontario to meet people who still speak regional dialects disappearing at home. In contrast to the predominant trend in the Netherlands, some people who grew up speaking a dialect—and later learned to speak standard Dutch—reverted back to their mother tongue in a Canadian context. This happened to Tony, a man who emigrated to Canada in 1973 from Tilburg, in Noord Brabant.

During Tony's childhood, people spoke a version of Brabants specific to that city; indeed, each parish had its own unique expressions. However, his parents and teachers discouraged him from speaking *plat* ("low") and to learn "proper" Dutch. At age 33, Tony emigrated to Canada.[15] The first place Tony was again exposed to his original, but now rusty, mother tongue was in Barrie, where he encountered Dutch-Canadians from Tilburg and Den Bosch.[16] A good friend of Tony's, who had known him when he first arrived in Barrie, later told me Tony spoke "very proper Dutch," but was no longer fluent in Tilburg Brabants. Tony only spent a month in Barrie before moving on to North Bay, where he worked for another couple of months. In 1976, he opened a fish restaurant in Sudbury, where he met more Brabanders. One day, when Tony went to visit his wife in the hospital and spoke to her in standard Dutch, a lady in the same ward addressed them in Brabants.[17] Tony soon got to know the rest of her family in Sudbury. Gradually he picked up more and more expressions in Brabants, as he met other families from his home province. His Tilburg version of Brabants was reinforced during a chance encounter with a man from his old neighbourhood during a transatlantic boat cruise. That man was proud of his home-town language and they conversed in Tilburgs during that trip. They became friends and have since made regular exchange visits.[18]

It would be misleading to give the impression that the Netherlandic languages are alive and well in Ontario. Those who speak a regional dialect with some level of fluency are a minority. Many Dutch immigrants who arrived as adults in the late forties have passed away or are spending their last days in nursing homes. Those who still know a regional dialect mainly consist of people who were young couples when they came in the fifties, or the Dutch-born children of older immigrants.[19] Few of their offspring or younger siblings, born in Canada, use their home dialect.[20] Nowadays, even people brought up in a regional dialect are much more likely to use English both inside and outside the home. It is not uncommon to hear young adults address their parents in English with the elders answering in Dutch or Frisian. When a Dutch film crew came to Ontario to film the Boekel reunion (see chapter 10), most people who spoke in front of the camera needed an evening's practice before they could again converse in their mother tongue. The revival of Dutch dialects among younger people is even more problematic, despite increased visits to Europe. Regardless of their level of understanding of Dutch, their Dutch cousins invariably want to practise their excellent beginners' English.

The Frisian Language

My impression is that Frisian is better preserved than most dialects. There is a growing movement internationally to maintain the Frisian language, and Canadians who speak Frisian have no trouble finding an opportunity to use their mother tongue on return visits. Even young people visiting their relatives are encouraged to practise their Frisian. Unfortunately, few Frisians who emigrated knew how to read or write their mother tongue. In its home province, Frisian has only been taught as a written language since the late fifties and did not receive official status as the second language of the Netherlands until about two decades ago.[21] In Ontario there are no heritage language classes, and few people have the training in the written language to offer such courses in Canada.[22] The Frisian language's gradual deterioration is reflected in the termination of Frisian plays once performed throughout southern Ontario (see chapter 10).

The Retention of Standard Dutch

Unlike dialects, or Frisian, standard Dutch is more likely to survive somewhat longer as a second language. Standard Dutch is more accessible since there is more reading material, even if there are few opportunities to converse. Some Dutch-Canadian immigrants who used their dialect, or Frisian, at home, thought it was important for their Canadian-born children to learn standard Dutch so that they could write to and read letters from their Dutch relatives. Others saw the utility of having access to another written language. Standard Dutch, albeit with some English admixture, was also still widely spoken in the sixties and seventies as a lingua franca among Dutch immigrants from diverse backgrounds. For example, in Reformed churches, "high" Dutch was used to read passages from the Bible, and for sermons. Anyone who came to Canada over the age of eight had learned some standard Dutch in school, and the versions of Dutch spoken in the Netherlands' western half, including Utrecht, are not that different from standard Dutch.

Broadcasting in the Dutch Language

For at least two decades, the influx of first-generation Dutch immigrants provided the stimulus for Dutch-language radio and television broadcasts. In the fifties, thousands of Dutch immigrants throughout southern Ontario listened to "Radio Nederland." Its broadcaster, Jan Van Bruchem, moved to Vancouver in the sixties to start his own multilanguage radio station.[23] However, many of the Dutch-language radio programs in Ontario did not last long; they first disappeared in small towns like Tilsonburg,[24] while others had to be scaled down. Throughout the sixties and seventies, Toronto's CHIN still had a daily 90-minute Dutch program. However, in the eighties it was cut down to a half hour, except for Saturday mornings which had an hour of largely religious music. In 1993, the daily CHIN program was still hosted every morning by Ada Wynston,[25] but in the summer of 1994 that was turned into a Sunday-afternoon-only talk show. Throughout these five decades, Dutch radio also received partial support directly from the Dutch government, and in 1972, the International Dutch Broadcasting Corporation (*Radio Wereld Omroep*) even employed Jack Brouwer in Scarborough to act as their representative in Canada. He still provides Dutch tapes to radio stations all over Canada, including Guelph.

Television programs operated in a more sporadic fashion. In the early seventies, Lisette van Gessel, a Dutch national, was hired to put on a Dutch television program for channel 46 in Toronto. Several years later she was put in charge of all ethnic programming on channel 84. Besides material from Europe, she produced Canadian shows featuring interviews with Dutch-Canadians.[26] Other cities that had television programs included Guelph (in the early eighties), Ottawa (until 1984) and Kingston.[27] The announcers and directors for these television programs were emigrants. However, they could not always find people who could speak "pure Dutch." The producer of the Toronto program had to turn down a young applicant because his Dutch was too "old-fashioned."[28] Instead, a recent Dutch immigrant with a non-Dutch name was hired. The person who ran the program for cable 8 in Guelph was Dirk Bod, who works as a university administrator. He and his wife emigrated in 1963, although he had spent some time in Guelph before that, when he was single. He was an ideal announcer because his Dutch was *zuiver* (pure), but the program was discontinued because no one could take over.[29]

Dutch television programs were not viable due to lack of support from the Dutch-Canadian community. There were not enough viewers and, even more important, insufficient financial backing from the business community. The numerous complaints I have heard about these cancellations indicates that they had a loyal, if small, following. Nevertheless, any Dutch-language television program would have a hard time getting broad-based support within its own ethnic community, unless the producers could find a Canadian equivalent of the Dutch pillar system. Someone whom I interviewed pointed out how the longer radio programs in the seventies and the more recent television programs in Toronto were run only along "neutral" lines. This person complained about the lack of any references to religion, and he complained about the coverage of topics like abortion. Such perceptions—that a Dutch-Canadian program represented a humanist or secular ideology—would inevitably mean a low level of support from the Reformed community.

Written Dutch

Unlike Dutch radio and television, which required greater institutional support and centralization, written Dutch served as a more effective vehicle for communication for a heterogenous and often dispersed population. The main publication of the Reformed community, the *Calvinist Contact*, was written in Dutch for the first ten years, as was a Catholic newsletter called *Kompas*. Written Dutch was also initially used for official correspondence in Dutch-Canadian organizations. For example, the minutes of meetings (*notulen*) of the Dutch-Canadian Credit Union in Toronto were written in Dutch until 1956,[30] and their newsletter, *Ducapost*, contained Dutch language columns and ads until the end of the 1970s.[31] Likewise, minutes of monthly board meetings of the St. Willibrord Credit Union were written sometimes in English and sometimes in Dutch prior to April 15, 1963, when a motion was passed that from then on all correspondence would be in English.[32] The Christian Farmers Federation of Ontario used Dutch for its internal correspondence up to 1968, when English was gradually introduced.[33]

Eventually, written Dutch was replaced by English in all organizations founded by Dutch immigrants.[34] Nevertheless, it survived as a language of personal correspondence outside the ethnic framework of Dutch-Canadian communities, and was even passed on to the next generation. While they might continue to speak a dialect at home, and not join any Dutch-Canadian organizations, some Dutch immigrants still wanted their children to learn standard written Dutch. Initially this was done at home. Frequently a mother would read to her children in Dutch as a way of passing on the language. This happened even in cases where the mother's home tongue was a regional dialect. Again I cite Hermina Joldersma, whose mother used to read to her from Dutch books and sing Dutch songs as she was growing up. For Hermina, who was exposed to two official languages plus a dialect, the standard form of Dutch represented a different cultural world: "Whether in sermons, books, or songs, Dutch seemed to be a highly dramatic language and opened up vastly different worlds."[35]

However, further development of standard Dutch by the offspring of immigrants required backup reading material, especially if family members did not use Dutch for daily conversation. Such reading material was usually provided by close relatives in Canada or the Netherlands. This was also the case for Hermina:

> One of my aunts gave us books every Christmas: *Gerdientje*, *Ouwe Bram*, *Om twee schitteroogjes* and, constituting my first awareness that Frisian was a different culture, *Beppe knapt het op*. But I did not confine my reading to children's books alone. I often read when I visited relatives and friends, and I consumed Dutch books and magazines indiscriminately: *Libelle* and *De Spiegel*, *Ben-Hur*, *Jij meisje*, *Moeder Ditta* and all of Luis Wessel's South African books.

Only constant reading, accompanied by some spoken Dutch, resulted in a second generation of Dutch-Canadians with at least an adequate understanding of standard Dutch.

Standard Dutch as a Second Language

Immigrants from Dutch urban centres were more likely to promote standard spoken Dutch at home. These parents had already made the transition to standard Dutch before emigrating. An example is the Van Amelsvoort family of Barrie. They arrived in Canada in 1955, as a young working couple in their mid-twenties. He grew up in Den Bosch (Noord Brabant) and she was originally from Deventer (Overijssel). They both finished the Dutch equivalent of high school, and studied English before emigrating.[36] Like many immigrants, they started conversing in English at home right away. However, the method they used to improve their English, and a decision to switch back to Dutch, were unique. The Van Amelsvoorts lived for five years in Port Colbourn and Welland in the Niagara peninsula. Although they had contact with their fellow countrymen, they made a conscious decision to speak only English at home. They designated a pot which acquired a penny for every new word they brought home, and used a similar system to help his brothers who joined them in Canada. These brothers spoke little English, so their hosts pinned English labels all over their house.[37] However, when their children started talking, this couple decided to teach them "good Dutch" by speaking Dutch only at home again. They continued to do so when they moved to Barrie in 1961. In 1991, their five children, all born in Canada, could understand Dutch (the youngest the least). The oldest daughter, who married a Frenchman and lives in Europe, gives Dutch lessons.

Dutch Language Classes

In contrast to these exceptional cases, the offspring of most postwar immigrants learned to understand, but not to speak Dutch at home. Starting around the mid-seventies, with the advent of heritage language classes, Dutch-Canadian parents became more aware of the impending loss of their national language. The motives for enrolling their children in Dutch language classes were a desire that their children learn to communicate with older relatives, and to preserve the Dutch heritage. However, the dropout rate was high.[38] Older children and young adults also took Dutch credit courses in high school or university but again, only a small percentage have persisted. Still, these programs keep attracting new pupils. In 1983, the language committee of the Canadian Association for the Advancement of Netherlandic Studies conducted a national survey. They found that Ontario had by far the largest number of classes, with the highest concentration of teachers and pupils in Toronto, Ottawa, St. Catharines, Hamilton and London (including Strathroy and Stratford). According to their survey, 31 teachers were teaching or had, in the past, taught Dutch. Interest in such classes had gone up in the previous four years.[39]

In 1988, the Netherlands consulate general in Toronto conducted its own survey.[40] The numbers cited in a report include university courses at Toronto, Carleton and Waterloo. University students who take credit courses are predominantly of Dutch background and would have previously been exposed to the language. This would also hold true for classes at the primary level under local boards of education, involving both the Catholic and public school systems. Some independent Christian schools also provide Dutch lessons, as do private teachers, sometimes in collaboration with a Dutch organization.

The most elaborate Dutch courses were mounted by the *Nederlandse school*, an educational program in Ottawa providing classes on Saturdays. Set up in 1983, this program offers heritage language classes plus three levels of Dutch study at Ridgemont High, the only secondary school to do so. These courses are available to students from across the city.[41] The program in Ottawa is unusual because its teachers and students are Dutch immigrants who came to Canada after 1970. In the rest of the province, the large Dutch-Canadian population who immigrated prior to 1960 shows less interest in heritage language classes. The teenagers and young people who emigrated at that time had little opportunity or incentive to keep up their Dutch, much less pass it on to their children (see also next chapter). My rough estimate is that more than half the Dutch-Canadians who originally had at least some schooling in the Netherlands would have difficulties initiating a fluent conversation in standard Dutch today. I have met numerous people who claim to have forgotten their Dutch because of lack of use, although they would certainly understand it. Such people would probably revive their spoken Dutch under the right circumstances, as we shall see later. However, many Dutch-Canadians who came to Canada as adults did keep up their standard Dutch through Dutch-Canadian publications.

The Dutch-Canadian Press

Two bi-weekly and one monthly Dutch-Canadian newspaper cater to both a Dutch-Canadian and Dutch-American readership, although the majority of subscribers live in central Canada. These newspapers, read in almost every Ontario county,[42] provide current news about the Netherlands, feature articles written by regular contributors, and advertisements. Their combined North American circulation is approximately 20,000,[43] although the actual readership is higher because people lend them to friends and neighbours. The first Dutch-Canadian bi-weekly, *De Nederlandse Courant*, was started in Scarborough (Toronto) in 1953 by the Schippers (see the next chapter). It was later taken over by Joseph Diening, who also bought the rights to publish a separate Dutch monthly, *De Nederlandse Post*, in the mid-sixties.[44] The *Nederlandse Courant* dwindled down to a low level of subscribers (under a thousand), before it passed into the hands of Thea Schryer, who was at that time still raising her children and working part-time. Over the next twenty years, she built up her paying readership to over four thousand subscribers.[45] In 1989 it was sold to Theo Luikenaar, a consultant and more recent immigrant who had just set up Dutch Heritage, Inc., in Burlington (see chapter 16).[46]

Dutch-Canadians also read the *Windmill Herald*, published in Surrey, British Columbia. That paper, owned and edited by Albert Vanderheide, has a larger circulation than the *Nederlandse Courant* with three editions: for Eastern Canada, Western Canada, and the States. He started that paper in 1971, after taking over an advertising sheet called *Good News*, which dates back to 1958. Several years later he also bought another newspaper, called *Hollandia News*, which started off in 1954, in Chatham.[47] Finally, the *Hollandse Krant*, a monthly paper that started a bit later, comes out of Langley, British Columbia. It is run by a retired Dutch schoolteacher, Gerard Bonekamp. Although all three papers are printed in Dutch, occasional articles in English do appear. The *Windmill Herald* has a four-page, English-language supplement called the *Windmill Post*.[48] *De Krant* has a somewhat different content and format, with more letters to the editor. Both the letters and longer editorials are more reflective, often comparing the Netherlands with Canada, as we will see later (chapter 18).[49] Their regular contributors are people who received higher education in the Netherlands and who came to Canada somewhat later. For example, one of their contributors is a speech therapist who came with her geologist husband to Calgary in 1965.[50]

Dutch Language Theatre

The Dutch language was also used in amateur performing arts. In the fifties and sixties amateur Dutch-language theatre groups (*toneelclubs*) sprang up in places with a larger concentration of Dutch-Canadians, such as Toronto, Aurora, Hamilton, Oshawa and Sarnia. Plays were performed in standard Dutch, although their content and style ranged from more serious dramas, including a Dutch version of Molière, to rural farces (*boerenkluchten*). Most of these theatre groups did not operate for more than a couple of years, although the FAMA theatre group in Toronto, which appealed to a more sophisticated audience, lasted until the late seventies. Its director, Henk Poesiat, an artist with professional theatre experience in the Netherlands, recruited players representing a broad spectrum of the Dutch-Canadian community in Toronto. They had a small but loyal audience, but had to quit due to a lack of players and declining turnout.[51]

In contrast, the folk theatre tradition, with strong roots in the rural Netherlands, survived longer. In 1996, the only Dutch-language folk theatre group operates out of the Woodstock area. The players are members of farm families, who live in Innerkip, Thamesford, Kintore and Woodstock. They come from a variety of religious backgrounds and represent a wide age range, from early twenties to their seventies.[52] However, they were all brought up and educated in the Netherlands. The actors and actresses practise at home and usually put on a comedy, although they once put on a drama dealing with the 1953 flood.[53] Their theatrical group is invited to perform throughout southern Ontario, in conjunction with Dutch cultural festivals. The turnout, consisting of a largely middle-age or older audience, is high; their annual performance at a high school auditorium in Woodstock is always sold out, with the proceeds going to charity. These plays, based on Dutch scripts, take full advantage of the different speech patterns of their players, who come from various Dutch regions.

The Social Context for Spoken Dutch

Despite a gradual decline in the use of different versions of the Dutch language, Dutch-Canadians unwittingly use more Dutch than they would be willing to admit. Furthermore, many older people are today reverting to their mother tongue (see chapter 17). Even rural middle-aged people who came to Canada when they were small are starting to speak more Dutch with the arrival of close to a thousand Dutch immigrant farmers in the eighties. Like the "old-timers" in the forties and fifties (see chapter 4), some rural postwar immigrants found that they had to revive their standard Dutch, since not all of the more recent Dutch immigrants come with fluent English. The revival of Dutch is also bound up with an increase in transatlantic travel.[54]

Return Trips

Prior to 1960, when most postwar immigrants had already been in Canada close to a decade, few families could afford to make trips back home. With the advent of cheap charter flights, traffic between the Netherlands and Canada grew exponentially (see chapters 14 and 16). Even people who have little interest in seeing Holland per se will still use the Netherlands as a springboard for trips to other parts of Europe; flights to Amsterdam are thus full of Dutch-Canadian passengers. The typical scenario is a plane full of passengers speaking mainly English with Dutch accents on the way to the Netherlands. On the way back one would hear those same passengers chatting away in Dutch. Although some Dutch-Canadians have initial difficulties switching back to their national language upon landing, renewed contact with relatives quickly brings out long- suppressed or unused Dutch. Upon returning to Canada, family members or friends are surprised to hear someone suddenly speaking fluent Dutch after so many years. Nonetheless, the Dutch again falls by the wayside after a few days. For young Dutch-Canadians who came to Canada when they were small children, or the second-generation Dutch-Canadians who learned some Dutch, their first trip back enables them to practise whatever Dutch they may have learned in Canada. However, unless reinforced in some fashion, such trips rarely lead to a long-term linguistic revival.

I have not exhausted all the sociolinguistics pertinent to postwar Dutch immigrants. This chapter has only provided an overview of the basic continuities and discontinuities of linguistic behaviour, albeit within a more general framework of ongoing contact with the Netherlands, immigrant adaptation, language policy and family dynamics. However, we have only touched on the topic of bilingualism, especially how or why most first-generation postwar Dutch immigrants still switch back and forth between Dutch or Frisian, Dutch dialect and imperfect English. A full explanation of that phenomenon requires an examination of the relationship between linguistic usage and social stratification among Canadians of Dutch descent.

Fieldnotes Interlude

11.1 *Excerpt from notes on a conversation (in Dutch) with the same retired physician as interlude no. 7.1*

I believe that a lot of emigrants did not want to speak much Dutch. They were ashamed because they used a regional language [*streektaal*]. . . . most patients who were simple [*eenvoudig*] people spoke mostly English with me when they came in for an appointment. Only when they could not explain something in English, like "*ik kan niet plassen*" [I cannot urinate], then they had to express that in their own language.

[And what language did you used to use with the Reformed ministers?]

They always spoke Dutch with me.

11.2 *Translation of an excerpt from an interview (in Dutch), with an investor holding a Dutch university degree, in Oakville, November 24, 1990*

My neighbours are a typical example of the emigrants who arrived in the fifties. They are a bit older and speak English with a thick accent, but they also have difficulty with Dutch even though they came from Leiden, where people are supposed to speak a pure form of Dutch. I have noticed that he can speak good Dutch when they have visitors from Holland. But when we converse in the backyard, it always has to be in English—that is when he goes into his Canadian mode; that is when Dutch doesn't fit [*past*]. Those kind of people have two souls.

11.3 *Translation from an excerpt of an interview (in Dutch) with a retired business manager, in Don Mills (Toronto), May 7, 1991*

We once had a cleaning lady who came in once a week. She was from Brabant and a couple of times I tried to speak Dutch with her, but she always answered in English. I wanted to hear her dialect because I am fascinated by regional variations of Dutch and I like listening to the way people from the south speak. But I could not even get her to try a few words in Brabants. That is too bad [*jammer*].

11.4 *Excerpt from an interview with the former employee of a Dutch-Canadian credit union, in Thornbury, March 12, 1991*

When we first went to a gathering to meet other Dutch immigrants, they did not want to speak Dutch, although my wife wanted to speak it again since it was tiring having to always use English . . . today our friend ______ who lives down the road from us always wants to speak Dutch to us because her husband is Swedish and she misses her mother tongue. . . . we used to conduct all of our credit union meetings in Dutch, but on occasion everyone would be speaking Dutch and someone would ask a question in English and they would then all switch to English and maybe back again.

I am writing my life history for my kids and I have got up to the War. I find I had to do that in Dutch. Then I started to translate it into English since my grandchildren don't read Dutch, but I found it was very difficult, even using the dictionary. A lot of words just don't have an exact equivalent so I had to use the Dutch words and explain them in English in brackets.

... I sometimes encounter difficulties speaking Dutch when I visit the Netherlands. Now the stupid Dutchies have a lot of new words, including English ones.

11.5 Excerpt from an interview (in Dutch) with a retired foundry worker, in Hamilton, January 28, 1990

Harry [their son] certainly understands Dutch and he can even speak it a bit—especially Limburgs [a dialect of Dutch]—but the rest of the kids understand very little. But they did take Dutch classes at the heritage program. They learned a bit there, but they speak it with a Canadian accent. We laughed ourselves silly when we heard that and that is why they don't practise their Dutch when we are around.

... I remember how one person at a meeting of our Holland-Canada Club insisted that we all use English as our official language. I thought that was terrible. I think there were a lot of Dutch immigrants who were ashamed [*beschaamd*] to maintain their Dutch identity because they were seen as DPs.

Chapter 12

Negotiating Class Standing

Long before this book was conceived, I was struck by an enigmatic phenomenon. First-generation postwar Dutch immigrants, including those who came to Canada when they were adults, invariably initiate a conversation with fellow Dutch-Canadians in English. Even if they speak broken English with a noticeably Dutch accent, Dutch-Canadians will switch into some form of Dutch (or the related language of Frisian) only after a lengthy period of conversation. I even found myself going back and forth between standard Dutch—which I still speak with my parents on occasion—and English. This pattern of linguistic behaviour is quite unique. It is my impression from observing and talking to people who came from other parts of Europe that first-generation postwar immigrants from other ethnic groups usually start speaking a home language other than English when they meet someone of the same national origin.[1] While conducting fieldwork, I became aware of a connection between linguistic usage and class status among Canadians born in the Netherlands, but the exact nature of that connection and its implications did not become evident until the last stages of my research.[2]

It was not immediately apparent that in refusing to start a conversation in Dutch and constantly switching back and forth between languages, Dutch-Canadians were negotiating their class standing. People engage in subtle day-to-day dickering not only over the meaning of words, but over what language or version of a language will predominate in any social situation.[3] This aspect of linguistic behaviour constitutes an integral part of the reproduction, as well as the reshaping, of the intersecting lines of age, ethnicity and class. For example, which language or "dialect" is spoken by whom, and under what circumstances, is an arena of contestation

Notes to this chapter are on p. 380-84.

over ethnic boundaries within a broader system of ethnic stratification. Such day-to-day struggles over language use can also alter class relations among bilingual people sharing a common national background.

This chapter will explore intra-ethnic class dynamics through an examination of the micro-politics of language. My framework of analysis is based on Pierre Bourdieu's model of a 'linguistic market,' whereby linguistic exchanges "are also relations of symbolic power in which the power relations between speakers or their respective groups are actualized."[4] However, unlike Bourdieu's examples, mainly taken from French society, my case study pertains to people situated in a more complex 'social space' resulting from international migration. The trajectory of Canadians whose mother tongue is Dutch exemplifies a process whereby a set of dispositions rooted in the class structure of Dutch society generated a range of social practices adjusted to a different type of society (see Introduction). I will specifically focus on the lingering effects of a European system of social stratification on the linguistic behaviour of bilingual Dutch-Canadians, as they renegotiated their class standing after learning sufficient English to function in a North American setting.

Chapter 3 examined the social class system of Dutch society, with its emphasis on the use of "proper" Dutch and the stigma attached to forms of speech associated with certain classes and regions. The last chapter showed how postwar Dutch immigrants adopted English as their main language within a decade of arrival in Canada, although both standard Dutch and other versions of Netherlandic languages continued to be used in specific contexts. The last part of this chapter will examine in more detail just how these immigrants, born and raised in the Netherlands, renegotiated their class standing, or status, through linguistic interactions with fellow Dutch-Canadians. However, first we need to look at how the dispositions ('habitus') of Dutch immigrants became modified as they coped with a society with a different hegemonic language and a distinct class system.

Continuities and Discontinuities in Patterns of Stratification

One of the first things newcomers learned in Canada is that employees no longer had to say "mister" to their employers. People who had occupied a low position in the Dutch system of social stratification initially felt they were free from the restrictions of their homeland. Moreover, they saw that Dutch immigrants with higher education or professional degrees often had to start a new life on the same footing as farmers and blue-collar worker. The apparent lack of class distinctions came as a surprise. One's family background, speech patterns and lack of schooling no longer seemed to stand in the way of climbing the socio-economic ladder. Occasionally someone who had been a rich farmer in Holland might recognize a person they had known at home as a *boereknecht* (a hired hand). However, they would not get away with making this too obvious in any but private conversations among very close friends and relatives. Dutch farmers also stopped looking down on factory workers when they found out that industrial workers not only earned good wages, but had social standing in Canada. However, it did not take long for newcomers in Canada to encounter new distinctions based on "accent" and immigrant status. Nor did old class distinctions become entirely irrelevant when interacting with other Dutch-Canadians.

In most locations in Ontario, Dutch status distinctions between small businessmen, farmers and workers rapidly disappeared. Higher wages and living standards reinforced the impression that "there were no social classes."[5] However a Dutch 'habitus' rooted in the social structure of Dutch society did not automatically disappear when people moved to North America. Dutch immigrants found it hard to accept egalitarian modes of interaction between members of different generations; their adult children were still not allowed to address their parents or in-laws by their first names even after marriage. Nor did immigrants feel comfortable when their children did not maintain the proper social distance with neighbours. If a Canadian neighbour insisted that everyone should address him as John, the Dutch parents would insist that their own children at least say "Mr. John."[6] Signs of respect and status among adults also lingered on. Dutch-Canadians with little education stood in awe of physicians and lawyers, especially those of Dutch background. Dutch Protestants in particular found it difficult to accept the informal manner in which Canadians interacted with their clergy, and ministers continued to be treated with great deference.[7]

Although working-class immigrants and farmers no longer accepted class distinctions among themselves, they did replicate other Dutch dispositions. While "Canadian" workers talked freely about how much they earned, and compared pay cheques in the beer parlour, their Dutch-Canadian counterparts usually went straight home, each one with his cheque carefully tucked away in an inner pocket, lest someone might find out how much he had earned. Dutch immigrants, particularly those who came from the same social background or region, were still highly competitive, and jealousies could erupt into personal disputes.[8] At the same time Dutch immigrants believed in the North American dream that anyone could become rich, if only they worked hard enough. Gradually, the old forms of stratification were thus replaced by new forms of 'symbolic violence'[9] associated with the North American myth of equality of opportunity.

The Mythology of Upward Mobility

In their conversations, farm immigrants often mention how they all came over as poor people. The standard version of the farm immigrant story includes the initial year of obligatory labour as hired hands. They all arrived penniless. Through hard work and luck, and with God's blessing, the immigrants established themselves as independent farmers, obtained good jobs or built up small businesses.[10] Like all myths, there is a grain of truth in such stories. There were cases of dramatic economic upward mobility. However, class background played a significant part in how quickly immigrants advanced. When interviewing full-time farmers, I always asked if they knew immigrant farmers who had been *landarbeiders* (day labourers) in the Netherlands. Invariably people had difficulty recalling specific examples.[11] Typically, Dutch immigrants who started farming on their own within two or three years after arrival had owned a farm in the Netherlands, or their parents had owned a farm. Many of the larger, more successful first-generation farmers I interviewed had been *grote boeren* ("big farmers"), or village notables.

Immigrants did not advance economically without hard work and perseverance. Nonetheless, prior education, experience in business and capital assets played a greater role than Dutch-Canadians would be willing to admit. For example, Jan Hendrikx, a farmer from Alphen in Noord Brabant, studied in a junior seminary until age 15, long before emigrating. There he learned French and Latin.[12] Upon his father's death, he inherited a good-sized farm.[13] When Jan emigrated to Canada in 1948, together with his wife and four children, their hired man also came along. They landed in Blenheim, Ontario, where he had a Belgian uncle who was a Capuchin priest. He helped Jan to find a landowner willing to enter into a sharecropping arrangement to grow vegetables. Jan Hendrikx is an example of a small but prosperous Dutch farmer with prior business experience and linguistic skills who bought his own farm within a year.[14] Such farmers got ahead much faster in Canada than poor, part-time farmers (*keuterboertjes*) or farm hands with no start-up capital.[15]

Like their rural counterparts, city immigrants also recount stories about starting in a menial job. A common theme is how they, or someone else, got cheated on their first car or house purchase. Such stories always have happy endings, with an emphasis on eventual success, despite insurmountable obstacles along the way. There are indeed cases of dramatic economic upward movement. For example, John Overzet, who became a successful developer in Toronto, arrived in Canada with only a mechanic's license and $38 in his pocket at the age of 18.[16] The ethnic literature tends to repeat such success stories to underscore a "rags-to-riches" mythology involving "self-made" men (rarely women!). The tale of the poor, struggling, but eventually successful immigrant must be put into a broader perspective. Upon investigating the background of other well-known Dutch-Canadians, it became apparent that most of them had prior business experience, special technical training or academic credentials. Some people who became rich or famous in Canada belonged to, or had married into, "good families" in the Netherlands with money and the right connections.

Matthew Gaasenbeek, one of the five Dutch-born men in the eightieth edition of *Who's Who in Canada*[17] can serve as an illustration of how even someone who emigrated without money—yet with the dispositions inculcated in a prestigious, upper-class setting—managed to climb the corporate ladder. He emigrated in 1948 after completing his secondary education, and was sponsored by his older sister, a war bride living in Hamilton. Matthew worked on a farm for a summer. In order to get admission to a business program at the University of Western Ontario in London, he entered grade 13. As a poor student, he had to put pieces of cardboard in his shoes to keep the icy water from seeping through the soles, and took a part-time job lifting bags of cement.[18] Yet his background was not that of a typical immigrant, since his father was a prominent stock broker and he had himself attended the prestigious *lyceum* (academic high school) in Baarn. While Matthew struck out on his own, he knew what he wanted. At the end of his interview he commented, "I knew exactly where I came from, and I wanted to get back to the same place."

Matthew Gaasenbeek was not the only immigrant of middle- or upper-middle-class background who came to Canada from places like Baarn or Bloemendaal, the preferred residence of the Dutch elite. Daniel Horn, an architect from Baarn, settled in Victoria, B.C., in 1952. His wife corresponded regularly with the Gaasenbeek family.[19] All their children became lawyers, financiers and university professors in Canada, regardless of whether they came on their own or with their parents. These immigrants already had lots of 'cultural capital,' and they were conscious of the higher status their families occupied in the Netherlands, which in turn influenced their relationships with other Dutch-Canadians as well as Canadians at large.

The Replication of Dutch Forms of Class Standing

The vast majority of people I interviewed initially denied the existence of class distinctions when asked if *standsverschil* (status differences) existed among Dutch-Canadians. People who had themselves been farmers and workers before emigrating went to great lengths to point out how no pretentious Dutch person would ever get away with such an attitude in Canada. Dutch immigrants from a middle- or upper-class background in turn emphasized how everyone should be "treated in the same way." They would lecture me on how "class" or "standing" have to do with honesty, personal integrity and good moral conduct. Yet the very denial of overt class prejudice is consistent with the stance of upper- and middle-class people in the Netherlands (see chapter 3). Despite public denials, Dutch status distinctions are revealed in conversations on other topics, and can be observed during social interactions.[20]

Even in talking about the absence of class, Dutch-Canadians invariably reveal their background, or "embodied" class dispositions, through facial expressions, subtle references and speech. For example, a woman from a prestigious Dutch family told me that the father of a real estate broker she knew had been a *lorreman* ("junk dealer") in the Jordaan, a working-class neighbourhood in Amsterdam. She was especially critical of the way he pronounced Dutch. She also portrayed the real estate broker, who completed a graduate program at a Canadian university, as being "deficient in general education." The term used was *algemene ontwikkeling*, although she hastened to add that people could be *ontwikkeld* even if they had never attended a university.[21] Class distinctions can also be detected in a range of social 'fields,' where those of Dutch background interact. For example, immigrants from a Dutch working- or lower-middle-class background are more likely to attend Dutch ethnic clubs. Middle-class professionals or people with higher education in turn refer to club members as *boeren* (farmers), even if such members are city immigrants who have white-collar occupations or operate small businesses in Canada. The most common reason cited for their lack of interest in such clubs is the "um-pa-pa" music played, and the "lack of sophistication."[22] Such lack of interest is in turn perceived as disdain and haughtiness by people involved in such clubs. One club executive confirmed that first-generation Dutch-Canadian doctors or lawyers were marginally involved in his club. He admitted that people considered more "*ontwikkeld*" might give donations or pay membership fees, but would rarely show up for dances or other club events.[23] Other middle- or upper-middle-class Dutch immigrants refused to have anything to do with Dutch social clubs because they did not consider themselves to be "club people." Yet these same Dutch-Canadians of Dutch middle-class background have their own all-Dutch private social gatherings and organizations. Such ongoing class distinctions among Dutch-Canadians, and their corresponding forms of social interaction, are especially apparent in Metropolitan Toronto.

Class Dynamics in Metropolitan Toronto

Since the early fifties, Toronto has been a pole of attraction for Dutch-Canadians. It has a consular office and serves as headquarters for Dutch companies and various Dutch institutions. According to the 1986 census, there were nearly 6,000 first-generation Dutch-Canadians in Metropolitan Toronto.[24] This figure swells to 15,000 when the municipalities of Peel (Mississauga and Brampton), York and Durham (Pickering and Oshawa) are included. A sizable Dutch-Canadian population facilitated the emergence of an ethnic community with a strong sense of identity, despite differences in religious and political ideology. Its leaders, many of whom are still first-generation immigrants, form a cohesive and close-knit group. At the same time, this urban ethnic community displays internal tensions and controversies, resulting in a constant realignment of friendships and social networks. Newcomers from the Netherlands and other provinces come and go frequently, adding fuel to an active gossip network. Toronto is thus an ideal setting to examine ongoing class dynamics among Dutch-Canadians.

The socio-economic make-up of the Dutch in Toronto is diverse. The area has more than its share of wealthy, nouveau riche Dutch-Canadians, plus those who had money and family connections before emigrating. Below this small economic elite—the "movers and shakers"—is a larger upper-middle-class network of professionals and business people, including older, retired people with good incomes; a somewhat smaller group still working and doing business; and a minority of professionals in their thirties or forties. The last two categories represent a mixture of first- and second-generation middle-class Dutch-Canadians. In the middle to bottom half of the socio-economic ladder we find a large group of people in other occupations: small entrepreneurs, skilled tradesmen, clerical workers and other salaried employees.

This system of social stratification is reflected in people's membership and level of participation in various organizations (see also chapter 16). The middle to upper-middle stratum of Dutch-Canadians in Toronto is the easiest to identify, since most of their names have at one time or another appeared in the membership lists of either the Netherlands Luncheon Club or the Canadian Netherlands Business and Professional Association (CNBPA).[25] Taking into account people cross-listed in both organizations, the total number of active members between 1987 and 1989 came to approximately 300. They represent the core of the Dutch middle class of the Toronto area.[26] As we will see later, the top economic elite is more likely to join much more prestigious non-Dutch organizations, but a few names have in the past also appeared in the membership lists of these two Dutch ethnic professional and business organizations.[27] While a few people from the lower-middle-class stratum also belong to these largely middle-class organizations, skilled labourers, owners of small family businesses and white-collar employees not in management positions are more likely to join other ethnic organizations, including card clubs and choirs.

It would be misleading to classify the class structure of the Dutch-Canadian community in too schematic a manner. The sociological categories presented form part of a continuum, ranging from the very wealthy and prestigious to hard-luck cases. In addition, both individuals and entire families are constantly moving up and down the socio-economic ladder. We must further take discrepancies between belief and behaviour into account. Dutch-Canadians, like people anywhere, tend to think in rigid and simplistic categories even though social relations are far more complex.[28]

Middle-class Immigrants and Expatriates

When Dutch immigrants came to Toronto in the fifties, middle-class people faced the same hardships and prejudices as workers and farm labourers. Sometimes former white-collar workers or professionals had to start off doing manual labour. Dutch professionals employed by big Canadian companies found that they too faced discrimination. One immigrant with a diploma from a Dutch *lyceum*, plus business experience in Indonesia, got a job with the Noranda Corporation. Apart from a French-Canadian, he was the only "ethnic" employee in the office.[29] For a long time he and his wife did not have close "Canadian" friends, and they sought social contacts within their own ethnic community. At the same time, the presence of Dutch nationals working for Dutch-based international corporations, such as Philips, Unilever, or Shell, resulted in tensions between immigrants and expatriates. The latter did not consider themselves to be "immigrants." They had close connections with the consulate, and knew they would eventually go back to Holland or expected appointments and tours of duty in other countries. Such upper-level employees, posted abroad, were referred to as *uitgezonden* ("sent out"). They reminded other middle-class Dutch immigrants that they had just "moved," and not emigrated. These *uitgezonden,* including former diplomats, were an integral part of the "upper-crust" of the Dutch-Canadian community.

Expatriates, as well as middle-class Dutch-Canadians with good jobs, had little social contact with their fellow countrymen if the latter did not have the same social standing in the Netherlands. For example, even the employee in Noranda mentioned above, and his wife, looked for friends who were "like-minded," with a similar Dutch middle-class background. However, such avoidance of more intimate social contact did not prevent considerable interaction with Dutch-Canadians from different backgrounds in other contexts. Initially, Dutch immigrants of lower-class origin, who often did not speak English upon arrival, depended on educated, middle-class community leaders to help them deal with Canadian institutions. Dutch working-class immigrants, no matter how much they might want to become "real Canadians," also sought services and products that could only be supplied by Dutch professionals. All these Dutch immigrants, especially those who arrived in Toronto prior to 1960, had to get along with one another, and found new ways of interacting. Some middle-class immigrants came to appreciate the life skills of people with whom they had previously had little in common. For others, involvement in the Dutch-Canadian community was an alternative way of getting prestige in a Canadian context.

Middle-class Dutch-Canadians trying to establish businesses catered to an immigrant clientele. This was especially true for travel agents, retailers of Dutch delicatessen products, insurance brokers, accountants and lawyers (see chapter 14). Initially, Dutch-Canadian business people had to be careful to not treat their clients or customers with the same formality and reserve as in the Netherlands. Despite such good intentions, not everyone succeeded. One Dutchman who had previously worked in Curaçao became a life insurance broker for Holland Life, a Dutch company that set up a branch in Toronto. According to another middle-class Dutch immigrant, this broker was "a real gentleman," but one who "had a hard time getting along with ordinary people." Nevertheless, such upper-class Dutch people ended up acting as advisors and helping out newly arrived immigrants. However, in many of their day-to-day social interactions, especially those revolving around formal organizations, Dutch-Canadians also inadvertently reproduced the Dutch ranking system.

The Class Dynamics of Urban Ethnic Institutions

The internally stratified Dutch-Canadian community in Toronto first developed an organizational structure by working together for a worthy cause. When a Dutch immigrant family who landed in a small village near Ottawa lost their belongings in a fire in 1956, middle-class women in the Dutch-Canadian community in Toronto initiated a campaign to collect money to help.[30] Laura Schippers, who, together with her husband, set up a Dutch-language newspaper, provided the publicity and helped with the organizing. This campaign led to the establishment of the Netherlands Bazaar, the main charitable fundraising institution of the wider Dutch-Canadian community.[31] Another Dutch-Canadian institution promoted by the Schippers and other Dutch immigrants of middle-class background was the credit union. Designed to help provide consumer loans for Dutch immigrants, the Dutch-Canadian Credit Union in Toronto (DUCA) eventually grew into one of the larger credit unions in Ontario (see chapter 15). This credit union illustrates the discrepancies between a simplistic perception of class and the reality of a Dutch-Canadian institution that involves a complex pattern of social interaction involving people of different backgrounds.

The founding father of DUCA is Mau Coopman. A tailor by trade, he was a Dutch socialist who grew up in a predominantly working-class neighbourhood in Amsterdam. He and several white-collar workers or small family business owners played an active role in DUCA from the start. The credit union recruited members from typical immigrant families struggling to get established. Later, when the credit union had its own building and some surplus funds, Dutch-Canadian clubs used its facilities rent free and/or received financial assistance. Such clubs had a broad membership, many of whom were blue-collar workers. For this reason, some big business people wanted nothing to do with the credit union. One snobbish Dutch-Canadian real estate broker stated categorically that the credit union was "for working-class people only." In fact, Coopman and other people who ran the credit union, or became board members, collaborated closely with Dutch-Canadian middle-class professionals. Poolman, a young Dutch-Canadian lawyer who acted as their part-time administrator, let the credit union use a room in his office.[32] A few *uitgezonden* also became involved.[33] Indeed, even the previously mentioned "gentleman from Curaçao," the one who had difficulties getting along with "ordinary people," served on their board.[34]

While Dutch-Canadians from diverse class backgrounds became active participants in the credit union and the bazaar, social interaction involving more intimate social contact followed the same class lines as in the Netherlands. At the start of the Dutch-Canadian population movement, expatriates and upper-middle-class immigrants organized patriotic events designed for all Netherlanders.[35] Together with the Dutch consul, they arranged public gatherings, to which they invited all Dutch immigrants, including young men then working on farms in the vicinity of Toronto. The agricultural attaché from Ottawa used to attend the festivities; he and the other organizers thought that the "boys" were enjoying themselves.[36] However, immigrants of middle-class background were scandalized by the rowdy behaviour and "foul language" of the *gewone mensen* ("common people") during such public parties.[37] Such class tensions reoccurred during subsequent large-scale events designed to provide entertainment and an opportunity for Dutch immigrants from a variety of backgrounds to socialize with their compatriots.[38] Again, Dutch people who considered themselves to be *ontwikkeld* (cultured) thought that these public events were "too noisy."[39] Thus while well-placed people from the *betere stand* (higher-status group) were instrumental in bringing the Dutch together, other immigrants of Dutch middle-class background—

who considered themselves to be "refined" (*beschaafd*)—were not interested in socializing with fellow countrymen not in their league.

The same group of Dutch expatriates (*uitgezonden*) and businessmen in Toronto who organized large public get-togethers also set up their own more exclusive social network. In 1951, the consul in Toronto, Ravensloot, set up *de Borrel Club*—a cocktail get-together—for alumni from the University of Delft.[40] Founding members included an employee of a Dutch insurance company and an expatriate who had lived in Indonesia. Others invited to attend were a Dutch war veteran and former student from Delft who had come to Toronto as an immigrant the same year that the *Borrel Club* was set up.[41] That man later played a leading role in setting up various clubs for Dutch upper- and middle-class immigrants. For example, together with the consul and Jan Heersink (a former mayor from the Netherlands)[42], he helped to found the Netherlands Luncheon Club.

The Luncheon Club still invites Dutch dignitaries, well-known business leaders and academics to give noon-hour speeches, followed by a sit-down lunch. Its membership includes professionals and business people, plus several leaders of other organizations, such as the bazaar or the Dutch-Canadian press. The Luncheon Club, which has a membership fee, was designed for middle-class Dutch-Canadians. However, Dutch middle-class people follow a subtle but elaborate internal "pecking order." In jockeying for better positions along a continuum of increasing exclusivity, some Dutch-Canadians objected to associating too closely with people a few notches down; they felt people from the same *lagen* (layers) of society should always seek out people "of their own kind."

The Sliding Scale of Exclusivity

The *Borrel Club*, originally set up for alumni of Delft University, expanded to include people deemed to be of a sufficiently high social rank by Dutch standards. Membership was by invitation only, and the implicit criterion was a university connection (*academische opleiding*) or a high-level management position in business or finance. To join, one had to be "an intellectual or an executive."[43] "Good family" connections, or illustrious ancestors, were also helpful.[44] The *Borrel Club* also had an agricultural connection: the son of a Dutch banker who had come to Canada in 1939 to become a gentleman farmer. The father had bought a farm close to Toronto, which specialized in Angus cattle; he sent his then sixteen-year-old son to study at the Ontario Agricultural College in Guelph.[45] Altogether there were about 40 members in the club, including several physicians, and Dutch consuls automatically became members. Since their gatherings were for men only, the wives organized their own book club (see chapter 13). Around 1954 the same Delft alumni, together with other members of this cocktail circuit, founded a Dutch-Canadian investment club, which existed in 1991 under the name "Golden Age Investment Club." Their membership list includes 23 names, including a *jonkheer* (a Dutch noble title) and several men with the title of Drs. (the Dutch equivalent of MA) or Dr.[46]

The men who initially joined the first investment club already knew each other from the *Borrel Club*. Some occasionally attended the Netherlands Luncheon Club. However, it was more difficult to move from that larger middle-class association into the smaller, more exclusive social clubs than the other way around. Several middle class immigrants with aspirations of upward mobility, who belonged to the Luncheon Club, wanted to enter the *Borrel* group too. When they did not succeed, they founded their own cocktail circuit, *Het Slokje*,[47] which was considered to be less prestigious by members of the *Borrel Club*.[48] Some people who used to attend *Het Slokje* in turn accused the *Borrel Club* of being discriminatory, as Catholics and Jews were not welcome. I suspect that the implicit criteria for selection to such smaller clubs were based more on *stand* (social status) than religion, since at least one member of the more prestigious social club has a Dutch Jewish connection. However, religion and status are to some extent intertwined in the Dutch class system (see chapter 3). Although the *Borrel Club* was officially *neutraal* (i.e., secular or "general"), its leading members were brought up in the *Hervormde Kerk*, or the more prestigious *protestantenbond*.[49]

Eventually *Het Slokje* petered out, to be replaced with *De Instuif*. The latter, designed to be less competitive and more open, was started by one of the main cheese importers. He persuaded the Dutch manager of the Skyline Hotel to host a monthly cocktail hour. This event, announced over the Dutch radio program on CHIN, attracted a subset of the same group of middle-class Dutch-Canadians who have known each other for years. Only Dutch is spoken. In theory open to everyone, I have heard comments along the lines that "ordinary" Dutch-Canadians would not feel at home. Over the past few years this event has also been held at the Constellation Hotel (located near Pearson Airport) and at the Brownstone Hotel in downtown Toronto, both of which had Dutch-Canadian managers.[50] More recently, they were planning to go back to a more informal get-together at peoples' houses.[51] At the same time, members of a younger generation of Dutch-Canadian businessmen and several recent Dutch immigrants have set up a new version of the *Borrel Club*. Most of their members, including executives for the Dutch ABN Bank and KLM, are the offspring of people who belonged to the old *Borrel Club*.[52] They wanted a separate and more exclusive club for the "younger crowd," although at least one member, who is middle-aged, also belongs to the Golden Age Investment Club.[53]

Although family background and formal education are important in the Dutch social ranking system, there is room for social mobility. Whether one goes up or down the prestige ladder partly has to do with success in the world of business and public administration, and not just university degrees. For example, a young graduate from the University of Amsterdam, who arrived in the fifties, first worked as a system analyst for the Ford Motor Company. He took out a membership in a Dutch credit union and had sporadic contact with the Dutch consul, who sometimes made enquiries about possible jobs for Dutch workers at Ford.[54] However, he "meant nothing" in the more exclusive Dutch-Canadian social network. This man later became a financial director for several international corporations, with postings in different parts of the world. When he returned to Toronto in 1979, he was immediately invited to join the *Borrel Club*. Other men were dropped off the lists of more exclusive clubs.[55] Such a sliding scale of prestige was apparent to a non-Dutch member of the *Florin* investment club. This man, an Eastern European married to a Dutch woman, learned about the importance of social standing among the Dutch after two members no longer showed up "because they were too busy."[56] He found out that these members had switched to the "more exclusive" investment club described earlier.

Such smaller and more exclusive clubs by no means represent the real "upper crust." Rather, the best-known Dutch-Canadian corporate executives prefer to avoid undue publicity.[57] One wealthy and prominent businessman who went "public" on a radio program was hounded by requests from fundraisers in the Dutch-Canadian community. Such people are more likely to have their own connections to more exclusive non-ethnic (or English Canadian) yacht clubs or other social networks.[58] For business connections, some might have links with the Netherlands Chamber of Commerce. Established in both Montreal and The Hague in 1978, this organization consists of Dutch and Canadian companies that have ties to the Netherlands.[59] There also used to be a Canadian-Netherlands Council in Toronto in the fifties. Its driving force was Major-General Albert Bruce Matthews, son of a former lieutenant-governor of Ontario.[60] A prominent business executive, he set up the Council to promote trade between Canada and the Netherlands. One of the founding members of the *Borrel Club* joined this Council. In the fifties, a few top Dutch business executives who had been involved in the military in Europe were also allowed to join the Royal Canadian Military Institute, which has few members with an ethnic connection. However, all the men who joined already knew Bruce Matthews. Otherwise, Dutch-Canadian "ethnics," no matter what their pedigree, would find it just as difficult as other immigrant groups to break into the more exclusive English-Canadian elite.

Internal (Dutch-Canadian) social ranking can be observed in other social contexts. A crowd of several hundred invited guests, some from out of town, gather in a downtown hotel once a year on the occasion of the birthday of Juliana, former queen of the Netherlands. Only a handful of the people who show up at this reception proceed to the less prestigious *oranjebal*, a dinner dance held in another part of the city. I once overheard a professional woman, who has a high profile in the Dutch-Canadian community and is portrayed as "someone without pretensions" grumble about how she had to put in an appearance with the "oom-pah-pah" crowd at the ball. Likewise, with one rare exception, professionals or business executives do not attend the large *klaverjas* tournament, where Dutch-Canadians play a popular Dutch card game. People of a "higher social standing" prefer to play bridge, preferably with other middle-class Canadians from a variety of European backgrounds.

The Dutch-Canadian community in Toronto is thus characterized by subtle class barriers. The main distinction is between "ordinary" Dutch-Canadians and those who are either top-level managers or people with Dutch university degrees. The same can be said for Ottawa, except that the top stratum includes high-ranking Dutch-Canadians in the federal bureaucracy. Still, while many first-generation, educated, middle-class Dutch-Canadian immigrants have a similar outlook on life, not all of them are interested in exclusive Dutch-Canadian social clubs. One businessman in Toronto, whose family used to own a castle in the Netherlands, has no interest "playing the status game."[61] Likewise, another Dutch immigrant with French aristocratic connections (but married to a Canadian commoner) declined an invitation to join the *Borrel Club*. Nonetheless, even these people still have close friends who are *ontwikkeld*, if not always high ranking in the business or professional community.

New Forms of Social Stratification

Prestigious Dutch-Canadians in other cities like Hamilton, Kingston and Ottawa likewise are mostly first-generation immigrants or former diplomats and expatriates who have retired in Canada. The latter were approaching middle age when they first came to Canada. In contrast, their offspring, who received their educations in North America, are less attuned to Dutch patterns of social ranking.[62] They also resent the perceived lack of democratic control in organizations like the Luncheon Club. Indeed, several such younger Dutch-Canadians, together with a few disgruntled older people, originally started the Canadian Netherlands Business and Professional Association.[63] Compared to the Luncheon Club, the CNBPA tends to use English rather than Dutch, which has become relegated to occasional symbolic use. They are more into networking, group outings and black-tie dinners.[64] This younger Dutch-Canadian middle class does not attach as much importance to speaking "proper Dutch," or to a broad education (*ontwikkeling*), as do their elders. The CNBPA is therefore somewhat more accessible to a broader range of immigrants, including those whose parents were lower class.[65] The only factors that might exclude someone are the annual fees and the cost of leisure activities that go hand-in-hand with being at the upper end of the middle-class scale. In the CNBPA the Canadian and Dutch social stratification systems thus blend together.[66]

New class distinctions also appeared in small cities where the Dutch ranking system had all but disappeared by the 1980s. It is usually well known which immigrants of humble background have become owners of medium-sized businesses. They usually portray themselves as "just one of the guys," like their Canadian counterparts. Nevertheless, Dutch-Canadians of more modest incomes see such upwardly mobile people as "big shots."[67] Sometimes, the offspring of such successful Dutch-Canadians may even marry into the local non-Dutch town elite. For example, in Blenheim, the daughter of a wealthy Dutch-Canadian farmer and entrepreneur of Catholic and Brabants background married the son of a very well-known English-Canadian Protestant family with money. Class distinctions and social segregation are also appearing in the otherwise fairly close-knit and largely endogamous Christian Reformed community. Not only has this sub-community generated a large number of businessmen and professionals, but marriage across class lines is now discouraged within some congregations by upwardly mobile families.[68]

The Dual Nature of Social Stratification

Status distinctions, whether old or new, are an integral part of the complex system of relations of power and unequal control over resources. However, it is important to disentangle the objective components of social stratification, such as income and property, from the subjective ones, including perceptions and the subtleties of linguistic interaction. We must also take into account the discrepancies among the viewpoints of different people.

To a large extent, one's standing in the Dutch-Canadian social status continuum depends on whether you are looking from the top down or the bottom up. For example, mainly rural members of a Dutch-Canadian theatre group in a small town referred to the Dutch-Canadian Club in the city of London as a place where *hoge lui* ("high folks") hang out after work. In contrast, the Dutch-Canadian owner of a restaurant, a more recent immigrant who was trained as a chef in Europe, and who would be considered *ontwikkeld*, had quite a different perspective; he thought that the people who frequented the London club were *kleinburgerlijk* (petit-bourgeois). Likewise a manager of an originally Dutch-Canadian credit union in London thought that his counterparts in a somewhat larger credit union in Toronto were "too uppity," because they held a formal, sit-down dinner and "spoke too much Dutch." Similarly, a Dutch-Canadian farmer who lives near Gananoque felt intimidated by the "fancy" people who frequented the Dutch-Canadian club in Kingston. Yet these "fancy" club members were classified as *onbeschoft* (ill-mannered) by a Dutch-trained professional in a nearby city in eastern Ontario.

Ongoing Tensions over Social Status

Class tensions and ambiguities can surface even between people who occupy similar objective class positions, but with very different dispositions reflecting their social background in the Netherlands. I came across an example while conducting an interview in Chatham. A man who came from a lower-middle-class family in Baarn emigrated to Canada in 1952 when he had finished his secondary education (HBS). His father worked as a sales agent for a medical supply firm. Like his father, he saw himself as an intellectual, but he felt he could not advance in the academic world without the right social connections. That is why he decided to emigrate to Canada to continue his education. Arriving in Canada as a poor student, this young man gained admission to McMaster University.[69] Today he is an author, educational book editor, and freelance consultant. I will refer to him as the writer, since he has had a half dozen books published. During my interview, he mentioned meeting another student while attending his first year of university. This other student, who later became a lawyer, belonged to a better-off, "upper-crust" Dutch family in his home town of Baarn.[70] It so happens I had met this lawyer only several months before. The discrepancy between the history of the lawyer's family and how they were perceived by the writer illustrates the continuity of deep resentment over former status inequalities, even among Dutch-Canadians who came to Canada when they were teenagers or young adults.

The writer, who lives in Kitchener today, mentioned how he used to "make deliveries to the doorstep" of the lawyer's family home as a young boy. He recalled how that family was not only rich and privileged, but how they had "blue blood connections." He pointed out that he would never have been able to get ahead in Baarn without such connections. The writer immediately assumed that the lawyer's family had emigrated to Canada with money. That impression was reinforced when the writer's daughter, who was studying music, met the lawyer's niece, who happened to be an opera singer. Being an opera singer is a prestigious and upper-class occupation, according to Dutch standards. In fact, both the lawyer and several brothers emigrated to Canada on their own and without money.[71] The two older brothers suffered the same hardships as the writer when they first came to Canada. When their parents joined them in Canada several years later, in the mid-fifties, the lawyer's father took a lowly clerical job and their mother turned the first home they bought into a boardinghouse to make ends meet.

I have also come across cases where women of a working-class or rural background in the Netherlands expressed great sympathy for the trials and tribulations of educated, middle-class Dutch immigrant women. Even such cases show how old status distinctions and class awareness were not completely obliterated in Canada. People do not alter their dispositions or ingrained attitudes and habits, formed during their formative years. For example, one middle-aged farm woman referred to a Dutch middle-class immigrant as a "lady who had to suffer terribly" because "she was not used to a hard way of life." The two women in question, both now elderly, enjoy the same living standard and they both live in lovely homes. In their minds, however, they still exist in separate worlds.

Renegotiating Class Status through Language

Most Dutch-Canadians in Ontario did not have much contact with their fellow countryfolk beyond a small circle of close friends and relatives. However, even if they did not join Dutch-Canadian clubs or Reformed churches, they were still likely to eventually meet someone of Dutch background whom they had not met before. Such encounters are particularly revealing for insights into the dynamics of class and language among immigrants. Educated middle-class immigrants, who recreated the Dutch system of social ranking in Canada, take great pride in their ability to speak "proper Dutch" (see chapter 3). In contrast, many working-class immigrants, with strong memories of the Dutch system of social ranking, no longer feel comfortable operating in a Dutch social environment charged with class distinctions. However, such an environment was automatically recreated whenever they had to speak standard Dutch with someone whose dispositions were formed in a Dutch middle-class setting. In such a social context, even inadequate English has more cultural currency—to use a phrase from Collins[72]— than a non-standard, or less than perfect, form of Dutch.

Ingrained class dispositions can explain why so many Dutch-Canadians who ranked low on the prestige scale of Dutch society refused to use standard Dutch in interacting with other Dutch-Canadians (see interludes of previous chapter). Dutch immigrants often lost their fluency in standard

Dutch, especially when couples from the same region continued to use their home dialect. Consequently, it was embarrassing when such Dutch-Canadians had to interact with Dutch "city slickers," who sometimes poked fun at people who spoke with a "low-class" or "country" accent. Verbal interactions among postwar Dutch-Canadians of different class background thus reinforced class distinctions. As soon as they had learned enough English, Dutch immigrants from farms and small villages preferred to communicate in broken English, rather than standard Dutch, with fellow countrymen from the western provinces or with people who had a higher socio-economic status. Such immigrants of working-class or rural background resented attempts by fellow immigrants to "show them up," by insisting on speaking "proper" Dutch. At the same time, they did not appreciate "old-timers" (prewar immigrants) criticizing them for not learning English fast enough.[73] Matters are more complicated, however; these same people might not mind speaking a slightly imperfect Dutch, or a modified regional dialect, with a Dutch-Canadian physician or a lawyer. Here the status distinctions are too obvious and self-evident to worry about losing out in the subtle game of status competition with fellow immigrants who are closer to one's own social standing.

In analyzing interclass encounters among Dutch immigrants, one cannot ignore the broader context of Canadian society, which has its own form of linguistic stratification. Immigrants of a lower-class background are subject to class prejudice regardless of which language they speak. People with more education, who studied English in the Netherlands, are more conscious about separating the two languages, although even they will occasionally use Canadian-English expressions when speaking Dutch. In contrast, people who used to speak a dialect of Dutch before emigrating are less likely to pay attention to the interference across different languages. Hence they often speak a form of English which is an amalgamation of English, dialect and Dutch. Their speech patterns make them subject to discrimination by both native-born Canadians—who tend to label people with accents as "immigrants"—and Dutch-Canadians of middle- and upper-class background who place equal emphasis on speaking "correct" English and "proper" Dutch.

The modified 'linguistic habitus' of Dutch-Canadians can explain why they almost invariably begin a conversation in English, even if both parties speak with a Dutch accent or have Dutch names. Given the range of variation in regional and class dialects, difficulties with speaking standard Dutch and the negative connotations of using dialects, it is safer to initially resort to English as a common language. The conversation will continue in English, even broken English, or turn into Dutch or a dialect, depending on a complex set of circumstances relating to both region and status. If two or more people are of similar Dutch class standing, and come from the same region, the conversation might continue in either standard Dutch or a regional dialect (or Frisian). For example, a Dutch-Canadian businessman in London, who originally came from Noord Brabant, said he has always spoken a form of standard Dutch with another businessman, although he did not want to use it with me. He commented, "I only feel comfortable speaking Dutch with someone who comes from the same region."[74]

It is difficult to shake off the legacy of linguistic stratification, even among middle-class Dutch immigrants undergoing linguistic assimilation. Prestige or status, the use of "proper Dutch" and a grammar and vocabulary reflecting social standing are too closely bound together in both the household and the public sphere. Even if they were interested in "keeping up" their mother tongue for motives quite different than status, the offspring of Dutch middle-class immigrants will discover that their parents are more likely to laugh at their mistakes or awkward pronunciation than to strongly encourage them to perfect it. Dutch people are critical, and native speakers find it hard to accept anyone speaking less than impeccable Dutch. In fact, when they visit the Netherlands, even first-generation immigrants who speak fluent, but old-fashioned Dutch, might face ridicule regardless of whether they inadvertently use a "foreign" (i.e., English) word or a perfectly good Dutch word that has since been replaced with an English equivalent in modern Dutch! The Dutch spoken in Canada is no longer the same as that used in the Netherlands today.

The ambiguities and complexities of linguistic interaction are endless. A high-status person may be reluctant to speak standard Dutch with someone they consider a potential rival or someone in a subordinate position (in the Canadian context), even if they both come from the same region in the Netherlands. This will happen if the high-status Canadians feel that their standard Dutch is not polished enough due to lack of use. Thus, when a reporter for a Dutch-Canadian newspaper arranged an interview with a recently elected Dutch-Canadian MP, his Canadian wife told the reporter not to try speaking Dutch because her husband had not spoken Dutch since he was a child. Indeed, during the interview, the MP mispronounced the newspaper's name. Nonetheless, when this MP discovered the number of Dutch-Canadians in some parts of his riding, particularly one senior citizens' home, he quickly brushed up enough to communicate with some of his ethnic constituents in their mother tongue. Dutch thus still serves a useful purpose in a political context or as an ethnic marker. This incident demonstrates that the same linguistic currency has a different value in different 'fields' (*champs d'action*), as indicated by Bourdieu. Despite the tendency to use English in order to maintain a neutral ground in the micro-politics of language in most social settings in North America, saying just a few words in Dutch is still valued as a means of eliciting a sympathetic response from another self-conscious Dutch-Canadian when a social setting, especially a political encounter, becomes "ethnicized."

Status distinctions are an integral part of a complex system of social stratification, in which language, the distribution of resources and power relations are closely intertwined. People's perceptions of social reality and the economic class structure constitute complimentary aspects of a single social reality. However, it is sometimes useful to analytically disentangle the objective components of that reality, such as inequalities in income and control over property, from values and perceptions. In studying linguistic behaviour—where the objective becomes internalized as the subjective, and the subjective in turn shapes the objective—we must be on the lookout for discrepancies and tensions between social structures and dispositions. Such discrepancies are more likely to occur as a result of large-scale migrations from one society to another.

As we have seen in previous chapters, postwar Dutch immigrants in Ontario reproduced many aspects of the social structure of the Netherlands, especially its pillar system, despite considerable linguistic assimilation. Similarly, at least some aspects of the Dutch system of social stratification was replicated, yet also modified, among Dutch-Canadians sharing a common linguistic heritage; people can, to a limited degree, negotiate their class standing. However, not everyone starts off with the same resources. Like familiarity with high-brow culture, or the nature and extent of social contacts, one's 'linguistic capital'[75]— accumulated through a combination of education and upbringing—is an important resource in the struggle over one's place in the structure of social positions. At the macro level, the lingering effects of the Dutch system of social stratification can account for the rapid rate of linguistic assimilation noted in first-generation Dutch-Canadians. However, that same system can also explain why a smaller segment of the same postwar cohort retained their language at least up until the second generation.

The politics of class at the level of interpersonal relations (on a micro scale) has the same indeterminacy as ethnic identity or the social construction of gender. Within certain limits, which vary by place and time, agents can renegotiate their class standing; the outcomes of each individual act cannot be predicted with a high level of accuracy. Relative prestige rankings and their corresponding differences in income and occupation never fully crystallize into a stable pattern, since social class involves ongoing struggles over both meanings and resources. International migration often leaves somewhat more room for manoeuvring one's way through the 'social space.'

Fieldnotes Interlude

12.1 Excerpts from an interview with a suburban couple in Mississauga, May 1, 1989 (translated from Dutch)

I know of one case in that community [a nearby Christian Reformed congregation] where a woman and a guy [*jongen* in Dutch] were planning to get married. She came from a rich and successful family. I think her father was an engineer. The guy was from a completely common [*gewone*] family. The mother told me she thought it was terrible that her daughter wanted to marry him. Not only are people supposed to marry someone from the same church [*kerk*, as in denomination] but also someone from the same social layer [*sociale laag*]. It is alright for a woman to marry a man from a better family, but not the other way around.

12.2 Excerpt from a series of conversations or interviews, with different people, at different times:

a. a woman with a university degree, in Toronto (in Dutch)

It is very different here in Canada. The distance [*afstand*] based on who your parents were or how much education you have is not as important, but how much money you earn *is* very important.

b. a retired janitor, in Brantford (in Dutch)

We thought it was certainly very strange [*gek*] that everyone, even your boss, used their first name. Even in the case of a Dutch minister, we noticed that a man would not have to take off his cap [*pet*] as in the Netherlands.

c. a retired manager of a Dutch-Canadian credit union (of farm background), in London (in English)

Class differences among the Dutch immigrants were not emphasized to the same degree as in Holland. However, after knowing someone for a little while, you could usually tell what type of family background they had. There was still a bit of standing.

d. a retired farmer (Dutch Catholic) in Arkona (in English)

When I first went to work in the Oost Polder to start farming on my own [in the Netherlands], there was a whole series of rungs on the social ladder—from larger farmers with 40 hectares, to those with 20 hectares, to day labourers. There, day labourers would not eat at the same table with the larger farmers. Those distinctions did not exist here in Canada where everyone could interact socially, even though some people do own more land than others.

e. *a retired factory worker in Kitchener (in English)*

There are no class differences between Dutch-Canadians here, although some people will still try to buy a bigger t.v. than somebody else. But it is much less than in Holland. Here I am on good terms with my boss [Canadian] and we are friends.

12.3 *Excerpt from an interview (in Dutch) with a woman married to the owner of a large business, in Mississauga, November 27, 1988*

I am aware there are class distinctions [*standsverschil*] among the Dutch in Canada, and I believe that is partly my fault [*schuld*] too. I would not just associate with anybody, but that just happens because people are interested in very different kinds of things. Those class differences [*standsverschillen*] are necessary [*nodig*]. My mother-in-law once explained to us that you should never invite the people who work for you to visit. Then they would be too close to you, or they might find out that you don't really have such nice furniture or that your house is really not that big. Then they would no longer have respect for you.

We also know very nice [*aardige*] people and we get along well, even though they are ordinary [*gewone*] workers. They even invited us to stay with them when we had to be evacuated because of that derailment [of a train with hazardous chemicals]. But we would never invite them to go with us to a dinner of the CNBPA or to the *Instuif* because they would not feel at ease [*op hun gemak voelen*]. We would not want them to be offended [*beledigd*] if someone were to ask them what they do for a living.

12.4 *Excerpt from "Becoming Canadian: An Immigrant's Journey" by Michiel Horn (professor at Glendon College)*

Unlike us, they did look for other Netherlanders. But not just anyone would do. Although Father was fairly flexible, Mother felt at ease only with people of her own milieu such as Philip van der Goes, son of a Dutch diplomat. Those from a lower class in Holland were kept at a distance. "*Goede mensen maar wel wat ordinair*," she would say: good people, but a bit common. She worked with some of them on Dutch flood relief in 1953; they did not become intimates. Not surprisingly she was delighted when friends from Baarn, Karel and Hansje van Voorstvader, arrived in Victoria in 1954.

Chapter 13

Gender and Dutch-Canadian Ethnicity

Most women from the Netherlands landed in Canada prior to the renewal of the women's movement in both North America and Europe. The impact of this movement was not noticeable in either country until at least a decade or two after the arrival of the first postwar immigrants. However, men and women raised in the Netherlands experienced the gradual process of female emanicipation and changing sex roles with a different set of expectations and values from their Canadian counterparts. Moreover, while they shared a common national origin and faced many of the same challenges of adapting to a new language and way of life, the immigration experiences of men and women were quite distinct. Women also had fewer opportunities for economic advancement and were less likely to fulfil their aspirations.

The sex role models associated with Dutch society (see chapter 3) were carried over and modified in a Canadian context. Gender dynamics at the household level, which was the most deeply ingrained, showed the greatest continuity. What struck Dutch postwar immigrants as odd, particularly in a working- or lower-middle-class Canadian setting, is how women would stay together in one part of the house during social get-togethers while the men gathered in the basement or another room. For the most part, the Dutch patterns continued for at least two generations, as did other aspects of home life. In contrast, immigrant women became more involved in the work force than their counterparts in the Netherlands. When women arrived in Canada, they often had to work part-time in house cleaning as well as in agriculture, largely out of economic necessity. A minority of Dutch immigrant women also developed professional careers or set up small businesses of their own, while still others played a

---

Notes to this chapter are on p. 385-89.

prominent role in Dutch-Canadian organizations. All of these working women faced gender stereotypes from Dutch and "Canadian" men, which presented special problems as well as unique challenges.

The "typical" Dutch-Canadian immigrant woman cannot be depicted. Like their male counterparts, differences in age, class position, marital status and religion moulded their lives on the farm and in the city. Yet one cannot assume that Dutch-Canadian women, even if they came from the same class background, had the same dispositions as men.[1] They had distinct expectations about what the future might hold in store, and also experienced their new life in a way quite different from that of their husbands or boyfriends. Even single women with career aspirations had to overcome different obstacles than their male counterparts. In previous interludes, we have seen examples of Dutch-Canadian immigrant women coping with the process of adaptation, including their economic roles. Women also contributed to the formation and maintenance of ethnic regional networks (chapter 10). However, women are consistently portrayed as shadowy figures in both popular and scholarly accounts. The gender dimension is difficult to fit into a kaleidoscopic picture when so much of the experiential world of women remains hidden from view.

Dutch Women as Portrayed in Dutch-Canadian Publications

Notwithstanding their diverse roles, Dutch women have been overlooked. In published accounts, they are too often misrepresented as playing a secondary, supportive role. In the book *To All Our Children*, which adorns the living rooms of many Dutch-Canadian homes, there are lots of pictures of women. However, both the text and pictures depict them in their roles as mothers, with babe in arms, or as hardworking housewives. In contrast, a chapter entitled "Making an Impact" deals almost exclusively with high-profile men.[2] The images of "typical" Dutch-Canadian woman thus helps to further reinforce gender stereotypes; the only chapter dealing mainly with women focuses on homesickness, with one reference to a man who had emotional difficulties adjusting to life in Canada. Dutch immigrant women are also depicted as lonely widows, and the reader gets glimpses of angry or helpless wives or women in distress.[3] Such meagre and one-sided coverage illustrates how written discourse contributes to the perpetuation of gender inequality, as reflected in the underrepresentation of women in public life.

What is less obvious is that most of the detailed descriptions of the life and thoughts of Dutch immigrants, especially first impressions, were taken from diaries or letters written by women.[4] Indeed, Dutch women have been writing about their immigration experience since well before World War Two. The best-known female author is Jane Aberson, who sent letters to a hometown newspaper in the province of Groningen on a regular basis.[5] Her main themes were ethnic diversity and cultural adjustment. After the War, many Dutch women in Canada likewise put their first impressions on paper, as shown by the excerpts in *To All Our Children*. In contrast, men were more likely to pen their thoughts later in life, usually during retirement. I encountered half a dozen older men who were in the process of writing memoirs or family histories, or had already done so. Unlike the sociological flavour in the dairies of younger immigrant women, these retired men seemed preoccupied with their own careers, or illustrious ancestors.[6] The reader gets a sense of partnership between husband and wife, but comments about women being both hard-working and frugal reveal stereotypical Dutch sex role expectations.

A more recent publication, dealing with the Holland Marsh, likewise mentions the endless hard labour of Dutch women, while acknowledging that their male counterparts were more likely to be "thrust into the limelight." The author includes the following quotes from anonymous Dutch growers: "They [the women] were the best labourers the farmer had. Without their help, the Marsh would have been quite a different place ... but behind every successful man stands a woman, and this is especially true in the Marsh."[7]

Despite the good intentions, the basic message that comes through is that women, no matter how valuable, were expected to play second fiddle. Apart from two short pages, plus a few references to the role of a Ladies Aid Society, the book on the Marsh throws more light on men than women. A total of 136 men were identified by name, compared to only 42 women.[8] Moreover, women were more likely to be depicted as dependents, as someone's wife or daughter. An examination of photographs illustrating the text is more revealing. In photographs showing groups,[9] I counted well over 200 men or boys, compared to only 100 women or girls; only two photos focused on groups of women by themselves, compared to numerous pictures of all male groups.[10]

A dozen or so other publications about Dutch-Canadians, both popular and academic, pay little attention to women,[11] with the exception of an essay dealing with the relationship between Dutch women and Canadian soldiers during World War Two.[12] Men have generally chosen to ignore the participation of women who did gain public renown for their achievements, and even female authors have written primarily about the man's world, thereby inadvertently ignoring Dutch immigrant women who broke into the world of business or politics.[13] Exceptional women were just that—exceptions who accommodated themselves to a male-dominated world.

This chapter takes a closer look at these career or professional women as part of a conscious attempt to right the balance. However, we must pay equal attention to the majority of largely invisible Dutch women immigrants who were unable or chose not to enter into professional careers.

The Immigration Experience of Dutch Women

The first postwar Dutch immigrants were women who fell in love with Canadian soldiers during the War. These war brides, who had little contact with other Dutch-Canadians, had to integrate rapidly. A common theme is the mismatch resulting from such marriages: the sophisticated city woman who agreed to marry a handsome young man in uniform, only to later discover that his home in Canada was a dilapidated shack in a remote region.[14] In cities, many Canadian husbands did not want their Dutch brides to establish contacts with their own ethnic community.[15] Other Dutch immigrant women came by themselves, sometimes with plans to meet up with a former sweetheart already in Canada. By law, they had to marry within several months of arrival to stay in Canada, unless they had a contract to work as a nanny. For many of these young women, like young couples, their immigration experience was an adventure, even though they might have had to "rough" it in Canada for a number of years.[16] Other young women did not have such a pleasant experience, especially if their male partners turned out to be abusive alcoholics.[17] Life could also be difficult for teenagers or young unmarried women who came as part of a larger family unit. Dutch parents demanded that their daughters, as well as their sons, contribute to the household budget. Young rural women harvested beets, worked in canneries, picked fruit and weeded gardens, with all the earnings going straight into the household economy. Older female siblings assumed additional household obligations if their mothers worked outside the home.[18]

The middle-aged immigrant woman with a large number of children took on the largest burden of responsibility as well as hard work. Apart from combining household duties with part-time work, she sacrificed luxuries to make ends meet, especially if her husband had low-paying jobs, with frequent layoffs, or if the family was trying to build up a business short in cash. Many such women had emigrated reluctantly or against their wishes. Already well established within a secure network of friends and relatives in the Netherlands, with easy access to shopping facilities, they landed in a strange land. There was little contact with other adults. Farm women in particular experienced physical isolation, although even in small towns or suburbs Dutch immigrant women no longer enjoyed the mobility previously provided by bicycles or efficient public transportation (see chapter 5). This made them more dependent on their husbands and other male relatives who usually secured a car within a year or two of immigration. Although the women, like other members of the household, might eventually enjoy the benefits of years of sacrifice, they still put in long hours of cleaning and cooking well into a period of relative affluence.

Joyce van der Vliet, who conducted a study of postwar Dutch Calvinist women, probed a little deeper to gain further insights into the immigration experience from the perspectives of women.[19] In a series of in-depth interviews with Dutch-Canadian women of different ages, she discovered some themes that are normally missed by male researchers. For example, in some cases, immigrant women had taken the initiative to emigrate, while the husband was reluctant to leave the comforts of the homeland.[20] Moreover, several informants learned how to drive a car contrary to their husbands' expectations and wishes. Some seemingly conservative women also questioned traditional gender roles. One orthodox Calvinist woman mentioned she was opposed to the ordination of female ministers because then the women would have to do everything, including running the church.[21]

Other stories unmask the male myth of the all-sacrificing Dutch-Canadian woman with strong maternal instincts, who prefers to stay at home with her children. Many immigrant women with education or prior job training in the Netherlands did not have the chance to pursue their previous careers, especially if they ended up in small towns or rural areas. The words of a Dutch-Canadian housewife, cited by Miep Verkley in an anthology about women immigrants, express the resulting feeling of frustration:

> As a nurse I would have made a good living. There was a shortage of nurses in Ontario in 1955, the year we came to Canada and it would have not been difficult to find a job. In those days, however, not many married women worked outside of the home. I followed the example of my older sisters and stayed at home. Not wholeheartedly, however; I longed to go back to my own profession. I missed the people, and I missed the challenge of a demanding job. I would have not been so lonely, I would have learned to speak English better, and would have made friends and a decent living. As it was, John found work at a farm, far away from a city, too far from a hospital. We owned one car, which was not very reliable, and my chances to go to work were slim.[22]

Dutch Immigrant Women as Wage Labourers

We saw earlier how postwar Dutch immigrant families arriving prior to 1952 had to be sponsored by Canadian farmers. Mothers and children, as well as men, worked in the fields at harvest time. Dutch women also performed domestic duties for their sponsors, especially for farm bachelors or hired hands.[23] At times young women went off to the city to earn additional income, while their parents and younger siblings stayed behind on the farm. Even women with experience in nursing or secretarial work had to do menial tasks well below their level of competence, just like their male counterparts. Apart from seasonal agricultural labour, and nanny work, Dutch women scrubbed, polished and vacuumed. The historical reputation for cleanliness associated with Dutch households (see chapter 3) enabled Dutch women looking for part-time work to occupy a niche created by the upper-middle-class demand for cheap and efficient cleaning ladies. For example, there was a high demand for Dutch domestics in Toronto in the fifties. However, many women discovered they could earn more money working in factories or canneries, even if only on a part-time basis. Yet a young woman still under her parents' authority was not given the same opportunities as a man to strike out on one's own. How much freedom she had varied greatly, depending on her family's background and inclination.

Gender Roles and Organized Religion

I did not detect significant differences in attitudes on gender between Catholics and orthodox Calvinist immigrants.[24] Both groups hold that the man is the head of the household, and religious leaders from both groups tried to persuade women to stop working outside the home through sermons or home visits. Yet I found a great variation in attitudes among both laymen and clergy, plus discrepancies between theory and practice. The following observation was reported by an English woman (also an immigrant) about her Dutch-Canadian neighbours:

> The Dutch people near where I live believe in the man being the head of the household. But I know that _______ [name of a woman] is the one who manages the farm business. She is really on the ball. It is funny because I saw them at church, where their minister gave a fire and brimstone sermon, and she sat very sedate and quiet. But her husband had to take his cue from what she did.

Although orthodox Calvinist men frequently espoused antiquated views on gender relations, male members of mainstream churches or men with no religious affiliation were not exempt from a male superiority complex. The most extreme case was recounted by a woman who once worked for the honorary consul in Hamilton. She described the attitude of one man who stepped into her office: "He was proud that his wife stayed at home with their children and that she also did not have her driver's license. He even claimed it was not necessary for her to learn English. How it that possible?"[25]

Notwithstanding such deep-rooted cultural norms, married women from all the pillars worked outside the home. I suspect that married orthodox Dutch Calvinists were more likely to do so than other categories of women. The most common reason they gave for working outside the home was that they needed to earn extra money to pay for their children's education in privately run Christian schools.[26] This still holds true today. Ironically, the same religious principles that emphasize that married women should not neglect their duties as wives and mothers force these same women into jobs and careers to finance the schools whose avowed function is to reinforce "healthy family values." An awareness of this discrepancy between norm and action is expressed by a woman writer in *Reformed Perspective*, a magazine published by a group of Canadian Reformed laymen.[27] That article criticizes the hypocrisy of Reformed men putting social pressure on young mothers with certificates in primary education to take teaching positions in their Christian schools.

While neither the Reformed Dutch nor Roman Catholic Churches allow women to play a prominent role in administration and decision making, the former institution has greater influence over the daily lives of women. The Catholic Church, headed by the Pope in Rome, does not allow women to become priests and is even stricter than most Reformed churches on such issues as birth control. Nevertheless, most Catholic parishes are big and impersonal, resulting in little effective recrimination of lay members who discreetly practise birth control or who criticize their church's gender bias. Clergy and lay religious leaders are frequently not that effective in exerting sanctions against women who do not conform to church rules regarding women's issues. In contrast, the close-knit and more tightly organized structure of Reformed churches results in greater social pressures to conform to the rules (see chapter 9). Direct intervention from elders or ministers often directly reinforces the authority of fathers and husbands. For example, one young woman commented:

> Right now we have an elder who is quite open and accepts the fact that women go to work. That is not the case for a lady in another church I know, who set up her own business in interior decorating. She has three children, ages six, four and a small baby. She takes the baby with her to work and the other kids go to a babysitter. On various occasions an elder has come to see her to suggest that she might be doing psychological harm to her children.[28]

Nevertheless, despite such social pressures, both Calvinist and Catholic women work full-time as secretaries, nurses, teachers, lawyers and storekeepers. This pattern stands in sharp contrast to the Netherlands, where fewer women have full-time careers or work outside the home (see chapter 3). Yet, unlike the Netherlands—where women in the larger Calvinist congregations can become ministers—until recently, members of sister denominations in Canada were still debating whether or not women should be allowed to serve as deacons or elders (see chapter 9). Compared to mainstream Protestant denominations, relatively few Reformed women are deacons, or even speakers, in Ontario. One young woman of American and English background, who became Christian Reformed after her marriage, made the following comparison:

> Last Sunday I was asked to address the congregation and the minister said I had done a fine job. It had been a long time, since I used to do that quite a bit in my old Presbyterian church. _____ [her husband] and I used to speak together in front of the congregation whenever we came to give talks about our work in Central America, but whenever we visited a Christian Reformed church ______ would go up front with the minister while I sat in the pews with the ladies and had coffee with them in a separate place.[29]

We saw earlier how controversies about the roles of women in this denomination resulted in a new schism in the early nineties.

Within the Reformed community, controversies surrounding gender issues do not cut across clear generational lines, of young versus old, or of first-generation Dutch-Canadian immigrant versus second-generation. One woman commented:

> I know a lot of young couples who are just as adamant about not allowing women a greater say in the church, although it is true that the older people generally are totally against the idea. But some people of my parents' generation are in favour of granting more rights to women. My mother is in favour of women becoming ministers, but she did not think the way she does now twenty years ago. I think my father hasn't really made up his mind.[30]

Notwithstanding such changes, women with an overt feminist perspective still comprise a tiny minority within the Christian Reformed denomination.[31]

Despite their exclusion from ecclesiastical office, Dutch-Canadian women are actively involved in various lay organizations. For example, in the Dutch-linked Reformed churches, volunteers in Ladies Auxiliaries provide the back-up services required for the day-to-day running of their many institutions. In the case of largely multicultural Roman Catholic parishes, Dutch-Canadian women make up a disproportionate number of active members in the Catholic Women's League.[32] Yet so far, women volunteers proceed to the highest levels of public office only in organizations outside of the churches. In 1990, Rennie Feddema, a first-generation Dutch-Canadian woman who belongs to the Christian Reformed church, was elected as national president of the Canadian Farm Women's Network.[33] In contrast, there are no Reformed female ministers of Dutch descent anywhere in Ontario. Nor have I encountered any examples of Dutch-Canadian female ministers in other mainstream denominations that have changed their rules concerning eligibility for ordination.

Ironically, only in the Catholic Church, which practises even greater gender segregation, did about half a dozen Dutch-Canadian women reach a higher level of authority in an ecclesiastical establishment, as nuns. Indeed, one Dutch-Canadian woman of both farm and immigrant background became mother superior of an order whose headquarters are located in the Netherlands.[34] However, even educated, professional Dutch women who came to Ontario as members of Catholic religious orders could be relegated to lower-status positions. An example is the assignment of a group of Dutch nuns with training and experience in social work to laundry duties and farm work for the Catholic establishment in the London area (see chapter 8).

Women in Regional Networks

Women-centred social networks are difficult to detect because they may not be revealed through a common surname. We must therefore have a closer look at the various Brabander connections described in chapter 10, and go back to Freda Leenders of Erin. Her circle of relatives, friends and in-laws link her not only to villages in eastern Brabant but to at least three different regions in Ontario. Her role in organizing the Boekel reunion illustrates how the personal skills and social networks activated by women play a major role in reinforcing ethnic bonds among Dutch-Canadians.

Freda Vander Zande (her maiden name) became one of the early pioneers of Mariahout when her father moved there in 1940. In 1949 her father's sister, then living in Veghel, emigrated to Ontario with her husband and their twelve children. Within a year this "clan," including in-laws and friends, moved into several houses on a large farm near Aurora. The aunt from Veghel, Hendrika Van Bakel, became the focal point for an extended family network that later spread out all over Canada.[35] Freda, whose family emigrated a few years later, was to maintain contact with them right up to the present. Freda met her future husband, Joe Leenders from Boekel, in Bronte. His parents, both from farm backgrounds, emigrated to Canada with nine kids when Joe, the eldest, was nineteen. Joe's sister in turn married Jan van Werde, who later took over a farm the Leenders had bought just outside Sarnia. They all knew Freda, who has since stayed in close contact with that part of the family. Freda did not lose touch with any of them after a move to Grand Valley and later Erin. Her main contact in Bronte was with the Brouwers family. Ted Brouwers, also from Mariahout, had married the oldest Van Bakel sister from Aurora. This is where the link between Freda and her aunt Hendrika from Veghel comes in. Bill Brouwers—we meet him here for the second time—later became involved in running the Mariahout reunions. Freda also kept in touch with the Leenders family, now located in Oakville, London and Sarnia. With her children grown up, Freda reactivated all of her old contacts and her in-laws from Boekel in preparation for their first hometown reunion. Today she is in touch on a regular basis with relatives and in-laws from Aurora, Wainfleet, Sarnia, Milton and Oakville.

Women were good at getting people in touch with each other, even if they were not embedded in a close-knit extended rural family network. In chapter 10 we saw how a group of men originally from Noordwijkerhout came together thanks to the organizational and networking skills of a career woman, even though she had previously never met any of her husband's father's old schoolmates. This woman was originally sponsored by a Toronto family to come and help with housework, then worked as a cashier, and later got a job in a personnel firm prior to setting up her own agency. She is typical of many Dutch immigrant women, both single and married, who developed careers after they came to Canada.

Dutch-Canadian Women in the World of Business

While not occupying a specific niche in the Canadian world of business, Dutch immigrants women entered into a variety of professional careers. Some received higher education in the Netherlands, while others completed or upgraded their schooling once they were in Canada. In many cases, they provided crucial services, which enabled family businesses to survive. However, Dutch-Canadian women also started businesses on their own or took over enterprises founded by men. Running a retail store was another option, although a single mother who ended up in Sudbury waited until her daughter was off to college before she bought a paint and decorating store.[36] Gender expectation made it easier for Dutch women to enter into occupations already identified as part of the "female" domain, such as hairstyling salons (interlude 10.2) or personnel agencies. However, Dutch immigrant women with a good business sense broke into the predominantly male world of money and politics in the fifties and sixties. In fact, I came across several cases of women who did much better than their male partners as real estate brokers.[37]

Some Dutch immigrant women did not become actively involved in business until after their husbands' deaths. For example, someone known in the Dutch-Canadian community as "the richest woman in Toronto" started her career as a partner in her husband's mortgage brokerage firm, which she took over after he passed away.[38] She further expanded the business and today lives in a large farm house, just outside Toronto. A Dutch widow in Sudbury introduced earlier (see interludes 5.1 and 13.7) developed a real estate business completely on her own. When her husband was still alive, she not only ran part of his business—while she was raising five children and taking university courses—but started selling houses on commission on a part-time basis. After her husband's death, she continued working in real estate to support herself and her children.[39]

While extremely varied in social backgrounds and career histories, Dutch immigrant women, most of them with family responsibilities, gravitated towards careers that gave them more flexibility in managing their time. As far as I know, no Dutch immigrant women with training in the Netherlands entered more prestigious professional careers as doctors, lawyers or engineers in the fifties or sixties—that was difficult enough for the men (see the next chapter). This scenario changed somewhat for second generation, Canadian-educated women of Dutch background who came closer to the norm of Canadian women in general. More recently highly educated Dutch women have emigrated to Canada and immediately entered prestigious careers.

We can get a better picture of the Dutch-Canadian female presence in the world of business by looking at the membership of the professional and business associations in Toronto (see chapter 12). Initially, all the professional or middle-class institutions set up by Dutch immigrants were for men only. We already saw how the wives of one social network (*Borrel Club*) had to set up their own book club.[40] The Netherlands Luncheon Club, which later allowed women to join, also started off as an all-male institution. For this reason, some Dutch-Canadian career women had no interest in getting involved: "We knew about the luncheon club from the beginning. I was a businesswoman but they said ladies were not allowed to become members. When they did allow women to enter I did not have enough time and I did not need them."[41]

In contrast, the Canadian Netherlands Business and Professional Association incorporated women from its conception.[42] Nineteen percent (or 17 out of 90) of the names in their 1989 membership list were women. The percentage of women involved in the much bigger 220-member Netherlands Luncheon Club that same year was lower (only 13 percent);[43] in addition, 18 of their 28 women members did not list a specific management position or business. Many of these women members were nevertheless actively involved in their husbands' businesses or had well-paid jobs of their own. One wonders if such jobs were deemed not prestigious enough to be mentioned in their booklet.[44] When a woman was finally chosen to take over as president, she did not last more than several months, and was replaced by yet another long-serving male!

The listed occupations of the women in both organizations do at least give a rough idea of what these Dutch-Canadian women do for a living. I counted six presidents of small or medium-sized companies (ranging from imports to fabrics); two executive directors (one for a private company and the other for a government agency); four lawyers (associated with private law firms); four managers (one in the public and the others in the private sector); and two real estate agents. One of each of the following occupations were also represented: teacher, supervisor in a government department, contractor, sculptor, travel agent, trustee, fashion consultant, publisher-editor, and finally, "designer-owner." This list illustrates the wide range of activities in which Dutch-Canadian women are involved. However, unlike the Dutch businessmen who have carved out a niche for themselves in specific sectors of the economy (see chapters 14 and 19), women entrepreneurs and professionals are more evenly distributed over a wide range of occupations.

Some Dutch immigrant women forged careers in the public sector. For example, the full-time president of the Ontario Folk Arts Council is Aleida Limbertie. Not only did she organize one of the first Dutch folk dance groups in Toronto in 1964,[45] but she coordinated all folk arts activities in the province with the advent of Trudeau's policy of multiculturalism.[46] Dutch-Canadian women also made careers in other branches of the public sector; Sophia Geenen, for example, became an administrator in the Homes of the Aged Division of Social Work for the Municipality of Metropolitan Toronto,[47] while others entered the male-dominated world of finance. Two large credit unions established by Dutch immigrants have had women managers (see chapter 15) and Toronto DUCA has had several women on their board of directors since the early sixties.[48] Numerous women have gone from working as real agent agents on commission to becoming completely independent real estate or mortgage brokers.

Dutch-Canadian rural women have played an equally active, but less visible role, in family farm businesses. For example, most women had full responsibility for poultry operations—which brought in cash income—while their husbands were busy doing other things. A man who later became the full-time manager for a small credit union in Milton admitted that his wife "has always looked after the chickens." Not only was she in charge of managing their quota of 800 laying hens (about two hours of work each day), but she and the children did all the grading. She also went around local stores in a van and made regular deliveries to supermarkets.[49] I also came across one case where a Dutch farm woman did all the carpentry and repairs.[50] This rural woman not only helped look after their 200 cows, of which 70 needed milking, but also raised ten children! Her oldest daughter, who also lived on the farm when I visited them in 1991, had her own barn with heifers, sheep and goats. Many wives of full-time commercial farmers also took care of the bookkeeping end of the business.

Dutch-Canadian Women in Leadership Roles

Immigrant women throughout Ontario combine busy careers as professionals and homemakers with active participation in the Dutch-Canadian community. Often their involvement continues throughout their lives. We have already noted the involvement of women in such diverse institutions as the Netherlands Bazaar, a biennial fundraising event (see chapter 12), and the ethnic press. Gee Spaans, who worked in her husband's landscaping business, served as president of the Dutch-Canadian Association of Greater Toronto for many years. The late Ruth Mesritz, a businesswoman mentioned earlier, was a founder and later the chairperson of the Bazaar, helped to establish the Dutch-Canadian Association of Greater Toronto and became its treasurer. Lia de Groot, who joined the Canadian Netherlands Business and Professional Association, served for many years on the board of directors of the DUCA credit union and was another long-standing member of the Bazaar committee. There are too many first-generation women leaders to name them all.[51]

Both full-time career women and those who spent more time in the informal economic sector played leadership roles as advocates or organizers for a variety of causes within the larger Canadian society. For example, Dutch immigrants women, originally from a society with an extensive network of programs and special facilities for children with disabilities, took the initiative to have such services instituted in Canada. Beg De Groot, now living near Trenton, emigrated to Canada with her husband, a physician, in 1949. When she realized there was no educational facility for her mentally handicapped child, she started her own program in Regina. She also became an advocate for more comprehensive care facilities for handicapped children in Canada.[52] I have met numerous other Dutch-Canadian women who have also done various kinds of volunteer work, especially for the Red Cross.[53]

Women from quite different backgrounds also worked together to implement a social vision. A good example is the establishment of Dutch Heritage Villa, a retirement home in Kingston (see chapter 17). Although a former Dutch-Canadian mayor of Kingston and other men were involved in this project, it was initiated by a woman who wanted to see a retirement home along the lines of what she had seen in a trip to the Netherlands.[54] A combination of housewives and professional women also did most of the legwork and planning. As someone explained in an interview:

> We saved a lot of money by not paying for a professional planning group. We did it all ourselves; it was really the women on the board of directors who did it, because the men just attended the meetings. We selected the rugs and furniture we wanted and went over all the details, even the types of tiles laid. The contractor used to say, "there come the ladies." I also had to sell the houses of some of the residents, although my only experience was being a housewife. We were quite fortunate that one of our board members [also a Dutch-Canadian woman] is a trained accountant, which our auditors really liked.[55]

Class and Gender

We cannot afford to exclude the dimension of class, which bisects gender and denominational bloc divisions. Dutch-Canadian women brought up in an upper-class Dutch environment were just as status-conscious as their male counterparts (see chapter 12). This Dutch class system is reflected in women's organizations. For example, the book club organized by the wives of men who formed more exclusive social clubs in Toronto was quite separate and involved different kinds of women from those who joined *Dames Welkom*, a less prestigious get-together for Dutch housewives.[56] We have already seen how middle-class women dominated the running of the Netherlands Bazaar. Wealthy Dutch-Canadian women also employed nannies and cleaners from their own ethnic group.

Despite such internal diversity, Dutch-Canadian women share a subordinate status as females, regardless of economic class. Not only were all Dutch immigrant women originally relegated to their own organizations, but they were underrepresented in the formal economy sectors and public life. Thus, no woman ever became president of the board of directors of a Dutch-Canadian credit union or mayor of a city. Moreover, all women assumed a much greater share of the responsibility of raising children, even if they were working full time.

Language, Gender and Ethnic Identity

Some Dutch women learned English prior to emigrating, but most picked it up after their arrival in Canada. Like many men, some women attended evening classes. However, married women who stayed at home took longer to learn the language (see chapter 5) although here too we find a lot of individual variation.[57] However, even women who made a rapid transition to English as a home language perpetuated other aspects of ethnic identity retention, since they prepared the Dutch type of cuisine[58] which both men and women were reluctant to give up despite all efforts to become "fully Canadian" (see chapter 18).

The almost imperceptible transition from Dutch to English among Dutch-Canadian couples (see chapter 11) stands in stark contrast to the identity and linguistic usage of immigrant women with non-Dutch spouses. Women married to non-Dutch men, including war brides, maintained their mother tongue throughout all their life stages. These women were middle aged or older when I encountered them. Despite their total immersion in Canadian life (and frequently, little contact with the Dutch-Canadian community), they responded in fluent Dutch when I phoned to set up interviews.[59] Their almost flawless Dutch indicates the total separation of the languages of husband and wife. Unlike women who form part of a larger Dutch-Canadian family unit, war brides did not undergo a gradual process of linguistic modification, in conjunction with their husbands, older children and other immigrant couples. Their mother tongue has in a sense been "frozen in time."

One Dutch war bride gave me an alternative explanation for this phenomenon. She pointed out how important it was for a married woman to maintain some personal autonomy.[60] In the case of Dutch women of intra-ethnic unions, thinking, writing and occasionally speaking Dutch was one vehicle for expressing or reaffirming their own personal identity. Ironically, while more closely integrated into the mainstream, English-speaking Canadian society, such women have remained more "Dutch" as far as their knowledge of the Dutch language and national identity is concerned. Thus, one Dutch war bride in Toronto, who declined to be interviewed, nevertheless spoke to me over the phone for forty minutes in fluent Dutch. During our conversation, she was adamant she did not consider herself to be Dutch since she was married to a Canadian and had little contact with other immigrants. Yet her final remark was "you can only truly be Dutch in Holland."[61]

The Politics of Gender and Dutch-Canadian Ethnicity

The links between gender politics and Dutch-Canadian ethnicity is complex and full of ambiguity. In the field of literature, Aritha Van Herk, a well-known feminist writer of Dutch descent, questions traditional gender roles in works of fiction.[62] Most of her writings do not deal with the Dutch immigration experience or the Dutch-Canadian presence. Yet she herself became part of that ethnic presence when she agreed to write the introduction to VanderMey's book, which also portrays her as a Dutch immigrant's daughter who influenced Canadian literature.[63] The connection between ethnicity and the politics of gender is more direct in the case of Dutch-Canadian academic women who are using a feminist perspective to examine Dutch literature.[64] Likewise, the depiction of Indo women in Dutch and Indonesian literature has come up as a topic at conferences or seminars organized by Dutch-Canadian scholars.[65] Yet, among the very diverse Dutch-Canadian population, feminism as a form of political action, as well as a perspective, is not monolithic.[66]

Gender politics—particularly the issues of homosexuality and human reproduction—has brought together sub-groups with hitherto diametrically opposed world views. During the eighties and nineties, orthodox Calvinists of Dutch descent and their counterparts in the more conservative wing of the Catholic Church became strong allies in the "real women" and pro-life movements.[67] Similarly, the movement to promote equity issues and a higher status and recognition for women, including lesbians, has united Dutch-Canadians of both genders from a variety of Dutch backgrounds. None of these political currents has anything to do with being Dutch, since Canadian men and women of non-Dutch background are as likely to be involved in such advocacy work as their Dutch-Canadian counterparts. However, we cannot leave out the broader symbolic significance of Dutch ethnicity for gender politics.

While the politics of gender has no obvious bearing on the politics of ethnicity, many Canadians equate "Dutchness" with a conservative position on gender issues. This connection reflects the high profile of the Reformed community (seen as "Dutch"). It so happens that the Christian Heritage Party, which is the strongest advocate for "traditional family values," was founded by Dutch Calvinists and is still largely run by Canadians of Dutch descent (see chapter 19). The Reform Party has similarly attracted more than its share of Dutch-Canadian adherents, and the best-known Dutch-Canadian spokesman for the anti-abortion movement is Bill Vander Zalm, the ex-premier of British Columbia, who can be easily identified by both his surname and accent. In contrast, for orthodox Calvinists, the "Dutch" (with European connotations) are more likely to be identified with radical feminism, given the current policies of the Dutch state and the liberal policies of most churches in the Netherlands. Class, generation, gender, religion and ethnicity are not separate spheres of contention. Counteracting images of what Dutch "culture" really stands for is but one example of a broader 'classification struggle' over social divisions.[68]

Fieldnotes Interlude

13.1 Excerpt from an interview with a woman in London [in Dutch], October 29, 1988

I did not want to go out and work like other women who had found factory jobs, so my neighbour asked me to look after her daughter for a dollar a day. Then another woman, who was Italian, asked if I could also babysit her children and then others did too. I had a whole bunch [*troep*] of kids and one of the mothers, a woman from Latvia, brought me her child with the chickenpox, whom I did not want. Then I gave that up. When those other women went on vacation, they got paid, but then I got nothing. After that I also started to work in a factory and that is what I still do. I work for Telecom and inspect telephone parts.

13.2 Excerpt from an interview with a Flemish-Canadian farm woman, near Warwick (near Strathroy), April 27, 1989

When my father bought his first farm in Canada, he started growing beets and other vegetables and all of the girls and my mother helped him . . . my three brothers all worked in Aylmer in the tobacco fields and they gave their pay cheques to my father to help him pay off the farm and expand. The boys used to take our old car to get to Aylmer, and we had to walk, or my mother would take the tractor to town to buy groceries. That is how we used to work then—the children all worked to support their parents' farm, but when they got older and wanted to get married and farm on their own, their father would in turn help them buy their own farms. But the girls usually got nothing. My father was an exception because he did leave something for the girls but he also used to say, "too bad they were born as girls."

13.3 Excerpts from an interview with the same Flemish woman from Sarnia in interlude 10.2

I was 38 years old when I emigrated from Belgium, and my husband, who was a millwright, was forty. I had my own café and also did hairdressing. My daughter also joined us in Canada.

. . . . my husband had a hard time getting a good job because his English was so poor. He already knew German and I thought he would easily be able to learn English but that was not the case . . . he was sometimes out of work for months at a time and I had to make the money. He also used to have to work out of town a lot, when he used to work for Ontario Hydro, which was his third job. He did that until he retired but he was already sick.

I was one of the first ones who started the credit union [St. Willibrord] here in Sarnia, together with some Dutch-Canadians. They came to my place and asked if I would represent the Belgians. At that time I was already a member of the board of a credit union of our church, St. Peter's parish. . . . I also started the Belgian-Canadian-Dutch Club in Sarnia.

13.4 *Excerpt from an interview with a woman, on her farm near Strathroy, April 28, 1989*

Many men in the Christian Reformed community are not in favour of their wives getting involved in wider community affairs. For example, I know of a woman in Chatham who didn't come to the workshop we organized in Ridgetown because she did not receive the invitation which came in the mail. It was sent in a brown envelope with the name of our organization but her husband took it and did not show it to her.

13.5 *Excerpt from* Sojourners (A Family Chronicle) *by Arie Verduijn (published in 1981 by the author), p. 116*

Busy as he was, most of the time my Dad was present when we had our meals. But when he was away, mother would sit in the middle of the oblong table in the kitchen, a thin rattan [cane] of about one and a half meters at her right hand. That way she did not have to get up to remind us of how we should behave; mother would not have had the time to start walking around. Once, before my oldest sister could also help out, mother had been so busy cutting slices of bread and preparing her sandwiches that at the end of the lunch she suddenly said to her helper: "Suus, I am so hungry; I wonder what happened; did you see me eat?" Suus was startled and stopped clearing the table. Then she said: "Come to think about it, no, I did not; you must have forgotten."

13.6 *Excerpt from an interview with a retired Dutch-Canadian farmer [Christian Reformed], on his farm in Simcoe county, May 30, 1991*

One of my granddaughters started coming home later and later—first 11, then 12, then 1, then 2. But her father said he would wait and see what happened, that everything would turn out OK. Only when she once came home at 3 did he tell her he thought girls shouldn't come home that late. But she asked, "Is it OK then for boys to come home so late?" But she turned out alright and she works hard. She still does not have a boyfriend, so who knows when she will get married. I helped her at one point to buy a new car, and my son-in-law was surprised when she was able to pull out a chequebook and write out a check for $2000. She had saved it. But she has a good sense of humour. We told her if she was a boy, lots of girls would want to have a ride in a car like that, and she said, "You mean girls can't pick up boys too?"

13.7 *Excerpt from an interview with the same real estate agent in Sudbury quoted in interlude 5.1*

I also started taking correspondence courses, mainly in English literature and composition and then enroled in English courses at Laurentian. At that time I bought an old car with no handbrake, for only $230. But my husband got pneumonia. Whenever I used to visit him in the hospital he used to ask me, "How is my business going?" I told him I didn't know because I was busy raising five kids and taking courses, but it was his way of hinting that he wanted me to work for the business. So I started taking bookkeeping courses, although I hated it. I learned all about invoicing and prices and eventually became better than the parts man. But that was not a job for a woman because men didn't like for a woman to know too much, or to know when they made mistakes. . . . At that time I also got a girl to do work for me at home . . . later in life, when the children were older, my husband and I started speaking a lot more Dutch again.

. . . . It has been 11 years since my husband died, and I have 5 children and 7 grandchildren.

Chapter 14

Dutch Business

There is a double connection between the world of business and ethnicity. Ethnically oriented businesses, which cater to Dutch-Canadian customers, involve a direct link between ethnic identity retention and economic viability. Such enterprises must be distinguished from those where the owners just happen to be Dutch. However, it would be simplistic to draw too hard a line between these two types of businesses. In some cases, the Dutch immigrant community served as a springboard, leading to commercial ventures geared to a broader clientele. In both cases, capital investment by Dutch corporations—plus the relationships between the Canadian business community and business in the Netherlands—must be taken into consideration. Finally, even in the pragmatic world of business, the Dutch pillar system cannot be overlooked; while Dutch people conduct business across denominational lines, the operation of social networks and loyalties based on religion or political ideology do have some influence on access to markets and the way in which business is conducted.

Dutch Investment in Canada

Postwar international migration was a major stimulus for increasing trade between Canada and the Netherlands, as well as for direct Dutch investment. Such investment goes back to before the War. For example, the Netherlands Investment Company, a Dutch mortgage corporation, was involved in land development in Manitoba prior to the Great Depression.[1] More substantial postwar Dutch business activity involved Holland-America Lines,[2] KLM and Holland Life. In the early fifties, Holland-America Lines set up an office in Toronto, as did Holland Life, which sold life insurance.[3] The managers of their respective offices in Toronto were Dutch nationals

Notes to this chapter are on p. 390-93.

(see chapter 12), but they employed Dutch immigrants in the field.[4] With the decline of transatlantic boat travel, Holland-America Lines decided to specialize in luxury cruises and their personnel were transferred to New York. KLM (Royal Dutch Airlines) became more prominent with the subsequent rapid expansion of air travel. They and other Dutch airlines, including Martinair, also set up administrative offices in Toronto and collaborated closely with Dutch-Canadian travel agencies (see below).

There was also Dutch investment in Canadian banking. In 1953, Henri Moquette, a former Dutch airforce pilot and son of a banker, founded the Mercantile Bank in Montreal, affiliated with the Dutch *Nationale Handelsbank*.[5] The trajectory of Dutch manufacturing companies is less well known. The biggest is Philips, which built an electronics plant in Scarborough where they employed many Dutch immigrants.[6] Philips set up factories in other locations; they modernized an old tube factory in London,[7] and manufactured wooden TV cabinets in Strathroy. That operation, which employed between 250 and 300 workers, was a major employer in the town. Their first employees were Dutch immigrants; later they started hiring more Portuguese and Italians.[8] Today, other Dutch companies operate in the Ontario market, including the ABN-Amro Bank, which set up branches in Toronto.[9] These corporations are injecting new blood into the small network of people in Ontario with connections to the Netherlands and to the Dutch-Canadian community. Smaller companies and wealthy individuals from the Netherlands are also investing in Ontario, either personally or through proxies.[10]

Loans from wealthy Dutch families sometimes provide financial backing to Dutch-Canadian entrepreneurs. A prime example is Roel Bramer, who came to Canada as a young man in 1959. His career, outlined in a Canadian investment magazine, illustrates the stimulus provided by Dutch capital. A member of the new *Borrel Club* (see chapter 12), he first came to Toronto for a holiday with friends. A year later his father helped to finance his studies in economics and political science at McGill. Roel used his Dutch connections to raise capital to develop novel restaurant/bar operations in prime downtown locations, and then sold the leases to banks or large corporations needing space for plaza complexes.[11] Young entrepreneurs like Bramer have been coming to Toronto and other parts of Ontario since the fifties. To what extent they stay in touch with Holland, and the links they have established with other Dutch-Canadians, to a large extent depends on the business they are in.[12]

Business for the Dutch

The postwar population movement provided opportunities for those with some capital and the ability to serve Dutch immigrants. A common way of making extra money in the early fifties was to set up a boarding house for newly arrived immigrants. Such small-scale investments enabled many immigrant couples to pay off their mortgages. Initial profits enabled others to branch off into other commercial activities. As the average income of Dutch immigrants went up, a correspondingly more diversified ethnic business sector catered to their consumer demands. The next challenge for these ethnic entrepreneurs was expansion into the broader non-Dutch market, as immigrants started to assimilate into the mainstream Canadian society.

Importers and Wholesale Distributors

When Dutch immigrants arrived in Canada, not everyone could get accustomed to Canadian household products, or find Canadian substitutes. Newcomers fancied Dutch-style peppermints and *zoute drop* (salted licorice), Dutch-style raisin bread and *speculaas* (spiced cookies), Dutch cigars and sliced horsemeat. To give flavour to mashed potatoes, the Dutch added kale and pieces of Dutch-style *rookworst* (smoked sausage).[13] Special scrubbing brushes, linen teatowels and cotton underwear from the Netherlands were considered superior. It is thus not surprising that in places with Dutch immigrants some enterprising man or woman would become a travelling salesman, going from house to house selling delicatessen products and Dutch wares.[14] Such retailers in turn bought their supplies from Dutch-Canadian importers.

How the business of importing Dutch goods started is a story in itself. Prior to 1940, there was little trade between Canada and the Netherlands. The only Dutch imports were tulip bulbs, rope (for agricultural combines), and herring.[15] The latter two were destined for western Canada, where herring was consumed by people from Poland or Ukraine. After the War, eastern Canada also became a recipient of Dutch goods, when importers introduced traditional Dutch products to Ontario. In 1946, Jan Overweel started promoting Dutch herring in Toronto, but there was little demand.[16] At that time there were few Dutch-Canadians.[17] To make a living, he started importing other types of fish, and obtained a concession for wholesale cacao. Once established, he obtained a licence to import cheese. However, Dutch cheese was even less well known than herring. He could not find customers until he happened to drive along highway 3 in the vicinity of Delhi. That is where the prewar Flemish provided his only customers until Dutch immigrants started to arrive en masse. Eventually

Overweel became the main wholesaler for cheese and other products to other Dutch-Canadian vendors.[18]

Other importers and distributors started off with their own capital. The Holtzheuser brothers, whose name appears on Dutch candies in the import section of supermarkets throughout Ontario, initially sold antiques and copperware. Jan and Joop Holtzheuser, then in their mid-twenties, emigrated in the early fifties.[19] Initially the store they jointly established in Toronto did not do well. They then realized more money could be made from the culinary nostalgia of the fast-growing Dutch-Canadian population. Eventually, they ran a fleet of trucks delivering goods to specialty shops across Ontario and beyond.

The growing Dutch-Canadian market had room for specialization. Overweel dealt in cheese, although he carried other products, including fish. Ebsel Van den Velde, operating out of Hamilton, started with cigars, cologne and household goods before branching out into foodstuffs, including his quota of cheese.[20] Vanden Top imported and distributed a bit of everything. Van den Velde and Vanden Top, both members of the Reformed community, initially tapped into that sub-segment of the Dutch market. However, all the importers also served the broader Dutch-Canadian community and branched out to reach a wider clientele. Over time, other Dutch-Canadians broke into the importing niche; the last ten years has seen a proliferation of new companies, including Triple "C," Scholten's and WMK, which operates out of Chatham. Another trend is the mail-order system, whereby Dutch-Canadians can obtain wall plaques and books.[21]

The Dutch Retail Stores and Delis

In 1993 there were forty retail outlets in Ontario that sold delicatessen products and dry goods to Dutch-Canadians. These "Dutch stores" (*Hollandse winkels*) sometimes include a butcher counter or a bakery outlet. Their owners usually started off selling Dutch goods from a car or van; in 1992 Piet Veurtjes, owner of a Dutch store in Ottawa, still made personal deliveries to farm households located off highway 31. John Niekerk, the owner of a Dutch delicatessen in Barrie, used to make the rounds of Floss township. Such retailer made their initial contacts and received credit from wholesale outlets. For example, one woman found out about a small Dutch wholesale operation on Dundas street, in downtown London, when she was out shopping. She and her husband, a furniture maker, had just arrived in Canada with their teenage son.[22] Initially all three worked in factories, and she started delivering Dutch groceries by bicycle. They were still living in a small apartment when she accepted an offer from the wholesale outlet to sell Dutch foodstuffs on commission in her spare time. When her son got a car, they started visiting their customers in the evenings. The business went well enough that they rented space for their own store and the father quit his job. They started buying directly from importers based in Toronto,[23] and also received goods directly from Holland.[24] After ten years they sold their operation and used their profits to buy a small house they had rented from another Dutch couple.

Dutch-Canadian business people had to be sensitive to their clientele's diverse social make-up. Some ministers of Reformed churches encouraged their congregations to give their business to someone who shared the same faith. Even if this was not the case, storekeepers had to be careful not to antagonize or offend orthodox Calvinists by using inappropriate language or openly declaring a Catholic allegiance. In some cases, Catholic vendors pretended to be Protestants. For instance, one man from the predominantly Catholic province of Noord Brabant sold Dutch goods in his spare time while working at the Ford plant in Oakville. His wife made french fries which they sold from a rented trailer during the summer. They soon realized that numerous customers, particularly in the Burlington-Hamilton area, were Dutch Protestants from the north. The man, who later became a prominent Dutch-Canadian entrepreneur, recalls how sometimes customers would approach their truck and ask with a *gronings* accent what church they attended. He would reply, "the one close to where I live."[25] A Reformed businessman in turn tried to woo potential clients away by telling them his Catholic competitor was a *Brabantse boer* (farmer from Brabant).

On the whole, Dutch-Canadian businesses cross denominational lines. Calvinist store owners have told me that their best customers are Dutch Catholics because they are less stingy with their money. For example, one couple who emigrated from the Netherlands in the early eighties took over a store and deli in Bradford. They found that the members of the church in Holland Marsh they attended had become quite Canadianized in their eating habits. During a conversation in Dutch, she told me "if we had to count on the Christian Reformed community, we would have been bankrupt by now."[26] In contrast, when members from the predominantly Calvinist Frisian community hold their annual picnic reunion near Paris (see chapter 10), they order their supplies from someone who happens to be Catholic.[27]

Dutch stores became centres for social interaction. People have told me how they first met other Dutch-Canadians while visiting such stores, and some Dutch store owners provided the stimulus for the formation of ethnic clubs. The perpetuation of a Dutch identity and ongoing contacts among Dutch-Canadians is a necessary condition for the viability of such specialty stores. At the same time, Dutch ethnic stores have diversified and expanded. The Dutch Toko shop in Guelph has a meat counter and also sells books, Dutch videocassettes, copperware and Delft blue ceramics.[28] While emphasizing its Dutch connection, the store tries to appeal to both Dutch and non-Dutch customers.

Dutch Bakeries and Butchers

Bakers represented one of many trades among the wave of immigrants in the mid-fifties. Every Dutch town or village used to have a myriad of tiny bakeries, which were being squeezed out after the War due to increased competition and a changeover to less labour-intensive technology. Consequently many bakers were put out of work, while others sold out to relocate in Canada. Initially bakeries started by Dutch immigrants served a Dutch clientele. However, unlike specialty retail stores, bakeries had a greater potential for attracting non-Dutch customers and expanding to huge proportions.[29] Here I will concentrate on specialty bakeries that make Dutch-style breads or pastries, albeit altered to suit the North American palate.

Ray Wiersma, a baker who had a thriving business in the old country, emigrated in 1951 and started off in Canada as an employee for a Canadian bakery in Stratford. His boss lent him the money he needed to assemble a pre-fabricated house he had shipped over from the Netherlands, but Wiersma did not realize that under the legal contract for the loan, he would never be allowed to open up his own bakery in the Stratford area. For that reason he and his family moved to Sarnia four years later to buy a bakery from another Dutch-Canadian baker.[30] Wiersma started off in Chatham with a single employee who was also Dutch, but he gave him permission to accept a better job offer working for a new Zellers outlet. Without his helper, Wiersma could no longer bake bread, but he found out that pastries and cakes were a more lucrative product. At first, most of their customers were fellow immigrants, but their bakery later ended up doing their best business with local caterers. A largely non-Dutch clientele always asked for Wiersma's European-style pastries with real whipped cream. Their best walk-in customers were also non-Dutch.[31]

Notwithstanding a largely non-Dutch clientele, the Wiersmas baked Dutch specialties, including *suikerbrood* (a Frisian sweet bread) on the weekends. Their bakery also supplied Dutch stores, including the Toko shop in Guelph. Empty delivery vans from the major Dutch-Canadian importers picked up Wiersma's baked goods on their way back to Toronto or Hamilton, after making deliveries of imported goods in Chatham. Store owners in places like London or Guelph paid the freight costs at a reduced rate. For 33 years, until he retired, Wiersma's bakery operated as a strictly family concern. His sons took over the business, with their father helping out. Their mother worked behind the counter until she was 83 years old. Today such Dutch family bakeries continue to operate throughout southern Ontario, and recent immigrants have followed in the footsteps of those who arrived in the fifties.[32] Many women also opened small Dutch bakeries in Ontario.[33]

At the other end of the spectrum are bakeries like Voortman's, whose windmill cookies and other baked goods represent a large share of a much broader market. That business, located in Hamilton, was developed by two brothers who started off helping their uncle. Other family members, including another brother, branched out into related enterprises, including English muffins. Today the name Voortman is well known to Canadian consumers, but in the early seventies, another bakery called Hollandia, started by the Bruinink family, actually surpassed Voortman's (see fieldnote interlude 14.1). In the end, Henk Bruinink was left with a small bakery in Strathroy, which he operated until cancer forced him to stop working. The dramatic decline of Hollandia illustrates the cyclical nature of businesses that depend on family dynamics. The fate of their enterprise also reflects the nature of links with Dutch capital. Not only did the Bruininks buy their first heavy equipment from a Dutch firm, but one family member sold the original bakery in Mount Brydges to Zeelandia, a Dutch corporation interested in promoting the sale of machinery to bakeries across Canada. However, with a recession and lack of familiarity with the North American market, the Dutch company cut back their operations in the eighties and dismissed a demonstration baker they brought in from Holland. That baker, in turn, set up a small specialty bakery in Norwich, a town with a high proportion of Dutch-Canadians.

The challenges and opportunities available for Dutch butchers were similar to those of bakers. People trained as butchers in the Netherlands set up family businesses in Ontario, most of which stayed small. At first, the cuts they provided appealed to a predominantly Dutch-Canadian market, although some meat businesses grew in size and expanded. For example, Simon de Groot ran a butcher shop in downtown Toronto during the fifties; it became a regular fixture in the Dutch-Canadian community. Today his sons operate a meat-packing plant in Brampton, with a factory outlet.[34] Their smoked sausages and other meat products, such as *rollades*, are shipped to Dutch stores as well as non-Dutch retail outlets.

Unlike the more specialized field of baking, owners of small abattoirs often learned their trade on their own. Luit Miedema, who runs a small slaughterhouse and meat outlet near Simcoe, came from a farm background and wanted to become a farmer in Canada. In 1950 he started working with a Canadian farm sponsor. One day, the Miedemas ordered smoked, sliced horsemeat from a Dutch-Canadian travelling salesman. His

Canadian employer was shocked, and questioned whether or not that was really a "Christian" thing to do.[35] So the farmer gave his Dutch farmhand piglets for them to fatten on the condition that they stop eating horsemeat. The farmer used to slaughter his own cattle, so when the pigs were ready, he showed Miedema how to cut up the meat. The family kept half the meat for themselves and sold the rest to other Dutch-Canadians who belonged to the same Christian Reformed church he attended. Four years later, Miedema bought a corner of the farm he was working on and built a small slaughterhouse. At that time (and prior to 1966) one did not need a special permit. Eventually he set up several small slaughterhouses in Norfolk and Oxford counties, where Dutch-Canadians still make up a significant proportion of the rural population.[36] In the last decade, other immigrants from the Netherlands have also set up abattoirs in Ontario, sometimes combined with a livestock farm.[37]

Physicians and Lawyers

Between 1946 and 1960, a large number of Dutch professional workers, with higher education, emigrated to Canada. The total numbers per year who came to Canada ranged from a low of 6 (in 1946) to a high of 504 (in 1953), adding up to a total of 3,596. If we look, during that period, at immigrants of all nationalities who were professionals, the vast majority (68.6 percent) came from Great Britain or the United States,[38] while only 3.9 percent of professional immigrants in Canada came from the Netherlands. Considering that the Dutch comprised 7.7 percent of total immigration during this period, professionals were certainly not overrepresented.[39] Like the bakers and Dutch retailers, the livelihood of these professionals, especially lawyers and doctors, initially depended on a Dutch-Canadian clientele. Consequently they were more closely bound, and contributed more, to the emerging Dutch-Canadian community. However, economic interests were not the only factor in the complex relationship between ethnic identity and occupation. Some Dutch-Canadian professionals kept up their heritage, or established close links with fellow Netherlanders, even when such links had little bearing to their work (see interlude 14.2).

There are relatively fewer first-generation Dutch immigrant lawyers in Ontario. Canada's legal system is completely different from its Dutch counterpart and former law students in the Netherlands had to requalify before they could set up a practice in Canada: two years of law school and an additional two years to article. Most of the first Dutch-Canadian lawyers actually emigrated when they were still students. For example, one Dutch-Canadian lawyer in Hamilton was sponsored by his older brother before he had finished high school in Holland.[40] Another initially worked as a bartender while he went back to school. He was one of only five or six Dutch immigrants who thus made a career in law in Toronto, either with their own practice or as partners with Dutch-Canadian or non-Dutch lawyers. Nevertheless, all but one of these lawyers became involved in Dutch-Canadian organizations, including the Dutch-Canadian credit union movement and several professional and business associations. They were still *the* lawyers for the Dutch-Canadian community in 1993 and advertised in the ethnic press. By that time there were more second-generation Dutch-Canadians lawyers, including women, some of whom have joined the Dutch-Canadian Business and Professional Association in Toronto (see previous chapter).

Unlike lawyers, Dutch physicians who arrived in the fifties only had to do a year of internship before they could start a practice. Such immigrant doctors, mostly retired today, ended up in places with a heavy concentration of Dutch immigrants. In almost all cases, they had contacts with Dutch-Canadian associations, and five became honorary vice-consuls (see chapter 4).[41] A typical story of the immigrant physician is that of H.L. van Vierssen-Trip. Member of a prestigious Dutch Mennonite family (his father was a judge), Dr. Vierssen-Trip emigrated in 1951 with his wife and six children.[42] Like other immigrants, they could only take a hundred dollars per person with them, plus personal belongings. The latter included an automobile, which they drove from Nova Scotia to Saskatchewan with the help of a car mechanic from Holland. Trip had already decided he wanted to set up a practice in Hamilton during a prior trip to southern Ontario with a Dutch friend who lived in Rochester. Initially Rem Jongbloed, fieldman for the Christian Reformed church, invited this doctor to set up his practice in Jongbloed's home.[43] Trip's clientele were the young immigrant couples who were having children; between June 1952 and November 1962, Trip delivered 800 babies.[44] While running his practice in Hamilton, he became actively involved in the Dutch-Canadian community, like most other Dutch-Canadian physicians. Similarly Hans Westerberg, who established a family practice in Kingston, was still serving as honorary vice-consul for the Netherlands in 1993 (see interlude 14.2).[45] Another Dutch-Canadian doctor who served as honorary vice-consul is Otto Ackerman, who had his medical practice in Chatham.[46]

The Travel Business

Every major city has at least one Dutch-Canadian travel agency. This ethnic travel business gradually evolved from one specializing in the transport of immigrants to Canada and return trips of established Dutch-Canadians, to bringing in European tourists who combine tours of North America with visits to relatives in Canada. A person whose career reflects the travel industry's metamorphosis is Rimmer Tjalsma, who emigrated in

1950. After little more than a year of farm work, he got a job as fieldman for the Reformed church, which required him to accompany people of *hervormd* background on their train trip to Ontario, arrange temporary accommodations and find farm sponsors (see chapter 9).[47] The next step in his career was as landing agent for Holland-America Lines, a position that put him in touch with newly arriving immigrants. In 1957 he was placed in Montreal, but soon returned to Ontario to live in Willowdale.[48] However, transatlantic traffic for the steamship lines declined rapidly in the sixties, when air travel became less expensive than travel by boat. At this point Tjalsma left the company to work for the Dutch Canadian Alliance (DCA), then actively involved in booking charter flights to Amsterdam (see chapters 15 and 16). When new regulations forced the DCA to get out of the charter business, a Dutch-based organization called *Wereld Contact* asked Tjalsma to be their representative in Canada.[49]

Other Dutch-Canadians, with prior experience in the travel business in the Netherlands, set up travel agencies almost as soon as they arrived in Canada. Thus in Chatham, a small agency run by the Vellinga family became the nerve centre of the largely Dutch Protestant community for Kent county.[50] One of the first Dutch-Canadian agents for KLM in the Toronto-Hamilton area was Mr. Koops, who established his business in his home in Burlington.[51] During the first two decades of the postwar era, such travel agencies, like other small businesses, were associated with different sub-segments of the Dutch-Canadian community—at least in the minds of Dutch-Canadians. For example, the owner of Valentine Travel in Toronto is Reformed,[52] while one of his early competitors, Bill Brouwers in Oakville, came from a predominantly Roman Catholic region in the Netherlands. Brouwers, who started the Dutch-Canadian Entertainment Club, set up his own travel agency (Burloak Travel) in the mid-seventies, as a sideline to several other business enterprises.[53] The travel agencies mentioned so far, plus many others started prior to 1960, maintained strong links with the Dutch-Canadian population. The case of Gerry Van der Kley, who came to Canada in 1973, is somewhat different. He was invited to come to Canada to work for a Dutch travel bureau with a Toronto office; he then started his own company, Guardian Tours.[54] However, with the lower value for the dollar, fewer people made trips abroad and his business went under. Van der Kley then moved to Whitby, where he started an agency specializing in bringing Dutch tourists to Canada. When the people who organized the Mariahout reunion (see chapter 10) approached a Dutch travel agency, the Dutch agent in turn contacted Van der Kley in Whitby. He likewise booked flights for people from Europe interested in attending the Frisian picnic in Paris or the Andijker reunion in Aylmer.[55] However, he had little contact with the large Dutch-Canadian community in the Whitby area, illustrating the lower level of social contact between more recent immigrants and the earlier cohort of postwar Dutch immigrants.

Printing and Publishing

Another business that once involved Dutch-Canadian workers as well as consumers is printing and publishing. In the early fifties, a Dutch firm, Bosch and Keuning,[56] bought a printing plant in the Hamilton area, with the expectation that they would publish all the Dutch-language papers in Canada. Mr. Bosch personally supervised this operation, and they hired Dutch-Canadian printers who had recently emigrated.[57] One of his employees was Al van de Veen, who had initially moved to Harriston. Al was in charge of printing *The Pioneer*, the magazine for the Reformed community in Canada. Bosch and Keuning likewise hired Dick Farnhout, who had close connections with the newly established *Calvinist Contact*. He, too, moved to Hamilton from Exeter to join this new firm, which changed its name to Guardian Press to better blend into an English-speaking environment. Initially they also printed *De Nederlandse Courant*.[58] This company then diversified to publish other publications that were not Dutch-Canadian. To reduce their costs, they laid off already established Dutch-Canadian printers, who earned $85 a week, to hire newly arrived Dutch printers willing to work for $50. However, the lower labour costs did not compensate for lack of connections and ability to work in a North-American business environment, and Guardian Press lost several Dutch-Canadian business customers. As a result of this business failure, Mr. Bosch went back to Holland and his operation in Canada was sold to a Dutch-Canadian immigrant.[59]

The only other publishing firms that still cater to a specifically Dutch-Canadian readership have been smaller outfits, like Paideia Press in Jordan Station. Such publishers have little potential for growth because of linguistic assimilation which leads to a shrinking market. The same can be said for the ethnic newspapers mentioned in chapter 11. While not a good outlet for investment from a purely business perspective, they are still viable as family-based businesses. In contrast, other Dutch immigrants with prior experience in this field and other fields have applied their expertise in the broader Canadian context.

The Influence of Religion

Although my study did not include a systematic comparison based on a survey, I did not come across any evidence that might suggest Dutch Protestants were more likely to own their own business than Dutch

Catholics. People of all religious backgrounds, plus those with no religious affiliation, seem to be represented among the handful of people of Dutch background who made it to the top in the world of agribusiness, finance and retailing. The same applies to medium and smaller businesses. Dutch Catholics may be somewhat stronger in some sectors of agriculture (hogs and cash-cropping), but they are underrepresented in large-scale retail, nurseries and bakeries. However, when it comes to dairy producers, housing construction or nurseries, I did not detect any differences. I doubt if a more systematic study would find any but minor variations.[60] However, we cannot dismiss religion entirely when looking at the world of business.

The Canadian Reformed Business Sector

The Canadian Reformed community, a sub-group among Dutch-Canadian Calvinists, represents a small minority (see chapter 9), which is characterized by a high level of institutional completeness plus geographic concentration in specific localities. The fact that its members form a close-knit network—even more so than their Christian Reformed counterparts—plus their rejection of labour unions, affects the way that they do business. Because any form of collective bargaining unit leads to expulsion from the church, the choice of jobs is limited. Hence, a higher proportion of Canadian Reformed are predisposed to go into business on their own.[61] At the same time, those who are not self-employed often seek employers who belong to the same denomination.[62] Despite an official emphasis on harmony and "worker participation," such a situation is not immune to internal frictions and abuse.

In some cases, especially in more labour-intensive businesses, a Canadian Reformed employer might have a competitive advantage because he has a captive labour force. If the business is well organized and operating in a favourable market, harmonious and cooperative relations between workers and employer can result in higher productivity. On the other hand, in a less favourable economic environment, the employers might be tempted to depress wages and provide poor working conditions in order to undercut competitors. Under such circumstances, even devout and conscientious employees might be forced to seek work elsewhere or try to go into business on their own.[63] I learned about a half dozen businesses in southern Ontario with Canadian Reformed owners: an egg-processing plant in St. Marys, a foundry in Orangeville, a ditch-digging operation in Smithville, a factory in Guelph and several home-builders or renovators in these and other localities. Although these businesses vary in size—from small family enterprises to businesses with up to 30 employees—in every case both employers and almost all the employees belong to the same ethnic as well as religious category. In one medium-sized firm, workers complained about the worst working conditions they had ever encountered.[64] In another case, involving a highly successful and innovative firm, the workers seemed content with their pay and working conditions. Thus, while one cannot generalize about all businesses owned by people of a particular religious persuasion, the beliefs and social networks associated with that denomination are not irrelevant to understanding their place in the broader economic system.

Over the past few decades, the nature of Dutch-Canadian businesses and professional practices has changed. While Dutch-Canadian customers became increasingly less important in most realms of endeavour, the proportion of self-employed people has gradually increased; many people who started off "working out" gradually build up family enterprises or farms. Throughout the seventies and eighties, most Dutch-Canadian businesses also relied less and less on Dutch-Canadian workers, with the rapid drop in Dutch immigration and the availability of cheaper sources of labour. Only in specific businesses catering to a Dutch-Canadian clientele can we still talk about a direct connection between ethnicity and the world of making money. However, we should not ignore a related topic—the relative importance of the image or reputation of the Dutch, either in general, or in specific sectors like agriculture and horticulture. The whole question of the extent to which such perceptions may provide a competitive edge to any business whose owner is seen as "Dutch" will have to wait until part three.

Fieldnotes Interlude

14.1 Observational and analytical notes (including a sketch of a family business), based on an interview with Henk Bruinink, in Strathroy, May 15, 1991

The history of another bakery, Hollandia, illustrates the transformation of a family-sized operation into a limited company.

Henk Bruinink came to Canada from Enschede, Holland, in 1951, but under different circumstances than the Wiersma family of Chatham. Bruinink also came from a family of bakers, but he was much younger. His father ran their family bakery in Holland, and the son first emigrated to investigate possibilities of relocating. Henk spent four months working for a farmer, near Brantford, until he persuaded the son of a Frisian farmer to take his place. When he found out about a long-term lease for a bakery in Chatham, he wrote to his father, who sold their family business. Another brother and Henk's fiancée joined him in Canada. They all came to

Chatham, where the bakery was located, but not enough capital remained, not even in their Dutch bank account. So they all started working as employees, an interim arrangement before the lease started, until the owner changed his mind. Another opportunity came up when the owner of a Greek restaurant asked the family to start a bakery next door, in extra premises which included a kitchen. Henk baked pies in his spare time and took a job working for a moving and storage company. When he lost that job, the family was ready to buy their own business. Henk's sister ran the store front for them. A few years later that bakery, located on King Street, was sold to another Dutchman, who in turn sold it to Wiersma [described in this chapter]. From here on their family business followed quite a different trajectory.

After selling their business, the senior Mr. Bruinink made a trip to the Netherlands to buy Dutch equipment to set up another bakery in Canada. In the meantime, Henk Bruinink moved back to Brantford and became a salesman of machines to make cookies. One day he passed by a small store owned by a woman in Mount Brydges. The store was in a run-down condition, but it was in a beautiful location, and Henk's father already had his eyes on it. Henk Bruinink bought that outfit for only 750 dollars and his father invested additional money to turn it into a bakery. They then invited Tony, his brother, who was washing cars in Chatham, to join the family business again. He was interested in going on the road to sell bread for them. A Christian Reformed minister they knew in nearby Strathroy helped them to get their first corporate customer, an IGA supermarket, and soon business was booming. Their Dutch-style baked goods were popular and they could hardly keep up with the demand. Soon they employed four young women recently arrived from Holland and then hired their first Dutch-trained pastry chef. Mr. Bruinink, Sr., made another trip to Holland to buy more equipment and next bought an old dairy bar in Mount Brydges. This became their new location after undergoing extensive renovations; the new bakery was equipped with two revolving ovens. At this point, Henk's brother-in-law, a bookkeeper in Toronto, joined the business as well.

In the sixties their business, called Hollandia, expanded, and they became a limited company with an additional partner, the Kannet Corporation in the Netherlands. Henk Bruinink spent six months in Europe learning how to operate new equipment capable of running twenty-four hours a day for months on end. This resulted in a "cookie explosion."

14.2 *Analytical note on the ethnic identity of first-generation physicians, and social contacts with their own ethnic constituency; based on an interview in Kingston, December 18, 1989*

Dr. Hans Westerberg came to Canada as a medical student in 1961 and started his practice in Kingston in 1964. Like other doctors, he has extensive contacts with other Dutch-Canadians professionals, including Dutch professors recruited at Queen's University. He has promoted cultural activities for Dutch-Canadians, ranging from the Canadian Association for the Advancement of Netherlandic Studies to a Dutch social club in Kingston. Unlike many other Dutch-Canadian physicians, most of Westerberg's patients are not of Dutch background, although he is under constant pressure to take on his fellow countrymen as patients.

Chapter 15

The Dutch Credit Union Movement

Unlike Quebec or western Canada, Ontario has no tradition of cooperative institutions. In the forties, people in the heartland of English Canada were still leery of credit unions; some saw them as an extension of trade unionism while others equated them with the Catholic Church.[1] Postwar immigrants from different parts of Europe were to play an important part in the subsequent building of a powerful network of credit unions in the province. Initially the Dutch were ignorant of this fledgling credit union movement in Ontario; they did not realize that any group of people (parish, ethnic constituency or company employees) could become incorporated as a savings and loan association with twelve signatures. Once they associated credit unions with the co-operative banking system started by Friedrich Raiffeisen in Europe, Dutch immigrants started joining existing credit unions. Others built up their own cooperative financial institutions. Such ethnically based credit unions served more than financial functions, since they were also a vehicle for social interaction, which generated choirs and ethnic clubs (see chapter 16).[2] Yet credit unions were not immune from class tension as we saw in the case of Toronto (see chapter 12).[3] The credit union movement also reproduced the Dutch pillar system.

The Development of Dutch-Canadian Credit Unions

The first credit unions founded by Dutch immigrants were shoestring operations, set up in someone's home or in a church basement.[4] They were run by volunteers, with prewar immigrants sometimes acting as cultural brokers and advisors.[5] Initially these credit unions provided mainly consumer loans for a used car, fridge or down payment on a house, while

Notes to this chapter are on p. 394-99.

farmers might borrow no more than what they needed to buy a young sow or calf.[6] They all experienced difficulties, often resulting from the contrasting visions of Dutch immigrants and government officials in charge of enforcing the rules. Such divergence in dispositions could create minor disagreements. For example, some inspectors insisted that each credit union started by Dutch immigrants include the adjective "Dutch-Canadian" in its name, whereas many local groups wanted a religious designation.

Not all Dutch immigrants were equally enthusiastic about forming their own credit unions. Many people did not like the idea of a neighbour or someone from the same congregation knowing about their earnings or what they owed. Moreover, members who were not successful in getting loans sometimes accused loan committees of personal bias. Even when such difficulties were overcome, some credit unions did not grow beyond several hundred members and continued to operate as strictly savings and consumer loan operations. Nevertheless, the rest slowly picked up momentum, until credit unions reached the point where they could offer more substantial loans, residential mortgages and eventually business credit.[7] They hired part-time and later full-time managers, thus providing employment for immigrants who had a background in accounting and management.[8] With the advent of credit union newsletters, which were also an avenue for advertising, Dutch-Canadian entrepreneurs saw the possibility of tapping into a larger network of potential clients.

The fifties was a decade of rapid growth, with the establishment of 15 Dutch-Canadian credit unions, spread out all over the province, from Trenton in the east to Sarnia in the west, from Toronto to Thunder Bay in the north.[9] During the seventies they became more inclusive, as ethnically based credit unions started recruiting a broader membership; their executive members, however, were still for the most part Dutch-Canadians. Most of these original Dutch-Canadian credit unions survived, sometimes with new names; in 1979 there were still 10, with a wide range in assets and type of membership.[10] At that time they were all still loosely linked together under a larger umbrella known as the Dutch-Canadian Alliance.

The Dutch Canadian Alliance (DCA)

The DCA was founded in 1965 as a way to coordinate "affinity" charters for travel abroad.[11] Two larger credit unions, St. Willibrord of London and DUCA in Toronto, were already organizing charter flights, in collaboration with Dutch-Canadian travel agencies.[12] However, other credit unions were too small to do so. The idea of an umbrella organization to coordinate charter flights for everybody came from a Dutchman who worked for Koop's Travel Agency in Burlington (see previous chapter). He approached Dick Gaasenbeek, at that time on the Hamilton Netherlands Credit Union's board of directors.[13] Consequently 13 Dutch-Canadian credit unions jointly set up a non-profit organization that could book flights to Europe, thereby attracting additional credit union members.[14] Interest was high enough that the DCA was able to hire a part-time and then full-time manager (one of whom, Tjalsma, we met earlier). The DCA, which had a board of directors with representatives from participating credit unions, also took over a funeral insurance scheme from the Toronto Dutch-Canadian Credit Union and made it available to other Dutch credit unions. This group life term insurance with a small death benefit was a typically Dutch plan.[15] However, starting in the seventies, the travel business witnessed a major transformation. New government regulations affected the charter flights, which had previously been intimately connected to travel or entertainment clubs. DCA sold its travel business, and continued to function under a new mandate—to support charitable activities within the sphere of influence of the Dutch-Canadian credit unions.[16]

Contraction and Expansion

In the early seventies, around the time the charter flights ended, smaller Dutch-Canadian credit unions disappeared.[17] The first to go were those associated with the Reformed community, in Thunder Bay, Clinton, Trenton, Brampton and Barrie. The Christian Reformed (Clinton) Credit Union, which had lasted for 16 years, simply dissolved.[18] Similarly, a tiny Christian Reformed church credit union in Sarnia, with about 120 members, folded in 1975.[19] Some Dutch credit unions amalgamated with larger ones. In 1976, the Hamilton Netherlands Credit Union, which had already changed its name to DUCA Hamilton, was amalgamated with the Hamilton Mountain Credit Union.[20] More credit unions succumbed to a rise in interest rates in the eighties, while others disappeared due to bad management or internal squabbling.[21]

The further evolution of the Dutch-Canadian credit union movement reflects broader economic trends. Between 1980 and 1990, additional credit unions folded. The once-successful Dutch Canadian (Kent) Credit Union, in Chatham, was the first to go. It had expanded up until the 1980s,[22] but ceased operations in 1991. The DUCA Credit Union (Peterborough), with about 400 members, also closed its doors. Of the smaller credit unions, only the Sydenham, formerly Dutch Canadian (Strathroy) Credit Union, with branch offices in Mount Brydges and Park Hill, was still operating in 1995. With that exception, only the "big players" remain. Today many non-Dutch members of these remaining credit unions are no longer aware of the Dutch connections and ongoing Dutch-Canadian control; yet the Dutch-Canadian credit union movement still has symbolic value, albeit open to different interpretations. For many Dutch-Canadians and their non-Dutch friends, the emergence of the Dutch credit unions in the past, and the survival of the high profile ones, epitomizes good business sense as a hallmark of *the Dutch*. A director of the DUCA board once pointed out how they have "gained the respect of the banking establishment." In contrast, a Dutch-Canadian from the financial "upper crust," who sits on corporate boards, told me he was ashamed that so many Dutch credit unions had folded. He claimed that gave the Dutch "a bad name" among members of Canada's financial establishment. It is hard to live up to a reputation!

While most of the original credit unions folded, the remaining ones expanded and took over non-Dutch credit unions; St. Willibrord had nine branches when they celebrated their fortieth anniversary in 1990.[23] Another successful credit union is DUCA of Toronto. After merging with the Dutch Credit Union (Oshawa) in 1988, the new DUCA counted 11 branch offices in the Greater Toronto area. According to its 1989 annual report, DUCA had over 300 million dollars in total assets with over 31,000 members.[24] With further growth came the acquisition of offices and the changeover to computerized operations. However, these two credit unions are quite different from each other and merit a closer look.

A Comparison of DUCA and St. Willibrord

While sharing common features, the two largest credit unions founded by Dutch immigrants exhibit different ethnic dynamics and styles of conducting business. They also operate in contrasting socio-economic regions. DUCA is a city credit union, today catering to a diverse metropolitan population. All its branches are located within or close to Metropolitan Toronto, and its members have always been urban workers or business people. In contrast, St. Willibrord has both city and rural members, and provides special services for farmers. Unlike the geographically more concentrated credit union in Toronto, its branch offices are located in four counties and its membership in nine counties.

Similarities and Differences

DUCA and St. Willibrord were each founded by Dutch-Canadians who shared a common vision of cooperative banking, and also had some prior business experience.[25] The men who have served over the years as their boards' presidents were small businessmen or professionals, although people from diverse occupational backgrounds (including farmers in the case of St. Willibrord) served as members of their boards of directors, supervisory and credit committees. Both credit unions recruited capable managers at crucial stages of their development. Each credit union also expanded from an ethnic constituency to include a sizable number of members not of Dutch descent as they became transformed into more general community credit unions. In other respects, they followed quite different trajectories.

St. Willibrord received its charter on January 25, 1951, under the name Dutch Catholic Immigrants (London) Credit Union Ltd. The name was changed to St. Willibrord (London) Credit Union on February 15, 1953. Apart from several Dutch priests who were involved in the beginning (see chapter 8), its most active members included a core of Dutch-Canadian farmers who had been independent operators and community leaders in the Netherlands. For a long time the credit union's centre of activity was the rural area of eastern Lambton and western Middlesex, although the head office was located in the city of London.[26] Initially there were some tensions between urban and rural members; the majority of the latter (originally borrowers) were interested in low interest rates, while the former (the depositors) wanted to get as high a rate of return on their money as possible. However, such strains were kept in check due to crosscutting linkages between farm and non-farm business operations.[27]

DUCA was founded on May 6, 1954 by 24 immigrants under the name Dutch Canadian Toronto Credit Union. The shorter acronym was proposed in 1962, but not ratified until 1971 when they became DUCA (Toronto) Credit Union.[28] At that time the credit union expanded to areas on the outskirts of Metropolitan Toronto.[29] Unlike St. Willibrord, this Toronto area credit union never developed the expertise or interest in doing business with farmers. Their mandate was to provide financial services to people working and doing business in a large urban centre. To stimulate savings, DUCA held draws for members depositing their family allowances. City businesses became important customers, and DUCA also had the advantage of being located in the fastest-growing market in North America. For several decades these two Dutch-Canadian credit unions were friendly rivals. In 1964, they each reached the one million dollar mark in assets, but during the seventies DUCA outstripped St. Willibrord.[30] By 1990, the gap in assets per member had narrowed, although DUCA was 35 percent greater in membership and monetary value.[31]

Contrasting Ethnic Symbols

DUCA and St. Willibrord displayed contrasting ethnic dynamics. The original DUCA was as much an ethnic club as a credit union, and its organizers held car rallies, dances and St. Nicholas children's parties. DUCA even had its own choir. When the credit union had enough space, several Dutch-Canadian cultural organizations used their facilities. Indeed, the group of people who ran the Toronto credit union strove to develop a cohesive working group based on their shared ethnicity.[32] In contrast, the credit union in London has always been quite separate from the Dutch-Canadian Society, which built its own club building (see chapter 16). While most club members joined St. Willibrord, only two people with a leadership role in the credit union were actively involved in that association.[33] St. Willibrord also developed a very different type of relationship with the broader, non-Dutch population.

Leaders of both credit unions decided to change their bond of association from a purely ethnic to a community-based one in the early seventies. DUCA was the first to get permission to open its membership to all people residing in North York, regardless of ethnic origin. They also hired their first non-Dutch employee in 1974.[34] Nonetheless, their bond with the rest of Metropolitan Toronto remained ethnically based. The opening of a branch office in Scarborough, inside the Philips plant, was based on an obvious Dutch connection, and the subsequent takeover of the former Christian Reformed Credit Union in Brampton again reinforced the Dutch link. According to the manager, Cees Bijl, DUCA remained very "Dutch" because the whole board and all but one staff member were Dutch-Canadians. Many business transactions were still conducted in Dutch despite their official community bond (see chapter 11). Not until 1983, when DUCA bought out the Torcity Savings and Credit Union Ltd, could they legally recruit more non-Dutch members in the city of Toronto. However, a takeover of the Dutch credit union in Oshawa in 1988 again brought in what had hitherto been an almost exclusively Dutch-Canadian institution. The opening of a new branch in Orangeville a year later, also served a predominantly Dutch-Canadian group of people. Nevertheless, with the rapid increase in non-Dutch and English-speaking second-generation members, the Dutch connection of DUCA became less noticeable to outsiders.[35] New non-Dutch members are unlikely to attend the annual meeting, where the ongoing Dutch nature of DUCA is more apparent. Moreover, with a shortage of established Canadians willing to work as tellers, the Toronto branches of DUCA started hiring newly arrived immigrants from Asia and other parts of the world. By 1990, only about 20 percent of the staff could still speak Dutch if necessary, another 20 percent were Dutch-Canadians who didn't really speak Dutch and the rest had no Dutch connection whatsoever.[36] The majority of branch managers (eight) also have no Dutch allegiance. Yet all but one board director is Dutch-Canadian, and DUCA maintains close ties with the Dutch-Canadian Association of Greater Toronto.[37] Given the multiethnic and cosmopolitan nature of Toronto, such ethnic traits are not unusual. This is not the case for small-town and rural Ontario.

St. Willibrord officially became a community credit union (at least for London) around the same time as Toronto's DUCA. The change in status occurred when the formerly Dutch and Flemish Catholic St. Willibrord merged with the Co-op Services (London) Credit Union in 1977 through a buy-sell agreement. That credit union, which had a large building with its own staff, became a full-fledged branch with its own delegates and a local council. An enlarged board received two new members, including a former director of Co-op Services, Nick van Osch, a Dutch postwar immigrant who had earlier belonged to St. Willibrord. However, the other new board member, Paul Cartney, had no Dutch connections. Additional executive positions were likewise filled by people not of Dutch background.[38] While Nick had no trouble fitting into St. Willibrord, the non-Dutch members of the former Co-op credit union felt apprehensive.[39] In order to fully integrate them, it became crucial to de-emphasize the Dutch connection. The London credit union's early "Canadianization" was thus accelerated by the incorporation of active executive members who were not Dutch.[40]

Notwithstanding an early transition to the use of English, and the influx of non-Dutch members, St. Willibrord still looks "Dutch" to many non-Dutch members. One member of a branch council reported the following during an interview:

> St. Willibrord was and still is Dutch-oriented. You can certainly tell that at the annual meetings; more than fifty percent of those who attend are of Dutch origin. The Dutch are also still the biggest depositors.... They are still trying to get away from that stigma but they havn't been able to change the name, except that they added the word "community." The people who keep on defeating the motion to change the name are the older Dutch people. They are still sticking against it.... At the annual meetings I have also noticed that the Dutch farmers form into their own little groups and speak their native language.[41]

The high profile of the Dutch-Canadian farmers, who were probably speaking the dialect of Noord Brabant, is due to the credit union's strong rural component. The area west of London has a significant concentration of Dutch-Canadian farmers (see chapters 6 and 8). Many were teenagers when they came to Canada and they married within their own ethnic community. Their elderly, but still influential, parents insisted that the name St. Willibrord be retained; in some cases, as their last wish before dying. Moreover, prior to 1983, people not of Dutch descent in the rural townships of Middlesex and Lambton counties were not eligible to join St. Willibrord, thus reinforcing the already large Dutch-Canadian rural contingent. The predominance of Dutch-Canadian farmers is thus the main factor underlying the continuing, albeit minor, ethnic tensions of St. Willibrord over a decade after the amalgamation.

In 1980, when St. Willibrord took over a former community credit union in Blenheim, there was increasing pressure to change their Dutch image. The Blenheim operation was originally called St. Mary's Parish Credit Union and had been set up under the close supervision of Flemish priests (see chapter 10). However, that credit union had long ago become a multiethnic institution, and their many non-Dutch and non-Flemish members were apprehensive about an amalgamation with a "Dutch" credit union.[42] After its incorporation, people living within a certain radius of Blenheim automatically became eligible to join St. Willibrord,[43] although the ethnic bond still applied to some other rural regions within the diocese of London. The last breakthrough occurred when the broader community bond, formerly applied only to London, Blenheim and Stratford, was extended to all of Middlesex and Lambton counties. This change in legal status allowed the largely non-Dutch downtown business community of Watford, previously without any bank services, to petition the credit union to set up a new branch in their town. Such new members were quickly integrated into St. Willibrord's decentralized system of decision making, consisting of a structure of local delegates who also sit on a regional board. Since an increasing number of professionals and business owners not of Dutch descent rubbed shoulders with their Dutch-Canadian counterparts, the Dutch-Canadian directors had to work harder to emphasize their community bond. Its directors are not ashamed of their Dutch heritage, but go out of the way to counteract any possible ethnic tensions resulting from the entry of people not of Dutch descent into their governing body.[44]

DUCA actually has more regular non-Dutch members, and a higher proportion of non-Dutch staff employees. Nevertheless, due to the low level of involvement of non-Dutch on the board of directors, they do not have to be as worried about how their credit union might be perceived. *Ducapost*, their newsletter, regularly advertises flights to Amsterdam and announces the currency exchange rate between Canada and the Netherlands.[45] As recently as 1988, the following public statement could still be made:

> Outside of the Cities of Toronto and North York, DUCA is "officially" a Dutch Credit Union. DUCA's Dutch background is the foundation on which this organization built its success and we pride ourselves in having a very important position and name in the Dutch-Canadian community. We particularly feel a strong obligation to the Dutch-Canadian seniors. . . . Our Brampton office, in Holland Christian Homes is specifically geared to this group, with personalized service available in Dutch, Frisian, and English.[46]

St. Willibrord's directors criticize such open displays of a Dutch connection. They feel DUCA is "too Dutch" because older members in Toronto speak so much Dutch among themselves.[47] Yet a much greater percentage of the managers and staff of St. Willibrord, especially those who are younger, have Dutch names. One could also point out that St. Willibrord's system of choosing representatives is almost identical to the way the members of the Dutch senate (*Eerste Kamer*) are elected by members of their provincial parliaments (*Provinciale Staten*); local credit union council members are elected by members of a particular branch, who in turn elect directors at the general annual meeting in London.[48] In addition, about half the staff members of local branches also have Dutch-Canadian spouses. So which institution is more "Dutch"? It depends on your point of view.[49]

Dutch-Canadians in Other Credit Unions

Dutch-Canadians also joined, and assumed leadership roles, in credit unions that did not have any ethnic connotations, especially in small towns where people had already set up credit unions. For example, in the Barrie area, Martin de Groot served for several years as an executive member of the Innisfil Farmers Credit Union in Stroud and was subsequently asked to take part in a parish credit union in Phelpston. Dutch Catholic immigrants who lived in Uxbridge also joined an already established credit union, where Bill Keyzers, a Dutch-Canadian printer and publisher, became one of their directors.[50] In other places, small parish credit unions even became de facto Dutch-Canadian organizations.

The Halton Community Credit Union

The former Holy Rosary Parish Credit Union in Milton can be used to illustrate a non-ethnic credit union that went through a "Dutch phase." This credit union was set up in 1958 by Scottish and Irish immigrants, many of whom worked in the factories of De Haviland, Ford and General Motors. Together with more established English-speaking Canadians, they dominated both the parish and its credit union.[51] Gradually a number of Dutch-Canadian parishioners also signed up to become members. In 1961, when the treasurer of the credit union was having problems with the books, Jules Fryters was asked to join their supervisory committee. Although he was working in the steel plant in Milton, Jules had received training as an accountant. He balanced their accounts, and was asked to become part-time treasurer. By 1964, the credit union was getting big enough to hire a full-time manager. Again, they recruited Jules Fryters, who quit his job at a plastics factory. Under his supervision, the credit union grew rapidly, but it also became dominated by Dutch-Canadians.

Jules realized the credit union operated in much the same manner as the *Boerenleenbank* in the Netherlands. He pointed this out when he recruited rural Dutch families in the Milton area. Although they did not make up more than 15 percent of the parish, within a couple of years half the credit union's membership was Dutch-Canadian.[52] The Dutch also displaced the Scottish and Irish on the board. While not eligible to join the Dutch Canadian Alliance, Jules Fryters had contact with other credit unions run by Dutch-Canadians. Indeed, some people spoke of the "Milton Dutch-Canadian credit union" (*sic*!). By 1969, the manager and directors of the Dutch-dominated parish credit union opened up their bond, against the wishes of the parish priest, thus turning it into the Milton (and later, Halton) Community Credit Union. The new community credit union later took over seven smaller credit unions in Georgetown and Acton. Most of them became branch offices and two of them ended up with managers of Dutch Protestant background. However, by 1997 there was only one director of Dutch background on their board.

The Dutch-Canadian Credit Unions and the Pillar System

The replication of Dutch patterns of social interaction and a pillar mentality applies as much to credit unions as it does to other facets of the Dutch Canadian experience. Of the fifteen Dutch-Canadian credit unions set up in the fifties, seven had a religious as well as an ethnic bond. The rest were non-denominational, although in some cases (such as Chatham) they were dominated by Christian Reformed members. However, none of the credit unions set up by Dutch immigrants were immune from the tensions, and the need for accommodation, between the various religious and non-religious segments of the Dutch-Canadian population. Nor did the legal or official status of institutions always correspond to the way they were perceived or even how they operated.

St. Willibrord Credit Union was originally set up only for Catholics of Dutch and Flemish descent in the diocese of London. While still operating under this religious bond, Dutch Calvinists or Dutch people without religious affiliation living in the same region had to set up their own Dutch-Canadian or Christian Reformed credit unions. Thus, in 1951, the same year that St. Willibrord received its charter, the largely Dutch Protestant community in Chatham established the Dutch Canadian (Kent) Credit Union Ltd. Although not officially defined in terms of church affiliation, both its founders and the majority of members were drawn from the several Reformed denominations in Chatham and its surroundings. Dutch Catholics in the Chatham area either joined St. Willibrord or smaller parish credit unions with Flemish connections, such as in Blenheim. An explicit religious bond was adopted in the case of the credit union set up by a group of Calvinist farmers in Clinton, and a small credit union was later organized by a group of Christian Reformed labourers in Sarnia.

Over time, religious labels, and the distinction between religious and secular, became less pronounced, though not irrelevant. When St. Willibrord was still officially Catholic as well as ethnic, some Dutch Protestants did join. However, the incorporation of non-Catholic members did not go without a hitch after the stipulation about being Catholic was dropped. In Sarnia, members of the Christian Reformed community were hesitant to join St. Willibrord, which they perceived as a typical Catholic organization. Only when a man belonging to the Christian Reformed Church was appointed manager of the Sarnia branch, did members of that denomination start joining. The directors in London were aware that the Sarnia branch would only grow if the much larger and more cohesive Dutch Protestant community became involved. Thus the new manager encouraged a local contractor in Sarnia, who was an informal leader within the Reformed community, to stand for election for the local board. The contractor persuaded fellow church members to join, with the argument that the person after whom the credit union was named had brought Christianity to the Netherlands prior to the Reformation.[53] When the issue of a name change was raised at the annual meeting of 1990, this board member argued that it not be altered because "at least it is a Christian name."[54]

Even when the credit unions abandoned their religious and ethnic bonds, first-generation immigrants thought and acted according to categories of the Dutch pillar system. When a group of Protestant Dutch immigrants formed the Dutch Canadian (Strathroy) Credit Union, in 1957, the Christian Reformed Church did not want to open an institutional account. While the majority on the board were church members, the minister and more traditional elders were hesitant to give their support to what was officially an ethnic and secular organization.[55] Yet meetings of the credit union, held in the Strathroy Christian Reformed church, were regularly opened with a prayer and the singing of psalms and hymns.[56] After much persuasion, the church and several church organizations did open up accounts the following year, in what was a de facto Dutch Calvinist credit union. The board of directors and employees were still predominantly of orthodox Calvinist persuasion after 1982, when it adopted a non-Dutch name (Sydenham) and became a community credit union. They also resisted amalgamation with St. Willibrord, which then opened a full-service branch in a nearby downtown location—a classic example of Dutch pillarization in a Canadian small-town context. Today the manager of Sydenham emphasizes its Canadian status and interdenominational character. But the world view and ongoing pattern of social interaction of their older, charter members is quite different. During an interview with one of their founders, who lives in a predominantly Dutch Calvinist home for the elderly, I came across the following depiction of the credit unions in Strathroy:

> We had three groups here: our credit union, St. Willibrord and also something resembling the SDAP or Workers Party in the Netherlands. Its director was——, yes a Canadian. That was for people who did not belong to any church. Yes, it also had Dutch-Canadian members—probably about ten percent—and some came from Amsterdam. That credit union doesn't exist any more.[57]

The third credit union in the quote, which he depicted as "neutral" (and by implication socialist and anti-religious), was a small employees' credit union, which included Dutch-Canadian workers from the furniture factory owned by Philips in Strathroy—a credit union later taken over by Sydenham.

Although individual members of the Christian Reformed Church took part in other Dutch-Canadian credit unions—in Chatham, St. Catharines, Hamilton, Peterborough and Oshawa—none came that close to becoming de-facto Dutch Protestant ones. For example, the Hamilton Netherlands Credit Union (see interlude 15.1) was founded by professionals from different religious backgrounds: a biology professor at McMaster who was a secular Jew; Viersen-Trip, the physician of Dutch Mennonite background whom we encountered in an earlier chapter; an atheist; and two Christian Reformed men.[58] What bound them together was their common ethnic identity; all but one of these charter members had earlier been involved in setting up a cultural organization called the *Nederlandse Vereniging*, and until 1962, all credit union members had to first join this organization. Soon after the credit union's founding, Dutch Catholics were also elected to sit on various committees and subsequently there was always at least one Catholic on the board. This emphasis on mutual respect and collaboration among diverse segment of the Dutch-Canadian community became a norm, as revealed in a statement in the 1976 annual report: "It's great to see Frisians and Amsterdammers work so closely and pleasantly together."[59]

Notwithstanding this ideal, the credit union had a stormy political history, which involved bids to oust board members, the resignation of a manager and internal factional struggles. However, these internal disputes, which cut across ideological or religious lines, more often reflected cleavages associated with the Dutch system of social stratification (see chapters 12 and 16) than with religious opposition. At one point, the original officers of the *Vereniging*, considered too "snobbish" by the membership at large, tried to dominate and take control of the credit union. They were defeated in 1962 when the by-laws for membership were changed so that one no longer had to be a member of their Dutch organization. Three years later Dick Gaasenbeek, the young Dutch-Canadian lawyer we met in the chapter on class standing, took over as president. He had joined the Presbyterian church, but considered himself "neutral." He collaborated closely with Arie Verduijn, an industrial engineer (without a university degree) who worked for Stelco, but who was an active member of the Christian Reformed community.[60]

The credit union in Peterborough was run more along the lines of the Dutch pillar system. The main founder of that credit union was Jack van Winssen, an engineer who worked for General Electric. He and his wife (of Frisian descent) attended the United Church and were involved in a credit union set up by the employees of the firm where he worked. However, in the early sixties Jack helped to organize a Dutch-Canadian credit union.[61] Catholics, Christian Reformed and those who attended mainstream Canadian Protestant churches or had no religious affiliation each comprised about a third of their membership, and they went out of their way to make sure all three were represented on their executive. Nevertheless the participation of the Christian Reformed members in both the membership and the executive went up over time.[62] This trend reflects the local Reformed community's greater institutional strength and cohesion.

Reformed members who have sat on the boards of Dutch-Canadian credit unions like the ones in Peterborough or Hamilton made it quite clear that such credit unions were not officially Calvinist and had no connection with the churches to which they belonged.[63] These statements are consistent with the practice of such credit unions to provide space for secular social activities, including card playing (e.g., *klaverjassen*), something frowned upon by orthodox Calvinists until recently. Nevertheless, in accordance with the mindset and dispositions of Dutch orthodox Calvinists, many people automatically associated such organizations with members of their own denomination as part of the network of Reformed institutions they label as "Christian." Likewise, Catholic or non-religious Dutch immigrants frequently assumed that any form of Christian Reformed participation automatically meant that "the *gereformeerden* have taken over." In the case of the Hamilton credit union, this impression was reinforced by the active role played by two Reformed men, including one long-standing manager and a former board president (who also acted as secretary).

The same pillar mentality operated within Toronto DUCA. Discussions reported in early minutes of board meetings stress the importance of recruiting both Dutch Catholics and the Christian Reformed community in order for the credit union to succeed. Indeed, special contact persons were appointed for both sub-segments of Toronto's Dutch-Canadian community.[64] Yet during the mid-sixties and early seventies, several DUCA board members expressed concerns about the credit union's religious connections, especially in regard to cooperation with *Wereld Contact*, the Dutch travel organization. In a typed summary of a discussion held in 1971 between the DUCA and the board of the Dutch Canadian Alliance, a Toronto representative raised the objection that religious affiliation with the Christian Reformed Church was stressed too much.[65] Christian Reformed members of DUCA in turn accused DUCA of becoming too "neutral," and complained that they no longer felt they "fitted in" because the credit union was not only non-denominational but becoming blatantly anti-religious.[66] Orthodox Calvinists also did not like it when the executive voted to allow the consumption of alcoholic beverages at their annual dinner and dance.[67] Other members were preoccupied with the notion that their organization was becoming dominated by Jews because of the involvement of several secular Dutch Jews and one orthodox Jewish Dutch couple.[68] Later, when several Catholics became more actively involved, DUCA was suddenly seen by some people as *rooms* ("Roman" [Catholic]). The hiring of a Protestant manager (who joined an evangelical congregation) and the election of someone who belonged to the Christian Reformed Church, brought forth rumours about a gradual takeover by the "*gereformeerden*."

The Dutch-Canadian credit union movement was truly representative of postwar Dutch immigrants. Apart from including people from a diversity of religious and political backgrounds, its Dutch-Canadian membership consisted of people from a wide range of city occupations, from janitors to company executives, although its more active core was solidly middle class (small business and professionals). It should thus not come as a surprise that these credit unions reflected the dispositions of people brought up within a society dominated by both accommodation and tensions among various pillars. Moreover, they were characterized by the same complexities and ethnic ambiguities typical of other 'fields' relevant to the lives of postwar Dutch-Canadians.

Fieldnotes Interlude

15.1 *Excerpts from* Sojourners (A Family Chronicle) *by Arie Verduijn (published in 1981 by the author)*

Having greatly benefited from belonging to Credit Unions, I felt strongly that such a cooperative financial enterprise should be chartered for the many people of Dutch descent in the Hamilton area, who otherwise had no chance to join one. Several times I suggested to Board members of the *Nederlandse Vereniging* to take the initiative. Dr. Trip, who himself had been helped by Credit Unions, finally persuaded his colleagues on the Board to do so. On 26 March 1956 Rem Jongbloed, the Secretary, sent out letters inviting members to do so.... The office was located in Dr. Trip's basement. It was a start of great things to come (p. 330).

... At the end of the first fiscal year, the Dutch Credit Union had a loss of $88.62. At a board meeting on 17 September a motion was accepted to pay the treasurer $200. I objected, since this money would have to be taken out of share capital (p. 338).

... At the annual meeting of the Credit Union in Robert's Restaurant on 13 February [1962] we learned that there were now 200 members, not all of whom were members of the *Nederlandse Vereniging*. Compulsory membership in this society had to be stricken from the Bylaws. Share capital was $15,000, deposits $38,888 and loans outstanding $16,000. A modest dividend could be paid (p. 374).

... As a member of the Credit Committee I started again to share the load in the Dutch Credit Union [1964]. Its first charter flight for $275 came two years too late for us (p. 386).

... As secretary of the Dutch Credit Union [1965], with now $100,000 assets, I made an analysis of its vulnerability. If only 29 out of the 634 members took their money out, the assets would be cut in half. 60% of the members were so in name only. Each one cost the Credit Union $2.29 per year. Clearly we needed more active members and so, with my friend ____ [in] Caledonia, we promoted the movement in the Chr. Ref. Church of York, signing up members (p. 391).

... I must admit that initially I was very upset about the outcome of this election in which I lost my seat on the Board. But when the interest squeeze in the following years got worse, I pitied the poor guys in charge. Of course, Klaas and I were blamed anyway for the many low interest rate mortgages still on the books, but we had not been the only Board members (p. 453-54).

15.2 *Excerpt from a transcription of a taped interview with Jose Cozijn, manager of the Stratford branch of St. Willibrord Credit Union, April 28, 1990 [names omitted]*

There were problems at the credit union and all of a sudden our Stratford office here was closed. So ____ hit the road to try to find a replacement. There had been a disagreement between the cashier here and London and they weren't going to open the doors again until the problem was resolved.

At the end of August, in 1969, ____ phoned and asked if we could come over. ____ and ____ had come over from London and we sat around the dining room table and talked about the credit union. ____ was all excited because he was fighting to keep the office here. You see, they had already gone to see several people, always male. I was the first woman they had interviewed; they had never had a woman cashier before. . . .

It was a tough decision to make because I had young children and one of them was going to kindergarten. I also already had an office job where I could set my own hours. I worked in the afternoons and was able to be home before the children came home from school. But _____ talked me into trying for at least six months. If it didn't work out, they would call it quits in Stratford. So I took it on. It was an opportunity to stay home with the kids and I liked working with figures and with people.

That time was still a difficult period; the credit union was still suffering growing pains. Yes, I was able to work at home. Like I said, we used our old kitchen table which was put in the family room, by the front door, and we had a roll-out vault that was sitting beside our bed. And the filing cabinet was in my daughter's bedroom. We had no other place to put it . . . it was quite an experience because lots of people—many of whom I knew from the Benelux Club—would come in to see me to tell me about how they had not been able to get loans in the past (while others did), and so had an opportunity to get a chip off their shoulder about the credit union. It seemed that for two years I did nothing else but listen to complaints. But still, we grew slowly. We stayed alive and gradually it got busier all the time.

Chapter 16

Dutch-Canadian Social and Cultural Associations

Dutch-Canadian organizations provide men and women with similar dispositions an opportunity to socialize with like-minded people. The crosscutting links among such organizations, some of which are still active today, tie together the diverse components that define the Dutch-Canadian community. Their members, most of whom came to Canada around the same time, experienced a gradual process of transformation from immigrants to Dutch-Canadians within the broader context of Canada's cultural policy. We will explore numerous connections between such organizations and the groups and institutions already covered elsewhere. This chapter will also outline the part played by Canadians of Dutch descent in forging the new 'sub-field' of multiculturalism.

With the exception of some privately owned ventures, Dutch-Canadian social and cultural associations were sustained through membership fees, contributions from local businesses (who advertised in club bulletins) and, to some extent after 1975, support from the Secretary of State.[1] These ethnic associations varied in origin and in organizational structures.[2] Nevertheless, one can generalize to some degree. Most would fall under the category of "clubs," in the sense of people gathering on a regular basis for some specific purpose.[3] Dutch-Canadian clubs with an ethnic label normally do not have anything to do with religion, although the majority of members often turn out to be Catholics or people of Catholic background.[4] The next largest membership categories would be Dutch Protestants affiliated with mainstream Canadian churches, and people without religious affiliation, with neo-Calvinists constituting a small minority. In terms of occupation or gender, professionals played a less prominent role (see chapter 12),[5] while all but one of the social clubs were

Notes to this chapter are on p. 399-408.

set up and controlled by men, with women playing a more prominent leadership role after 1970.[6]

The Emergence of Ethnic Clubs (1950 to 1965)

Prior to 1950, newly arrived immigrants were too busy making a living to come together on a regular basis except for soccer, which provided an outlet for young men.[7] Dutchmen chose names such as Hollandia or Neerlandia to compete with players from other ethnic groups. In this early period, only the Dutch clergy or embassy personnel organized other activities.[8] Around 1950, expatriates employed by Dutch companies, together with a handful of professionals, established the first ethnic organizations in larger urban centres. They invariable used the name *Nederlandse Vereniging* ("Netherlandic Association"). We have already come across two such associations, one in Toronto (chapter 12) and the other in Hamilton (chapter 15).[9] Its members arranged St. Nicholas parties for children, sponsored dances and showed films, in collaboration with the consulate. However, not all Dutch immigrants appreciated their subservient stance vis-à-vis Dutch-educated middle-class organizers, while strict Calvinists objected to what they considered the "non-Christian" nature of such occasions. Tensions based on class differences and religious divisions plagued all broad, ethnically defined organizations from the beginning. Except for strict Calvinists, Dutch immigrants felt public events should be organized along "neutral" lines. However, immigrant reception centres had already been established according to the pillar-model (see chapter 4). Hence it is not surprising that Dutch people in Toronto should found a similar pillar-type association, the *Nederlandse Centrum*, to coordinate the activities of various social clubs and cultural organizations.[10]

In contrast, in numerous farms, villages, and smaller cities, Dutch gatherings initially took place exclusively within the confines of a particular pillar. For example, throughout the London diocese—in Stratford, Strathroy, Mitchell and a hall along highway 81 (outside Arkona)—the Sacred Heart priests set up clubs for Catholic youths and married couples.[11] Dutch Catholics in regions where the Flemish had settled prior to the War were more inclined to join clubs originally established under the auspices of the Capuchins (see chapter 10). The main purpose of all of these clubs was to hold dances under the supervision of a priest (see chapter 8), but they soon freed themselves of ecclesiastic control.[12] The increasing separation of church and secular life also paved the way for the entry of non-Catholics; for instance, the Stratford Club was officially Catholic until a Dutch Protestant from Mitchell, married to a Catholic, launched a formal protest.[13] Within a couple of years, and against the bishop of London's wishes, all the Dutch Catholic social clubs became ethnic clubs open to all Dutch-Canadians. Sarnia and Chatham already had secular Belgian-Dutch organizations while Catholics in the rest of Ontario founded social clubs without religious connotations, together with Dutch immigrants from other backgrounds.

Initially orthodox Calvinists did not need such social clubs, since their churches organized their own social activities within the Reformed network (see chapter 9).[14] They also frowned upon dancing and card playing, and thus mainly organized community picnics, or only celebrated Dutch national rituals, such as the annual St. Nicholas party. Yet Calvinists from an urban background did accept invitations to attend activities organized by secular ethnic clubs. Nevertheless, increasing contact with secular clubs resulted in disagreements. Catholics, liberal Protestants and those with no religious affiliation held meetings on Sundays to accommodate people who worked on Saturdays. In contrast, orthodox Calvinists opposed playing soccer or having meetings on the Christian Sabbath.[15] Thus, in St. Catharines, orthodox Calvinists left a fledgling cultural organization set up by a group of Dutch immigrants who saw themselves as "neutral." In a few places, the Calvinists established their own ethnically defined cultural organizations. For example, in Chatham a group of people already involved in a de facto Dutch Protestant credit union set up the Dutch-Canadian Culture Club. Originally founded as a service organization in 1957, the club showed films, had talent nights, and organized tours.[16] Some events were also held in nearby towns, such as Wallaceburg or Dresden. This club maintained close ties with the Christian Reformed community, and opened all events with prayers.[17]

Prior to 1960 most ethnic organizations had links with either consular officials or church leaders. Most immigrants did not have the time or inclination to do the organizing, draw up membership lists, and act as peacemakers. Indeed, clubs run by local volunteers often failed. For instance, a Dutch Canadian Alliance in London, founded in 1951, lasted less than a year. Instead, privately owned, commercial clubs appeared. Several entrepreneurs (one of whom later became a prominent businessman) built an entertainment hall in Stoney Creek, where people could pay to attend dances, while a group of Dutchmen in Etobicoke and in Whitby set up similar commercial clubs. The presence of such privately run clubs gave impetus to the formation of Dutch bands whose leaders (Nick de Rooy, Pierre Fransen, Roly Klasen)[18] became household words among Dutch-Canadians. Notwithstanding the bands' popularity, some people complained about club owners making a profit from people's need to socialize and have a good time, especially if a club presented an image of being a "community" organization. Following a more cooperative philosophy, immigrants then established non-profit clubs, with constitutions stipulating annual elections of executive officers.[19]

The first clubs to be incorporated in this manner, in the early sixties, were the Neerlandia Club in Windsor, Club "the Netherlands" in St. Catharines, Stratford's Benelux Club and the Dutch Canadian Country Club in Milton. These clubs contracted Dutch-Canadian musicians themselves and rented halls or used space provided by a Dutch-Canadian credit union. People in London used a different approach. In 1960, 10 men—over a couple of beers after a soccer game—decided they wanted to have their own clubhouse. After holding several dances to raise funds, they set up the Dutch Canadian Society.[20] Nine members signed a personal guarantee for the mortgage on behalf of their 351-member association.[21] Their building was officially opened in 1965 by the mayor of London and the consul general of the Netherlands. It underwent renovations and enlargement several years later. The clubhouse, managed by a board of directors, was used by a card club, a Dutch Canadian Carnival Society (The Dykehoppers) and other "subsidiaries."[22] The Dutch Canadian Society (DCS) involved a cross-section of immigrants, including small business people such as the couple who set up the Dutch imports store mentioned in chapter 14. The majority of the founding members were at least nominally Catholic, many of whom also belonged to St. Willibrord Credit Union.[23] However, there has always been a minority of non-Catholics actively involved in this club.

The Charter Flight Connection

Group booking of charter flights was one way the London club raised funds in the early sixties.[24] All over Ontario people likewise started joining clubs or credit unions in order to become eligible for bargain flights to the Netherlands (see previous chapter). Since each club received 5 percent for each seat sold, the travel business became an important source of revenue for financing Dutch entertainers and cultural events. Although technically non-profit, such charter transactions also represented a potentially lucrative venture for entrepreneurs.

The Dutch Canadian Entertainment Club

The first person to set up a network of travel clubs was Bill Brouwers, whom we came across in earlier chapters.[25] His first involvement in setting up a Dutch-Canadian organization goes back to the mid-fifties when he and a group of friends started the Dutch Canadian Charity Agency in Oakville to raise funds after a fellow immigrant lost his house in a fire.[26] The charity ceased operations several years later, but their legal charter was maintained. This organization evolved into the Dutch Canadian Entertainment Club (DCEC), which was registered under that name in 1966.[27] Their members, shareholders of a non-profit organization, were distinguished from associated members, an idea that inspired the Dutch Canadian Society of London to adopt a similar legal structure. However, unlike the London Club, the Dutch Canadian Entertainment Club organized charter flights and shows for people across Ontario, and they had affiliates in cities all over the province.[28] Their first charter flight to Amsterdam was organized in 1964, two years before the club received its new name.[29] With the increasing popularity of charter flights, the Dutch Canadian Alliance (DCA) and other organizations also took part, creating a friendly rivalry. Nonetheless, Brouwers' network of clubs maintained the lion's share of bookings and the DCA had to participate in joint flights.[30]

Although Dutch in name, and run by Dutch-Canadians, the DCEC attracted a broad membership that went beyond the Dutch-Canadian community. Apart from non-Dutch spouses, people from other ethnic groups joined up. Germans and Czechs, in particular, took advantage of this opportunity to get access to charter flights. There was also a chapter composed of Filipinas and their Dutch-Indonesian friends (see chapter 10). The Entertainment Club served all segments of the Dutch-Canadian population, including the orthodox Calvinists,[31] and stimulated the formation of numerous chapters in the sixties and early seventies. Someone in each chapter did the bookings, and was rewarded for his or her efforts with free flights.[32] Commissions on bookings were likewise disbursed by the head office to finance big gala events in Oakville. Dutch-Canadian couples from as far away as Sudbury used to drive to Oakville to listen to big-name Dutch entertainers.

The Holland Canada Club

The social network originating from the Oakville Charity Agency included a Dutch-Canadian technician who lived in Milton. He was a close associate and partner in the DCEC until he went his own way. In 1968 this man set up a rival network of travel clubs. His Holland Canada Club had local chapters, some of which originally came out of the DCEC.[33] The new charter club also arranged charter flights for independent clubs, including the one in St. Catharines. Like the DCEC, the Holland Canada Club was registered as a non-profit organization with a board.[34] Yet executive members obtained prestige and had access to such perks as free trips, although the division of "spoils" could result in internal bickering or even shady business dealings.

The control of large sums of money collected as deposits for scheduled charter flights tempted some people to fudge the rules. In the case of the Holland Canada Club, for example, these funds were sometimes invested in risky high-return loans.[35] The first time this was done, the club generated a profit. However, their next speculative venture involved a large sum of money to finance a supposedly miraculous cancer treatment centre. That deal turned out to be a hoax, and the backers from the Holland Canada Club lost their investment. Consequently there were insufficient funds to cover the cost of chartering a plane, and the passengers were almost left stranded.[36] The discovery of this debacle led to a series of crises which resulted in the dismantling of the Holland Canada Club, as relations between the head office and local affiliates soured. Thus Guelph no longer wanted anything to do with the head office,[37] and formed an independent club in 1970, keeping the name Guelph Holland Canada Club. Other local chapters similarly cut off all ties. For the Golden Triangle Area Club, the scandal associated with the charter fiasco resulted in an internal split. Their president, who sat on the Holland Canada Club's board of directors, was one of eight businessmen who bailed out the club by pitching in five thousand dollars from their own pockets. However, when he tried to recover his money, by keeping back part of the commissions on subsequent flights, some club members became suspicious.[38] This dispute resulted in the formation of a new club for Cambridge, now officially affiliated with the DCEC. Such conflicts reflected the underlying tensions and jealousies that emerged as status-conscious Dutch immigrants juggled for positions within a network of social interaction involving both old and new ways of gaining prestige, while simultaneously struggling to get ahead economically in a highly competitive North American market society.[39]

The Revival of the Dutch Heritage

Controversies over money and power did not lead to the demise of Dutch associations. The growth of clubs and the Dutch Canadian Alliance reinforced a sense of group identity among Dutch-Canadians trying to find their place in a pluralistic society. The trips back to the old country cured some people of homesickness, and made Dutch-Canadians aware that they were no longer the same as people living in the Netherlands. A sense of belonging to Canada can be illustrated by the involvement of a broad range of Dutch-Canadian organizations in the celebration of Canada's centennial in 1967.[40]

Operation Thank You Canada

The momentum of public involvement by Dutch-Canadians, as one of Canada's immigrant ethnic groups, continued after Expo '67. Anticipating the twenty-fifth anniversary of the liberation of the Netherlands, Dutch-Canadian organizations across Canada mounted Operation Thank You

Canada. The initiative came from the Dutch Canadian Alliance, which contacted groups across Canada with a proposal to donate a Dutch-built baroque concert organ to the National Arts Centre in Ottawa. The operation, which took several years of planning and fundraising, culminated in a huge celebration, with a gala dinner and interdenominational church service in the capital on Victoria Day, 1970.[41] Operation Thank You Canada involved a broad range of Dutch-Canadian social and cultural associations, Reformed community representatives and numerous Dutch-Canadians who had hitherto not been involved in formal ethnic organizations.

The Dutch-Canadian Committee, 1945-1970, set up to execute this project, was the first and only national organization representing all Canadians of Dutch descent.[42] Their coast-to-coast effort even resulted in a short-lived, albeit unsuccessful, attempt to make the Dutch more visible in the broader political arena through a new national committee. One of its main promoters, Nick Meulmeester, who had been actively involved in Operation Thank You Canada, wrote a proposal for a Dutch-Canadian coordinating organization in 1971.[43] He recruited Peter Speelman, a prominent member of the Christian Reformed community and owner of a publishing and distribution firm specializing in Dutch and Reformed literature. Their newsletter, *Dutch Canadian Co-ordinator*, appeared for three years. However, despite all good intentions, attempts to turn the ideal into reality did not succeed. Leaders within the diverse and heterogenous Dutch immigration population could act in concert on matters of collective concern, especially on issues evoking a shared national symbol; but Dutch-Canadians did not have enough in common to sustain a national institution.[44] Nevertheless, the bonds of friendship created by involvement in Operation Thank You Canada did reinforce the cohesion of ethnically defined cultural clubs on the local level, resulting in additional activities of a multicultural nature.

Dutch Heritage Clubs

Inspired by the 1970 national project, Dutch-Canadians, including orthodox Calvinists, initiated heritage events in many towns and cities in Ontario. The committee representing Sarnia in Operation Thank You Canada became the Windmill Club. The two most active members were a Roman Catholic insurance agent and a Christian Reformed contractor who still organizes bi-annual gatherings of people from Friesland (see chapter 10). Their activities ranged from putting on plays to taking part in joint remembrance day celebrations with the Legionnaires. The Dutch in Ottawa formed an *oranjecomite* (in charge of celebrating Dutch national holidays). Dutch clubs in other cities stepped up their activities after 1970, including celebrations of *koninginnedag* (the queen's birthday) and the traditional St. Nicholas day (*sinterklaas*) on December 5. The Kingston Dutch Canadian Club was started anew.

Under Canada's new multicultural policy (initiated under Trudeau in the mid-seventies), the emphasis shifted from Dutch national holiday celebrations to participation in town parades, heritage language classes and Dutch folk dances. Such activities attracted a variety of Dutch-Canadians regardless of region of origin or religion, and some Dutch-Canadians who had come to Canada as teenagers in the fifties enroled their Canadian-born children in Dutch language classes. More recent Dutch immigrants also took part. For example, in 1975, a recently arrived electrician from the Netherlands (of *hervormd* background) became a representative in the Sarnia Multicultural Council. He and a group of older immigrants set up the Dutch Heritage Club, which coordinated language classes, organized food displays and a float for multicultural gatherings, and formed a Dutch-Canadian choir.[45] Although separate from the Windmill Club, which had more Reformed members, they and other Dutch-Canadians cooperated during public events.

Cultural clubs became officially incorporated in other places. The Whitby-Oshawa region saw the founding of the Dutch Canadian Club of Durham region on September 4, 1975.[46] A renewed Hamilton Holland Club drafted a constitution in 1977, and people in Mitchell and Seaforth, previously affiliated with the Stratford Benelux Club, started the New Canadians Club for Huron and Perth Counties in 1978. Such clubs combined social dances with multicultural activities. A characteristic feature was their Canadianization and internationalization. Many Dutch-Canadians had married non-Dutch spouses, and such mixed couples also joined Dutch Clubs. In some cases, non-Dutch women even became more involved in club affairs than their immigrant husbands. Such clubs changed their names from "Dutch" to "Dutch Canadian," as in Brantford's Dutch Canadian Windmill Club in 1984.[47] Although some non-Dutch spouses picked up a bit of Dutch, English started being used more and more, and club bulletins began to be written in English. Couples from other European ethnic groups also started attending club dances whenever a good band was featured.[48] In fact, social events organized by Dutch-Canadians even came to the attention of Canadians descended from English, Scottish or Irish settlers. A good example of someone involved in such cross-cultural contact is Charley Indewey, a former Guelph Holland Canada Club president, who simultaneously served as vice-chairman of the entertainment committee of the Canadian Legion. He had first landed on Prince Edward Island in the fifties, when he was 19 years old,[49] later meeting his future wife, also a Dutch immigrant, after moving to Guelph. His "Dutch dances," featuring the band of Nick de Rooy, were a real hit among middle-aged and older "Canadian" couples, who also attended dances sponsored by the Dutch club.[50] His dual role further demonstrates the early integration of liberal Protestant Dutch immigrants in a small-town environment (see also chapter 7).

While Canadians from diverse backgrounds become integrated into Dutch organizations during the seventies and eighties, intergroup tensions soon resurfaced. An organizer of the Heritage Club in Sarnia, an ardent supporter of multiculturalism, admitted to me that there were sometimes tensions inside the Windmill Club between Catholics from Noord Brabant and Reformed Frisians. But he added: "As Hollanders, you have to know how to play the game (*moet je spelen*). For example, if people start criticizing, you give them something to do."[51]

In other cities, collaboration across religious and regional lines resulted in open wrangling. For example, the ethnic club in Brantford split into opposing factions. Reformed members wanted to preserve their Dutch heritage, but not take part in New Year's parties or dances where liquor was served. When the Multicultural Council organized an annual festival, there were two separate Dutch "villages."[52] Between 1975 and 1977 two ethnic organizations competed for members and local business support: the Reformed-linked Dutch Cultural Society and their rival Brantford and District Dutch Social Club, "The Windmill."[53]

Dutch-Canadians not of Reformed background were as likely to avoid gatherings organized by orthodox Calvinists as the other way around. Starting in the sixties, a committee composed of Christian Reformed Church members held a Dutch Day (*Hollandse Dag*). Their biggest gatherings were held in Moorefield (near Drayton).[54] Throughout the seventies, such Dutch days attracted big crowds who came to take part in races and singalongs, watch performances and drink coffee with Dutch *koek*. However, the organizers were not successful in persuading Catholic families in nearby Ayton to join them.[55] This failure to attract a broader range of Dutch-Canadians can be explained by the same religiously based cultural differences that caused divisions and splits in some city heritage clubs. While Dutch Catholics and liberal Protestants kept religious and non-religious affairs quite separate, neo-Calvinists applied Reformed ("Christian") principles to all areas of life, including rules that set limits on which social activities were acceptable (see chapter 9).[56] Consequently, members of other segments of the Dutch-Canadian community did not "feel at home." People who were not strict Calvinists were as likely to avoid "*gereformeerde*" (Reformed) Dutch days as non-Catholics were to stay away from the annual Dutch picnics in Delaware, which were organized by Catholic priests.[57]

Umbrella Organizations

Toward the end of the seventies, the Dutch Canadian Entertainment Club, the DCA and the remains of the Holland Canada Club had been either disbanded or existed only on paper. However, many of their former chapters still operated on the local level. With renewed contact among club members, and the need for coordination, 12 clubs in southwestern Ontario came together to form the Dutch Canadian Cultural Organization of Ontario (DCCOO) in 1978.[58] Their first joint activity was to resurrect a queen contest among various clubs.[59] However, despite this coming together of Dutch-Canadian clubs from different places, the DCCOO never included the various Dutch clubs of Toronto. We saw in chapter 12 that Metropolitan Toronto has myriad organizations, ranging from Dutch senior clubs to a biannual bazaar which draws visitors from a large area. Like Ottawa, Toronto also has a consular office, and various middle-class and more exclusive associations. Indeed, the presence of such high-profile Dutch-Canadian institutions, typifying the ranking system of Dutch society, caused tensions when representatives of the Dutch-Canadian community of Toronto came into contact with their counterparts in smaller urban centres.[60]

For many Dutch-Canadians in the rest of the province, their counterparts in Toronto (and Ottawa) look "more Dutch." Nevertheless, even in the bigger cities like Toronto, the process of Canadianization gradually transformed Dutch immigrants into Dutch-Canadians, or "ethnics." This transition point was formally acknowledged as early as 1968 when the *Nederlandse Centrum* became the Dutch-Canadian Association of Greater Toronto.[61] However, although technically encompassing all Dutch-linked organizations, the unity of the various Dutch-Canadian associations in Toronto is more symbolic than real.[62] The member clubs operate quite independently and their executive members maintain a cordial but somewhat distant relationship with the Dutch consulate, which no longer has much of a say in the running of Dutch-Canadian affairs. The leadership of the Toronto umbrella organization has also become transformed over the past decade. Its last two presidents (one a woman, the other a man) were of working- or lower-middle-class immigrant background, rather than Dutch expatriates or high-profile professionals. We encountered Martin Van Denzen, the most recent president, in connection with a hometown reunion (chapter 10). The Toronto association he heads today more closely resembles many other ethnic organizations in the province. He has also established informal links with Dutch clubs in other parts of the province, including those affiliated with the DCCOO.

Decline in Club Membership and Specialization

By 1989 the DCCOO's treasurer indicated that their year-end balance had never been so low. Some clubs had dropped out of their association. Almost all Dutch-Canadian social and cultural clubs saw a similar drop in membership towards the end of the eighties and early nineties. First the Milton club was dissolved and remaining monies were donated to charities. A few years later other clubs went dormant or were reduced to a small number of active members (Guelph, Woodstock, Kitchener-Cambridge, then Stratford), putting the DCCOO in further jeopardy. The remaining members of Dutch-Canadian clubs lamented the decline in interest and support among the broader Dutch-Canadian population. Club bulletins openly expressed a feeling of malaise, illustrated by the following comments from the Dutch Canadian Club of Kingston: "This year again was very successful, in spite of so many Dutch-Canadian people being uninterested in our activities. . . . I am still wondering why so many Dutch-Canadians are not willing to participate . . ."[63]

Club organizers recognize that the disappearance of Dutch clubs reflects the process of integration and assimilation which they themselves have personally undergone. They are well aware that ethnic identity and language retention within Dutch social clubs has become largely symbolic. They also know that the second generation no longer needs special ethnic clubs, and doesn't share the same tastes in music and recreational activities as their elders.[64] Nevertheless, despite the decline in club membership, specific events or activities are still popular with middle-aged and older Dutch-Canadians. The early nineties saw a resurgence of tournaments for a Dutch card game called *klaverjas*, bringing together players from London, Toronto, Hamilton, Georgetown and other places.[65] Heritage language programs also continued to attract new people who might not have anything to do with any particular club or association.[66] Family gatherings and dances designed to attract a broad range of people of Dutch descent are being replaced by more specialized activities. This trend from an origin-specific to an interest-specific orientation was also noted by Lowensteyn for the Dutch in Montreal.[67]

The long-term viability of ethnic clubs is partly dependent upon demographic factors. Even an enthusiastic and energetic organizer needs a minimal level of support from a Dutch-Canadian constituency. In the nineties, only those clubs in urban areas with a critical mass of postwar Dutch immigrants survived. It also helped if most immigrants originally came around the same time, as in the cases of St. Catharines, London or Toronto. In contrast, Dutch clubs in small towns have always been short-lived. Bradford is a prime example.[68] Its Dutch club had already disbanded in the early seventies. In 1989 the owners of a new Dutch delicatessen store, who came to Canada in 1983, tried to resurrect the older ethnic club after they organized a dance to raise money for charity.[69] A steering committee drafted a constitution for a new "Club The Dutch Tulip," which held an inaugural meeting in March 1990.[70] Despite an auspicious beginning, the club was disbanded two years later.[71]

Heritage Festivals

A more successful format for promoting a Dutch-Canadian presence in smaller towns consists of yearly or biannual festivals. For over a decade, Clinton had a yearly *klompenfeest* ("wooden shoe festival") which attracted Dutch-Canadians from all over southern Ontario and beyond.[72] The three-day event featured a parade, souvenir stands and ethnic food, an interdenominational service, and family entertainment.[73] The Clinton festival also incorporated non-Dutch participants, including local service clubs.[74] Indeed, the festival idea was originally conceived by someone not of Dutch background: Bob Campbell, owner of a downtown clothing store and member of the Clinton Retail Merchants Association.[75] That business group wanted to promote regional development and attract more summer visitors. Several of their members had served in the Netherlands during World War Two in the Canadian army, and they were quite aware of the Dutch immigrant presence in their home town and its surroundings. In 1979, Bob invited the Dutch community to take part in the organizing of a festival, and it took two years for the proposal to be put into place.

Initially, Bob Campbell was not aware of the tremendous differences among Dutch-Canadians, nor did he know the religious affiliation of the Dutch people with whom he had interacted. A Dutch Catholic couple (de Groot)[76] were actively involved from the beginning, and Mrs. de Groot became the festival committee's first secretary. Gradually more Dutch-Canadians, including Reformed people, became involved.[77] Clinton's *klompenfeest* also illustrates that Canadians not of Dutch background are not the only ones ignorant of the Dutch immigration population's heterogeneity. Dutch-Americans, mostly of Reformed background, drive up from nearby Michigan, which also hosts Dutch heritage festivals. These Americanized Calvinists of Dutch descent often assume that the Dutch-Canadians they see on parade in Clinton must all be Reformed.[78] However, they do not realize that the Dykehoppers and a majority of the Dutch band from St. Catharines, who provided most of the entertainment, are Catholic Brabanders!

A similar festival appeared in Peterborough. When a committee for multiculturalism was started in 1987, a few Dutch-Canadians got together to establish a cultural association. There had never been a Dutch club, and cultural events were previously held under the auspices of Peterborough's Dutch credit union.[79] The Dutch Canadian Cultural Association's first organized event, for which they printed 600 tickets, was a Netherlands Night. When an unexpected 1,400 visitors showed up, they decided to plan a larger, two-day festival in 1989, for which they sought support from the Ministry of Citizenship.[80] The 1993 Netherlands Day was again a resounding success.

The Peterborough festival shows a fluctuating interest in ethnicity. The recent revival of Dutch heritage events can be attributed to the fact that older, retired Dutch-Canadians, who used to be so busy with their jobs and careers, now have more time to get involved in ethnic activities (see chapter 17). In Peterborough, the involvement of first-generation retired Dutch-Canadians coincided with a revival of a second-generation ethnic identity. In Peterborough and its surrounding area (including Lindsay), 110 Dutch-Canadian families signed up for membership in the new Cultural Association. Of these, 85 people serve as volunteers during their triannual festival. Although the average age was above 50, 10 percent of their active members are young adults (between 20 and 30) born in Canada. Almost all the younger members have taken over a family business, thus indicating that ethnic identity retention among the Dutch is becoming a middle-class phenomenon.[81]

Dutch Heritage Incorporated

The market potential of a growing population of retired Dutch-Canadians, and the revival of heritage events, was not lost on Theo Luikenaar. An entrepreneur who grew up in the Netherlands, he first worked in Edmonton for a company specializing in air flight simulations. When this company shut down the office where he worked, he moved to Burlington, Ontario, where he became a consultant and professional organizer. He put his organizational skills to work when he coordinated the Dutch queen's 1988 visit to Hamilton, where she held a public reception in the botanical gardens. Several years later, Theo founded Dutch Heritage Inc., an enterprise for coordinating Dutch-Canadian festivals, club events and other activities on a commission basis.[82] In order to obtain a mailing list for publicity purposes, and as a way of reducing his advertising costs, he bought the *Nederlandse Courant* when that newspaper came up for sale.[83] Theo approached Dutch ethnic clubs to persuade them to adopt the paper instead of their own newsletters, with a subscription as part of their membership fee.[84]

The first events promoted by the new *Nederlandse Courant* were a financial success; one alone netted over a $1000 in profits. The first disaster occurred when its owner collaborated with the Hamilton Holland Club to host a Dutch festival. He had already approached the city of Hamilton and the Dutch embassy for funds to organize the festival, which included a conference with workshops for representatives of Dutch clubs. The latter was cancelled when no one registered, but the biggest debacle occurred when not enough spectators showed up for a soccer match of retired professional players from Holland.[85] Before this financial disaster occurred, relations between the *Nederlandse Courant* and some Dutch clubs were already becoming strained. Long-time club members resented the loss of their own bulletins, did not agree with paying fees for attending the workshops in Hamilton, and complained that the written material they submitted did not always get printed the way they liked. The newspaper owner in turn felt that the clubs were "letting him down" by not showing up for the workshops.[86]

Special Purpose Organizations

We have already seen how educated middle-class Dutch immigrants in Toronto set up exclusive social clubs. Such people also founded or joined Canadian chapters of Dutch university alumni clubs. Every October, University of Groningen alumni meet for a reunion at the Royal York Hotel in Toronto. Most but not all of their members are physicians, some of whom we encountered in chapter 14. The person who started up what became the Niagara district chapter is Dr. Verster of Beamsville, Ontario. Dr. Emile Campioni, organizes similar alumni reunions for anywhere from 50 to 70 graduates from Leiden. As well as physicians practising in Toronto, Ajax and other places, their group includes other professionals.[87]

Dutch Veteran Associations

Former Dutch marines have an association (*Kontact Oud Mariniers*). A special Canadian branch (Royal Netherlands Marine Corps Veteran Association) was set up by Ben Hendriks who came to Canada in 1974 to work for a Dutch import company.[88] Together with some friends who already belonged to a Dutch marine veteran organization, he set up a branch in 1990. About 100 members receive a newsletter from the Netherlands, and meet annually to vote for a local executive. They also hold annual picnics, hosted each year by a different member.[89] Another veteran association includes former members of other Dutch armed forces, plus former Dutch resistance fighters. Its history is somewhat different. Initially a handful of Dutch-Canadians in Chatham, who were members of a Dutch veteran organization in the Netherlands, planned to send a list of names to obtain official recognition as a chapter. However, in 1981, a retired officer representing the Dutch organization moved to Brantford, Ontario. His former commander asked this man and his wife to organize war veterans living across Canada. In 1985, Mr. and Mrs. Roosegaarde-Bisschop placed ads in various Dutch-Canadian newspapers. Their membership grew quickly, from six members to 30 in the first year. By 1988, they had more than 120 members, mostly in Ontario.[90] Just a year earlier the organization in the Netherlands had chosen a new name, *De Bond van Wapenbroeders* (Association of Brethren-in-arms).[91] Members, who range in age from their sixties to over 80, organize tours and outings, and they take part in parades side by side with the Canadian Legion.[92]

The Dutch veterans' recent history illustrates the tensions that can arise when earlier and later Dutch immigrants interact within the same organization. One objective of the *Bond* was to act as a support network for veterans who had suffered psychological trauma, especially those who had witnessed atrocities in the former Dutch East Indies. Other simply wanted to share memories. Their organization's new head also introduced a political discourse consisting of a strident anti-communist ideology and expected the veterans to not only attend remembrance day celebrations but to march in uniform side by side with militant nationalists from Eastern Europe.[93] He also insisted that the organization's executive members speak only "proper" Dutch. These policies did not sit well with the majority of Dutch-Canadian veterans, most of whom had emigrated to Canada in the forties or fifties. They also did not feel comfortable speaking standard Dutch, especially at public gatherings (see chapter 12).[94] The possible exclusion of veterans' wives was a potential impediment to the new organization's growth.[95] The misgivings of the women were allayed when it became clear that they were welcome to attend meetings and participate in the organization's social events. However, problems associated with language usage and the political tenor of the *Bond* remained unresolved.[96]

Matters came to a head during a meeting in Ancaster in 1989 to elect a new executive. A majority of the members wanted greater autonomy for their local chapters, and a new chairperson. Someone from a Dutch-Canadian newspaper was invited to attend the meeting and report on the outcome of their deliberations. The meeting in Ancaster was conducted in Dutch, with the chair and other executives sitting on a podium at the front. Half a dozen ladies were busy preparing an Indonesian-style meal in the kitchen opening up into the meeting hall, although several women sat among the predominantly male audience. The meeting started with the chairman reading a long list of regulations in impeccable Dutch. The reporter, who sat near the back, noticed a growing impatience among the people sitting in his vicinity. Some grumbled in English and others in Dutch about the long speeches. They wanted to get down to business. Finally a man stood up to interrupt one of the speakers, triggering off a heated round of debate, with motions and counter-motions.[97] After the debate, ballots were distributed for a formal vote. Unity and decorum were quickly restored.[98] Following a formal announcement of the results,[99] everyone agreed to "forget and forgive." In subsequent years, more outings were organized and there was greater collaboration between the two Dutch veteran organizations (just like in Holland). As one member commented: "The advantage of our organization, and the reason it is more successful, is because we come together not just because we are Dutch, but because we are all old soldiers. That is what gives us cohesion."[100]

CAANS (The Canadian Association for the Advancement of Netherlandic Studies)

The last special-purpose organization that should be mentioned is CAANS. Originally conceived and promoted by non-Dutch academics,[101] most of its executive members on the national level have positions in departments of languages (including Germanic studies) or fine arts.[102] However, CAANS also has local chapters, which are open to anyone interested in promoting the study of Netherlandic culture or history.[103] The eighties saw a mushrooming of activities of local chapters across Canada, including Vancouver, Windsor, Ottawa, Waterloo and Toronto.[104] Officially, CAANS is not a Dutch-Canadian organization and the official languages of communications are English and French. However, it has at times had both support and extensive contact with Dutch consular officials in Canada. More importantly, the local chapters operate as de facto Dutch-Canadian organizations. Ninety-nine percent of their dues-paying members, or the people who attend meetings, are Dutch-Canadians. A brief comparison of Waterloo and Toronto can offer some insights into the internal dynamics of such local chapters.

For a long time, the Toronto chapter consisted of a diverse group of people, all born in the Netherlands and interested in Dutch history and literature. Most had at least a high-school education and were not overtly religious. The local chapter was thus "neutral" in one Dutch sense. The level of participation has fluctuated over time. For several years, Nick Badenhuizen (a biology professor) kept the chapter alive almost single-handedly. At other times, two younger professors of fine arts and literature respectively worked closely with non-academic members to organize local meetings. In the early nineties, with both professors away on sabbatical, a new group of people took charge of the chapter. Two new executive members belonged to Dutch-Canadian business and professional associations, but had no connections with a university. Due to a combination of personality clashes and a different style of operating, most of the earlier members stopped attending meetings of the local chapter. They felt the Toronto CAANS chapter was turning into another social club or business association. The gap in communication between the new CAANS group and the original membership led to misunderstandings and a rift between the local chapter and the national executive. In the minds of many people, there were two separate CAANS in Toronto.[105] In 1997, the original group was again in charge and their membership growing.

The Waterloo chapter started off in a similar fashion. Like Toronto, two professors who taught Dutch language and literature courses were involved from the beginning.[106] In contrast to Toronto, their level of membership and rate of participation was fairly stable over the years, in part due to an unofficial connection with the Christian Reformed community. Initially only a handful of people were involved in the Waterloo chapter. They represented a diverse group of people: a Dutch professor in Slavic studies who had become a Catholic; a tour guide and partner in a book-keeping business who was brought up as a Dutch Mennonite; a couple who were humanists without any religious affiliation; and a retired Christian Reformed minister. Another person who became actively involved in the local chapter was both a minister (Christian Reformed) and a professor.[107] He recruited a large contingent of members from the Reformed community, including faculty at the University of Waterloo. Announcements of chapter activities are always sent out to the Christian Reformed churches in Kitchener-Waterloo and nearby towns and villages, thereby giving their chapter greater exposure to at least one segment of the Dutch-Canadian population.[108]

Despite such variation in the make-up of local chapters, the patterns of social interaction are similar. Business meetings are invariably conducted in English, even if everyone present can understand and speak the Dutch language. Not only is English the official language of CAANS, but I speculate that the use of English lends the proper aura of formality to a public gathering of people from different backgrounds and ideological perspectives.[109] Whenever official business is finished, people invariably switch to Dutch for private conversations.[110] However, in such an informal setting a larger crowd tends to cluster into small sub-groups according to their class background, present occupation and religion (or level of secularism). One can thus detect the same pillar mentality, Dutch class dispositions and linguistic 'habitus' found among people belonging to most other Dutch-Canadian organizations.

Dutch-Canadian social or cultural organizations initially served recreational functions or provided an ethnic niche for specialized activities in such fields as sports, folk dancing, travel or education.[111] Dutch alumni or veteran associations represent Canadian transplants of Dutch-European forms of interaction involving specialized groupings. Over time, most of these organizations also took on a special symbolic significance as one way of drawing ethnic boundaries vis-à-vis similar ethnic 'classes' within the context of Canadian society. However, compared to other postwar immigrant groups, Dutch-Canadians were overall less committed to such ethnic associations for reasons that will become more apparent in part three.

Fieldnotes Interlude

16.1 *Excerpts from an interview with a retired postwar farm immigrant, in Holland Landing, March 18, 1990*

In Hoorn [Holland] I was a member of a mandolin assembly, but it was an all-Catholic group. Later I formed a small band, with mandolins, here in the Marsh as well. A man who knew me recommended that a friend of his who had also emigrated look me up when he got here. He had quite a few children and I trained them and put together a small group and we performed in various places. We mainly played in each others' homes, but also went to Toronto and played in Bradford when KLM was advertising and put on a show. The other players were all members of the same family and they had come to work for the Verkaiks. Their father was Christian Reformed and he died soon after from cancer. After that the group fell apart, because the kids used to complain about getting callouses or having to do so much practising and their father was no longer there to direct them.

16.2 *Excerpts from* Hendrika and Her Family, *a family history written and printed by John van Bakel (Quadville, 1980)*

By now [1952] there were many Dutch people around, who could always find a friendly home to visit or just to spend some time there. . . . Everyone still called it St. Michael's farm (p. 60).

. . . We were never at a loss for excuses to have a party. We either said the haying was completed, the wheat was harvested or the fall ploughing was done. All of the people that lived on the farm would come over and sit with us. A couple of cases of beer would do most of us, and a bottle of Bols for the older folks. These get-togethers would often end up in a singsong or a joke-telling session (p. 64).

. . . When we took over the farm and the buildings, we turned the big room in the cottage into a recreation hall. Frank Gerrits put his pool table in it, and there was always a group of people showing off their skill at playing pool. We often set up tables for card playing, a game everybody seemed to enjoy. This hall was used for several wedding receptions, including my parents' twenty-fifth wedding anniversary (p. 67).

. . . Bert and Martin Van Schyndel helped George Van Knoot to organize the Dutch Players Theatre Group, which I also belonged to. We performed Dutch plays at Vandorf, where we rented the community centre on a yearly basis. We played in Ajax and Whitby when invited to. Unfortunately, all these three men have now passed away (p. 68).

16.3 *Excerpt from an interview [in Dutch] with a folk-art specialist, in Toronto, February 16, 1990*

I also know two university professors of Dutch descent. They are both specialists in Folk Art and they are dancers too, but only for other ethnic groups, particularly East European. They find that more stimulating [*opwekkend*]. They are not interested in Dutch folk dancing or the folk art of the Netherlands .... I also know someone from the Netherlands who is a puppeteer, and another who makes doll houses, but they also have no contact whatsoever with the Dutch-Canadian community.

Chapter 17

The Elderly

The Dutch who emigrated to Canada between 1947 and 1960 as adults are today close to or past retirement age. In many cases, their friends and relatives, if still alive, are spending their last days in retirement or nursing homes, many of which specifically cater to Dutch-Canadians. Regardless of whether or not a term referring to their Dutch heritage is included in the names of such ethnic homes, the Dutch language is extensively used.[1] However, many older people born and raised in the Netherlands remain active and financially independent. Frequently they are still helping out or providing financial assistance to their middle-aged offspring, whose children refer to their grandparents affectionately as *oma* and *opa* (in Dutch) or *paka* and *beppe* (in Frisian). For at least one more decade, the remainder of this postwar cohort, the embodiment of the Dutch pillar system, will continue to shape the Dutch-Canadian presence.

Homes for the Aged

Today's Dutch-Canadian senior citizens themselves starting planning for retirement homes as early as the sixties. One of the early projects of the Dutch Canadian Alliance was the founding of a home for the rapidly ageing parents or grandparents who had joined their adult children in Canada.[2] At various times the Dutch-Canadian community at large discussed plans for this project, but nothing materialized due to the fragmented nature of the Dutch-Canadian population. Nonetheless, two segments of the postwar Dutch-Canadian population did finally set up such retirement homes, with some assistance from the Alliance.[3] The first retirement homes were built in the early seventies. Seniors who were members of the Christian Reformed churches of Sarnia were able to move into Pineview, a 25-unit,

---

Notes to this chapter are on p. 409-11.

no-care facility in 1972, and a year later a similar 51-unit home (Sunset Homes) went up in St. Catharines.[4] By 1990 such Reformed senior homes were found in 15 different cities throughout Ontario, and many had already undergone expansions. The biggest and best known, with both extended care and a special wing for Alzheimer's patients, is Holland Christian Homes in Brampton. The only retirement home set up by the Dutch Roman Catholic community is Windmill Gardens, in Stratford. The people who set up that home came out of the de facto Dutch Catholic parish in Kinkora (see chapter 8). The preponderance of homes for the aged set up by Calvinists, as opposed to Catholics, is consistent with the degree of institutional completeness of their respective communities (see chapter 7).

Since most of these homes were established with partial government funding, they had to make some spaces available for people from the community at large, though the percentage of non-Dutch seniors is minuscule. Moreover, the Dutch inhabitants of retirement homes continue to lead their lives within the confines of the same pillars in which they were originally brought up in the Netherlands. In some Christian homes in smaller cities, there are no Dutch Catholics whatsoever, while the big Holland Christian Home complex in Brampton has a mini-version of the pillar system under Reformed supervision. The overwhelming Reformed presence is evident in the name of this complex, with its "towers" (the high-rise wings added over the years): Covenant, Faith Manor, Trinity and Providence. Frequent choir performances also provide a Dutch Calvinist flavour.[5] However, the home's directors go out of their way to point out that special religious services are available for Catholic residents.[6] The only home for the aged I would classify as "general" (*algemeen*) is Dutch Heritage Villa, established in Kingston in the late eighties. Not only does its name emphasize its ethnic (national) character, but that institution is representative of a broader spectrum of Dutch-Canadians.

One of the founders of Dutch Heritage Villa is John Gerritson, former mayor of Kingston and chair of the Villa's board of directors.[7] Another key promoter, and later a board member, is a woman who belongs to the Christian Reformed Church.[8] They got together with a group of Dutch-Canadians of different backgrounds, all of whom had elderly parents who were having difficulty coping with living alone and maintaining older houses.[9] We saw earlier (in chapter 13) how the women on the committee did the planning and selected the furniture. John Gerritson knew how to pull the strings at Queen's Park in order to facilitate the inevitable red tape. When the 35 units in the Dutch Heritage Villa were ready, both Dutch and non-Dutch people moved in, although over the last couple of years most of the non-Dutch residents have been replaced by Dutch-Canadian seniors.[10]

Dutch Heritage Villa is similar to other Dutch-Canadian homes for the aged in terms of the ethnic composition of the residents and board members. Yet it is different because of the contested nature of its identity. The organizing committee's Christian Reformed members would have preferred to set up a home for mainly Reformed people, with greater support from their own community. Since this was impractical, they agreed to cooperate with a broader group of Dutch-Canadians. Their main spokesperson, who represents a senior's group within the Christian Reformed community, allayed the fears of the members of her own church who worried that they might not feel at home in a "non-Christian" setting.[11] In contrast, the non-Calvinist board members were afraid that the Dutch Calvinist establishment might want to "take over." They did not want the home to officially sponsor specific religious events, Catholic or Reformed, although they were willing to host interdenominational services. However, the compromise solution involved in setting up the retirement home was not immune to misunderstanding and competing interpretations. Outside of Kingston, many Dutch-Canadians assumed that Dutch Heritage Villa was an integral part of a network of Reformed institutions.[12] Yet one of the board members assured me that religious background or affiliation had absolutely no bearing in either the founding or running of Dutch Heritage Villa. Still other people in Kingston pointed out how the home was a collaborative effort between the Christian Reformed community and the "neutral" Dutch club. However, at least one Reformed board member did not realize that the club member on the board, whom she thought did not belong to any religion, was in fact a practising Catholic.

There was additional ambiguity about the ethnic nature of the home, which resulted in minor frictions. The all-Dutch planning committee wanted to set up an ethnic home for the aged, which is why they chose the name Dutch Heritage Villa. Yet at least one member, as well as some other people who got involved in the project, wanted to maintain a balance between Dutch and non-Dutch residents to avoid forming an ethnic ghetto. They assumed that the non-Dutch residents would not object to some elderly Dutch people speaking Dutch among themselves, and pointed out that Dutch-Canadians were fairly careful to use English whenever a non-Dutch person was present. In spite of such good intentions, at least one resident, a widow born in England, complained bitterly about not being able to understand what people in the lounge were saying to each other. A potentially more damaging incident occurred with the visit of the honorary vice-consul of Kingston. This consul, a physician, had not been included in the setting up of the home, notwithstanding his strong interest in all Dutch activities in the region.[13] Dutch-Canadians who wanted to play down the Dutch nature of the home objected when the consul and his wife visited the home dressed up as *sinterklaas* and *zwarte piet*. When one of the board members returned from a vacation, she discovered that the consul had hung up a portrait of Queen Beatrix of the Netherlands, and the next day she put up a portrait of Queen Elizabeth as well. Several board members objected to the daily hoisting of the Dutch flag.[14] They felt that the Dutch Heritage Villa represented a Dutch-Canadian and not a national Dutch institution: "It's alright to have a Dutch touch and to display the Dutch flag on the queen's birthday, but every day is too much."[15]

The Dutch-Canadian homes for the aged, like the credit unions, illustrate the complex make-up and ambiguous nature of Dutch-Canadian institutions. Both institutions were set up by first-generation Dutch immigrants, yet for the most part they evolved into de facto rather than officially Dutch-Canadian establishments. Moreover, most retirement or nursing homes were dominated or controlled by the Dutch-Canadian Reformed component. The opposite is the case for the "real" (ethnically defined) clubs and cultural organizations we saw in the last chapter, where other parts of the Dutch-Canadian community were more prominent. However, while the pillar mentality common to all postwar Dutch-Canadians generated a diverse set of institutions, one cannot ignore the common linguistic dispositions of elderly Dutch-Canadians, which resulted in a revival of home languages within a changing set of social circumstances.

Language and the Process of Aging

The Dutch elderly, some of whom have not used their mother tongue for decades, are once again speaking Dutch, especially in Dutch retirement homes. For example, the use of Dutch is quite noticeable in Holland Christian Homes, located in Brampton. A Dutch-Canadian woman in Holland Marsh mentioned during an interview that her friends living in that home, many of whom had come to Canada prior to World War Two, were starting to lose their English.[16] Another retired Dutch-Canadian, now living in an apartment in Bradford, made a similar remark about people who have moved into that Brampton seniors' home: "There, if a husband says something to his wife in English, you get a lot of funny looks."[17]

However, this phenomenon is not restricted to people who emigrated when they were already beyond middle age, since many people reverting to Dutch have not spoken it since they were teenagers or in their early twenties.

The transition from English back to Dutch is also happening among retired couples living in their own homes. In some cases, a degenerative disease may result in the loss of a second language. However, the reversion to mother tongue—or to standard Dutch—is not primarily associated with the "second childhood" ascribed to the elderly. Many older Dutch-Canadians are in excellent health, travel and pursue lifelong hobbies. Rather, when the children are gone, people who originally emigrated as adults simply slip back into speaking more Dutch with each other. This process can be just as gradual and unplanned as the original transition from Dutch to English or an English peppered with Dutch. This language reversion is accelerated if one's best friends are also Dutch immigrants. For older Dutch-Canadians, the language they use also depends on who they are talking to. Most Canadian-born grandchildren would not understand their grandparents if spoken to in Dutch only. During family visits, younger grandparents therefore have to use English. Even when talking to their children, or their peers, about Canadian politics or business, such people will immediately switch into accented English. However, when reminiscing about their upbringing or the Netherlands, Dutch comes to the fore.[18] People brought up in the Netherlands also find it easier to talk in their mother tongue about matters relating to the household, family relations and illness. The "choice" of language thus depends on the topic of conversation as well as social context (see also chapter 11).

Older Dutch-Canadian couples usually start interacting more and more with fellow Dutch-Canadians of similar background after retirement, even after years of dealing with non-Dutch employers or customers. Although well integrated into other aspects of Canadian society, they are not as likely to have intimate friendships with Canadian families who have been in Canada for generations. In numerous interviews, Dutch-Canadians who are adamant about being Canadian rather than "Dutch," also confessed that those with whom they socialize on a regular basis are other Dutch immigrants. This is as true for Catholics or people who have no specific religious affiliation as for Calvinists. In almost all cases, Dutch-Canadians felt that they had "more in common" with fellow immigrants.[19] Increasing interaction with other postwar Dutch immigrants after retirement from the workplace reinforced the tendency to revert to speaking Dutch, especially if such fellows were "like-minded" people of approximately the same age, social standing and religious affiliation (see chapters 11 and 12).

The tendency to revert back to speaking Dutch can also be seen as an indirect effect of the Canadian system of ethnic stratification, with its subtle distinctions. Dutch immigrants of lower- or even middle-class origin often felt "excluded" by their non-Dutch neighbours, especially if the latter were well educated or came from families with strong local roots. Many people confided to me that their "Canadian" acquaintances, though always "friendly," also "kept their distance" and that they had rarely been invited to Canadian homes. At the same time we should not overlook the national dispositions shared by people who grew up in the Netherlands. First-generation Dutch-Canadians, even those from a rural background, looked down upon and disapproved of the Canadian working-class lifestyle. They thought Canadians "drank too much beer," did not have "a wholesome family life" or "were not clean enough." Working-class (blue-collar) Canadians in turn accused the "Dutchies" of being too strict or opinionated and too concerned with "making money." Given such subtle social barriers between established and new Canadians, it is not surprising that the Dutch language should be revived in a context of more intense socializing among Dutch-Canadians once they leave the work force.

I have observed or heard about the recreation of a Dutch-speaking social environment in both urban and rural settings. Aylmer, in Elgin county, is but one example. In this predominantly rural county, Dutch-Canadians make up 6 percent of the total population.[20] According to the 1986 census, 275 Dutch-Canadians lived in this small town and 385 more in surrounding Malahide township. Of those of Dutch descent in town, the ratio of people speaking Dutch was higher than average; 60 percent of them reported Dutch as their mother tongue. Initially, a number of elderly Dutch-Canadians joined the Leisure Club, which had already been established by residents whose original background was predominantly English and Scottish. As Dutch-Canadians joined, they started speaking more and more Dutch among themselves. Eventually the non-Dutch Canadian members, who could not understand what was being said, left the organization.[21]

Involvement in Ethnic Associations: Travel and Nostalgia

In the last chapter we saw how retirement often resulted in a revival of interest in club activities. In fact, the majority of Dutch, Frisian, Indo or Flemish ethnic clubs are increasingly becoming "old folks" clubs. For example, the key people in the 12-person organizing committee for the Peterborough Dutch festival are recently retired Dutch-Canadians (see previous chapter). In some cases, newcomers also stimulated earlier immigrants to raise their ethnic profile. Thus, Maria Toonen, who came to Canada in 1980, started a folkdance group, De Brabanders, whose performances have been been reported in numerous local newspapers, including *The Toronto Sun*.[22] Similarly, a group of women of retirement age in Clinton formed the Festival Singers, to hold old-fashioned Dutch singalongs. Many retired Dutch-Canadians regularly include ethnic festivals in their travels or spend more time making out-of-town trips to visit old friends and acquaintances. They also make frequent trips to the Netherlands, as long as their health holds out, which further reinforces the use of Dutch or Frisian.

Most older immigrants told me they liked such return visits, but "would never want to return." However, in some cases, people who had disowned their original homeland for decades, and saw themselves as "100 percent Canadian" did go back for good. I was already acquainted with several such cases and more were mentioned in the course of interviewing people. For example, one couple in Toronto, who had sworn they would never go back and live in Holland, ended up doing just that soon after retirement. This phenomenon of return-migration happened more often than acknowledged.[23] Indeed, between 1980 and 1990 ten of thousands of elderly return migrants flooded back to the Netherlands from various countries, including Canada. While some did so because it was more economical and personally rewarding to retire in Europe, many were motivated by a deep-seated nostalgia.[24] However, the elderly immigrants who returned after several decades to the Netherlands to "wait until they die" still represent a small proportion of the hundreds of thousands who emigrated after the War. A larger proportion of Dutch-Canadians are enjoying their last years in their Canadian homes or going back and forth between Canada and Florida.

Along with the revival of mother tongues comes a resurgence of ethnic identity among elderly Dutch-Canadians. Often people who refused to speak Dutch to their children as young adults are quite willing at a later stage in life to teach some Dutch words to their grandchildren or tell them about Dutch history. I have also come across a dozen cases of retired people who were either in the process of writing, or had just completed, their family or life history. They all wrote in English, often with the help of younger family member educated in Canada, so that their grandchildren would be able to read their account. The stories inevitably remind their readers of the Dutch background of their ancestors and the country they came from. Several writers of such memoirs have died during the writing of this book, but their message remains. This link between elderly Dutch immigrants and their more distant offspring is bound to influence the ethnic identity of third- and fourth-generation Dutch-Canadians.

Fieldnotes Interlude

17.1 Excerpts from an interview with a Christian Reformed woman who lives just outside of Kingston, December 20, 1989

My Dutch heritage is very important to me.... some of the government people called me a dreamer when I told them about my vision of an integrated residence for both senior citizens and younger people, just like the one I had seen in Holland when I went there for a trip. Since 20 years ago, I have been dedicated to the ideal of getting decent accommodations for Dutch elderly.

One English lady [resident of Dutch Heritage Villa] complained about how Dutch the Heritage Villa had become and I had to remind her that we did call it by that name because of the fact that a lot of Dutch people were going to be living there. I've told her that the Dutch have a sense of humour and that next time someone speaks Dutch—or she can't understand what others are saying among each other—that she should ask them "would you please translate that for me".... it's natural that people would use Dutch inadvertently. For example, when they are putting together puzzles, someone will often say, "*ja, waar gaat dat stukje nu*?" [Yes, now where does that piece go?]

17.2 A case study of a retired artistic Dutch-Canadian couple (based on my fieldnotes, plus other sources)

[Analytical note: Rarely does one encounter such a clear-cut illustration of long-term disjuncture between dispositions and social structure; yet the life trajectory of this immigrant couple exemplifies how social energy can be channelled to restore the equilibrium between 'habitus' and various overlapping social 'fields'.]

Henk Poesiat and Leida Van Vliet emigrated in 1956 with two children. Originally from Amsterdam, he studied art in Utrecht and became a member of the Surrealist school.[25] He had already mounted half a dozen exhibitions in Europe before landing in Toronto. In Canada he supported himself and his family for twenty-two years with a job at Simpson's, doing advertising, window displays and fabric designing. However, apart from several commissioned portraits, his artistic talent lay dormant, to be resumed after retirement. The Poesiats spent the last part of their life in the cooperative housing complex for artists located at Queen's Quay near Harbourfront,[26] where his earlier and more recent paintings received public attention. Surrounded by non-Dutch artists and writers, this couple exemplifies how people can simultaneously live in different worlds: the heterogenous urban Dutch-Canadian community and the world of art and counterculture in downtown Toronto. The social background of Henk Poesiat, in particular, defies classification in accordance with clear-cut sociological categories: sophisticated urban (Amsterdam), educated middle class (his father was an architect), Calvinist (*gereformeerd*) and socialist; even his entry into the artistic field took place in the largely Catholic and conservative city of Utrecht.[27]

Before emigrating, the Poesiats were immersed in a vibrant intellectual and artistic environment, quite distinct from the atmosphere of Toronto in the fifties. The changeover was traumatic. In Poesiat's own words,

> The transition had, creatively, the effect of a paralysis. The lack of the cultural climate I was used to in Europe, of an age-old history and tradition, made me feel as if I had landed in a vacuum. It would take me years to get over this trauma and to come to creative labour again.[28]

The Poesiats were welcomed to Toronto by a Christian Reformed fieldman, and joined his congregation.[29] Apart from disappointment with what they saw as the sterility and materialism of a North American city, they found the Dutch Calvinism practised in North America stifling and dated. In that early period of immigrant adaptation, this artistic couple had not yet been exposed to the small bohemian circle in downtown Toronto where they would have felt more at home.[30] In the absence of the right social atmosphere, the Poesiats channelled their energies in other directions. Drawing on their earlier theatrical experience, Henk and Leida used to travel to various cities in southern Ontario, doing skits for Dutch immigrant audiences. These skits, recorded live, were part of an unsuccessful attempt to develop a Canadian branch of the *Christelijke Nederlandse Radio Vereniging*, a Dutch Calvinist Radio Network.

Involvement in the world of amateur acting reconnected them with non-Calvinist middle-class people, as this denominationally linked theatre group evolved into a more diverse, non-religious acting club called FAMA (see chapter 12).[31] Their lives were nourished through contact with an evolving, heterogenous, Dutch-Canadian network, which included Catholics, Jews, Reformed and atheists. This ethnic network formed the basis for lasting friendships.

Their relationship with the Reformed pillar was more ambiguous. From the beginning, the Poesiats were criticized and even ridiculed for their lifestyle and political views. People objected to the content and language associated with the plays they put on, and they were ribbed for being "communists" because they supported the NDP, the closest equivalent in Canada to the Dutch Labour Party. Although theirs was an oddball position within the Calvinist fold, the Poesiats maintained contact with the Reformed community even when they stopped attending church. A more tolerant minister used to keep them informed of what was happening. However, Henk was ostracized when he spoke out against pro-life activists during a televised debate shown on the Dutch-language program. Former friends no longer talked to them, and they were not welcome in a Dutch seniors' club. They lost all contact with the Dutch Calvinist community after moving into the artist co-op. Despite the manner in which they were treated, Henk does not bear a grudge. He told me that they still liked a small minority of Reformed intellectuals, although they disagreed with them.[32]

Part Three

From Immigrants to Dutch-Canadians

Chapter 18

Dutch-Canadian Dispositions: Identity and Culture

Anyone interested in how Canadians of Dutch background portray themselves is bound to be bewildered. Even postwar immigrants with similar religious and regional backgrounds have different identities, partly depending on what stage they have reached in their life cycle: people may deny being "Dutch" while speaking the Dutch language, and someone who may represent himself or herself as Dutch in one context may not do so in another. The combinations and permutations are endless. Indeed, Dutch-Canadians, who express quite strong opinions about other topics, are quite ambiguous when talking about who they are. Nor do they seem to do what they say. Moreover, the way the postwar immigrants from the Netherlands talk about themselves is quite different from the way they represent themselves to others. Nevertheless they do have some things in common, including several "myths" jointly constructed after coming to Canada.

This chapter will present an objectivist account of Dutch-Canadian "culture" along the same lines as an earlier one dealing with Dutch society (see chapter 3). I am using the concept of culture to refer to something shared by postwar Dutch immigrants, regardless of religious affiliation, class, regional background, gender or education. Such an exercise assumes that one can discover a set of unwritten "rules" to reveal the underlying logic of both identities (how Dutch-Canadians view themselves) and a wide range of behaviours.[1] One can also think of Dutch-Canadian "culture" as the values and expectations that emerged after a period of exposure to Canadian society. In Bourdieu's terminology, I will examine the modified dispositions, or 'habitus,' shared by an entire cohort of postwar immigrants,[2] which generate the varied and sometimes contradictory actions and attitudes of Dutch immigrants as they interact with one another and with other Canadians.

Notes to this chapter are on p. 411-13.

Some readers, especially those for whom my analysis rings true, might read this chapter as a definitive statement on the essence of Dutch culture in North America, instead of as a tentative interpretation of a historically specific myth/reality. The task of explaining what constitutes *Dutchness* in contemporary Canadian society is not easy, given the dual nature of ethnicity. The "reality" side of the Dutch-Canadian equation is complex and still changing while the "myth" component gives the false impression of stability and timelessness. Indeed, my mythologizing objectification, also known as social science analysis, runs the risk of eliminating the inherent tensions and diverging viewpoints that are part of the ongoing construction of social reality. The seemingly stable, albeit complex relational structures uncovered by the outsider (or historian) can easily become part of the process of replication of the phenomenon under investigation, by giving the impression that the object of enquiry represents a natural state of affairs rather than a temporary outcome of prior contestations. I want to avoid this interpretation of my representation.

To prevent a reading which could transform what I write into a self-fulfilling prophesy, I should clarify from the outset that this chapter does not apply to Dutch immigrants who have come to Canada in the past 15 to 20 years. Instead I will primarily concentrate on the people who emigrated between 1947 and 1960. However, my "scientific" construction of their shared dispositions is the construct of a construct, and should not be taken as the timeless essence of Dutch-Canadians. In order to incorporate some sense of a process over time, this chapter will include a short section dealing with the very different dispositions of the children and grandchildren of the postwar immigrants, who have in turn become yet another kind of Dutch-Canadian. We should always keep in mind that any social reality, whether we call it "culture" or "society" is a multifaceted and dual phenomenon. I will also go back and forth between the present and past tense as a way of overcoming the pitfalls of separating a diachronic and synchronic analysis. Although my representation of Dutch-Canadian culture refers to something created in the fifties and sixties, many of the people whose dispositions embody this culture are still alive today and continue to influence the ongoing, albeit imperfect, reproduction of the Dutch component of Canadian society.

The Dilemma of Being Dutch-Canadian

One way to uncover Dutch-Canadian "culture" at any time is to pay close attention to discourse, or verbal interactions. Dutch-Canadians tend to emphasize the importance of integration. Almost all the postwar immigrants I interviewed stated that they or their parents emigrated in order to "become Canadians." The norm is one of fitting in. Dutch-Canadians distinguish themselves from other immigrant groups who supposedly either "stick together" too much, do not want to learn English or are too attached to their homeland. They believed, and still believe, that people from the Netherlands are better adapted to Canadian society. Many informants used the analogy that the "Dutch are like water," with reference to the historic myth of the Dutch going abroad and blending in. One man compared the Netherlanders' adaptability to the clannishness of the Germans.[3] Dutch-Canadians see their ability to become "good Canadians" as a logical outcome of the perseverance and work ethic forged by the Dutch nation's long struggle against the sea. Nonetheless, in defining the ability to integrate as a typical "Dutch" trait, Canadians of Dutch descent unconsciously created a group identity. Such an unintended consequence is a classic example of how too-ardent a pursuit of an ideal can lead to its opposite. There is no simple one-to-one correspondence between self-image and the so-called objective side of social reality.[4]

Equating *Dutchness* with being an "ideal Canadian" is fraught with danger. Dutch immigrants inadvertently maintained many habits and much of their mindset, notwithstanding linguistic assimilation. Although they quickly adopted a new homeland, they held strong opinions and freely "spoke their mind" (as opposed to the English Canadian emphasis on compromise and keeping one's distance). In true Dutch fashion, Dutch immigrants would never admit that they wanted to become rich[5] in the land of opportunity. Instead they loudly proclaim that they emigrated "to make a contribution" to their new fatherland, and "to provide a better future for their children." There were other differences between the new Dutch-Canadians and their neighbours. Even after many years in Canada, Dutch immigrants were stricter with their children, and argued among themselves and with others about religion or politics. A growing awareness of such differences in values engendered an implicit contrast between "Dutch" and "Canadian."

Most Dutch immigrants liked the seeming lack of class distinctions (see chapter 12) in Canada. However, they were ambivalent about other facets of Canadian society. Although ready to reject many aspects of the "old country," immigrants brought up in the Netherlands also criticized the Canadian way of life. Indeed, they saw it as their mission to work for a "better" Canada: rural people would show Canadian farmers how to "farm properly"; orthodox Calvinists planned to make Canada into a "Christian country"; Dutch Catholics wanted more separate schools and to show Canadians how to sing better (and in Latin!); business people yearned to introduce more efficient management and implement the metric system; and most Dutch immigrants thought that Canada needed better social assistance (although they complained about the socialistic tendencies of postwar Netherlands). Many postwar Dutch-Canadians also saw *the Dutch* as born leaders. As the Dutch-Canadian owner of a prominent architectural firm put it, "In my business and my travels I have met many Dutch people. The Dutch for the most part play leading roles. They are real leaders."[6]

Several people brought up the theme of leadership when talking about other topics. Yet living up to an ideal is not easy. Dutch immigrants had problems learning English and many suffered homesickness (see chapter 5). Some never adjusted to a different way of life, much less took on leadership roles. Notwithstanding such difficulties and disappointments, many did eventually buy farms, hold steady jobs or establish small businesses (see the next chapter). The vast majority became Canadian citizens and dropped the Dutch language for all but symbolic or occasional use. Nevertheless, although postwar Dutch immigrants and their immediate descendants have seemingly become "invisible" or "silent," they continue to make comparisons between "the Dutch" versus "the Canadians." The ways these labels are used reflect alternate tactics for reconciling Dutch Canadians' status as "immigrants" or "ethnics" (see also chapter 20) with a desire to be "good Canadians."

After 30 or 40 years in Canada, Dutch immigrants portray themselves as Canadians. Yet these same Dutch-Canadians may confide to close friends (or sympathetic researchers) that only their children or grandchildren will be "true Canadians." This opinion is most frequently expressed when reflecting on the experience of adapting to Canada. First-generation Dutch-Canadians are self-conscious about the fact that they "will never lose their accent." Many feel resentment about perceived prejudice or condescension on the part of Anglo-Canadians. While speaking English, they may socialize mainly with fellow Dutch-Canadians. Even those who get along well with their non-Dutch neighbours, or who have as many "Canadian" as "Dutch" friends, reluctantly admit that they will never feel "completely at home."[7] Feelings of ambivalence also come out when Dutch-Canadian writers try to summarize the Dutch immigrant experience: two different authors use the adjective "bittersweet" in book titles.[8] How then do people reconcile such tensions with their strong belief that the Dutch make "ideal Canadians"?

One way of dealing with the dilemma is to deny one's ethnic heritage. Such a response is not uncommon among immigrants. One can change the spelling of one's name, lie about where one was born (or where one's parents were born) and associate with as few members of one's own ethnic group as possible. For some first-generation Dutch-Canadians, such a response borders on the pathological, such as when someone pretends they cannot speak their native language after only two months in Canada. Such self-denial can last for several decades, until a repressed sense of nostalgia and homesickness finally erupts (see chapter 17). However, in most cases Dutch-Canadians developed a compromise position. Many people interviewed stated that they were foremost Canadians, but that they were also proud of their Dutch heritage—that they were not ashamed of being born and raised in the Netherlands. I once overheard a Dutch Canadian dairy farmer say to the man who picked up his milk, "I'm lucky—you only have a fatherland, but I have a motherland as well as a fatherland." Some people make a clear distinction between their Dutch heritage and their Canadian citizenship and loyalty to Canada. They may prefer Dutch food or occasionally listen to old Dutch records, yet show no interest in keeping up with current political events in the Netherlands.[9] Even people who identify strongly with Holland, or with Dutch culture, still emphasize that "the Dutch make good immigrants."

Admitting that one can be simultaneously "Dutch" and "Canadian" is not always easy. Some immigrants underwent an internal struggle before they could feel "at peace with themselves." Many feel that they are neither Dutch nor Canadian. I heard people making comments such as, "I do not fit into either place." Identical remarks were made to VanderMey when he was doing interviews for his book, *To All Our Children*.[10] Grant Cassidy, who conducted a study of Dutch-Canadian identity in Toronto, made the same observation that first-generation Dutch-Canadians feel "somewhere in between."

> Most respondents in our sample . . . admitted they were Canadians from a Dutch perspective, but from a Canadian perspective they were Dutch. A typical response would be paraphrases such as, "In Holland, I know I'm Canadian, but in Canada I realize I'm still Dutch.[11]

Still, these same people preferred, and most of them still prefer, to live in Canada rather than in Europe.

The level of Dutch—as opposed to Canadian—identity has little bearing on linguistic usage. I have heard vehement denunciations, in fluent Dutch, of the Dutch way of life. Others, speaking English, may express great admiration and praise for the Netherlands, and denounce Canada. Nor is a strong sense of loyalty to Canada incompatible with visiting the old country. Most trips (like letter writing) are undertaken to maintain family ties, sometimes the only link that still ties Dutch-Canadians to the Netherlands. Moreover, during trips to Holland, Dutch-Canadians are forced to confront how much the Netherlands has changed since they emigrated. The inevitable contrasts and comparisons create a greater awareness of differences between Dutch-Canadians and the European Dutch.

A good illustration of such awareness comes from a series of letters in the Dutch-Canadian newspaper *De Krant*. The letters (written in Dutch) were submitted in response to an editorial and, more revealing, in reaction to another letter from someone representing the "odd-ball" position. The editorial compared immigration in North America and the Netherlands.[12] The main point was that newcomers in the Netherlands (in contrast to Canada) had never been fully accepted, and could never feel at home. In contrast, Canada was portrayed as a "real immigration nation," which encourages acceptance of newcomers in a setting that allows the harmonious blending of people from all parts of the world. Readers immediately responded to that editorial article and their opinions were printed in subsequent issues. Most agreed with the criticism of the old country, although many added that they were proud to be of Dutch background and had warm feelings for the Netherlands, despite its shortcomings.

The dissenting opinion came from a Dutchman who maintained his citizenship after living abroad for 50 years.[13] His published letter attacked the editor for daring to slander the Netherlands, calling Canada a "more or less third world county" with many problems. He also mentioned living in Canada only for tax advantages and family reasons. This letter brought vehement rebuttals[14] from Dutch-Canadians who reiterated the themes outlined earlier: how Canada has been good to them, how much better things are in Canada than in Holland (although Holland "is still a nice place to visit") and how the children of Dutch immigrants have done well because they have inherited their parents' energy and vision to build a better Canada. These and other readers reiterated another editorial opinion, namely that Dutch people in the Netherlands are "too pushy," "fussy," "conformist" or "narrow-minded."

The content of such items in the Dutch-Canadian press resemble statements of people interviewed in my study. Yet it became apparent that the words "Dutch" (*Nederlands*) and "Canadian" have different meanings, depending on the context in which they are used. When comparing the Netherlands to Canada, "Canadian" is used in a more comprehensive sense to refer to all Dutch-Canadians whether or not they can speak Dutch. Being a "Canadian" in this sense is better than being "Dutch." "Dutch" in the negative sense is used whenever Dutch-Canadians make comparisons among themselves. Other Dutch-Canadians are seen as "too Dutch," if they fall short of being well-integrated citizens. Then the word "Dutch" connotes being cliquish, short-tempered, overly opinionated, too liberal or too conservative, depending on one's own political orientation. But when comparing Dutch-Canadians to other members of Canadian society (including those of British descent), the term "Dutch" takes on quite a different and more positive meaning. "Dutchness" in that context epitomizes the best of Dutch traits: hard work, perseverance, tidiness, strong family bonds and an ability to "fit in."

The term "Dutch" in this second (positive) sense stands in silent (implied) opposition to "Canadian" (*de canadezen*), which becomes a negative term. The pejorative and exclusive use of the label "Canadian" only occurs when Dutch-Canadians make invidious comparisons between themselves and their non-Dutch neighbours. Thus, one hears such comments as "the Canadians don't know how to farm," or "the Canadians don't work as hard" or "Canadians do things in a different way." In that context, the contrast between "Dutch" and "Canadian" becomes part of a "we" versus "them" mentality. More commonly found among first-generation immigrants, the usage lingers on in the second- and even third-generation. Dutch-Canadians know implicitly when "Canadian" is used as a negative label, although they might not be consciously aware of how its usage contradicts their tendency to equate "being Dutch" with "being a good Canadian." When confronted, Dutch-Canadians who have used the term "Canadian" in such an exclusive way will deny they themselves are somehow not Canadian.[15]

It takes an outsider to pick up such inconsistencies. I encountered a prime example during a visit to a small settlement in the Ottawa region. In that settlement the original farmers had long ago been bought out by several Dutch brothers. They were Catholics and, like so many Dutch Catholics in Canada, both brothers had sons who were married to Catholic but non-Dutch spouses. One of their wives indicated to me that she had no trouble getting along with her in-laws because they always spoke English and accepted her. She compared her own situation to that of an old school friend who had married into another ethnic group, with disastrous results due to cultural clashes. However, at the end of the conversation she commented that she found one thing puzzling: her Canadian-born, completely English-speaking husband occasionally used the expression "those Canadians."

The quite different usage of the terms "Dutch" and "Canadian," as polar opposites, has to be seen in the overall context of any conversation. Dutch-Canadians living in eastern or Northern Ontario make disparaging remarks about the Dutch in southwestern Ontario (including those living in Toronto!). They say that the Dutch in southern Ontario are cliquish and "too Dutch" because they have their own business and professional associations. They also criticize them for being too involved in Dutch clubs and multicultural events. However, I have heard members of largely secular Dutch clubs and organizations in southern Ontario in turn accuse the Reformed Dutch of being "too Dutch" because so many married within their own ethnic category, and because they are less involved in organizations such as Rotary or Kiwanis. Members of the Christian Reformed Church will in turn criticize each other and members of smaller Dutch Calvinist sects in the same manner. In other words, the negative connotations of the term "Dutch" are associated with a continuum that goes from completely Dutch to just a "touch of Dutch." By implication, the more Canadian you are, the better.

One consequence of this emphasis on being "a good Canadian" is a discrepancy between the way Dutch-Canadians portray themselves, as opposed to how they are perceived by neighbours. In a big-city context (like Toronto), with rapid geographical mobility, many first- (and certainly second-) generation Dutch-Canadians blend into the mainstream culture. Canadians not of Dutch descent are largely oblivious to the existence of close-knit Dutch-Canadian networks, ethnic associations or the yearly Dutch consular reception for hundreds of people in a downtown hotel (see chapter 12). Urban "ethnic ghettos" never developed or dispersed quickly. However, in small towns, or rural areas, long-term residents (going back several generations) are quite aware of "outsiders" in their midst. Here the "Dutch" will remain visible for several generations to come.

A classic illustration of a place that has come to be seen as "Dutch" is Delaware (close to London). Delaware was the centre of a seminary founded by Dutch priests (see chapter 8). For twenty years "Dutch picnics," and the annual meetings of the (at that time) Dutch St. Willibrord Credit Union took place there. Many Dutch families settled in and around Delaware (and in the nearby villages of Mount Brydges and Komoko), including the Roks. Their son, John, who came to Canada with his parents when he was eighteen years old, later played a prominent role in local politics. He first became a councillor and in 1990 was elected reeve of Delaware. Three other Dutch-Canadians also became members of the township council that same year. Canadians in Delaware not of Dutch descent, and Dutch-Canadians in other regions, referred to Delaware as having a "Dutch council." However, in an interview with the reeve himself, he presented a different image:

> The Dutch Catholics integrated well and more so in Delaware than in other places. The Sacred Heart fathers came to set up a Canadian parish, not a Dutch parish. . . . It is true that three out of five members of the [township] council are of Dutch background, but they were nominated by non-Dutch Canadians. Some people have commented that the Delaware council is Dutch, but I always respond, "I have a paper to prove that I am Canadian. Can you show me one?" I think this label of "Dutch" will soon disappear.[16]

This discrepancy between visible ethnicity and a self-perception that plays down a Dutch connection also holds true for the Reformed community. While Dutch-Canadian Calvinists emphasize the "Christian" and not the "Dutch" part of their identity, their non-Dutch neighbours continue to talk about "Dutch schools" and "Dutch churches" when talking about Reformed institutions. It does not matter that the people who attend these schools or churches deny such ethnic labels. No matter how many times Reformed Dutch-Canadians reiterate that they no longer have Dutch-language services and that they do not teach Dutch or anything about Holland in these schools, their non-Dutch Canadian neighbours will continue to see them as "Dutch." Given their high rate of endogamy and the fact that the overwhelming majority of that religious community is of recent Dutch immigrant background, it is not surprising that they should be labelled as "Dutch." After all, many Canadian communities going back many more generations are still referred to as "Irish" or "Scottish." First-generation Dutch-Canadians do not fully appreciate this tendency of "real Canadians" to use ethnic labels about themselves.

The Impact of Multiculturalism

The complex dynamics of ethnic identification by Dutch-Canadians is a product of two clashing sets of cultural values and expectations: those the immigrants brought with them from Holland, and those that already existed in Canada. Moreover, since the postwar wave of Dutch immigration, Canada's official position on cultural pluralism has changed. We must take into account the effects of such changes on the process of ethnic identification. This is especially true for Canada's official policy of multiculturalism and bilingualism, which did not appear until the early seventies, under Pierre Trudeau. The development of multicultural festivals and folk-art councils occurred when most postwar Dutch immigrants were already well integrated into Canadian society. Dutch-Canadians involved in politics or local service organizations discovered that they were now supposed to preserve or portray their heritage in order to contribute to a "better Canada." The minority who maintained a strong interest in their language, history or other aspects of their culture came out of the closet. Other Dutch-Canadians, anxious to conform to the ideal of multiculturalism (because that was the "proper Canadian thing to do") had to start apologizing to their non-immigrant neighbours that they no longer spoke their native tongue at home, and that they did not putter around their backyard in wooden shoes, or display a decorative windmill. Still others felt confused. Someone in Guelph told me that "I've told Canadians that they give us immigrants contradictory messages. When I first came here I was supposed to become Canadian as quickly as possible. But now we are supposed to preserve our own identity, with the emphasis on multiculturalism."[17]

Dutch-Canadians, like Canadians on the whole, are divided in their opinions on multiculturalism. Some see it as a potentially divisive force and a waste. They see nothing wrong with people keeping their native languages or putting on folk dances, as long as this is done with one's own money, on one's own time. In contrast, other Dutch-Canadians see government-supported heritage language classes and ethnic festivals as an essential ingredient of what makes Canada a unique country. During a visit to Sarnia, I heard a Dutch-Canadian who had come in the mid-sixties express such an opinion to his brother from Holland who was in Canada for a short visit. The brother (speaking in Dutch) thought it was ridiculous for people who had emigrated to maintain their own language and traditions. His Canadian brother argued that Canada's multicultural policy encourages all immigrants to preserve their ethnic heritage while also becoming integrated into Canadian society. Others hold the view that Canada can only be strong and united if its government and people develop a cohesive Canadian identity and foster the intermingling of people, without ethnic distinctions. I have heard such opinions expressed, in fluent Dutch, by older people who are proud of the fact that their children have found spouses from other ethnic backgrounds. One man asked, "In what category do my grandchildren fit if they have English, Jamaican and Polish, plus Dutch grandparents?" He did not like the notion of hyphenated Canadians and argued that people should have the choice to put "Canadian" down when answering the question about ethnic ancestry on the census form.[18] Yet the same informant conceded that he was being consistent with his Dutch ancestry by having such outspoken opinions. He also regretted that his youngest children had not learned Dutch.

The minority of Dutch-Canadians who are involved in multicultural events lament the disappearance of the Dutch language and the lack of a national organization. They complain about the low level of interest of fellow Dutch-Canadians in "their culture," although they recognize that otherwise apathetic Dutch-Canadians have occasionally rallied around the flag. We have already seen how, in 1970, Dutch-Canadians from all across Canada organized a "Thank You Canada " committee to commemorate the role played by Canadian soldiers in the liberation of the Netherlands at the end of World War Two. On the local level, Dutch-Canadians who normally keep a low profile have successfully organized their own parade floats and displays (see chapter 16). When they set their mind to do something, Dutch-Canadians do it well. In one multicultural event organized in Renfrew, non-Dutch Canadians jokingly commented that their Dutch friends were "showing off a bit."[19]

The apparent contradiction between sporadic public displays of ethnic pride and an overall low ethnic profile is consistent with the dispositions already outlined—especially the strongly held belief that Dutch immigrants are superb at adapting to Canadian society. What constituted "Canadian culture" during the heyday of massive Dutch immigration (the early 1950s) did not include a Dutch component, since few native-born Canadians were aware of the Dutch origin of some of the United Empire Loyalists. Hence it was not consistent that postwar immigrants would bring forth or publicly display their Dutch heritage at that time. Only later was it possible for some Dutch-Canadians to become leaders in the 'field' of multiculturalism. Regardless, few Dutch-Canadians are likely to follow in their footsteps because that is not an area in which the "Dutch" (in a positive sense) are supposed to excel. Those who openly display their Dutch heritage are still perceived to be "too Dutch" (in the negative sense).[20]

Second- and Third-Generation Dutch-Canadians

Although postwar Dutch immigrants developed a unique "immigration culture" of their own, while simultaneously reproducing much of the Dutch pillar system, their Canadian-born offspring are as different from their parents as they are from younger people who remained in the Netherlands. Dispositions tend to change from one generation to the next, and more so in cases of international migration or colonization (see Introduction). Hence, quite apart from the process of ethnogenesis resulting in the creation of a new form of *Dutchness* in North America, the identities of Dutch-Canadians became transformed in the second and third generation.[21] Dutch-Canadians born in Canada, or who were still very young when their parents emigrated from the Netherlands, are considered to be "real Canadians" (usually in the positive sense) because they do not speak with an accent. They also feel more "at home" if they have grown up and gone to school in Canada. Unlike immigrant groups with a different skin colour, most Dutch-Canadians are not subject to racial prejudice. However, it is impossible for second-generation Dutch-Canadians to hide their origins from close friends and relatives. A common theme in the ethnic literature is how the offspring of low-status immigrants are often ashamed of their ethnic heritage. Intergenerational differences in moral values and attitudes towards spending money may compound the resulting confrontations between parents and children. Such intergenerational tensions, common to all immigrant groups, are lower for Dutch-Canadians whose parents have already gone to considerable efforts to "fit in." Yet Dutch-Canadian children are bound to feel resentment if they feel their parents are "too strict" or "too stingy."

The children of Dutch immigrant parents might be tired of hearing how "some things were better in Holland." However, they are also likely to hear non-Dutch Canadians pointing out how Dutch immigrants have done well in adapting to and prospering in the Canadian context (see the next chapter). Such discrepancies are bound to give rise to feelings of ambivalence, whose salience depends on various factors. If a Dutch immigrant couple experienced upward social mobility, their children are more likely to be proud to be Dutch-Canadians. In contrast, those whose parents did not improve their social and economic position might find emphasizing their Dutch heritage to be painful because it reminds them that their family "failed." If such "failure" resulted in not getting access to the farm they were promised or in a lack of education, the rejection of the Dutch label is all the more likely.

Ethnic identity retention among second- and third-generation Dutch-Canadians shows a great deal of variation. The offspring of Dutch immigrants may or may not understand their mother tongue, and they may have greater or fewer Dutch connections. Regardless, they have one thing in common: while growing up in a completely Canadian context and learning to speak fluent English with a "Canadian" accent, they are aware that one or both parents or grandparents are different (speak with an accent, have "different ideas," etc.). Some Canadian-born children of Dutch immigrant parents try to hide their ethnic background as they go through the school system. However, the fact that they are "Dutch" often strikes home when young people grow up and approach marriage. At that point the offspring of immigrants are more likely to develop a new form of Dutch-Canadian identity, and certainly a strong awareness of their Dutch-Canadian origin, if both parents are of Dutch descent, if they have Dutch surnames or if many close relatives are still "Dutch."

A comparative study of three generations within the postwar Reformed community was carried out by Harry Van Belle.[22] He sees the changes in identity and behaviour from the first to the third generation as a process whereby Dutch-Canadians as a group made the transition from a Dutch model based on religious pluralism (the pillar system) to a North American one based on ethnic pluralism. Only then (in the third generation) does the word "Dutch" become used in a more descriptive manner to mean simply Canadians who happen to be of Dutch descent. At that point we can say they have truly become North Americans or Canadians whose "culture" includes a different use of racial and ethnic distinctions. When used by second-, and especially third-generation Dutch-Canadians, the term "Dutch" simply becomes one of several ethnic labels with various connotations, depending on the social context.[23] When interacting with other people (especially in the workplace) such ethnic labels are used in a joking manner to underscore both group solidarity[24] and status differences (a sense of superiority or inferiority).

The label "Dutch" may also be used to express a specific Canadian regional or local community identity among second- or third-generation Canadians. I have found this phenomenon in several places. For example, in dropping in at a fast-food restaurant near Forest, a young female attendant whom I assumed had no Dutch connections mentioned that she was from Arkona, where a lot of Dutch Catholics settled in the fifties. She replied to my enquiries about whether or not she knew about any Dutch-Canadians in that village with the answer "Yes, there are a lot of Dutch farmers around there. We are all Dutch."[25] Similarly a woman of Dutch descent in Ottawa (who does not speak Dutch and is married to someone of Scottish descent), jokingly referred to a "Dutch mafia." I thought she meant a close-knit network of mainly first-generation Dutch-Canadian immigrants in the capital city, but it turned out she was referring to a group of young couples, most of whom speak little or no Dutch. What they have in common is the fact that their parents or grandparents are all first-generation Dutch immigrants with similar attitudes and beliefs, many of whom have a Dutch Calvinist background (though some had since joined other congregations). These couples also shared similar views on how to raise children and established a food co-op where they can buy Dutch delicatessen products.[26]

To return to an earlier theme, we cannot get away from the influence of the Dutch pillar system when discussing the identities of second- and third-generation Dutch-Canadians. Because of a higher rate of endogamy, orthodox Dutch Calvinists are more likely to retain a Dutch identity after several generations than other Dutch-Canadians (with notable rural exceptions). Chapter 9 demonstrated how members of that religious denomination continue to foster social contact with other people who happen to be of Dutch descent. It should come as no surprise, then, that third- and fourth-generation Dutch-Canadians brought up in a Reformed denomination should show a higher level of Dutch ethnic identity.[27] We would also expect such an ethnic identity retention to show up in the use of the term "Dutch" to refer not only to individuals but collectivities. In contrast, Dutch-Canadian Catholics, or people with no religious affiliation, who are not nearly as likely to marry within their own ethnic group, will disappear much faster into mainstream society without reactivating ethnic ties. However, even among such groupings one would find variations in personal or individual identity depending on the class background of their parents (see chapter 12), gender and occupation.

It is harder to generalize about new dispositions for the offspring of smaller sub-groups. Dutch Jews (particularly orthodox Jews) are numerically too small to maintain a distinct ethnic sub-identity within Judaism abroad. The children and grandchildren of racially mixed Indonesian Dutch are also not likely to continue to identify as either Dutch or *Indisch* in the Canadian context for the same reason. The only sub-category that may survive is Frisian, if the offspring of Frisian couples marry others of Frisian descent. Again, that is more likely to occur among Dutch Frisians who belong to a stricter Calvinist congregation that also happens to have a high percentage of such immigrants. In Ontario it is more likely to happen in rural pockets around Waterford (near Simcoe) or in the Bowmanville area. However, categories associated with such sub-groupings are more likely to eventually blend into a broader Dutch category as defined in North America.[28]

A Dutch identity may not develop until later in life among second- or third-generation Canadians, often as a result of renewed contact with grandparents who themselves have become more open about their heritage (see chapter 17). "Discovering one's roots" may also take place while attending a college or university with other young Canadians of Dutch background, such as Redeemer, a liberal arts college in Ancaster founded by the Reformed community. About 80 percent of the students attending the college (and a higher percentage of faculty) are Dutch-Canadians and have Dutch (or Frisian) surnames. Most of the students come to that college without a strong Dutch identity, until they hear such expressions as, "You're not much if you're not Dutch."[29] Only when their non-Dutch friends point out the occasional use of a Dutch household word or comment on their impressions when visiting the homes of such Dutch-Canadian students, do these students start seeing themselves as Dutch.[30] This process of ethnogenesis in turn influences the perception of non-Dutch students. A foreign student (from India), who spent several years living at a residence at Redeemer College, wanted to know if all Canadians were Dutch![31]

The different uses of the word "Dutch" represent one of the subtleties of English-Canadian discourse. Visitors from the Netherlands cannot understand such subtleties, even if they are fully conversant in English. Newly arrived immigrants from Holland cannot accept that someone who does not speak Dutch and who knows almost nothing about contemporary life in the Netherlands could be "Dutch." They are having a hard enough time relating to the Dutch-born immigrants who have been in Canada for several decades or longer. Such new immigrants prefer to organize their own get-togethers. They also do not consider themselves to be "real immigrants," with the connotation of leaving one's homeland on a long journey by ocean liner. Nor are they likely to be as worried about "becoming good Canadians." Their dispositions are quite distinct from the earlier postwar immigrants because they have grown up in a different kind of Dutch society, and are now adjusting to a new kind of Canada.

The continuation of old ethnic identities and the creation of new ones affect historical memories and interpretations. Dutch-Canadians are now writing about how Dutch settlers helped in the building of Canada in the eighteenth and nineteenth centuries. One postwar immigrant who became a history buff not only discovered that Dutch-Americans constituted a segment of the United Empire Loyalists, but that a "real" Dutchman, Anthony Van Egmond (mentioned in chapter 2), was involved in opening up the Huron tract.[32] No doubt second- and third-generation postwar Dutch-Canadians will uncover further historical connections and use this information to write new versions of Canadian history.[33] From the viewpoint of a social scientist or a historian, attempts to demonstrate a process of historical continuity tracing contemporary Dutch-Canadians back to earlier pioneers is dubious. However, past portrayal of Dutch-Canadian historical figures as "British" is equally open to criticism.[34] Such exercises in historiography are no different than attempts by family historians to trace their ancestry back to some illustrious figure of Dutch descent, while ignoring those ancestors who are less interesting, less noble or unrecorded. That is the way new identities and cultures are forged.

Chapter 19

The Invisible Minority in the Vertical Mosaic

Prior population movements and the subsequent interactions among people originating from different countries resulted in Canada's "vertical mosaic" (see chapter 4). For the most part, people of Dutch descent became entrenched somewhere in the top half of this mosaic, jumbled between other tiles of largely European derivation. Although the reader encountered hard-luck stories, the Dutch-Canadian population as a whole has not fared too badly in economic terms, even in the first generation. Taking into account both obstacles and opportunities, Dutch immigrants and their descendants are neither disadvantaged nor privileged, if regarded as a whole. *The Dutch* are also well regarded by other Canadians. However, it is not so easy to disentangle "objective" traits, such as material wealth and level of income, from "subjective" ones, including the ranking of ethnic categories based on reputation. "Scientific" surveys, based on random sampling techniques, average out individual differences in income to come up with a number representing the "typical" state of affairs for a specific ethnic group. Yet the publication of such numbers can change people's subjective perceptions as much as gossip and rumours. Highly variable perceptions are in turn again measured to generate the "normal" or "average" ranking of different ethnic categories. This chapter will tackle both of these dimensions of how the Dutch "fit" into Canadian society.

Dutch immigrants had to compete with other immigrants and native-born Canadians in the same economy. Taking into account many characteristics of their country of origin, it is easy to explain the geographical dispersal, linguistic assimilation and economic integration of postwar Dutch immigrants. The postwar Dutch immigrants were relatively well educated

Notes to this chapter are on p. 413-18.

compared to their counterparts from some other parts of Europe. With the exception of some racially mixed Dutch Indonesians or Dutch Jews, postwar Dutch immigrants were not subject to overt racial or ethnic discrimination. It should then not come as a surprise that these postwar immigrants and their offspring entered a wide range of occupations or professions. Furthermore, those dispositions forged in the Netherlands which were in tune with specific aspects of mainstream Canadian society provided Dutch immigrants with a comparative advantage within many existing 'fields' of endeavour. Like other newcomers, Dutch immigrants were able to carve their own niches in certain sectors of the economy, as well as in the worlds of religion or music, where their presence in turn affected how the Dutch as a whole were perceived. Nor can one leave out the reputation of their country of origin.

A few postwar Dutch immigrants eventually became millionaires. It would be easy to reinforce an already existing positive image of *the Dutch* by dwelling on success stories, especially those resulting in brand names or companies familiar to the average consumer.[1] Such "big names," which inevitably crop up in Dutch-Canadian publications, are used to underscore "the special contribution" made by people of Dutch descent.[2] However, in focusing on famous entrepreneurs, the much larger number of Dutch-Canadians who did not achieve the same notoriety are overlooked. People whose businesses went bankrupt, and those who once had thriving careers, only to founder in Canada, can easily be forgotten. People proud of their ethnic heritage might not want to dwell on the Canadians of Dutch-Canadian ancestry who ended up with mundane and unglamorous jobs, or on those who depend on welfare. Yet we cannot leave out an examination of individual or sub-group variations. Not all Dutch immigrants started off with the same level of education or have the same class background. Those who "made it" in Canada usually had some start-up capital or other advantages (see chapter 12). Yet even if there had been more middle- or upper-class Dutch immigrants, it is not that easy to "rise to the top" in another country, much less displace existing economic or political elites.

The "Place" of the Dutch

No statistical study of ethnic groups has specifically compared Dutch-Canadians with other postwar immigrant groups in Ontario. However, in at least one research project, Dutch-Canadians living in major Canadian urban centres were included as a sub-component of the category "Northern Europeans," together with Scandinavians and Germans. Overall, the North Europeans had relatively high levels in job status and income compared to Eastern and Southern Europeans.[3] This finding is consistent with other studies focusing on subjective rankings, which show that Canadians place the Dutch above other ethnic groups of European descent, but below charter groups such as British, Scots or French.[4] Another way of making comparisons is to examine to what extent members of ethnic categories are over or underrepresented in various occupational groupings. Such a measure of occupational dissimilarity reveals the proportion of a particular population which would have to be redistributed in order for it to be the same as the population at large. For example, compared to Canadians as a whole, Canadians of Dutch descent were only slightly underrepresented among professional and financial occupations in 1961 (−.9). People of German descent were only a bit more underrepresented compared to the Dutch in this category of occupations (−1.8), while for Italian-Canadians the underrepresentation became much larger (−5.2).[5] The group differences are accentuated when we focus on primary and unskilled occupations. Dutch-Canadians are again slightly underrepresented (−2.0), indicating that they are almost as likely to be unskilled workers as the Canadian population as a whole. In contrast, Canadians of Italian descent (with a value of +11.5) were much more likely to work as unskilled labourers.[6] Yet Canadians of Dutch descent are not as "average" or "invisible" as they would like to think, especially if we focus on certain occupations.

The Dutch in Ontario Agriculture and Construction

In chapter 6 we saw that nearly half of all Dutch-Canadians in Ontario live in rural townships, especially in the southwestern corner of the province. Indeed, as early as 1961, people of Dutch descent involved in agriculture were highly overrepresented (+10.3) compared to the Canadian population as a whole. By 1970 over a third of all Canadians of Dutch origin still lived in rural areas. Technically the Dutch were at that time still the least urbanized of all ethnic categories, not counting native peoples.[7] This strong rural presence rises in Ontario, where people of Dutch background today make up the largest ethnic component of its agricultural heartland.[8]

It seems that Dutch-Canadian farmers have been successful (i.e., commercially viable) farmers.[9] The proportion of Dutch in different parts of rural Ontario, as reported in the 1986 census, lends credence to this image. Generally speaking, rural townships with more Dutch-Canadians also show higher average numerical values for standard indicators of economic success: gross sales per hectare of improved farmland, amount of land and number of buildings per farm, machinery and equipment per hectare, tons of fertilizers, and number of farmers reporting hired labour.[10] For example, Oxford county (around Woodstock) is one of the most fertile agricultural regions, with both a dairy industry and cash cropping; here Dutch-Canadians comprise more than 3 percent of the population in all townships, ranging from a low of 3.2 to a high of 19.56.[11] Names of prominent Dutch-Canadian dairy producers frequently appear in dairy magazines.[12] Dutch-Canadians are also prominent in horticulture and in the hog industry.[13]

Almost all full-time Dutch-Canadian farmers came from a farm background, although those who excelled in Canada were usually more prosperous or enterprising agriculturalists back home, albeit on a smaller scale (see chapter 12). No data is available to enable us to make a similar rough estimate of how Dutch-Canadians who came from towns and cities in the Netherlands did in comparison. I suspect that if a comprehensive survey of occupational distribution were done it would show that first-generation postwar Dutch immigrants (like the Germans) were more likely to be skilled craftsmen, such as carpenters and tool-and-die makers. The proportion of immigrants who got white-collar jobs within a reasonably short period of their arrival would also be higher for the Dutch for reasons to be outlined later on.[14] Numerous Dutch immigrants of working-class background later became supervisors or foremen in industrial plants. Many postwar Dutch immigrants also ended up in the construction industry, just like the Italians. However, the Dutch found a niche in a specialized subsector, that of framing and building houses. Indeed, approximately a fifth of the membership of the Canadian Home Builders Association is of Dutch descent.[15] The bigger builders were city immigrants, although people with a farm background also became contractors in Canada.

The Dutch in Other Fields of Endeavour

The Dutch are also well represented in the world of politics, especially at the local level. A surprisingly large number, many in the first generation, have become mayors, part-time mayors or reeves, not to mention the numerous councillors and school board officials of Dutch background. For example, in the 1992 Ontario municipal elections, nearly 50 Dutch-Canadians (including three women) ran for posts on city and town councils and school boards, and many won.[16] In Perth county alone, three out of 11 townships have had Dutch-Canadian reeves, and in two cases (Durham and Ottawa), first-generation Dutch-Canadian mayors chaired regional municipalities.[17] However, these elected Dutch-Canadian officials, who come from different backgrounds in term of religious upbringing or region of origin,[18] do not form a coherent network based on common ethnic affiliation. Nor do they represent a specific ethnic constituency, although many are aware of each others' existence. Such invisibility as an ethnic group in the political arena is again consistent with statistical data on the high level of integration of Dutch-Canadians as a whole.

In other 'sub-fields,'[19] such as the musical world, the active involvement of the Dutch is likewise significant, although not obvious. For example, the Canadian armed forces bands recruited musicians from the Netherlands during the fifties, and again in the mid-sixties. Dutch-Canadian musicians, stationed in places like Camp Borden and Petawawa, at one point constituted over half the members in several regimental bands providing concerts across Canada. At least one Dutch-Canadian writer has brought this fact to light, thereby modifying the definition of *the Dutch* in terms of their "contribution" to Canadian society.[20] However, most people who used to attend such musical events would be oblivious to the bands' Dutch-Canadian composition; band members sometimes wear Scottish kilts! Numerous cases of such economic and social integration can be found in other aspects of Ontario society. For example, at least a dozen Dutch-Canadians took over and ran established community newspapers with no Dutch connections.[21]

The Pitfalls of Comparison

It is customary in ethnic research to include a comparative analysis. However, comparisons can be problematic; differences among ethnic groups, no matter how narrowly such groups are defined, usually turn out to be less significant than those based on gender or region. Social and economic inequalities within an ethnic category may be larger than those between people of two distinct ethnic categories. Nevertheless, the very portrayal of differences among ethnic groups can create self-fulfilling prophesies.[22] The social perception of ethnic groups affects how people interact with one another, which may in turn reinforce individual inequalities related to ethnicity.[23] Even the "scientific" act of measuring differences in average income, status or level of education among people who happen to come from another country (or who have the same skin colour or a shared religion), could perpetuate such differences.[24] It is unethical to compare ethnic categories, without at the same time dispelling the myths surrounding such inequalities.[25]

Statistics on average income or differential status relating to *the Dutch* in Canada are subject to misinterpretation. Some people, including most Dutch-Canadians themselves, explain such differences in terms of a stronger work ethic, religious values or other cultural factors. Such explanations do not take into account the influence of the overall level of social and economic development in the Netherlands at the time of emigration. Dutch immigrants who entered the Canadian world of business and politics came from a country where they had already been exposed to a highly urbanized, industrial society with a good educational infrastructure.[26]

Dutch society was also characterized by a social structure capable of recruiting family labour and by a cultural tradition emphasizing both cooperation and individual competition (see chapter 3). The relatively greater success rate of first-generation Dutch-Canadian immigrants (on average) is the outcome of opportunities that matched their level of education, work experience and class background, with cultural values playing a secondary role.

Compared to postwar immigrants from southern Italy or Portugal, the "typical" Dutch immigrant had a relatively high level of education and technical training.[27] Given the Dutch educational system, which produced large numbers of skilled craftsmen, it is not surprising that Dutch-Canadians entered a variety of economic and other fields. Dutch immigrants who wanted to become financially independent also arrived at the right time, during the economic boom of the fifties and sixties. In contrast to German-speaking political refugees from Eastern Europe, the Dutch had more personal belongings and greater possibilities of bringing at least some money into Canada (see chapter 4). The overall ranking of the Dutch as a national grouping thus makes sense in the light of studies which have tried to sort out the relative importance of educational background, class background, parents' economic status and ethnicity. Such studies demonstrate that ethnicity per se plays only a small part in determining the differential rates of socio-economic mobility among various categories of people.[28] Chapter 12 already argued that family connections and schooling could explain the most dramatic cases of upward mobility among first-generation Dutch immigrants. Here I will provide additional background information concerning postwar Dutch immigrants to highlight the opportunities available in Ontario in the fifties.

Competitive Advantage

Dutch dispositions related to schooling, work experience, family structure and level of urbanization "fitted" the postwar economy of Canada. In fact, in all these respects, postwar Dutch immigrants had a long-term competitive advantage. We have already seen (chapter 8) how some capital got transferred directly from the Netherlands, as "black money," in the case of some agrarian immigrants. More importantly, farm immigrants came at the right time, when prices of land and farm operations were very low (see chapter 4). Many a Canadian farmer, about to retire and with no family members interested in taking over, provided private mortgages at low interest rates. For example, the Reinders, who have a farm in Moorefield (near Drayton) gave a $500 down payment in 1952 and received a 4 percent mortgage from the previous non-Dutch owner.[29] In the region of Simcoe, Dutch immigrants obtained farms for a down payment as low as $100, with a 3 percent private mortgage![30] In many cases, immigrants could pay off the money they owed by continuing to work for the previous owner. Canadian landowners also helped Dutch immigrants buy farms by co-signing loans at local banks. According to a study conducted by Tuinman in the mid-fifties, almost half the Dutch immigrants of agrarian background who arrived between 1946 and 1952 started their own farm operations.[31]

We cannot overlook the hierarchical and close-knit nature of the Dutch family, which enabled Dutch immigrant farmers to save on labour costs. This is one reason why so many were able to displace established Canadian farmers. Traditionally, in the Netherlands, offspring of both sexes helped their parents prior to getting married (see chapter 3). Dutch parents, in turn, had a moral obligation to assist their children in setting up a farm or business once they were older. Hence able-bodied sons and daughters sent off to work were expected to hand over their earnings to their parents, enabling Dutch-Canadian families to quickly save up the money to buy their first farm. Once the family farm was established, the children would work on the farm or continue to work elsewhere to help pay off debts. Although the custom of unpaid labour was modified after a decade of immersion in Canadian society, this disposition provided an important competitive advantage to the Dutch-Canadian farmers.[32] Farmers who emigrated to Ontario in the forties and fifties also came during a period of economic expansion, with the possibility of off-farm employment for both city and country immigrants.

City immigrants, especially skilled tradespeople, had the advantage of previous training and experience. However, in the late forties and early fifties many did not have the chance to immediately pursue the career of their choice. Consequently, people often learned new trades or took jobs they would have never considered at home. The theme of immigrants having to adjust to a completely different line of work comes out in immigration stories—how the baker had to become a butcher or vice versa. However, it would be misleading to overemphasize this turbulent side of the immigration experience associated with initial adaptation. In the long run, Dutch immigrants gravitated towards careers and social positions that most closely corresponded to their expectations. Whenever possible, they entered careers where they were more likely to succeed, given their prior dispositions.

Ethnic Reputation

We have already seen how Dutch dispositions, including prior training and expertise originally obtained in the Netherlands, influenced rates of success in different economic and social 'fields.' How well individual Dutch-

Canadians did in business, politics or the world of education or art also depended in part on the reputation of the Dutch as a whole. Just as a negative image can impede the social mobility of members of a stigmatized ethnic group, a reputation for excellence attached to an ethnic 'class' or an entire nation has real social consequences. For example, in the case of Dutch farmers, Holland has an international reputation for its horticulture, greenhouses and dairy industry.[33] Indeed, this reputation was one factor that prompted the Canadian government to allow the immigration of agricultural workers and prospective farmers from the Netherlands just after the War (see chapter 4). The arrival of thousands of agrarian immigrants, especially in regions like southwestern Ontario, reinforced the image of the Dutch as frugal and enterprising agriculturalists in the popular imagination, thereby augmenting the reputation they had already achieved earlier in the Holland Marsh (see chapter 2). Once numerous postwar Dutch immigrants became established in parts of rural Canada, their presence simultaneously reinforced the image and well as the reality of *the Dutch* as a separate ethnic group, whether Canadians of Dutch descent liked it or not. This particularly holds true for horticulture.

Nurseries and Flowers

In people's minds, the Dutch and Holland are so strongly associated with this sector of the economy that even non-Dutch businesses frequently adopt names like "Dutch Mill Nursery" or "Holland Gardens." Indeed, the commercial growing and transportation of flowers in particular is a business dominated by Dutch-Canadians, who control 80 percent of the greenhouse operations in Ontario. About 70 percent of the growers and at least 10 percent of the retail florists in Ontario are of recent Dutch descent.[34] This Dutch presence is noticeable in the flower auction in Mississauga, which uses a clock system introduced from the Netherlands.[35] While only a small proportion of the Dutch immigrants went into horticulture, Dutch-Canadians as a whole are still best known as farmers or people who run nurseries. This image is both reflected and perpetuated by the novels of award-winning, Dutch-Canadian writers, such as Hugh Cook, and even Aritha Van Herk, who have written about growing up or working on farms.[36] To some extent, the image corresponds to "reality" as shown in this and earlier chapters. However, we must be careful in making sweeping generalizations. For example, in Essex and Kent counties, the Italians and not the Dutch have become foremost in the greenhouse business.[37] Other ethnic groups, such as the Slovaks and the Swiss, have also carved out niches in commercial agriculture. Yet the very fact that I singled out the Dutch-Canadians reinforces popular expectations, making it even more likely that Dutch-Canadians (or Canadian businesses assuming Dutch symbols) will maintain their competitive advantage.

The World of Art

Almost every popular book dealing with *the Dutch* inevitably includes some references to visual artists, since almost everyone will have heard of Rembrandt, Van Gogh, Hals, Vermeer and Escher. Although the artistic 'field' operates according to its own rules,[38] the world of art still intersects with the ethnic dimension, in so far as ethnic identity may provide at least one of the social conditions under which works of art become recognized. The international reputation of Dutch artists throughout the past three centuries cannot help but shape the self-image and strategies of artists of Dutch descent, as well as how they are perceived by, and relate to, other Canadians. Any well-known artist of Dutch descent in Canada can become a symbol for *Dutchness*, regardless of the actual connections of the artist with other Dutch-Canadians. For example, the Canadian Netherlands Business and Professional Association sponsored a special art exhibit of Dutch-Canadian artists at Harbourfront in Toronto in the summer of 1980.[39] Similarly, at the 1991 annual CAANS conference held in Kingston, a Dutch-Canadian bronze sculptor and a visual artist were invited as guest speakers, even though they had little contact with other Dutch-Canadian or Dutch-Canadian organizations. Other visual artists, both professional and amateur, have become well entrenched in a Dutch-Canadian network of social interaction.[40]

The "Dutch" in Public Life

In exploring the theme of ethnic reputation, one cannot ignore the unintended consequences of a strong Dutch-Canadian presence in other 'fields,' including politics. We have already seen how postwar Dutch immigrants entered local political life without drawing much attention to themselves (see above). However, even political organizations with no ethnic agenda or labels are not immune from being perceived in ethnic terms. A prime example is the Christian Heritage Party (CHP). While Dutch-Canadians are found in all political fringe groups, the CHP fields more Dutch-Canadian candidates than any other party.[41] Indeed, that political party, founded by a group of Dutch immigrants who belonged to the Canadian Reformed Church, is sometimes referred to as a "Dutch" party (see chapter 13). The high profile of Dutch-Canadians in that party is bound to effect how *the Dutch* are perceived by Canadians at large. Matters get more complicated once we look at cases where Dutch-Canadians, regardless of religious affiliation, almost completely dominate non-Dutch institutions. We saw a case in the chapter on language, where a community senior citizen's club was taken over by Dutch-speaking people. Any one of the three formerly Dutch credit unions still controlled by Dutch-Canadians, long after they have lost their official ethnic bond, can serve as another example. Such organizations are all de facto rather than de jure Dutch-Canadian institutions (see also next chapter).[42]

Dutch immigrants have also left their imprint in 'fields' other than agriculture, the credit union movement and organized religion. For instance, individual Dutch-Canadians with no connections to credit unions rose to positions of prominence in other branches of the cooperative movement. One could ask to what extent their success, or failure, in that socio-economic sector is explainable in terms of prior dispositions inculcated in the Netherlands or in a Dutch-Canadian environment. That question would apply to any prominent person in the world of business or politics who happens to be of Dutch descent, regardless of whether or not they identify with the ethnic category into which they are slotted. Another issue is the symbolic effect of raising such questions in the first place. To further explore this dimension, I will cite the case of a postwar Dutch immigrant who became a high-ranking official in the cooperative insurance empire.[43]

This former official, whose name will not be revealed, first came to my attention during an interview with a former employee of DUCA.[44] Originally from the Veluwe, in the Netherlands, our nameless man emigrated in 1951 at the age of 19. His involvement in the co-operative movement started as a result of a claim involving a car accident.[45] However, while he has kept in touch with old Dutch friends abroad, going back to his college days, he no longer has any connections with other Dutch-Canadians. He left the Christian Reformed Church a long time ago, and does not have a clue about the presence of other Dutch-Canadians or Dutch-Canadian organizations in the town where he has lived for several decades. In that regard he is typical of many former immigrants who have no interest in Dutch-Canadian affairs, in other Dutch immigrants, or in promoting a Dutch presence in Canada. Yet he cannot get away from the fact that other Dutch-Canadians do know him. His career inevitably put him in touch with a handful of Dutch-Canadians in charge of running credit unions.

Some Dutch-Canadian ethnic historian may one day recognize this official's name, which appears in at least two publications,[46] and then turn him into yet another example of the contribution of *the Dutch* to Canadian society. People who want to remain anonymous might be thus incorporated into the ethnic myth/reality against their will. I too, could be accused of such manipulation just by virtue of writing this paragraph. No scholarly treatment, regardless how "objective," can avoid the place of the writer or social scientist in the very social reality of which he or she is a part. The thoughts and actions of people, including social scientists, revolve around a complex constellation of economic and symbolic interests which may or may not be compatible with the survival of specific ethnic identities. Indeed, the collective outcome of the actions of even isolated individuals sharing a common national origin can make a difference in how ethnic aggregates are perceived. In the very process of interacting with their non-Dutch neighbours, Dutch immigrants and their immediate descendants inadvertently helped to reinforce an image of *the Dutch* even if they saw themselves as "true Canadians" (see previous chapter). Ethnic categories, and the notion that every ethnic group makes its special contribution to Canadian society, is an integral component of the everyday discourse that constitutes the myth/reality called Canada.

A Counterimage

Despite their good reputation, not all Dutch immigrants prospered or even managed to keep their head above water. There were numerous cases of immigrants who did not have the nerve to start a business for themselves, even if they had one in the Netherlands. Such people preferred steady, albeit not always lucrative jobs, and channelled their energies into hobbies, community involvement or family affairs. More than half of the agrarian immigrants did not became full-time commercial farmers, nor did they all "live poor and die rich." Such cases contradict the picture so far presented. As we saw in the case of the greenhouse industry in Essex county, the Dutch are not always "the best." Similarly, the highest concentration of rural Dutch is in the less fertile land on the Lake Erie side of the Niagara escarpment, not in the vineyards and fruit orchards along the coast of Lake Ontario.[47] It is also important to examine why so many agrarian immigrants from the Netherlands did not enter the agricultural sector at all, and what happened to those who did not succeed.

We have already seen how Dutch immigrant farmers were dependent on unpaid family labour. Consequently, many Dutch immigrant farmers discouraged their offspring from completing or continuing their studies (see chapter 5). This was especially true in the fifties, when Dutch rural families still relied on the earnings of their teenage children. Dutch parents also kept teenage children on the home farm as long as possible to ensure that they would carry on the family tradition of independent farming. Indeed, even fathers who had received extensive agricultural schooling in the old country were worried that higher education might tempt young people to pursue city careers and thus follow the example of many young rural Canadians who were no longer interested in farming. However, if a Dutch immigrant couple did not manage to eventually buy a farm to pass on to their offspring, or if they went bankrupt, such children, without education or specialized skills, could only enter the work force as unskilled manual labourers. Few people are likely to talk about these cases, and their children are less likely to identify with their Dutch heritage (see last chapter).

More so than agrarian immigrants, newcomers from a city background often experienced downward mobility or never fulfilled their life's ambitions. A woman in Guelph commented,

> We came to Canada in 1952. My father was a city person and had a good business in Holland. Just like my husband's family, we arrived in Montreal and then moved to Brantford. There my father had various odd jobs but he never got very far. He went down a notch in Canada. I have a brother who was in his late twenties when I left. He has done OK for himself. He later emigrated because he had four boys and did not see a future for them in Holland, but emigration also did not do that much for him.[48]

I also heard such expressions as "going a step down" in talking to people about their emigration experience. Another woman told me a story about how her parents had a paint and chemist's supply outlet in Den Helder (Noord Holland), with sixteen employees. Her father did "odds and ends" in Canada before setting up a paint and wallpaper store in Ottawa, while her mother worked as a cleaning lady. Their business later went under. That man spent his last ten years in the work force as a "maintenance engineer" (janitor) at a local civic hospital. She added, "Dad bought a winterized cottage but we used to have to go out and get pails of water to fill the baths."[49]

Contrary to their image as a "successful" ethnic group, lots of Dutch-Canadians have ended up in dead-end jobs or are chronically unemployed; many women in particular ended up as poor widows and single mothers dependent on a combination of government cheques, meagre pensions and sporadic earnings. According to the 1990 population census, over 7,000 women of Dutch descent belonged to households with a total annual income of less than $10,000.[50] We can get some indication of the extent to which these women's families have some link with the broader Dutch-Canadian ethnic network by taking into account the 400 packages sent out to needy families or individuals each year with money raised at the Dutch Bazaar. The number of needy children of Dutch descent sent off to summer camp has gone up from 12 in 1975 to 150 in 1993.[51]

Dutch-Canadian Crooks

Like all social groups, the postwar Dutch had their fair share of con-artists and crooks, and people who engaged in "shady dealings." We encountered such a case when examining chartered flights. A more infamous example, which came to the attention of the broader public, involves the owner of a national car dealership franchise. His company was charged with fraud (including setting back odometers). However, not all cases of "white collar crime"—mainly known among Dutch circles—have been detected. For example, in my conversations and interviews with Dutch-Canadians, people consistently recounted stories about an otherwise well-known and respected member of the Dutch-Canadian community (now deceased) who made his money through crooked deals in the field of agribusiness.[52] The Dutch tiles on the mosaic have smudges.

Conclusion

We cannot completely disentangle Dutch dispositions, the structure of opportunities in Canada available to immigrants and ethnic reputation. Surveys comparing ethnic groups lead to meaningless generalizations if they leave out other 'class' differences. Even if researchers use sophisticated statistical techniques (like multiple regressions) to control for such variables as social class and gender, we are still left with a quandary. The very act of comparing people of different ethnic or national categories—especially those already ranked in the wider society—can perpetuate the socially constructed hierarchies that are part of the process of social stratification. Social systems are embodied as dispositions (including those of academics) that continually produce and reproduce social systems. It does not matter if the statistical comparison of ethnic groups involves prejudiced opinion or "scientific" investigation. Social reality and the perception of social reality exist in a state of constant tension and recursive causal loops; what journalists and scholars write about is an integral part of the dialectic between discourse and relations of power involving struggles for both reputation and access to resources.

Chapter 20

A Reinterpretation of Immigration and Ethnicity

> ". . . theoretical progress presupposes the integration of new data at the cost of a critical challenging of the bases of the theory that the new data put to the test."[1]

Research on the migration of people from one country to another presents a challenging task to social scientists. This task is all the more complicated because immigration is invariably connected to ethnogenesis and multiculturalism, as well as to social mobility and stratification. Ethnic categories resulting from immigration are an integral part of a multifaceted social reality that critical investigators need to scrutinize. Yet academic researchers use the same habitual language, and often take for granted the same ethnic labels, as the rest of society. This familiarity with the phenomenon under investigation presents epistemological problems; even empirical scholars are prone to replicate taken-for-granted categories in their formal, "scientific" discourse unless they systematically conduct a prior critique of ordinary language.[2]

Methodological Implications

My research on postwar Dutch immigrants in Ontario was originally motivated by an interest in ethnic identity and immigrant adaptation.[3] However, as someone considered to be a member of the "Dutch-Canadian community," I had to be doubly vigilant. The advantage of having an insider's knowledge made it more likely that I might reproduce the social phenomenon under investigation instead of discovering "the relationships and connections that remain hidden within the wealth of appearances and actions of everyday life."[4] To avoid making such an error requires an epis-

---

Notes to this chapter are on p. 418-19.

temic break with common sense,[5] as well as what Pierre Bourdieu calls "scientific common sense."[6]

Initially I was tempted, time and time again, to focus on the neo-Calvinists, who displayed such a high level of institutional completeness. They had already been given semi-official recognition in the Canadian ethnic literature through Ishwaran's case study of *the Dutch* in the Holland Marsh,[7] not to mention numerous university dissertations (see bibliography). Another strategy would have been to focus only on Dutch-Canadians who were more "visible" in terms of ethnic identity retention, especially the "club people," many of whom happened to be Catholics. However, even a combination of these approaches would have resulted in a one-sided study, since at least half of the postwar Dutch immigrants might have been excluded. Instead, I opted to look at everyone, including Dutch immigrants affiliated with other churches, as well as people with no religion at all. I wanted to get the "whole picture," yet it was disappointing to find out that members of other sub-groups had not set up their own organizations, nor did they necessarily display signs of a unique spatial clustering. I was still hoping to find the "essence" of *the* "cultural group," using the traditional anthropological notion of a holistic study. My work could not proceed further until I confronted the basic assumptions in ethnic studies, which were getting in the way of my investigations.

Assumptions in Ethnic Studies

An unacknowledged assumption is that ethnically defined populations are homogeneous entities with well-defined boundaries. People with links to a common country of origin are usually treated as if they shared some important, essential trait. Until recently, most experts in ethnic studies and government census officials alike thought it was possible to divide the entire Canadian population into mutually exclusive categories defined in terms of national origin. The same logic is reflected in the official lists of "ethnic groups" put out by the Multicultural Branch of the Secretariat of State. Such notions of ethnic categories are consistent with taken-for-granted folk categories. Comparative statistical research, which uses nationally defined ethnic categories, further contributes to this common-sense notion of ethnic homogeneity, by emphasizing inter-ethnic differences at the expense of intra-ethnic diversity (see previous chapter). This is as true for ethnic studies as it is for the work done by sociologists interested in stratification and social mobility.[8] Social science research, in turn, can shape the mentality of people exposed to higher education or government policies promoting multiculturalism. Stereotypes, officially sanctioned labels, self-representation, and the portrayal of ethnic and racial groups by scholars thus reinforce each other in the social construction of reality.

A second, though not corollary, assumption is the equation of ethnic identity retention with continuities in pre-immigration cultural values or social institutions. According to that assumption, the salience of ethnic phenomena depends on cohesive communities whose members preserve the values and institutions of their homeland. At the same time, ethnicity is no longer considered a crucial variable after a transitional period of assimilation and integration into the "mainstream."[9] Of course most researchers would acknowledge that Canadian society does continue to display some ethnic diversity. Past immigration resulted in the establishment of several long-lasting ethnic communities, usually with religious connotations. Their members are supposed to maintain a unique language or other ethnographic traits. The best-known examples are the Old Order Mennonites in southern Ontario, Doukhobors in Western Canada, and even Irish or French Catholics enclaves in rural regions where the population is of predominantly Protestant Scottish and English origin. The continued existence of ethnic minorities is associated with a high level of "institutional completeness." This term, coined by Raymond Breton, refers to the existence of various institutions founded by immigrants (including ethnic churches). Nevertheless, contemporary scholars specializing in Canadian ethnic studies tend to focus on recent immigrants,[10] thus reinforcing the impression that ethnicity remains at best a token, part-time aspect of the lives of the majority of English-speaking Canadians beyond the immigration stage. In their everyday language, "mainstream" Canadians usually equate "ethnics" with immigrants and their immediate descendants.

The assumptions just outlined reflect the ambiguous nature of ethnicity. Social scientists and non-academics alike simultaneously use the notion of ethnicity in both a more restricted and in a broader, more inclusive, sense. Depending on the social context, we either see all Canadians as "ethnics," or else equate "ethnics" with specific sub-groups. The discourse of ethnicity becomes even more ambivalent when we turn such ethnic labels into hyphenated names: Franco-Ontarian, African-Canadian, Italian-Canadian or Dutch-Canadian. Moreover, the phenomenon of ethnicity, itself subject to different interpretations, is but one component of a complex process involving both continuities and discontinuities. In order to achieve a deeper understanding of the outcome of large-scale international migration, it is crucial to analytically distinguish ethnic identity retention from other forms of social continuity. In so doing, social scientists must discard the common-sense assumption of homogeneous ethnic groups. An alternative approach, illustrated through my case study of

Canadians of Dutch descent, is to pay more attention to internal diversity within both the immigrant population and that of the country of destination.

Going Beyond Common Sense

In order to come to grips with the link between immigration and ethnicity, I had to make a concerted effort to go beyond the taken-for-granted world of everyday reality reflected in ordinary language.[11] Failure to do so would have resulted in an incomplete, and even distorted, analysis. In the case of postwar Dutch immigrants, studies based on the twin assumptions of ethnic homogeneity and of the equation of ethnic identity retention with socio-cultural continuity have been particularly prone to inconsistent findings. The whole notion of a homogeneous cohort of postwar Dutch immigrants, or the idea of a single Dutch-Canadian community, is a myth. However, like most myths that become part of common sense, this myth has become an integral part of social reality. Despite considerable internal diversity, we cannot ignore the fact that the various sub-groups originating in the Netherlands were nevertheless perceived as a single entity by their non-Dutch neighbours. Nowadays *the Dutch* are considered by most Canadians of both Dutch and even non-Dutch descent to be one of Canada's discrete, well-bounded, nationally defined ethnic groups. This image is in part the outcome of a process of ethnogenesis, worthy of investigation by itself. That topic is certainly covered in various parts of this book. However, the formation of Dutch ethnic associations was not very relevant for the majority of Canadians of Dutch descent (see chapter 18), although Dutch-Canadians did form many other kinds of institutions. The contested and even indeterminate nature of what it means to be "Dutch-Canadian" becomes especially apparent when talking about such institutions that may not carry ethnic labels.

Many "Dutch," or Dutch-Canadian, institutions, especially Reformed ones, are not defined in ethnic terms by their own members.[12] Yet both professional researchers and the general public continue to consider churches and religious organization set up by Dutch Calvinist immigrants as an ethnic phenomenon.[13] Such religious institutions are also deemed ethnic within Canada's multicultural bureaucracy. For example, a recent directory of the Hamilton and District Multicultural Council lists eight different Reformed churches as well as the secular Hamilton Holland Club under the category "Dutch."[14] Most organizations that carry the label "Christian" are similarly treated as Dutch-Canadian institutions if they were started by Dutch immigrants. Canadians not of Dutch background similarly label such denominationally based institutions as "Dutch schools" and "Dutch churches" (see chapter 18). Even the Christian Heritage Party (CHP) gets depicted as "Dutch," although most of its members and supporters would reject such a label.

A Dutch presence becomes clear cut in those cases where people openly display their *Dutchness* through ethnic symbols, especially within Canada's "multicultural" establishment. However, that social 'field' has little immediate or practical relevance for the majority of Dutch-Canadians. Dutch ethnic clubs involved mainly newly arrived immigrants and became relevant again only as Dutch-Canadians approached retirement. For most other men and women, such ethnic activities were at best marginal and part-time. Nevertheless, Dutch ethnic organizations, either homegrown or directly transplanted from the Netherlands, carried a symbolic significance much broader than their numerical size. Hence the periodic revival of support for local Dutch museum exhibits[15] or such Dutch-Canadian ethnic institutions as the Operation Thank You Committee or Netherlands Days (see chapter 16).

The extent to which postwar Dutch immigrants retained a separate group identity is open to debate; it depends in part on whether we use a "subjective" or an "objective" approach. Chapter 18 showed how Dutch-Canadians do not go out of their way to emphasize their *Dutchness*. They are indeed "silent," or "invisible." Yet if ethnic identity retention is equated with observable behaviour—or membership plus level of participation in Dutch-Canadian institutions—we might get quite a different picture; but that too depends on the definition of what is a Dutch institution. If we were to count only ethnically defined associations, the participation rate of Dutch-Canadians in their own ethnic institutions shows great variation over time. Membership grew slowly throughout the forties and fifties, reaching a crescendo in the late sixties and early seventies. That period was the heyday of the Dutch-Canadian credit unions and many social and cultural associations. At least 50,000 Dutch-Canadians in Ontario belonged to organizations that had the label "Dutch Canadian," based on a conservative estimate of total Dutch membership in all Dutch-Canadian credit unions,[16] plus the people in Dutch clubs whose members did not belong to credit unions.[17] With a marked decline in club memberships, and the loss of an ethnic bond for a shrinking number of credit unions, the number of people with a connection to Dutch ethnic organizations dropped to insignificant proportions by the late eighties. The complete list of members of such organizations in 1990 would not exceed 3,000.[18] This optimistic estimate represents 5 percent of the roughly 60,000 first-generation postwar Dutch immigrants who came to Ontario during the past four decades. If we take the total figure of approximately

200,000 people of Dutch descent in Ontario, the proportion dwindles to less than 2 percent.

However, such estimates concerning participation in ethnically defined Dutch-Canadian organizations must be put into a broader perspective. Although Dutch immigrants and their offspring have assimilated in terms of language and other visible cultural traits, at least one subsegment of the Dutch-Canadian population refuses to become fully integrated into the social and political institutions of mainstream Canadian society. That segment of the Dutch-Canadian population consists of orthodox Calvinists (or the Reformed group), who have created their own schools, churches and a myriad of organizations described in chapter 9. If these religious establishments were counted as de facto Dutch-Canadian institutions, the proportion of Canadians of Dutch descent involved in "ethnic" organizations in Ontario would probably rise to close to 30 percent (or 65,000).[19] The number rises even higher if we add the combined Dutch-Canadian memberships of the St. Willibrord and DUCA community credit unions, counting only those people of Dutch descent not already associated with a Reformed church. That procedure would bring the ethnic identity retention of Dutch-Canadians well above that of other European ethnic groups. The strength and visibility of the Dutch presence thus depends on the claims or assumptions of people of both Dutch and non-Dutch descent, which in turn affect the way statistics are generated and interpreted.[20] The Dutch-Canadian reality is thus more complex and varied than a purely objectivist or subjectivist approach would indicate.

Migration and Ethnicity: Continuities and Discontinuities

We cannot link ethnicity and immigration in a simplistic fashion. If we look at postwar Dutch immigrants as a whole, the replication of social structures and cultural values originating in the country of origin did not always go hand in hand with the retention of a strong ethnic identity. On the contrary, if we compare various sub-components of the Dutch-Canadian population, strength of ethnic identity has little bearing on levels of group endogamy or institutional completeness. Immigrants from the Netherlands and their immediate descendants ended up joining a diverse set of overlapping communities in Canada. Some of these communities were founded by, and still consist primarily of, Dutch-Canadians; others could not be described in ethnic terms by any stretch of the imagination. Yet, regardless of whether they have kept in touch with institutions set up by fellow immigrants, or have blended completely into the political and religious world of North America, many postwar Dutch immigrants still maintain an individual sense of Dutch identity based on national origin, region or mother tongue.

In examining some specific topics or social issues, like economic specialization or overt discrimination, it is still useful to group together all postwar Dutch immigrants (see previous chapter). However, it does not make much sense to treat all Canadians of Dutch descent as a single category when it comes to identity, group cohesion or integration into the Canadian "mainstream." People who came from the Netherlands did not share a common religion, home language or political philosophy.[21] Indeed, one could argue that, with the exception of a few small, but still heterogenous, urban-based ethnic communities, Dutch-Canadians do not really comprise a single ethnic group in a sociological sense.

Nevertheless, people of Dutch origin do make up an identifiable "group" in a different way. They could even be considered a 'class' in the unique way Bourdieu defines this term. The multicultural branches of various governments do view the Dutch as one of Canada's official ethnic constituents, with their own language and "culture." This Dutch-Canadian "fact" is evident in the abundance of written documents housed in several government archives; hence the Dutch ethnic group exists on paper as well as in the popular imagination. Yet Dutch-Canadian ethnicity is not just an "object" for literary analysis, to be treated as a cultural myth by social scientists; the Dutch-Canadian social reality includes flesh-and-blood people who sit on multicultural councils. The process of ethnogenesis, as manifested in the institutionalization of a single *Dutchness*—including the title of this book—is synonymous with the transformation of a group of diverse, predominantly first-generation immigrants, most of whom shared a common national citizenship, into an ethnic unit within Canadian society. Yet the criteria used to define Dutch-Canadians, including the connections among national origin, language and religion, continues to be subject to an ongoing struggle over meanings.

Previous students of ethnic studies have been exclusively preoccupied with the process of ethnogenesis associated with immigration. Such an approach led to portrayals of *the Dutch* in Canada, as well as many other groups, as single homogeneous entities, thereby ignoring intra-ethnic diversity. This tendency applies to scholars, to journalists and even to Dutch-Canadian writers. The notion of a single, essential *Dutchness* has become part and parcel of taken-for-granted categories, or "common sense." Apart from unmasking such everyday assumptions based on the simplistic notions of homogeneous, and thus comparable, ethnic groups, my research further questions the utility of ethnic studies as a separate field of studies. The overspecialization of academic labour means that scholars neglect many aspects of the history of immigrants not connected to ethnicity.

The migration of a large number of people originating in the same country or region can result in considerable social continuity even when these immigrants do not exhibit a strong national or ethnic identity. In the case of the postwar Dutch immigrants, much of the behaviour and many of the values prevalent in the Netherlands at the time of emigration re-emerged in a Canadian context. Many of these social patterns were passed on to the next, Canadian-born, generation. Yet Dutch-Canadians who do not identify with their ethnic heritage might be oblivious to such continuity. If we include both the first and second generations, the majority of Dutch-Canadians never joined ethnic clubs, credit unions founded by Dutch immigrants, de facto Dutch-Canadian parishes or Reformed denominations. Normally, these people would be of little interest to scholars specializing in ethnic studies. However, these other Dutch immigrants usually joined organizations or churches most closely resembling their equivalents in the Netherlands. Despite their low level of either religious or ethnic identity, their incorporation into Canadian society was still shaped by the social structures of their homeland. Their children's dispositions and corresponding social trajectories likewise echo those of their parents.

My case study demonstrates the need to clearly distinguish between the replication, or even reformulation, of nationally defined ethnic identity and other forms of social continuity resulting from large-scale migration. Institutions and values can be reproduced in 'fields' other than the realm of ethnicity or ethnically linked religion. Focusing on the internal diversity (or intra-ethnic heterogeneity) of any immigrant population can provide researchers with better insights into both continuities and discontinuities associated with the movement of large numbers of people from one country to another. A scientifically rigorous, yet critical, perspective in research on international migration can reveal the continuities in relational structures which may not be discovered in studies that place too much faith in common sense categories.

Chapter 21

Conclusion

A central theme of this book has been the ambiguous nature of ethnicity. Ethnic groups are not homogeneous entities, except in our minds. All ethnic groups display internal diversity and have fuzzy boundaries. In Canada the label "Dutch" has been applied to all sub-groups of Netherlandic origin (Frisians, Hollanders, Dutch-Indonesians, or Brabanders). Dutch in turn merges into Flemish and "Pennsylvania Dutch" (which is close to German). The shifting nature of ethnicity calls into question the validity of long-term longitudinal studies comparing ethnic groups, however defined. Intermarriage and acculturation make it meaningless to ask whether the children and grandchildren of any ethnic category will, "on average," surpass, or at least keep up with, other kinds of Canadians in terms of status and economic power. The categories keep shifting.

Human agents have stakes in both changing and maintaining group boundaries as they jostle for better positions in the hierarchies of power, prestige and control over resources. We have seen how Dutch immigrants renegotiated their class standing as well as their ethnicity through linguistic interactions in bilingual situations (see chapter 12). Both class and ethnicity must be placed in a broader context. The ability to get ahead in a new country had a lot to do with prior training and whether or not an individual had any business experience. Connections—what Bourdieu calls 'social capital'—helped. Even the people who "made it" did not all reach the peak in their careers in the same length of time; gender, stage of family development, age of children and ties with extended family all played a role. Unattached single people, as well as large families with older children, were able to save up more money than couples with young children.

Notes to this chapter are on p. 420.

Yet most Dutch-Canadians would probably deny the determining influence of such "objective" social and economic factors.

Constantly contested, shifting, always fuzzy social boundaries make it difficult for social scientists to completely separate ethnicity from social class, gender, region or other types of social relations. Indeed, following the praxeology of Bourdieu, the very distinctions between social class and ethnicity, or between ethnicity and religion, are constantly open to question. The complex intertwining of various dimensions of social life becomes even more convoluted in the case of large-scale migration from one country to another. I thus had to modify and creatively apply Bourdieu's conceptual framework and methodology in order to examine a situation where the 'habitus' of one group of people no longer "fit" a new configuration of social positions.

The Fragmented Nature of the Dutch-Canadian "Community"

As an ethnic category, Dutch-Canadians are defined as much by internal divisions as by cultural symbols based on a shared national origin. There has never been a national association representing all Dutch-Canadians. Only on the local or regional level do we find ethnically defined clubs and organizations which include, and purport to represent, all people of Dutch descent. The closest to an umbrella organization in Ontario would be the Dutch Canadian Alliance of credit unions, but today the Alliance exists only on paper. The lack of official representation on the national level reflects the Dutch-Canadian population's fragmented nature, generated by dispositions reflecting the Dutch pillar system. Members of various subcomponents of Dutch society each went their own way in the Canadian context, either founding their own institutions or joining North American equivalents of Dutch organizations.

Most Canadian women and men of Dutch descent today have little social contact with each other beyond family circles or close friends, a specific church denomination or specialized associations. Yet most Reformed churches, as well as Dutch clubs consisting of veterans who fought in the Dutch armed forces or graduates of Dutch universities, are quite cohesive. Together, all of these elements of the Dutch-Canadian "community" can be conceptualized as a series of overlapping social networks, to some extent linked together through ties of friendship as well as pragmatic business dealing among people from various Dutch-linked institutions. Most of these institutions, which are still dominated by first-generation immigrants, quickly became bilingual in Dutch and English. With a few exceptions, they are losing Dutch as a common language for all but symbolic purposes. However, it is the divided nature of the Dutch-Canadian population, not its low level of language retention, that accounts for its weak presence as an ethnic constituency in Canada's multicultural establishment. This divisiveness in turn reflects the society from which they came.

To fully comprehend any group of immigrants, it is essential to understand their country of origin. The Netherlands, with its pillar system and tradition of tolerance, was born in a struggle of an already diverse group of people against Spanish domination. Those people, most of whom spoke some form of Dutch or Frisian, forged a common national identity. A low level of overt internal strife over the subsequent three centuries was an accident of history and geography. For a long time the Dutch regents, a ruling class of merchants, required peace and stability to further their economic interests. While nominally Calvinists, they saw the advantage of maintaining good relations with people of other religious persuasions and thwarted the doctrinaire tendencies of more radical ministers within the Dutch Reformed Church. The ruling classes in the Netherlands have always preferred compromise and accommodation to confrontation. A spirit of tolerance on the part of the ruling regents set a precedent for the compromises that formed the basis of the Dutch pillar system towards the end of the nineteenth century. The system became consolidated prior to World War Two, survived a short period of Nazi occupation, then reemerged intact after being liberated by Allied forces in 1945.[1]

Postwar Dutch immigrants, at least in Ontario, inadvertently reproduced much of the pillarized social structure of the Netherlands. However, structural continuity was manifested in ways that went far beyond the confines of a small, largely urban, ethnically defined social network. To recognize such continuity, I had to examine Dutch-Canadians in a broader context, regardless of the languages they use or their level of ethnic identity. Traditionally, ethnic and immigration research has focused on the survival of a visible ethnic presence. Ethnic researchers are generally interested in people who "look different," and who act in ways that create a unique ethnic space. They study how ethnic traits or ethnic networks are perpetuated over time. People who assimilate quickly or who no longer associate with "their own kind" can be ignored or else recalled to illustrate the process of acculturation marking the end of ethnicity.

Dutch-Canadians do not seem to be an ideal case study for research on "ethnicity" or "multiculturalism," since so many of them portray themselves as "typical Canadians" (see chapter 18). Previous studies have applied such labels as "silent" and "invisible" (see introduction), and even first-generation postwar Dutch immigrants adopted English as their main language (see chapter 11). Immigrants from the Netherlands also tend to represent themselves in terms of religion, or political ideology, rather than ethnicity. Nevertheless, the reputation of their country of origin and the process of ethnogenesis that led to the development of an ethnic 'class' of Dutch-Canadians affected, and will continue to affect, the trajectories of all Dutch immigrants.

Applying Bourdieu's Notions of 'Field' and 'Habitus'

Because so many postwar Dutch immigrants did not seem to act or look like "ethnics," my research examined the social interactions of people of Dutch descent in many different social 'fields.' I wanted to find out how the 'habitus,' or different dispositions corresponding to the Dutch pillar system as it operated in the Netherlands of the fifties and sixties, generated much of the behaviour of Dutch-Canadians in areas of social life not normally associated with ethnicity. Southwestern Ontario, in particular, had the critical mass to allow this process to coalesce. It is where I found my strongest evidence of Dutch dispositions regenerating many of the features of Dutch society,[2] albeit in a Canadian context. Yet, no matter how strongly embedded in people's personality, Dutch dispositions were gradually modified to "fit" a Canadian social structure which was not the same as that of the Netherlands.

The postwar Dutch immigrants and their descendants formed social networks within institutions most closely resembling those in which they were involved in the old country. Such institutions ranged from organized religion to the co-operative credit union movement. Some of those institutions, especially the larger Reformed churches, had been set up by earlier Dutch immigrants, but no longer carried an ethnic label. Those Dutch immigrants who could not find the institutions or organizations they expected, started their own, together with non-Dutch people, or joined whichever "Canadian" institution most closely resembled the one they knew at home. The various institutions and other aspects of Canadian society in which Dutch immigrants were immersed in turn shaped Dutch-Canadian expectations, values and habits, resulting in altered dispositions.

Institutions created by Dutch immigrants, either by themselves or with the help of other Canadians, are still linked to *the Dutch*, even though these institutions never did, or no longer, carry ethnic labels. Dutch Catholics, especially those from the south, left behind a thriving regional financial institution—the St. Willibrord Community Credit Union. The more ethnically self-conscious, but diverse, Dutch-Canadian community of

Metropolitan Toronto built up an equally large co-operative financial institution which now serves a broader Canadian population. These two credit unions are quite different; each reflects the region into which they are now firmly embedded. Contrary to the expectations of most social scientists, however, it is the big city and not the more rural-oriented institution that has kept a "touch of Dutch" (see chapter 15).

My study of postwar Dutch immigration also explored the relationship between the 'fields' of formal, institutionalized religion and ethnic politics. The Reformed sector of the postwar Dutch-Canadian population has partly succeeded in moulding Canadian society in its own image by creating their own version of Protestantism, including a separate school system. This segment of the Dutch-Canadian population also influenced the way some labour unions are run. Today they are slowly incorporating Canadians not of Dutch background into a new form of faith-ethnicity, itself subject to internal diversity and controversy. The Reformed presence represents yet another interpretation of what it means to be Dutch. The tension between religion and ethnicity as two interrelated yet also competing aspects of social reality continues.

Together with other postwar immigrants, Dutch-Canadians helped to transform Ontario into a less Anglo-Saxon, less Royalist and—in the case of almost half of the Dutch immigrants—a less Protestant society. At the same time, they have become one of the official ethnic groups of Canadian society, thanks to the official recognition of *the Dutch* by state archives and other institutions linked to multiculturalism. However, a precise definition of *Dutchness* in a North America context has not yet crystallized, and different aspects of the Dutch heritage may yet come to the forefront. Whether Dutch-Canadians will even survive as a viable ethnic constituency, as well as a cultural "fact," is still up in the air. My examination of postwar immigrants from the Netherlands has at least provided insights into the complex process whereby immigrants were transformed into "ethnic" Canadians.

My case study brings home the dangers associated with generalizing about any immigrant ethnic group. Not only were Dutch immigrants divided along religious and ideological lines, but the postwar immigrants from the Netherlands who came to Ontario in the fifties were not the same as their prewar counterparts. Different cohorts have different dispositions. Likewise, the newcomers who arrived between 1946 and 1958 were not the same as the small number of Dutch immigrants who arrived later, although members of both groups came into contact with earlier arrivals. Together they further dismantled, yet also partly reassembled, the Dutch pillars, most of which had already starting crumbling at home. Some of the broken pieces were rearranged in the same colour patterns, while the colours of others quickly faded to match an already existing Canadian mosaic. The kaleidoscopic picture keeps changing.

Glossary

Glossary of Dutch Words and Acronyms (English)

afscheiding	secession (or schism) [refers to first split in Dutch Reformed Church in nineteenth century]
algemeen	public or general
ARSS	Association for Reformed Scientific Studies (later became ICS)
beschaafd (on-)	cultured or polite (not—)
beschaving	culture or civilization
boer(en)	farmer or peasant
boerenleenbank	farmer's bank (i.e., cooperative or credit union)
bond	union or confederation
brabander	a person from the province of Brabant
indisch	Indo (Dutch-Indonesian)
burger(lijk)	burgher (petit-bourgeois)
CAANS	Canadian Association for the Advancement of Netherlandic Studies
CFFO	Christian Farmers Federation of Ontario
CLAC	Canadian Labour Association of Canada
CNBPA	Canadian Netherlands Business and Professional Association
CNIC	Canadian Netherlands Immigration Council
CPJ	Citizens for Public Justice
CRC	Christian Reformed Church
CRCBPA	Canadian Reformed Christian Business and Professional Association
DCA	Dutch Canadian Alliance (of credit unions)
DCCOO	Dutch Canadian Cultural Organizations of Ontario
DCEC	Dutch Canadian Entertainment Club (was based in Oakville)
DCS	Dutch Cultural Society (in London, Ont.)
doleantie	mourning [refers to second split in Dutch Reformed Church in nineteenth century]
doopsgezind(en)	Dutch Mennonites
DUCA	Dutch-Canadian (name of credit union)

gereformeerd(en)	Reformed (Orthodox)
gezellig	cozy or comfortable
graaf(schap)	count(y)
hervormd(en)	Reformed (as in the original old Dutch Reformed Church)
ICS	Institute for Christian Studies (formerly known as ARSS)
kaats(en)	a type of Frisian sport
katholiek (rooms)	Catholic (Roman)
kerk	church
klaverjas(sen)	a Dutch card game resembling bridge
landarbeider	agricultural day labourer or hired hand
landverhuizer	migrant
Nederland	The Netherlands (as a country)
nederlands(e)	the Dutch language (or Dutch in general)
OACS	Ontario Alliance of Christian Schools
ordinair(e)	common or uncouth (as class term)
ontwikk(eld/eling)	educat(ed/ion)
RC	Roman Catholic
RCA	Reformed Church in America
remonstrant(s/en)	a liberal Calvinist offshoot of the old Reformed Church in the Netherlands
rijsttafel	an elaborate rice-based Indonesian dish
sinterklaas	St. Nick (Dutch Santa Claus)
stand(sverschil)	status (difference)
vereniging	association
verzuiling	pillarization (as a process)
zuil(en)	pillar(s) or column(s) [to refer to principal "segments" of Dutch society]
zwarte piet	"black Peter" (St. Nick's helper)

Notes

Notes

Chapter 1

1 According to the Ministry of Social Affairs and Public Health of the Netherlands, 184,150 sponsored emigrants left for Canada between 1956 and 1982 (cited in Albert VanderMey, *To All Our Children* [Jordan Station: Paideia Press, 1983], p. 57). This figure does not include people who emigrated to Canada directly from Indonesia and other countries, nor the subsequent arrival of Dutch immigrants between 1982 and 1990.

2 This political culture, rooted in the collective memory of a "Golden Century" (the 1600s), includes a sense of loyalty to the House of Orange (see chap. 2).

3 See Will van den Hoonaard, *Silent Ethnicity* (Fredericton: New Ireland Press, 1991), p. 9-10; Jeffrey Reitz, *The Survival of Ethnic Groups* (Toronto: McGraw Hill, 1980), p. 91; and Robert Hoogendorn, "Miners against Their Will, The Netherlanders in Northern Ontario: A Study of an Invisible Minority," *Laurentian Review*, 15 (1982): 83. The term "invisible ethnic" has even crept into the popular press; see article by Linda Shutt in the (St. Catharines) *Standard*, 24 May 1996, p. A1 and A4.

4 See Report of the Royal Commission on Bilingualism and Biculturalism, *The Cultural Contribution of the Other Ethnic Groups*, Vol. 4 (Ottawa: Information Canada, 1970), p. 7.

5 Van den Hoonaard, *Silent Ethnicity*, p. 12.

6 This term was first introduced by Raymond Breton in his article "Institutional Completeness," *American Journal of Sociology*, 79 (1964): 193-205.

7 Conversation with John Russell (during a visit to the museum), 8 July 1996. The gathering of information and artifacts, as well as much of the writing for this exhibit, was carried out by Miep Verkley from Thedford, Ontario. She provided me with copies of a series of short biographies which form part of the exhibit. See also article by Noel Gallagher, *London Free Press*, C2, Saturday, 24 August 1996.

8 My book does not fall under the Secretary of State-sponsored "generation" series, which already includes a work on the Dutch in Canada. See Herman Ganzevoort, *A Bittersweet Land* (Toronto: McClelland and Stewart, 1988). A more popular book, VanderMey's *To All Our Children*, which deals mainly with

the immigration experience, also appeared several years ago. There is also a case study of the Dutch in Quebec (focusing on Montreal) (Johanna H. Lowensteyn. "A Social History of the Dutch in Quebec," MA thesis in sociology and anthropology, Concordia University, 1986). A book about New Brunswick appeared while I was doing research in Ontario (van den Hoonaard, *Silent Ethnicity*). There are numerous case studies dealing with Dutch Calvinists, including one focusing on British Columbia (see chap. 9).

9 His writings on class distinctions, language and education are frequently cited in the scholarly literature. One of Pierre Bourdieu's earlier theoretical works is *Outline of a Theory of Practice* (Cambridge: University of Cambridge Press, 1977). For a useful overview of the development of his thinking and research, see Derek Robbins, *The Work of Pierre Bourdieu* (Buckingham: Open University Press, 1991); Nicholas Garnham and Raymond Williams, "Pierre Bourdieu and the Sociology of Culture: An Introduction," in Richard Collins et al., eds., *Media, Culture and Society* (London: Sage Publications, 1986). Even his critics have admitted that Bourdieu has developed a useful set of "working" concepts that can facilitate empirical research. See Nicos Mouzelis, *Sociological Theory: What Went Wrong?* (London: Routledge, 1995), p. 117.

10 Bourdieu's work is also suitable for the interdisciplinary field of cultural studies. See Scott Lash, "Modernization and Postmodernization in the Work of Pierre Bourdieu," in Scott Lash, ed., *Sociology of Postmodernism* (London: Routledge, 1990), p. 237-83.

11 Especially Johan Goudsblom, whose works on the Netherlands are frequently cited in Part One of this book. What characterizes the theoretical orientation of the Dutch social scientists influenced by Elias is their interest in mentality and historical contextualization. See Jeremy Boissevain and Jojada Verrips, eds., *Dutch Dilemmas* (Assen: Van Gorcum, 1989), p. 3; and Norbert Elias, *The Symbol Theory* (London: Sage Publications, 1991), p. ix-x. There is a more direct influence, since Bourdieu's work has also been brought to the attention of the Dutch sociological establishment. See Johan Heilbron and Benjo Maso, "Interview met Pierre Bourdieu," *Sociologisch Tijdschrift*, 10, 2 (1983): 307-34.

12 For an extended definition, see Bourdieu, *Outline of a Theory of Practice*, p. 72, where he refers to 'habitus' as "the strategy-generating principles enabling agents to cope with unforeseen and ever-changing situations." When using specialized terms used by Bourdieu, I will place them in single quotation marks.

13 A Mexican anthropologist refers to "intimate local class culture" in a way which resembles the use of the notion of 'habitus.' (Claudio Lomnitz-Adler, *Exits from the Labyrinth* [Berkeley: University of California Press, 1992], p. 18, 28-29).

14 Bourdieu refers to 'habitus' as a "mediating concept." His perspective is similar to Anthony Giddens' structuration theory. See Christopher Bryant and David Jary, eds., *Giddens' Theory of Structuration* (London: Routledge, 1991), p. 22. For a discussion of how Bourdieu differs from Giddens, see Richard Harker et al., eds., *An Introduction to the Works of Pierre Bourdieu* (London: Macmillan, 1990), p. 201-203.

15 See also Jay Lemke, *Textual Politics* (Discourse and Social Dynamics) (London: Taylor and Francis, 1995), p. 32-34.

16 Such 'fields,' a term with the connotations of a force field, as in physics, attracts or repels the individuals under its sphere of influence. Each field of

action (*champs*) is examined in terms of the relative distribution of different species of power (or capital): economic (money), social (connections) and cultural (knowledge acquired through both formal and informal education), all of which define the logic of social practice in "relatively autonomous social microcosms" such as art, religion, education and sport (Pierre Bourdieu and Loïc Wacquant, *An Invitation to Reflexive Sociology* [Chicago: University of Chicago Press, 1992], p. 97-98). The historical development and dynamics of each separate 'field' or 'subfield' must be empirically discovered.

17 For a more elaborate exposition of his game metaphor (as an analogy for his notion of 'field'), see ibid., p. 98, and Robbins, *The Work of Pierre Bourdieu*, p. 85-89. Bourdieu also sees 'fields' as different markets, each with its own law of supply and demand, and subject to degrees of monopoly versus open competition. People's dispositions are adjusted to the various social 'fields' just as players in different sports develop a "feel for the game."

18 For his treatment of social class, see Pierre Bourdieu, *Distinction* (Cambridge: Harvard University Press, 1984); for gender, see "La domination masculine," in *Actes de la recherche en sciences sociales*, 84 (1990): 2-31; and Bourdieu and Wacquant, *Reflexive Sociology*, p. 170-74.

19 Bourdieu tends to use the term 'class' in this broader sense to include gender and ethnicity, although he pays more attention to socio-economic classes.

20 That is why Bourdieu refers to 'habitus' as a "structured structure predisposed to function as structuring structure." See Pierre Bourdieu, *The Logic of Practice* (Stanford: Stanford University Press, 1990), p. 53.

21 While not ignoring the importance of economic class interests (objectively defined), Bourdieu recognizes different 'species' of power (or capital) that define the logic of social practice in "relatively autonomous social microcosms" (see also note 16).

22 Bourdieu analyzed social transformation, from a more traditional rural society to modern capitalism, in both his research on Algeria, during its war for independence, and in his native region of Béarn. See Robbins, *The Work of Pierre Bourdieu*, chaps. 2 and 3. For a more critical analysis of his treatment of social change, see Harker et al., *An Introduction*, p. 212-13, 216.

23 For a definition and analysis of the process of ethnogenesis, see E. Roosens, *Creating Ethnicity: The Process of Ethnogenesis* (Newbury Park: Sage Publications, 1989), p. 46.

24 G. Carter Bentley has applied his theoretical perspective in a study focusing on ethnic dynamics in the Philippines. See "Ethnicity and Practice," *Comparative Studies in Society and History*, 29 (1987): 24-55; and Kevin Yelvington, "Ethnicity as Practice? A Comment on Bentley," and Bentley's "Response to Yelvington" in ibid., 33 (1991): 158-75.

25 For a summary of all the different ways of conceptualizing ethnicity, including religious-based ethnic groups, see Bradley Breems, "'I Tell Them We Are a Blessed People': An Analysis of 'Ethnicity' by way of a Dutch-Calvinist Community," PhD dissertation in sociology, University of British Columbia, 1991, chap. 2

26 Thomas K. Fitzgerald, "Media, Ethnicity and Identity," in Paddy Scannel et al., eds., *Culture and Power* (Newbury Park: Sage Publications, 1992), p. 112-33.

27 Frederick Barth, *Ethnic Groups and Boundaries* (Boston: Little Brown, 1969).

28 Pierre Bourdieu, *Language and Symbolic Power* (Cambridge: Harvard University Press, 1991), p. 220-23.

29 For an example of a sophisticated Marxian approach to the influence of class position on ethnicity, see Orlando Patterson, "Context and Choice in Ethnic Allegiance: A Theoretical Framework," in Nathan Glazer and Daniel Moynihan, eds., *Ethnicity* (Cambridge: Harvard University Press, 1975), p. 305-49.

30 In a previous research project, I explored the relationship between ethnicity and class as two interconnected yet independent factors. Ethnic distinctions were treated either as a manifestation of class opposition (particularly in the national arena) or else as alternative (parallel) expressions of class domination and class resistance. See Frans J. Schryer, *Ethnicity and Class Conflict in Rural Mexico* (Princeton: Princeton University Press, 1990), chap. 17.

31 Bourdieu also advocates an eclectic use of various techniques of data collection, including statistical analysis of survey data. See Pierre Bourdieu, Jean-Claude Chamboredon and Jean-Claude Passeron, *The Craft of Sociology* (New York: De Gruyter, 1991), p. 254.

32 Inventory of the Multicultural History Society of Ontario Papers (F 1405, series 5B, Dutch Canadian Papers), prepared by Jan Liebaers, Archives of Ontario (1990). Henceforth referred to as MHSO.

33 Almost all were Dutch-Canadians, although I also talked to a handful of people not of Dutch background to get their impressions.

34 About a dozen chance encounters and short casual talks were also included.

35 See H. Russell Bernard, *Research Methods in Anthropology* (Thousand Oaks: Sage Publications, 1994), p. 97-98; and Robert Stake, "Case Studies," in Norman Denzin and Yvonna Lincoln, eds., *Handbook of Qualitative Research* (Thousand Oaks: Sage Publications, 1994): 244.

36 Often I did not know beforehand which language would be used or at what point the conversation might switch over from one language to another.

37 I also examined to what extent I had had previous contact with the people with whom I interacted, no matter how sporadic. I was acquainted with 30 people and there were 34 more (7.9 percent) who knew about me via close relatives or friends, even though I had never met them before. Over 85 percent of my interviews were conducted with complete strangers. That proportion had gone up by the final stage of field research.

38 For example, 16 informants (4 percent) were Frisians, while a dozen were Dutch-speaking people of Chinese, Arabic or Javanese descent (*Indisch*). Although I had heard about and once met a former Dutch citizen of African descent (from the Caribbean) in Canada, I was not successful in contacting anyone from that category in Ontario.

39 See Janice Morse, "Designing Funded Qualitative Research," in Denzin and Lincoln, eds., *Handbook of Qualitative Research*, p. 229.

Chapter 2

1 Numerous articles about Dutch historical figures in North American history have appeared in the *Windmill Post*, the English-language supplement of the *Windmill Herald*. For an example of a two-part instalment on Samuel Holland, see Janny Lowensteyn's contribution in the newspaper mentioned above, vol. 35, issues 729 and 730 (March 8 and March 23, 1993).

2 Some writers trace the development of a distinctive Netherlandish civilization back to the thirteenth century, with the development of *Dietsch* as a wider literary language. See Pieter Geyl, *The Revolt of the Netherlands (1555-1606)* (Lon-

don: Ernest Benn, 1962), p. 28; and William Shetter, *The Pillars of Society* (The Hague: Martinus Nijhoff, 1971), p. 33.

3 The region under this count (*graaf*) is known as the *graafschap* of Holland.

4 This is seen in English publications put out by the Dutch government. See Frank Huggett's books, *The Dutch Connection* (The Hague: Ministry of Foreign Affairs, 1982), p. 43-46; and his *The Dutch Today*, 3rd ed., (The Hague: Government Publishing House, 1983), p. 42.

5 The region of Burgundy is located in the eastern part of what is today France. The House of Burgundy lost control over most of its French territories and was basically left with the more prosperous sections of the Low Countries.

6 For a brief synopsis of this earlier historical period, see Geyl, *The Revolt*; his *History of the Low Countries* (London: Macmillan, 1964); and Bernard Vlekke, *The Dutch Before 1581*, in Bartholomew Landheer, ed., *The Netherlands* (Berkeley: University of California Press, 1940), chap. 2.

7 The Burgundians had already brought together the various provincial councils of the Low Countries in a States-General (*Staten Generaal*), a kind of parliament. Charles V persuaded the German Diet at Augsburg to reorganize all of his Netherlandic possessions into a single administrative unit in 1548. A year later the States-General agreed that henceforth rules of succession would be identical all over the Low Countries. See John Fitzmaurice, *The Politics of Belgium* (London: C. Hurst, 1983), p. 10-13.

8 For an overview of the Dutch Revolt see Geyl's *The Revolt of the Netherlands* or Geoffrey Parker, *The Dutch Revolt* (Harmondsworth: Penguin, 1985).

9 Their base of power was Amsterdam, while the nobles tended to live in The Hague.

10 These cultural variations within the borders of the Dutch republic reflected the outcome of earlier migratory movements, which resulted in the regional predominance of Frisians (in Friesland), Saxons (mainly in the east) and Franks (to the south).

11 One of several tribes described by Tacitus, a Roman historian, the Batavians were rediscovered by Dutch writers in the sixteenth century. See Simon Schama, *The Embarrassment of Riches* (np: Fontana Press, 1988), p. 54.

12 See Henry Lucas, *Netherlanders in America* (Grand Rapids: Eerdmans, 1989), p. 27. Their Holland Land Company was used as a model by the Scottish writer John Galt, who founded the city of Guelph, when he opened up the Huron tract in southwestern Ontario.

13 Orange was a principality in the heart of France, which was inherited by William I ("The Silent") together with sections of the Netherlands; Nassau refers to the German county Nassau-Dillenburg, where William was born. William of Orange's parents were Lutherans, but he was brought up as a Catholic in Charles V's court in the southern Netherlands. See C.V. Wedgewood, *William the Silent* (London: Jonathan Cape, 1946), p. 9-12.

14 This William of Orange (the son of Prince William V of the Netherlands), was then living in exile in England.

15 For Canadians of northern Irish origin, the name William of Orange (King "Billy") represents Protestantism, a hatred of the Pope and loyalty to Great Britain. The Dutch prince William of Orange III (1650-1702) married Mary Stuart of England in 1677. When her father, King James II of England, was overthrown, William and Mary became joint sovereigns after leading a Protes-

tant revolt, and subsequently shaped the foreign policy of both countries. See Gerald Newton, *The Netherlands* (London: Ernest Benn, 1978), p. 37-38.

16 This form of Protestantism, started by John Calvin (in Switzerland) spread to other parts of Europe and took strong roots in the Low Countries. Some Calvinists in France, known as Huguenots, later fled north. See William Monter, *Calvin's Geneva* (London: John Wiley and Sons, 1967), p. 171-72, 233.

17 The most famous early Dutch writer, Joost van den Vondel, was a patriotic Dutchman and a practising Roman Catholic, as were several other well-known intellectuals, artists and architects such as Philip Vingbooms, Vermeer and Jan Steen.

18 Those residing abroad maintained full citizen rights, although Jews living in Holland were subject to legal restrictions. See Schama, *The Embarrassment of Riches*, p. 587-94.

19 For the United States, see Philip Gleason, "American Identity and Americanization," in William Petersen, Michael Novak and Philip Gleason, eds., *Concepts of Ethnicity* (Cambridge: Harvard University Press, 1982), p. 57-143.

20 Except for several periods of foreign occupation, these boundaries have remained virtually the same until today. This Dutch nation is known in English as the Netherlands.

21 Until recently, the full title was *algemeen beschaafd nederlands* (general, civilized Dutch), which implied the superiority of one form of Dutch. Today the official form of Dutch is referred to as the "standard" Dutch language.

22 Initially there was much confusion between Dutch and *Deutsch* in North America. See Ganzevoort, *A Bittersweet Land*, p. 1-2; and Lucas, *Netherlanders in America*, p. 580. Even today Dutch-Canadians are puzzled by the term "Pennsylvania Dutch," which refers to people who are mainly of German descent.

23 The use of these terms depends on the social context in which they are used. Frisians, or people who speak a regional dialect of Dutch, do not mind using the term *hollands* in referring to the national language. In contrast, the Flemish in Belgium resent it when people from the north say that the Flemish speak *hollands* as opposed to *nederlands*; yet the Flemish (*Vlaams*) in Belgium do not refer to themselves as *nederlands* when it comes to national or ethnic identity. Words are likewise not used in the same manner in academia as in everyday life. Specialists in art history and literature classify the Netherlands and northern Belgium under the common rubric of "Netherlandic." However, in most other contexts, even scholars use the word "Netherlands" (or *nederland),* to refer only to a specific nation state, separate from Belgium. See E. H. Kossman, *The Low Countries* (Oxford: Oxford University Press, 1978), p. 1.

24 However, they did exclude native leaders from key public posts. For a comparison of the Dutch presence and "race" relations in these different parts of the world, see Christopher Bagley, *The Dutch Plural Society* (London: Oxford University Press, 1973), chap. 6.

25 Such difference in "race" relations is in part the consequence of a distinct pattern of emigration. Unlike the state-sponsored migration to the East Indies, most of the Dutch settlers in South Africa emigrated on their own, as individuals. See Bagley, *The Dutch Plural Society*, p. 173.

26 These Afrikaans-speaking people of either African or Asian descent have a different identity from the descendants of the Dutch settlers who were transformed into the "Boers," and who portray themselves as *Afrikaaners*. See Sheila Patterson, *Colour and Culture in South Africa* (London: Routledge and Kegan Paul, 1953), p. 15.

27 When Dutch-speaking African-Americans emigrate to the Netherlands they are labelled as *Surinamers* (referring to a former Dutch colony on the South American continent). In a survey on racial prejudice in the Netherlands, Bagley found that attitudes towards Moroccans were more hostile than against Surinamers. There was also greater acceptance of coloured Dutchmen than of most white foreigners (Bagley, *The Dutch Plural Society*, p. 198, 212).

28 See van den Hoonaard, *Silent Ethnicity*, p. 20; and Albert VanderMey, *And the Swamp Flourished* (Surrey: Vanderheide Publishing, 1994), p. vii.

29 See Lucas, *Netherlanders in America*, p. 7.

30 For example, the name Harlem, the equivalent of the Dutch city of Haarlem, and Stuyvesant, the last of New Netherlands' governors. However, the Dutch presence lingered on for at least another hundred years after the British took control of this part of North America. All services of the Reformed Church in America were conducted in Dutch until 1770, and even ministers of Scottish descent studied their theology in the Netherlands.

31 For example, Anthony Van Egmond, who died in the Don Jail in Toronto after getting mixed up in the Mackenzie revolt. See John Martens, *Making Waves* (Waterloo: Waterloo Printing, 1988), p. 23-25; G.H. Needler, *Colonel Anthony Van Egmond* (Toronto: Burns and MacEachen, 1956).

32 Henri van Stekelenburg, *Landverhuizing als regionaal verschijnsel* (Tilburg: Stichting Zuidelijk Historisch Contact, 1988), p. 82-110; see also Mary A. Corry, *The Story of Father Van den Broek, O.P.* (Chicago, 1907); and Jacob van Hinte, *Nederlanders in Amerika*, vol. 1 (Groningen, 1928), p. 189-94, 203-204, 320-24.

33 See Yda Saueressig-Schreuder, "Dutch Catholic Immigration Settlement in Wisconsin," in Robert Swierenga, ed., *The Dutch in America* (New Brunswick, NJ: Rutgers University Press, 1985), p. 105-24.

34 The colonies they set up consisted exclusively of Dutch Calvinists, although some followers came from Bentheim, a region in Germany (Lucas, *Netherlanders in America*, p. 104-10).

35 See Robert Swierenga, "Dutch Immigration Patterns in the Nineteenth and Twentieth Centuries," in R. Swierenga, ed., *The Dutch in America*, p. 39.

36 For example, records show largely Dutch neighbourhoods, including the *Groningsche Hoek* ("Groningen Quarter") just outside Chicago in 1859. See Lucas, *Netherlanders in America*, p. 232.

37 See ibid., p. 529-41.

38 For a more comprehensive treatment of Dutch and Flemish Catholics in North America between 1880 and 1940, see H.A.V.M. van Stekelenburg, "*Hier is alles voorvitgegang*" (Landverhuizing van Noord Brabant naar Noord-Amerika, Tilburg: Stichting Zuidelijk Historisch Contact, 1996).

39 See Ganzevoort, *A Bittersweet Land*, p. 39-41, and Klaas de Jong, *Cauliflower Crown* (Saskatoon: Western Producer Book Service, 1973). Flemish immigrants also ended up in Manitoba and Saskatchewan, going back to as early as the 1870s. See Vermeirre, "Aspects de l'Immigration Neerlandophone au Canada," *Canadian Journal of Netherlandic Studies*, 7(1986): 52, 58.

40 Apparently that urban, ethnically mixed neighbourhood kept a Dutch presence right up until the 1940s (Lucas, *Netherlanders in America*, p. 457). St. Willibrord was an Anglo-Saxon missionary who set out from Ireland in 692 A.D. to convert the Frisians and Saxons in the Low Countries.

41 Most of these Dutch Catholic immigrants came from Noord Brabant. See van Stekelenburg, *"Hier is alles voorvitgegang,"* p. 79-114.

42 Ganzevoort, *A Bittersweet Land*, p. 47. Attempts to establish Dutch Protestant congregations in Windsor and Toronto were less successful (Lucas, *Netherlanders in America*, p. 465-66).

43 See Joan Magee, *The Belgians in Ontario* (Toronto: Dundurn Press, 1987).

44 A well-known example is Bill Vander Zalm's father, who lived in Canada while his son (the former premier of British Columbia) was with his mother in Holland.

45 A memorial statue provided by the Dutch army was erected in Stratford (corner of William and Mornington Streets) in 1959. In 1992, the fiftieth anniversary of their stay in Stratford was given extensive coverage in the Dutch-Canadian press. See *De Nederlandse Courant*, November 7, 1992, p. 9-11.

Chapter 3

1 See Arend Lijphart, *The Politics of Accommodation* (Berkeley: University of California Press, 1968), p. 17; and Shetter, *The Pillars of Society*, chap. 1. The Dutch term *verzuiling*, as part of a sociological model, originated with J.P. Kruyt in the early 1960s. The process of depillarization, i.e., the gradual disintegration of the system is known as *ontzuiling* (depillarization).

2 There is ambiguity around the use of such terms "general" and "neutral." According to one interpretation, "neutral" means completely secular and non-religious (and hence also not sensitive to the viewpoint of orthodox religious groups). Another interpretation sees "neutral" as the capacity to accommodate all religious and non-religious groups under one umbrella, precisely by going out of one's way not to offend any group.

3 Some authors refer to this as the secular bloc or blocs; however the term "neutral" comes closer to the Dutch connotations of the word *neutraal*, and is used by at least one author. See Huggett, *The Dutch Today*, p. 58.

4 Any classification of the pillar system is an approximation of the extremely complex social structure of the Netherlands. Some scholars consider the liberals and the socialists as two distinct units. Not only did these two groups vie for control over public institutions, but they each had their own organizations. This is particularly true for the socialists, who tended to operate as a separate bloc.

5 For a precise overview of nineteenth-century Dutch political history, see Willem Verkade, *Democratic Parties* (Leiden: Universitaire Pers Leiden, 1965), p. 38-42.

6 At the same time, Calvinism has had a strong influence on the development of the unique form of Catholicism found in the Netherlands. This has been demonstrated by L.J. Rogier, *Geschiedenis van het Katholicisme in Noord-Nederland in de zestiende en zeventiende eeuw*, vols. 4 and 5 (Amsterdam: Elsevier, n.d.); and A. Chorus, *De Nederlander innerlijk en uiterlijk: Een characteristiek* (Leiden: Sijthoff, 1964). Dutch Catholicism was particularly prone to Jansenism, a moralistic school of thought that resembled Protestantism in spirit but not in form.

7 By law, public worship could only take place in the Reformed Church, although no restrictions were placed on private forms of worship. See Schama, *The Embarrassment of Riches*, p. 60.

8 See Shetter, *The Pillars of Society*, p. 82-83; and Schama, *The Embarrassment of Riches*, p. 215.

9 Since their founding, the *remonstranten* have gradually moved further to the "left," and they now feel akin to the Congregationalists in North America. The Remonstrants have existed as a separate Calvinist religious organization up until today. See C.N. Impeta, *Kaart van kerkelijk nederland* (Kampen: J.H.Kok N.V., 1964), p. 161-68.

10 The new spirit of the times emphasized the primacy of reason even in religious matters, resulting in a gradual marginalization of the orthodox religious faction.

11 The new Reformed Church, which resembled a similar Prussian state-sponsored Lutheran church, was now subject to a new set of regulations contradicting the canons (*leerregels*) originally established by the orthodox faction in 1618-19, during the general synod of Dordrecht. See Impeta, *Kaart van kerkelijk nederland*, p. 45.

12 See Gerrit ten Zijthoff, *Sources of Secession* (Grand Rapids: Eerdmans, 1987).

13 They called themselves the *Christelijke Afgescheiden Gemeenten*, which became the *Christelijke Gereformeerde Kerk* (Christian Reformed Church) in 1869. By that time the Dutch constitution had been revised, and the established Netherlands Reformed Church (*Hervormde Kerk*) was no longer under the government's control, except through its links with the Orange monarchy.

14 The orthodox Calvinist social movement, leading to secession, must be put in the broader context of a more general European *reveil* (religious awakening) originating in Geneva, which swept across Europe at the end of the Napoleonic Wars.

15 The main critic of secular schooling was Groen van Prinsteren. In 1886, he and other religious leaders, still loyal to the established church, openly declared their unconformity. Unlike the earlier seceders, these new protesters did not initially portray the established church as false, but rather as one in need of renewal.

16 Some English writers have translated the Dutch name of this church as Re-Reformed. See Bagley, *The Dutch Plural Society*, p. 5. They actually resurrected the adjective *gereformeerde*, originally used in the seventeenth century.

17 See Harry Kits, "World Views and Social Involvement: a Proposal for Classification of Canadian Neo-Calvinist Social Involvement, 1945-1988," master's thesis in Philosophical Foundations, Institute for Christian Studies, 1988), p. 5.

18 The latter are concentrated in rural Zeeland and among former fishing villages in what was once known as the Zuider Zee.

19 The exact percentage in 1960 was 28.3 percent. See Lijphart, *The Politics of Accommodation*, p. 16. The Dutch monarch still has an official link with the *Hervormde Kerk*, similar to the role of the Queen of England as head of the Anglican Church. However, at least one more conservative but loosely affiliated group under the *Hervormde* umbrella uses the name *De Gereformeerde Bond*.

20 These include the *Waalse kerken* (Walloon churches) and the *Nederlandse Protestantenbond*, both of which also emphasize their historical continuity going back to Holland's "Golden Era."

21 See Herman Bakvis, *Catholic Power in the Netherlands* (Kingston: McGill-Queen's University Press, 1981), p. 10-19.

22 Between 1946 and 1980, its official name was *Katholieke Volks Partij (KVP)* (Catholic People's Party).

23 While remaining loyal to the Pope, they reorganized their parishes with little outside help or interference. See J.M.G. Thurlings, "The Case of Dutch Catholicism," *Sociologica Neerlandica*, 7 (Spring 1971): 118-36.

24 Ever since the 80-year war against Spain, when the Dutch republic became a mission region in the eyes of Rome, Dutch Catholic clergy have gone their own way and kept their distance from the religious orders dominated by non-Dutch priests, including the Jesuits. See Bakvis, *Catholic Power*, 23.

25 See Michel Van der Plas, *Uit het rijke Roomse leven* (Utrecht: Ambo, n.d.); cited in Bakvis, *Catholic Power*, 15. Catholics began to more closely identify with the Dutch state and the monarchy when their schools received full state funding in 1917.

26 Unlike other European countries where some bishops turned a blind eye to the Holocaust and antisemitism, the Dutch hierarchy took a unified stance against National Socialism. During five years of German occupation, the Catholic clergy worked in close co-operation with orthodox Calvinists in the underground resistance movement.

27 Unlike the eighteenth and nineteenth centuries, there were just as many Catholic lawyers and engineers in the middle of the twentieth century who were also well represented in local governments (see Lijphart, *The Politics of Accommodation*, p. 89-92).

28 According to a study of nine countries conducted in the 1960s by UNESCO, both class feelings and inequality of income distribution were higher than in Britain, France and the U.S. Only in the Netherlands was class cleavage perceived as more significant than national allegiance. See Lijphart, *The Politics of Accommodation*, p. 20-23; and Bagley, *The Dutch Plural Society*, p. 12-13.

29 Within the original state church (*Nederlandse Hervormde Kerk*), itself somewhat more prestigious because of its association with royalty, such loosely affiliated groupings (*aanhangsels*) as the *Nederlandse Protestantenbond*, and the *Waalse kerken* (Walloon churches) represent up-scale versions of Dutch liberal Protestantism. The *Remonstrantse Broederschap* is also considered to be more "upper class."

30 Even in the sandy regions, where family farms predominated, someone with more windows in their barn—and thus more cows —snubbed a poor farmer (*keuterboer*), who would be discouraged from marrying the daughter of a *grote boer* ("big farmer"). For an example of how the major soil regions in the Netherlands affected the class composition of rural emigrations going back to the nineteenth century, see Robert Swierenga, "Dutch Immigration Patterns in the Nineteenth and Twentieth Century," in R. Swierenga, ed., *The Dutch in America*, p. 36-38; and Hille de Vries, "The Labor Market in Dutch Agriculture and Emigration to the United States," in ibid., p. 89, 92.

31 For a discussion of a similar dynamic of rural-urban status distinction in France, and how these effected patterns of marriage, see Bourdieu, "Célibat et condition paysanne," *Études rurales*, 5/6 (1962): 32-136; and "Reproduction interdite. La Dimension symbolique de la domination économique," *Études rurales*, 113/114 (1989): 15-36.

32 Surnames associated with such families, often hyphenated or of foreign derivation, are well known in the Netherlands.

33 In his analysis of the class system of French society, Bourdieu identified a similar division between two fractions of the bourgeoisie, depending on the different distribution of 'cultural' versus 'economic' capital. He refers to intellectuals

and bureaucrats who derive most of their income from salaries as "the dominated fraction of the dominant class" (see Boudieu, *Distinction*).

34 The upper class of Dutch society, one of the oldest bourgeois nations, was smug and secure, with a somewhat aloof yet paternalistic attitude. The middle class, including professionals and white-collar workers, had a similar "burgher mentality," quite distinct from the working class. See Johan Goudsblom, *Dutch Society* (New York: Random House, 1967), p. 70.

35 In the 1940s and 1950s, social class was a tabooed subject among politicians in the Netherlands, and in Dutch sociological literature. See ibid., p. 63, 67; and Lijphart, *The Politics of Accommodation*, p. 20.

36 Family status very much defined how much 'cultural capital' a person acquired in growing up. As in the case of France, students from more "cultured" families had higher rates of academic success, after controlling for economic position and social origin. See Bourdieu and Wacquant, *Reflexive Sociology*, p. 160.

37 A strong bias against upward social mobility was revealed in the verbal expressions usually directed against the nouveau riche or anyone who was accused of climbing a few too many notches up the social ladder. For example, one might hear the comment *als niets komt tot iet, kent hij zich zelven niet* ("if a nobody become a somebody, he no longer knows himself").

38 This word cannot be translated as "ordinary"; the closest English equivalents would be "vulgar" or "crude," although in some contexts it could also be translated as "common." This adjective is often qualified in such expressions as "good people, but *ordinair*." The terms *onbeschaafd, gewoon* ("ordinary"), *onfatsoenlijk* (bad-mannered) or *vulgair* (vulgar) have similar connotations.

39 See Raymond Williams, *Marxism and Literature* (Oxford: Oxford University Press, 1977), p. 108-15.

40 Frisian was again recognized as an official language of the Netherlands in the late 1950s. However, the different regional variations of Frisian continued to have their respective internal prestige rankings.

41 The word *bekakt* refers to pretention and affectation usually used in reference to *deftige lui* ("respectable" or "fashionable" folk).

42 There was considerable streaming of students, who were groomed to become either workers or professionals from as early as age twelve. Prior to the education reform, it was next to impossible to upgrade or go back to school when one was older.

43 The two academic programs were often combined in a single *Lyceum*. Only the latter, similar to the grammar schools of England, allowed students to continue their educations at a university. The new (reformed in 1968) education system is somewhat less hierarchical (see Newton, *The Netherlands*, p. 70, 227).

44 While upward mobility through the educational system was not impossible, family background played an equally important role (see Frank Huggett, *The Modern Netherlands* [London: Pall Mall Press, 1971], p. 75).

45 The Netherlands have had fewer strikes than other industrialized countries. See Lijphart, *The Politics of Accommodation*, p. 108; for a brief summary of the development of a moderate socialist movement in the Netherlands, see Newton, *The Netherlands*, p. 86-98.

46 Lijphart, *The Politics of Accommodation*, p. 15, 211.

47 See Anna Aalten, "The Accidental Businesswomen: Gender and Entrepreneurship in the Netherlands, 1950-1975," in Jeremy Boissevain and Jojoda Verrips, eds., *Dutch Dilemmas* (Assen: Van Gorcum, 1989), p. 153-63.

48 I remember my mother reminiscing about her job as telegraph operator, from which she had to resign as soon as she got married. Today such rules no longer apply, but the participation of women in the work force still lags far behind that of other countries. For a nuanced analysis of why this is the case, see Gisela Kaplan, *Contemporary Western European Feminism* (London: UCL Press, 1992) p. 158-61.

49 Goudsblom, *Dutch Society*, p. 46-49. See also Lien van der Leij, "Talking about Our Generation," *Holland Horizon*, 2, 3 (1991): 6-10.

50 For the concept of overlapping (as opposed to completely separated) experiential worlds, and how the degree of overlap varies over time as well as across cultures, see Eleanor Cebotarev, "Households, Gender and Sustainability," in John Bryden, ed., *Towards Sustainable Rural Communities* (Guelph: University School of Rural Planning and Development, 1994), p. 108.

51 All of these comparisons—as the use the north/south distinction itself—are relative. For example, northern Limburgers also fall under the category of all southerners, including their Flemish neighbours in Belgium, who are deemed to be more outgoing and friendly compared to the *stijve* ("formal" or "stuffy") northerners.

52 A sense of cohesion may be associated with even smaller areas corresponding to a specific polder, such as the Wieringermeer (in Noord Holland).

53 Folk costumes were still widely used in many rural areas prior to World War Two and continued to be worn in rural area of Zeeland and many fishing villages. In many villages, Catholics and Protestants even wore different costumes or variation of the same costume (but with different types of hats or positioning of buttons).

54 The government has set up a special commission to strengthen and protect Frisian, which is now one of the official languages. See Newton, *The Netherlands*, p. 27. Not everyone in the province of Friesland speaks Frisian and those who do are all bilingual in Frisian and in Dutch. There are also dialectical variations. The Frisian of the city of Leeuwarden (referred to as *stadsfries*) is not the same as that spoken in the countryside, which in turn differs from the island of Terschelling.

55 There are people with typical Frisian names in other parts of the Netherlands as well, who would not identify as Frisians. For an anthropological study of Frisian ethnic identity, see Cynthia Keppley Mahmood, *Frisian and Free* (Prospect Heights: Waveland Press, 1989).

56 See Goudsblom, *Dutch Society*, p. 28-29, 59-60. People living in this southern region distinguish "those living above the rivers" from "those below the rivers."

57 The main differences are in the persistence of distinct speech patterns, religious values and a stronger resistance to the overall cultural dominance of the western region (Holland). See I. Gadourek, *Riskanten gewoonten en zorg voor eigen welzijn* (Groningen: J.B. Wolters, 1963), p. 312; and John Dortmans, *Brabanders in Canada* (Burlington: Sportswood, 1994), chap. 1.

58 See Tineke Hellwig, "The Asian and Eurasian Woman in the Dutch East Indies, in Dutch and Malay Literature," *Canadian Journal of Netherlandic Studies*, 14 (1993): 20-26.

59 For a comprehensive treatment of "race" relations in the Netherlands, see Bagley, *The Dutch Plural Society*, p. 25.

60 See Jean Gelman Taylor, *The Social World of Batavia* (Madison: University of Wisconsin Press, 1983).

61 For a description of the social position and cultural values of Javanese, especially Javenese women, in The Hague prior to World War Two, see Bagley, *Dutch Plural Society*, p. 71-76.

62 Even Dutch-Indonesian creole families spoke *maleis* (a lingua franca) as well as Dutch, and had adopted oriental customs, such as the use of a round cushion for sleeping and the use of water (usually stored in bottles) instead of toilet paper.

63 Bourdieu rarely uses the word "culture" in this sense, and instead uses the term to refer to "high-brow" or elite culture (knowledge of literature, "cultivated manners," etc.). However, in an earlier article he even suggested that the anthropological term might be even better than 'habitus' were it not for the risk that the concept of culture "risks being misunderstood." See Bourdieu, "Structuralism and Theory of Sociological Knowledge," in *Social Research*, 34 (1968): 706 fn23.

64 Within cultural anthropology the concept of culture is gradually giving place to such substitutes as 'habitus,' hegemony or discourse. However, earlier anthropologists did use the original term in a more nuanced manner, allowing for contestation and heterogeneity (see Robert Brightman, "Forget Culture: Replacement, Transcendence, Relexification," *Cultural Anthropology*, 10 (1995): 509-46.

65 Bourdieu also talks about 'objectification' in *The Logic of Practice*, p. 14-15.

66 Frank Huggett, the author of two books about the Dutch put out by the Dutch Ministry of Foreign Affairs (and quoted in both this chapter and the last), was born and educated in Britain.

67 See Pierre Bourdieu, *In Other Words* (Stanford: Stanford University Press, 1990), p. 118. Anthony Giddens' structuration theory also posits that "the 'findings' of the social sciences very often enter constitutively into the world they describe." See Philip Cassell, ed., *The Giddens Reader* (Stanford: Stanford University Press, 1993), p. 150.

68 Shetter, *The Pillars of Society*; Huggett, *The Modern Netherlands*; and Schama, *The Embarrassment of Riches*.

69 I took the liberty of slightly modifying their analysis to incorporate the insights of Dutch-Canadians. Like outsiders visiting the Netherlands for the first time, Dutch emigrants can appreciate the peculiarities of Dutch culture because they can compare the behaviour and attitudes of the people they left behind with those of North Americans.

70 Bourdieu's concept of 'habitus' refers to dispositions that are shared by people who lead similar lives; the concept can thus be quite specific (e.g., rural Dutch-Canadian women brought up as Catholics prior to World War Two) as well as very general (e.g., all postwar immigrants who grew up in the Netherlands). See also Lemke, *Textual Politics*, p. 33.

71 Bourdieu shows how spatial organization, especially the arrangement of the house, contributes to "durable imposition of the schemes of perception, thought and action," which reproduces the subordinate position of women in Kabyle society. He uses this as an example of "the dialectic of objectification and embodiment in the privileged locus of the space of the house and the earliest learning processes" (see *Outline of a Theory of Practice*, p. 90). Johan Goudsblom makes a similar point when he makes the connection between the

primness and neatness of the Dutch home and how women in particular were "enveloped in the bourgeois family" (see *Dutch Society*, p. 138).

72 Goudsblom, *Dutch Society*, p. 139.

73 There are also fewer cafés and cinemas in the Netherlands. See ibid., p. 138; and Huggett, *The Dutch Today*, p. 16.

74 Schama, *The Embarrassment of Riches*, p. 399-400. Even today, affordable housing is a priority for the Dutch government.

75 For a summary of accounts of socialization and the family in three different Dutch regions (and different classes), see Bagley, *The Dutch Plural Society*, p. 26-29.

76 Although the offspring of professionals were expected to pursue further studies, they, too, were supposed to help earn money for the household if their parents were experiencing financial difficulties. I came across two such cases during my interviews with immigrants whose professional parents emigrated when the interviewees were teenagers or young adults.

77 Schama, *The Embarrassment of Riches*, p. 377-84.

78 One immigrant who made a return visit after 20 years made the following comment in Dutch: *De ruiten blinken, de mensen stinken* (i.e., "the window panes shine, but the people stink").

79 Huggett, *The Dutch Today*, p. 23.

80 His analogy of social life as a "game," with culture as the "rules," is similar to an anthropological approach to culture. In chapter 7 of his *The Politics of Accommodation*, Lijphart likewise suggests a number of "unwritten" rules in his explanation of Dutch political life.

81 Shetter, *The Pillars of Society*, p. 12.

82 Dutch parents are supposed to be addressed by the more formal *u* (like vous in French) even after the children are married.

83 For more extensive treatment of the context that determines which of the two styles of speech are used, see Shetter, *The Pillars of Society*, p. 24-26.

84 I have heard this from many non-Dutch people, including my wife, who has observed many Dutch family gatherings.

85 In Canada people who don't know each other very well or who belong to different social classes or religions are supposed to be friendly and informal with each other. First names are more commonly used. At the same time, the Canadian norm is not to discuss politics or religion with either strangers or family members. In contrast, in the Netherlands, among friends and family members, people are not only allowed but almost expected to discuss religion and politics and express their views.

86 There are exceptions. Inter-pillar friendships were prevalent during World War Two and are more likely to occur when Dutch people meet abroad. In such situations people still cement their friendship through a frank exchange of viewpoints. I have come across cases where an orthodox Calvinist became close friends with an atheist or a socialist with a liberal. Such people told me what "wonderful" arguments they had had. However, Dutch people are not likely to publicly admit feelings of warmth and sympathy for such friends.

87 In a similar vein, the Dutch are leery of easy praise.

88 See Bourdieu et al., *The Craft of Sociology*, p. 74-77.

Chapter 4

1 Unlike Western Canada, which had already seen a steady inflow of East European and Asian immigrants, Ontario remained the stronghold of United Empire Loyalists, Orangemen and "the English." The religious establishment was still Anglican. For a brief overview of the ethnic mix in Ontario prior to 1945, and its historical precedents, see Jean Burnet and Howard Palmer, eds., *"Coming Canadians": An Introduction to a History of Canada's Peoples* (Toronto: McClelland and Stewart, 1988), p. 18-20, 30-39.

2 See Ruth Frager, *Sweatshop Strife* (Toronto: University of Toronto Press, 1992), p. 13.

3 John Porter, *The Vertical Mosaic* (Toronto: University of Toronto Press, 1956).

4 In 1961, 170,177 people in Canada reported having Dutch as mother tongue (compared to 563,713 Germans, 361,496 Ukrainians and 339,626 Italians). See Dominion Bureau of Statistics, *1961 Census Bulletin*, Population—Citizenship and Immigration, Cat. No. 92-548, Vol. 1, part 2.

5 Ministry of Social Affairs and Public Health of the Netherlands, *Verslag over the werkzaamheden van de organen voor immigratie*; chart shown in VanderMey, *To All Our Children*, p. 52-53.

6 See Anthony Sas, "Dutch Migration to and Settlement in Canada: 1945-1955," PhD dissertation in geography, Clark University (Massachusetts), 1957, p. 63-68.

7 William Petersen, *Planned Migration* (Berkeley: University of California Press, 1955), p. 10-12.

8 Abe Sybe Tuinman, *Enige aspecten van de hedendaagse migratie van nederlanders naar Canada* (Wageningen: Ministerie van Landbouw, Visserij en Voedselvoorziening, 1952). For a Petersen-Tuinman exchange, see *Tijdschrift voor Economische en Sociale Geografie*, 43, 12 (1957).

9 Prior to 1945, policy makers used pseudo-scientific language to cover up blatant discrimination against immigrants not of European origin (see Petersen, *Planned Migration*, p. 180, 237).

10 A. Tuinman, "The Netherlands-Canadian Migration," *Tijdschrift voor Economische en Sociale Geografie*, 47 (1956): 182.

11 Industrialists and English Canada were in favour of increasing immigration, while French Canada and labour unions were opposed (Petersen, *Planned Migration*, chap. 6).

12 This pattern of proportional increase holds for the two other major occupational categories—construction and services (A. Sas, "Dutch Migration to and Settlement in Canada," fig. 9, p. 52).

13 In the interwar period, the Dutch had the highest standard of living in Europe after Switzerland. See Colin Clark, *The Conditions of Economic Progress* (London: Macmillan, 1940), p. 39-41.

14 Petersen, *Planned Migration*, p. 35.

15 See Newton, *The Netherlands*, p. 169-70.

16 Henry van Stekelenburg, "The Quest for Land: The Movement of Roman Catholic Dutch Farmers to Canada (1947-1955), *Migration News*, 34 (October-December 1985), p. 24.

17 Personal communication (via a letter from Vucht) with H. van Stekelenburg, October 7, 1992.

18 Ministry of Social Affairs and Public Health in the Netherlands, *Verslag over the werkzaamheden van de organen voor emigratie*, a chart shown in VanderMey, 52-53.
19 Forty years later, some of these emigrants used the biblical story of the exodus of the Israelites from Egypt as an analogy for their trials and tribulations before and after their arrival in the newly chosen land of Canada. See articles by William Lensink and Stan de Jong in *Christian Courier* (January 15, 1993), p. 11, 13.
20 See van Stekelenburg, "The Quest for Land," p. 23.
21 Anthony Sas, "Dutch Migration," fig.7, p. 45.
22 See table in VanderMey, *To All Our Children*, p. 52-53.
23 See Aritha Van Herk's "Writing the Immigrant Self: Disguise and Damnation," *In Visible Ink* (Crypto-frictions) (Edmonton: NeWest Press, 1991), p. 185.
24 The following section is based on data from my typed fieldnotes; there were 75 entries on the theme of the immigration experience in general, and 40 which specifically referred to factors influencing emigration from the Netherlands to Canada.
25 See VanderMey, *To All Our Children*, chap. 4; Ganzevoort, *A Bittersweet Land*, p. 64-66; and Margaret Vanderschot and Mary A. Smith, "Netherlands Research Project (A Study of Postwar Immigration to the St. Marys Area)," a report of St. Marys Museum, 1990). For an official Dutch perspective on the motives for Dutch emigration, see the Dutch government publication *de gaande man* (gronden van de emigratie beslissing) (The Hague: Staatsdrukkerij, 1958); and N. H. Frijda, *emigranten nief emigranten* (The Hague, Staatsdrukkerij, 1960).
26 Such as the memoirs written by John Hendrikx of Park Hill, March 1984 (unpublished manuscript); see also VanderMey, *To All Our Children*, p. 63-64.
27 The percentage of immigrants who fall under this category would be very difficult to establish; those who actively resisted the Nazis constitute a small minority but the majority of Dutch citizens offered some measure of passive resistance during the occupation through foot-dragging or minimal cooperation.
28 Bagley, *The Dutch Plural Society*, p. 76; also, interview on November 8, 1989, with George Matern, Woodstock; and conversation with Huibert Sabelis and Theo Teveen, Mississauga, November 8, 1989.
29 See also VanderMey, *To All Our Children*, p. 64; and Ganzevoort, *A Bittersweet Land*, p. 62-63.
30 A new Labour Party, incorporating left-liberal middle-class groups, put less emphasis on class strife than prewar socialists. However, the Dutch communist party enjoyed a short-lived boom in the 1946 election (Petersen, *Planned Migration*, p. 71).
31 Dutch socialism could be labelled "pragmatic." See ibid., p. 68.
32 Ibid., p. 77, 91, 100.
33 Several people I interviewed had initiated proceedings to emigrate, with their elderly parents joining them in order not to break up the family unit.
34 The books most often mentioned were: S. Hovius and T. Plomp, *Canada: Een land met grote mogelijkheden* (Groningen: Niemeijer, 1948); and T. Cnossen, *Canada: Land van Vrijheid, Ruimte en Ontplooiing* (Wageningen: N.V. Gebr. Zomer en Keunings Uitgeverij, 1952). There were also numerous propaganda tracts published by the Canadian government. See also Petersen, *Planned Migration*, p. 173.

35 A Dutch-Canadian author, specializing in this aspect of Canadian military history, has pointed out some negative aspects of the Canadian presence. See Michiel Horn, "Canadian Soldiers and Dutch Women after the Second World War," in Herman Ganzevoort and Mark Boekelman, eds., *Dutch Immigration to North America* (Toronto: Multicultural History Society of Ontario, 1983), p. 187-195.

36 Ganzevoort, *A Bittersweet Land*, p. 70-71.

37 Ibid., p. 68; and VanderMey, *To All Our Children*, 49-51.

38 This was a common theme in many of my interviews. See also ibid., p. 129-52; and VanderSchot, "Netherlands Research Project," p. 1-2.

39 Starting in the mid 1960s, the CNIC administered a Young Farmers Program, which brought young people from farm background to work for several months on Canadian farms. These temporary workers often decided to become immigrants themselves. Interview with Lambert Huizing, Aurora, Ontario, May 5, 1989. The correspondence for the CNIC is housed in the Archives of Ontario: MHSO (F 1405, series 58, "Dutch Canadian Papers").

40 Real estate agents not only made the travel arrangements and found farms for Dutch immigrants, but organized social get-togethers as well. Interview with Mr. and Mrs. Veldman, on their farm near Embro, July 9, 1990.

41 Another task is making local arrangements for tours by the Dutch monarch (at first Queen Juliana, who was succeeded by her daughter Beatrix). Such royal visits to Ontario took place in 1952, 1967 and 1988. The consul also bestows special recognition to prominent Dutch-Canadians on behalf of the Dutch queen through the granting of medals of honour and induction as honorary knights into the Order of Orange (*ridder van order van oranje*). This annual award is given to so many Dutch citizens and former Dutch citizens abroad that many Dutch people jokingly refer to the ceremony as a "rain of *lintjes*" (ribbons). At least a dozen Dutch-Canadians have been granted this award over the past decade.

42 By 1971, such prewar immigrants and their descendants represented 26 percent of the people in Ontario of Dutch descent. See John Kralt, "Netherlanders and the Canadian Census," *Canadian Journal of Netherlandic Studies*, 3 (1982): 40, 44.

43 They often use the Dutch word *landverhuizers* (literally, "people moving from their county"); technically this is the Dutch term for any kind of emigrant, but I have heard older Dutch-Canadian postwar immigrants use it to distinguish themselves from more recent Dutch immigrants.

Chapter 5

1 Between April 1945 and March 1953, 165,000 displaced persons were admitted under a special program. Their presence gave rise to the derogatory term "DP," which was also used to label all European postwar immigrants. See Petersen, *Planned Migration*, p. 153; and Burnet and Palmer, *"Coming Canadians,"* p. 41, 74, 94.

2 These observations are based on numerous anecdotes recounted in my interviews, as well as my recollections as a young immigrant who arrived at the age of 11 in 1957.

3 An article in the December 2, 1950 issue of the *Hamilton Spectator* described the wretched conditions under which some Dutch immigrants had to live. That

article, based on an interview with Bob Gosschalk, a life insurance agent who worked among Dutch immigrants, resulted in a political controversy. See commentary by Ger Graaskamp in *Dutch-Canadian Courant,* English-language insert in *De Nederlandse Courant,* July 4, 1992, p. 7; and VanderMey, *To All Our Children,* p. 171-74.

4 Canadian banks were hesitant to lend money to newcomers who had little or no collateral, and finance companies charged outrageous interest rates.

5 While they read, and even spelled English, they could not necessarily understand, much less conduct, a conversation. Moreover, very young Dutch immigrants would have attended high school during the Nazi occupation of the Netherlands, when English was not offered in most schools.

6 This is a theme in books written on the immigration experience. (see VanderMey, *To All Our Children,* p. 256-57). Apart from an "accent," older Dutch-Canadians inadvertently use Dutch words or phrases, such as *ik* instead of I.

7 This was the standard contract in the later 1940s. The pay varied from region to region and increased over time.

8 Interview with Jaap De Boer on his farm near Innerkip, November 30, 1989.

9 Interview with an elderly Dutch lady in Brampton (in the presence of her son), July 6, 1991.

10 Interview with Gerry Van Bussell, on his farm near Lucan, July 9, 1990.

11 One person recalled seeing one big family's children crawling out through a car's back window. Interview with Mr. K. Rietkerk, Guelph, January 7, 1992.

12 See "Canadian Perception of the Immigrants," in Vanderschot and Smith, "Netherlands Research Project," p. 49-52.

13 This estimate is extrapolated from interviews with several people who were personally acquainted with this part of Simcoe county. Stroud is located in Innisfil township, where Dutch-Canadians still represented over 4 percent of its rural census units in 1986.

14 Interview with Martin de Groot, Phelpston, April 23, 1990.

15 For references to postwar Dutch immigration farmers on Wolfe Island in published material, see J.W. Hofwijk, *Canada (Reis met Onbekende Bestemming)* (Utrecht: N.V. Uitgeverij de Lanteern, n.d., ca. 1954), p. 116-20; Petersen, *Planned Migration,* p. 178; and Ad Wijdeven, *Oogsten op vreemde velden* (Zutphen: Uitgeverij Terra, n.d., ca. 1985), p. 48.

16 One woman expressed such reservations to a Dutch television crew who visited her farm in the summer of 1988, around the time Queen Beatrix of the Netherlands was touring Canada. I saw this farm woman interviewed on television during a trip to the Netherlands.

17 This was a common theme in interviews with or about Dutch-Canadian farmers. Starting in the mid-1960s, Dutch immigrant farmers started to appreciate the value of high school education (followed by an agricultural college) for children interested in becoming independent farmers.

18 See also Huggett, *The Modern Netherlands,* p. 84.

19 I conducted several interviews with older Dutch-Canadian farmers in the Drayton area and also had conversations with rural extension officers and people working at the University of Guelph who are well acquainted with this part of Wellington county.

20 This percentage was slightly higher than for the townships of Maryborough to which the village of Drayton belongs, although the absolute number of people

of Dutch background in Drayton was only a third that of the township. For source of statistical data, see next chapter.

21 This picture of the movement of Dutch farm hands from the Guelph area to the northern part of Wellington county, based on several interviews, is consistent with 1986 census data showing a much lower percentage of Dutch-Canadians living in the rural parts of the townships of Guelph, Puslinch, Eramosa and Nichol.

22 I have encountered few Dutch Catholics in the city of Guelph (even among those who joined their largely secular Dutch club) and at least one person whom I interviewed in the London area told me that she and her husband moved away from Guelph in the early 1950s precisely because they felt they did not "fit in."

23 Interview with John C. Derksen, Kitchener, September 9, 1990. See also 25th Year Anniversary Yearbook of the First Christian Reformed Church of Guelph (1953-1978).

24 Interviews with Dirk Bod, Guelph, February 23, 1990; the Reverend John C. Derksen, Kitchener, September 9, 1990; and Bill Joukema, July 29, 1992.

25 Money resulting from the sale of their belongings was set aside for supporting missionary work abroad. Interview with Dr. Piet Haayen, Eden Mills, September 9, 1990.

26 This group evolved into a close-knit non-denominational evangelical congregation and their leader obtained credentials as a minister. They established a church-run school in 1981 and today about half of their membership has no Dutch connections. Interview with Henk Katerberg (by phone), April 2, 1997.

27 I conducted interviews or had conversations with 36 Dutch-Canadians in Guelph, most of whom were immigrants. My general name file, which includes people not interviewed, contains another 104 names of Dutch-Canadians who had some sort of a Guelph connection (not including people who were students at the university).

28 This in my impression from various interviews with people who had extensive contact with Dutch immigrants in the 1950s and 1960s. The occupational breakdown is consistent with other data on overall patterns of the occupational distribution of Dutch immigrants after 1953.

29 I extrapolated this from the 1986 census data.

30 For another reference to the higher level of education of Dutch immigrants who came from urban areas after 1950, and their subsequent career paths in Canadian cities (in particular Windsor), see Joan Magee, *A Dutch Heritage* (Toronto: Dundurn Press, 1983), p. 67.

31 I interviewed a half-dozen bakers or former bakers, both working for wages and self-employed. My index on the topic of Dutch immigrants in this branch of the Canadian economy has 20 entries.

32 These figures were taken from the 1986 population census; there was a slight decline in these percentages for 1991.

33 I conducted nine extensive interviews with Dutch-Canadians in Sudbury (and nearby communities); my file of Dutch immigrants with a Sudbury connection contains 92 additional names.

34 Much of the land close to Sudbury consists of slag heaps; a lot of the original forest cover was destroyed through a combination of wood cutting, burning and pollution, leaving outcroppings of blackened rock.

35 Dutch immigrants came close to forming an inner-city ghetto along Elgin Street. The history of the Dutch in Sudbury is based on a conversation with Rena Bishop, November 5, 1989; interviews with Piet van de Henne, Chelmsford, July 4, 1990; and Adrian Smits, Sturgeon Falls, April 16, 1991.

36 Interview with Henk de Bruins, Whitefish, April 4, 1991. People driving from Espanola to Sudbury along highway 17 can see the full-sized replica of a Dutch windmill at the entrance to this camp.

37 See file of newspaper clippings (1952-1958) and personal papers donated by Klaas Kamstra to the MHSO, housed in the Archives of Ontario, MSR No. 4987, sub-series No. 85-107, MU No. 9417.

38 This settlement was mentioned in several interviews. A congregation in Cochrane with only 11 families was still listed in the 1987 Yearbook of the Christian Reformed Church.

39 Interview with Father Kaptein, Coniston, December 19, 1990.

40 Although he was later sent off to other parts of Northern Ontario, Father Kaptein kept in touch with these Dutch parishioners and later returned to Sudbury. Another Dutch priest was stationed in Whitefish during this early period of adaptation.

41 Interview with Anthony Pel, November 5, 1989. This social club, which operated in Sudbury from 1972 to 1976, was a branch of the Dutch-Canadian Entertainment Club, with headquarters in Oakville (see chap. 16).

42 Interviews with Robert Hoogendorn, October 9, 1988; Gerda Runia, July 3, 1990. See also Hoogendorn, "Miners against Their Will," p. 85-86.

43 In the meantime he had already gone back to the Netherlands, first to play amateur soccer and then to get married. His variety stores stock strictly non-Dutch items.

44 See Jean Burnet and Howard Palmer, *"Coming Canadians,"* p. 37.

Chapter 6

1 See Bronwen Walter, "Tradition and Ethnic Interaction: Second Wave Irish Settlements in Luton and Bolton," in Colin Clarke, David Ley and Ceri Peach, eds., *Geography and Ethnic Pluralism* (London: George Allen and Unwin, 1984), p. 259.

2 The 1986 short population census counted only one out of every 20 people. All of the numbers cited are statistical estimates (with a small margin of error). A system of random rounding was used in the census, which made it equally likely that any number between 1 and 5 would be assigned a value of either 0 or 5.

3 After this book was written, a more up-to-date census became available. However, for all practical purposes, the figures pertaining to Dutch-Canadians in 1991 were identical for all but a few places, and I doubt if any dramatic changes have taken place between then and now. Most of the minor changes in numbers between 1986 and 1991, especially for some of the census divisions with few Dutch-Canadians, were as likely to be the result of the random rounding techniques used, as proportional increases or decreases in population.

4 Data were taken from the *1987 Yearbook of the Christian Reformed Church in North America* (Grand Rapids: CRC Publications, 1987), the *1987 Yearbook of the Canadian and American Reformed Churches* (Winnipeg: Premier Printing, 1987) and the 1987 Annual Statistical Report of the Classis of Ontario of the Reformed Church in Canada. Adding up the totals for congregations in the

same counties, Dutch Calvinists represent anywhere from zero to 70 percent of the total Dutch-Canadian population.

5 Most of these are the same townships where Dutch-Canadians have held elected public posts (see chap. 19).

6 Timiskaming, Sudbury, Algoma and Cochrane; the top portions of Renfrew and Victoria counties; and more than half of the townships in Parry Sound, Nipissing, Muskoka and Haliburton. In the counties of Lanark, Frontenac, Lennox-Addington, Hastings and Peterborough, where Dutch-Canadians did settle, nowhere do they comprise more than 5 percent of inhabitants.

7 The number of people of Dutch descent found in such centres on weekends would far exceed those who actually live there.

8 For example, there are only 130 people of Dutch descent in the township of Uxbridge, which constitutes less than 3 percent of total population. In contrast, rural Uxbridge, a separate census division, has 295 Dutch-Canadians (or 4.03 percent).

9 The proportion of Reformed in the county is 60.4 percent of Dutch-Canadians, one of the highest for the province.

10 The 115 people of Dutch descent who live in Athens, of whom a quarter can speak Dutch, make up over 10 percent of a total population of about a thousand inhabitants. Although almost all Dutch-Canadians in the village of Athens are Christian Reformed, the Reformed Dutch only constitute 37.7 percent of the total population of Dutch descent in the county.

11 There are well over two thousand Dutch-Canadians in these three townships, most of whom came from the Dutch province of Noord Brabant (see chap. 8).

12 Wyoming has a Dutch store, a Christian Reformed Church and a Catholic church and school with a strong Dutch presence. Indeed, the Catholic school, originally located on the 6th line of Warwick township, was founded by Dutch immigrant families in 1954, against the protests of local Orangists. Another village that has about an even distribution of Protestants and Catholics is Wainfleet, in the Niagara peninsula.

13 Although the Dutch represent less than 10 percent of the population of these villages, they all have at least 50 Dutch-Canadian inhabitants.

14 The ones that came up in conversations, or that I visited, include the predominantly Catholic settlements of Kinkora in Ellice township (Perth county), Kerwood in Adelaide township (Middlesex), Caledonia (Haldimand-Norfolk), Thamesford and Kintore (Oxford) and Phelpston in Floss township (Simcoe county). Rural villages with a significant Reformed Dutch presence include York (Haldimand-Norfolk), Maitland and Spencerville (both in Leeds-Grenville) and numerous places in the Niagara peninsula, such as Smithville (part of Grimsby), Fenwick (in the rural portion of Pelham) and Attercliffe and Wellandport (in the rural part of West Lincoln township). Almost all of these villages have one or more Dutch Calvinist churches, although there is always a smattering of Dutch Catholics in the surrounding countryside. Ansnorveldt and Springfield, both in the Holland Marsh, deserve special mention, not only because of their Dutch presence today, but because they were founded by Dutch immigrants just prior to World War Two. They are located respectively within the boundaries of East Gwillimbury (York regional municipality) and West Gwillimbury (Simcoe county). In eastern Ontario, in the united counties, I have come across Williamsburg and Lancaster (in townships with the same name) and Iroquois (in Matilda), all of which have mixed Dutch populations.

15 Table 2 does not include every small town with a visible Dutch-Canadian presence. Rural towns with an even smaller number of Dutch inhabitants, such as Blenheim in the township of Harwich (Kent county), Seaforth in the township of McKillop (Huron), and Alliston in Essa township (Simcoe) all serve as gathering points for rural Dutch-Canadians. For example, apart from its Catholic church, Seaforth is the meeting place for a social club of new Canadians of largely Dutch descent, while Alliston is the site for a Christian Reformed church. Blenheim has a branch of St. Willibrord Credit Union, which took over a parish credit union initially founded by Flemish immigrants (see chaps. 8 and 15).

16 This impression, based on observations made during fieldtrips, is consistent with what people told me in numerous interviews. My fieldnote file contains information (i.e., at least two entries) for 149 localities with Dutch-Canadian connections.

17 At least one medium-sized town, Bowmanville, also serves as a service centre to a large number of Dutch-Canadian farmers, many of whom work part-time in the city.

18 Industrialized belts are growing around the core of London and St. Thomas; in the eastern tip of the Niagara peninsula, around Welland, St. Catharines and Niagara Falls; and in a region encompassing Guelph, Kitchener-Waterloo and Cambridge.

19 Port Hope, Cobourg and Cornwall were excluded from table 4 since they have only 150, 240 and 350 Dutch-Canadians respectively (less than 2 percent). However, Cobourg has a Dutch store and a Christian Reformed church serving several hundred people in the townships of Hope, Hamilton and Haldimand. Cornwall has a Christian Reformed church and acts as a centre for the Dutch in the townships of Charlottenburgh and Lancaster.

20 The most prominent ads for contractors in the 1990 phone book for Chatham and region included the names Bruinsma, Heyink and Westhoek. The city of London also has several prominent contractors of Dutch descent (including the Loyens), some of whom specialize in custom-made homes.

21 According to the records of *De Nederlandse Courant*, 33 households in Guelph subscribed to this newspaper in 1990. The main rival newspaper, The *Windmill Herald*, had at least the same number of subscribers, and a smaller number of people read *De Krant* on a regular basis. A lot of other Dutch people without subscriptions regularly borrow these papers from friends or neighbours, or buy one of these papers on a less regular basis in a Dutch shop in Guelph.

22 In London, 6,700 people were of Dutch descent, and more than a third of these reported Dutch as their mother tongue.

23 All ads for Dutch specialty stores located in Ontario that appeared in each of the *De Nederlandse Courant* (*Dutch-Canadian Bi-Weekly*), the *Windmill Herald* (Central Canada/Maritime Edition) or *De Hollandse Krant* were tabulated for two consecutive years.

24 Ontario Ministry of Citizenship and Culture, *Ethnocultural Data Base Materials*, series 2 (Population Data 12), Hamilton Census Metropolitan Area, 1981 (released in 1986).

25 Various churches and schools founded by Dutch Calvinist immigrants can be seen in both Ancaster and Dundas (just outside of Hamilton), and near the entrance to Sarnia, coming off the 402. The proportions of those speaking

Dutch in neighbouring urban and rural areas is similar in both regions, indicating a balance between young and old.

26 Arkona, mentioned above, is an exceptional case. Not only do its various Dutch-Canadian businesses and institutions provide opportunities for better-educated, younger people, but the tiny overall size of this service centre makes its predominantly Dutch-Canadian population proportionately more significant.

27 Lambeth is an ideal place of residence for young couples who have steady jobs in London and want to live outside the city proper, but within short commuting distance. Telephone interview with John Feron, February 28, 1991.

28 It came as no surprise to learn in 1993 that two of six candidates vying for a seat on London city council for the former town of Westminster, were Dutch-Canadians. See "Two Dutch-Canadians Vie for Seat," The *Windmill Herald*, March 23, 1993, p. 14.

29 London has two Christian Reformed congregations, and one each of a Reformed Church (in Canada) and a Canadian Reformed congregation.

30 Telephone conversation with Mrs. Guichelaar of Brantford, February 7, 1992.

31 On the basis of several phone calls, I surmised that a large proportion of the adult children of both groups have stayed close to home, given that they already have access to jobs and shopping facilities in several nearby urban centres.

32 Sudbury has 325 Dutch-Canadians (of whom few live downtown); the combined Dutch-Canadian population of the surrounding towns (Walden, Onaping Falls, Rayside-Balfour and Valley East) comes to 320. Unlike southern Ontario, the number of Dutch people in the rural portion of all these census divisions is tiny.

33 The same proportions are found for Bracebridge and Huntsville (same district municipality); in Victoria there are as many Dutch in Bobcaygeon as in the corresponding township of Verulam.

34 The cottage and vacation areas had the usual proportion of two people of Dutch descent for every one whose mother tongue is Dutch. The Calvinist presence appears to be absent, since there are no Reformed churches in this part of middle Ontario.

35 I have come across feature articles in Dutch-Canadian newspapers advertising lodges or resorts established by more recent Dutch immigrants (usually young couples). These newcomers are likely to have another residence somewhere in Europe or in a larger urban centre in North America.

36 These patterns seem to be repeated at different scales, similar to fractals in science and mathematics.

37 See also Bourdieu, *The Logic of Practice*, p. 54.

38 We will see later (chap. 18) how Dutch national dispositions, based on cultural expectations, prior work experience and overall level of education, matched the 'field' of economic activities they encountered in Canada. Such a match made it more likely that Dutch immigrants ended up settling down in their places of choice.

39 In 1976, Metropolitan Windsor had 2,785 Dutch residents, which represented less than 1 percent of the total population. This number declined in the 1986 census.

40 R. A. Helling, "Dutch Immigration to the Tri-County Area (Essex, Kent and Lambton Counties, Ontario)," *Canadian Journal of Netherlandic Studies*, 3 (Fall 1981): 13.

41 Officials in the Canadian immigration and citizenship department were aware of this Dutch cultural preference. In 1951 a minister announced that Dutch artisans would be brought in and sent to small towns "which the Dutch seem to prefer" (see Petersen, *Planned Migration*, p. 176).

42 In a study of the city of London in the early 1960s, Una Elliott found that the Netherlanders occupied "the suburban newer areas especially in the N. East, East and South." The areal distribution of the Dutch was almost the inverse pattern of that of the Italians, although the two groups were comparable in terms of length of stay in Canada. See Una Elliott, "Comparative Roles of the People of Italian and Netherlandish Origin in the Creation of a Homogenous Population in the City of London," MA thesis, Faculty of Graduate Studies, University of Western Ontario, 1964, p. 19.

43 This pattern also shows up for the Hamilton area, where the percentage of Dutch-Canadians who report Dutch as their mother tongue in the town of Ancaster is higher than that for the city of Hamilton (46.81 versus 40.23).

44 Further evidence for the tendency for first-generation Dutch immigrants to move to the suburbs comes from data in "a Report on the Ethnic Origins of the Population of Toronto" put out by the Toronto City Planning Board in 1960, which shows that in 1950, 46 percent of the 12,500 people of Dutch origin in Metro Toronto lived in the suburbs (i.e., outside the city of Toronto proper), the highest percentage of eight ethnic groups listed in that report. An estimate for 1960 in that same report shows an even higher percentage of 60 percent out of a total of 25,000 Dutch-Canadians (still in first place). This data (and its corresponding table) are mentioned in a fourth-year University of Toronto history paper, "Dutch Acculturation in Metropolitan Toronto: 1947 to 1960" by J. Bruce Forrest (July 1974).

45 Helling, "Dutch Immigration," p. 13. The author of this article comments "lower-middle to upper-middle class" Dutch-background residents (identified as craftsmen and small businessmen) "live in the newer sub-divisions which were often established by Dutch contractors."

46 These finding are based on numerous comments in interviews about where different religious groups were located, personal observations based on trips and archival research on the distribution of Dutch Calvinist churches.

Chapter 7

1 Life/food section of the *Daily Mercury*, Wednesday, December 7, 1988.

2 The Dutch version of St. Nick with his helper, "Black Peter."

3 See also an article on the Dutch community in section C3 of *The Ottawa Citizen*, Tuesday, July 8, 1985.

4 Another newspaper article dealing with the Dutch in the Niagara peninsula, which was published in the May 24, 1996 issue of the (St. Catharines) *Standard* (section A), did mention that postwar Dutch immigrants represented at least three different religious groupings as well as five different Reformed churches. However, the emphasis in the article, written by Linda Shutt, is on individual immigration stories, a Dutch store and the successful assimilation of the Dutch in general. Moreover, the article does make any connections among these different sub-components of the Dutch-Canadian population; the story of a resident of Shalom Manor, a Dutch Calvinist retirement home, is interspersed with references to an ethnically defined Dutch social club in St. Catharines largely run by Dutch Catholics and to "internecine squabbles and the outspoken opin-

ions of more conservative elements of various Dutch-based Reformed churches."

5 See also Ganzevoort, *A Bittersweet Land*, p. 78.

6 Margaret Vanderschot and Mary Smith, "Netherlands Research Project," p. 39.

7 A Dutch Catholic immigrant might marry someone who was a "Canadian" Protestant, but never someone who was *gereformeerd*.

8 It was founded in 1925 with the amalgamation of Presbyterian, Methodist and Congregational churches.

9 The unexpected outcome of the 1980 census is the unusually high proportion of Dutch-Canadian Presbyterians in Hamilton (i.e., 13.3 percent of those reporting Dutch as mother tongue).

10 On the national level, the 1980 census showed slightly higher percentages for both Dutch Catholics and Dutch-Canadians with no religious affiliation.

11 See Sas, "Dutch Migration to and Settlement in Canada," p. 47, table xi.

12 I came across several such examples in my fieldwork; in such cases, the couples mentioned that what they had "in common" was their religious background, even though they had not practised their religion for some time prior to dating.

13 I was not able to find any examples where Dutch-Canadians constituted a noticeable minority or "clique" in United Church congregations, after making enquiries (from both Dutch and non-Dutch members and ministers) in numerous localities.

14 A dozen or so ministers were born in the Netherlands. For example, Johannes Huntjes, now a senior minister, arrived in the Maritimes with his parents at the age of 15. After serving as port chaplain and on Indian reserves, he was minister in several United churches in Ottawa and later in downtown Toronto.

15 I am not aware of any students enrolled in Dutch-linked "Christian" high schools or colleges where the Dutch immigrants parents belonged to the United Church. For the few cases of intermarriage, the couple was engaged prior to emigrating.

16 In the Netherlands, the older Reformed Church is roughly the equivalent of the Anglican church in Ontario, in terms of prestige or class status. Indeed, some *hervormden* of middle-class background became Anglicans in Ontario.

17 Alternatively, these *hervormden* might learn to adapt themselves to a more conventional Presbyterian church.

18 Mrs. Koeslag's brother, an officer in the Dutch underground, was beaten to death by the Gestapo after he was caught spying on the movement of German army units. A year after his arrival in Canada, Albert Koeslag received the King's Medal for Courage for helping 60 Allied airmen shot down over Holland. The award was personally presented by then-lieutenant-governor for Ontario, the Hon. Ray Lawson, in Durham Park.

19 See G.W. Koeslag papers (1949-1975), in Dutch-Canadian papers series of MHSO, housed in the Archives of Ontario (Toronto), Acc. No. 21210, MU series 9418, MSR No. 6267. This collection of newspaper articles, which covers a thirty-year period, can provide a glimpse into the process of rapid incorporation of a liberal Protestant Dutch immigrant family in rural Ontario. Information obtained from the newspaper clippings was supplemented by additional background provided in a telephone interview with Mr. John Koeslag (Quadville, Ont.) on April 25, 1993. He also pointed out some minor factual errors in the Durham newspaper articles.

20 All but three of 11 children who came to Canada, married "Canadians" and ended up in small towns—Durham, Wiarton and Petersburg (near Kitchener)—or on farms in areas that have had few other Dutch residents. Bill Koeslag, a Guelph graduate and farmer, became the local co-op board's vice-president and chairman of the Clifford Medical Building committee.

21 This pattern of involvement in Canadian public affairs also applied to their parents. Mr. Albert Koeslag returned to the Netherlands in 1957 when he became ill, but his wife returned to Canada after his death in 1962. Despite her advanced age, she was an active member in the Knox United Church and its women's organization, the Rocky Saugeen Federated Farm Women's Club and the Royal Air Force Escape Society.

22 Some of the Koeslags have also kept up their native language; the high-school couple taught Dutch to all six of their children. Some of them can read and write Dutch.

23 Based on an interview with Dr. A. Verster, Beamsville, October 22, 1989.

24 In 1988, the proportion of Dutch-Canadians in Toronto with no religious affiliation was twice the provincial average.

25 For example, Dutch humanists, originally members of the *Humanistisch Verbond*, had greater difficulty finding an equivalent grouping in Ontario, and often did not even know of each others' presence in Canada. But eventually Dutch humanists started or joined their own chapters, together with Canadians of other backgrounds. This did not happen until a minimum critical mass allowed for the emergence of a fledgling humanist movement, several decades after the peak period of Dutch immigration. In 1992 about a quarter of the approximately 30 members of a small humanist chapter for the region of Kitchener-Cambridge-Guelph—and half of its executive members—were Dutch-Canadians. Similarly active NDP-supporters of Dutch descent had been socialists in the Netherlands during their youth. Similarly, Jesse Vorst, a Dutch academic and socialist in Holland who ended up in Manitoba, is the driving force behind the Society for Socialist Studies.

26 Dutch Mennonites (*doopsgezinden*), many of whom were professionals, were not unaware of their historical connections with Canadian Mennonites. I met one educated Dutch Mennonite postwar immigrant who joined a "modern" (non-orthodox) Mennonite congregation in the heart of Toronto. However, many postwar Dutch immigrants of Dutch Mennonite background had become completely secular prior to emigrating.

27 Prior to the War, Jews were an integral part of Dutch society, with roots going back to the sixteenth century; Sephardic Jewish merchants arrived in Amsterdam in the sixteenth century, when the Low Countries were still part of the Spanish empire (see Schama, *The Embarrassment of Riches*, p. 593). In the Netherlands, the distinction between a "Portuguese" (Sephardic) Jewish community, found only in Amsterdam, and a *Nederlands* (Dutch) Jewish community who use the slightly different Ashkenazic pronunciation of Hebrew in reading passages of the scriptures, still exists today. See C.N. Impeta, *Kaart van kerkelijk nederland*, p. 216-23.

Unlike their counterparts in other parts of Europe, who continued to speak Yiddish, Jews in the Netherlands spoke and continue to speak the Dutch language. They likewise adopted many of the customs of the Dutch population. Nevertheless, antisemitism returned with a vengeance in the first half of the twentieth century. The occupying German forces registered those of Jewish descent, culminating in massive deportation to concentration camps and gas chambers in different parts of Europe. Prior to 1940 there were 130,000 Jews in the Netherlands; by 1960 there were only 25,000. However, the German Nazis did not exterminate the Dutch Jewish population all on their own, since only Dutch Nazi collaborators could distinguish the largely Dutch-speaking Jews from the rest of the population.

28 Judaism took on great symbolic importance in Dutch culture. Calvinist writers compared the new nation of the Netherlands as a new kind of Israel, depicting the Dutch struggle against the king of Spain with the flight of the ancient Hebrews from the clutches of the Egyptian pharaoh. Dutch Calvinists thus portrayed themselves as heroic reborn Hebrews. However, these same Calvinists were more ambiguous when they had to confront the reality of Jews living in their midst. More humanistically inclined Calvinist scholars, interested in reviving the study of Hebrew as one of the important classic languages, came to admire the Jewish intellectuals and writers of their day. In contrast, more dogmatic Calvinists pressed for draconian measures that would extend the restriction against Jews which already existed on paper. During the peak of the "golden age," a major Jewish publisher was only allowed to print books in languages other than Dutch by the official Church Council of Amsterdam. Indeed, prior to the Batavian republic of 1796, Dutch Christians were not allowed to marry Dutch Jews and Jews were excluded from some guilds and trading houses. The more pragmatic Calvinist leaders of the Dutch republic successfully counteracted the intolerant and hostile attitudes of these more hard-line and purist Calvinist ministers towards both Jews and clandestine Catholics. See Schama, *The Embarrassment of Riches*, p. 587-96.

29 The Dutch language contains expressions stereotyping Jews as conniving and untrustworthy.

30 Few Dutch Jews survived the atrocities of World War Two. Those who escaped to North America before or during the war ended up mostly in New York City, although some later moved to Canada or emigrated directly to Canada after the War. Interview with John Mesritz, Toronto, September 16, 1989.

31 This figure seems reasonable in light of estimates provided by several people concerning the number of practising Jews in Toronto who are postwar Dutch immigrants.

32 In my interviews with Dutch-Canadians on this topic, several Jews and non-Jews all came up with a number close to this estimate.

33 Canada also had a very restrictive policy about allowing Jews to enter the country during the War. See Royal Commission on Bilingualism and Biculturalism, *The Cultural Contribution of the Other Ethnic Groups*, p. 28.

34 Conversation with Harry Bromet (from Oakville), Toronto, December 7, 1988.

35 Based on an interview held in Toronto. The Anglican affiliation became useful when he started selling life insurance to Dutch-Canadian farmers. Being affiliated with a Canadian church meant he could not be pigeon-holed into the usual Dutch religious categories with their pillar connections.

36 For instance, for the last decade a Dutch Jewish woman has hosted one of the weekly Dutch radio programs. She also writes a column for one of the Dutch-Canadian bi-weekly newspapers in her spare time. For a short biographical sketch, see the article about her by Ine Scheper, in *De Nederlandse Courant*, May 7, 1988, p. 10-11. A Jewish man, actively involved in the Dutch-Canadian

community, is an insurance broker. He also started writing a column in that newspaper a couple of years ago.

37 Interview, Eddy van der Sluis, Toronto, December 13, 1990.

38 One orthodox Dutch Jewish man, whose family roots in the Netherlands go back several generations, recounted how it took him a long time before he could work his way into a leadership position in his synagogue.

39 Interview with a non-Dutch accountant, in Toronto, April 12, 1989. Some Jewish Dutch people are as prone to being labelled stubborn or rationalistic as are Dutch Calvinists.

40 André Stein, *Quiet Heroes* (Toronto: Lester & Orpen Dennys, 1988), p. 7.

41 A paper on Dutch Holocaust literature was presented by Basil Kingston at a CAANS Conference, Waterloo, November 11 (also in Laval, May 28); a session dealing with the history of the Jews in the Netherlands was organized by the Toronto CAANS chapter, February 25, 1988. See ad in *De Nederlandse Courant* (February 8, 1988). A series of newspaper articles by Krystyna Henke, about Victor Kugler, a Toronto resident who hid Anne Frank, and about a retired Dutch rabbi in Toronto who worked in Japanese prisoner-of-war camps, appeared in the *Nederlandse Courant* (October 21, 1989, September 21, October 7, October 21, 1988). For a historical article dealing with Dutch Jews in New York, see Swierenga's article in the *Windmill Post*, the English-language supplement of the *Windmill Herald*, April 23, 1993, p. 13. The persecution of Dutch Jews under the Nazis is a theme in John Terpstra's novel, *The Homecoming Man* (Oakville: Mosaic Press, 1989).

42 Two men whom I interviewed mentioned that they had previously not told their children or friends about their Jewish background or upbringing.

43 This institutional presence is reflected in the wealth of documents in Ontario's multicultural historical archives that pertain to this sub-group of Dutch-Canadians.

44 Bradley Breems has referred to the orthodox Calvinist community as an example of "faith ethnicity." See his "'I Tell Them We Are a Blessed People,'" p. 80. See also Harold Coward and Leslie Kawamura, eds., *Religion and Ethnicity* (Waterloo: Wilfrid Laurier University Press, 1978), p. viii.

45 Other former orthodox Dutch Calvinists have told me that they prefer to belong to churches that have a greater mixture of people of different ethnic and racial backgrounds. For these and many other reasons, many orthodox Dutch Calvinists who joined a Dutch-linked Reformed church upon arrival later switched to a non-Dutch denomination.

46 There is even a Canadian historical connection, since ministers in the early history of Canada's Presbyterian Church were Dutch-American ministers from the Reformed Church in America. William Gregg, *History of the Presbyterian Church in the Dominion of Canada* (Toronto: Presbyterian Printing and Publishing, 1885), p. 67.

47 In the Dutch language, degrees of orthodoxy or strictness are classified in terms of *zwaar* ("heavy") versus *licht* ("light").

48 Interview with George DeKleer, Jr., February 17, 1990.

49 Interview with Marinus Mol, Ayton, March 12, 1991.

50 I met three in the course of doing my fieldwork.

51 Initially the Presbyterian representatives sent to Europe did not like the orientation of the ministers they met who belonged to the *hervormde* or the *gereformeerde* version of Dutch Calvinism—until they discovered in Hans Segerius a man whom they felt was compatible with their Canadian vision. This minis-

ter, who later retired in Guelph, was a member of a small Dutch denomination called the *Vrije Evangelische Gemeente* (another small offshoot of the *Hervormde Kerk*). Interview with the Reverend Hans Segerius, Guelph, February 27, 1990.

52 Another connection between the Presbyterian and Christian Reformed Church is Stanford Reid, a Canadian minister who did historical research on the Reformation in the Netherlands while on sabbatical from the University of Guelph. He was one of the first non-Dutch Presbyterian ministers who preached to Dutch-Canadian congregations.

53 The Canadian Catholic Church, which already had a large number of members not of British descent prior to 1940, became even more diversified after World War Two, with the influx of southern European, and later Latin American, immigrants.

54 I came across several Dutch-Canadian community leaders, especially in Catholic enclaves near London and in the Ottawa Valley, who were actively involved in the Liberal Party (federal and provincial).

55 Various Dutch traditions and folk customs (Carnival, Dutch card games, dances) were frowned upon or forbidden by orthodox Calvinists in the 1950s.

56 See Will Herberg, *Protestant-Catholic-Jew* (New York: Anchor, 1960). Each of these blocs or segments is diverse enough to allow for varying degrees of secularism or orthodoxy. For most North Americans, especially those of European background, these wider spheres of social identity are still an indicator of where one is likely to go to school, who one will marry and who will be your best friends. However even the North American form of pillarization is being eroded by increasing interreligious marriages. See Richard Alba, *Ethnic Identity: The Transformation of White America* (New Haven: Yale University Press, 1990).

Chapter 8

1 Actually, there were at least 85 priests of Dutch origin working in Canada in 1959, but most of them worked in remote northern communities (see Ganzevoort, *A Bittersweet Land*, p. 97). Father Van Wezel, a Dutch priest who worked with Dutch immigrants in Ontario, mentions a figure of 104 Dutch priests in Canada in the early 1950s in an interview with Henry van Stekelenburg (tape-recorded in Dutch in Dommelen, in the Netherlands, on August 7, 1979). This tape (henceforth to be referred to as the Van Wezel tape) was then housed in the Queen's Crescent offices of the Multicultural History Society of Ontario (MHSO).

2 Canadian priests considered Dutch parishioners, with their emphasis on church attendance and desire for separate schools, more committed than their Canadian-born counterparts.

3 Interviews with Mr. Adrian Bruijns, near Ilderton, August 27; with Mrs. Katrien de Groot, Strathroy, August 28; and with Martin Strijbosch, just outside Strathroy, October 20, 1990.

4 Here Dutch Catholics were served by a group of Dutch priests associated with Milhil, a Catholic missionary organization originally founded in England. Interview with Father Falke, in the rectory of St. Joan of Arc Church, Toronto, December 13, 1990.

5 Interview with Father Falke, December 13, 1990; and Mr. Douwinus Horst, St. Marys, May 14, 1992.

6 Interviews with Peter and Betty Poel, on their farm near Thamesforth, March 16, 1989; Maria Aarts, near Kintore, April 13, 1989; Jack Verhulst, Guelph, March 3, 1990; Martin de Groot, Phelpston, April 23, 1990; and Ralph Bakker, Watford, July 7, 1990.

7 The Dutch Catholics presented an enigma to the established Canadian families who had always thought that all Dutch were Protestants.

8 Interview with John Hendrikx, Park Hill, December 16, 1988.

9 Estimate based on a conversation with Mr. and Mrs. John Arts in Arkona, November 21, 1988.

10 Interview with Piet Gouweleeuwen, Uxbridge, February 3, 1990.

11 I went over this yearbook with Mrs. Ann van Boxmeer, Wyoming, June 4, 1991.

12 Conversation with Julie Straatman, together with her brother Paul, in their home near Warwick (near Watford), July 7, 1990.

13 This neighbour is a woman of Dutch Belgian (i.e., Flemish) descent; interview with Mrs. Margaret Hendrickx, in her home near Warwick, April 27, 1989. We sat at her kitchen table and together examined the church yearbook for 1989.

14 This historical information is included in the 1989 parish yearbook entitled *Our Family Parish* (St. Christopher's Church).

15 The founding of this school was recorded in four pages of handwritten minutes of meetings held between November 24, 1953 and December 27, 1954. This first meeting was held at the home of Mr. Jack Boere. The expected enrolment was 40.

16 These rural Dutch and a few Flemish families represent the older, more established core of the parish; the non-Dutch members, who live in the towns of Thedford, Forest or the village of Camlachie, moved in after 1980, with the gradual expansion of suburban development.

17 All names mentioned in the yearbook, plus maiden names obtained in my interview in Warwick, were added to an existing file of people compiled on the basis of all previous oral interviews and other documentary sources in this area. My file, which contained information on region of origin, indicates that even rural Dutch Catholics came from a number of different Dutch provinces.

18 Unmarried offspring living at home have been left out. The kinship diagrams were constructed on the basis of information on all Dutch-Canadian individuals listed in the yearbook. Interview with Mrs. Margaret Hendrickx, April 27, 1989.

19 This is not unusual; I came across several such cases among rural Dutch families in this region.

20 One of these villages, Park Hill, is part of a different parish altogether. Dutch-Canadian Catholic families in nearby Watford, Strathroy and Stratford, and even beyond the diocese of London, have similar social bonds. In some smaller parishes, such as St. Patrick's in the hamlet of Kinkora, parish members of Netherlandic descent constitute about 70 percent of the parish. I perused the parish list around a kitchen table, on April 26, 1989, together with several members of the Willems family, who live near Kinkora.

21 This diagram was constructed on the basis of an interview with Mrs. Ann van Boxmeer, Wyoming, June 4, 1991, in which she provided kinship information about all the Dutch-Canadian families listed in the 1987 yearbook of the parishes of St. Philip (Petrolia), St. Anne (Oil Springs) and Holy Rosary (Wyoming).

22 The priest in charge was Jan van Buren, originally from Amsterdam. Much of the information about this order and its activities in Ontario was obtained from the van Wezel tape, MHSO.

23 Father White had escorted Father van der Vorst, who was invited by the Canadian bishops to come and visit Dutch immigrant families, throughout the London area.

24 In return for permission to found a minor seminary, van Buren agreed to take on the responsibility of looking after postwar immigrants.

25 Interview with John Roks, Delaware, May 3, 1990.

26 Other dioceses where the Sacred Heart priests were later invited to come included Toronto and Ottawa. About a half dozen children of Dutch immigrants, having received their training in Canada, also became priests in this order.

27 In Windsor, and the hamlets of Bornish (near Park Hill), Kennilworth (south of Mount Forest) and Carlsruhe (near Hanover).

28 Interview with the Reverend John Meendering, in the rectory of St. Patrick's, Caledonia, January 30, 1990.

29 He was ordained in London, Ontario, two years after his arrival in Canada. Interview with Father Falke, Toronto, December 13, 1990.

30 Although known by some people as the "Dutch church," this parish in Toronto never had more than a few Dutch families, even during the height of the postwar Dutch migration. However, there is an indirect Dutch connection; by the early 1990s about 400 out of the 1500 members of the parish were ethnic Chinese who fled political persecution in Indonesia. The older people within this group of refugees, who were educated in the former Dutch East Indies prior to coming to Canada, could still speak Dutch. A Catholic Indonesian organization, which organizes an annual bazaar in the parish, used to advertise this event in the *Nederlandse Courant*, the Dutch-Canadian bi-weekly published in Toronto at that time.

31 He also edited the magazine called *Compass* (*Kompas* in Dutch) for several years. Taped interview (in English) with the Reverend Martin Grootscholten, conducted by Elsie E. Murphy at the former immigration centre, 150 Kent Street, London, on May 4, 1979. In the archives of the Multicultural History Society of Ontario in Toronto.

32 The Dutch immigrants thought the currency restriction in the Netherlands might be enforceable in Canada. Various people I interviewed corroborated the existence of this misconception in the 1950s; it was also mentioned in the van Wezel tape.

33 In 1956, this bank, which formed part of the Dutch Catholic pillar, extended a 10-year loan for $100,000 to assist Dutch immigrants in Canada (Ron Kenyon, *To the Credit of the People* [Toronto: Hunter Rose Company, 1976], p. 155).

34 Another Dutch priest, eventually van Wezel's superior, was Piet Renders who was involved in setting up a similar Catholic immigration centre in Antigonish, Nova Scotia. That centre operated for seven years in the 1950s, but many of the Dutch farm immigrants who started in the Maritimes gravitated to southwestern Ontario. Father Renders had a great deal of day-to-day contact with Dutch Catholic rural immigrants. His own rural background—one of his own nephews settled in rural Ontario—enabled him to establish especially good rapport with farm immigrants from his home province of Noord Brabant. See also Dortman, *Brabanders in Canada*, p. 184.

35 There his presence met with vehement opposition from local people, who did not want anything to do with any foreign priest. The Irish-Canadians of the Ottawa Valley were particularly afraid of the increasing encroachment of French-speaking Catholics.

36 He persuaded a new deputy minister of immigration to cover the cost of boarding Dutch immigrants stranded in Ottawa.

37 Consequently, there was no more work for van Wijk, who became general manager of the Dutch Catholic credit union for London alone.

38 This official was William Jaffray who had been appointed Inspector of Credit Unions for the Department of Agriculture (see Kenyon, *To the Credit of the People*, p. 94). Not being Catholic, he had not realized that the diocese of London was so big and hence felt deceived (according to van Wezel's account).

39 Canadian immigration officials were also leery of promoting further ethno-religious enclaves. See also Burnet and Palmer, *"Coming Canadians,"* p. 9.

40 Van Wezel made a trip to the Netherlands to attend a session of the Dutch parliament, when its members had to debate whether or not to retract a letter expressing Dutch government opposition to the expansion of St. Willibrord Credit Union of London to other parts of Canada (based on van Wezel tape).

41 A book written of the history of the credit union movement in Ontario suggests at least approval on paper by the Ontario government to "organize five new diocesan 'St. Willibrord' type credit unions in various regions" (see Kenyon, *To the Credit of the People*, p. 155).

42 This was done since any interest payments to non-residents were subject to a withholding tax except when made to a sovereign government. Personal communication from Dick de Man.

43 At that time the diocese of Toronto included St. Catharines and other parts of the Niagara peninsula which were connected to Toronto via a ferry across Lake Ontario. That is how Sacred Heart fathers ended up in places like Caledonia and Hagersville.

44 Technically it was in charge of all Catholic immigration policy on the national level.

45 He did not like the fact that the French-Canadians wanted Catholic immigrants to come to Quebec, but without being willing to provide special assistance to Dutch newcomers.

46 Toward the end of side A of cassette 3 of the van Wezel tapes, MHSO. Handwritten documents referring to disagreements between Father van Wezel and Quebec delegates at the International Roman Catholic Migration Congress in Assissi are also included among the Catholic Immigration Services Papers collection in the Dutch-Canadian papers of the MHSO, MU. 9429.1. The main opponent of van Wezel at various international congresses was Msgr. Armand Malouin, the spiritual advisor of the SCER in Montreal. Personal communication from Dr. Henk van Stekelenburg, who also sent me photocopies of correspondance, written in 1957, between Father van Wezel and Bishop Cody of London and with a fellow clergyman in the Netherlands involved in these political intrigues. Copies of these and several policy documents written in the late 1940s were provided to van Stekelenburg by Ann van de Valk of London, Ontario.

47 See also Henry van Stekelenburg, "Tracing the Dutch Roman Catholic Emigrants to North America in the Nineteenth and Twentieth Centuries," in Ganzevoort and Boekelman, ed., *Dutch Immigration to North America*, p. 73.

48 Here they replaced the Sisters of St. Joseph, an order of Canadian nuns who had previously provided instruction at both the primary and secondary levels in the diocese of London. Interview with Anthony van den Heuvel, Sarnia, June 4, 1991.

49 One of them, who specialized in social work, participated in multicultural events and sat as a Dutch representative on a committee to commemorate the Canadian liberation of the Netherlands from the Nazis.

50 Interview with Brother Anthony van den Heuvel, Sarnia, June 4, 1991. There are two other small religious orders for women (Peter Claver and Kostbaar Bloed) that operate in Ontario and have their "mother houses" in the Netherlands. However, the latter is actually German and the former does not include any Dutch members.

51 Interview with Martin de Groot, Phelpston, April 23, 1990; taped interview with Dirk and Jeltje Mous, Smithville, November 8, 1993.

52 They are promoting his canonization by Rome as a saint, meeting every year for a mass and picnic in Niagara Falls, where they are usually joined by a group of Carmelites, the religious order to which Brandsma belonged. About a hundred people attended their fifth annual picnic on July 29, 1990. A committee also puts out its own newsletter, *The Lighted Candle*, from Welland, Ontario.

Brandsma was a Frisian-Dutch priest in the resistance movement who died in Dachau, a concentration camp in Germany. One of the St. Louis brothers in Sarnia translated a Dutch version of a life history of Titus Brandsma for this small group of Dutch-Canadians. See Anthony van den Heuvel, "Titus Brandsma, a Modern Martyr for the Truth" (adapted from the Dutch version by H. Audes, *Het Leven van Titus Brandsma*), Welland, 1990.

53 One of them told me in an interview that they represented the "middle-class Dutch Catholics in Toronto." Based on a conversation in Toronto. The names he mentioned as part of this network were corroborated by several other people.

54 Based on several interviews or conversations with Dutch Catholics who live or lived in Aurora.

55 Many of their children and grandchildren are likely to have stopped practising their religion, or have changed their religion altogether. The older Dutch Catholic population is quite aware of this trend of increasing secularism, and will openly admit this even to an outside observer. However, their children generally continue to offer a token level of support to, or at least refrain from openly criticizing, the Church to avoid open confrontations with their parents or grandparents.

56 Their priests hold mass in private chapels in barns or people's houses, including in the hamlet of Hyde Park, also near London.

57 I interviewed one of the principal lay leaders, who is a retired Dutch-Canadian dairy farmer, as well as one of his Dutch-Canadian neighbours who did not join the group. Both live in Perth county.

58 In the village of Arkona there is still a predominantly Dutch St. Joseph's Club for Dutch Catholic seniors and the majority of inhabitants of a retirement home are also of Dutch Catholic background.

Chapter 9

1 The basic organization structure of all Reformed churches vests authority in the hands of the presbyters, or ministers, who serve on local church consistories together with lay elders who act as deacons. The elders play an important role in the church since they regularly visit all of the families, to ensure that church members conform to community standards of conduct based on ascetic values, sobriety and self-discipline.

2 See also Reginald Bibby, *Fragmented Gods* (Toronto: Irwin, 1987), p. 185.

3 One Reformed sociologist calls the Reformed community a form of "faith ethnicity." See Breems, " 'I Tell Them We Are a Blessed People,' " p. 4.

4 It is not always possible to draw a hard-and-fast line between liberal and orthodox Calvinists. For example, both more liberal and very orthodox *gereformeerden* joined the Presbyterian church in Canada (see chap. 7).

5 The *Gereformeerde Kerken* in the Netherlands resulted from a union in 1892, under Abraham Kuyper, of the *afscheiding* and the *doleantie*. The neo-Calvinist trend, which emphasized political engagement, was always stronger in the Netherlands, although they did have some influence on American Orthodox Calvinism, which was the product of the earlier *afscheiding* that took place in 1834. This earlier Dutch-American church has also been labelled as "Confessional Reformed." See Harry Kits, "World Views and Social Involvement," chap. 1.

6 Any group interested in becoming part of the CRC needed a minimum of twelve families. Such small congregations would rent the basement of a local Canadian church until they had saved up sufficient funds to build their own place of worship.

7 The Reverend H. Moes covered eastern Canada, from Kingston to Nova Scotia, while Adam Persenaire, also a home missionary, was in charge of the entire Niagara peninsula. John van der Vliet, who welcomed Dutch immigrants when they disembarked in Halifax, worked as pastor for both Hastings and Prince Edward counties. Interview with Andrew Schaafsma, Waterdown, September 10, 1990. Initially, even "resident" ministers served more than one congregation, as with the Reverend S.G. Brondsema, who visited groups in Brampton, Dixie and Toronto. All of these ministers appear in VanderMey's *To All Our Children*, p. 309-10.

8 For example, a small congregation in Trenton called their first minister in 1950, but families who lived further away, east of Trenton, established their own church in Belleville four years later. Subsequently, rural families living to the west started attending a new church in Brighton. Interview with Joe Dibbits, Wooler (near Brighton), July 3, 1991.

9 See W.W.J. Vanoene, *Inheritance Preserved* (Winnipeg: Premier, 1978), appendix 1.

10 Other Dutch Calvinist sects, resulting from much earlier church splits, included the *Oud Gereformeerde Gemeenten* (Old Reformed) and *Christelijke Gereformeerde Kerken* (see figure 6). The presence of people of such different denominational backgrounds within a single church presented quite a challenge, especially to the often bewildered Christian Reformed ministers from the States working among new Canadians.

11 For a short biography, see VanderMey, *To All Our Children*, p. 282-83.

12 When he came to Canada as a young man in 1950, he worked on farms and ended up in Whitby, Ontario. A recently appointed Reformed minister from the States then hired him to escort newly arrived immigrants disembarking at pier 21 in Halifax. Interview with Rimmer Tjalsma, Mississauga, May 1, 1989; see also ibid., p. 469-70.

13 VanderMey, *To All Our Children*, p. 457.

14 Interview with John Reinders, at his farm near Moorfield, January 18, 1992.

15 *1987 Yearbook of the Reformed Church in Canada*. The Reformed Church in Canada tended to attract more orthodox members of the *Hervormde Kerk* in the Netherlands. In a telephone interview [to Surrey, B.C.], on August 19, 1994, Albert Vanderheide, the publisher of the *Windmill Herald*, suggested other people likely to join this North American denomination were those who closely associated this formerly official state church with Dutch nationalism and royalty (*kerk en vaderland*, or "church and fatherland"), or people who wanted an ethnic church (to associated with fellow Dutch immigrants), as long as they were not *gereformeerd*.

16 Overall, the Christian Reformed churches represented only .3 percent of the Canadian population, and Canadian Reformed .05. See Bibby, *Fragmented Gods*, table 2.1, p. 28. If we include all the other Reformed denominations in Canada, the total would still not go above 1 percent of the total Canadian population.

17 *1987 Yearbook of the Christian Reformed Church*. In addition, several other Christian Reformed churches in Northern and eastern Ontario belonged to classes that included areas outside Ontario.

18 In Sarnia, an early CRC minister was dubbed *de dominee met het emmertje zand* (the minister with the little pail of sand), because he always went around "putting out fires of controversy." Interview with Mr. and Mrs. Gerrit de Boer, Sarnia, August 29, 1990.

19 The smaller denominations initially "called" their own ministers from the Netherlands, who in turn recruited additional members among newly arrived immigrants or people who had hitherto attended services in CRC or Reformed congregations.

20 Services are still conducted in both Dutch and English in some of these churches, largely because they are receiving new Dutch immigrants.

21 As they expanded in the United States, they chose the name "American Reformed," although in Australia they adopted the name "Free Reformed."

22 My figures refer to the state of affairs around 1991. Churches were instituted in Orangeville (1950), Hamilton (1951), Smithville (1952), Watford (1954), Toronto (1954), Brampton and Fergus (1956), Guelph (1974). See Vanoene, *Inheritance Preserved*, p. 294-97.

23 Some newly arrived members include Dutch *oud gereformeerden*, although some members of this very small Dutch sect have also entered the Free Reformed Church.

24 That church, founded by former *oud gereformeerden*, is called the Old Netherlands Reformed Congregation.

25 In his study of a Christian Reformed congregation in British Columbia, Breems emphasizes such heterogeneity, focusing on the very diverse motives people have for maintaining group membership, and the multiple criteria for defining such membership, despite a common world view. However, while he treats a single religious community as a unit of analysis, my study treats all

Reformed churches with Dutch connections as a single "faith ethnicity," which is in turn a sub-unit of a broader Dutch-Canadian network. We thus apply concepts such as Barth's notion of ethnic boundaries at very different levels of analysis. See Breems, "'I Tell Them We Are a Blessed People,'" p. 243-44.

26 See Gary D. Bouma, "Keeping the Faithful: Patterns of Membership Retention in the Christian Reformed Church," *Sociological Analysis*, 41 (1980): 259-64.

27 See Henry Stam, "Effectiveness of Formal Socialization Processes within the Christian Reformed Church," MA thesis in sociology, University of Windsor, 1987.

28 K. Ishwaran, a non-Dutch sociologist, analyzed a similar close-knit rural kinship network in Ansnorveldt and Springfield, two villages in the Holland Marsh that date back to the thirties. See K. Ishwaran, *Family, Kinship and Community* (Toronto: McGraw-Hill Ryerson, 1977).

29 According to a 1992 survey, about 80 percent of the CRC, including its American wing, is still of Dutch background. Reported in the *Windmill Herald*, February 23, 1993, p. 16.

30 *1991 Directory of the Hamilton Area Christian Reformed Churches* (Ancaster: Guardian Press, 1991), p. 132-46. Similar tendencies are revealed in CRC directories for Toronto (especially Scarborough). The percentage of couples with non-Dutch surnames listed in the Ottawa church directory of 1989-1990 is around 15.

31 Similarly, an elderly couple in Brantford, members of the Reformed Church in Canada, had a son who joined the CRC in Brantford and a daughter who entered the Free Reformed Church in Dundas after her engagement. I have also met prominent CRC ministers with blood relatives or in-laws from rival denominations.

32 The Reformed tradition that emerged in Canada, and particularly in Ontario, is not the same as its counterpart in the United States. This contrast between Dutch-Canadian and Dutch-American is as important as variations in the level of orthodoxy.

33 The theological tenet underlying this model of society is the notion of Christ's kingdom including all areas of life. According to this tenet every social institution should be based on biblical principles, yet run by laymen (Abraham Kuyper, *Christianity and the Class Struggle*, translated by Dirk Jellema [Grand Rapids: Piet Hein Publishers, 1950]). Kuyper referred to "separate spheres of sovereignty" to distinguish between state, church and other aspects of civil society.

34 Harry Kits has classified such neo-Calvinism (or Calvinism that believes in societal involvement) into three "streams": antithetical, radical and engaged. See his "World Views and Social Involvement," p. 24.

35 For example, they resemble other American Protestant denominations in incorporating such symbols as the stars and stripes and the bald eagle into their places of worship.

36 Dutch-American Calvinists set up their own denominationally based liberal arts colleges, but their children for the most part attended public schools. Even religiously based private primary schools were designed to help Dutch-American children conform to American society, albeit in a protected environment. Unlike the immigrants themselves who wanted to establish both

churches and schools, the American home missionaries who worked among postwar Dutch immigrants were not in favour of immigrants with few resources setting up their own Christian schools right away. See Aileen Van Ginkel, "Ethnicity in the Reformed Tradition: Dutch Calvinist Immigrants in Canada, 1946-1960," MA thesis in history, University of Toronto, 1982, p. 59.

37 Unlike Calvin College, its American counterpart located in Grand Rapids, Michigan, Redeemer has no official connection with the CRC, although almost all board members, administrators and faculty belong to Dutch-linked Calvinist denominations. Similarly, a Canadian Reformed newspaper (originally published in Dutch) is owned and operated by independent laymen, unlike *The Banner* put out by CRC headquarters in Grand Rapid, Michigan. The name of the Canadian publication, which used to called *Calvinist Contact*, was changed to *Christian Courier* at the end of 1992. See *De Nederlandse Courant*, 37, 25 (1992): 22.

38 Van Ginkel, "Ethnicity in the Reformed Tradition," p. 82-110.

39 Harro Walter Van Brummelen, "Molding God's Children: The History of Curriculum in Christian Schools Rooted in Dutch Calvinism," PhD dissertation (in Education), University of British Columbia, 1984, p. 419.

40 Dutch-Canadian Calvinists subsequently played a leadership role in the broader Ontario Alliance of Christian Schools (OACS), whose headquarters are today based at Redeemer College, in Ancaster. In the 1950s this Alliance sponsored a Dutch-Canadian publication, the *Christian School Herald*, which advocated a Kuyperian vision. See Adriaan Peetoom, "From Mythology to Mythology: Dutch-Canadian Orthodox Calvinist Immigrants and Their Schools," MA thesis in history and philosophy of Education, University of Toronto (OISE), n.d., ca. 1988, p. 106-108.

41 These non-Dutch students include Baptists and Pentecostals, although parents affiliated with other churches also send their children to these schools.

42 Interview with the acting principal, Corrie Bootsma, June 15, 1989. She showed me a list indicating that 11 out of 97 students enrolled were not of Dutch background. Schools in Strathroy, Burlington and Georgetown are also predominantly "Dutch."

43 Unlike other Christian schools, these are officially denomination schools.

44 Interview with Cees Bijl, Willowdale, February 5, 1990. In Clarkson, Mississauga and Ottawa, the percentage of non-Dutch pupils is closer to 60, and a minority of teachers is neither Reformed nor Dutch-Canadian.

45 In Puslinch, south of Guelph, about half the parents who founded a Christian school were Reformed Dutch-Canadians and the other half were evenly divided between Baptists and Presbyterians. Interview with Bill Brunsveld, at his farm near Puslinch, December 5, 1990.

46 Dutch Calvinists tend to be more legalistic, and put greater emphasis on reason than emotion.

47 At least a half a dozen first-generation Dutch-Canadians with whom I spoke corroborated this analysis, which was first suggested to me by a former teacher in the system.

48 This period is referred to as "the wild years."

49 Such differences in attitudes towards alcohol is even noticeable between the Canadian and American branches of the CRC itself. During religious conventions or synod meetings held in Grand Rapids, the "Canadian" (Dutch) ministers would occasionally go up to someone's room for some "Dutch chocolate"

(a euphemism for alcohol), to the horror of their American colleagues. Interview with one of the instructors at the Institute of Christian Studies, Toronto, November 18, 1988. Van Ginkel refers to similar differences in attitudes towards smoking, and the influence of Methodists on the American Calvinists (Van Ginkel, "Ethnicity in the Reformed Tradition," p. 60-62).

50 See Peetoom, "From Mythology to Mythology," 110; and Breems, "'I Tell Them We Are a Blessed People,'" p. 226, 228-29, 253-54.

51 This pattern of isolation is further reinforced through a dozen or so Christian high schools with Dutch connections. The first such high school was inaugurated in Woodbridge, north of Toronto.

52 Reformed colleges located in Western Canada and the Mid-western United States give young educated Calvinists access to an even more extensive social network, leading to further in-group endogamy. These include King's College in Western Canada, and Dordt College in Sioux City, Iowa. All of these colleges are de facto "ethnic" institutions, further reinforcing group solidarity.

53 They chose an executive and invited a high school teacher, who had been an agricultural consultant in the Netherlands, to act as their advisor. This federation, then called the Federation of Christian Farmers Associations (FCFA) of Ontario, fell apart in 1956 when only 14 people showed up at a meeting held in the CRC in London. Additional chapters were formed in Exeter, Jarvis and Aylmer. Minutes of meetings of the FCFA of Ontario (for March 6, 1954) in a notebook in the office of the CFFO in Guelph. Other historical information was also obtained from this notebook.

54 Their advisor also used his contacts at the University of Guelph to organize several "Dutch" days in order to provide information to immigrant farmers. Interview with Jan Bakker, Hamilton, April 21, 1989.

55 New locals were also established in Listowel and Owen Sound. During this interim period, the federation stopped referring to the Reformed and Protestant character in their constitution and opted for a broader Christian label.

56 The son of a farmer, Elbert van Donkersgoed attended Calvin College, and took courses in economics at the University of Waterloo. At the time of his hiring he was employed as a teacher in a Christian school. As spokesman for the Federation (now called the Christian Farmers Federation of Ontario or CFFO), he has since become well-known for his articles and speeches on agricultural policies. His position was later renamed Reseach and Policy Director.

57 This change is reflected in official correspondence and minutes of meetings, written in English rather than Dutch since 1969 (see also chapter 11).

58 This vision is described in their 1993 booklet *CFFO Backgrounder*, p. 2-3. Their research director supports the notion that agricultural workers in Ontario should be allowed to unionize; they are also concerned with the plight of third-world peasants and the need to find ecologically more friendly agricultural technologies, which they express in the concept of stewardship. Interview with Elbert van Donkersgoed, Guelph, October 21, 1988.

59 These members represent a minority within the approximately 2,000 Dutch-Canadian Calvinists involved in full-time commercial farming in Ontario. I derived this rough figure by adding up half of the total of all members of predominantly rural-agricultural congregations. I came up with this average proportion after some checking in specific locations.

60 Although other Dutch-Canadian farmers may have heard about the CFFO, they would not necessarily agree with its policies, perceived by some as "too radical." Several Dutch-Canadian farmers who believe in free and unbridled free enterprise are adamantly opposed to CFFO policy statements. Two founding members quit after they moved well beyond a family-farm scale.

61 Interview with Hans Vanderstoep, Burlington, June 18, 1989.

62 Commercial farmers can join the CRCBPA, and several commercial chicken or turkey operators have done so. This potential overlap in membership, plus a difference in philosophy, has caused tensions with the CFFO, which openly criticizes big business farming. I have also heard members of the CRCBPA who are small business people accuse their own organization of "being dominated too much by the big guys."

Like any Reformed organizations, there is internal diversity in both ideology and denominational ties. Some members have signed collective agreements with employees affiliated with the CLAC, while Canadian Reformed members are opposed to any labour union—even a Christian one—and would expel unionists from their church.

63 They obtained advice from a similar Dutch-linked Christian labour organization which had been set up in the U.S. in the thirties. Interview with Ed Pyper and Hank Beekhuis, St. Catharines, November 27, 1989. Other Dutch Calvinist immigrants started meeting at regular intervals in Vancouver and in four other urban centres in Ontario.

64 These and other cases are discussed by Michael Fallon in an unpublished paper entitled, "The Narrow Way: A Study of the Christian Labour Association of Canada" (1991), p. 29-37.

65 See ibid., p. 66-72. See also Kits, "World Views and Social Involvement," p. 48, 52.

66 The decision was made by Chief Justice J.C McRuer on May 2, 1963, overturning a lower court's refusal to give certification rights for the Trenton Construction Workers Local No. 52. The original petition dated from September 1960.

67 Interview with Ed van den Kloet, November 17, 1988.

68 The CNV was the strongest member of the International Federation of Protestant Workers and he became their general secretary following the War ("In Memoriam: F.P. Fuykschot," *The Voice*, February 1961, p. 2). Fuykschot started working as a messenger for a Dutch bank in 1928 and later ended up as an post office employee. This and other aspects of his career are based on interviews with his two daughters, Jacoba Fuykschot, Ottawa, June 30; and Cornelia Fuykschot, Gananoque, August 28 (both in 1991). I was also able to consult some personal records of Frans Fuykschot in their possession.

69 Fuykschot, who was conversant in English, joined a Presbyterian church and became close friends with a Baptist minister who was interested in his union work. No doubt, this social contact with non-Dutch Christians must have modified the original outlook of Fuykschot, who came to Canada with some misconceptions about an evil and supposedly "communistic" mainstream union movement in North America.

70 The strongest support for the CLAC came from local chapters, which included sympathetic supporters as well as potential workers. Dutch Calvinists saw this institution as an integral part of the Reformed community.

71 According to Fuykschot's annual report for 1955 (p. 5), there were more than 50 "locals," and the circulation of *The Guide* had increased to 4,000 copies a month.

72 They were worried that they would lose the opportunity to organize Christian workers who would all end up in mainstream non-religious unions, unless they got certification. Fuykschot knew that most of the union locals in British Columbia, where certification was also turned down, had turned into mere study groups.

73 Gerard Vandezande, "Which Way," *The Guide*, 7 July-August, 1958, p. 1-2. Harry Kits interprets these opposing sides of the debate over CLAC's relationship with the Ontario government as an example of the differences between more "engaged" neo-Calvinists (exemplified by Fuykschot) and "antithetical" Calvinists. See Kits, "World Views and Social Involvement," p. 66, 77.

74 The tension was exacerbated by a personality conflict between Fuykschot, the polished gentleman, and Vandezande, the young militant immigrant worker. The problem might have been that they were too much alike. Although a generation apart, they were both self-educated, both started as white-collar workers in banks, and they both became involved in public affairs.

75 Twenty years later, in 1979, it was reunited with the CLAC ("Christian Labor Unions Merge," the (St. Catharines) *Standard*, February 16, 1979).

76 This version asked members to uphold the constitution, rather than agree with the union's religious principles.

77 According to one informant to whom I spoke in 1991, Mr. Bosch, the owner of the printing firm which first tried to get certification in the early 1950s, was very much involved in setting up the union.

78 Interview with Ed Pyper and Hank Beekhuis, St. Catharines, November 27, 1989.

79 Although they believe in a non-adversarial approach, they are militant. The union even participated in its first strike involving safety issues in a stamping plant, showing that they certainly do not function as a "company union." Indeed, some Dutch-Canadian employers prefer to deal with the Teamsters, who don't insist on workers' participation in management decision making. Individual members are allowed to have their dues remitted to a charity of their choice—if they do not agree with having a union at all—but they can also have their dues transferred to another union that comes closer to their own principles. So far only a small percentage of the workers in CLAC have taken advantage of this option. This policy reflects the vision of Harry Antonides, the director of research and education of the CLAC. See his *Multinationals and the Peaceable Kingdom* (Toronto: Clarke, Irwin, 1978).

80 See Kits, "World Views and Social Involvement," p. 80-81. When CPJ was started as an offshoot of the CLAC, its was called the Committee for Justice and Liberty (CJL). See ibid., p. 48; and feature article by Bert Witvoet, *Calvinist Contact*, February 5, 1988, p. 12-13.

81 Interview with Gerald Vandezande, in Toronto, November 18, 1988.

82 See Gerald Vandezande, *Christians in the Crisis* (Toronto: Anglican Book Centre, 1983). A young man who remembered Vandezande as an open supporter of the Vietnam war in the 1960s was surprised to see him espouse quite a different political stance in the early 1980s.

83 The second-generation Dutch-Canadians involved in the Citizens for Public Justice committee include John Althius, a lawyer who negotiated land claims for the Dene people. He too served as CPJ director.

84 Its earlier name was the Association for Reformed Scientific Studies (ARSS), which held its first study conference in 1959. One of its main speakers, who also became the "spiritual father" of a generation of young neo-Calvinist leaders in Canada, was Dr. H. Even Runner. Although not of Dutch or Calvinist background, he became an active promoter for the Dutch neo-Calvinist vision, and his lectures particularly affected Dutch-Canadian students at Calvin College who started a "Groen" club. See Kits, "World Views and Social Involvement," p. 44, and Peetoom, "From Mythology to Mythology," p. 127-32.

The most avid supporters of the ICS were all Calvinist intellectuals, including Speelman, the owner of a publishing house in Toronto. Another founder, Bernard Zijlstra (who later became director) was an academic before he emigrated.

85 It can only grant an MA, but has a collaborative PhD program with the Free University of Amsterdam.

86 Kits refers to them as representative of the "radical activist view" within neo-Calvinism. Their main spokesman, Michael Welton, resigned from the CJL (forerunner of CPJ) board of directors in 1972. See Kits, "World Views and Social Involvement," p. 71-75.

87 Zijlstra, who maintained good contacts with a diversity of Dutch-Canadians, acted as mediator. The last two directors have been older, non-Dutch Protestant men who give an aura of respectability to the Institution.

88 The Institute, which is a "think tank" for the Reformed intelligentsia, has close ties with the Free University of Amsterdam (the *VU*), the original *gereformeerde* university today no longer considered to be "truly Christian" by orthodox Calvinists.

89 Many were also influenced by the thinking of a modern Dutch theologian called Herman Dooyeweerd. See Kits, "World Views and Social Involvement," p. 34. A Dooyeweerd "chair" was even set up at Redeemer College.

90 See Nicholas Wolterstorff, "The AACS in the CRC," *Reformed Journal* (December 1974).

91 Such critics think that Dutch Calvinists should have made their presence known by becoming an integral part of the public school system. See Arie Verduijn, "Sojourners: A Family Chronicle," published by the author, Burlington, 1981), p. 308 and 385. Some CRC members criticized the Christian school system for becoming too complacent, too elitist and "too dull." The most vocal critic is Peetoom, "From Mythology to Mythology," p. 147-49. Every denomination has such a dissenting minority.

92 Witvoet later assumed the editorship of the *Calvinist Contact.* For a discussion and references to this controversy, see Peetoom, "From Mythology to Mythology," p. 140-41, 145; and Kits, "World Views and Social Involvement," p. 49.

93 This controversy was intrinsically tied up with existing tensions between established business leaders who sat on the board and university graduates associated with the ICS. The latter, who criticized the old curriculum, had links with the teachers who sat on the high school's education committee. See Peetoom, "From Mythology to Mythology," p. 132-34; 139-41.

94 Non-Dutch Canadian social activists working within some mainstream Protestant denominations respect and admire the Institute of Christian Studies. In contrast, the majority of Dutch-Canadian Calvinists prefer to adapt to North American Christianity—either a more secular version or one that sees a breakdown of sexual morality and traditional gender roles as the primary cause of the modern world's social and economic problems.

95 At the time of immigration, orthodox (*gereformeerde*) Dutch Calvinists from an urban background saw nothing wrong with theatres, social dancing or watching television. Their more worldly attitudes put them at odds with the predominantly rural members of more conservative congregations. However, it would be too simplistic to reduce everything to lifestyle preferences and levels of orthodoxy. Equally strict and orthodox Reformed members can be divided along political lines, while more "lax" or "liberal' Calvinists may take opposite sides on how, or even if, they should apply neo-Calvinist principles.

96 However, in the late 1970s about 100 Dutch-Canadians joined a Christian and Missionary Alliance Church in Rexdale after a period of particularly nasty disputes.

97 For example, in St. Catharines, the Trinity congregation was conservative, while Jubilee was considered to be progressive.

98 Their paper, called *Christian Renewal*, received financial backing from a conservative faction in the United States. Some of their opponents dubbed this paper "Christians Be Cruel." Their Dutch-Canadian publisher, Jan Hulting of Jordan Station, continued to be actively involved in a more conservative CRC in St. Catharines.

99 They discouraged their members from sending their children to the same Christian schools as CRC students and established their own schools. They even set up a separate minor hockey league, and strict sanctions are applied against dating outside their own religious community.

100 Dutch orthodox Calvinists believe that even the best of men are sinful creatures, and thus internal divisions are likely to be the outcome of selfishness or pride—which may lead to schism.

101 This is the situation with the *gereformeerde bonders* within the *Hervormde Kerk* in the Netherlands. People from this same splinter group have also become affiliated with the Reformed Church in Canada, but as separate community congregations.

102 Another possibility is for the dissenting minority to temporarily cut off all ties, while continuing to recognize the original church to which they belonged. They will rationalize such a move by saying that they are only waiting for the established church—now in error—to mend its ways. This is what happened with the *Doleantie* in 1886.

103 On various occasions, reunification has taken place, such as when congregations resulting from both the *Afscheiding* and the *Doleantie* came together to form the *Gereformeerde Kerken* in 1892. On such occasions, a new name is usually chosen, precisely to avoid the type of problems mentioned above. A similar reunification took place in 1869, when the *Christelijke Afgescheiden Gemeenten* joined together with those secessionists who had previously refused to become registered as a separate church. They called themselves *Gereformeerde Kerk onder het kruis*. As a result of this union, the *Christelijke Gereformeerde Kerk* came into being. But not every attempt at reunion is successful. For example, in 1952, an act of union was signed between the Protes-

tant Reformed Church and the Canadian Reformed Church in Hamilton, Ontario. Nevertheless, they split only a few years later. Even when an amalgamation takes place, not all congregations may go along with the union, resulting in yet another new label, as in the case of the *Kruisgemeenten* after the reunion of 1869. The number of new Reformed churches, with new names, thus far exceeds the number of new names resulting from amalgamation (see figure 6).

104 People dissatisfied with the larger denomination's policies are not likely to follow the suggestions made by a Christian Reformed professor at Redeemer College that they should seriously consider such a move. See article by Theodore Platinga, *Christian Renewal,* March 23, 1993, p. 11-12.

105 The 1994 synod again voted down a motion to allow women to be ordained and the issue cannot be discussed again for another 10 years.

106 However, at least one Reformed denomination obtained new members when a similar division took place within the United Church after it allowed the ordination of women and gay men. Conservative dissidents in several United congregations, including one in Peterborough, joined the Reformed Church in Canada because they felt that it more closely resembled the United Church they remembered. While some former United members were first-generation Dutch immigrants who had been *Hervormd* in the Netherlands, many non-Dutch Canadians from about a half dozen congregations also joined. However, the new Reformed congregation in Peterborough was dissolved in 1994. At the time this book went into print, some of these groups had left the Reformed Church in America to become independent.

107 Contrary to common misconceptions, the evangelistic churches have not been that much more successful in winning new converts than mainstream churches. They have consistently stayed at around 7 percent of the Canadian population. However, some of these churches have been able to woo away members from other conservative Protestant sects (including the Reformed denominations). See Bibby, *Fragmented Gods*, p. 24-30.

108 Even people who are marginal or alienated from the Reformed community maintain links for nostalgic reasons. Furthermore, Dutch-Canadian couples who no longer associate with a Reformed church still send their children to the same schools and colleges they attended when they were younger.

109 Even members of the supposedly more liberal Christian Reformed Church look "typically old-fashioned Dutch" to visitors from the Netherlands, where the Calvinist churches have become even more unorthodox. In the Netherlands, the *gereformeerden* and the *hervormden* are now in the process of amalgamating.

110 Very orthodox splinter groups are now attracting new Dutch immigrants who represent the few remaining arch-orthodox Calvinists remaining in the Netherlands.

111 Bourdieu would say that orthodox Dutch Calvinists have succeeded in creating a new 'field,' with its own 'subfields,' within an even broader (macro) religious 'field' transcending political borders.

Chapter 10

1 Informants commented that they felt more at ease with people from their region of birth because "you know them better."

2 This region had already provided the bulk of Dutch emigrants to Wisconsin during the nineteenth century (Stekelenburg, "Landverhuizing als Regionaal Verschijnsel").

3 Since immigration statistics are not broken down by region of origin, such generalizations can only be based on general observations and informed speculation.

4 Interviews with Mrs. Korrie Krabbe, in her home near Alma, January 14, 1990; Mr. John Reinders, on his farm near Moorfield, January 18, 1992.

5 Interview, Mrs. Maria Aarts, on her farm near Kintore, April 13, 1989.

6 Interviews with Case Smeekens, on his farm near Thedford, and with Mrs. Wilma Bastiaansen, Arkona, both on May 3, 1990; Chris van Loon, Watford, July 7, 1990.

7 Interview, Gerry Van Bussell, Lucan, July 9, 1990. Before he went into business for himself, Gerry's father used to work for the Loyens.

8 Interview with Dr. Otto Ackerman, Chatham, December 2, 1989; and telephone conversation with Marion Bruinsma, August 20, 1992. Halber Taekema, a contractor in Sarnia involved in house building, came from the same region in Friesland as the Bruinsma family in Chatham.

9 Many people in the Chatham construction business came from towns in a region of Friesland called the Friese Wouden, especially Drachten. Interview with, Dr. Ackerman, Chatham, December 2, 1989; telephone conversation with Marion Bruinsma of Chatham, August 20, 1992.

10 In the 1976 census, many Frisians probably reported Dutch as their mother tongue, assuming that the federal bureaucrats would not know the difference between Frisian and Dutch. John Kralt, "Netherlanders and the Canadian Census," *Journal of Netherlandic Studies*, 3 (May 1981): 40.

11 Many Catholic Frisians came from a region of Friesland known as Het Bildt, which includes St. Annaparochie and St. Jacobsparochie.

12 He was born in his mother's village in Groningen and his mother tongue is actually the Dutch dialect of that province. However Luit Miedema grew up in his father's village of Buitenpost (Friesland) where he learned Frisian.

13 Including visitors from Friesland; about 10 percent of those who attend come from the States. Interview, Luit Miedema, June 12, 1989.

14 In Vineland, Chatham, Sarnia, Bowmanville, the Ottawa Valley, Picton and Toronto. Apparently a group of immigrants also used to put on Frisian plays in Brockville.

15 Some of their old programs are included in the "Jarvis Frisian Club Papers (1972-1976), located in MHSO (Acc.#21210, Mu# 9411, MFN# 031, Subseries# 058-079, MSR# 1583).

16 There is a small pocket of Catholic Frisians (also farmers), in the area around Smithville.

17 In the last population census, the Frisian language was dropped as a category. However, at least one reference library in Metro Toronto does have some catalogues of Frisian books for both adults and children. See *1989 Guide to the Multilanguage Collections in the Public Library Systems of Metropolitan Toronto* (Languages and Literature Department).

18 In Sarnia, Halber Taekema, a contractor, organizes "Frisian evenings" every second year. About fifty couples come from Chatham, Wyoming, Clinton, Wallaceburg and Forest, and, at one gathering, from as far away as Woodstock. Interview with Halber Taekema, Sarnia, August 29, 1990.

A group of Frisians in Lambton county also put up a small display, showing the Frisian flag including a short summary of the history of the Frisians as part of an exhibit of Dutch-Canadians at the Lambton County Heritage Museum held in 1996.

19 The game is similar to *Jeu de pelotte*, played in Belgium, France and Spain. There is a short description of the game and its survival in Ontario in an article written in Dutch (no author) in *De Nederlandse Courant*, April 21, 1991, p. 16.

20 Most of them were farmers originating from the town of Mantgum, and one of the players worked in the GM plant in Oshawa. Interview with Piet Boersma, in Ingersoll, August 27, 1994.

21 There are also strong links between the *kaats* tournaments in Ontario and their counterparts in Friesland. When the Halton tournament disbanded in the early 1970s, their trophy and all of their game schedules were sent to a sports museum in Franeker, Friesland. The current Ontario federation is also affiliated with the KNK (*Koninglijke Nederlandse Kaatsenbond*).

22 It was started by Piet van der Werf, one of the original players from the Halton group. Piet made a conscious attempt to teach the game to the younger generation after the original Halton group lost many of its original members when they moved to the States to buy farms. These players had contact with a group of Frisians from an old established Frisian community in New Jersey who used to come to play *kaatsen* with postwar immigrants in Ontario. Based on a telephone interview with Piet van der Werf [from Stoney Creek], August 16, 1994, followed by an interview, during a game held on August 27 in Ingersoll. I also read the minutes of past meetings of their organizing committee, membership lists and financial ledgers.

23 For example, for the Ingersoll tournament, the Salverda family, who run various Tim Horton outlets (in Aylmer, Simcoe, Ingersoll and other towns), provided the prizes and donuts.

24 Eight of those players are younger second-generation men, and one woman (a recent immigrant from Friesland) is also a regular player. Her Canadian-born husband, who won the trophy in 1994, is of Italian descent. A few younger women from the Netherlands have also competed in Paris from time to time, but most women come only as spectators.

25 Other ex-Netherlanders in Canada have told me how such nationalistic Frisians refused to speak Dutch or would declare they were Frisian, not Dutch.

26 Interview with Mr. De Voogd, Sr., Chatham, July 7, 1989; December 2, 1992.

27 They suspended their reunion in the early 1980s; it became too difficult for the older people to attend, some of whom had settled further away, in the Trenton, Frankford and Belleville area. Interview with Marinus Mol, on his farm near Ayton, March 12, 1991.

28 Interview with Harry Klungel, in Rockwood Park, June 17, 1989. See write-up in *De Nederlandse Courant*, July 15, 1989, p. 8.

29 People race to a finish line, shuffling along on two small wooden boards, which must be lifted up with a rope looped in one's hands.

30 Conversation with a woman from Twenthe, at a Dutch exhibit in St. Marys museum, December 1, 1990; also interview with Peter Poel, on his farm near Thamesford, March 16, 1989.

31 See announcement in *Calvinist Contact*, July 1, 1989. This reunion used to be organized by Klaas Dekens in Drayton.

32 Interview with Gerry Van der Kley, Whitby, May 7, 1991.

33 Such events are advertised in ethnic newspapers and club bulletins. A special *Achterhoekavond*, is sometimes organized in both St. Catharines and in Woodstock. Interview with Thea Wensing and Frank Niesink, St. Catharines, October 27, 1988; also *De Nederlandse Courant*, September 7, 1990, p. 9.

34 There is also a network of Limburgers in the Ajax-Whitby area.

35 These rural immigrants, with less education, were moving into town from other parts of Wellington county around the same time (see chapter 5). Interview with Hans Jansen (originally from Amsterdam), Guelph, September 14, 1988.

36 A network of about a dozen people in the Toronto area, who originally came from the city of Rotterdam (mainly from Rotterdam Zuid), kept in contact after they emigrated. Interview with Jan Hendriks, in Whitby, December 12, 1988.

37 Most of the Catholics who attended the reunion were farmers from the London area. Interview with Mr. De Voogd, Sr., in Chatham, December 2, 1989.

38 I know various people in the Toronto area who at one time or another were invited to attend these evenings. Their fifth gathering in St. Catharines took place in the fall of 1992. See *De Nederlandse Courant*, November 7, 1992, p. 8.

39 See Dortmans, *Brabanders in Canada*, p. 64.

40 For example, North Dumphries (which includes Ayr and Galt) became a pole of attraction for a number of Brabanders, many of them from Schijndel, the home town of Frank Den Ouden (who sponsored many relatives and friends). They formed their own soccer team. See article by Ger Graaskamp in *De Nederlandse Courant*, October 24, 1992, p. 8.

Another area with a heavy concentration of rural Brabanders is the township of Bosanquet, where a group of couples raised the public profile of their province by setting up a group of folk dancers who performed in many parts of southern Ontario (see chap. 17).

41 They even have their own informal leaders and spokesmen, one of whom wrote and published his own book, which is part biography and part history of the Brabanders in Canada. John (Jan) H. Dortmans, whose book was already cited, grew up on the outskirts of St. Oedenrode, where his parents owned a farm and also ran a small cafe. He continued his higher education in Canada and eventually worked his way up the corporate ladder of a "major financial services company" (mentioned on book cover).

42 This also comes out in Dortmans' book (p. 2 and elsewhere).

43 They not only shared a common dialect, but people from Noord Brabant liked playing a card game called *rikken*, quite different from *klaverjassen* which is played "above the rivers."

44 People from this region have shown me examples of newsletters or booklets about their home towns; for example, *Heem Son en Breugel* (*Driemaandelijkse uitgave van de heemkundekring Son en Breugel*) (1986) number 3.

45 At that reunion in the Netherlands, the Dutch-Canadians presented a totem pole to Mariahout which now stands in its central square. Various interviews

plus phone calls with Mrs. Freda Leenders, on her farm near Erin, 1992 and 1993. For picture and write-up of the totem pole memorial see *De Nederlandse Courant*, June 10, 1993, p. 24.

46 See write-up and invitation (in Dutch) in the "Community Calendar" section of the *De Nederlandse Courant*, April 23, 1994, p. 17.

47 Members of an organizing committee live in Milton, Cambridge, and Oakville. They recruit people from all over Ontario and have organized bus tours, with stopovers at farm homes. Such trips always culminate in a general reunion at a single location. They have met in a hall and at someone's farm (both near Milton) and at a Burlington golf and country club.

48 The conversion of the Dutch video into the North American system was done by Winnie Van de Berlo.

49 Many were children of immigrants who had emigrated sometime between 1946 and 1954. All the people interviewed by the Dutch team spoke the Boekel version of Dutch, which they had either learned while growing up in Boekel or from immigrant parents and older siblings. Many were introduced by traditional personal names, which coexisted with the official system of surnames. For example, Morris van den Baar, an ex-Brabander from another town who today lives in Pembroke today, was known in Braband as Marinus van Jan van Drieke. Interview in Pembroke, July 15, 1990.

50 They came from the counties of Wellington (1), Perth (1), Halton (1), Lambton (6), Elgin (1), Haldimand-Norfolk (1), Niagara (2), Hastings (1) and Dundas-Stormont (3). However, not all of them were full-time farmers or retired farmers in 1990. Two brothers in Niagara-on-the-Lake had worked the day shift at a large factory for over thirty years, while building up vineyards and fruit farms in their spare time with the help of family members, while a man in Chesterville had quit farming ten years earlier to become a small contractor. An additional dozen people who were briefly interviewed during the reunion included a bricklayer and someone who owns a small welding shop.

51 See advertisement in *De Nederlandse Courant*, April 21, 1991, p. 13; and pictures of a Boekel display in issue 13, 10. The year before, the Hamilton Holland Club organized a *Brabantse Bonte Avond* (Brabant Variety Evening) in collaboration with the Boekel reunion. See *De Nederlandse Courant*, September 7, 1990, p. 8.

52 Noordwijkerhout in located on the edge of the bulb-growing region south of Haarlem.

53 Interview with Martin Van Denzen, North York (Toronto), May 9, 1991.

54 For instance, when Vander Zalm's father, a businessman who had to stay in Canada during the War, returned in 1945, the village threw a party for him.

55 In Canada he worked for nurseries, in the shipping department of Tamblyn's drug stores and did freelance gardening. Even after he was married, Martin sent part of his earnings to his mother.

56 The people who came to the reunion resided in Unionville, Stoney Creek, St. Catharines, Toronto, Uxbridge and London. Only one lived in the countryside, along highway 5 west of Toronto. These men had been agricultural day labourers in Holland, like Martin's father, yet only one worked as a farm labourer in Ontario. The rest include a house painter, a hospital worker, a gardener, a superintendent of an apartment building and a former travelling salesman.

57 I have come across examples of very large family reunions in Ontario, running into the hundreds, for the following families: Scholten, Pel, Beukema, Van Donkersgoed, Horling and Verhoeven.

58 Interview with Adriaan Rodenburg, on his farm near Thamesford, November 30th, 1989.

59 I was shown a copy of this first edition during a visit to a farm near Kintore, Ontario: "Keep in Touch," *Rodenburger Courant*, summer edition, September 1989.

60 For a comprehensive historical account of the Flemish Belgians in southwestern Ontario, see Magee, *The Belgians in Ontario*.

61 Interview with Marcel Lannoo, Delhi, October 24, 1989. This period of Netherlandic cultural activity in southwestern Ontario coincided with the florescence of a Flemish cultural revival in Belgium.

62 Smaller pockets of Flemish tobacco farmers were also established in Port Elgin, near Lake Huron and around Port Hope. See map in Magee, *The Belgians in Ontario*, p. 100. Many of these farmers later sold their tobacco rights to Delhi. Interview with Peter Schep, near Alliston, May 30, 1991.

63 See ibid., p. 8, 246.

64 In terms of recreation activities, the rural Belgians have a preference for archery, pigeon racing and their own bowling game.

65 An example is Michiel de Groot, who became the owner of Laidlaw. He is considered to be a Belgian because of where he lived prior to emigrating to Canada, but technically he is Dutch, since he was born in the Dutch city of Maastricht.

66 One Dutch immigration historian points out that the original founder of a Capuchin house in Blenheim was a Theophilus van de Heuvel, a member of the Dutch branch of the order. He was originally invited by Bishop Fallon in London to work among Dutch-speaking Catholic farm workers, using Chatham as his base of operations. However, after the Flemish Capuchins were sent in in 1927, he did not "feel at home" among the Belgians. He then moved to Toronto (which at that time had very few Dutch Catholics), and eventually ended up in Winnipeg. See Stekelenburg, *"Hier is alles vooruitgang,"* p. 102.

67 Interviews with Marcel Lannoo, Delhi, November 24, 1989; with Angelina van Leugenhagen, Sarnia, June 3, 1991.

68 Those who arrived in the Chatham or Wallaceburg areas were still sponsored by the Dominion Sugar Company, and they usually worked under six-month contracts. See Magee, *A Dutch Heritage*, p. 63-64.

69 Interview with Andy Veldman, on his farm in Embro, July 28, 1990.

70 He had also recently arrived with his parents. Interview with Jose and Bill Cozijn, Stratford, April 28, 1990.

71 In contrast, the majority of her Dutch husband's seven brothers and sisters married Dutch-Canadians. Interview with Madeleine and Harry Visser, Stratford, October 23, 1989.

72 For example, when several brothers from the Strijbosch family from Liessel (Noord Brabant) settled in the Strathroy area, two married recent Belgian immigrants, and another the daughter of an older, established prewar Flemish-Canadian family. Interview with John Strijbosch, London, November 20, 1988.

73 Interview with Angelina Leugenhagen, Sarnia, June 3, 1991.

74 By 1991, the Belgian-Canadian-Dutch club only had a few mixed Dutch-Belgian couples, while a combination of Dutch Catholics and Dutch Calvinists completely dominated the management of the now officially non-ethnic credit union (see chap. 15).

75 They also had one prewar Dutch member. Interview with John Cowan, Blenheim, July 10, 1990.

76 At one point he performed the same function in Sarnia. Interview with Harry Wijsman, Blenheim, May 2, 1990.

77 A second-generation Dutch-Canadian then took charge, and today the majority of Blenheim delegates and directors are Dutch-Canadians. By 1990, Dutch-Canadian farmers, who are still its major depositors, represented nearly half the full-time farmers in Harwich township (to which Blenheim belongs). Interview with the new manager, John de Bruyn, Blenheim, May 2, 1990.

78 Based on a conversation with Agnes Feryn, St. Marys, December 1, 1990.

79 Vanderschot and Smith, "Netherlands Research Project."

80 Interview with Jerry Yzinga, Brantford, November 14, 1988.

81 In Toronto, few of the postwar Flemish immigrants who arrived in the early 1950s became involved in the Dutch-Canadian community of Toronto. Only one Belgian couple and several Flemish spouses of postwar Dutch immigrants joined the more middle-class-oriented Netherlands Luncheon Club (see chap. 12).

82 Interview with Roger de Bakker, Hamilton, October 18, 1988.

83 Interview with Jan Liebaers, Toronto, November 25, 1990.

84 The Dutch and Belgian, as well South African ethnic business associations, occasionally host joint events. See *De Nederlandse Courant*, 1992, p. 14; November 13, 1993, p. 9; and 38 (1993), p. 28.

85 Interview with Roger de Bakker, Hamilton, October 18, 1988. Such Flemish-Canadians argue that "pure Dutch" has been better preserved in Flanders than in Holland.

86 Interview with Joan Magee, Windsor, January 9, 1989. This is ironic, considering the fact that the enemy of the more nationalist Flemings were the French-speaking Walloons.

87 The other researcher is André Vermeirre. See Magee, *Belgians in Ontario*, p. 145.

88 Nor can one go by surnames: a typical Dutch surname, like Van Dam, might belong to a Eurasian born in Java, while someone who "looks European" might have a Chinese or Arabic name. Moreover, many Dutch-Indonesian immigrants who spoke standard Dutch and *maleis* had typically French or German surnames.

89 On several occasions, when asking people how many Dutch-Canadian *Indisch* they knew, they wanted me to clarify whether I meant "mixed blood" (*gemengd bloed*), or "pure" (*zuiver*) Dutch-Indonesian.

90 For the limitations inherent in survey research based on questionnaires, see Bourdieu et al., *The Craft of Sociology*, p. 44-46.

91 This number was based on his extrapolation from an extensive network of people whom he had met. Interview with Huibert Sabelis, Mississauga, November 8, 1989. His estimate, which represents less than 2 percent of the total 200,000 Dutch-Canadians in Ontario (according to the 1986 census) seems low.

92 This generalization, drawn from various conversations and interviews, is consistent with my impressions based on past and ongoing contacts with the Dutch-Canadian community.

93 Another popular dish is *nasi goreng,* which consists of rice, vegetables and small pieces of meat flavoured with *sambal oelek* and other condiments. Men who served in the Dutch marines in particular acquired a taste for these Indonesian dishes. Dutch people in Holland were introduced to Indonesian cuisine through relatives who had been abroad or by exposure to the Indonesian restaurants that expanded with the influx of Dutch-Indonesian refugees to the Netherlands in the early 1950s (see chap. 3).

94 Some of these Dutch-speaking Indonesians had served in the KNIL (the Dutch colonial army) or in an underground group within the Dutch marines (the VDMB). Interview with Ben Hendriks, Oakville, June 20, 1989. I spoke to several Dutch-Indonesian veterans at one of their reunions, held in Embro.

95 Based on a conversation with Mr. Businger, at the Dutch Embassy on Slater Street in Ottawa, November 17, 1989.

96 During an interview, she explained how she considers the Dutch language and the Dutch culture her own, without strongly identifying as either Dutch or Indonesian. Interview with Winnie Olenroot-Macaré, Toronto, December 7, 1988.

97 The older family members usually spoke Dutch more fluently than English. However, they also spoke modern Indonesian (*Bahasa*) while their children, and some young couples did not know any Dutch at all. Interview with George Matern, Woodstock, November 8, 1991; with Mr. Klaring, Willowdale (Toronto), May 30, 1989.

98 This drop-off in attendance was interpreted by some as evidence of a three-way split among "Dutch," "racially mixed Dutch" and "Indonesians."

99 Mrs. Van der Griff had to learn Dutch when her husband took her to the Netherlands after the War. There they lived in a small village near Utrecht. Based on conversations with both Mr. and Mrs. Van der Griff, during a picnic in Pelco Park (near Milton), June 19, 1989.

100 On July 17, 1991, the Dutch-Indonesian picnic was held in the same place, but as a potluck type lunch organized by Louise Opdenkelder. See *De Nederlandse Courant*, 36, 12, p. 8.

101 Interview with Mr. G. Klaring, Thornhill, May 30, 1989.

102 Personal communication from Robert Siebelhof (Toronto). The ongoing association between the Indonesian community (even the Indonesian consul) and the Dutch-Canadian community is reflected in the reporting of local events in the *De Nederlandse Courant*, September 7, 1990, p. 9.

103 He was born in the Netherlands during the War, but at the age of seven his Dutch mother and stepfather took him to Indonesia. His mother was an opera singer.

104 Yet several Dutch-Canadians who know him told me this man is a *half-bloed* ("halfbreed"); When I interviewed him in 1990, he was living in Mississauga, not too far from the Corner Rouge restaurant run by a Dutch-Indonesian friend.

105 This description matches a photograph of her which I saw during my interview with Huibert Sabelis, at his home in Mississauga, November 8, 1989.

106 He had taken art lessons at a technical school in the Netherlands when he was young.

107 He did this together with an Indo woman who had only recently immigrated together with her husband. They decided to call their gathering *Picnic Kumpulan Indo* and make it into a potluck-style meal, in the tradition of Javanese food-sharing. They have since met twice at a farm in Greenwood owned by a Dutch-Indonesian man whose uncle was once mayor of Batavia (in Java). See their ad in *De Nederlandse Courant*, August 7, 1993, p. 17.

108 Interview with George Matern and his brother Willy Matern, Woodstock, November 8, 1989.

109 See *De Krant*, 246 (January 1990): 22. That paper also has a regular column called *Tempo Doeloe*, which reminisces about life in the former Dutch East Indies.

110 Another author has used the metaphor of kaleidoscopic change (as opposed to mosaic or melting pot) to characterize the complexity, ambivalence and contradictions of ethnic group formation. See Timothy Smith, "Religions and Ethnicity in America," *American Historical Review*, 83 (1978): 1185.

Chapter 11

1 This also holds for the use of French in most places outside the province of Quebec, where French for the most part functions as a dominant language.

2 These figures are consistent with the 34 percent in 1971 for the Dutch on a national level. See table 1.2 in Breton et al., *Cultural Boundaries and the Cohesion of Canada* (Montreal: Institute for Research on Public Policy, 1980), p. 24.

3 The percentages of other ethnic groups were 43 for Germans, 53 for Ukrainians and 74 for Italians.

4 The corresponding figure for Flemish, reported as a separate language, was –77 percent. The only ethnic groups with a higher decline were, again, Scandinavians and people speaking Gaelic. See table 11 in Alan Anderson and James Frideres, *Ethnicity in Canada* (Toronto: Butterworths, 1981), p. 120.

5 In conducting research on this aspect of Dutch-Canadians, I took special note of linguistic interactions involving the use of both "high Dutch" and various dialects. I have nearly 800 separate entries in my fieldnotes regarding different aspects of language use by Dutch-Canadians in the context of Ontario.

6 Wsevolod Isajiw, "Ethnic-Identity Retention," in Raymond Breton et al., *Ethnic Identity and Equality* (Toronto: University of Toronto Press, 1990), p. 44.

7 Many Dutch immigrant parents forbad their children from using their mother tongue. This policy, based on the premise that children "would not learn proper English" if they spoke their mother tongue, sometimes backfired. Instead of learning English from native speakers, some Dutch-Canadian children picked up faulty English speech patterns, and sometimes an accent, from their immigrant parents.

8 This example was taken from Hermina Joldersma, "The Convergence of Three Worlds: Post-Immigrant Dutch Culture in Canada," an unpublished manuscript, n.d..

9 "I am the daughter of Trui, [daughter of] Willem from [the place of] Lambooy."

10 Joldersma, "The Convergence of Three Worlds," p. 2.

11 The few prewar families of Flemish background they met had already become quite Canadianized. Interview with Bert Segeren, Blenheim, July 10, 1990.

12 I was able to ascertain that most of the offspring of the Dutch immigrants who arrived in the mid-1950s picked up a bit of their parents' language. In contrast, his 21-year-old daughter does not know any Dutch whatsoever.

13 This new language has also become a source of humour and mockery (see VanderMey, *To All Our Children*, p. 253).

14 Standard Dutch is today rapidly gaining ground in the Netherlands, where Dutch dialects have been modified by standard Dutch to a much greater extent than their counterparts in Canada have been influenced by English.

15 He had worked his way up in the food business, and become a purchasing agent for Albert Hein, a large Dutch company. Their main motive for emigrating was so that their second oldest child could get medical treatment at the Hospital for Sick Children in Toronto. Interview with Tony Teklenburg, Sudbury, April 18, 1991.

16 At least one family in Barrie still speaks real Tilburgs at home; their 16-year-old, Canadian-born daughter knows English and *plat Tilburgs*, but not standard Dutch. I was told about this Tilburg family in an interview with Gerald Van Amelsvoort, Barrie, April 25, 1991.

17 It turns out that this other patient had known, and even worked for, Tony's father!

18 Tony and his family go to celebrate carnival with them in the Netherlands and their Dutch friends park a rented trailer in Tony's backyard in Sudbury when they come for visits to Canada.

19 Even these people are now middle-aged or approaching retirement.

20 Their limited knowledge is mainly passive and they are not likely to pass it on to their children. Marriage to spouses of non-Dutch background will further accelerate this process of language attrition.

21 See Newton, *The Netherlands*, p. 26-27. The promotion of the Frisian language is being carried out by a Frisian Academy (*Fryske Akademy*).

22 In 1992, Fetje Benoit-de Boer, coordinator of the *Nederlandse School* in Ottawa, announced that she was willing to start a Frisian-language course in the evenings. See *The Link,* the newsletter of the Dutch-Canadian Association, Ottawa Valley, 6 (April 1992). As far as I know, this never got off the ground. The only publication in Frisian in North America I have heard about was a newsletter which used to come out of Grand Rapids, Michigan. Professor Ridsma, who used to teach Frisian in Calvin College, prepared a language manual.

23 See write-up in *De Nederlandse Courant*, June 7, 1989, p. 8.

24 A private commercial radio program was also broadcast from Niagara Falls for two years, in the early 1960s, by Arie Klein. Interview, May 9, 1989.

25 In part financed through advertising from Dutch-Canadian businesses, her program featured music, announcements for community events plus interviews, interspersed with a running commentary.

26 For her Dutch-Canadian guests, she sometimes had to do extra editing to eliminate excessive use of English words. Interview with Lisette van Gessel, Toronto, August 15, 1989.

27 Lini Grol, a retired registered nurse and writer in Font Hill, had a Dutch program in Welland, which lasted for one winter, in 1974-75. All of her guests had recently arrived from the Netherlands. Interview with Lini Grol, Font Hill, September 17, 1989 (with a follow-up telephone conversation on April 5, 1993).

28 I interviewed the job applicant, about a year later, in Burlington.

29 Interview with Dirk Bod, Guelph, February 23, 1990.

30 At that point English started to be used, since their documents were subject to inspection. I read through all of the minutes of the board meetings, and other

miscellaneous documents, up until 1977. These are located in the archives of the headquarters of DUCA, located on Yonge St.

31 For example, articles entitled "bazaar" and "Nederlandse voetballers naar Toronto," *Ducapost* (May 1977): 21-23.

32 Minutes of board meetings, in the archives of St. Willibrord Credit Union, at the head office in downtown London.

33 Notulen boek van de FCFA of Ontario, located in their head office in Guelph.

34 Henceforth Dutch lingered on in a purely symbolic fashion, such as the "Dutch" page in *Calvinist Contact* until 1989. A rival (more orthodox) Calvinist newspaper, *Christian Renewal*, still had a full-page Dutch section (see 8, 4 [1989]: 16).

35 Joldersma, "The Convergence of Three Worlds," p. 2-3.

36 In Canada she worked as a nurse and he as electrician prior to building up his own electronics shop. Interview (in Dutch) with Gerry Van Amelsvoort, Barrie, April 25, 1991.

37 These labels were gradually removed, one by one, as the word for each object was mastered.

38 Parents found there were too many competing activities on Saturday mornings; and although children might have been exposed to some form of Dutch at home, they discovered that learning standard Dutch was not easy.

39 Twenty-two were teaching children, the rest adults. See "Survey of Dutch Language Teaching in Canada" (ca. 1984), without author. In 1987 a language consultant from the Netherlands visited these various schools. His report, which recommended further exchange visits by students and additional pedagogical material from Holland, describes a high level of interest. A report written by Drs. W.A.J. Godschalx, "Het onderwijs van het Nederlands als vreemde taal op enkele plaatsen in Canada," 1987.

40 "Overzicht Nederlandse Taallessen in Canada—per 1 december, 1988," a listing made by Mrs. Schnitzler (chancellor). A year later, the Netherlands consulate general in Toronto published a listing of Dutch-language courses at all levels, based on a questionnaire sent out to various institutions. They reported a total of 777 students at various levels in both credit and non-credit courses.

41 The *Nederlandse School* also gives courses on such topics as the Dutch cabaret tradition. Today they have about a hundred pupils, with a growing interest in credit courses. I visited the school on November 17, 1989, and the following day interviewed one of the former coordinators, Miriam Sutorius-Lavoie. Their program was started in January 1982 by Dimmy Riverin and Odile Waslander. See article by Fetje Benoit-de Boer, coordinator, in 1992 issue of *The Link*. In November of 1993, the school organized a symposium for Dutch language teachers in Canada. See also *De Nederlandse Courant*, 38, 26 (1993), p. 12.

42 In the case of the *Nederlandse Courant*, the province of Ontario had 2,613 subscribers in 1990. These were found in all counties, regional municipalities and districts, except for Rainy River. The largest number of subscribers (587) lived in Metropolitan Toronto. The breakdown for the rest of the province was as follows: 14 administrative divisions had less then 10 subscribers, 20 had between 11 and 50, six between 51 and 100, and six more between 101 to 200. The proportion of subscribers generally reflected the numbers of Dutch-Canadians present in each county (as indicated in chap. 6), with the exception of Kent county (with Chatham) which was underrepresented. This last case can be

explained by the fact that one of the Dutch-Canadian newspapers, which was later moved to the West Coast, already had a large number of loyal subscribers in that city, who would more likely read the *Windmill Herald* (which has an insert of what used to be the local Chatham newspaper).

43 The figure of a combined circulation of 22,000 (in the 1980s) given on page 119 in Ganzevoort's *A Bittersweet Land* seems reasonable.

44 That monthly had been published in Montreal, and was the first of the smaller Dutch publications that ceased to exist.

45 The paper won the ethnic press award in 1987.

46 *De Nederlandse Courant* started becoming increasingly bilingual, with both ads and articles in Dutch after around 1992.

47 For a short while in the early 1950s, Chatham also had another Dutch-Canadian newspaper, called the *Free Press*. *Hollandia News* was started by John Vellinga, who also ran a travel agency and was instrumental in setting up a Dutch-Canadian credit union in Chatham (see chap. 15). That same man had also put out *Contact* (which later became part of *Calvinist Contact*), while he worked as fieldman of the CRC.

Between 1975 and 1984, *Hollandia News* was still printed and distributed out of Ontario (from Tilbury), with the text, virtually identical to the *Windmill Herald*, created in British Columbia. After that date, the name Hollandia only appears at the top of several pages of the slightly different Eastern Canada edition of the *Windmill Herald*. Telephone interview with Albert Vanderheide, Surrey, B.C., August 16, 1984.

48 That section includes articles about Dutch history and the Dutch in North America. It also reports on anyone of Dutch birth or Dutch origin, whether famous or infamous, who appears in the news in Canada or the United States (see chap. 2).

49 That monthly also features longer articles written by Dutch-Canadians on a wide range of topics.

50 Another writer, whose articles appear in *De Krant*, worked as a stewardess before settling in southern Ontario in the early 1970s. Such information of specific people, here as well as in other chapters, was obtained from a name file (part of my fieldnotes), which were updated and sometimes revised with the addition of information obtained from other written sources, as well as any notes about these people in the context of other conversations or interviews.

51 FAMA even put on a few plays in English, and Poesiat and his wife became more involved in the English-language theatrical scene after the Dutch group disbanded (see interlude 17.2).

52 Their director emigrated in 1949, while the younger players are more recent agrarian immigrants. I obtained most of this information during a visit to Innerkip and Thamesford at the end of November 1989, where I attended the first rehearsal of one of their plays.

53 An earlier group was started in the Woodstock area in 1973, but the present *toneelclub* originated in 1983. Interview with Jaap de Boer, near Innerkip, November 30, 1989.

54 For example, the recent owners of Delft Blue, Inc. in Cambridge, frequently travel back and forth for business and technical advice. Their veal operation employs both recent Dutch immigrants and Dutch-Canadians, and it is not rare to see them all speaking Dutch together in the workplace. Personal communique.

Chapter 12

1 This is certainly a commonly held belief among Dutch-Canadians, as well as members of other ethnic group with whom I am acquainted. More systematic research would have to be carried out to validate this observation.

2 Even then I had to reinterpret the type of data illustrated in the fieldnote interlude following the previous chapter.

3 See also Lemke, *Textual Politics*, p. 7.

4 Bourdieu, *Language and Symbolic Power*, p. 37-38. For a synopsis of the differences between Bourdieu's social context approach versus Chomsky's structural linguistics, as well as Austin and Habermas' approaches to language, see John Thomson's introduction to that book, p. 7-10.

5 This first impression came up time and time again in my interviews about first impressions of Canada. See also Ganzevoort, *A Bittersweet Land*, p. 95, 114.

6 Overcoming the stigma of inferiority connected to the use of regional dialects of Dutch was also more difficult, as we shall see later.

7 Only in newer congregations, with younger, North American-trained ministers, have I noticed a more casual style of social discourse. Dutch Catholics, who were already used to addressing priests as "father," did not find many changes in Canadian churches.

8 A series of such disputes, which happened in Sudbury, were mentioned in chapter 5. The same jealousies and competition were partly responsible for the squabbling that took place within Dutch-Canadian social clubs (see chap. 16). Even middle-class immigrants had to compete in an environment fraught with uncertainties and the potential for exploitation.

9 This term, coined by Bourdieu, refers to a form of domination "which is exercised upon a social agent with his or her complicity" (see Bourdieu and Wacquant, *Reflexive Sociology*, p. 167).

10 In accordance with this myth, only differences in individual effort or exceptional luck would result in differential success. Another common theme is the rich immigrant farmer losing everything because he did not "learn" how to farm properly in Canada by first working as a hired hand.

11 For cases I was able to document, people usually "worked out" for many years before they could buy their own farm or business.

12 Interview with Jan Hendrikx, Park Hill, December 14, 1988. Before his death, several years later, he finished writing his personal memoirs.

13 His 20-hectare farm in Brabant at that time would be big by Dutch standards.

14 At that point Jan returned to the Netherlands to sell his home farm, although the money from the sale had to be sent in instalments due to monetary restrictions (see chap. 4). With this additional income, plus the profits from farming in Canada, he was able to buy additional land. Other successful Dutch-Canadian farmers who came from the south smuggled in *zwart geld* ("black money") via the Catholic church (see also chap. 8).

15 In cases involving agrarian immigrants from the north, wealthy landowning farmers or storekeepers at home would pay the passage for poor villagers in the form of a loan. These poor immigrants later repaid their debt in Canadian dollars, allowing the money lenders who subsequently emigrated themselves to get ahead much sooner.

16 See "Ex-Mechanic Found Fortune North of 401," *Toronto Star* (February 28, 1990). His mother had been a teacher and his father was a police inspector.

Upon arriving in Canada, Overzet worked in a garage before turning to real estate. Telephone interview with John Overzet, Richmond Hill, March 15, 1990.

17 See the 1989 edition, put out in Toronto by Global Press. He is listed as president and director of Northern Crown Capital Corporation.

18 Interview with Matthew Gaasenbeek, in his office, downtown Toronto, November 7, 1989.

19 Interview with Jack and Michiel Horn, Guelph, March 21, 1993. See also Michiel Horn's "Becoming Canadian: An Immigrant's Journey," a paper presented at the Annual Meeting of CAANS (during the Learned Societies Conference), held at Carleton University, June 5-6, 1993.

20 My fieldnote files contain almost 200 entries regarding class/and or status distinctions.

21 A typical remark is that "common" people show no interest in "culture," especially classical music or literature. Dutch immigrants also used such terms as *gewone mensen* ("ordinary people") in referring to people with working-class or rural backgrounds. Moreover, Dutch-Canadians from middle- or upper-middle-class background frequently make comments about how they would not have chosen to interact with some Dutch people they met in Canada had they not emigrated.

22 A suggestion that such comments imply class distinctions inevitably brings denial; on two occasions I heard the rationalization that "some colours simply clash," indicating that lifestyle differences are a matter of personal preference with no status implications.

23 One club member of working-class background complained that such professionals would only show up for official functions when they could "appear in the limelight."

24 I am using declaration of Dutch as mother tongue as a rough yardstick for measuring the number of first-generation Dutch-Canadians (see chap. 6).

25 I did not conduct a formal survey of the socio-economic background of every member listed in membership booklets. The analysis of the dynamics involving members of these organizations is based on selected in-depth interviews with both executive and regular members as well as non-members. My fieldnotes contain 27 entries on the Luncheon Club and 39 on the CNBPA.

26 At least a dozen Dutch-Canadian professionals who have close contact with the Dutch-Canadian community did not join either organizations, or quit before 1987. Official membership lists also include a few people who live out of town.

27 One of them is Matthew Gaasenbeek, who also served as their president for one year. He has since left the CNBPA.

28 To find out what is "really going on," one would have to measure actual income, property ownership and level of formal education as well as people's official accounts of how they perceive their own places (and those of others) in an elaborate system of prestige rankings.

29 Although this educated immigrant eventually worked his way up to a top management position, it took a long time to get promoted. While he had a perfect command of written and spoken English, he was constantly reminded of his "foreign accent." Interview with this man's wife, in Toronto, September 9, 1988.

30 Interview with Corrie Hiel, Toronto, November 28, 1988.

31 This bazaar, which attracts several thousand visitors to Toronto every second year, is organized by a combination of career women and spouses of professionals or businessmen. Women from working or lower-middle-class families rarely form part of the organizing committee.

32 According to the 1959 minutes of the board meetings of DUCA, Poolman agreed to sublet one room with telephone to the credit union, at 200 Bay Street.

33 The first chairman of the board was a booking agent for the Holland-American Lines. Interview with Dolf Hiel, Toronto, November 28, 1988.

34 While it is true that some of the earlier middle-class members later quit, often because they moved away, their places were taken by other businessmen and professionals. This information, obtained from various interviews, is also recorded in the minutes of the board meetings (*notulen*) in the archives of the head office of DUCA on Yonge Street.

35 In 1946 two prominent Dutch businessmen, recently established in Toronto, started a Dutch cultural organization, called the *nederlandse vereniging* (see chap. 16). One of them was the father of Robert Korthals, future president of the Toronto-Dominion Bank. Interview with Frans Sayers (in Dutch), in his office in Toronto, February 5, 1990.

36 One of the organizers used the Dutch term *hospartij* to refer to the happy but noisy atmosphere of these parties.

37 I heard such negative impressions from several people who remember attending such events.

38 For example, a Dutch-Canadian civil engineer started organizing dances and parties to celebrate the birthday of the Dutch queen a couple of years after the big party of 1946.

39 Not only did the "more sophisticated" Dutch immigrants have a hard time relating to fellow immigrants who were farmers and working-class people, but they even looked down upon hard-working, well-behaved, petit-bourgeois immigrants. They found them *burgerlijk* (see chap. 3).

40 At first they gathered at the Royal York Hotel in downtown Toronto, and later met at people's houses. Interview with Frans Sayers, Toronto, February 5, 1990.

41 The Delft graduate started his career in Holland in 1939, working for an export company. In Canada he initially held a junior position in a Canadian export company, but eventually worked his way up the corporate ladder to become vice-president of a large food importing firm (no Dutch connection).

42 Jan Heersink was a businessman and a consultant who lived in Burlington, where he served as the honorary vice-consul for the Niagara region.

43 Interview with Sander Schimmelpenninck van der Hooyen, Oakville, November 24, 1990. *Het Heren Logement*, a similar club of about a dozen Dutch-Canadian intellectuals and professionals, have monthly meetings in Ottawa.

44 One of their members, a consultant with a prestigious hyphenated Dutch surname, was born in Bloemendaal. He had also lived in Baarn, where he knew Matthew Gaasenbeek. Another member (now deceased) was Baron van der Feldz, an agent for a Dutch firm that sold agricultural equipment in Ontario. Interview with his widow, Yvonne van der Feldz, Moffat (near Guelph), December 14, 1988.

45 This son and his brother (another Guelph graduate) eventually took over the family estate, which specializes in breeding purebred cattle for export to South

America. Interview with Francis Redelmeier, at his farm near Toronto, January 30, 1990. Visitors to their farm include the Dutch royal family.

46 One man, who has been associated with this club from the beginning called this the *deftige* (respectable) investment club, a notch higher than three other Dutch-Canadian investment clubs.

47 Like the *Borrel Club*, they met at each other's houses, where the host's wife was kept busy in the kitchen preparing *hapjes* (Dutch snacks) and hors d'oeuvres.

48 A spokesman for the *Borrel Club* whom I interviewed explained how they had simply become too big to admit new members.

49 A similar social network based on a combination of social standing and religious affiliation consists of a group of Catholics within the Luncheon Club (see chap. 7). That network includes the executive in Noranda introduced earlier. An unofficial spokesman referred to them as the "middle-class Dutch Catholics" of Toronto.

50 I attended several of these gatherings, including one in early December, where a well-known member of the Dutch-Canadian community appeared as *sinterklaas*.

51 In theory, everyone who wants to come is still welcome. See invitation in an article by Ada Wynston, in *De Nederlandse Courant*, 36, 6 (1993), p. 7.

52 Their official membership list has the names of thirty men. This list (*borrellijst—een vergadering van de zaak*), which I received from one of their members, indicates that they have an interim *penningmeester* (treasurer).

53 In typical Dutch fashion, one of the members of the old *Borrel Club* told me that these younger men no longer wanted to associate with the *ouwe zakken* (the "old jerks"). Members of the new *Borrel Club* meet regularly at the Amsterdam and Rotterdam bar in downtown Toronto.

54 Interview with Jan Lusink, Don Mills, May 7, 1991.

55 One civil engineer with a degree, who works for a large corporation, was not invited to come back to the club after a period of temporary absence in the Netherlands. This man, who later became an active member of the Canadian Amateur Musical Association, told me this during an interview.

56 Based on a conversation with Raymond Burka, in Guelph, April 30, 1991.

57 However some of them do appear in *Who's Who in Canada* or *Who's Who in Canadian Finance*. Some prominent and already well-known Dutch-Canadian businessmen might express their allegiance to the broader Dutch-Canadian community by providing financial contributions or goods for community events.

58 Some of this information was based on conversations with someone who has acted as consultant to some of these Dutch-Canadian top-level managers or entrepreneurs.

59 Known in Dutch as *De Canada-Nederland Kamer van Koophandel*, they have since established branches in Vancouver and Toronto. See article in *De Nederlandse Courant*, February 7, 1990, p. 10.

60 As commander of the 2nd Canadian division operating in the Netherlands in 1944-45, he was named an officer of the Order of Orange Nassau. *Who's Who in Canada* (1989), p. 555-56.

61 Even the refusal to join such "exclusive" clubs could be seen as consistent with the Dutch status system which would consider it below the status of any member of the aristocracy (even poor aristocrats) to join a "nouveau-bourgeois" group.

62 Younger middle-class Dutch-Canadians, even in Toronto, find their middle-class elders too "snobbish," too "stuffy" or too preoccupied with ritual and etiquette.

63 One of the founders of the CNBPA told me they modelled their organization after similar ethnically based professional organizations in Toronto. Other members explained how they were too busy to take off two hours a month to attend the luncheon club.

64 The CNBPA, which also invites guest speakers and organizes art exhibitions, boat races and other get-togethers, usually gets extensive write-ups in the Dutch-Canadian press. Their 1993 Sinterklaas/Christmas gala dinner, jointly sponsored by the somewhat larger Belgian Canadian Business Association, was held in the University Club on University Avenue. Their yearly business meeting that year was held in the "exclusive Royal Military Institute" (quoted in write-up of meeting). See *De Nederlandse Courant* 38, 26 (1993), p. 28.

65 They have also been attracting the more recent young professional immigrants from the Netherlands.

66 The membership of the CNBPA and the Luncheon Club still overlaps to a large degree; however, neither organization has been able to attract Dutch-Canadian academics, who tend to operate in social circles composed of other university people.

67 Dutch-Canadians whom I interviewed would refer to "big shots" as people who could afford to make frequent trips abroad, and "think nothing of spending two hundred dollars in a restaurant."

68 We have already seen (in chap. 9) how a group of such middle-class Calvinist professionals and businessmen (but not women) formed their own parallel organization (the CRCBPA). It was founded by a second-generation Dutch-Canadian. In terms of their special religious connection, they follow the very "Dutch" pillar system, but in terms of internal social stratification, they are very North American.

69 For the first few years he owned one pair of good trousers, and had to find a job before he could proceed to obtain an MA from the Ontario Institute for Studies in Education in Toronto.

70 I spoke to this writer on four separate occasions between 1989 and 1993.

71 The lawyer and his brother (who is listed in *Who's Who in Canada*) belong to the same Gaasenbeek family that was mentioned earlier in this chapter. All of these brothers emigrated to Canada after they had either completed, or almost completed, the more prestigious *lyceum* (high school) of Baarn.

72 Randall Collins, *The Credential Society* (New York: Academic Press, 1979), p. 62.

73 A former Dutch farm worker, who first landed in the Holland Marsh, made the following comment: "Our bosses wanted us to learn English as quickly as possible when we joined their [Christian Reformed] church, but they used to tell us off in Dutch when they thought we were not working hard enough in the fields." Interview, in Dutch, with a retired Dutch-Canadian farmer in March of 1989.

74 Occasionally a particularly nationalistic (pro-Holland) Dutch-Canadian, or newcomer, will insist on speaking only Dutch, but that will usually not bring about the desired response.

75 In Bourdieu's terminology, this would be a sub-type of 'cultural capital.'

Chapter 13

1 For Bourdieu's analysis of gender, in terms of 'habitus' and 'symbolic violence,' see his *Outline of a Theory of Practice*, p. 93-94; also, Bourdieu and Wacquant, *Reflexive Sociology*, p. 170-74.

2 The only professional Dutch-Canadian women mentioned in that book are two nurses and Aritha Van Herk, the daughter of a Dutch immigrant who became a well-known Canadian writer and professor in English literature. Two Dutch-Canadian women who became teachers also appear in a page of photographs of the "Impact" chapter, but with no further elaboration. See VanderMey, *To All Our Children*, p. 445, 448.

3 The presumably funny, but actually embarrassing and humiliating situation, involved a woman and an outhouse. The only incident in the book where a Dutch immigrant is depicted as angry and shouting also portrays a woman. See VanderMey, *To All Our Children*, p. 35, 165.

4 The part played by Dutch immigrant women as keen observers could have been given more explicit recognition. Chapter 6 ("The Crossing") has lengthy excerpts from diaries written by three women, as well as numerous recollections based on interviews with women. Sections from these same diaries appear again in subsequent chapters. Chapter 1, which gives a background description of the Netherlands, was written by an Dutch-American woman.

5 A woman of upper-class background who followed her husband to the Canadian prairies in the 1920s, Jane Aberson was a pioneer, living on a small homestead. She witnessed the Great Depression, and supported the CCF, for whom she acted as scrutineer. See Mark Boekelman, "The Letters of Jane Aberson, Everyday Life on the Prairies during the Depression: How Immigration Turns Conservatives into Social Democrats," in Ganzevoort and Boekelman, eds., *Dutch Immigration to North America*, p. 111-29.

6 I came come across at least one set of memoirs (including a family genealogy) written in English by an 80-year-old woman (a mother, grandmother and great-grandmother).

7 VanderMey, *And the Swamp Flourished*, p. 25-26.

8 Moreover, the number of women's names is inflated with the inclusion of several members of the Royal Dutch family.

9 After the exclusion of pictures showing groups of schoolchildren or large crowd scenes (such as people on deck an ocean liner, or blending into the background of a street scene).

10 The prominence of men comes out even more in photographs showing individuals or couples. Sixteen men, compared to only two women, were singled out in larger pictures. Similarly, only five individual women appear in smaller, less conspicuous photos, compared to 43 men.

11 All included in the bibliography at the end of the book.

12 Michiel Horn, "Canadian Soldiers and Dutch Women after the Second World War," in Ganzevoort and Boekelman, eds., *Dutch Immigration*, p. 187-96.

13 This applies to all but one of the MA dissertations written by women, which are also listed in the bibliography. The only anthology dedicated exclusively to immigrant women (including Dutch women) is Miep Verkley's *A Particular Path* (Thedford: Swans Publications, 1993).

14 Andy Boekema, who came to Canada in 1952, came across several such cases when he used to travel to remote northern regions as an employee of Imperial Oil. Interview with Andy Boekema, in Kingston, December 19, 1989.

15 Thea Schryer, former editor of the *De Nederlandse Courant*, heard such stories from various Dutch war brides, often many years after they had been in Canada.

16 This theme came out in many interviews and conversations with women who had come to Canada just after they were married.

17 I came across several such cases. A woman in Hamilton, with whom I spoke over the phone, told me she used to be married to an executive for a large multinational corporation with a $500,000 home in Toronto. She left him because he was abusive, and she complained that he still came along now and then to beat her up. Another Dutch-Canadian woman in Hamilton, now living in poverty in a run-down downtown neighbourhood, came to Canada in 1965 when she was 13 years old. In 1991 she was raising three teenage daughters by herself, while attempting to upgrade her education by attending McMaster University. Earlier in life, that woman was abused by her stepfather but her mother would not recognize it.

Another tragic story about a woman called Martha is included in Verkley's *A Particular Path*, 17-23.

18 Young men who were interested in becoming farmers often deliberately sought out such Dutch partners because women brought up in a rural Dutch setting not only had farm experience but were thought to share a propensity for working hard and saving money.

19 See Joyce G. van der Vliet, "Women, Church and Society: The Christian Reformed Church Case," a graduate thesis in Sociology, University of Guelph, August 1994.

20 Joyce van der Vliet, "Women, Church and Society," p. 69.

21 This same woman remarked that the men would refuse to take on the tasks of cleaning, making sandwiches and other volunteer labour, which were essential in the smooth operation of church activities (ibid., p. 89-91).

22 Miep Verkley's *A Particular Path*, p. 1. Dutch immigrants women whom I interviewed expressed similar sentiments: "I have noticed that a lot of Dutch women, especially those who came from big cities, went out to work. They usually became cooks or waitresses. Some did that out of sheer necessity, but I believe that they also wanted to do that . . . It was a good experience for them because that is how they learned English. They were also not as bored as if they would have stayed home all day."

Adapted from fieldnotes based on interviews with two women (both living on farms in southwestern Ontario).

23 I came across several such cases. See also VanderMey, *To All Our Children*, p. 174.

24 Men from both groups quoted the Bible or other religious texts to underline the God-ordained place of women.

25 Interview (in Dutch) with a Dutch-Canadian couple, Burlington, November 24, 1988.

26 The burden is even greater for women in the smaller and stricter Canadian Reformed denomination, whose members have set up another, parallel Christian school system in some locations.

27 See article by Femmie VanderBoom, "Reformed education—at all costs?," *Reformed Perspective*, October 1990, p. 30-31.

28 Conversation with young woman, Guelph, December 9, 1988.

29 This quote is a close-to-verbatim reconstruction of a conversation I had with a young woman of non-Dutch background, Guelph, November 29, 1988.

30 Interview with a young Christian Reformed woman working as social worker in a government-run group home in downtown Hamilton, May 10, 1989.

31 There are two streams of feminist theology within Western forms of Christianity: evangelical feminism and mainstream or reformist Christian feminism. There are also post-Christian or post-biblical feminists who have forsaken Christianity altogether because they see it as inherently contradictory to feminist theory. See van der Vliet, "Women, Church and Society," p. 44-46. All four streams are found among Dutch-Canadian feminists.

32 Several Dutch-Canadian Catholics (both men and women) pointed this out to me; confirmation would require more systematic research involving statistical analysis.

33 Dutch-Canadian farm women from various backgrounds make up about a third of the membership of this organization in Ontario. In my fieldwork in rural Ontario I came across several of their members.

34 Interview with John Van Werde, Sarnia, July 11, 1990; Telephone conversation with Wilhelmina Verhoeven, in Toronto, Dec. 11, 1990. This "Dutch" order actually has no other Dutch members in Ontario. Other Dutch-Canadian nuns ended up in religious orders (such as St. Joseph's) with no ethnic links. In my fieldnotes I encountered about half a dozen names.

35 John Van Bakel, "Hendrika and Her Family," (printed at home, in Bancroft), 1980.

36 The daughter of a prosperous Dutch Calvinist immigrant who became established in Chatham before the War, she left an abusive husband—against the wishes of their Christian Reformed minister—after he started hitting her daughter. Her father did not allow her to receive any money from her estranged husband, but eventually she received help from a woman not of Dutch descent, who helped her find a job in Sudbury. As a single, working mother, she worked for a radio station, and did some cleaning in the apartment building where she lived with her daughter. Later she combined a day job in a government department with part-time work in a bar. Based on two interviews, conducted in English, with a store owner in Sudbury, on July 4, 1990 and March 6, 1991.

37 For example, Ruth Mesritz became a well-respected and successful real estate broker in Toronto. While her career prospered, her husband encountered difficulties, first as broker for a firm that imported textiles and later as someone who sold ready-made clothing on assignment for a manufacturer in Winnipeg. He closed his showroom in 1974 to take early retirement, but outlived his wife. Based on an interview with her husband in Toronto, September 16, 1989; see also a summary of her career in an obituary in *Ducapost* (March 1975), p. 11.

38 She is listed in the 1990 Luncheon Club membership booklet, but without any reference to her former occupation (she was then already retired). Her name came up numerous times in the course of conversations or interviews in Toronto.

39 Interview at her home, Sudbury, July 3, 1990.

40 Interview with Yvonne van der Feldz, Moffat (near Guelph), December 14, 1988.

41 Interview with a retired career woman, Toronto, October 27, 1990. This woman used to write a business column for a Dutch newspaper in Amsterdam and later worked for a Dutch-Canadian credit union. Another postwar Dutch immigrant woman thought about setting up a Dutch-Canadian professional association just for women, but that idea never came to fruition.

42 Interview with one of its (male) founders, an agent for a larger real estate broker in Mississauga, November 1, 1988.

43 Women members were easy to identify because most entries included first names. Some women were also identified by the prefix Mrs. or Ms. There was a great deal of overlap in the membership of the two associations, although 10 women were only members of the Luncheon Club, but not the CNBPA.

44 I obtained much of the information about what these women did through cross-referencing names already in my own files and then asking a key informant who knew many of these women.

45 She founded the Netherlands Cultural Association in 1978.

46 Interview with Aleida Limbertie, Toronto, October 11, 1988.

47 The Netherlands Luncheon Club, List of Members (1989), p. 13.

48 Fenny Bloemink (B.A. Econ, University of Amsterdam) served on the DUCA board of directors until she moved away in 1965. She was succeeded by Mrs. Wil Braaksma, wife of Ale Braaksma, founder of the "House of Viking." When she passed away in the later 1970s, she was replaced by Lia de Groot. A list of members of the board of directors (between 1954 and 1988) also mentions the names of Mrs. W. Hak, Mrs. F. Bloemink, Mrs. A. la Bastide, Mrs. T. Stewart and Mrs. E. Krygsman (*The Duca Story* [1988 Annual Report], p. 18).

49 Interview with Jules Frijters, Acton, February 21, 1990.

50 She even built the roof of one of their barns. I first heard about this woman on Wolf Island through a mutual acquaintance, and subsequently paid a personal visit and interviewed both the man and the woman, which confirmed the validity of original information.

51 To continue this short list, Wil Braaksma, who emigrated in 1952, assisted her husband in his furniture company while raising a family, and was elected to the board of directors of the DUCA Credit Union in 1965. She also served as president of the Netherlands Bazaar and director of the Netherlands Centre Charitable Foundation Inc., (see 1977 Annual Report the DUCA Credit Union, p. 15). Moreover, she sat on the board of directors of a Dutch senior citizen's group long before she herself was ready to retire.

52 The De Groots initially had difficulty getting immigrant status because of their handicapped child, but Tommy Douglas (to whom they were introduced via a United Church minister) interceded on their behalf. She resumed her advocacy and volunteer work for handicapped children when they moved to Ontario in 1963. Her commitment won her certificates of honour, including a "New Canadian Mother of the Year" award in 1960. Interview with Dr. and Mrs. De Groot, in their home near Carrying Place (near Picton), December 18, 1989.

53 Another Dutch immigrant couple, actively involved in the Salvation Army (both in Holland and in Canada), adopted numerous handicapped children in Conestogo, a small village near Kitchener. Their operation (including the additions to their house) grew so large that the government had to take it over. Although the husband (a craftsman by trade) received most of the publicity, his wife in fact did most of the work.

54 She was impressed with an example of an integrated complex, which allowed young and old to live together within a single housing estate.

55 Interview with Joyce Groot, in her home just outside of Kingston, December 20, 1989.

56 The latter includes a fairly broad range of Dutch-Canadian immigrants women, but has not been able to attract either young professional second-generation women nor postwar immigrant women of an upper-middle- or upper-class Dutch background.

57 It depended on age, prior exposure to English, and whether or not they had school-age children. For example, it took married women with small children who did not enter the work force longer since they did not have as many opportunities to talk and listen to English-speakers on a daily basis.

58 The Dutch ate boiled potatoes with every meal, and lunches consisted of homemade vegetable soup with sandwiches covered with thinly sliced meat or chocolate sprinkles. Breakfasts invariably included Dutch rusks (*beschuit*) and *koek* (a kind of spiced sweetbread). The demand for such food products stimulated a thriving import and delicatessen business (see chap. 14).

59 The three Dutch war brides with whom I spoke all used fluent Dutch over the phone, even though they had all lived in Canada for over three decades.

60 Interview with Ellen Chamberlain (nee Van Praag), in Scarborough, May 31, 1991.

61 In Dutch, "Maar je kan alleen echt Hollands zijn in Holland." From a telephone conversation with a war bride in Toronto, February 19, 1990.

62 Her published novels include the award-winning *Judith*, *The Tent Peg* and *No Fixed Address*.

63 A well-known man would rarely be publicly acknowledged as his mother's successful son.

64 A whole issue of the *The Canadian Journal of Netherlandic Studies* (Fall 1990) was dedicated to women writers in the Netherlands and Flanders, although some of the writers are men and not all the writers use a feminist perspective. See Hermina Joldersma, "Women Writers," "Writing by Women" and "The Female Voice," in ibid., 11, 2: 1-3. A 1992 issue of the same journal opens with an introductory essay about the controversial Anna Bijns literary prize set up by Dutch feminist writers.

65 See Tineke Hellwig, "Change in the Colonial Society of the Dutch East Indies: Literature in Dutch and Malay," a paper presented at the annual meeting of CAANS, held at Carleton University, June 5-6, 1993. See also her "The Asian and Eurasian Woman of the Dutch East Indies in Dutch and Malay Literature," *The Canadian Journal of Netherlandic Studies*, 14 (Fall 1993): 20-26.

66 For instance not all women of Dutch descent who advocate gender equity have allied themselves to the pro-choice movement, particularly if they have close links with people belonging to a Dutch Calvinist or a Catholic denomination.

67 This tendency is very noticeable in many small towns in southwestern Ontario with a Dutch-Canadian presence.

68 Bourdieu, *Distinction*, p. 479-82.

Chapter 14

1 In collaboration with its North American counterpart, this financial institution also put money into reclaiming the Pit Polder in British Columbia, to earn dollar dividends by selling land to Dutch farmers. Neither project was a success, although several thousand acres of the Pit Polder were again drained and developed after the War under Jan Blom's direction. Interview with F. Jensma, Nepean, November 18, 1989. See also VanderMey, *To All Our Children*, p. 449.

2 They did a booming business shipping immigrants from all over Europe from the port city of Rotterdam to North America.

3 The company's name did not help to attract a broader clientele, and they eventually sold out to an established North American insurance company.

4 Holland Life even had an agent in Wellandport. Interview with a former employee of the company, Jack van Marrum, Chatham, December 1, 1989.

5 He had to lobby the federal government for two years to get the legislative changes allowing Canada's first foreign-owned bank. For a brief outline of the history of the Mercantile Bank and its founder, who died in 1992, see article, "Dutch-born Banker Dies in Montreal, Quebec," *Windmill Herald*, June 8, 1992, p. 14.

6 Interview with Jan Lusink, Don Mills, May 7, 1991. Their employees started a branch of an originally completely Dutch-Canadian credit union (DUCA) (see chap. 15).

7 They put a Dutch expatriate in charge of this operation.

8 A regional director who oversaw this Strathroy operation for nine years belonged to the Dutch-Canadian "upper crust" in Toronto. This same man was a member of the *Borrel Club* (see chap. 12).

9 Its president, Eduard Merbis, is chairman of the Canadian-Netherlands Chamber of Commerce, which also moved its head office from Montreal to Toronto in 1992. See article by Wim van Duyn in *De Nederlandse Courant*, March 20, 1993, p. 1.

10 A member of the Canadian Netherlands Business and Professional Association (see chap. 12) manages money for Brenninkmeyer, a wealthy Dutch investor whose name cropped up on various occasions in the course of interviews.

11 Bramer was the brains behind such well-known drinking establishment as the Boiler Room, the Coal Bin, and later the Gasworks & Chimney and the Amsterdam Brasserie & Brewpub. By the 1970s he had bought out his Dutch shareholders, whom Bramer identified as "wealthy Dutch families who wanted to invest money in Canadian mortgages which were a particularly attractive investment from a tax point of view" ("The Dutch in Canada," *Invest Canada*, February 1987, p. 32-33).

12 During the 1970s and 1980s the number of investors from the Netherlands who emigrated to Canada increased, when having capital became a requirement for emigration. Some invested in luxury resorts and tourism operations in the Muskokas or remote parts of Northern Ontario. They make frequent trips to the Netherlands but have limited or no contact with older postwar Dutch immigrants or with its institutions.

13 Another must for the Dutch palate is *applestroop* (a type of apple butter), chocolate sprinkles and a sugar-coated confection (*hagelslag*) for sandwiches.

14 See also Ganzevoort, *A Bittersweet Land*, p. 90-91.

15 Telephone interview with Jan Overweel, Toronto, April 6, 1993.

16 The only way he could find customers was to look for a church with an onion-shaped dome, which indicated the presence of Ukrainians.
17 Before arriving in Canada, he had sailed with the Holland-America Lines and worked in South Africa, where he met and married a Canadian nurse. That is how he was able to get immigrant status—a war bride in reverse! Telephone interview with Jan Overweel, Toronto, April 6, 1993.
18 Initially, Overweel worked on commission and did not have his own car. When profits increased, he purchased products directly from abroad, to become one of the biggest importers.
19 One came to Toronto while the other went to Chicago to open up a store, but soon joined his brother in Canada. Conversation with Joop Holtzheuser, Toronto, December 7, 1988.
20 His company, Van's Importing, was a subsidiary of Hagemeyer, a Dutch import consortium.
21 This has become a sideline of Vanderheide, the owner of the *Windmill Herald* published in British Columbia (see chap. 11).
22 Interview with Mrs. Van Greuningen, London, November 20, 1988.
23 They became one of the first customers of the Holtzheuser brothers in Toronto.
24 He made several trips to the Netherlands to make contacts, but most shipments were received as postal packages.
25 Conversation with Bill Brouwers, Oakville, June 20, 1989.
26 Conversation with Mrs. Medendorp, Bradford, September 14, 1989.
27 Many of his regular customers are also Reformed Dutch-Canadians. Interview with Bill Weinen, near Sheffield, June 28, 1989.
28 Its owner later opened up two other stores in Hamilton to capture the ethnic market there. See also VanderMey, *To All Our Children*, p. 240-41. But Ontario has not yet seen a large Dutch-style department store cum wholesale operation, such as the Holland Shopping Centre, in New Westminster, B.C.
29 Although running a bakery requires prior experience and training, this skill can be transferred to other forms of commercial baking. Dutch-Canadian bakers with donut shops that are linked to North American chains, or who work for supermarkets, are too numerous to mention.
30 Interview with Ray Wiersma, Chatham, December 4, 1989.
31 Unlike the typical Dutch-Canadian consumer, who would only buy cakes or pastries for birthday parties and other special events, their Canadian counterparts would buy such treats for their regular dessert.
32 For example, the Jansen family, who operate a specialty bakery in Delhi, arrived in 1981; two other bakers have since set up shop in Norwich, south of Woodstock. Like the Netherlands in the 1950s, they are now facing increasing competition from mass-produced baked goods sold in corner groceries and drugstores. Conversation with Frans Jansen, Delhi, December 29, 1992.
33 For a larger bakery developed by a woman, with outlets in several cities, we have to turn to another province. The mother of Simon de Jong, federal MP from Saskatchewan, started running her own pastry shop, a trade she had learned in Holland, when she came to Canada. Initially she made her pastries at home, but later expanded her business and brought over a couple of bakers from Holland to work under her. Not only did she run two bakeries in Regina, but she bought a third in Calgary. One of her employees became her partner in that third business, and she sold it to him in the late 1950s. Based on a conver-

sation with Simon de Jong, in Guelph, March 22, 1990; followed up with a telephone interview (to Ottawa) the following day.

34 See article by Wim van Duyn, "Simon de Groot Opent 'Factory Outlet' in Brampton," *De Nederlandse Courant*, February 6, 1993, p. 7. See also VanderMey, *To All Our Children*, p. 442.

35 Interview with Luit Miedema, near Simcoe, June 12, 1989.

36 The nearby villages of Hagersville and Caledonia have resident Dutch Catholic priests who used to buy their meat from him on a regular basis. His customers also included numerous people not of Dutch background.

37 Several Dutch meat producers, who also operate stock farms, have at one time or another set up stands in the Kitchener, Waterloo or Guelph farmer's markets.

38 "Migration of Professional Workers into and out of Canada, 1946-1960," Professional Manpower Bulletin no. 11 (October 1961). Research branch of the Department of Labour in Ottawa. Found in archives of MHSO (Queen's Park); 3533-HVI.

39 However, as a proportion of professionals recruited from abroad, the Dutch were only preceded by the British and the Germans. See Burnet and Palmer, *Coming Canadians*, p. 71-72.

40 This lawyer, Dick Gaasenbeek, did not have much contact with other Dutch-Canadians until he set up his law practice 10 years after he immigrated, when he renewed his ties with the Dutch-Canadian community. First, his Dutch-Canadian family physician nominated him as a board member of the Hamilton Netherlands Credit Union. Gaasenbeek later became the director, as well as president of the Dutch Canadian Alliance, and was actively involved in the Operation Thank You Canada committee to commemorate the twenty-fifth anniversary of the liberation of the Netherlands (see chap. 16). Initially around 40 percent of Gaasenbeek's clients were Dutch-Canadians; this number declined to about 20 percent by 1989. Interview with Dick Gaasenbeek, Dundas (near Hamilton), November 17, 1989.

41 Like lawyers, some Dutch-Canadian doctors became involved in the broader Dutch-Canadian world of business through membership in an ethnic investment club or, in at least two cases, buying farm land for investment purposes.

42 Dr. H.L. van Vierssen-Trip, "The Trip Family, An Outline of Five Centuries," 4th ed., 1989, p.246 (a manuscript written in Ottawa during retirement).

43 Later that summer, Trip bought a 16-room mansion on Main Street East and took in a Latvian doctor as a partner. Since few patients were referred to him by other physicians, he started a maternity clinic and surgery in his home.

44 When OHIP came in, business declined, and a son, then working for Health and Welfare in Ottawa, brought to his father's attention an opening in Manitowaning, on Manitoulin Island. Here Trip served as physician for a largely native population until he retired in 1971 and moved to Ottawa. Interview with Dr. Vierssen-Trip, Ottawa, November 17, 1989.

45 Interview with Dr. Hans Westerberg, Kingston, December 18, 1989.

46 When he came to Canada in 1959, the regulations for immigrant doctors had changed, and Ackerman had to complete two years of internship. Most of his clients were Dutch-Canadian, and he received patients from as far away as Petrolia. Interview with Dr. Otto Ackerman, Chatham, December 2, 1989.

47 He used to meet newly arrived immigrants at Pier 21 in Halifax, where most immigrants from Europe landed in Canada.

48 Before that he had lived in Whitby. Interview with Rimmer Tjalsma, Mississauga, May 1, 1989.

49 Since 1973, *Wereld Contact*, which dates back to 1959, has had representatives in Canada who oversee the reception of relatives of Dutch-Canadians who are visiting Canada in increasing numbers.

50 Its original owner was a co-founder of the former Chatham Dutch Canadian Credit Union and started a Dutch-Canadian newspaper, *Hollandia News* (see chap. 11).

51 He booked the first flights to Amsterdam for the Dutch-Canadian Entertainment Club, which started organizing charter flights on a large scale (see chap. 16). Koops later sold his business to Baldwin Verstraete, the owner of Valentine Travel.

52 He originally started off working for an established Canadian travel business, but eventually bought out his boss. Verstraete's travel agency, called Valentine Travel, eventually did most bookings in the Toronto area for Martinair.

53 By the late 1980s, he accepted an offer to amalgamate his travel agency with the larger Valentine Travel. Yet despite a declining influence of the Dutch pillar mentality, some Dutch-Canadian Catholics expressed both surprise and disapproval when that deal was made.One person commented, "How is it possible for a Catholic and a *gereformeerde* to become business partners?" Others made glib remarks like "Bill better watch his language around those people."

54 In the Netherlands he worked for a travel business that used to arrange all the bookings for *Wereld Contact*. Interview with Gerry Van der Kley, Whitby, May 7, 1991.

55 Van der Kley also arranged special tours for groups of farmers and people specializing in flower growing.

56 This was also the first company whose workers signed a contract with the Christian Labour Association of Canada (see chap. 9).

57 Interview with Douwinus Horst, St. Marys, May 14, 1991.

58 Schippers, the first owner and editor of *De Nederlandse Courant* used to write his editorial articles in the offices of Guardian Press in Hamilton, so that they could come hot off the press.

59 Guardian Press, which has since changed hands on several occasions, prints for a general clientele; but all its owners and some of its workers have always been Dutch-Canadians.

60 Even then, differences in religious background would probably be more indicative of region of origin and level of education than religious ideology per se.

61 This theme came out in various interviews with members of this religious community, as well as conversations with people who had done business with, or worked for, members of this denomination. I had over 80 separate fieldnote references to this sub-segment of the Dutch-Canadian population.

62 From the workers' viewpoint, not only will they be assured a "safe" place of employment—because they will not be pressured into joining a union or be subject to ridicule—but they will have the advantage of working with like-minded individuals.

63 Alternatively, workers could try to put moral pressures on their employers through the church, to make them live up to their own paternalistic discourse.

64 I heard such complaints from both members of the same denomination and local non-Dutch, non-Canadian Reformed workers.

Chapter 15

1 In Canada, credit unions were first introduced by Catholic clergy, especially in Quebec, which has long had a strong presence of *caisses populaires*. In Ontario, the small credit unions that existed prior to the War, some without official charter, operated in isolation from one another (see Kenyon, *To the Credit of the People*, p. 16).

2 My fieldnotes on Dutch-Canadian credit unions included 13 categories, each of which contains between seven and 180 individual entries. Additional archival research was also conducted.

3 One credit union was started by a Dutch farmer who dabbled in real estate; he sold farms to the same immigrants whom he helped to get loans. Dutch-Canadian insurance agents and car salesmen utilized their links with a credit union to gain access to customers. Such observations are based on reading the minutes of board meetings as well as conversations with people mentioned in those minutes. Because of the confidential nature of some of those documents and conversations, it would be inappropriate to refer to specific names in many instances.

4 The idea was to pool people's resources so that some could get a higher rate of return on their savings while others had access to cheaper credit. Initially, the money collected to form a basic capital fund was as low as 25 or 50 cents per person.

5 Time and time again, during interviews with charter members, I came across the name Visser, who must have been of Dutch background because he could speak Dutch. Several people also referred to a Dutch-speaking inspector by the name of Fisher. I assume this must have been the same person (who possibly Anglicized his name).

6 Some Dutch credit unions were also able to offer health insurance, prior to the introduction of OHIP, through CUNA (Credit Union National Association). Part of the U.S. network of co-operative institutions, this organization set up their own Mutual Insurance Society, which provided loan protection and life insurance for credit unions in both countries. This corporation was in turn connected to CUMBA (Credit Union Mutual Benefits Association), first set up in Toronto in 1946 as an alternative to the Blue Cross plan. See Kenyon, *To the Credit of the People*, p. 13-14, 61, 79-80, 237.

7 Working capital did not become available until later, with loans from Dutch banks, as in the case of St. Willibrord in London (see chap. 8) or with access to loans from the Ontario Co-operative Credit Society. In the 1960s and 1970s, in Toronto, the DUCA Community Credit Union also financed the building of some (mainly Christian Reformed) churches by having a number of members of a congregation each guarantee a portion of the mortgage loan.

8 However, credit union managers were also subject to dismissal whenever financial difficulties arose, regardless of whether these were brought about by personality clashes, human error or factors beyond control (downswings in the economy or increasing interest rates).

9 This number does not include parish credit unions that were not started by Dutch immigrants, but where Dutch-Canadians played a leading role.

10 The small Quinte (Community) Credit Union, in Bloomfield, had 223 mainly Dutch members and total assets of $193,876. The biggest was DUCA Community Credit Union Ltd. (in Toronto), with 17,500 members about half of whom

were Dutch-Canadians. Their assets were $64,555,000. See also Ger Graaskamp, *Dutch Canadian Mosaic* (Niagara Falls: Decker, ca. 1980), p. 25-27.

11 Travel agencies and KLM recognized the business potential of such charters. However, according to Canada's Air Transport Commission, organizations eligible to arrange "affinity charters" had to have a purpose other than travel by chartered aircraft and their members had to pay dues. This meant drafting a special set of by-laws. As one of the early DCA organizers commented, "between DCA and their credit unions, some financial contortions were made in order to meet the appearance of membership dues."

12 St. Willibrord provided travel service for its members as early as 1953, in cooperation with a Mr. Boerkamp. This arrangement developed into Wibo-Travel Service. See St. Willibrord Credit Union, "25 Years of Service (1950 to 1975)" (Annual Report).

13 Interviews with Dick de Man, Willowdale (Toronto), June 9, 1989; Dick Gaasenbeek, Dundas, November 27, 1989; and Bert Kruithof, Thornbury, March 12, 1991.

14 The only Dutch-linked credit unions that did not want to participate were Chatham, run by someone who owned his own travel agency, and Oshawa.

15 In the Netherlands, almost all Dutch households had a state-issued *begrafenis kaart* ("burial card") hanging near the front door. In Canada, an insurance agent with connections to St. Willibrord kept the records. The DCA also instituted scholarships to reward essays written by credit union members, and engaged Dutch variety artists. Personal communication from Dick de Man.

16 By the time they discontinued their travel business, the DCA still had a surplus, part of which was then donated to Dutch-Canadian senior citizens' centres (see chap. 17).

In 1983 Dick de Man, a past president and former executive of DUCA, was elected to head the board of DCA. He had left DUCA in 1975 to become the treasurer-manager of the LCBO Employees Credit Union. With the travel business out of the way, DCA had scaled down its activities limited to administering the group life insurance plan, scholarships and modest funding of seniors' housing. DCA Travel (which had a separate board of directors) continued to function as a separate, now privately owned company, and eventually passed into the hands of a consultant/advisory company owned by a Dutch-Canadian.

17 With a tight money market, interest rates became more volatile. Many credit unions did not build up reserves or had an unprofessional approach to lending. In 1969 Ontario counted 1,500 credit unions, which had dwindled to around 500 by 1994.

18 All members got back their original investment and deposits and all outstanding loans were paid back within six months, sometimes by getting a new loan from the Clinton Community Credit Union. Interview with Kees Buurma, in his home near Homesville, May 14, 1992.

19 Their members joined other credit unions, including St. Willibrord. This credit union dated from 1967. Interview with Gerrit de Boer, Sarnia, August 29, 1990.

20 It in turn sold its remaining assets to Avestel Credit Union, previously the Steel Workers Credit Union at Stelco. Interview with Dick Gaasenbeek, Dundas, November 27, 1989.

The Dutch Canadian (Lincoln and Welland) Credit Union, which first changed its name to DUCA Niagara Credit Union with special permission from the DUCA in Toronto, was eventually taken over by the large Niagara Credit Union Ltd.

21 Many Dutch-Canadian credit unions, particularly the ones in Hamilton and later a much bigger one in Chatham, made costly errors. When such credit unions went into the red, their depositors were bailed out by OSDIC (Ontario Share and Deposit Insurance Corporation).

22 See Kenyon, *To the Credit of the People*, p. 131.

23 At that time it had nearly 20,000 members and $186 million in assets (*Fortieth Annual Report, St. Willibrord Community Credit Union* (London: Hearn/Kelly Ltd.). See also article in the *Windmill Herald*, October 23, 1989, p. 16.

24 See 1989 Annual Report of DUCA, "Better 'Banking' for Everyone," p. 8-9.

25 St. Willibrord witnessed its most spectacular growth and expansion under the management of John Strijbosch, a Dutch accountant of rural background who was the general manager from 1969 until 1988. He became the undisputed "kingpin," of their operation. The principal founder and moral leader of DUCA is Mau Coopman. Although he served only one term as president of the board, he became their longest-serving member.

26 The village of Arkona (in Middlesex) was the second major branch that offered full-time service as early as 1964. See Peter de Groot, "St. Willibrord Credit Union in the East Lambton West Middlesex Area," an internal report written in 1981.

27 In the long run, the involvement of farmers strengthened St. Willibrord, since the monetary value of farm assets and agricultural land consistently outstripped the rate of inflation. Consequently, early farm members made huge deposits when they sold their farms upon retirement.

28 While a deliberate attempt to appear "less Dutch," Dutch-Canadians liked the new name because it reminded them of an old Dutch coin called a *ducaat*; an earlier mimeographed newsletter of the credit union had been called *ducaatje*.

29 According to DUCA minutes of January board meetings [notulen], in their head office in North York they were allowed to take on "members in good standing of bona fide Dutch-Canadian Associations operating within the county of York, the county of Halton, the county of Peel or the county of Ontario west of King's highway 12." This expanded definition of their membership goes back to an amendment of their by-laws in 1962. See John Hees, "A Short History of Our Credit Union," *Ducapost*, July-August 1978. The original wording in the September 4, 1962 minutes reads "persons of Dutch extraction residing in. . . ."

30 The credit union drew in people who had steady and well-paid jobs, especially those who worked for large companies, including the Philips electronics plant in Scarborough (see previous chapter). Like St. Willibrord, DUCA also obtained capital funds from the Netherlands with a loan arranged through the Dutch embassy around the beginning of the 1960s.

31 I arrived at these calculations by comparing the figures in their respective annual reports for that year, as well as data included in various other information bulletins.

32 They also spoke standard Dutch among themselves, and continued to write sections of their newsletter in Dutch.

33 When asked why they showed so little interest in the Dutch Canadian Society of London, several former directors told me they had a greater interest in

implementing ideals or affecting social policy than in "partying and having a good time" for the sake of being Dutch.

34 Hans Grotheer, a German-Canadian, worked as an accountant between 1974 and 1977. Personal communication from Dick de Man.

35 DUCA is a contraction of DUtch-CAnadian, but that word by itself does not indicate a Dutch origin to people who do not know about its derivation.

36 According to "A Brief History of DUCA" written (by a GW) in 1988, of 60 people on staff, roughly 25 were of Dutch descent, with 15 of those reasonably fluent in Dutch.

37 The cultural component of DUCA included a youth club called "The Tulip Trampers," whose parents were all active in the Toronto credit union. Such social activities, and a sense of common national origin, held together a diverse group of people, including Dutch-Canadians with Indonesian connections (see chap. 10). People in this core group were also an integral part of the close-knit network of Dutch-Canadians in Toronto who belonged to the Netherlands Luncheon Club and who later joined the Canadian Netherlands Business and Professional Association (see chap. 12).

38 Fred Gale and Dan McDonald.

39 Taped interview with Nick van Osch, London, April 30, 1990.

40 According to the written excerpts from a discussion at the board of directors meeting of the DCA, held on March 11, 1969, the DUCA Toronto representative argued in favour of expanding DCA's mandate to include a broader range of organizations (nation-wide) whose members shared a common Dutch background. In contrast, the London (St. Willibrord) representative is quoted as saying, "The members of the London Group would simply not be interested in any efforts to preserve a strong Dutch image."

41 Taped interview with Dan McDonald, during visit to Dundas Street branch office, in London, June 29, 1990.

42 Interview with John Cowan, Blenheim, July 10, 1990. Moreover, the predominantly non-Dutch Canadian owners of small businesses in downtown Blenheim, interested in joining St. Willibrord since it would give them to a broader range of financial services, were not in favour of stressing the Dutch connections.

43 Likewise the inhabitants of the area surrounding the city of Stratford could join that branch of St. Willibrord regardless of ethnic or religious background.

44 A good example of a non-Dutch executive member is Chris Nanni, a Canadian of Italian background who grew up in a largely ethnic neighbourhood in Windsor. Chris became an avid supporter of credit unions in Thunder Bay, and later became involved in the Blenheim branch of St. Willibrord. Interview with Chris Nanni, at the University of Guelph, June 19, 1990.

45 DUCA also offers a payment service for pensions and other payments from and to the Netherlands.

46 From the concluding paragraph of "A Brief History of DUCA," 1988.

47 In 1992, St. Willibrord and Sydenham Credit Unions withdrew from the DCA and designated their capital shares to the Ontario Credit Union Charitable Foundation and DUCA, leaving DUCA Toronto as the sole member of that association. St. Willibrord is also not interested in placing ads in Dutch-Canadian newspapers.

48 This similarity in structure was pointed out to me by Dick de Man. In contrast, Toronto accepted nominations for candidates for the board of directors from the

floor at the annual meetings prior to the mid-1980s. Since then they have moved to mail-in balloting and the posting of candidates in a newsletter that goes out to all of their members. However, most DUCA members eligible to vote do not send in their ballots and those who do have little information to go by and may have never met the candidates. That system of elections is more typical of other North American organizations.

49 Despite the emphasis on the importance of "Canadianization," and the need to recruit more non-Dutch members, executive positions of originally Dutch ethnic credit unions will continue to be dominated by Dutch-Canadians for at least another decade, no matter how hard they try to recruit directors or board members not of Dutch descent. The more active older members, who always show up at annual meetings, continue to nominate and vote for their fellow Dutch-Canadians. Dutch-Canadian networks, whether based on family loyalties, a common religious bond or ethnic identity, are also bound to influence in which places the Dutch-based credit unions will expand in the future. Such networks operate in a different manner in the rural versus urban environments. St. Willibrord will probably expand precisely in those areas that have a large clustering of postwar Dutch Catholic farm immigrants. DUCA's growth and expansion will be more diffuse and unpredictable, given Toronto's Dutch-Canadian population's dispersed and heterogenous nature.

50 Interview with Bill Keyzers, Uxbridge, February 18, 1990.

51 Interview with Jules Fryters, Acton, February 21, 1990.

52 Although the credit union office was located in Milton, Dutch Catholics who belonged to a parish credit union in Acton switched to the one in Milton. Jules himself lived in the town of Acton at that time. He also invited his Reformed Dutch-Canadians neighbours, interested in a family insurance plan, to join the credit union.

53 The local Christian Reformed church also transferred its bank account with St. Willibrord.

54 He mentioned this to me during a conversation held in his home in Sarnia.

55 Perhaps they did not like the fact that one high-profile member of the credit union, a dairy farmer, had recently left the church to join a non-Dutch Protestant congregation. This historical sketch was reconstructed on the basis of a combination of their official records and various conversations and interviews with charter members.

56 From the records of Sydenham Credit Union; see *notulen* of the meeting of the board of directors, February 25, May 6, 1957.

57 Interview with Jan Tamming, Strathroy, April 21, 1989.

58 This sketch of the Hamilton Netherlands Credit Union is based on interviews with several former board members and managers, plus many short written references in *Soujourners*, an autobiographical account written by Arie Verduijn (see also fieldnotes interlude 15.1).

59 "Annual Reports & Financial Statements (1975/1976)," DUCA Hamilton Credit Union Limited, about ninth page (not numbered).

60 See Arie Verduijn, *Sojourners: A Family Chronicle*. Dutch Calvinists did not always vote the same way. In one dispute that pitted a manager (with no religious affiliation) against the board, the Christian Reformed board members found themselves on opposite sides. Interview with Dick Gaasenbeek, Dundas, November 27, 1989.

61 Interview with Jack van Winssen, Peterborough, December 20, 1989. A list of newspaper clippings, correspondence and other archival material pertaining to this credit union is available in the Dutch-Canadian Papers collection of the MHSO in the Archives of Ontario (MU 9406, SER 058-042, MSR 0394).

62 During an interview in 1989, we went over the list of all former board members and supervisory or credit committees. The subsequent change in proportions was later confirmed through a conversation with several Christian Reformed members.

63 I interviewed or spoke to several of them, in different localities.

64 Official approval from the Catholic clergy came in 1955 when Father Lannoye, the Canadian pastor of a parish with Dutch immigrants, addressed an open letter to all Dutch Catholics in the region, urging them to support the credit union. In 1956, A.N. Noordam agreed to act as an official representative and credit union promoter in Weston, which was the Christian Reformed community's focal point in the Toronto region; and in 1959 the Reformed Church in America's support was assured when the Rev. Van Kuiken arranged to have his church guarantee loans given to new immigrants who did not yet have any collateral. From *notulen* (minutes) of board meetings of DUCA, April 16, 1956.

65 Photocopies of this and other papers were given to me by someone I interviewed. The incident is also mentioned in the 1971 minutes of board meetings of DUCA, located in their head office in North York.

66 Many orthodox Calvinists did not feel comfortable with the secular ideology fostered by the DCA and many core members of DUCA. They particularly objected to the bringing of well-known Dutch cabaret performers. Based on several conversations or interviews with such members in Toronto.

67 Actually the strongest opponent of opening a bar following the Annual Meeting was a secular man who grew up in the socialist youth movement in Amsterdam.

68 I often overheard these and other such comments while I was growing up, as well as during recent fieldwork in the Toronto area.

Chapter 16

1 Many Dutch-Canadians shied away from government funding and the control that went with it. For example, the Woodstock theatre group (see chap. 11) refused to join a Dutch cultural club to be eligible to receive government assistance. Even under multiculturalism, towards the end of the 1970s, operating costs were generated from a combination of private sector sponsorship and the sale of dance tickets and liquor.

2 The information in this chapter is based on numerous interviews with members of clubs and organizations. My fieldnote file contains 384 separate entries on this topic. In addition, I examined numerous club bulletins either given to me during interviews or housed in the MHSO at the Archives of Ontario.

3 The same word in Dutch (*club*) has a slightly broader set of connotations, ranging from "association" (*vereniging*) to "gang" (*troepje*).

4 I asked various club members to do a rough calculation of the breakdown of their membership in term of religious affiliation or background. Although the first reaction was that they would normally not discuss religious affiliation, when asked to think about it, the replies were fairly consistent. Many active

club members would say, "Now that I think about it, most of the people I know in the club are Catholics." Not only were the replies fairly consistent, but they were consistent with a rough head count I did of the religious background of all the club people I interviewed, and of all club founders and executive members in my much longer file of names obtained from various sources.

5 For example, in its heyday three quarters of the members of the Guelph Holland Canada Club had steady jobs while the rest were owners of small businesses. Interview with Charles Indewey, Guelph, April 17, 1989. None of the university professors at Guelph had anything to do with this club, although a physician trained in the Netherlands did take part in some activities.

6 When I did my fieldwork between 1988 and 1993, I found women in charge of Dutch or mixed Dutch-Belgian clubs in Toronto, St. Catharines, Ottawa, Stratford and Kingston. For the only woman founder of a club in Sarnia, see fieldnote interlude nos. 10.2 and 13.3.

7 In the mid-1950s, some of the same men who played soccer also organized *kaats* tournaments if they were of Frisian descent (see chap. 10).

8 The Canadian Women's Institute occasionally sponsored special events for newly arrived Dutch immigrants. In conducting interviews, various Dutch-Canadian women who first landed in farms or small villages (near Chatham and Uxbridge, and in Onondaga near Brantford) mentioned being invited to join or take part in activities of the Women's Institutes. On at least one occasion I heard about, a specifically ethnic or Dutch-related event was set up.

9 Several Dutch engineers in Peterborough also founded a *vereniging* in the early 1950s.

10 This umbrella organization was started in 1964 by the same group of middle-class people referred to in chapter 12. Several Reformed churches joined the *Centrum*, which held monthly get-togethers, and coordinated charitable activities. A proposal for an actual building for the Centre never came to fruition.

11 These priests also ran a youth centre located on Kent Street, in downtown London, called St. Willibrord Club (like the credit union). Rural youth clubs were Dutch offshoots of the Roman Catholic Regis clubs. Married couples in Middlesex county joined St. Joseph's Club, which still exists today.

12 Young couples did not want to listen to lectures on sex and morality in a club context, or to start dances with prayers.

13 Interview with a former executive member of the Stratford Benelux Club.

14 Since the Dutch language was initially used both for church services and other public events, people had no difficulty finding someone with whom to speak the same language or dialect.

15 We have already seen how even nationalistic Frisians held separate *kaats* tournaments (either on Sundays or Saturdays) prior to 1978 (see chap. 10).

16 See Dutch Canadian Culture Club File, in Dutch Canadian Papers, Archives of Ontario, MHSO, SER. 058-129, MSR # 3421.

17 While several hundred people showed up at a St. Nick's party or evening concerts, the dues-paying membership was small. In the mid-1960s, the club amalgamated with the Christian Burial Society, although the club itself was never officially incorporated. An official typed list for 1966 shows 31 members. By the early 1970s it had ceased to function.

18 These bands were still performing for Dutch-Canadian audiences in the 1990s. See reference to Roly Klasen in an article by Wim van Duyn in

"Dutch-Canadian News," a section of the *De Nederlandse Courant*, February 25, 1992, p. 7.

19 Usually such institutions stated that all surplus revenues collected should go to worthy charitable causes.

20 The moving force behind the idea was Simon Theeboom, a contractor who was to oversee the construction.

21 The association was legally constituted as a corporation, in which members had the option of obtaining "shares" worth a dollar per hour of labour. Thirty volunteers worked a total of 6,439 hours, with some skilled craftsmen working close to 1,000 hours each.

22 *Dutch Canadian Society of London & District Incorporated, Silver Anniversary: 1960 to 1985*, a booklet edited by Ted Smeenk, Sr.

23 Only two club members were credit union executives (see chap. 15). John Strijbosch, who later become the general manager of St. Willibrord, lived outside London at the time of the club's founding. Although he never had much to do with the DCS, John did establish a co-operative-owned clubhouse in Arkona, which he named Taxandria—after a Celtic tribe that once inhabited the southern Netherlands. The Taxandria Club served as a gathering place for Dutch-Canadian, and non-Dutch, rural people, and the club still hosts huge wedding receptions and anniversary celebrations. However, unlike the London club, which joined the London Folk Arts Council, Taxandria was never defined as an ethnic organization.

24 One of their presidents did all of the bookings and paperwork together with his wife, with the proceeds going to the Society.

25 Together with the Leenders, he organized the Mariahout reunions in the 1980s (see chap. 10). Originally from a farm background, he was trained as a tool-and-die maker and became a jack-of-all-trades and entrepreneur in Canada. His outgoing personality also made him an ideal organizer. I did two interviews with Bill Brouwers, in Burlington on June 20, and in his home near Bronte on June 21, 1989.

26 They held a dance, which was a big success. However, the Christian Reformed people who took part were not interested in holding another dance where liquor was sold. The Calvinists were subsequently outvoted and left the organization.

27 Its set-up was similar to the earlier Charity Agency, but a new constitution stipulated that Bill Brouwers was to act as chief organizer. The DCEC also organized the first Dutch-Canadian queen contest.

28 Guelph, Brampton, Drayton, Kitchener, Barrie, Peterborough, Belleville, Kingston, Galt, Scarborough, Thunder Bay, Sudbury, Sault Ste. Marie, Pembroke and Petawawa. There was also a club chapter across the border, in Buffalo. Already existing clubs, such as the Dutch Canadian Society of London and the Stratford Benelux Club, became affiliated as a way of getting access to charter flights. The DCEC also arranged charter flights for private Dutch clubs, like the one set up in Stoney Creek.

29 Members had to fly via Buffalo, since the Canadian government did not allow direct flights from Toronto to Europe for charters.

30 John Bosch, announcer for the Toronto Dutch radio program, accompanied all DCA passengers, while Bill Brouwers flew back and forth with his own members three times a week. All passengers were given a travel bag with bro-

chures prior to departure. One former member recalled, "they made us feel important."

31 Bill Brouwers arranged Saturday and Wednesday flights for them so they would not have to fly on Sundays. Some orthodox Calvinists with no credit union (and hence DCA connections) joined local chapters of the DCEC to become eligible for charter flights to the Netherlands.

32 The founding members in Oakville had separate business ventures, which provided real profits and not just perks. Together with one of his associates, Bill Brouwers invested money in the private Dutch club in Stoney Creek, which they took over. They subsequently sold the clubhouse (on Battlefield Drive) to the Canadian Legion, making a profit. As Bill put it, "we gambled but we won." There were also kinship connections between the DCEC and Bill's private business: a DCEC associate married Bill's maintenance company superintendent.

33 Milton, Guelph, Hamilton, Brantford, Woodstock and the Golden Triangle Club (Kitchener, Cambridge and Galt). The headquarters for this rival club was also located in Oakville.

34 According to a former member, the technician was well liked and helpful, but sometimes acted as if he "owned" the club.

35 The money collected from members was deposited in a credit union in Milton run by Dutch people (see chap. 15).

36 This affair was reconstructed on the basis of about a half-dozen interviews or conversations with people in Guelph, Scarborough, Burlington, Kitchener and other places. I also found a legal document relating to a countersuit in which the technician (who will remain anonymous) accused other club members of breaking into his office and of breach of character. The technician later ended up spending some time in jail, although some of the people involved in the scam managed to extricate themselves and were never formally charged.

37 The founder and interim president of the Guelph chapter actually did some work as paid assistant to the technician in Oakville. He helped to uncover the plot, but Guelph members were still suspicious of his involvement and voted not to keep him on as their president.

38 Others, including a member from Waterloo who was a close personal friend of the technician, accused the local president and other directors in the head office of unfair treatment in sacking the technician. Legal documents and a lawyer's report regarding the 1970-71 dispute are included in the file of Golden Triangle Dutch Canadian Papers (1965-1978) in MHSO papers, in the Archives of Ontario, F 1405, series 58-161 (MSR 2388, 3734).

39 We came across another example in Sudbury (see chap. 5).

40 Toronto's umbrella organization established a special committee to involve Dutch-Canadians in these celebrations. As a result of their efforts, a maze of hedges (*doolhof*) was planted on Toronto Island. A chronology of this and other events are included in a long poem, written in Dutch, written by members of the Dutch-Canadian Association of Greater Toronto in 1976. See "Ter Herinnering aan 3 April, 1976," located in the archives of the Multicultural Historical Society, on Queens Crescent in Toronto (in a box classified as DUT-003-SPA; this item was not transferred to the Dutch-Canadian collection in the Archives of Ontario).

41 See also VanderMey, *To All Our Children*, p. 424-29.

42 Their initial chair was Dick Gaasenbeek of Hamilton, whom we have met before (see chaps. 14 and 15). Jan Van Bruchem, a member of the Toronto Dutch-Canadian community who later moved to Vancouver (see chap. 11), carried the project to its successful completion.

43 See Dutch Canadian Federation papers, in the Archives of Ontario, MHSO, SER 058-097 (MSR #3394); and J. Lowensteyn, "A Social History of the Dutch in Quebec," MA thesis, Concordia University, 1986, p. 128-29. Meulmeester was also on the board of directors of the DUCA.

44 The geographical breadth and regional divisiveness of Canada presented further obstacles. Dutch-Canadians in Western Canada and other parts of the country were envious of the powerful Dutch Canadian Alliance in Ontario which, in turn, vetoed one of their own members' suggestion to purchase their own plane to fly charters for Dutch people all across Canada. Interview with Dick Gaasenbeek, Dundas, November 27, 1989.

45 The heritage club's 40-odd members also came together to play a Dutch card game (*klaverjassen*) in a friendly atmosphere (*gezellige Hollandse avonden*). Interview with Gerry van Hoorn, Sarnia, June 3, 1991.

46 Its members started folk dancing groups for both juniors and seniors, and established a heritage language program. Their executives sat on the board of directors of the Oshawa Folk Arts Council, and their club received various awards: the President's Trophy for Fiesta Week in 1976, the best float in 1978 and best ethnic float in 1979 and 1981. Interviews with Piet van der Pol, December 11; and with Jan Hendriks, December 12, both in Whitby (1988). I also read through various club bulletins.

47 Interview with Jerry Eyzinga, Brantford, November 14, 1988.

48 Groups of Dutch couples would not only drive a car to a nearby town to visit another Dutch club, but also attended dances hosted by German or Belgian clubs.

49 After a stint of farm work, where he worked side by side with his father, he moved to Guelph, where he delivered bread from door to door, worked for Royal Dairy and was caretaker for the Board of Education until the time of his retirement. Interview with Charles Indewey, Guelph, April 17, 1989.

50 An older brother who spent five years in the navy and became a member of the Canadian Legion arranged to have Charley become a social member. Prior to organizing similar events for the Dutch club, Charley also helped the Knights of Columbus with their dances, although he has no Catholic connections. On the contrary, he occasionally attended a Presbyterian church, although he did not consider himself "a church-going type."

51 Interview with Gerry van Hoorn, Sarnia, June 3, 1991.

52 I attended one club meeting and spoke to several club members. Documents relating to both of these clubs are located in MHSO at the Archives of Ontario. See REF 058-98 and 058-131.

53 The Dutch "village" display run by the Reformed community pulled out altogether when their minister disapproved of the beer tents and the rowdy behaviour that occurred during one festival.

54 The chief organizer and chairman for 17 years was Ralph Spikman, who set up a co-operative feedmill for Dutch farmers in Drayton. When he could no longer organize the Dutch Days, the song books were handed over to a group of Reformed men in Strathroy to organize a "Christian" ethnic reunion in that city.

55 Interview with Ralph Spikman, Guelph, February 26, 1990.

56 Although theoretically open to everyone of Dutch descent, the Dutch Days in Moorefield, Blythe, Strathroy and Stayner were explicitly instituted along "Christian lines" (*op een christelijke grondslag*).

57 Orthodox Calvinists clearly distinguished such Dutch Days from annual summer reunions held for people from specific Dutch regions or provinces (see chap. 10), regardless of the religious make-up of the people attending such regional gatherings. An organizer of the Dutch Days, who also used to attend the annual picnic organized by his brother-in-law for people from the Wieringermeer Polder, referred to that regional reunion as one of "*losse mensen*" (people who are disconnected).

58 Their founding president, Bill Wynen, originally from Mariahout (in Noord Brabant), also served as president of the Milton Dutch-Canadian Country Club for 15 years. He was in charge of the DCCOO for eight years. Representatives from member clubs initially held their business meetings in Bill Wynen's Brown Barrel Restaurant, which is located close to Sheffield. Two clubs (St. Catharines and Sarnia) were qualified members; they only received the minutes of the meetings, but were eligible to provide candidates for their queen contests.

59 For the first 10 years there was enough demand for tickets to cover the costs of their annual banquet and queen pageant. The minutes of their meetings indicate sponsorship by CP Air (which provided free trips to Holland for winning queens) and Amstel beer. The DCCOO also introduced a Dutch-style obstacle race, called a *zeskamp*, twice a year, and there was correspondence with the Dutch consul requesting a greater exposure of their club activities to potential visitors from the Netherlands.

60 Such class tensions are revealed in some of the minutes of meetings of the DCCOO. According to their records, its executive resolved "to forget becoming a member of the Toronto group of businessmen" in 1981. From handwritten minutes of meetings of DCCOO, April 27, 1981 (shown to me in the Brown Barrel Restaurant).

61 The Association's membership included four different Reformed denominations, a Dutch priest to represent the Dutch Roman Catholic community, the Dutch radio program, DUCA, *De Nederlandse Courant* and a folklore group.

62 The Association mustered enough people to take part in Toronto's multicultural Caravan (with an Amsterdam exhibit) on only a few occasions. An article in *De Nederlandse Courant* (September 7, 1988), p. 11, "No Dutch," lamented the absence of Dutch and Belgian representatives in Toronto's multicultural council.

63 Note from Klaas Stoker, from the Entertainment Committee, in the July 1987 issue of the "News Bulletin" (centrefold).

64 On several occasions Dutch clubs tried to put on dances for both young and old, but the combination did not work. Another reason commonly cited for the drop-off in club membership was the increasingly strict regulation of alcohol permits and the growing awareness of the dangers of drinking and driving.

65 They even have parallel sessions for those preferring to play according to either the Amsterdam or Rotterdam rules. Some card groups are still affiliated with Dutch clubs, while others are linked only to their own federation (Klaverjassers United).

66 Those interested in folk dancing tend to maintain their membership in cultural organizations because access to financial assistance from the government requires an affiliation with a broader ethnic association.

67 See Lowensteyn, "A Social History of the Dutch in Quebec," p. 134. The Dutch-Canadian clubs that have survived tend to organize activities for different age groups and people with different tastes and interests. The success of such clubs also hinges on the leadership abilities of a handful of people who have taken on the task of keeping such clubs or associations alive over the years.

68 With a total population of less than 10,000 people, it is technically a rural population centre (see chap. 6), although the couple of hundred people of Dutch descent who live there represent close to 4 percent of its inhabitants.

69 See "Club The Dutch Tulip: A proposed Club for people of Dutch heritage headquartered in Bradford, Ontario," a photocopied report, 1989. I attended their inaugural meeting on March 16, 1990, and spoke to various members and the newly elected president of their club. He had recruited former members of the old club (many of Catholic background) and couples from a wide range of ages who belonged to nearby Christian Reformed congregations.

70 It was attended by representatives from Dutch clubs in Hamilton and Oshawa, and the Dutch-Canadian Association of Toronto. Their second-generation Dutch-Canadian part-time mayor also joined in.

71 Apart from their small numerical base, their membership was too diverse: prewar, immediate postwar and more recent Dutch immigrants, orthodox Calvinists and Catholics and a wide range of ages. Their dispositions were too discordant to generate a stable social structure.

72 The Clinton *klompenfeest* has not been held since 1993.

73 Their 1992 program included a grandstand show featuring the Dykehoppers, a carnival band affiliated with the Dutch Canadian Society of London; the Brabanders, a folk dance group of seniors from the Strathroy area; and folk dancers from various localities. I attended this event on May 14, 1992, and examined several back issues of former printed program booklets. See also write up and photos by Wim van Duyn in *De Nederlandse Courant*, 37, 12 (June 20, 1992): 15.

74 They have also featured the Central Band of the Canadian Air Force, and the Royal Canadian Mounted Police have put on performances. A longstanding Dutch band which took part, *Hollands Glorie*, includes a non-Dutch member, Roy Adams, the former mayor of St. Catharines. See also VanderMey, *To All Our Children*, p. 482-83.

75 Bob Campbell had sporadic contact with Dutch immigrants when he returned home after the War. His wife's family, who owned a farm, sponsored several Dutch families, and he met more when he opened up a men's clothing store. Interview with Bob Campbell, Clinton, May 14, 1992.

76 An immigrant craftsman with Dutch training, he had been recruited to teach home economics and shop at the local high school.

77 When the *klompenfeest* started, two thirds of the organizing committee was Dutch-Canadian, but by 1992 the involvement of non-Dutch organizers was down to about a fifth.

78 In reality, their religious counterparts in rural Ontario tend to keep a low profile during big secular public occasions. This impression was further confirmed during a subsequent conversation with someone not of Dutch

background who married into a Dutch family that belongs to the Christian Reformed Church. One member of that family was involved in organizing the *klompenfeest*, but other members of her congregation kept a low profile and did not quite "feel at home" during the festivities.

79 Joint interview with John Andela and Frank Meevis, Peterborough, May 13, 1989.

80 The program included a Dutch carnival band flown in from the city of Nijmegen, and a dance, all in the local arena. A variety of other activities, such as an old-timers' soccer tournament and a bicycle tour, were held outdoors. Additional attractions, similar to those that can be seen at other multicultural gatherings, included a wooden-shoe carver, a Dutch accordion player from Pickering and De Hagenaar, a Dutch Concert Street Organ, which was bought and restored by Franklin Foly from Belleville, Ontario. Its non-Dutch owner is one of many people who travel the festival circuit throughout the province. See write up in *De Nederlandse Courant*, June 7, 1989, p. 10, 15.

81 Members of the Peterborough Association who are first-generation immigrants represent almost 10 percent of the approximately 1,000 Dutch immigrant families who arrived in the region since 1945. Their participation rate, at least during the festival's duration, is thus higher than places like Guelph or Kitchener, which have larger Dutch-Canadian populations. One organizer told me that "everyone wanted to become Dutch again."

82 I had a long conversation with him in his office in Burlington, July 12, 1990.

83 Full-page ads for a KLM-sponsored golf tournament, an evening of Brabant-style entertainment, and a Dutch-Indonesian evening started appearing. To play down the commercial aspect, the name Dutch Heritage Inc. appeared in small print in publicity posters.

84 He told me about his plans during an long conversation in his office in Burlington in July of 1990. The subsequent events were reconstructed through reading his newspaper and various conversations with other people who had dealing with him, or who attended various festivals or other events he coordinated.

85 Poor turnout for that event alone meant a loss of over $50,000. See "Hamilton Holland Festival: Cultural Success, Financial Failure," *De Nederlandse Courant*, 36, 12 (June 26, 1991): 7.

86 Some club organizers did not like the commercial aspects of Dutch Heritage Inc., which reminded them of similar private ventures in the 1950s. The Dutch-Canadian Association of Greater Toronto did not join forces with Dutch Heritage Inc. at all, and some affiliated clubs later broke off ties to proceed on their own—just like they had done earlier. A modest version of this enterprise (including the newspaper) continues. One of its more successful yearly events is a Canadian version of the Dutch *Avondvierdaagse* (a four-day walk).

87 Calgary has a similar alumni reunion for several Dutch universities. Most of them are geologists who came to Canada in the 1950s and 1960s.

88 He had already travelled extensively and at one point owned a shoe factory in Zaire, Africa. After being in Canada for several years, Ben again went into business for himself. Interview with Ben Hendriks, Oakville, June 20, 1989.

89 I attended a gathering at a farm in Embro on June 10, 1990, at which Ben Hendriks received a medal of honour (naming him member of the order of *ridder van oranje*, or Knights of Orange) from the Dutch consul (see chap. 4).

Their organization includes several Indos who belonged to the Netherlands' former colonial armed forces.

90 Interview with Mr. Roosegaarde-Bisschop, Brantford, October 13, 1988.

91 By the early 1990s, that organization, whose Canadian members also use the English name Dutch Veterans, was the most active Dutch-Canadian association in Ontario, with four divisions (Chatham, London, Hamilton and Toronto).

92 Like the Dutch Marine Corps veterans, their membership is drawn from a wide variety of backgrounds although they sometimes have difficulty recruiting more traditional members of the Reformed community. This I was told by several members who are themselves Reformed.

93 He wanted his members to show their support for Ukrainian- and Estonian-Canadians lobbying for recognition of their homelands (prior to the collapse of the former Soviet Union).

94 While proud to wear the blazers and pins indicating their affiliation with the *Bond*, Dutch-Canadians disliked the militaristic implications of wearing full army uniforms during parades. They also rejected the formality associated with the Dutch style of conducting business meetings.

95 Dutch-Canadian women were worried that the *Bond* might give their husbands an excuse to spend more time away from home, "carousing with the boys."

96 Potential recruits to the *Bond* felt uneasy about the strident tone of the numerous letters that their official representative and his wife kept sending to newspapers across Ontario. The first sign of contention appeared during the *oranjefeest* held in honour of the Dutch Queen's Canadian visit in 1988. Roosegaarde-Bisschop and several *Bond* members wanted to appear in full militaristic regalia, but the Dutch Marine veterans objected.

97 At one point, someone whispered to the reporter that he had perhaps come too early, and that he should not take notes on what was being said. A woman sitting at the back made a comment about females being excluded from the debate. Her neighbour replied in English, "Yes, we could do this a lot better." The reporter only took mental notes and did not mention any of the disagreements in the article for the *De Nederlandse Courant*, July 15, 1989, p. 9.

98 While the ballots were being counted, several people sitting on the podium told some funny stories to break the ice. The stories all started in Dutch and ended in English.

99 The list of newly elected candidates was later forwarded to the head office for ratification, resulting in the final official recognition of a *gewestraad* (regional council) for Canada with four autonomous chapters or divisions (*afdelingen*).

100 My translation of a comment made in a conversation (in Dutch) by a member of the *Bond* who lives in Scarborough. Since the time this book was written, VOMI (*Vereniging Oud Militairen Indiëgangers*), another Canadian chapter of Dutch veterans who served in the former Dutch East Indies between 1945 and 1951, was formed. Their first meeting in Port Perry brought 60 people together. See *De Nederlandse Courant*, Christmas 1993, p. 11.

101 The vision of an organization giving greater exposure to Dutch and Flemish literature, and other aspects of Netherlandic culture, was the brain child of Christopher Levenson of Carleton University. An English professor with an interest in Dutch literature, he placed a notice in a new journal of comparative literature in 1969, suggesting steps to make Dutch texts available to both university and public libraries. His initiative resulted in the founding of CAANS

in St. John's, Newfoundland, in 1971. See Joan Magee, "CAANS: An Overview of the First Decade, 1971-1981," *Canadian Journal of Netherlandic Studies*, 3, 1 and 2 (Fall 1981 and Spring 1982): 3-7.

For the next eight years, CAANS was kept alive by a handful of supporters, first in Ottawa and Kingston and later in Windsor, which became the organization's nerve centre. Sporadic issues of a newsletter were sent out across Canada and the membership grew from 75 to a couple of hundred, with a corresponding increase in attendance at the annual meetings. Their efforts culminated in the first issue of the *Canadian Journal of Netherlandic Studies* in 1979.

102 CAANS is affiliated with the Learned Societies, which hold a yearly conference at some Canadian campus. Two key members not of Dutch descent are Basil Kingstone of the French Department at Windsor and Joan Magee, a librarian at the same university. Together with Hendrika Ruger, Joan Magee set up the Netherlandic Press in Windsor, which publishes works of fiction by well-known Canadian writers of Dutch descent (some of whom had already received awards as "Canadian" writers).

103 However, few people who belong to local chapters opt to join the national organization, nor are they likely to attend the national meetings.

104 In Ontario, local chapters in St. Catharines, London and Kingston never got off the ground.

105 My version of events was pieced together from various sources, including conversations with members of the national executive (of which I was then a member), as well as people in Toronto. For a report on the annual meeting of the local (Toronto) CAANS in 1992, see article and photos by Wim van Duyn in *De Nederlandse Courant*, June 20, 1992, p. 8. In 1994, after a period of inactivity, the old members started their own local chapter again.

106 They recruited members among former students or Dutch-Canadians who worked in the library, to attend meetings, see a film or hear an out-of-town speaker.

107 Remkes Kooistra, who served as the chaplain for Reformed students at the University of Guelph, and later at the University of Waterloo.

108 The Waterloo chapter is not what the Dutch would call *gereformeerd*, since both executive and regular members include people with no connection to the Reformed community. Nonetheless, at least two or three people refused to renew their membership due to a strong Reformed presence. I acted as their local secretary for a couple of years, and had an opportunity to talk to several founding members, as well as to read previous minutes of all local meetings. However, with an aging membership, attendance was rapidly declining after 1996.

109 I see this as a Dutch-Canadian equivalent of the strong division between informal and formal ("written") Dutch in the Netherlands (see chap. 3).

110 People of Dutch background, including CAANS members, always expect to be served free coffee and cookies halfway through any public presentation. At the same time, Dutch-Canadians occasionally provide generous contributions to cover the cost of renting a hall or showing a film.

111 For a European Dutch perspective on Dutch-Canadian organizations, see the article "De functie van de Nederlandse verenigingen" (no author) in the travel magazine *Elders*, 1986 (1), p. 41-48.

Chapter 17

1 The units I visited in different towns were all furnished in a typical Dutch fashion. Those homes which serve meals also prepare traditional Dutch dishes, even if their Dutch-Canadian occupants had already become used to a more Canadianized diet. Personal communication from Joanne van Dijk, whose elderly mother lives in such a home.
2 These much older people had rarely achieved fluency in English.
3 A small sum of money came from the funds left over after the DCA got out of the travel business (see chap. 15).
4 Members of the Free Reformed denomination set up a 70-unit home, called Elim Villa, in Waterdown around the same time. See appendix in Joanne G. van Dijk, "Ethnic Identity Retention and Social Support: A Comparative Analysis of First-Generation Elderly Dutch-Canadian Catholics and Calvinists," MA thesis in sociology, University of Guelph, 1990.
5 Much of the music piped into various wall outlets is of a religious, Protestant nature.
6 One volunteer worker whom I interviewed mentioned that a group of Catholic occupants sat together at what the Calvinists called the *roomse tafel* ("Roman table").
7 He came to Canada when he was a teenager and married an Italian woman.
8 Although the congregation she belongs to is becoming Canadianized, she is proud of her Dutch heritage. Another female board member, an accountant, is a Catholic and an active member in the Kingston Dutch Canadian Club. I interviewed both of these women, in Kingston, on December 20 and 21, 1989, and spoke to various residents of the home (one of whom is also a board member) in the home itself.
9 Approximately a third of the original organizing committee were members of the Christian Reformed community; another third were members of the Kingston Dutch Canadian Club, which has both Catholic and non-Catholic members; and the rest were Dutch-Canadians whose only connection with each other was their concern for elderly parents.
10 Initially about a third of their units were rented to residents with no Dutch connection, including a young couple (recent immigrants) who were about to have a baby. One of the more recent residents is a retired Dutch Jewish couple from Montreal. He was a tailor.
11 She pointed out that the home would present an opportunity to witness their faith. Indeed, after the home was set up, the Christian Reformed members initiated the custom of hosting a reception for all residents after they returned from church.
12 Even a graduate student writing a paper on the Christian Reformed community incorrectly made this assumption and included the Kingston home in a list of "Reformed" homes in that paper.
13 Indeed, his involvement and interest in the Kingston Dutch Canadian Club is exceptional for Dutch professionals educated in the Netherlands (see interlude 14.2).
14 The consul was particularly concerned that the Dutch flag must hang beside and not below the Canadian one, following standard diplomatic protocol.
15 From an interview (in English), with a member of the Kingston Dutch Canadian Club, December 1989.

16 Interview with Wilma Oosterhuis, Arsnorsveld (Holland Marsh), September 19, 1989.
17 Interview with Dorothy Middel, Bradford, September 14, 1989.
18 In collecting life histories from first-generation immigrants, people would frequently slip into Dutch without prodding as soon their recollections went back into time.
19 Even when non-Dutch friends are mentioned, they are more likely to be other European immigrants (e.g., German or Italian) rather than native-born Canadians.
20 This figure represents the average of the town itself, where 5 percent of the population is Dutch-Canadian, and the surrounding countryside with over 7 percent.
21 Based on an interview with John Hendrikx, then president of the Leisure Club in Park Hill, Park Hill, December 16, 1988.
22 By 1990 they boasted 10 dancing pairs. Although they stopped dancing in 1996, they made an appearance to show their costumes and demonstrate collected antiques at the inauguration of the Dutch exhibit held that year at the Lambton Heritage Museum (close to Grand Bend). A short write up of their history and their founder, Maria Toonen (who had already passed away in 1989), formed part of that exhibit.
23 Younger immigrants have also gone back to the Netherlands. For a report on return migrants, see J.H. Elich and P.W. Blauw, *... en toch terug* (een onderzoek naar de retourmigratie van Nederlanders uit Australië, Nieuw-Zeeland en Canada), report from Erasmus University, Faculteit der Economische Wetenschappen (Vakgroep Sociologie), Rotterdam (November 1981).
24 See also "Terug naar Nederland," an article written by Michiel Willems for a Dutch newspaper, which was then reprinted with additional comments as "Remigratie met Bas Opdenkelder," *De Nederlandse Courant*, Christmas 1993, p. 23. Many of these return migrants had problems adjusting.
25 See "Reflections of H.B. Poesiat," with foreword by Stephen Riggins, a 1983 catalogue of pictures printed in Toronto by Schryers' Graphics Inc. I interviewed both of them in their apartment in Toronto in 1991. See also an article in the *De Nederlandse Courant*, March 26, 1994, p. 18.
26 He died in March of 1994.
27 During the war, he refused to register with the German authorities, thus becoming part of the underground resistance. This meant he could not buy paint supplies or exhibit his work. His creative talents were also constrained both during and after the War, when he made his living drawing cartoons for three regional newspapers belonging to different pillars; he was supposed to satirize current events, but was not allowed to antagonize either right or left. At that point in their career, they lived in the Dutch town of Woerden. As a commercial artist, he drew cartoons for the *Woerdense Dagblad, de Rijn* and the *Bodengraafse Dagblad*. See the March 26, 1994 article in *De Nederlandse Courant*.
28 See "Reflections," p. 5.
29 At that time, they started living in the High Park area of Toronto. Based on an interview in their apartment, Toronto, May 8, 1991.
30 That circle included Albert Franck, a prewar Dutch immigrant artist of Jewish background who had almost no connections with postwar Dutch immigrants. For a description of Albert Franck's background and references to many of his

Dutch habits, see Harold Town, *Albert Franck, Keeper of the Lanes* (Toronto: McClelland and Stewart Ltd., 1974), p. 9, 20, 22. Much later, the Poesiats became acquainted with Franck's widow (his second wife, a Canadian).

31 They also joined DUCA, which enabled them to meet other educated, middle-class, left-wing Dutch immigrants in a largely Dutch-speaking environment. Henk and Leida later put on more plays and made presentations to CAANS.

32 In talking in Dutch about his Reformed friends, he described them as at least "understanding" (*begrijpend*) and "principled" (*principieel*).

Chapter 18

1 Describing a culture in this anthropological sense can be compared to drawing a map of possible routes which people may follow, even though such a "map" has no existence for them. The anthropologist's map "may make explicit the implicit parameters within which agents make their strategic choices." According to Pierre Bourdieu, agents (people) make strategic choices in terms of which routes to follow. See Robbins, *The Work of Pierre Bourdieu*, p. 83.

2 Focusing on the commonalities of a cohort of postwar Dutch immigrants does not preclude looking at the more circumscribed dispositions shared by any subgroup (or 'class') of that cohort whose members share the same occupation, gender, age or region.

3 This informant used the crude expression, "the Germans stick together like shit." Actually social science studies indicate that the Germans have assimilated as much (if not more) than the Dutch.

4 The discrepancy between values (or beliefs) and actions (observable behaviour) is a central theme in Robert Murphy's writings. See his *Dialectics of Social Life* (New York: Columbia University Press, 1971), p. 5.

5 This is one of the central themes of Schama's *The Embarrassment of Riches*.

6 Interview in Dutch (for newspaper article), with Fred Reinders, Brampton, October 31, 1988. See also, "F.J. Reinders: Een traditie van bouwkunde," *De Nederlandse Courant*, December 7, 1988, p. 5.

7 In return, non-Dutch Canadians who marry "Dutch" spouses may feel "excluded" or "uneasy" in Dutch-Canadian company, or have a hard time adapting to their in-laws.

8 See both Ganzevoort's *A Bittersweet Land*; and VanderMey's *And the Swamp Flourished*.

9 Some do not even feel a lingering loyalty to the Dutch state or its monarchy.

10 See VanderMey, *To All Our Children*, p. 433.

11 Grant Cassidy, "Multiculturalism and Dutch-Canadian Ethnicity in Metropolitan Toronto," in Ganzevoort and Boekelman, *Dutch Immigration to North America*, p. 204.

12 Gerard Bonekamp, "Onder Ons," *De Krant*, October 1991, p. 2.

13 Letter from P.H. Aten to Bonekamp, in *De Krant*, November 16, 1991, p. 16. I suspect, but cannot confirm, that this "oddball" writer might be an expatriate or someone who had lived in many other countries, rather than a postwar immigrant to Canada. If that is the case, the heated exchange of letters that followed would represent a clash of quite different dispositions moulded by constrasting life trajectories.

14 See *De Krant*, January 1992, p. 16, 22; and February 1992, p. 18.

15 My analysis of this aspect of Dutch-Canadian discourse represents what anthropologists call a semiotic analysis, which Bourdieu would still classify as 'objectivist.'
16 From an interview with John Roks at his home, Delaware, May 3, 1990.
17 A conversation with a Dutch-Canadian truck driver in his home, Guelph, March 27, 1990.
18 Indeed, this is now an option in Canada's population census.
19 Interview with Bill Winters, on his farm near Renfrew (Horton township), July 1, 1991.
20 Even the president of the Dutch-Canadian Association of Greater Toronto qualified his enthusiasm for his largely symbolic Dutch heritage in the following statement: "You can see that I have my *klompen* [wooden shoes] at the front door and my windmill in the back yard, but when I walk out I leave them behind. I believe in integrating into Canadian society. During our last bus tour I said that they should change our name from 'Dutch-Canadian' to 'Canadian Dutch.'" From an interview with Martin van Denzen at his home, North York (Metropolitan Toronto), May 9, 1991.
21 I count people who were born in the Netherlands but spent most of their childhood in Canada as part of this category of second-generation immigrants.
22 See Harry A. Van Belle, "From Religious Pluralism to Cultural Pluralism: Continuity and Change among the Reformed Dutch in Canada," a paper presented at a conference entitled "The Dutch in North America: Their Immigration and Cultural Continuity," held at Middelburg, Netherlands, June 7-10, 1989.
23 The term "Dutch" is but one of many possible ethnic labels, such as "Italian," "Polish," "Armenian" or "Jewish," since most people in Canada are ultimately descended from some "other." When interacting with English-speaking descendants of other European nationalities, Dutch-Canadians might emphasize that all Canadians except for the native peoples are ultimately "immigrants," in order to counteract status claims concerning the main charter groups (see also chap. 20).

    However, in other contexts a reference to *Dutchness* as part of a broader European heritage can become a way of underlining distinctions based on racial categories. For the development of a more generic European identity, as part of a strategy of middle-class whites in America, see Alba, *Ethnic Identity*, p. 47-74. In his study of the Capital region, where the Dutch have been an ethnic group of long residence, a large percentage of people dropped their Dutch identity altogether (among a choice of various identities as a result of increasing intermarriage in the past). Alba relates the ability to talk about one's European ethnic ancestry as one component of 'cultural capital,' reinforced through formal education. He thus uses one of Bourdieu's key concepts, as introduced into American sociology by Paul DiMaggio, who is also cited by Alba (p. 58).
24 Ethnic distinction can also linger on as a means of preserving ethnic boundaries in specific social situations, as when the "Irish" celebrate St. Patrick's day by wearing green while pub-hopping, or the "Germans" wear funny hats during Oktoberfest. A Dutch equivalent in the United States are the tulip festivals in Michigan. The proportion of third-generation Dutch- Canadians is still too small for this phenomenon to become part of an established "Canadian" tradition.
25 A conversation with a young woman behind the counter of a Kentucky Fried Chicken outlet, just outside Forest (Lambton county), May 3, 1990.

26 Based on an interview with Diana Brebner, Ottawa, August 29, 1991. She is also part of a broader and more public Dutch-Canadian presence as an author in several anthologies of poetry published by the Netherlandic Press of Windsor.

27 For a historical study showing higher rates of ethnic assimilation among Catholics than orthodox Calvinists in North America, see Y. Schreuder, "Ethnic Solidarity and Assimilation among Dutch Protestants and Catholics in the State of Wisconsin, 1850-1905," a paper presented at the conference "The Dutch in North America: Immigration and Cultural Continuity," held at Middelburg, Netherlands, June 7-10, 1989.

28 An example of such a new (more "Canadian") use of the label "Dutch" comes from the Holland Marsh, where I have met several second-, third- and in one case, fourth-generation Canadians of Dutch descent who still refer to themselves as "Dutch." This new meaning of "Dutch" struck home during an interview with a woman living in the Marsh who had come to Canada as a young girl, with her parents, in the 1920s. She did not shop at a Dutch delicatessen run by a Dutch couple from her own Christian Reformed church, nor did she have any emotional attachment to the Dutch royal family. At one point she recounted how "the immigrants" (from Holland) arrived to the Marsh after the World War Two. Yet later during the interview, she commented, "But you know we Dutch can be quite clannish." Interview with a woman in Ansnorveld (Holland Marsh), county of York, in her home, September 19, 1989.

29 I have heard about similar comments being made in Ontario agricultural colleges (e.g., Ridgetown or Kemptville) which have a high percentage of Dutch-Canadian students.

30 Interview with Professor Dick Kranendonk, Redeemer College, Ancaster, regional municipality of Hamilton-Wentworth, May 10, 1989. He suggested that the non-Dutch students acted as a kind of "mirror" that reflected the Dutch image projected by the Dutch-Canadian students.

31 Based on a conversation with Bill Ubbens, Rexdale (Metropolitan Toronto), September 2, 1989.

32 His sons later set up businesses in what is now Egmondville (near Seaforth, Ontario). See John Martens, *Making Waves* (Waterloo: Waterloo Printing, 1988), p. 23-25. This book, edited by John Henry Mellor, contains many articles earlier published in various local newspapers.

33 Dutch-American scholars have written about a similar role played by the Dutch at various times in the history of the U.S. Their works, which are often reprinted in the *Windmill Post*, the English-language supplement of the *Windmill Herald*, are reinforcing a process of ethnogenesis among Dutch-Canadian readers.

34 This would hold for the case of Samuel Holland (see chap. 2).

Chapter 19

1 E.g., Canada Cup, Inc., set up by Tom Thomas; Nautavac, the rug-cleaning rental firm built up by the Nauta family of Stouffville; and Hudson Movers, Inc., owned by Henry Van Remortel. Other successful Dutch-born entrepreneurs include Cornelius de Kort of Kobe Fabrics Inc., one the biggest importers of quality fabric in Ontario; and Anne De Boer of De Boer's furniture. We came across the name Voortman, of Voortman's Cookies, in chapter 14.

2 See "Making an Impact," chap. 24 of VanderMey, *To All Our Children*. Any time now, a fully illustrated "who's who" of Dutch-Canadians, entitled *The Dutch Touch in Ontario*, will appear (Toronto: Mol Publishing, forthcoming).

3 See Reitz, *The Survival of Ethnic Groups*, p. 162.

4 See John Berry et al., eds., *Multiculturalism and Ethnic Attitudes in Canada* (Ottawa: Ministry of Supply and Services, 1977), p. 106.

5 Peter Pineo, "The Social Standing of Ethnic and Racial Groupings," in Jay E. Goldstein and Rita M. Bienvenue, eds., *Ethnicity and Ethnic Relations in Canada* (Toronto: Butterworths, 1980), p. 189, 196.

6 From Table 1 in Porter's *Vertical Mosaic*, reproduced and discussed in A. Gordon Darroch, "Another Look at Ethnicity, Stratification and Social Mobility in Canada," in ibid., p. 208-09.

7 In 1970, 23.8 percent of all Canadians were rural. Other more rural-oriented ethnic groups, with percentages only slightly lower than the Dutch on a national level, were Scandinavians, Germans and Russians. See Anderson and Frideres, *Ethnicity in Canada*, p. 175 (chart 3).

8 This is true even for counties like Dufferin, not mentioned in chapter 6. See Stan Barrett, *Paradise* (Toronto: University of Toronto Press, 1994), p. 176. Dutch farm children also form a majority in 4-H clubs in places where Dutch farmers predominate. For example, in Bosanquet township, they constituted between 80 and 90 percent of the 4-H group in Thedford throughout the 1970s. Interview with Miep Verkley, July 8, 1996.

9 One could easily write a "who's who" of Dutch-Canadians in Ontario agriculture. For example, Barend Flinkhert, a now-retired first-generation Dutch immigrant in Drayton, had one of the largest dairy quotas in the province. See VanderMey, *To All Our Children*, p. 457. Dutch-Canadian agriculturalists have also done well in tender fruits and vegetables. There are even prominent Dutch-Canadians in the grape-growers' association, one of whom, Peter Buis, won the "grape king" award in 1987. See article by John Schofield inside the front cover of the Bulletin of Club the Netherlands (October 1987). Prominent full-time commercial farmers of recent Dutch descent are found all over Ontario.

10 See Philip D. Keddie and Julius A. Mage, *Southern Ontario, Atlas of Agriculture (Contemporary Patterns and Recent Changes)*, Occasional Papers in Geography No. 7 (Guelph: University of Guelph, 1985).

11 Oxford county ranks among the highest in numbers of rural Dutch-Canadians, and is only surpassed by Middlesex county (the area around London) and Niagara regional municipality, each of which has well over 2,000 rural Dutch-Canadians (see also chap. 6).

12 For example, see booklet by Everett Briggs, *The Challenge of Achievement*, published by the Ontario Milk Marketing Board, 1991.

13 In Perth county, almost half the members of the Association of Pork Producers have Dutch surnames, and Dutch-Canadian farmers frequently win prizes or receive special recognition. At the 1990 Royal Ontario Winter Fair, both first and second prizes went to Dutch-Canadian hog farmers: one from Woodstock and the other from Lindsay. Conversation with Mr. Maninveld (one of the winners), Pembroke, July 15, 1990.

14 Such observations are consistent with the overall ranking of the Dutch in comparative surveys mentioned earlier in this chapter.

15 Interview with Ben Schuurmanhess, Guelph, October 6, 1988.

16 See "Dutch-Canadians Active in Ontario Municipal Elections," *Windmill Herald*, 34, 698/699 (December 9, 1991): 15. In that election, all three elected councillors in Goderich township were Dutch.

17 Gerry Herrema, who ran a farm near Uxbridge, was elected reeve and then mayor, before becoming chairman of a newly created Durham regional government; Anton Wijtenberg, who used to own a bakery in Ottawa and then moved outside the city to buy a farm, became mayor of Goulbourn and was then elected to chair the Ottawa-Carleton regional government council. Both of these men still had these posts when I interviewed them in 1992 or 1993. In my research I also discovered former or present Dutch-Canadian reeves or mayors in Strathroy (twice), Arkona, Bradford, Osgood, Goulbourn, Chesterville, Kingston, Fruitland, Drayton, Delaware, Westminster, West Nissouri, North Dumphries and Loughborough.

18 Based on the breakdown of politicians whose names appeared in my fieldnotes, there were about an equal number of Roman Catholics, Reformed (orthodox Calvinist) and "others" (including mainstream Protestants affiliated with Canadian denominations). Largely orthodox Dutch Calvinists who run as candidates for the Christian Heritage Party probably have the highest profile in federal electoral campaigns. For a breakdown of Dutch-Canadians who ran in the federal election on 1993 across Canada, see *Windmill Herald*, November 8, 1993, p. 16.

19 I am using the term 'field' in the same way that Bourdieu writes about *champ*, as a type of "force field" in social space with its own "species" of symbolic and cultural capital (see Introduction).

20 van den Hoonaard, *Silent Ethnicity*, p. 67-69. Several musicians born in the Netherlands whom I interviewed in Ontario also came to Canada in this manner and at one point they even had their own credit union called Del Signo. Interview with Fred Rusticus, Windsor, August 31, 1990.

21 I spoke to one who ended up buying up small-town newspapers in Keswick, Sutton, Beaverton and Markham, together with a non-Dutch partner. In 1974 he also teamed up with the Norwegian owner of a newspaper in Port Perry and together they also bought the Uxbridge paper, which they had already been printing since 1960. He came to Canada at the age of 20, but had learned the printing trade before coming from his father who had been a printer and publisher in Deurne, near Eindhoven. Interview with Bill Keyzers, Uxbridge, February 18, 1990.

22 For Bourdieu, the representation any social 'class' (i.e., grouping) is based on distinctions, which act as mechanisms for social differentiation (see Introduction). See also "Distinction," in Robbins, *The Works of Pierre Bourdieu*.

23 Ethnic discrimination is similar to racism, which can be seen as simply a "device" or a "lie" used by some people to oppress others. However, the lie becomes part of social reality and takes on a life of its own. In that case, one cannot simply ignore the "device" because it is a lie; both lie and reality must be examined. See Stephen Steinberg, *The Ethnic Myth* (Boston: Beacon Press, 1989), p. 170-72. Even the analytical distinction between "lie" and "reality" is problematic because the concepts are part of a single social reality in which objective and subjective phenomena are intrinsically interrelated in complimentary fashion (see Introduction).

24 There is a danger that stereotypes will be reinforced, even though such studies are done in the spirit of attenuating inequality. This possibility places a greater

responsibility on social scientists to explain the reasons for differences in average income or overall status among groups, and the mechanisms whereby such inequalities are perpetuated.

25 See Steinberg, *The Ethnic Myth*, p. xiv.

26 My interpretation of the national level statistical analysis as one reflecting an already higher average level of education and income in the country of origin is compatible with the argument presented by Steinberg in his book, *The Ethnic Myth*.

27 For a discussion of the relationship between education of immigrants and subsequent job opportunity and mobility in Canada, see Reitz, *The Survival of Ethnic Groups*, p. 158-62. In the metropolitan census area of Montreal in 1971, 71 percent of those of Dutch origin had from six to 13 years of schooling, compared to 47.4 percent of Italians and 51.1 percent for the Portuguese (Statistics Canada. Special Report No. 6001-00175AC-2B. 1971).

28 Gordon Darroch, "Another Look at Ethnicity," p. 221-22. For a more recent discussion, see Breton et al., *Ethnic Identity and Equality*, p. 4.

29 Interview with John Reinders, on his farm near Moorefield, January 18, 1992.

30 Interview with Luit Miedema, near Waterford, June 12, 1989.

31 The average sale price was $7000. See A.S. Tuinman, *Enige aspecten van de hedendaagse migratie van Nederlanders naar Canada* ('S-Gravenhage: Staatsdrukkerij, 1952), p. 77. Tuinman's figures on success rates were adjusted in a 1956 publication, which indicated that about a quarter of the 16,500 Dutch farm immigrants up to the end of 1955 had bought their own farms. See Abe Tuinman, "The Netherlands-Canadian Migration," *Tijdschrift voor Economische en Sociale Geografie*, 47 1956).

32 This cultural trait not only helped Dutch agrarian immigrants to become more quickly established as independent operators, but also helped them expand operations with a minimum of hired hands. The technical skills and strong family bonds were in turn passed on to the next generation.

33 The first part of the well-known name Frisian-Holstein refers to a Dutch province. Tulips have been associated with Holland for several centuries.

34 One can get a sense of their numerical importance by examining the membership lists of the Flower Association of Canada. Interview with William Vermeer, Grimsby, November 28, 1989.

35 A travel agent who used to include this auction in his tours commented that one could conduct business in Dutch almost as easily as in English at this permanent auction house. Interview with Gerry Van der Kley, Whitby, May 7, 1991.

36 See Hugh Cook, *The Homecoming Man* (Oakville: Mosaic Press, 1989); and Aritha Van Herk, *Judith* (Toronto: McClelland and Stewart, 1978). However, apart from this one novel, the latter writer is not primarily known for her work on either ethnic identity or a farming way of life (see references to her in the chapter on gender).

37 I discovered this during a visit to Essex county in the summer of 1993.

38 See Pierre Bourdieu, "Outline of a Sociological Theory of Art Perception," *International Social Science Journal*, 10 (Winter, 1968): 589-612.

39 A catalogue published on that occasion lists 30 contemporary artists of Netherlandic Heritage now living in Canada. Huibert Sabelis had organized a similar Dutch-Canadian art exhibition in Toronto a few years earlier. For an example of

coverage of other art exhibitions with Dutch connections in the Dutch-Canadian press, see *De Nederlandse Courant*, December 11, 1993, p. 6.

40 The Dutch-Indonesian painter mentioned in chapter 10 developed his artistic career in a Dutch-Canadian ethnic context, where he gained at least part of his reputation. His name appears in the Netherlands Luncheon Club membership booklet, and his art exhibitions have also been announced in the Dutch-Canadian press. See *De Nederlandse Courant*, April 21, 1988, p. 10. Amateur artists in Ontario who are known to Dutch-Canadians in Ontario include Lini Grol, Gerard Brender à Brandis, Ann Pompili, Jan Schoumans and Jake Mol.

41 In the federal election held in October 1993, 20 out of 59 CHP candidates were Dutch-Canadians. See *Windmill Herald*, November 8, 1993, p. 16. Ironically, a highly specialized sociological study carried out by a non-Dutch researcher using an ethno-methodological perspective (one focusing almost exclusively on worldview and subjective experience), completely ignored the very strong Dutch connections between this political party and the values and social structures associated with Dutch Calvinism. This omission illustrates the distortions that result if one does not combine a subjectivist and an objectivist approach in the study of human society. See Charles Scott Grills, "Designating Deviance: Championing Definitions of the Appropriate and the Inappropriate through a Christian Political Voice," PhD dissertation in sociology, McMaster University, 1989.

42 Even the de facto ("real") versus de jure (real "on paper") distinctions should be questioned given the multitude of transitional states of "Dutch-Canadian" institutions which are neither full-fledged ethnic associations nor their mere remnants. In the realm of human affairs it is impossible to separate the material from the symbolic. It is more useful to talk about an ongoing, dual process of hegemony and contestation.

43 He became the secretary and general manager of one of the larger confederations of co-op insurance companies. Although now retired, his name came up on several conversation with Dutch-Canadians in different parts of Ontario.

44 I made an appointment and did a short interview with the former official in question. To respect his anonymity, and his desire not to be portrayed as an "ethnic," his name will not be revealed.

45 His father, who happened to be in Ontario for a short family visit from the Netherlands, was involved in the accident that resulted in damage to his son's car.

46 He is one of many people whose name appears briefly in the Kenyon book, but without mention of his Dutch background. I have since come across another book that contains quite a bit of biographical information about this highly successful man in a chapter dealing with Canada's insurance industry. That book does refer to his Dutch background and early immigration experience, which involved the usual stint of farm work and hard (and sometimes humiliating) physical labour for a CNR section gang. The last sentence in that book also confirms the desire of the person in question to play down his Dutch identity: "I'm a prouder Canadian than a native-born Canadian. Once you get the feeling that you do belong, all the rest leaves you."

47 Similarly, Wolfe Island, which has a high proportion of farmers of Dutch descent, is not the best location for commercial agriculture, even though it is flat and surrounded by water. In contrast, there are relatively few Dutch in the

more prosperous districts of Essex and Waterloo counties in southwestern Ontario or in Russell county near Ottawa.

48 From an interview in Guelph, July 29, 1992.

49 Interview with a woman in Ottawa, July 12, 1991.

50 According to figures extracted from the individual public user data tapes relating to the 1991 population census. My figures relate to women reporting Dutch as either single or multiple ethnic origin. These absolute numbers, representing 3 percent of the total of all women of Dutch descent in Ontario, goes up to close to 17,000 (or nearly 8 percent if the cut-off point is raised to $15,000.

51 See article by Wim van Duyn in *De Nederlandse Courant*, Christmas 1993, p. 13.

52 I have heard numerous stories along these lines, even from people who strongly believe that *the Dutch* are generally honest, hard-working people, with no criminal elements.

Chapter 20

1 Bourdieu et al., *The Craft of Sociology*, p. 29.

2 Ibid., p. 21.

3 My research project does not tackle the issue of racialization associated with the more recent waves of immigrants coming to Canada—our new "ethnics." Nevertheless, many of the main themes in this book, such as the internal diversity of any ethnic group, multiple identities, the arbitrary nature of group boundaries and the complex interrelationships among economic relations, ethnicity, gender dynamics and even religion, are relevant to a much broader range of social phenomena connected to overseas migration.

4 Bourdieu et al., *The Craft of Sociology*, p. viii.

5 The notion of an epistemic break was first coined by Gaston Bachelard, a philosopher of science whose writings influenced not only Bourdieu, but other well-known scholars including Louis Althusser, Michel Foucault and Thomas Kuhn. See Mary Tiles, *Bachelard: Science and Objectivity* (Cambridge: Cambridge University Press, 1984), p. xi.

6 See Beate Krais's interview with Pierre Bourdieu et al., *The Craft of Sociology*, p. 257.

7 Ishwaran, *Family, Kinship and Community*.

8 Some authors combine ethnic categories based on national origin with racial categories, although people of European descent are usually classified only in terms of national origin. See Peter C. Pineo, "The Social Standing of Ethnic and Racial Groupings," *The Canadian Review of Sociology and Anthropology*, 14 (1977): 147-57. Even sociologists interested in demonstrating the importance of education and occupation over ethnicity, still tend to use statistical data based on questions about national origin. See Gordon A. Darroch, "Another Look at Ethnicity, Stratification and Social Mobility in Canada," *Canadian Review of Sociology and Anthropology*, 4 (1979): 1-25, and Reitz, *The Survival of Ethnic Groups*, p. 3.

9 My argument applies primarily to English-speaking regions of Canada, although it could easily be extended to Quebec, which has a Francophone "mainstream."

10 All one has to do is check any recent issues of such journals specializing in ethnic relations in North America. The fact that the bulk of overseas immigration

today comes from continents other than Europe has also brought the issue of racial inequalities to the forefront of discussion.

11 Scholars of ethnicity have come up with logical distinctions, such as that between ethnic groups and ethnic categories, to distinguish between objective and subjective aspects of ethnicity. See Wsevolod W. Isajiw, "Definitions of Ethnicity," *Ethnicity*, 1 (1974): 111-124. However, such formalization can still end up reproducing common-sense assumptions. See also Bourdieu et al., *The Craft of Sociology*, p. 54.

12 However, we should not underestimate the extent to which individual Calvinists have attempted to preserve the Dutch national heritage outside the church context.

13 Ishwaran's Holland Marsh study is a classic case. Canadian students of Reformed background or persuasion writing university dissertations (van Ginkel, Breems, Peetoom) have also learned to define their own faith community in ethnic terms (see many ethnic titles in bibliography).

14 "Ethnocultural Directory of Hamilton-Wentworth," (n.d., circa 1989), p. 24-27. Ethnically defined cultural organizations, plus religious institutions with the label "Reformed," are likewise lumped together in official archives. See also "Inventory of the Multicultural History Society of Ontario Papers," prepared by Jan Liebaers, Archives of Ontario, February 1990.

15 Special exhibits on postwar Dutch immigrants, involving the collection of objects and immigation stories, were carried out in 1991 by St. Marys Museum and by the Heritage Museum of Lambton County in 1996. In both cases, most of the research was carried out by first-generation Dutch immigrant women, and the non-Dutch curators who coordinated these projects were surprised as how many people of Dutch descent lived in their respective counties (Perth and Lambton).

16 Total memberships in credit unions still in operation in 1979, plus an indication of proportion of ethnic composition, are listed in Graaskamp, *Dutch Canadian Mosaic*, p. 26-27.

17 The highest level of membership in the province-wide Dutch Canadian Entertainment Club alone (whose members generally did not belong to credit unions) was 20,000 people (personal communication from Bill Brouwers).

18 This is a rough estimate, combining the total membership of all Dutch-Canadian clubs (including their special-purpose sub-groups, such as bands or choirs), Dutch veterans' organizations operating in Canada, the Frisian *kaats* federation, hometown reunion committees and the various Toronto-based, Dutch-Canadian professional and business organizations.

19 Adding up all church memberships with a subtraction of 10 percent (to exclude non-Dutch spouses and other converts who have been increasingly joining such denominations since about a decade ago).

20 Bourdieu has criticized survey-based research, based on the use of such "naturalized preconstructions" (or any form of social taxonomy), precisely because the questions often determine the outcome. See his *Distinction*, p. 245.

21 For a discussion of the importance of worldviews as constitutive of ethnic groups, with reference to the Calvinist sub-component of Dutch-Canadians, see Breems, "'I Tell Them We Are a Blessed People,'" p. 45-49.

Chapter 21

1 One of the ongoing debates among Dutch sociologists and historians is whether the term *zuil* (pillar) should be used only as a useful metaphor to characterize a historically specific phenomenon (found in the Netherlands only in the second half of the nineteenth and the first half of the twentieth century), or as a sociological concept referring to a broader social process going back much further in Dutch history. See J.C.H. Blom's review of S. Groenveld's book, *Was de Nederlandse Republiek verzuild?* (Leiden: Rijksuniversiteit Leiden, 1995), p. 237-38.

2 Dutch-Canadians who have travelled to visit friends or relatives in Australia frequently comment on the virtual absence of the Dutch-style system of parallel and segregated institutions there.

Bibliography

Bibliography

Primary Sources

Public Archives

Archives of Ontario
Multicultural History Society of Ontario (MHSO)

Private Archives or Collections

Claus van Banning (miscellaneous papers)
DUCA (head office)
St. Willibrord Community Credit Union (head office)
Sydenham Credit Union (head office)
VanderMey papers (miscellaneous papers)

Newspapers and Magazines

Calvinist Contact
Christian Courier (formerly *Calvinist Contact*)
Christian Renewal
Ducapost
The Guide
Holland Horizon
De Hollandse Krant
De Nederlandse Courant
De Nederlandse Post
Reformed Perspectives
Windmill Herald
Windmill Post (English language supplement of the *Windmill Herald*)

Secondary Sources

Aalten, Ana. 1989. "The Accidental Businesswomen: Gender and Entrepreneurship in the Netherlands, 1950-75." In *Dutch Dilemmas: Anthropologists Look at the Netherlands*, edited by Jeremy Boissevain and Jojada Verrips. Assen: Van Gorcum.

Alba, Richard. 1990. *Ethnic Identity: The Transformation of White America*. New Haven: Yale University Press.

Anderson, Alan B., and James Frideres. 1981. *Ethnicity in Canada*. Toronto: Butterworths.

Antonides, Harry. 1978. *Multinationals and the Peaceable Kingdom*. Toronto: Clarke, Irwin & Company.

Bagley, Christopher. 1973. *The Dutch Plural Society*. London: Oxford University Press.

Bakvis, Herman. 1981. *Catholic Power in the Netherlands*. Kingston: McGill-Queen's University Press.

Barrett, Stanley R. 1994. *Paradise: Class, Commuters, and Ethnicity in Rural Ontario*. Toronto: University of Toronto Press.

Barth, Frederick. 1969. *Ethnic Groups and Boundaries*. Boston: Little, Brown and Company.

Bernard, H. Russell. 1994. *Research Methods in Anthropology: Qualitative and Quantitative Approaches*. Thousand Oaks: Sage Publications.

Berry, John et al., eds. 1977. *Multiculturalism and Ethnic Attitudes in Canada*. Ottawa: Ministry of Supply and Services.

Bibby, Reginald W. 1987. *Fragmented Gods*. Toronto: Irwin.

Bissoondath, Neil. 1994. *Selling Illusions: The Cult of Multiculturalism in Canada*. Toronto: Penguin Books.

Blom, J.C.H. 1996. Book review of S. Groenenveld's *Was de Nederlandse Republiek verzuild? Over segmentering van de samenleving binnen de Verenigde Nederlanden*, in *Bijdragen en mededelingen betreffende de geschiedenis der Nederlanden* 11(2):237-38.

Boekelman, Mark. 1983. "The Letters of Jane Aberson: Everyday Life on the Prairies during the Depression: How Immigration Turns Conservatives into Social Democrats." In *Dutch Immigration to North America*, edited by Herman Ganzevoort and M. Boekelman, p. 111-29. Toronto: Multicultural History Society of Ontario.

Boissevain, Jeremy, and Jojada Verrips, ed. 1989. *Dutch Dilemmas: Anthropologists Look at the Netherlands*. Assen: Van Gorcum.

Bouma, Gary D. 1964. "Keeping the Faithful: Patterns of Membership Retention in the Christian Reformed Church," *Sociological Analysis* 41(3):259-64.

Bourdieu, Pierre. 1962. "Célibat et condition paysanne." *Études Rurales* 5/6(April):32-136.

________. 1968. "Outline of a Sociological Theory of Art Perception." *International Social Science Journal* 10(winter):589-612.

________. 1977. *Outline of a Theory of Practice*. Translated by Richard Nice. Cambridge: Cambridge University Press.

________. 1984. *Distinction: A Social Critique of the Judgement of Taste*. Cambridge: Harvard University Press.

________. 1989. "Reproduction interdite. La dimension symbolique de la domination économique." *Etudes Rurales* 113/114(January-June):15-36.

________. 1990. "La domination masculine." *Actes de la recherche en sciences sociales* 84:2-31.

________. 1991. *In Other Words*. Stanford: Stanford University Press.

________. 1991. *The Logic of Practice*. Stanford: Stanford University Press.

________. 1991. *Language and Symbolic Power*. Edited and introduced by John B. Thompson, translated by Gino Raymond and Matthew Adamson. Cambridge: Harvard University Press.

________, Jean-Claude Chamboredon, and Jean-Claude Passeron. 1991. *The Craft of Sociology*. Edited by Beate Krais, translated by Richard Nice. New York: Walter de Gruyter.

________, and Loïc J.D. Wacquant. 1992. *An Invitation to Reflexive Sociology*. Chicago: University of Chicago Press.

Breems, Bradley Gene. 1991. "'I Tell Them We Are a Blessed People': An Analysis of 'Ethnicity' by Way of a Dutch-Calvinist Community," Doctoral dissertation, Department of Sociology and Anthropology, University of British Columbia.

Breton, Raymond. 1964. "Institutional Completeness." *American Journal of Sociology* (79):193-205.

________, Jeffrey Reitz and Victor Valentine. 1980. *Cultural Boundaries and the Cohesion of Canada*. Montreal: Institute for Research on Public Policy.

________, Wsevolod W. Isajiw, Warren E. Kalbach and Jeffrey Reitz, 1990. *Ethnic Identity and Equality: Variations of Experience in a Canadian City*. Toronto: University of Toronto Press.

Breugelmans, Rene. 1970. "Dutch and Flemings in Canada." *Canadian Ethnic Studies* 2:83-115.

Brightman, Robert. 1995. "Forget Culture: Replacement, Transcendence, Relexification." *Cultural Anthropology* 10:509-46.

Bryant, Christopher G. A., and David Jary, eds. 1991. *Gidden's Theory of Structuration: A Critical Appraisal*. London: Routledge.

Burnet, Jean R., and Howard Palmer. 1988. *"Coming Canadians": An Introduction to a History of Canada's Peoples*. Toronto: McClelland and Stewart.

Carter, G. Bentley. 1987. "Ethnicity and Practice." *Comparative Studies in Society and History* 29:24-55.

Cassell, Philip, ed. 1990. *The Giddens Reader*. Stanford: Stanford University Press.

Cassidy, Grant R. 1983. "Multiculturalism and Dutch-Canadian Ethnicity in Metropolitan Toronto." In *Dutch Immigration to North America*, edited by Herman Ganzevoort and M. Boekleman, p. 197-219. Toronto: Multicultural History Society of Ontario.

Chadburn, Nancy L. 1993. "Kristien Hemmerecht's *Brede heupen* and the Social Construction of Woman." *Canadian Journal of Netherlandic Studies* 14(2):27-32.

Chorus, A. 1964. *De Nederlander innerlijk en uiterlijk: Een characteristiek*. Leiden: Slijthoff.

Clark, Colin. 1940. *The Conditions of Economic Progress*. London: Macmillan.

Clarke, Colin, David Ley, and Ceri Peach, eds. 1984. *Geography and Ethnic Pluralism*. London: George Allen and Unwin.

Cnossen, T. 1952. *Canada: land van vrijheit, ruimte en ontplooing*. Wageningen: N.V. Gebr. Zomer en Keunings Uitgeverij.

Coleman, Thelma, and James Anderson. 1978. *The Canada Company*. Stratford: County of Perth and Cummings Publishers.

Collins, Randall. 1979. *The Credential Society*. New York: Academic Press.

Collins, Richard et al., eds. 1986. *Media, Culture and Society*. London: Sage Publications.

Cook, Hugh. 1989. *The Homecoming Man*. Oakville: Mosaic Press.

Corrigan, Philip, and Derek Sayers. 1980. *The Great Arch: English State Formation as Cultural Revolution*. Oxford: Basil Blackwell.

Corry, Mary Alphonsa. 1907. *The Story of Father Van den Broek, O.P.: A Study of Holland and the Story of the Early Settlement of Wisconsin*. Chicago: n.p.

Coward, Harold, and Leslie Kawamura, eds. 1978. *Religion and Ethnicity*. Waterloo: Wilfrid Laurier University Press.

Darroch, Gordon. 1980. "Another Look at Ethnicity, Stratification and Social Mobility in Canada." *Canadian Review of Sociology and Anthropology* 4:1-25.

De Groot, Jan, and A. de Groot. 1995. *Separation and Inheritance*. Windsor: Electra Press.

De Jong, Klaas. 1973. *Cauliflower Crown*. Saskatoon: Western Producer Book Service.

Denzin, Norman K., and Yvonna S. Lincoln, eds. 1994. *Handbook of Qualitative Research*. Thousand Oaks: Sage Publications.

De Vries, Hille. 1985. "The Labor Market in Dutch Agriculture and Emigration to the United States." In *The Dutch in America: Immigration, Settlement, and Cultural Change*, edited by Robert P. Swierenga, p. 78-101. New Brunswick: Rutgers University Press.

Dortmans, John. 1994. *Brabanders in Canada: Their Heritage in the Netherlands, Their Experiences in Canada*. Burlington: Sportswood.

Driedger, L. 1989. *The Ethnic Factor: Identity in Diversity*. Toronto: McGraw-Hill Ryerson.

Elias, Norbert. 1991. *The Symbol Theory*. With introduction by Richard Kilminster. London: Sage Publications.

Elich, J. H., and P. W. Blauw. 1981. "En Toch Terug (een onderzoek naar de emigratie van Nederlanders uit Australië, Nieuw-Zeeland en Canada)." A report published by Erasmus Universiteit, Faculteit der Economische Wetenschappen, Vakgroep Sociologie. Rotterdam.

Elliott, Una. 1964. "Comparative Roles of the People of Italian and Netherlandish Origin in the Creation of a Homogenous Population in the City of London." MA thesis, Faculty of Graduate Studies, University of Western Ontario.

Fallon, Michael. 1991. "The Narrow Way: A Study of the Christian Labour Association of Canada." Unpublished paper.

Fitzgerald, Thomas K. 1992. "Media, Ethnicity and Identity." In *Culture and Power*, edited by Paddy Scannel et al. Newbury Park: Sage.

Fitzmaurice, John. 1983. *The Politics of Belgium: Crisis and Compromise in a Plural Society*. London: C. Hurst.

Forrest, Bruce. 1974. "Dutch Acculturation in Metropolitan Toronto." Unpublished paper.

Frager, Ruth A. 1992. *Sweatshop Strife: Class, Ethnicity, and Gender in the Jewish Labour Movement of Toronto, 1900-1939*. Toronto: University of Toronto Press.

Gadourek, I. 1963. *Riskanten gewoonten en zorg voor eigen welzijn*. Groningen: J. B. Wolters.

Galema, Annemieke. 1990. "Se binne nei Amearika tein (Aspekten van Friese landverhuizing naar de Verenigde Staten rond de eeuwwisseling)." *It Beaken* (tydskrift fan de fryske akademy) 52(2):45-58.

Ganzevoort, Herman. 1988. *A Bittersweet Land: The Dutch Experience in Canada, 1898-1908*. Toronto: McClelland and Stewart (in association with the Multicultural Program, Department of the Secretary of State, and Canadian Government Publishing Centre, Supply and Services).

________, and Mark Boekelman. 1983. *Dutch Immigration to North America*. Toronto: Multicultural History Society of Ontario.

Garnham, Nicholas, and Raymond Williams. "Pierre Bourdieu and the Sociology of Culture: An Introduction." In *Media, Culture and Society*, edited by Richard Collins et al. London: Sage.

Geyl, Pieter. 1962. *The Revolt of the Netherlands (1555-1609)*. London: Ernest Benn.

________. 1964. *History of the Low Countries: Episodes and Problems*. London: Macmillan.

Glazer, Nathan, and Daniel P. Moynihan, eds. *Ethnicity: Theory and Experience*. Cambridge: Harvard University Press.

Gleason, Philip. 1982. "American Identity and Americanization." In *Concepts of Ethnicity*, edited by William Petersen, Michael Novak and Philip Gleason, p. 57-143. Cambridge: Harvard University Press.

Goldstein, Jay E., and Rita M. Bienvenue, eds. 1980. *Ethnicity and Ethnic Relations in Canada*. Toronto: Butterworths.

Goudsblom, Johan. 1967. *Dutch Society*. New York: Random House.

Graaskamp, Ger W. n.d. (circa 1980). *Dutch Canadian Mosaic*. Niagara Falls: Decker Printing.

Graumans, Joe. 1973. "The Role of Ethno-Religious Organizations in the Assimilation Process of the Dutch Christian Reformed and Catholic Immigrants in Southwestern Ontario." MA thesis, University of Windsor.

Gregg, William. 1885. *History of the Presbyterian Church in the Dominion of Canada*. Toronto: Presbyterian Printing and Publishing.

Groenenberg, A. L. 1966. "The Social Geography of the Netherlanders in Southwestern Ontario with Special Reference to the Role of the Churches in the Integration of Immigrants." MA thesis, University of Western Ontario.

Harker, Richard, Cheleen Mahar, and Chris Wilkes, eds. 1990. *An Introduction to the Work of Pierre Bourdieu: The Theory of Practice*. London: Macmillan.

Hartland, J. A. 1959. *De Geschiedenis van de Nederlandse emigratie tot de tweede Wereld Oorlog*. The Hague: Minister van Sociale Zaken en Volksgezondheit en de NED.

Heilbron, Johan, and Benjo Maso. 1983. "Interview met Pierre Bourdieu." *Sociologisch Tijdschrift* (Stichting Amsterdam) 10(2):307-34.

Helling, R. A. 1982. "Dutch Immigration to the Tri-County Area (Essex, Kent and Lambton Counties, Ontario," *Canadian Journal of Netherlandic Studies* 3(1-2):12-15.

Hellwig, Tineke. 1993. "The Asian and Eurasian Women of the Dutch East Indies in Dutch and Malay Literature." *Canadian Journal of Netherlandic Studies* 14(2, Fall):20-26.

Hendriks, Milton. 1963. "L'immigrant hollandais au sein de la Confédération canadienne." Thèse de maitrise en arts (histoire), l'Université Laval.

Herberg, Will. *Protestant-Catholic-Jew*. 1960. New York: Anchor.

Hofstede, B. P. 1964. *Thwarted Exodus: Post War Overseas Migration from the Netherlands*. The Hague: Martinus Nijhoff.

Hofwijk, J. W. n.d. (circa 1954). *Canada (reis met onbekende bestemming)*. Utrecht: N.V. Uitgeverij De Lanteern.

Hoogendorn, Robert. 1982. "Miners Against Their Will, the Netherlanders in Northern Ontario: A Study of an Invisible Minority." *Laurentian University Press* 15(1):83-92.

Horn, Michiel. 1983. "Canadian Soldiers and Dutch Women after the Second World War." In *Dutch Immigration to North America*, edited by Herman Ganzevoort and M. Boekelman, p. 187-95. Toronto: Multicultural History Society of Ontario.

Hovius, S., and T. Plomp. 1948. *Canada: een land met grote mogenlijkheden*. Groningen: Niemeijer.

Huggett, Frank E. 1971. *The Modern Netherlands*. London: Pall Mall Press.

________. 1982. *The Dutch Connection*. The Hague: Ministry of Foreign Affairs, Government Publishing Office.

________. 1983. *The Dutch Today*. The Hague: Ministry of Foreign Affairs, Government Publishing Office.

Huizinga, Johan. 1962. *Homo Ludens: A Study of the Play-element in Culture*. Boston: Beacon.

Impeta, C.N. 1964. *Kaart van kerkelijk nederland*. Kampen: Uitgeversmaatschappij J.H. Kok.

Information Canada. 1970. *The Cultural Contribution of the Other Ethnic Groups*. Book 4 of the Report of the Royal Commission on Bilingualism and Biculturalism, Ottawa.

Isajiw, W. W. 1980. "Definitions of Ethnicity." In *Ethnicity and Ethnic Relations in Canada*, edited by Jay E. Goldstein and Rita M. Bienvenue, p. 13-26. Toronto: Butterworths.

Isajiw, Wsevolod. 1990. "Ethnic-Identity Retention." Chap. 2 in *Ethnic Identity and Equality*, edited by Raymond Breton et al. Toronto: University of Toronto Press.

Ishwaran, K., ed. 1971. *The Canadian Family*. Toronto: Holt, Rinehart and Winston.

________. 1971. "Family and Community among the Dutch Canadians." In *The Canadian Family*, edited by K. Ishwaran, p. 225-47. Toronto: Holt, Rinehart and Winston.

________. 1971. "Calvinism and Social Behaviour in a Dutch-Canadian Community." In *The Canadian Family*, edited by K. Ishwaran, p. 297-314. Toronto: Holt, Rinehart and Winston.

________. 1977. *Family, Kinship and Community: A Study of Dutch-Canadians—A Developmental Approach*. Toronto: McGraw-Hill Ryerson.

Joldersma, Hermina. 1990. "'Women Writers,' 'Writing by Women' and 'The Female Voice.'" *Canadian Journal of Netherlandic Studies* 11(2, Fall):1-3.

________. 1992. "The Anna Bijns Prijs (1985-)." *Canadian Journal of Netherlandic Studies* 13(2):29-34.

Kaplan, Gisela. 1992. *Contemporary Western European Feminism*. London: UCL Press.

Keddie, Philip D., and Julius A. Mage. 1985. *Southern Ontario: Atlas of Agriculture (Contemporary Patterns and Recent Changes)*. Occasional papers in Geography, No. 7. Guelph: University of Guelph.

Kenyon, Ron. 1976. *To the Credit of the People*. Toronto: Hunter Rose (for the Ontario Credit Union League Limited).

Keppley Mahmood, Cynthia. 1989. *Frisian and Free: Study of an Ethnic Minority of the Netherlands*. Prospect Heights: Waveland Press.

Kits, Harry J. 1988. "World Views and Social Involvement: A Proposal for Classification of Canadian Neo-Calvinist Social Involvement, 1945-1980." MA thesis in philosophical foundations, Institute for Christian Studies (Toronto).

Kossman, E. H. 1978. *The Low Countries, 1780-1940*. Oxford: Oxford University Press.

Kralt, John. 1981. "Netherlanders and the Canadian Census." *Canadian Journal of Netherlandic Studies* 3(1-2):40-44.

Kruithof, Bert. 1974. *Twenty Years: Dutch (Toronto) Credit Union*. Toronto: Canadian Offset Company, Ltd.

Kruyt, J. P., and W. Goddijn. 1962. *Verzuiling en ontzuiling als sociologisch process*. In *Drift en koers: een halve eeuw sociale veranderingen in Nederland* edited by A. N. J. del Hollander et al., p. 231-53. Assen: Van Gorcum.

Kuyper, Abraham. 1950. *Christianity and the Class Struggle*. Translated by Dirk Jellema. Grand Rapids: Piet Hein Publishers.

Lambert, Audrey M. 1971. *The Making of the Dutch Landscape: An Historical Geography of the Netherlands*. London: Seminar Press.

Landheer, Bartholomew, ed. 1940. *The Netherlands*. Berkeley: University of California Press.

Lash, Scott. 1990. "Modernization and Postmodernization in the Work of Pierre Bourdieu." In *Sociology of Postmodernism*, edited by Scott Lash. London: Routledge.

Lemke, Jay L. 1995. *Textual Politics: Discourse and Social Dynamics*. London: Taylor and Francis.

Lijphart, Arend. 1968. *The Politics of Accommodation: Pluralism and Democracy in the Netherlands*. Berkeley: University of California Press.

Lomnitz-Adler, Claudio. 1992. *Exits from the Labyrinth: Culture and Ideology in the Mexican National Space*. Berkeley: University of California Press.

Lowensteyn, Janny. 1981. "Dutch Ethnicity in Montreal: Its Persistence, Meaning and Uses." *Canadian Journal of Netherlandic Studies* 3(1-2):24-33.

________. 1992. "Samuel Holland, Canada's First Surveyor General." *Canadian Journal of Netherlandic Studies* 13(2):1-4.

Lowensteyn, Johanna H. 1986. "A Social History of the Dutch in Quebec," MA thesis in sociology and anthropology, Concordia University.

Lower, Arthur R. 1971 (first edition 1946). *A History of Canada: Colony to Nation*. Don Mills: Longmans, Green.

Lucas, Henry S. 1955. *Netherlanders in America: Dutch Immigration to the United States and Canada, 1789-1950*. Grand Rapids: William B. Eerdmans.

Magee, Joan. 1982. "CAANS, an Overview of the First Decade." *Canadian Journal of Netherlandic Studies* 3(1-2):3-7.

________. 1983. *A Dutch Heritage: 200 Years of Dutch Presence in the Windsor-Detroit Region*. Toronto: Dundurn.

________. 1987. *The Belgians in Ontario: A History*. Toronto: Dundurn.

Martens, John. 1988. *Making Waves*. Waterloo: Waterloo Printing.

Moberg, David O. 1966. "Social Differentiation in the Netherlands." *Social Forces* 39(4):333-37.

Monter, William. 1967. *Calvin's Geneva*. New York: John Wiley.

Morse, Janice. 1994. "Designing Funded Qualitative Research." Chap. 13 in *Handbook of Qualitative Research*, edited by Norman Denzin et al. Thousand Oaks: Sage.

Mouzelis, Nicos. 1995. *Sociological Theory: What Went Wrong*. London: Routledge.

Moyer, David S. 1984. "Sinterklaas in Victoria: St. Nicholas as a Symbol of Dutch Ethnicity," a paper presented at the annual meeting of the Canadian Association for the Advancement of Netherlandic Studies (at Guelph).

Murphy, Robert. 1971. *Dialectics of Social Life: Alarms and Excursions in Anthropological Theory*. New York: Columbia University Press.

Needler, G.H. 1956. *Colonel Anthony van Egmond: From Napoleon and Waterloo to Mackenzie and Rebellion*. Toronto: Burns and MacEachen.

Ng, Roxana. 1991. "Sexism, Racism and Canadian Nationalism." In *Race, Class, Gender: Bonds and Barriers*, edited by Jesse Vorst et al. Toronto: Garamond Press.

Newton, Gerald. 1978. *The Netherlands: An Historical and Cultural Survey, 1795-1977*. London: Ernest Benn Limited.

Parker, Geoffrey. 1988. *The Dutch Revolt*. Rev. ed. Harmondsworth: Penguin.

Patterson, Orlando. 1975. "Context and Choice in Ethnic Allegiance: A Theoretical Framework." In *Ethnicity: Theory and Experience*, edited by Nathan Glazer and Daniel P. Moynihan, p. 305-49. Cambridge: Harvard University Press.

Sheila Patterson. 1953. *Colour and Culture in South Africa*. London: Routledge and Kegan Paul.

Paus-Jenssen, Arne Louis. 1966. "Immigration to Canada from the Netherlands, 1946-1963," MA thesis, Queen's University, Kingston, Ontario.

Peetoom, Adriaan. n.d. (circa 1986). "From Mythology to Mythology: Dutch-Canadians Orthodox-Calvinists Immigrants and their Schools," MA thesis in history and philosophy of education, University of Toronto.

Petersen, William. 1955. *Planned Migration: The Social Determinants of the Dutch-Canadian Movement*. Berkeley: University of California Press.

________, Michael Novak, and Philip Gleason. 1982. *Concepts of Ethnicity*. Cambridge: Harvard University Press.

Pineo, Peter. 1980. "The Social Standing of Ethnic and Racial Groupings." *The Canadian Review of Sociology and Anthropology* 14:147-57.

Porter, John. 1956. *The Vertical Mosaic: An Analysis of Social Class and Power in Canada*. Toronto: University of Toronto Press.

Price, J. L. 1974. *Culture and Society in the Dutch Republic During the 17th Century*. London: B. T. Batsford.

Rees-Powell, Alan Thomas. 1964. "Differentials in the Integration Process of Dutch and Italian Immigrants in Edmonton," MA thesis in sociology, University of Alberta.

Reitz, Jeffrey. 1980. *The Survival of Ethnic Groups*. Toronto: McGraw-Hill Ryerson.

Robbins, Derek. 1991. *The Work of Pierre Bourdieu: Recognizing Society*. Buckingham: Open University.

Rogier, L. J. n.d. *Geschiedenis van het Katholicisme in Noord-Nederland in de zestiende en zeventiende eeuw*. Vol. 4 and 5. Amsterdam: Elsevier.

Roosens, E. 1989. *Creating Ethnicity: The Process of Ethnogenesis*. Newbury Park: Sage Publications.

Sas, Anthony. 1957. "Dutch Migration to and Settlement in Canada: 1945-1955." PhD dissertation in geography, Clark University (Worcester, Mass.).

________. 1958. "Dutch Concentration in Rural Southwestern Ontario during the Post War Decade," In *The Annals of the Association of American Geographers* 48(3): 185-94.

Saueressig-Schreuder, Yda. "Dutch Catholic Immigration Settlement in Wisconsin." In *The Dutch in America: Immigration, Settlement, and Cultural Change*, edited by Robert P. Swierenga, p. 105-24. New Brunswick: Rutgers University Press.

Scannel Paddy et al., eds. *Culture and Power*. Newbury Park: Sage Publications.

Schama, Simon. 1988. *The Embarrassment of Riches: An Interpretation of Dutch Culture in the Golden Age*. New York: Knopf.

Schreuder, Yda. 1989. "Ethnic Solidarity and Assimilation among Dutch Protestants and Catholics in the State of Wisconsin, 1850-1905," a paper presented at the conference "The Dutch in North America: Their Immigration and Cultural Continuity," held at Middelburg, Netherlands, June 7-9.

Schryer, Frans J. 1990. *Ethnicity and Class Conflict in Rural Mexico*. Princeton: Princeton University Press.

Sedoc-Dahlberg, Betty, ed. 1990. *The Dutch Caribbean: Prospects for Democracy*. New York: Gordon and Breach.

Shetter, William Z. 1971. *The Pillars of Society: Six Centuries of Civilization in the Netherlands*. The Hague: Martinus Nijhoff.

Smith, Timothy L. 1978. "Religion and Ethnicity in America." *American Historical Review* 83(5):1155-85.

Stake, Robert. 1994. "Case Studies." Chap. 14 in *Handbook of Qualitative Research*, edited by Norman K. Denzin and Yvonna S. Lincoln. Thousand Oaks: Sage Publications.

Stam, Henry. 1987. "Effectiveness of Formal Socialization Processes within the Christian Reformed Church." MA thesis in sociology, University of Windsor, 1987.

Stein, André. 1988. *Quiet Heroes: True Stories of the Rescue of Jews by Christians in Nazi-occupied Holland*. Toronto: Lester & Orpen Dennys.

Steinberg, Stephen. 1989. *The Ethnic Myth: Race, Ethnicity and Class in America*. Boston: Beacon Press.

Steiner, Ingrid. 1984. "Differences in Cultural Heritage between Dutch and Swiss: with Implications for Emigrants." MA research paper (unpublished), Department of Sociology, University of Waterloo.

Stokvis, Pieter R.D. 1985. "Dutch International Migration, 1815-1910." In *The Dutch in America: Immigration, Settlement, and Cultural Change*, edited by Robert P. Swierenga, p. 43-63. New Brunswick: Rutgers University Press.

Swierenga, Robert P. 1985. "Dutch Immigration Patterns in the Nineteenth and Twentieth Centuries." In *The Dutch in America: Immigration, Settlement, and Cultural Change*, edited by Robert P. Swierenga, p. 15-42. New Brunswick: Rutgers University Press.

________, ed. 1985. *The Dutch in America: Immigration, Settlement, and Cultural Change*. New Brunswick: Rutgers University Press.

Tait, Lyal. n.d. *The Edisons of Vienna*. St. Thomas: Elgin County Library.

Taylor, Jean Gelman. 1983. *The Social World of Batavia*. Madison: University of Wisconsin Press.

Ten Zijthoff, Gerrit J. 1987. *Sources of Secession: The Netherlands Hervormde Kerk on the Eve of the Dutch Immigration to the Midwest*. Grand Rapids: Wm. B. Eerdmans.

Thurlings, J. M. G. 1971. "The Case of Dutch Catholicism." *Sociologica Neerlandica* 7:118-36.

________. 1978. *De wankele zuil: Nederlandse Katholieken tussen assimilatie en pluralisme*. 2nd ed. Deventer: Van Loghum Slaterus.

Tiles, Mary. 1984. *Bachelard: Science and Objectivity*. Cambridge: Cambridge University Press.

Tuinman, Abe Sybe. 1952. *Enige aspecten van de hedendaagse migratie van nederlanders naar Canada*. Wageningen: Ministerie van Landbouw, Visserij en Voedselvoorziening.

________. 1956. "The Netherlands-Canadian Migration," *Tijdschrift voor Economische en Sociale Geografie* 47(8):181-89.

Van Belle, Harry, 1989. "From Religious Pluralism to Cultural Pluralism (Continuity and Change among the Reformed Dutch in Canada)," paper presented at the conference "The Dutch in North America: Their Immigration and Cultural Continuity," held at Middelburg, Netherlands, June 7-9.

Van Brummelen, Harry Walter. 1984. "Molding God's Children: The History of Curriculum in Christian Schools Rooted in Dutch Calvinism." Doctoral dissertation (in Education), University of British Columbia.

van den Hoonaard, Will. 1991. *Silent Ethnicity: The Dutch of New Brunswick*. Fredericton: New Ireland Press.

VanderMey, Albert. 1983. *To All Our Children: The Story of the Postwar Dutch Immigrants to Canada*. Jordan Station: Paideia Press.

________. 1994. *And the Swamp Flourished: The Bittersweet Story of Holland Marsh*. Surrey: Vanderheide.

Vanderschot, Margaret, and Mary A. Smith. 1990. "Netherlands Research Project: A Study of Postwar Immigration from the Netherlands to the St. Marys Area." A report from St. Marys Museum.

Vander Vliet, Joyce G. 1994. "Women, Church, and Society: The Christian Reformed Church Case." Graduate thesis in sociology, University of Guelph.

Vandezande, Gerald. 1983. *Christians in the Crisis: Towards Responsible Citizenship*. Toronto: Anglican Book Centre.

Van Dijk, Joanne G. 1990. "Ethnic Retention and Social Support: A Comparative Analysis of First Generation Elderly Dutch-Canadian Catholics and Calvinists." MA thesis, University of Guelph.

Van Ginkel, A. M. 1982. "Ethnicity in the Reformed Tradition: Dutch Calvinist Immigrants in Canada, 1946-1960." MA thesis, University of Toronto.

Van Herk, Aritha. 1978. *Judith*. Toronto: McClelland and Stewart.

________. 1991. *In Visible Ink: Crypto-frictions*. Edmonton: NeWest Press.

Van Hinte, Jacob. 1928. *Nederlanders in Amerika: een studie over landverhuizers en volksplanters in de 19de en 20ste Eeuw*. Two-volume PhD dissertation.

Vanoene, W. W. J. 1978. *Inheritance Preserved*. Winnipeg: Premier Printing.

van Stekelenburg, Henry. 1982. "Tracing the Dutch Roman Catholic Emigration to North America in the Nineteenth and Twentieth Centuries." In *Dutch Immigration to North America*, edited by Herman Ganzevoort and M. Boekelman, p. 57-83. Toronto: Multicultural History Society of Ontario.

________. 1985. "The Quest for Land: The Movement of Roman Catholic Dutch Farmers to Canada (1947-1955)." *Migration News* 34(October-December):23-27.

________. 1991. *Landverhuizing als Regionaal Verschijnsel*. Doctoral dissertation (*proefschrift*) for Catholic University of Brabant. Tilburg: Stichting Zuidelijk Historisch Contact.

van Stekelenburg, H. A. V. M. 1996. *"Hier is alles vooruitgegaan": Landverhuizing van Noord-Brabant naar Noord-Amerika*. Tilburg: Stichting Zuidelijk Historisch Contact.

Verduijn, Arie. 1981. *Sojourners: A Family Chronicle*. Burlington: published by the author.

Verkade, Willem. 1965. *Democratic Parties in the Low Countries and Germany: Origins and Historical Developments*. Leiden: Universitaire Pers Leiden.

Verkley, Miep. 1993. *A Particular Path: A Collection of Stories about the Experiences of Women Immigrants*. Thedford: Swans Publications.

Vermeirre, André. 1986. "Aspects de l'Immigration Neerlandophone au Canada." *Canadian Journal of Netherlandic Studies* 7(1-2):44-62.

Vlekke, Bernard H. M. 1940. "The Dutch Before 1581." Chap. 2 in *The Netherlands*, edited by Bartholomew Landheer. Berkeley: University of California Press.

Vorst, Jesse et al., eds. 1991. *Race, Class, Gender: Bonds and Barriers*. Toronto: Garamond Press.

Walter, Bronwen. 1984. "Tradition and Ethnic Interactions: Second Wave Irish Settlements in Luton and Bolton." Chap. 11 in *Geography and Ethnic Pluralism*, edited by Colin Clarke, David Ley, and Ceri Peach. London: Allen and Unwin.

Weber, Max. 1952. *The Protestant Ethic and the Spirit of Capitalism*. London: Allen and Unwin (first published 1904-5).

Wedgewood, C. V. 1946. *William the Silent: William of Nassau, Prince of Orange, 1533-1584*. London: Jonathan Cape.

Wijdeven, Ad. n.d. (circa 1985). *Oogsten op vreemde velden (over het leven van emigranten in Canada)*. Zutphen: Uitgeverij Terra Zutphen.

Williams, Raymond. 1977. *Marxism and Literature*. Oxford: Oxford University Press.

Wolterstorff, Nicholas. 1974. "The AACS in the CRC." *Reformed Journal* 24(December):9-16.

Yelvington, Kevin A. 1991. "Ethnicity as Practice? A Comment on Bentley" (plus a response by Bentley). *Comparative Studies in Society and History* 33(1): 158-75.

Index

Index